THE **Building Christian English** SERIES

Building
Christian English

Communicating Effectively

Grades 9 and 10

Book Two

Rod and Staff Publishers, Inc.
P.O. Box 3, 14193 Hwy. 172
Crockett, Kentucky 41413
Telephone: (606) 522-4348

Acknowledgments

We are indebted first and most of all to God, whose blessing made possible the writing and publishing of this book.

We express gratitude to each one who was involved in this work. Bruce Good wrote the text. Samuel Hoover and Lester Miller illustrated the book. Marvin Eicher and Ernest Wine were the editors, and various other brethren were reviewers. We are also indebted to the teachers who used the material on a laboratory basis in their classrooms, as well as to numerous people who assisted along the way by providing finances, by encouraging those directly involved in the work, and by interceding in prayer for the work.

Various reference books were consulted in accomplishing this task, such as English handbooks, other English textbooks, encyclopedias, and dictionaries. For these too we are grateful. We have chosen to favor the more conservative schools of thought that are considered authoritative in correct English usage.

—The Publishers

Crockett, Kentucky 41413

Printed in U.S.A.

ISBN 0 7399 0536-8

Catalog no. 12902.3

3 4 5 6 — 17 16 15 14 13 12 11 10

Table of Contents

(Stars indicate lessons on editing skills, writing style, or speaking style.)

Chapter 4 Writing an Expository Essay

Chapter 5 Glossary of Usage

Chapter 6 Writing a Short Story

Chapter 7 Substantives

Chapter 8 Improving the Style of a Story

Chapter 9 Verbs

Chapter 10 Writing Description

Chapter 11 Modifiers

Chapter 12 General Reference Sources

Chapter 13 Connecting Words, Interjections, and Idioms

Chapter 14 Parliamentary Procedure

Year-end Reviews

Introduction

New Features in Grades 9 and 10 of *Building Christian English*

Welcome to a new level in the study of English. In previous years of the *Building Christian English* series, you focused mainly on grammar—things like sentence structure and parts of speech. Now in Books One and Two, you will find several things that are different from the earlier books in the series.

One difference is that Books One and Two place a stronger emphasis on composition than the earlier books did. Instead of studying several lessons on grammar and then one on composition, you will have entire chapters on composition (alternating with chapters on grammar). The lessons in these chapters will give you practical help in effective listening, speaking, reading, and writing.

Another difference is that Books One and Two are parallel rather than consecutive. That is, Book Two does not build on Book One. Instead, each book reviews grammar concepts from grade 8 and previous years, and each book deals with different kinds of composition. For this reason, you may study either Book One or Book Two first, and grades 9 and 10 can be in the same English class.

A third difference is the three new kinds of lessons distributed throughout Books One and Two. They are called "Improving Your Writing Style," "Improving Your Speaking Style," and "Improving Your Editing Skills." These lessons will give you regular practice with writing, public speaking, and proofreading. In the writing and speaking lessons, the focus is on the style rather than the mechanics of a written or an oral presentation. That is, instead of teaching you how to gather and organize information, these lessons will teach you how to make your oral and written compositions more interesting and effective.

May God bless your study of English this year.

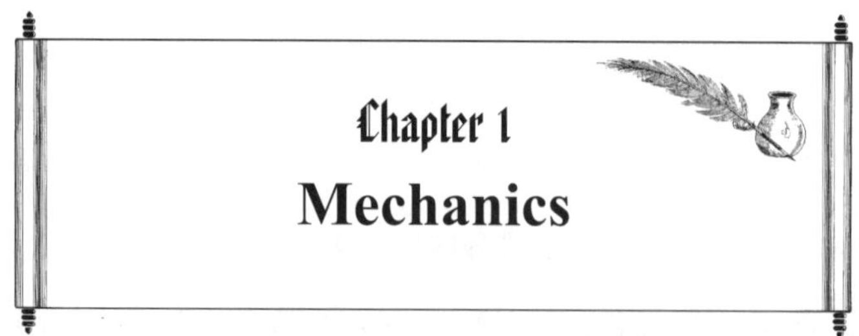

Chapter 1
Mechanics

1. Capitalization and End Punctuation

The mechanics of English relate primarily to the rules of capitalization and punctuation. Like road signs, these rules help a reader to understand where the road of thought turns, pauses, or stops.

Capitalization

1. *Capitalize the first word of every sentence, direct quotation, and line of poetry.*

   My father says, "Don't count the minutes; just make the minutes count."

   Have more than thou showest,
   Speak less than thou knowest.

2. *Capitalize all proper nouns.*

   a. Names of persons, including titles, abbreviations, and initials. Capitalize a title only if it is used as part of the name or in place of a name. Capitalize the word *president* when it refers to the current president of the United States.

   Dr. Lloyds
   Brother Robert; a faithful brother
   Daniel J. Hoover, Sr.
   the President; former presidents

   b. Names that refer to God, and words that refer to the Bible or to parts of it. Also capitalize personal pronouns that refer to God.

   our Shepherd; the shepherds of Palestine
   Psalm 23; a beloved psalm
   the Pentateuch
   the Major Prophets
   the Epistle of James; an epistle

   c. Names of geographical features, such as rivers, lakes, and mountains; and of political units, such as cities, states, provinces, and nations. Capitalize words like *north* and *southwest* only when they name specific geographical regions, not when they name directions.

   Mount Robson; a high mountain
   came from the South; south of the equator

   Ontario
   Brazil

d. Titles of stories, poems, songs, and publications. Capitalize the first and last words and other important words. Do not capitalize articles, coordinating conjunctions, and prepositions of fewer than four letters.

"Bring the Seekers In" (story) *A Home for Grandma* (book)

e. Names of specific organizations, businesses, institutions, groups, races, and languages.

Glendale Mennonite Church
American Cancer Society
Harris Plumbing and Heating
the United States Supreme Court
Africans and Europeans
an Italian family

f. Names of specific ships, airplanes, trains, buildings, monuments, natural phenomena, and heavenly bodies.

the *Orient Express*
the Washington Monument
Old Faithful (geyser)
Saturn
Jupiter
Earth

Note: Capitalize *earth* only if you use it as a proper noun to name the planet on which we live. Omit the article *the* in such a case.

The next planet beyond Earth is Mars. (proper noun)
The surface features of Mars can be seen from the earth. (common noun)

g. Names of parks, historic sites, events, eras, and documents.

Sequoia National Park
the Flood
the Reformation
the Treaty of Versailles

h. Brand names and registered trademarks. Do not capitalize a common noun that follows the brand name or trademark, even if it is capitalized in a label.

Vicks cough drops
Holsum bread
Toyota car
Rockwell table saw

i. Names of school subjects derived from proper nouns or followed by numbers.

Canadian geography Typing II bookkeeping class

j. Calendar items, but not the names of seasons.

September
Thursday
Ascension Day
spring

3. *Capitalize most words derived from proper nouns.* A word may become so common that it is no longer capitalized. Check a dictionary if you are not sure.

Jewish customs Alaskan winter macadam road

4. *Capitalize the pronoun* I *and the interjection* O. The word *O* occurs mainly in poetry and in archaic English, such as that in the King James Bible. In modern prose,

it signifies a solemn appeal and always precedes a noun of direct address. Do not confuse *O* with the interjection *oh.*

> "Unto thee, O LORD, will I sing."
> Stand firm for the right, O youth; oh, how the church needs faithful young people!

5. *Capitalize the greeting, closing, and signature of a letter.*

> Dear Sirs:
>
> . . . .
>
> Sincerely,
> Louella Unruh

6. *Capitalize abbreviations of proper nouns and of many other common terms.* Check a dictionary or an English handbook when you are not sure.

> 9:15 A.M.   650 B.C.

End Punctuation

7. *Use a period after a declarative sentence, an indirect question, and an imperative sentence.*

> The Bible is God's unchanging Word.
> Some people actually question whether the Bible is true.
> Hold the Bible in highest reverence.

8. *Use periods with initials and with many abbreviations.* Common exceptions include the two-letter abbreviations for states and provinces and the abbreviations for organizations and government agencies. Check a dictionary or an English handbook when you are not sure. Avoid most abbreviations in formal writing.

> Mrs. Donna A. West
> 6 yd.
> 8 bu.
> BC (British Columbia)
> FDA (Food and Drug Administration)

9. *Use a question mark after an interrogative sentence or quotation.* For emphasis, you may use question marks between items in a series within an interrogative sentence.

> "Is it time for lunch already?" asked Warren.
> Have you read the entire lesson? answered all the questions? learned the memory verse?

10. *Use a question mark within parentheses to indicate uncertainty about the preceding information.*

> Abram Martin moved from the Jura Mountains (?) to Lancaster in 1725.

11. *Use an exclamation point after a strong interjection and after an exclamatory sentence or quotation.*

> "Behold! What a wonderful Saviour is Jesus!" declared Brother Amos.

Applying the Lesson

A. Write correctly each word or abbreviation that has a capitalization error.

1. our heavenly father tenderly cares for his children.
2. the lord has preserved the bible unto our generation.
3. Because the canaanites served false Gods, israel was commanded to destroy them.
4. Even in the days of the Apostles, many false Christs were trying to undermine the gospel.
5. For many years, New York city depended heavily on Ferries.
6. A dutchman named cornelis dircksen started the first ferry line between manhattan and brooklyn in 1638.
7. Cornelis lived on Manhattan island and ferried people across the east river to Brooklyn, where a fast-growing dutch settlement was located.
8. During the 1800s, the City swelled with european immigrants.
9. According to the october 1959 *american heritage,* scores of ferries served the Region by 1910.
10. Yes, i enjoyed the story "apple on my conscience" in aunt Norma's book *short stories and illustrations*.
11. A nabisco shredded wheat biscuit soaked in hot milk makes a delicious Breakfast on a chilly Winter morning.
12. Our neighbor bought a honda riding mower at White Corner equipment last saturday.
13. Yesterday i attended ascension day services at Mount Dillborn Mennonite church.
14. In closing, Brother Harvey said, "consider well, o Youth, that your present choices will deeply influence your future character."
15. In Science class, we discussed some recent discoveries about jupiter, as reported in the *daily times of Lockesburg*.
16. We had our first snow before thanksgiving day; by christmas, the snow was here to stay until Spring.
17. Yesterday the president announced that the head of the epa had resigned.
18. In our History class on monday, we learned about the treaty of ghent.
19. On our trip to visit my Grandparents in the south, we met a swiss family.
20. The president toured the northeast to see the damage inflicted by hurricane edna.
21. We saw a picture of the *allegheny climber* in *reminiscences of early trains*.
22. The Doctor gave father an informative pamphlet from the aha.
23. When grandfather prayed, he said, "help us to remember, o Lord, that our Christian Heritage is a priceless blessing."
24. Carlton's country market is running a special on mueller's noodles the Week of the nineteenth.

B. Copy each word that should be followed by end punctuation, and add the correct mark.

1. What a privilege it is to know a heavenly Father's care

2. Do you truly trust His care when peace rests on your life's sea when storms of trouble threaten to sink your ship of faith when undercurrents of temptations pull you toward the rocks of sin
3. "How thankful we can be that God will never forsake His children" declared Father
4. Curtis wondered why we often tend to worry rather than trust
5. "Do you suppose it's because we tend to look at ourselves too much and at God too little" Carol asked
6. "If only we could readily see the folly of trusting in ourselves" she mused
7. Can you name examples of self-confident people from the Old Testament from the New Testament from recent times
8. Gerald asked if King Asa was one such example

C. Write a correct abbreviation for each word or phrase.

1. United Parcel Service
2. before midday *(ante meridiem)*
3. page
4. Company
5. Monday
6. ounce
7. Pacific Standard Time
8. northeast
9. Alaska
10. miles per hour

Review Exercises

Copy each numbered word, and write the abbreviation for the part of speech that it is.

noun—n.	adjective—adj.	conjunction—conj.
pronoun—pron.	adverb—adv.	interjection—interj.
verb—v.	preposition—prep.	

Is the Sea of Galilee a sea [1]or a [2]lake? [3]Well, [4]since [5]this body of water is not part [6]of an ocean, geographers [7]actually classify [8]it as a lake. It is also [9]known as the Lake of Gennesaret and the Sea of Tiberias. [10]With its clear, [11]sparkling waters and its soft, balmy [12]breezes, [13]this is one of the [14]most beautiful lakes in the world. [15]Jewish [16]rabbis wrote long ago, "The Lord [17]created [18]seven seas, [19]but the Sea of Gennesaret is His [20]delight."

---

2. Commas

1. *Use a comma before the coordinating conjunction that joins the clauses of a compound sentence.* (The common coordinating conjunctions are *and, but, or, for, nor, yet,* and *so.*) If the clauses are very short and closely related, you may omit the comma. If one or both of the clauses are long and already contain several commas, the comma between the clauses is often changed to a semicolon to make the division between the clauses more clear.

Youth is a time of great energy, but that energy must be directed properly.

Seek the Lord and He will direct you.
Three important virtues are faith, hope, and love; and of these three, love is the greatest.

2. *Use commas to separate items in a series.*

a. A series of words, phrases, or clauses. If a pair within the series is joined by a conjunction (as *chicken and rice* in the second example below), no comma is used between those two items. If a writer wishes to emphasize the number and variety of the things listed, he may connect all the items with conjunctions and omit the commas.

Stephen mowed the lawn, trimmed the hedge, and washed the car.
Mother suggested that Kathryn could make baked beans, chicken and rice, or pizza for lunch.
Bethany cooed and squealed and laughed and waved as the children played with her.

b. A series of descriptive adjectives that have equal rank. When two adjectives have equal rank, (1) you generally pause as you read them, (2) you could place *and* between them, and (3) you generally could switch their order. Sometimes the adjective immediately before the noun is closely related to the noun (almost like a compound noun) and should not be preceded by a comma.

A crooked, gnarled apple tree stood forlornly beside the deserted shack. (*Crooked* and *gnarled* have equal rank, but *apple* is closely related to *tree*.)

3. *Use commas to set off certain introductory material.*

a. Words of response and mild interjections.

No, I did not know the answer.
Oh, Velma has the dictionary now.

b. Verbal phrases.

Painted in large letters, the Gospel sign catches many people's attention.

c. Long prepositional phrases or a series of prepositional phrases. Do not use a comma, however, if a sentence has inverted word order.

To the salt lick beside the brook, many deer come regularly.
To the salt lick beside the brook come many deer.
(inverted word order—no comma)

d. Adverb clauses.

If we sit quietly behind these bushes, we should see a number of deer within an hour.

4. *Use commas to set off nonrestrictive and parenthetical elements.*

a. Nonrestrictive words, phrases, and clauses used as adjectives. Whereas a restrictive adjective limits the meaning of a substantive by telling *which one,* a nonrestrictive adjective merely gives additional information. Because it is not needed to make the meaning of the sentence clear, it is set off with commas.

Harlan and Wilmer, tired and thirsty, deserve a break.
(words are nonrestrictive—set off with commas)
The boys <u>inside</u> are resting from their hard work.
(word is restrictive—no comma)

Mabel, humming softly to herself, snapped the green beans.
(phrase is nonrestrictive—set off with commas)
The girl humming softly to herself is Mabel.
(phrase is restrictive—no commas)

b. Nonrestrictive appositives. Like an adjective phrase, an appositive is nonrestrictive if it merely gives additional information about the substantive it follows. It is restrictive if it is necessary to the meaning of a sentence and restricts that substantive. A restrictive appositive generally consists of only one or two words and is closely related to the substantive it follows.

Paul, the apostle to the Gentiles, wrote many New Testament epistles.
(appositive is nonrestrictive—set off with commas)
The apostle Paul wrote many New Testament epistles.
(appositive is restrictive—no commas)

In the phrase "the apostle Paul," you may think *apostle* should be capitalized because it is a title. But consider that *the* does not normally come before a title of respect; "the Brother Paul" would not be correct. So "the apostle Paul" must be a phrase in which the noun *apostle* is followed by the appositive *Paul*.

c. Titles of family relationship or of professional rank that follow names.

Lloyd Smith, Jr., lives next door to us.
Our family physician is Dr. George Wampler, M.D.

d. Nouns of direct address.

Clara, this pie is delicious! Your answer, Lyle, makes a good point.

e. Parenthetical expressions such as explanatory words, transitional expressions, and contrasting ideas.

The truth of the matter, no doubt, will become known eventually.
Furthermore, we know that God will settle all accounts.
God's will, not public opinion, should govern our decisions.

5. *Use commas in certain conventional situations.*

a. To separate the parts of addresses and dates.

Route 4, Box 113
Souderton, PA 18924
September 9, 20—

On July 15, 2000, the Witmers moved to 5245 Snow Avenue, Akron, Ohio, to help with the church work there.

b. To separate large numerals into periods of thousands, millions, and so forth.

186,000 miles per second 4,122 people

c. To follow the greeting of a friendly letter and the closing of any letter.

Dear Aunt Lucy, Sincerely yours,

d. To separate a direct quotation from the rest of the sentence unless some other punctuation is used.

"Gertie is quite a mischievous little goat," commented Sandra.
"It seems that every time we turn around," continued Alice, "she is finding a new kind of mischief."

6. *Use a comma if it is needed to prevent misunderstanding.* Only rarely should you use a comma that is not clearly required by one of the basic rules. Using too many commas is just as undesirable as omitting necessary commas.

This spring, housecleaning the church will be quite a task.
(comma needed to prevent reading *This spring housecleaning* as a phrase)

Applying the Lesson

A. Write the number and letter of the rule illustrated by each comma. If two commas have the same letter, one rule applies to that pair.

1. Hear us,[a] heavenly Father,[a] and grant us Thy blessing,[b] free and abundant.
2. Because we trust our heavenly Father's care,[a] our hearts are not filled with anxious,[b] unsettled thoughts.
3. Standing on the promises of God's Word,[a] we are truly secure,[b] for God's Word never changes.
4. Jesus Christ,[a] who endured strong temptations Himself,[a] is well able to understand,[b] comfort,[b] and strengthen those who are tempted today.
5. Francisco Gomez,[a] Juan's uncle,[a] was a gentle,[b] respectable man.
6. He was not,[a] however,[a] a Christian,[b] so we prayed daily for his salvation.
7. "After we helped him rebuild his fire-damaged house,[a] he started coming to church,"[b] Ramon recalled.
8. "Well,[a] sometimes God does use adversity to lead men to repentance,"[b] stated Aunt Dora.
9. In any event,[a] we all rejoice to see him serving the Lord,[b] desiring to be baptized,[b] and taking his place as a Christian father.
10. Around the outside of the cottage,[a] several flower beds,[b] Mrs. Stutzman's handiwork,[b] flaunt their rich colors and fragrances.
11. Inside,[a] the windowsills are loaded with flowers that are planted in the unique boxes built by Abraham M. Stutzman,[b] Sr.

12. Having admired his handiwork before,[a] I wonder,[b] Mrs. Stutzman,[b] how your husband did such good work despite his handicap.
13. On Uncle Laban's farm in Maryland,[a] migrant workers harvested 50,000[b] pounds of watermelons by August 1,[c] 20—.
14. Above,[a] the dark clouds rolled in threateningly as we entered the office of Malcolm S. Gruber,[b] M.D.,[b] of Fairview,[c] Alberta.

B. Copy each word or number with which a comma should be used, and put the comma where it belongs.

1. Yes God has blessed us abundantly but we are too often ungrateful.
2. From the Bible principles can be applied to every temptation every trial and every task.
3. By the power of the Gospel you can surely live consistently O youth.
4. If we cultivate a respectful outlook we can experience contrary to the ideas of many a truly satisfying relationship with those in authority.
5. Flourishing in the cooler ocean waters several species of Laminariales better known as kelp serve as a significant resource for man.
6. Growing as long as two hundred feet the giant kelp which grows only in the Pacific Ocean is the largest of the kelps.
7. Because the ocean waves and currents are constantly moving God has designed these large kelps with holdfasts rootlike structures that attach the kelp to the ocean floor.
8. The Japanese have gathered kelp for food for centuries and various kinds of kelp important resources yet today are still harvested in large quantities.
9. Kelp is used for example in manufacturing ice cream mayonnaise aspirin and skin lotions.
10. Well Cindy kelp is also used extensively as fertilizer and as a valuable concentrated source of iodine.
11. At our barn yards of concrete were poured on July 15 20— to make a smooth spacious holding area.
12. After five hours of driving we finally arrived at Uncle Glen's farm near Markham Illinois.

Review Exercises

Write correctly each word that should be capitalized. If no capital letter is needed, write *correct.* [1] (Turn to the lesson number in brackets if you need help.)

1. at rocky springs country store
2. a letter from aunt susan
3. for thy service, o lord
4. a french family from the west
5. a lutheran family at church
6. a large river of sandy valley
7. between spring and autumn
8. both spanish and typing II
9. my uncle's book, *in all things*
10. the edict of [illegible]

3. Improving Your Writing Style, Part 1: Originality

You have had many lessons on writing with good content and organization. This is important, for writing must say something meaningful and say it logically if readers are to understand it.

But content and organization alone do not produce effective writing. How many times have you started to read something, decided it was not interesting, and laid it aside without finishing it? You can be assured that people will do the same thing with your writing if it fails to capture their interest. The challenge is to write in a way that gets and keeps the reader's attention.

How can we accomplish this? These lessons on writing style will give a number of helps for making our writing more interesting and enjoyable to read.

A major element of an effective and forceful style is ***originality.*** Do not always settle for the first thing that comes to your mind. Seek rather to be creative, to express your ideas in a way that is fresh, a way that the reader will enjoy. For example, in describing some unusually warm weather, you could write the following sentence.

> On July 15 the temperature reached 101 degrees, breaking a 75-year record.

This sentence expresses its thought clearly. Anyone who knows English should be able to understand it. But stop and think. Can you say this in a more appealing way, a way deliberately designed to be interesting? One writer stated it like this:

> On July 15 the temperature reached 101 degrees, melting a 75-year record.

To speak of *melting a record* is a surprising twist that we can hardly fail to notice—and enjoy. As a matter of fact, heat does generally melt things rather than break them! And whether a record is *broken* or *melted,* it no longer stands. By the skillful choice of one unusual word, the writer has stated his point in a way that sparks our interest.

Here is another example to consider.

> By the end of the hike, my knees were aching terribly.

Most of us have experienced something like this. If our knees were not aching, then our feet or ankles were. We understand the sentence clearly. Now compare the following way of saying the same thing.

> By the end of the hike, my knees were begging for relief.

Which way of writing carries more force? Most people will agree that the second example is more interesting. To say that knees are begging for relief clearly conveys the agony felt by the writer. His knees did not beg with words, of course, but they did beg with cries of pain. We enjoy this kind of writing because the writer has given careful thought to expressing himself creatively.

In your effort to be creative, be careful that you do not merely use descriptive phrases that most people have heard before. The following sentence has a phrase like that.

> I felt uncomfortable because he was watching me like a hawk.

Hawks have extremely keen eyesight, and to speak of *watching like a hawk* is quite descriptive. However, we have heard this phrase so many times before that it now lacks the force that it once had. A phrase like this is a ***cliché*** (klē·shā′). You have heard many such expressions.

> After all is said and done, Jeremy usually accomplishes more than Curvin does.
> With diligent application, my scores improved by leaps and bounds.
> Your hands are as cold as ice.
> Eleanor proved quite equal to the occasion.

Clichés are common in speech, when people have little time to think of original expressions. But in writing you usually have plenty of time to express yourself creatively. Put that time to good use, and let your readers enjoy the results.

In striving for originality, you need to beware of two pitfalls. One of these is the temptation to step over the bounds of propriety. You must never stoop to using slangy expressions or expressions that treat sacred subjects lightly or irreverently. This kind of originality cheapens your work and weakens its power to convey a worthwhile message.

The other pitfall is to try so hard to be original that your writing sounds strained. If a student writes expressions that he would consider too pretentious for speech, he has probably fallen into this trap. You do not need to write something unusual in every other sentence. Originality is truly effective only when it flows from an active, imaginative mind.

No originality:

> The June sun shone brightly through the hazy sky as we slowly picked strawberries. In the heat we sweated profusely.

Strained:

> The June sun blazed relentlessly through the hazy gases that surrounded us and the strawberry beds. As we slowly advanced down the extensive rows, our faces were drowned in oceans of perspiration. The salty substance caused burning sensations as it poured down our faces and necks.

Creative:

> The June sun beat us mercilessly as we inched down the long strawberry rows. With rivers of sweat coursing down our necks, we writhed along under its lashes.

For these lessons on writing style, you will write various compositions that your teacher will likely evaluate by using the chart below. The element introduced in this first lesson is *Originality,* so this assignment will be evaluated only for that point of emphasis. The element introduced in the next writing style lesson will be *Active Verbs,* and then you will be evaluated on both originality and active verbs.

Each of the third through fifth writing style lessons will introduce another point of emphasis, and each will add one more item to the number of points on which your writing is evaluated. The last lesson is a review of the five elements of effective writing style.

Evaluation of Writing Style

Part	*Points of Emphasis*				
	Originality	*Active Verbs*	*Active Voice*	*Poetic Devices*	*Sentence Rhythm*
1.	———	....	....	....	....
2.	———	———	....	....	....
3.	———	———	———	....	....
4.	———	———	———	———	....
5.	———	———	———	———	———
6.	———	———	———	———	———

G = Good **F** = Fair **P** = Poor

Now read the following sample compositions. Especially compare the underlined words in the first one with the way the same thought is expressed in the second one. Can you appreciate the originality that is evident in the second composition? Do you see how a writer's thought and effort can greatly improve the style of his composition?

Perils Among the Poles

Lacks originality:

Our pole lima beans were bearing a very heavy crop. Father was away for a meeting in another state. Mother was caring for baby Brian, and the older boys were busy in the fields. That meant that I, the only girl in the family, had to pick those beans all alone! Even before nine o'clock, the air was shimmering with heat waves. I sighed as I glanced at all those big bean tepees standing around me in the garden.

Already tired of the boring job, I reached down to pick some fat beans near the ground. A warty toad, disturbed from its position under the leaves, hopped across my hand. I jumped but sighed with relief as it hopped out of sight.

After picking from a few more stalks, I reached into a spider web, nearly touching a big black spider. The spider disappeared.

Illustrates originality:

Our pole lima beans were bearing quite well—too well, it seemed to me. Father was away for a meeting in another state. Mother was caring for baby Brian, and the older boys were busy in the fields. That meant that I, the only girl in the family, was stuck in the bean patch by myself! Even before nine o'clock, the air was shimmering with heat waves. I sighed as I glanced at all those bean tepees standing like green giants around me.

Already aching with the monotony of the job, I reached down to pick some fat beans near the ground. A warty toad, surprised from its hideout under the leaves, hopped across my hand. I jumped but sighed with relief as it hopped out of sight.

A few stalks later, I reached into a spider web, nearly touching a big black spider. The spider quickly retreated. I shuddered

(Lacks originality)

I shuddered and stifled a scream. I did not pick any more beans on that part of the stalk!

I had barely moved away from that spider when I felt something land on my shoulder. Turning my head, I saw a big grasshopper. My bucket flew out of my hand as I swatted the ugly thing away.

For a while I picked beans in peace. The sun bore down hotter and hotter. My back ached. The shade of the big oak tree was a very inviting sight. Then I spotted a praying mantis, almost invisible on a green stalk. Fascinated, I watched it slowly swivel its triangular head. But the beans were waiting to be picked, so I reluctantly left the praying mantis behind.

My job was almost finished when I had the worst fright of all. I thrust my head into a tepee to see if any beans were in there. Suddenly I saw a beady-eyed garter snake! With a terrified screech, I jumped back, landing right on top of my bucket. I did not pick any more beans on that stalk either!

After I had finally circled the last tepee, I pulled the wagonload of beans over to the back yard. What a relief to sit down under that old oak!

(Illustrates originality)

and stifled a scream. The beans on that part of the stalk stayed right there for the spider!

I had barely escaped from that spider when I felt something land on my shoulder. Turning my head, I found myself eye to eye with a great green grasshopper. My bucket flew out of my hand as I swatted the ugly thing away.

For a while I picked beans in peace. The sun bore down hotter and hotter. My back cried for relief. The shade of the big oak tree beckoned invitingly. Then I spotted a praying mantis, almost invisible on a green stalk. Fascinated, I watched it slowly swivel its triangular head. But the beans were waiting to be picked, so I reluctantly left the praying mantis to guard that tepee.

My job was almost finished when I had the worst fright of all. I thrust my head into a tepee to find any beans hiding there. Suddenly I was peering into the beady eyes of a garter snake! With a terrified screech, I jumped back, landing right on top of my bucket. The beans still on that stalk ripened some more too!

After I had finally circled the last tepee, I pulled the wagonload of beans over to the back yard. What a relief to gain the safety of that old oak!

Applying the Lesson

Write a composition of 150–200 words, telling about an interesting experience you had this past summer. Can you incorporate originality and creativity that will make your writing interesting to read? Do your best!

4. Colons, Semicolons, and Ellipsis Points

Colons

1. *Use a colon to separate the numbers in Scripture references and in expressions of time.*

Ecclesiastes 12:1 3:45 P.M.

2. *Use a colon after the salutation of a business letter.*

Dear Sir: Gentlemen: Dear Mr. Irvington:

3. *Use a colon to introduce something that is to follow.* What follows may be a list, an explanation, a question, an appositive, or a formal quotation. In this use, the colon is a literary arrow: it points to the information that follows, directing the reader's attention there.

Our congregation has scheduled street meetings on the following dates: June 3, July 1, and August 5.
Our street meetings serve one basic purpose: spreading the Gospel.

If a complete sentence follows a colon, that sentence may begin with a capital letter, especially if it is long.

Many ask a simple but profound question: Who are you people, and why do you dress as you do?

A formal quotation is a notable statement made by a respected or high-ranking person. If it is introduced by a colon, it must be written with quotation marks and proper capitalization.

Calvin Coolidge made this worthwhile statement: "There is no dignity quite so impressive and no independence quite so satisfying as living within your means."

The words before a colon must express a complete thought. Therefore, a colon should never separate a verb from its complement or a preposition from its object.

Incorrect:
The electric eel lives in rivers of: Peru, Colombia, Brazil, and Venezuela.
Correct:
The electric eel lives in rivers of Peru, Colombia, Brazil, and Venezuela.
Correct:
The electric eel lives in rivers of the following countries: Peru, Colombia, Brazil, and Venezuela.

Semicolons

4. *Use a semicolon to join independent clauses in certain cases.*
   a. When no conjunction is used.

More than half of an electric eel's body contains organs that produce electricity; the snakelike creature can deliver a powerful charge.

b. When a conjunctive adverb is used.

No other fish can deliver a greater electric shock; indeed, it produces enough electricity to turn on eleven 100-watt light bulbs.

c. When commas are already used in one or more of the clauses. Sometimes either a comma or a semicolon is correct, depending on the degree of separation intended by the writer.

With a discharge of over six hundred volts, the electric eel can paralyze humans; [*or* humans,] yet neither the eel itself nor other eels suffer any apparent effects.

5. *Use a semicolon to separate items in a series when individual items contain commas.*

On our trip we visited Uncle Seth Krahn, Mother's oldest brother; Calvin Witmer's family; and Wayne Nolt's family.

Ellipsis Points

6. *Use ellipsis points to show an omission within a quotation.* Such an omission may be desirable when space is limited or when the omitted words do not apply specifically to the subject under discussion. But you need to guard against changing the meaning of a quotation by a careless omission. And you must *never* change the meaning deliberately by omitting certain words.

Original:

And be not conformed to this world: but be ye transformed by the renewing of your mind, that ye may prove what is that good, and acceptable, and perfect, will of God. [Romans 12:2]

Unacceptable quotation:

"And be not conformed to this world: . . . that ye may prove what is that good, and acceptable, and perfect, will of God."

(May suggest that merely being different from the world, without an inner change, is God's will.)

Acceptable quotation:

"And be not conformed to this world: but be ye transformed, . . . that ye may prove what is that good, and acceptable, and perfect, will of God."

When omitting words within a sentence, you may choose to retain or omit the punctuation immediately before or after the omission. If you retain punctuation, place it directly after the first part (before the ellipsis points). Study the following example, which shows three possible ways to punctuate the same quotation.

Original:

Do violence to no man, neither accuse any falsely; and be content with your wages. [Luke 3:14]

Quotations:

"Do violence to no man,... and be content with your wages."
(comma retained)

"Do violence to no man;... and be content with your wages."
(semicolon retained)

"Do violence to no man... and be content with your wages."
(no punctuation retained)

When you quote two sentences and omit the ending of the first sentence, place the appropriate end punctuation directly after the first part if it makes a complete sentence. Then use ellipsis points to show the omission, and continue with the quotation.

Original:

Wherefore the king said unto me, Why is thy countenance sad, seeing thou art not sick? this is nothing else but sorrow of heart. Then I was very sore afraid. [Nehemiah 2:2]

Quotation:

"Wherefore the king said unto me, Why is thy countenance sad?... Then I was very sore afraid."

Do not use ellipsis points at the beginning or end of a quotation. Remember: Ellipsis points indicate an omission *within* a quotation. They are not necessary at the beginning or the end.

Incorrect quotations:

"Wherefore the king said unto me, Why is thy countenance sad... ?"

"... Why is thy countenance sad... ?"

Correct quotations:

"Wherefore the king said unto me, Why is thy countenance sad?"

"Why is thy countenance sad?"

(No ellipsis points are needed even though the beginning and ending of the verse are omitted.)

7. *Use ellipsis points to indicate that a sentence trails off without a proper ending.* Do not use any end punctuation with these ellipsis points.

Well, the kitchen floor still needs to be mopped, but...

Applying the Lesson

A. Write the number and letter of the rule illustrated by each colon, semicolon, or set of ellipsis points. If two marks have the same letter, one rule applies to that pair.

1. "Lay up...[a] treasures in heaven," our permanent home;[b] but while you sojourn on this earth, be a good steward of material possessions.
2. After giving His model prayer, Jesus emphasized one point: forgiveness.
3. The Lord's Prayer, as we commonly call it, gives us an important pattern for prayer; Jesus surely did not intend that it be repeated meaninglessly.

4. "Not every one that saith . . .[a] Lord, Lord, shall enter into the kingdom of heaven";[b] indeed, many in our day profess to know the Lord but deny Him by their lives.
5. Grandmother must take these pills at the following times:[a] before breakfast, at 2:00[b] P.M., and at bedtime.
6. On Sunday we had visitors from the following places:[a] West Liberty, Kentucky;[b] Versailles, Missouri;[b] and Columbiana, Ohio.
7. Someone must have left the gate open, and now . . .
8. After being off for over four hours, our electricity came on at 5:20 P.M.
9. The teachers at our school are Sister Ada Mae Hoover, grades 1–3; Sister Betty Zehr, grades 4–6; and Brother Alvin Yoder, grades 7–10.
10. The snow is falling very thickly now;[a] Father must have . . .[b]

B. Copy each word or number with which there is a punctuation error. Place the correct mark where it belongs, or omit the unnecessary mark.
1. The doldrums, vast areas of the ocean near the equator, have little wind, so early sailors, who depended on wind power, feared these regions.
2. Sometimes ships drifted aimlessly in the doldrums for weeks until
3. Man conquered the doldrums when ocean travel was changed by one major invention, the steam engine.
4. The doldrums form where the trade winds on the two sides of the equator meet, the winds are forced upward, leaving the area below calm.
5. The sun shone brightly, however, a brisk north wind kept the temperature cool.
6. Heavy snow fell during the morning hours, moreover, by 200 P.M. a strong wind began to blow.
7. We had expected Grandpa's to arrive by 430 P.M., but since it's 600 now, we
8. Mr. Lawson has orders for chairs on: Monday, June 16, Wednesday, July 16, and Friday, August 15.
9. The only people named in the Bible as lifelong Nazarites were: Samson, a judge of Israel, Samuel, another judge, and John the Baptist, the forerunner of Christ.
10. Because God is all-wise, He can best choose the way for us, and because He is all-gracious, He can choose the best way for us.

C. Copy these quotations, using ellipsis points correctly to indicate omissions.
1. "But he that is an hireling seeth the wolf coming, and leaveth the sheep" (John 10:12).
2. "Looking unto Jesus; who for the joy that was set before him endured the cross" (Hebrews 12:2).
3. "And the LORD said unto Cain, Why art thou wroth? If thou doest well, shalt thou not be accepted?" (Genesis 4:6, 7).
4. "His name shall endure for ever: all nations shall call him blessed" (Psalm 72:17).

Review Exercises

For each underlined word, write *yes* or *no* to tell whether it should be followed by a comma. [2]

1. Our thoughts the source of our conduct, must be guarded with strict constant care.
2. In your mind set patterns of thinking become entrenched and strongly affect your entire life.
3. "Consider carefully, dear friend what the quality of your thoughts reveals about your character" Brother Fred exhorted.
4. If we fill our minds with good thoughts we can develop the noble character that pleases God.
5. Lo God provides for us through His Word, His Spirit and His people.

---

5. Quotation Marks and Italics

Quotation Marks

1. *Enclose a direct quotation in quotation marks.* In a divided quotation, capitalize the second part only if it begins a new sentence.

> "Standing firmly for what you know is right," observed Father, "is not always the easiest thing to do."
> "But it is always the right thing to do," added Mother. "And God will surely bless you if you have a good purpose of heart."

In a quotation of more than one paragraph, place quotation marks at the beginning of each paragraph. Do not place quotation marks at the end of a paragraph, except the last one.

2. *Enclose a quotation from a printed source in quotation marks.*

> In *Doctrines of the Bible,* Daniel Kauffman writes, "The tempter has hard work making inroads into the lives of those who habitually wrestle with God in prayer."

If a quotation is long, it may be printed in smaller type as an indented block without quotation marks.

3. *Enclose the title of a minor work in quotation marks.* Minor works include songs, short stories, sections of books, and poems less than book length. Generally, a comma is unnecessary before such a title.

> In the book *Selections for Oral Reading,* I especially enjoyed the story "Strange Tracks on the Hill" and the poem "Winter Winds."

4. *Use single quotation marks for a quotation within a quotation.* For the rare

occasion when another quotation occurs within the inner quotation, use another set of double quotation marks.

> "The apostle Paul could declare, 'I have learned, in whatsoever state I am, therewith to be content,' " commented Brendon.
>
> "I think I heard Wanda say, 'I like the other tune of "Jesus, Lover of My Soul" better,' " said Dorothy.

5. *You may use quotation marks to enclose an expression you wish to call into question.* If you use *so-called,* however, do not also use quotation marks.

> Apostate churches often try to cover up their disobedience to the Scriptures with "spiritual" activities.
>
> Apostate churches often try to cover up their disobedience to the Scriptures with so-called spiritual activities.

Be careful not to overuse quotation marks for this purpose. They tend to make writing look cluttered.

Other Punctuation With Quotation Marks

6. *If a quotation is followed by a comma or period, place that mark inside the quotation marks.*

> "For reading class on Monday," said Brother James, "practice reading the poem 'A Fence or an Ambulance.' "

Note this exception to the rule above: If a reference follows a quotation from a written source, place the reference in parentheses after the quotation marks, and place the comma or period after the parentheses.

> "The Lord is risen indeed" (Luke 24:34), and we rejoice in the salvation that He has wrought.

7. *If a quotation is followed by a colon or semicolon, place that mark outside the quotation marks.*

> When life goes smoothly, we can easily pray, "Thy will be done"; when life is full of difficulty, however, that prayer becomes much more difficult.

8. *If a quotation is followed by a dash, a question mark, or an exclamation point, place that mark inside the quotation marks if it applies to the quotation, and outside the quotation marks if it applies to the whole sentence.*

> Suddenly James shouted, "Watch those top bales!"
> (The exclamation point applies to the quotation.)
>
> Did Fanny Crosby write the words to "Safe in the Arms of Jesus"?
> (The question mark applies to the whole sentence, not to the quotation.)
>
> Jesus said, "Blessed are the poor in spirit"—a direct contrast to human philosophy. (The dash applies to the whole sentence, not to the quotation.)

9. *If a sentence contains a quotation within a quotation, place the question mark or exclamation point with the part of the sentence that is a question or an exclamation.*

"Was Mother saying, 'Dinner is ready'?" asked Elton.
(The inner quotation is not a question, so the question mark is outside the single quotation mark. But Elton's words are a question, so the question mark is inside the double quotation marks.)
"Was Mother asking, 'Are you ready for dinner?' " asked Elton.
(Both the inner quotation and Elton's words are questions, so the mark is inside both the single and the double quotation marks.)

Italics

Italics are not actually punctuation marks. But since they help us to communicate clearly, they are part of the mechanics of English just as capitalization and punctuation are. In handwritten or typewritten material, italics are indicated by underlining.

10. *Use italics for the title of a major work.* Major works include books, newspapers, pamphlets, book-length poems, and periodicals such as church papers, magazines, and newsletters. Italicize and capitalize an article (*a, an, the*) when it begins a book title, but not when it begins the title of a newspaper or periodical.

For my birthday, Grandfather gave the book *The Valley Between.*
I was inspired by the article "Lord, Teach Us to Pray" in the *Christian Contender.*
(not *The Christian Contender,* even though that is the actual title of this periodical)

11. *Use italics for the specific name of a ship, an airplane, a train, or another vehicle.*

Our veterinarian, Dr. Jansen, calls his van the *Vet Express.*
(*The* is usually not part of the specific name.)

12. *Use italics for a word, phrase, letter, number, or symbol that is the subject of discussion.* Such an item is not being used in its normal sense, but is being discussed as a word, phrase, letter, or other symbol.

Your *e* is so tall that this word looks more like *quilt* than *quiet.*
When you use *for example* as a parenthetical element, set it off with commas.
The # symbol can mean "pounds."

13. *Italicize foreign words that have not been adopted into the English language.*

The common abbreviation *e.g.* comes from the Latin words *exempli gratia.*

14. *You may occasionally use italics for emphasis.* Use italics sparingly for this purpose; otherwise, they will lose their effectiveness.

You must *learn to study* before you can *study to learn.*

Applying the Lesson

A. If the underlined part of the sentence has a punctuation error, write it correctly. If it is correct, write *correct.*

1. "Have you considered Jesus' words, 'Out of the abundance of the heart the mouth speaketh?' " asked Brother Dale.
2. "How wonderful that we can say, 'The Lord is my helper!' " declared Mother.
3. Brother Lavern said, "Let's practice the slurs in 'All Hail, Immanuel!' "
4. "Plutarch said, 'Nothing is cheap which is superfluous, for what one does not need, is dear at a penny,' " quoted Father.
5. Many things are promised to "him that overcometh:" hidden manna, a white stone with a new name, and other rewards.
6. Jesus plainly taught, "Swear not at all"; therefore, we refuse to give a legal oath.
7. Charles Wesley, who wrote thousands of hymns, wrote "A Charge to Keep I Have".
8. "Did Mr. Griggs ask, 'Will you folks come back to sing for us again'?" asked Mae.
9. William exclaimed, "What a shock to hear the man shout, 'Get out of here!' "
10. "I want you to read the story 'Is That All'?" said Martha.
11. "Jeremy Taylor wrote to be proud of learning is the greatest ignorance,' " said Sister Arlene.
12. You should meditate on the words of "Love and Help Each Other."

B. Copy the words with which there are errors in the use of punctuation or italics (underlining), and put the missing marks where they belong. Do not punctuate words as a direct quotation unless the sentence has explanatory words.

1. Have you read the chapter The Bible in Doctrines of the Bible? asked Mark.
2. This Christian nation is actually notorious for its evil.
3. The Christianity preached by many is a disgrace to the Name of Christ.
4. Did you think about it, Aaron, asked Brother Stoltzfus that you repeated the word and four times in this sentence?
5. The motto of Arizona is ditat Deus, meaning "God enriches."
6. The Bible clearly teaches that God created the world ex nihilo (out of nothing).
7. The second syllable in respite rhymes with fit.
8. The book I am reading, Insect Parables, has an intriguing chapter titled The Maker of Ping-Pong Balls.
9. The first Mennonite immigrants to the Lancaster area noted Grandfather arrived in Philadelphia on September 22, 1710, aboard the Maria Hope.
10. My cousins named their rowboat the Cocalico Cruiser.

Review Exercises

Write correctly each word that should be capitalized. If no capital letter is needed, write *correct.* [1]

1. to the gateway arch last summer
2. saw the president in washington

3. the poem "an answer to the cry"
4. saw chinese foods in wan's grocery
5. with father and my uncle
6. bought knapp shoes and some stanley tools
7. went west to the living desert state park
8. mr. watt of memphis, tenn.
9. visited a province farther east
10. science in the dark ages

---

6. Dashes, Parentheses, Brackets, Apostrophes, and Hyphens

Dashes

1. *Use a dash to show a sudden interruption or change in thought.*
   a. A sudden break in thought.

   "What do you think—well, I sure didn't expect that!" exclaimed Brent.

   b. Parenthetical matter that is abrupt or that has commas within it.

   I like to use *The Treasury of Scripture Knowledge*—a thorough cross-reference resource—when studying Scripture verses.

   If you want to know the original meaning of a Bible word, check *Strong's Exhaustive Concordance*—widely recognized as a thorough, dependable reference book.

   c. Interrupted speech. Ellipsis points can also indicate interrupted speech. Ellipsis points suggest hesitancy or uncertainty; a dash shows abruptness.

   "Did you hear what—" Galen stopped, remembering his resolve to avoid gossip.

Parentheses

2. *Use parentheses to enclose a parenthetical element that is relatively unimportant.*

   My parents lived near Mercersburg (James Buchanan's birthplace) for several years.

Note: Commas, dashes, and parentheses are all used to set off parenthetical elements. You must choose which to use according to the meaning you want to convey.

a. Commas make the parenthetical element a part of the sentence. Therefore, they cannot set off elements that are complete sentences or that have other punctuation. Of these three marks, commas are by far the most common in normal writing.

Amigo, our mixed-breed dog, certainly earns his keep around our farm.

b. Dashes sharply emphasize the parenthetical element. Sometimes they set off an exclamation or a question.

> Amigo—an outstanding cattle dog—certainly earns his keep around our farm.
>
> Amigo—what an outstanding cattle dog he is!—certainly earns his keep around our farm.

c. Parentheses minimize the importance of the parenthetical element, making it somewhat beside the point of the sentence.

> Amigo (someone dropped him off here when he was a puppy) certainly earns his keep around our farm.

3. *Use parentheses to enclose supplementary or illustrative matter, such as a Scripture reference or a short explanation.*

> "Can two walk together, except they be agreed?" (Amos 3:3).
>
> We looked in the Franklin County (Georgia) Courthouse for information.
>
> This issue of the *Christian Pathway* (June 15, 1997) has a story that challenges us to be kind to mentally handicapped people.

4. *Use parentheses to enclose figures or letters used for enumeration within a sentence.* If letters are used for this purpose, they should be italicized.

> We had these writing assignments during the past six weeks: (1) a story for English class, (2) a report for history class, and (3) a report on a book from the required reading list.

Brackets

5. *Use brackets to enclose a comment or correction within a quotation.*

> On the need for growth, Edward Gibbon wrote, "All that is human must retrograde [go backward] if it do not advance."

6. *Use brackets as parentheses in material already enclosed by parentheses.*

> Thailand (formerly known as Siam [sī·am′]) covers an area of 198,247 square miles.

7. *Learn the correct use of other punctuation marks with dashes, parentheses, and brackets.*

a. If a dash ends a sentence fragment, omit any end punctuation.

> "What was—" Father dashed out the door as Jonathan screamed in pain.

b. Place other punctuation marks inside these marks if they apply to the enclosed matter, and outside if they apply to the whole sentence.

> We certainly enjoyed the picnic (it was your father's idea, wasn't it?) that we had beside the pond. (question mark inside parentheses because the enclosed matter is a question)

What do you plan to do about the situation (if the report is really true)?
(question mark outside parentheses because the whole sentence is a question)

Apostrophes

8. *Use an apostrophe to form the possessive case of a noun or an indefinite pronoun.* For specific rules and examples, see Lessons 61 and 63.

9. *Use an apostrophe to show an omission in a contraction or other shortened form.* Contractions are acceptable for informal writing, such as friendly letters and the dialogue in stories. You should generally avoid them in formal writing.

isn't we're o'clock a '96 yearbook

10. *Use an apostrophe to form the plural of a letter, a figure, an abbreviation followed by a period, or a word used as the subject of discussion.* No apostrophe is needed in the plural form of a number with several digits or of an abbreviation with several capital letters (1900s, POWs). Remember to italicize (underline) such an item when it is the subject of discussion, but do not italicize the *'s.*

Change the *&*'s to *and*'s and remove the *etc.*'s.
Your essay has too many *then*'s and *so*'s.
The COs had no Th.D.'s, but they knew the Bible well.

Hyphens

11. *Use a hyphen to join some compound words.* Pay special attention to the following groups of compound words.

a. Compound number words from twenty-one through ninety-nine.

forty-two three hundred ninety-nine

b. A fraction written in words. (A hyphen joins the numerator and denominator unless either one already has a hyphen.)

one-fifth twenty-one hundredths two and two-thirds cups

c. Words ending with *-in-law.*

mother-in-law brother-in-law

d. Compound words beginning with *great-* that refer to relatives, those beginning with *self-*, and many beginning with *all-*.

great-uncle self-contained all-knowing God

e. Many compound adjectives, in which two or more words form a unit that modifies a substantive.

a four-lane highway a bad-tempered dog

f. A proper noun or adjective with a prefix.

inter-Caribbean trade anti-Biblical

12. *In a series of hyphenated adjective–noun combinations, with the noun included in only the last one, use a hyphen after each adjective.*

fifty- or sixty-hour weeks two-, five-, and ten-pound bags

13. *Use a hyphen to divide a word between syllables at the end of a line.* Observe these three rules: (1) divide only between syllables, (2) never leave a single letter at the beginning or end of a line, and (3) divide a hyphenated word only at the existing hyphen. The following words illustrate permissible divisions.

def-i-ni-tion iden-ti-cal cu-rio

14. *Use a hyphen to show a series of connected numbers, as in Scripture references or dates.*

Romans 12:1–3, 9–16 1921–1987

Applying the Lesson

A. Copy enough words to show where commas, dashes, parentheses, and brackets are needed, and add the missing marks. Some sentences have notes telling you how to treat the parenthetical elements.
   1. The Ten Commandments God Himself gave them to man express timeless principles. (sharp emphasis)
   2. The principles of the Ten Commandments which are not directly binding today have been restated in the New Testament. (part of the sentence)
   3. The Ten Commandments found in Exodus 20 reveal God's standard for man's faithfulness to Him and for man's relationships with others. (somewhat beside the point)
   4. Jesus' Sermon on the Mount here are high standards indeed! sets the spiritual tone for the New Testament church. (sharp emphasis)
   5. "And this your heave offering shall be reckoned unto you, as though it were the corn grain of the threshingfloor" Numbers 18:27.
   6. "In my Father's house are many mansions dwellings: if it were not so, I would have told you" John 14:2.
   7. "Let's get out to oh, the telephone is ringing," said Father.
   8. We shall plan to have Mrs. Wilson's vanilla pies did you know she had stopped in? for dessert. (somewhat beside the point)
   9. These loaves of bread which Karen just baked look and smell delicious. (part of the sentence)
   10. "I believe that's yes, it is Uncle Mahlon's!" exclaimed Fern.

B. Write correctly the items that have errors in the use of apostrophes or hyphens. If an item needs to be italicized, show it by underlining.
   1. When Lamech, Noahs father, was born, his great grandfather Jared had not yet lived one half his total life span.
   2. Although Noahs great grandfather Enoch lived only three hundred sixty five years, his grandfather Methuselah lived nine hundred sixty nine years.
   3. The world promotes its self expression philosophies, but the Bible teaches the humanly unpopular but soul satisfying doctrine of humility.

4. Weve a tremendous privilege to trust in Gods all sufficient grace.
5. Today Im making four, six, and eight foot stakes.
6. The post World War II era saw a marked increase in anti God attitudes.
7. My neighbors father in law still drives his original car, a 45 Buick.
8. People with Ph.D.s are not necessarily wiser than self taught people.
9. For art class, we made large scale maps of the area around the school.
10. My sister in law makes beautiful three dimensional bulletin boards for several teachers.
11. The pre Reformation years are often called the Dark Ages.
12. Mr. Garvers speech is freely punctuated with yes, wells.
13. Mrs. Steffy puts an extra line in her 7s, and they look almost like backward capital Fs.
14. In Spanish, js are pronounced like English hs.
15. As Sister Rose revealed the long awaited surprise, the younger students responded with ohs and ahs of pleasure.
16. Martha makes jelly, cream, and custard filled doughnuts to sell.
17. A two thirds majority is required for this proposal to pass.
18. We picked two and one half bushels of green beans.
19. Six, eight, and ten legged creatures are included in the group known as arthropods.
20. A lop eared rabbit stood on its hind legs and watched us.

Review Exercises

A. Write whether each underlined word should be followed by a *colon,* a *semicolon,* or *ellipsis points.* If none of these marks are needed, write *none.* [4]

1. "Mind not high <u>things</u>" (Romans 12:16).
2. Haman's character is well summarized by one <u>word</u> conceited.
3. Haman fully expected to receive the king's honor <u>himself</u> therefore, he was rudely shocked at the king's command to honor Mordecai.
4. Either wittingly or unwittingly, Haman was fighting <u>against</u> Mordecai, Esther, the Jewish nation, and God Himself.
5. "The day of the LORD of hosts shall be upon every one that is proud and <u>lofty</u>, and he shall be brought low" (Isaiah 2:12).

B. Write the letter of the sentence in which the boldface part is correct. [5]

1. a. "Was Leona talking about the poem 'Seek Him **Still'?"** asked Barbara.
   b. "Was Leona talking about the poem 'Seek Him **Still?' "** asked Barbara.
2. a. We wanted to sing "Glory Be to **God;"** however, we had no good bass.
   b. We wanted to sing "Glory Be to **God";** however, we had no good bass.
3. a. "The man on the bridge is shouting, 'Come **quick'!"** Keith exclaimed.
   b. "The man on the bridge is shouting, 'Come **quick!' "** Keith exclaimed.
4. a. I read **"Palestine Before the Conquest"** in *Baker's Bible Atlas.*
   b. I read ***Palestine Before the Conquest*** in Baker's Bible Atlas.
5. a. We crossed the lake on the **"Lake Cruiser."**
   b. We crossed the lake on the ***Lake Cruiser.***

7. Improving Your Editing Skills, Part 1

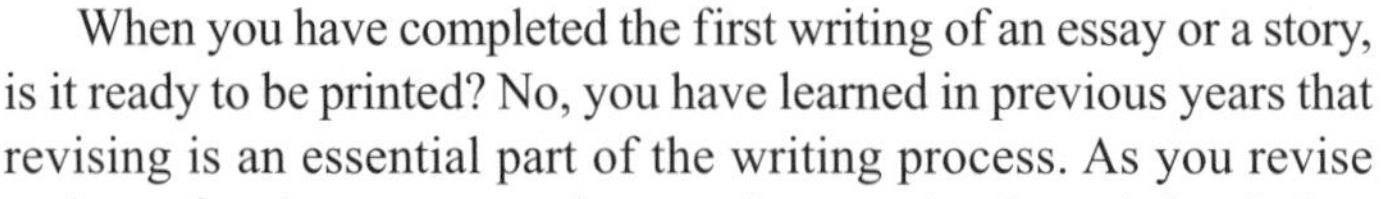

When you have completed the first writing of an essay or a story, is it ready to be printed? No, you have learned in previous years that revising is an essential part of the writing process. As you revise and proofread, you can mark your changes clearly and simply by using the standard symbols that most publishers use.

Throughout this textbook, you will find a series of lessons entitled "Improving Your Editing Skills." These lesson exercises are printed both in this textbook and in a separate booklet of tests and editing sheets, on which you can easily make your proofreading marks. The editing lessons have the following three general purposes.

1. To stimulate critical reading so that you will be able to catch errors in grammar, mechanics, and spelling.
2. To give practice in correct usage of grammar and mechanics.
3. To give practice in the use of proofreading marks.

Study the following table of proofreading marks. The sample manuscript below the table shows how the marks are used.

Marks Used in Editing and Proofreading

∨ or ∧ insert (caret)	delete	.... stet (let it stand)
¶ begin new paragraph	lc change to lowercase (small letter)	uc change to uppercase (capital letter)

Explanations	Sample Manuscript
Delete symbol has loop so that deletion is not overlooked.	Suppose you were a custommer of a
Caret shows exact point of insertion.	bank that credited your acount with
Comma after *used* is unnecessary.	$1,440 every day, and every night it canceled any amount you had not used,
Loop of delete symbol may curve down, especially if deleted item is replaced by item above.	that day. What would you do? You wood (would) make sure you used every doller, of
Any inserted punctuation is marked by a caret. Question mark or exclamation point is inserted above the caret.	course! Who would do otherwise? ¶ Well, you do have such a bank, and its name
Time is to be capitalized because it is used as a name.	is time. Every morning this bank credits you

Comma or period is inserted below the caret.
The word *stet* and the dots mean deleted item is to be retained.
Apostrophe or quotation marks are inserted above inverted caret.
Caret helps to assure that inserted hyphen is not overlooked.
Time is a common noun here.
Parentheses are inserted above carets.

```
with 1440 minutes, and every evening it
cancels any amount that you failed to
                   stet
to invest for a good purpose. It is no
one's loss but your own, for you must
                                  lc
say good-bye forever to lost Time.
Moses wrote, "So teach us to number our
days, that we may apply our hearts unto
wisdom" (Psalm 90:12).
```

Observe carefully how the proofreading marks are made, and pattern your marks after them. In this way, both you and others can easily tell what changes you intended.

Editing Practice

A. Use the proper proofreading marks to correct the errors in the sentences below. Each sentence needs one insertion and one deletion or replacement.

1. **The fear of the Lord is the begining of wisdome.**
2. **If you want be wise, fear God, obey the Bible, and respect the your parents.**
3. **Who would ever regret, any effort put forth in developing noble Christian ideals**
4. **When Josephs brothers sold him, they did not no that they would meet him in Egypt many years later.**
5. **The many plants in Grandmothers house reveal her love for growing thengs.**
6. **"How many busshels of apples did you pick? asked Kevin.**

B. Use the proper proofreading marks to correct the errors in capitalization. In each sentence, one letter should be changed to uppercase and one to lowercase.

1. **The Lord chose Paul to be the Apostle to the gentiles.**
2. **How many Sufferings he would need to endure as a christian!**
3. **Paul traveled through Asia minor and Parts of Europe, spreading the Gospel.**
4. **Do you know how many Missionary journeys are recorded in the Book of acts?**

5. **Just as I finished reading "Dreams of no Value," my Mother called.**

C. Now try your editing skills on the selection below. You will need to do the following things.
   a. Make five insertions.
   b. Make five deletions or replacements. (Be sure to read the note following the selection.)
   c. Make five corrections in capitalization.
   d. Mark two places where a new paragraph should begin.
   e. Show that one word already deleted should be retained.

This means that eighteen corrections are needed. Can you find them all?

Solar eclipses have long struk fear in the hearts of men and have given rise too many myths and superstitions. For example, the ancient chinese thought a dragon was swallowing the sun. They held ~~noisy~~ ceremonies to make the Dragon sick and cause him to spew the sun out again. Chinese astronomers were responsible to to predict coming eclipses so that the people would be ready to rescue the sun. The same kind of ignorance still exists today. Before a total eclipse occurred over south America on July 11 1991, warnings were circulated that looking any part of the sky during the eclipse could cause the blindness. Therefore, all people and livestock—especially horses—were suposed to stay inside ~~all~~ during the whole event. Another report indicated that rocks and dirt mite fall from the sky if the son and the moon rubbed against each other. How much better is knowledge than Ignorance! When a solar eclipse occurs, those living in ignorance prepare to protect themselves from imaginary dangers. But those who know the truth can appreciate the event as one the most awesome examples of God's Handiwork.

Note: In the editing lessons, you will proofread a number of paragraphs on the subject of astronomy. You will not be expected to check the spelling of proper nouns or to verify technical information, such as the distance to a star.

---

8. Chapter 1 Review

A. Use proofreading marks to correct the errors in capitalization and end punctuation.

1. **the theme for our Bible School studies this Summer is "Lessons from Bible youth"**
2. **"are you developing, o youth," asked brother Seth, "The qualities that god can use to build his kingdom"**
3. **in Math class we calculated the approximate distance that the israelites traveled from egypt to canaan.**
4. **What a surprise i had when grandfather invited me to go along to the writers' meeting at Glendale Mennonite church.**
5. **Although king Solomon gave much good advice in proverbs and ecclesiastes, he apparently did not follow it all himself.**

B. Use proofreading marks to add the missing commas.

1. "Do we my brethren have the faith, fortitude and fidelity" asked Brother Amos "to face any persecution that may come?"
2. Knowing the perils of these end times we must stay close to God's Word which is our source of spiritual direction.
3. At our church services are held on the third Sunday evening of each month and we have a song service whenever there is a fifth Sunday.
4. Mr. Alton F. Young Jr. paid $450000 for a productive well-maintained farm near Harrisonburg Virginia.
5. In the vicinity of Clarkdale a cloudburst it is reported dumped over five inches of rain.

C. Use proofreading marks to correct the errors in the use of colons, semicolons, and ellipsis points. Place ellipsis points below the caret, and colons and semicolons above the caret.

1. "This wisdom descendeth not from above, but is earthly, sensual, devilish. But the wisdom that is from above is first pure . . ." (James 3:15–17).
2. When we feel a lack of wisdom, we should remember one important fact, God gives His wisdom freely to those who sincerely ask.
3. "Surely God is good to man, but how often" Grandfather sighed.
4. Since God has blessed us richly, we should serve Him faithfully, but too many people, proud and selfish by nature, ignore God.
5. Examples of ingratitude in the Scriptures include: the children of Israel, who murmured frequently in the wilderness, Solomon, who turned to idolatry after God had enriched him supernaturally, and Jonah, who complained bitterly because God spared Nineveh.

D. Use proofreading marks to correct the errors in capitalization, punctuation, and italics.

1. Did you expect to hear Mother say, We are having vanilla pie and ice cream for dessert?
2. Get the book The Christian Short Story, and read Chapter 4, entitled Style suggested Brother Weber.
3. Mr. Reed quoted the saying, God helps them who help themselves; however, Father pointed out that this statement does not apply to salvation.
4. Uncle Ben wonders if we would like a ride on his sleigh, Queen of the Snow, which he has restored, announced Galen.

5. **Before you leave, would you folks sing Footprints of Jesus? asked Mrs. Lee.**

E. Use proofreading marks to add the missing dashes, parentheses, and brackets.
   1. **"When tribulation or persecution ariseth because of the word, by and by immediately he is offended" Matthew 13:21.**
   2. **"I don't quite oh, now I see what you mean!" exclaimed Donna.**
   3. **Our strawberries they surely produced abundantly this year! have sold well.** (give sharp emphasis)
   4. **Aunt Regina she really isn't related to us spends much time knitting.** (minimize the importance)
   5. **"Well, I certainly would not" Timothy gasped as a bolt of lightning struck the tree behind the barn.**

F. Copy each phrase, using apostrophes and hyphens correctly. If a word needs to be italicized, show it by underlining.
   1. twenty one nows in his story
   2. three, five, and ten speed bikes
   3. broke an all time record
   4. isnt a sharp tongued person
   5. wont be here before two oclock
   6. our great grandfather Newswanger
   7. my self confident sister in law
   8. a mid March snowstorm

G. Write the correct word for each blank.
   1. A good writing style helps to capture and hold the reader's ———.
   2. If writing has originality, it contains creative expressions that come from an ——— mind.
   3. A ——— is a descriptive phrase that lacks its original force because it has been used so often.
   4. In striving for originality, one pitfall is the temptation to use slang or expressions that treat ——— subjects lightly.
   5. A second pitfall is to try so hard to be original that the writing sounds ———.
   6. You should generally avoid an expression in writing if you would not consider using it in ———.

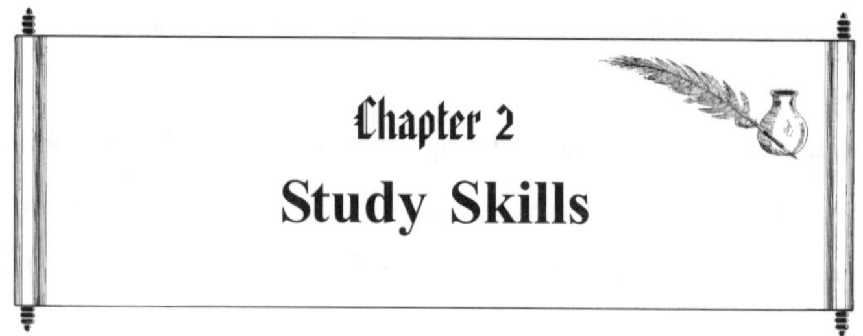

9. Preparing to Study

You have spent thousands of hours studying in school. Certainly you know how to study. But do you know how to study effectively? Do you work merely to finish your assignments, or are you striving to *learn*? Do you view your school lessons as so many tasks to toil through, or do you see them as building blocks of a productive life?

In your earliest school years, your teachers closely guided your studying. As you developed in your capacity to know and in your ability to pursue knowledge, you became more and more responsible to study on your own. You have learned much about study skills, both directly (as your teachers gave specific pointers) and indirectly (as you observed your teachers' methods and as you learned by trial and error). Now, as you stand near the end of your formal schooling, a closer look at these study skills can benefit you greatly. Although you may soon leave the formal school setting, you will never graduate from study and learning.

Proper Attitudes

Proper attitudes are the foundation of effective study skills. You cannot hope to do your best in studying if you do not think properly about it. What attitudes will a good student have toward study and learning?

1. *Interest.* This is the one most important attitude you must have. If you are interested in your work, you will apply yourself to it. If you are not interested, you simply will not do as well.

Some students will say, "I'm not really interested in this subject, but I do my lessons carefully. I don't see how I could possibly do any better than I am doing now." We might compare this with eating at the table. A well-mannered person will eat the food he is given, even when it is not his favorite dish. But will he take as much as the person who really enjoys it? Will he chew it as thoroughly? Will he ask for a second helping? No, of course not. Just as surely, the uninterested student will never dig into a subject as effectively as the interested one.

Now you may ask, "But what if I don't like a subject? I can't *make* myself like it, can I?" The answer is "Yes." But you must want to be interested.

So what can you do to spark an interest in a subject? Ask yourself, "What would I do if this were really interesting?" Of course, you would dig in with enthusiasm. You would enjoy the challenge of finding the treasures in the lesson. So do that very thing. Dig in just as you would if this were your favorite subject. You may be surprised at how quickly your attitude changes. We find meaning and satisfaction in the things we do with our might.

2. *Self-discipline.* Probably all students (and older people too) depend to some degree on outside influences for motivation to do their work. As a person matures, however, he depends less upon external motivation and more upon the internal motivation of personal self-discipline.

In what areas must you exercise self-discipline in your study? First of all, set to work immediately. Refuse to dawdle with your pen, a library book, or even your textbook. (Did you ever waste five minutes looking at future lessons?) Also, be prepared to work hard. Real studying is not easy. You simply must buckle down and work. Unless you are ready to give yourself to your studies without resentment and without fear of difficulty, you will not learn much. Finally, stick to your work. If you find your mind wandering, rein it in! If surrounding activities or noises distract you, force your mind to concentrate. Without self-discipline, very little learning can occur.

3. *Purpose.* Any undertaking in life becomes easier when we sense a wholesome purpose. What is the true reason for your study? Is it to please your teacher and your parents? to use your time wisely at school? to complete all your assignments promptly and correctly? These are not bad reasons, but true studying has more noble ends. As you study, adopt for yourself the following purposes.

a. *To master the material.* Yes, you want to obey and please your teacher. You do want to use your time well and receive good grades. But beyond that, determine that you will *learn* what you are studying. To go to all the effort of study and fail to learn is a great waste of time!

b. *To develop your mind.* As you study, you are training your mind to think logically. Appreciate this benefit, especially when the work seems unnecessary and difficult. Logical thinking is essential to "rightly dividing the word of truth," to understanding other studies, and to facing many of life's experiences.

c. *To glorify God.* "Whether therefore ye eat, or drink, or whatsoever ye do, do all to the glory of God" (1 Corinthians 10:31). Is God glorified by lazy students? by students who do only as much as necessary to get by? Obviously not. Remember this; and when your studies press you down, rise up to honor God by doing your best. "Study [give diligence] to shew thyself approved unto God."

These purposes should provide you with a strong motivation to develop good study skills.

Study Schedule

A definite study schedule contributes to effective studying. To be a good student, you must make good use of your time. Here are several suggestions to help you manage your time well.

1. *Do your lessons as soon as possible after class.* The rate at which you forget is highest immediately after you have studied something. Later, you forget more slowly, so that the things you remember an hour after class, you will probably remember the next day. By doing a lesson right after class, you review what you have learned and

reinforce it in your mind. This helps to keep you from forgetting in those first critical minutes.

2. *Have a regular time to study.* By maintaining a scheduled study time, you can prevent a very common problem: forgetfulness. If the time after supper, before bedtime, or after breakfast is regularly devoted to study, you will be far less likely to forget to do your lessons than if you try to study whenever it suits.

A regular study schedule is also important because of the time-habit it establishes. When lunchtime nears, your body begins to get hungry. When your regular bedtime arrives, your body begins to shut down for sleep. And when your regular study hour approaches, your mind is conditioned to study at that time.

3. *Be mindful of deadlines.* Tackle first what is due first. This is especially important if your time is limited. It is helpful to list your work in three different groups at the beginning of a day or a study period: the things that you *must do,* those that you *should do,* and some that you *could do* if you have time. Include in the last group a few things you would especially enjoy doing. Then do first what must be done. As time allows, work on your "should do" things. Usually, the "could do" things are more enjoyable, so try to get some of them done too.

4. *Start with the hardest and least enjoyable assignments.* If you have a list of physical chores, do you save the worst and hardest ones for last? Probably not, if you can help it. You want to get them out of the way and off your mind. Treat a list of study chores the same way. Do the hardest and least enjoyable ones while your mind is fresh. This enables you to give your best mental energy to these tasks. Save something enjoyable and easy for last, when you are more tired. In addition to having something easy when your energy is least, you will have something to look forward to throughout your entire study period.

5. *Take occasional breaks.* Study is work, and you can keep your mind functioning at its best by periodically relaxing the brain, exercising the muscles, and recharging your body with fresh oxygen. A five-to-ten-minute break after an hour of study will probably allow you to study more effectively when you return to your work.

Suitable Environment

A suitable environment definitely contributes to effective study. What are some qualities of such an environment? First, have a regular place to study. If you have a definite *time* to study and a definite *place* to study, you have habits of both time and place to aid you. Just as your mind turns to food when you enter the dining room at mealtime (even if no food is in sight), so your mind will turn to study when you go to your desk at study time.

The place of study should be as quiet and free from distractions as practical. The more you can shut out family noise and activity, the better. At the same time, you need to free yourself from distractions of your own making. Remove any pictures, magazines, or hobby items that may divert your attention from your work.

Be sure to have your study tools near at hand. You should not need to interrupt your work to look for basic items like a pencil or pen, a dictionary, or a Bible. Also provide good lighting and ventilation. Such physical comfort is not a mere luxury; it aids your ability to concentrate.

Finally, keep your work station organized. Clutter kills motivation and wastes time.

Good Posture

Good posture plays an important role in effective study. Sit erect on a firm, straight-backed chair that allows your feet to rest comfortably on the floor and your arms on the table. In contrast to a slouching posture, this allows natural breathing that supplies the brain with plenty of oxygen for clear thinking.

In addition to its physical benefits, good posture has the subconscious effect of telling your mind and body that you truly intend to study. Imagine the difference if you should allow yourself to slouch down in a soft, padded chair. Ahh. How relaxing. And relaxing is just what you would tend to do rather than studying diligently.

Good study skills involve a number of attitudes and practices. Although some people are more inclined to study than others, no one performs at his best without diligent cultivation of these skills. And no one is such a poor scholar that he cannot develop these skills and benefit from them.

Applying the Lesson

A. Write *true* or *false*.

1. If a student is interested in a subject, he tends to work hard at it.
2. Taking interest in something helps to make it more appealing.
3. If you truly enjoy your work, it will be easy.
4. You are better able to study at the beginning of a study period than near the end.
5. You should avoid doing your hardest work first because that will tire you out right at the beginning of your study period.
6. A good student needs no external motivation to get his work done.
7. It is best to leave the easier studies for last.
8. Studying for God's glory applies only to Bible study.
9. The primary value of a suitable environment is to make study more pleasant.
10. Slouching has negative effects on your body and your mind.

B. Write the letter of the best answer.

1. If you are not interested in a certain subject, you probably
   a. will never be interested in it.
   b. cannot do anything to become interested.
   c. will not study it as well as you could.
   d. have a good reason for not being interested.
2. By studying like an interested student even if you are not really interested, you are likely to
   a. satisfy your teacher.
   b. actually become interested.
   c. lose what interest you do have.
   d. fool your teacher.

3. Of the following things, the best purpose for studying is
   a. to get a good report card grade.
   b. to meet the expectations of teachers and parents.
   c. to make good use of your time at school.
   d. to learn the material and remember it.
4. You forget the most rapidly
   a. immediately after studying something.
   b. one hour after studying something.
   c. the next day after studying something.
   d. in none of these periods; there is little difference.
5. The best time for you to study is
   a. when you feel like studying.
   b. when you find time to study.
   c. at the same time each day.
   d. early in the morning.
6. When you make a list of things you have to do,
   a. list only the most important things.
   b. decide which of the things are most important.
   c. list only the things you can do that day.
   d. list the things in the order you will do them.

C. Do these exercises.
   1. Make three lists of your school-related work that is now waiting to be done. Use these headings: *Must Do, Should Do,* and *Could Do.*
   2. Describe the time and the place where you did your homework most recently. Underline any details that should be improved.

Review Exercises

For each underlined word, write *yes* or *no* to tell whether it should be followed by a comma. [2]

1. The Gila (hē′·lə) monster, which lives in the <u>southwestern</u> United <u>States</u> is a poisonous lizard.
2. This <u>colorful</u> <u>scaly</u> creature grows to a length of about twenty inches.
3. Although it often appears <u>slow</u> and <u>awkward</u> the Gila monster can move rapidly.
4. Its diet consists largely of small <u>animals</u> bird <u>eggs</u> and reptile eggs.
5. The Gila <u>monster</u> and its close relative, the beaded <u>lizard</u> are the only venomous lizards in the world.
6. Produced in glands in the lower <u>jaw</u> the poison travels up the fanglike <u>teeth</u> when the Gila monster bites a victim.
7. Its poison is fatal to small animals but it rarely kills humans.
8. <u>Carla</u> please see if this publisher in <u>Chicago</u> <u>Illinois</u> has a book about desert animals.

10. Using the SQ3R Method

Which person is more efficient at doing his tasks—the one who develops a system or the one who works haphazardly? Obviously, the systematic worker is much more efficient than the haphazard one.

The same principle applies to study. By having a definite system, our study will be much more fruitful than if we have no system. This lesson presents a particular system of study known as the *SQ3R method.* The letters in this name stand for five steps that a good student should follow: **S**—Survey, **Q**—Question, **R**—Read, **R**—Recite, **R**—Review.

Survey

Suppose your father gives you the responsibility of painting all the woodwork on the front porch. How will you approach your job? Will you immediately open a paint can and start painting in one corner? Hardly. You will probably look over the whole porch first to gain a good idea of what the job involves. Then you will be ready to start the actual painting.

Apply the same principle to studying a lesson in history, science, or your Sunday school quarterly. The first step is to *survey* the material. Get a bird's-eye view of it. A survey of the lesson helps you to gain a sense of direction that will guide you as you read. It helps you to see the various parts of the lesson in relation to the whole. It also helps you to understand the logical connection between the present lesson and adjoining lessons.

How can you gain such an overall picture? First, consider the lesson title, which usually states the main point of the lesson. Then look at all the boldface headings. They will help you see the various main parts of the lesson. If there are any pictures, graphs, maps, or charts, look at them briefly and read the captions.

Be sure to keep this survey brief. Look for the main points of the lesson, and ignore the smaller details for now.

The study of a new book, a new unit, or a new chapter should also begin with a brief survey. See how the book is organized; read the unit and chapter titles. If a book has a preface, read it to discover the author's purpose for writing. All of this will help you get a general picture of the material you will study. This might be compared to mapping the general route for a trip before beginning to plan the specific details along the way.

Question

The second step in this study method is to *question.* That is, ask questions for which you expect to find answers in the material you will be reading. Many times you can do this by turning each heading into one or more questions. For example, suppose one of the headings in a science lesson is "Pollination by Insects." You would ask, "What insects help with pollination? How do insects help with pollination?" In history, the heading "Christianity Begins to Spread Rapidly" gives rise to several questions: "Why did it begin to spread rapidly? How rapidly did it spread? How far did it spread? To what regions did it spread?"

What is the value of forming these questions? By asking questions, you stimulate your mind to seek answers. You will have something to look for as you read, and you will be able to recognize the important points as you encounter them.

Read

The third step is the part that you usually do anyway: *read* the material. "Simple enough," you might say. But this is not a mere going through the sentences and paragraphs to "get these pages done." Rather, you are looking for answers to your questions. You are reading to find something specific. This is active reading—something that requires careful thought and attention. It is the heart of meaningful study.

As you read, make sure that you are comprehending the material. Reread a paragraph if you do not understand what it is saying. Look up unfamiliar words. Study the pictures, graphs, maps, and charts. They have been included to clarify the text. Take notes on significant points. Remember, you are reading so you will learn, not just so you can say you have completed your assignment.

Recite

After you have read each section, you should stop and *recite* the main points of the section. You can do this by answering the questions you asked before beginning to read. This tests whether you have read with comprehension. If you cannot state the main points, you have not learned the material. And if you have failed to learn, you must go back and find those answers. You have truly mastered a lesson only when you can repeat the main points in the lesson.

In most of your school studies, recitation also involves completing written assignments. Ideally, you should be able to do much of the written work without turning back to the lesson text. Whenever you must look back, put special effort into remembering that detail. Remember, the whole point of studying a lesson is to master the material.

Review

After you have worked through a lesson, completing the previous four steps, you are ready to *review.* Mentally go back over what you have read and recall the main points. Answer again the questions you asked before reading the lesson. This is the final check, the proof that you have really learned the material.

Do this review actively. Do not merely look at the lesson or your notes and think, "Yes, I remember that." Rather, recall the main points without looking at the text or your notes. Use those helps only if you cannot remember something. You will master the details much more effectively in this way.

Review as soon as possible after the learning experience. Do you remember from Lesson 9 that the rate of forgetting is greatest in the first several minutes after you have studied something? Your most effective review, therefore, is immediately after you have worked through a lesson.

Reviewing is not something that you can do once and then leave. Before class discussion, review the lesson again. Can you still answer your questions? Can you still recite the main points of the lesson? And, of course, you should review before test time. If you have studied the lessons effectively, this final review will not prove burdensome. And it will produce much better results than if you cram for a test.

True study is hard work. The SQ3R method does not make it easy, but it does help to make your study effective and beneficial.

Applying the Lesson

A. Write *true* or *false*.
   1. To study a lesson most effectively, you should first read it carefully.
   2. When surveying a lesson, you should study each map and chart in detail.
   3. One good way to make questions is to transform main headings into questions.
   4. The most effective review is done right after you have studied a lesson.
   5. If you have used the SQ3R method faithfully, you should not need to review before taking a test.

B. Write the letter of the best answer.
   1. Surveying a lesson can help you
      a. to understand how the individual sections of a lesson fit into the whole lesson.
      b. to sense where you are going as you read.
      c. to understand the connection between the present lesson and adjoining lessons.
      d. in all the ways given above.
   2. You should ask questions before you read a lesson
      a. so that you can read the lesson with less effort.
      b. so that you have specific goals as you read.
      c. so that you will be encouraged to spend more time with the lesson.
      d. for all the reasons above.
   3. Active reading
      a. means that you read to find something.
      b. allows you to think about other things as you read.
      c. is what you naturally do when studying a lesson.
      d. includes all the things above.
   4. A good way to determine whether you have read with comprehension is to
      a. see if you can recall the main ideas of the lesson.
      b. answer by memory the questions you raised before reading.
      c. do much of the written assignment without looking back at the lesson.
      d. do all the things above.

C. Write two questions that each of these headings could suggest.
   1. American Colonies Build Prosperous Trade
   2. Inventions Fuel Industrial Growth
   3. Creating a Partial Vacuum
   4. The Conduction of Heat
   5. The Hindu Caste System
   6. Migratory Patterns in Birds

D. Study the following selection, using the SQ3R method. First, *survey* the selection. Next, turn every heading into at least one *question;* and write those questions on your paper, leaving enough room to fill in your answers. Then *read* through each section, *recite* the answers to your questions, and write them on your paper. Finally, *review* by writing from memory on another paper the main points you have learned.

Modern Times

By Robert Darrow

"The thing that hath been, it is that which shall be; and that which is done is that which shall be done: and there is no new thing under the sun. Is there any thing whereof it may be said, See, this is new? it hath been already of old time, which was before us" (Ecclesiastes 1:9, 10).

We are all aware that the times are changing; things are not the same as they used to be. Each year that goes by brings new events and developments in man's condition on earth. But sometimes, looking backward, we seem to discern a period marked by changes more significant and more profound than those preceding or following—a watershed division between the "old days" and the "new times."

Events That Ushered in Modern Times

History writers recognize such a division in the change from the Middle Ages to modern times, which occurred about five hundred years ago. At that time, a number of events took place—related to each other in many complex ways, and all together making remarkable changes in the course of history. Let us examine some of these events that mark the end of the Middle Ages and the beginning of modern times.

In 1453, the Hundred Years' War between France and England came to a close. After that, France and England began to develop into modern nations with strong central governments, with fairly definite boundaries, and with citizens who thought of themselves as being French or English. Portugal and Spain, meanwhile, were also developing. In a lengthy struggle called the *Reconquista,* they drove the Moors (Arabs) out of Europe and back into Africa. This *Reconquista* was completed in 1492.

Something else happened in 1453: the fierce, hostile Ottoman Turks finally conquered Constantinople after decades of fighting. This city is now Istanbul in modern Turkey. The emperor Constantine had made Constantinople the eastern capital of the Roman Empire in A.D. 330, so its fall actually represented the end of the Roman Empire in the East. (The fall of Rome in A.D. 476 marked the end of the empire in the West.) But more important, the fall of Constantinople shifted the focus of Europe westward to the newly developing nations.

Long before the city fell, thousands of refugees from Greece and Asia Minor had been coming to western Europe to escape the Turks. They brought with them various books and manuscripts containing knowledge long since forgotten or neglected in the West. The influx of this knowledge contributed to an upsurge of learning called the Renaissance (rebirth). People in western lands took a new interest in art, science, and learning in general.

In 1454, Johann Gutenberg printed a Bible on a press with movable type, the first known book printed in this way. Equally important was the development of good-quality paper and ink. The Gutenberg Bible marked the beginning of a new access to literature; before this, books had to be laboriously written out by hand. Such materials contributed to the explosion of knowledge so necessary in modern times.

The hostility of the Turks in the eastern Mediterranean cut off Europe from a highly desirable trade with India and China. The main products of this trade were spices, silk, cotton, and sugar. Spain and Portugal began searching for new routes around Africa or directly west across the Atlantic. The great explorations of Christopher Columbus (1492), Vasco da Gama (1498), and Ferdinand Magellan (1519) opened up new worlds and provided new things for the people of Europe.

Beginning in 1517, the Protestant Reformation resulted in the establishment of national Protestant churches. These churches undid the monopoly of the pope and the Roman Catholic Church, but they did not establish freedom of religion or Scripturally sound, New Testament churches. At the same time, however, the Swiss Brethren and related Anabaptist churches sprang up. The first recorded rebaptism took place in Zurich in 1525. God's guiding hand is seen in the chain of events leading to the rise of His Holy Word and His people, the church!

Results of These Events

The result of all these events was a period of extensive growth. The population increased. The ancient cities began to grow again, and new towns and cities sprang up. Commerce and industry prospered, stimulated by new explorations and new products. More land in Europe was brought under cultivation, and the production per acre increased. Some people accumulated enormous private fortunes.

By 1600, there seemed no end to the things that man could do. Every passing day brought news of fantastic discoveries. People were gazing out into the universe with telescopes, and with microscopes they were discovering the secret worlds hidden in a drop of water. They looked forward with great expectation to the time when all of man's problems would be solved by man himself!

Well, now we know otherwise. We know that this world was corrupted by sinful man, and it will not be saved by him. The more that things change, the more they stay the same! A proper understanding of history teaches us to see both the differences and the constants of all ages.

E. Use the SQ3R method to study your next lesson in science, history, or geography. Do not stop with that, but try to develop the habit of using this method in all your studies.

11. Developing the Art of Skimming

Generally, when you want to gain something from a lesson or an article, you expect to read and study it carefully. Depending on circumstances, however, detailed study may be unwise, unnecessary, or even impossible. Then you may wish to employ the art of skimming.

Have you ever skipped a stone across a still pool of water? One, two, three, and possibly more times the stone came down, briefly touched the water, bounced upward, and again hit the water. That is a picture of skimming—spot reading or briefly glancing over the material for specific ideas.

Purposes and Methods of Skimming

1. *Skimming to gain a bird's-eye view of a book or an article.* You wonder what a new book contains, so you pick up a copy and skim it. You check the table of contents and then page through the book quickly, noticing the information given on the beginning pages. As you proceed through the book, you stop here and there to read a paragraph or two. You pay particular attention to how the book begins and how it ends. When you lay the book down a few minutes later, you will have gained a fairly accurate impression of the kind of book it is and the kind of material it contains.

The following illustration gives a good picture of the pattern you should follow in skimming, especially with an item such as a magazine article.

You should usually read the whole first paragraph (and sometimes the second one) at normal speed. These opening paragraphs often contain an introduction or overview of the material you will skim.

You probably do not need to read the whole third paragraph. . . . .
. . . .
. . . .

Read the first sentence of each paragraph. . . . .
. . . .
. . . .
. . . .

However, main ideas occur in various parts of paragraphs. . . . .
. . . .
. . . .
. . . .
. . . .
. . . . sometimes in the middle . . . .
. . . .
. . . .
. . . . Sometimes the main idea comes in the last sentence of a paragraph.

Besides the first sentences, try to pick up other details in the middle of the paragraphs. . . . .
. . . .
. . . . names . . . .
. . . .
. . . .
. . . . . . dates . . . .
. . . .

Try to keep up a very fast rate . . . .
. . . .
. . . .
. . . . . . don't forget yourself. . . . .
. . . .
. . . . don't start to read everything
. . . .
. . . .

Sometimes the first sentence does not give the main idea. Then you must read the whole paragraph more slowly.

You can omit much of the next paragraph. . . . .
. . . .
. . . .
. . make up time. . . . .

Don't worry that you don't get anything from many of the paragraphs. . . .
. . . .
. . . .
. . . .

Some paragraphs merely repeat ideas. . . . .
. . . .
. . . .
. . . . restated points
. . . .
. . . .

This paragraph has nothing important. . . . .
. . . .
. . . . . . minor details. . . . .
. . . .

Skimming takes definite effort. . . . .
. . . .
. . . .
. . . . worthwhile skill . . . .
. . . .
. . . .
. . . .
. . . . easier with practice. . . . . .
. . . .
. . . .

For the last two or three paragraphs, again read at normal speed. These paragraphs often contain a summary of the composition.

Remember, when you skim to gain an overall view, you need to find the main ideas.

2. *Skimming to find information.* Suppose you have an assignment to write an essay on the migratory habits of North American birds. You have several books about birds. Do you read each book from cover to cover? No. First, you check the table of contents and the index to see if there is any entry on your subject. Then you turn to the page or pages indicated and let your eyes skim each page quickly as illustrated under Point 1 above. You read each heading and subheading. Your eyes may catch something that seems to be on the subject, possibly a word or a phrase, and you read a sentence or a paragraph. In a short time, you can decide whether the book has the information you want.

Or perhaps you have heard a friend mention some information that he read in a gardening magazine that you also subscribe to. You do not begin reading from the beginning of the magazine until you find the information he mentioned. First, you check the table of contents. If this gives you no clues, you quickly leaf through the magazine, page by page, looking at the headings and titles. When you come to an article that you think might contain the information you are looking for, you let your eyes run quickly down the page, reading headings and subheadings (if there are any), reading the beginning and ending sentences of paragraphs, and moving from page to page until you either know you have found the right article or are sure you need to look further.

This is the type of skimming you do to find information. Indexes, titles, headings, and beginning and ending sentences of paragraphs are all clues in finding the needed information quickly.

3. *Skimming to evaluate a book or an article.* Is the material worth reading? A quick skim can often give you a good idea. Again, as with skimming to gain a bird's-eye view of the book, check the beginning pages. Who is the author? Is his purpose for writing the book found in a preface or an introduction? What is that purpose?

Suppose you have a storybook to evaluate. Notice how the story begins. Does the main character appear to be an upright person? Skip back through the book, spot reading here and there. Is the language free of slang and coarse expressions? Do the characters—especially the main character—express hatred, anger, dishonesty, or other ungodly traits? If the book presents unchristian attitudes and conduct, you can reject it without wasting much of your time and without absorbing the wrong influence of the book.

Do you have a nonfiction book or an article to evaluate? Many nonfiction books have a preface or an introduction that indicates the main purpose of the book. The table of contents of a book or the headings in an article often indicate whether the material develops a subject from a worthwhile perspective. From this, you can usually tell whether the material is worth reading.

4. *Skimming to review material you have previously studied.* Are you refreshing in your mind the points of a lesson before class time? Are you reviewing for a test? Skim through the material page by page. Note the headings and the beginning sentences of paragraphs. This skimming will reinforce what you already know and bring it to your active consciousness. It also will reveal if there is something you should read more fully to rivet important information that you have not yet mastered.

Skimming fills a definite place in study. But you must not merely skim a lesson to find answers to the exercises when you have not actually studied the lesson. That is not the way to master facts and concepts. Neither should you use skimming to cram for a quiz or a test when you failed to diligently study the material earlier. Learn to use this study tool, but keep it in its proper place.

Summary of Skimming Skills

You cannot skim lazily if you expect to accomplish anything worthwhile. You must keep your mind alert and observant. You must be quick to sort out and evaluate what you read. The following list summarizes the techniques to use in skimming.

1. Check the table of contents and the index of a book.
2. Read the headings and subheadings.
3. Read the beginning and ending sentences of paragraphs.
4. Read a sentence or two here and there, or even a full paragraph occasionally.
5. With a quick eye, pick out significant words and phrases.

Applying the Lesson

A. Write *true* or *false*.

1. Skimming is the art of looking material over briefly for specific ideas.
2. When you skim to gain a bird's-eye view, you should pay closer attention to the beginning and ending paragraphs than to the middle paragraphs.
3. You should avoid reading any whole paragraphs as you skim.
4. To skim a book for information, you should first page through it to check the chapter titles.
5. When you skim a book to evaluate it, you need not consider the author's preface or introduction.
6. One reason for evaluating a book by skimming it is to avoid absorbing errors that the book may contain.

7. When you review by skimming, information that you had mastered earlier is brought to your active consciousness.
8. By perfecting the art of skimming, you may be able to master your school lessons without reading them closely.

B. Answer these questions by using the table of contents and the index of this English book.
   1. In which lesson will you study note-taking for writing an expository essay?
   2. In which lesson will you study methods of portraying characters in a story?
   3. On which pages would you look for the rules of italicizing words?
   4. On which pages would you look for information about conflict in stories?
   5. On which pages would you look for information about the mood of verbs?

C. Use a Bible with page headings for this exercise. Skim the headings in the Bible, and write the numbers of the chapters in which the following information is found.
   1. The chapter in Matthew that tells of Jesus' death.
   2. The chapters in Acts concerning Stephen's trial.
   3. The chapter in Revelation describing the heavenly Jerusalem.
   4. The chapters in Genesis that tell about Joseph's life in Egypt.
   5. The chapters in Judges that tell about Gideon.

D. Be prepared for a class drill in skimming.

Review Exercises

A. Name the punctuation that should follow each underlined word: *colon, semicolon, ellipsis points,* or *none.* [4]
   1. Especially large amounts of snow fall at Marquette, Michigan; Sault Ste. Marie, <u>Michigan</u> and Buffalo, New York.
   2. Marquette, Michigan, can expect an annual snowfall of over 171 <u>inches</u> that is more than 14 feet!
   3. The amounts of snowfall expected at Sault Ste. Marie and at Buffalo <u>are</u> 160 inches and 115 inches.
   4. People living in these areas had better enjoy one <u>thing</u> snow.
   5. "Well," Nevin said, "I like snow, <u>but</u>"

B. Write the letter of the sentence in which the boldface part is correct. [5, 6]
   1. a. "If we seek God's will," Father stated, **"The** Lord will direct our way."
      b. "If we seek God's will," Father stated, **"the** Lord will direct our way."
   2. a. I read the book **"Bernese Anabaptists"** for my report.
      b. I read the book ***Bernese Anabaptists*** for my report.
   3. a. Jesus said, "I am the light of the **world";** however, He also said, "Ye are the light of the world."
      b. Jesus said, "I am the light of the **world;"** however, He also said, "Ye are the light of the world."
   4. a. "Which disciple boldly declared, 'Though I should die with thee, yet will I not deny **thee?'"** asked Lisa.
      b. "Which disciple boldly declared, 'Though I should die with thee, yet will I not deny **thee'?"** asked Lisa.

5. a. The word ***adult*** may be accented on the first or second syllable.
   b. The word **"adult"** may be accented on the first or second syllable.
6. a. We sang for Sister Laura—how cheerful she **is!—on** her ninetieth birthday.
   b. We sang for Sister Laura—how cheerful she **is! on** her ninetieth birthday.
7. a. "We are ready to leave **if" The** rest of the sentence was lost in a thunderous crash.
   b. "We are ready to leave **if—" the** rest of the sentence was lost in a thunderous crash.
8. a. Several students' descriptions contained too many ***and*'s.**
   b. Several students' descriptions contained too many **"ands."**
9. a. Thessalonica (also known as **Salonika, sə•lon′•i•kə**) is a seaport of Greece.
   b. Thessalonica (also known as **Salonika [sə•lon′•i•kə]**) is a seaport of Greece.
10. a. My father is a **self employed** mechanic, who works at home.
    b. My father is a **self-employed** mechanic, who works at home.

---

12. Taking Notes and Summarizing

Study is primarily an activity of the mind. However, there are things we do with our hands which contribute to our study. Note-taking and summarizing are two valuable study skills that involve such physical activity.

Note-taking and summarizing are somewhat similar study skills. Both involve identifying main ideas, and both have several important values.

Values of Note-Taking and Summarizing

Note-taking and summarizing are valuable because they promote concentration. The discipline of taking notes from what you read or hear helps to keep your mind active. Furthermore, the discipline of being alert for the next main point to write in your notes helps you to grasp those points more firmly than a casual listening or reading would do. Likewise, the discipline of reducing a lesson or an article to a summary forces you to concentrate closely on what you are reading.

In the second place, these skills promote logical thinking. You cannot take meaningful notes on a lecture, a sermon, or an article in a haphazard manner. If the notes are to be an accurate representation, they must reflect the logical development followed by the speaker or writer. Similarly, to write an accurate summary, you must grasp well the logic of the original article.

Both of these skills are also valuable because they provide a good source of review material. In fact, this likely would be the primary reason for taking notes or summarizing specifically as a study skill. The brevity of notes and summaries makes them useful for quickly reviewing the main points of what you have studied.

Guidelines for Note-Taking

1. *Write down main ideas, not minor details.* Unless you are skilled at shorthand, you cannot possibly write down every detail in a lecture or sermon. And unless you plan to write an article based on the presentation, there is no good reason to do so. To realize the three values suggested above, you must write down only the main points.

2. *Write down significant subpoints.* Sometimes a listing of only the main points is hardly satisfactory. Other details may be essential to explain the main idea. How can you tell when details are significant enough to write down? The following three points will help to answer that.

3. *Write down things the speaker emphasizes.* Sometimes your teacher may say, "This will be on the test." Be sure to write it down, for it is something you must remember. Or he may say, "Be sure to remember this." Again, you can tell it is important. Write it down. Be especially alert whenever your teacher writes something on the chalkboard. That is another sign that he considers a point important.

Speakers use various other means to emphasize important points. They may use transitional words to signal the movement from one point to another. They may speak in a more emphatic tone than usual, and they may repeat a point several times. Whenever a speaker emphasizes a point, however he does it, be sure to get it in your notes.

4. *Write down important definitions, figures, dates, names, and so forth.* For example, a science lesson titled "Sanitary Living" includes these italicized terms: *sanitation, sterile, antiseptics, germicides, disinfectants, quarantine.* The same lesson includes figures such as boiling an object for *20 minutes* to sterilize it and heating milk to *144°F for 30 minutes* to pasteurize it. Your notes would include the italicized terms and their definitions, along with the figures given.

A history lesson, of course, would include more dates and names for your notes. An English lesson may have rules, and an arithmetic lesson may have formulas that you should write in your notes. Whatever the subject, note the types of information that you should definitely remember and that you can expect to find on a test.

5. *Be especially alert for information that is new to you.* Writing down such information will reinforce it in your mind right away. You remember much more of what you write than of what you simply hear. You also will need to review more frequently those things that you have never learned before. Sometimes that new information is material that your teacher brings in from outside your normal text material. Those details, of course, you cannot review from your book; you must rely on your notes for help to remember them.

6. *Keep your notes neat and orderly.* Because you must write rapidly, you must often sacrifice neatness as you take notes. It is therefore a good idea to organize and rewrite your notes soon after class. Do not be satisfied with scribbled notes, for you will find it discouraging to decipher your scribbles later. At a certain point, disorganized and illegible notes become totally useless.

Steps for Writing a Summary

A summary is a condensed review of the main points of an article or other composition. Writing a good summary requires that you be thoroughly familiar with the original writing. Follow these steps to write a summary.

1. *Skim the composition.* Put to practice the points in Lesson 11.
2. *Read the composition carefully for a thorough understanding.* Read as you were taught to read in Lesson 10. Reread a paragraph if necessary to understand it fully. Reread the whole composition if that is necessary.
3. *Write down the main points of the composition.* This list of main points will serve as a guide for your actual writing.
4. *Write the summary.* Use an appropriate heading, stating the title of the original piece and the author's name. If you are summarizing an article from a periodical, include the name and date of the periodical.

Use your own wording as much as possible. Copy from the original only if you want to preserve some unique style or wording of the author. Remember to enclose any exact quotations in quotation marks.

Include all the main points in their original order. Since you are merely summarizing another person's writing, you should not include your own thoughts and opinions. And stick to the *main* points. Include an example or illustration only if it is essential to explaining a point.

Make the summary of an appropriate length. A summary may range from less than one hundred words to about one-third the length of the original composition. Its length is affected by the length of the original composition, the number of main points, and the thoroughness of the summary.

Check the summary for accuracy and clarity. Be sure your summary conveys the same meaning and gives the same slant to the subject as the original does. Review the main points of the original. Does your summary include them in the correct order? Make sure you have properly credited all quotations. And consider whether your summary reads smoothly. Do the thoughts flow well from paragraph to paragraph? Or should you add some transitional expressions to improve it?

Read the following summary of the article that appears in Lesson 10. The original article contains 853 words; this summary contains 280 words, which is about one-third the length of the original.

A Summary of "Modern Times"

By Robert Darrow

Although times constantly change, certain eras bring dramatic changes that mark definite boundaries in history. Beginning in the middle 1400s, various events that were "related to each other in many complex ways" so altered the world that historians call this the beginning of modern times.

The Hundred Years' War between France and England ended in 1453. Soon these two nations were taking on the characteristics of modern nations. Spain and Portugal also were becoming distinct nations. By 1492, these nations had pushed the Arab Moors back into Africa.

In 1453, the Ottoman Turks overthrew Constantinople, the Roman Empire's eastern capital. A flood of refugees from Greece and Asia Minor poured into western Europe, bringing writings and knowledge that helped to spark the Renaissance.

Johann Gutenberg developed a movable-type printing press and printed a Bible in 1454. Because of Gutenberg's invention, it became much cheaper and easier to spread knowledge by the printed page.

Because the Turks controlled the eastern Mediterranean, Europeans could not trade directly with India and China. This spurred an interest in finding other routes to the East. The resulting explorations brought Europe into contact with new worlds and new products.

The Protestant Reformation, which began in 1517, greatly weakened the power of the Roman Catholic Church. Although this movement itself did not bring a revival of true Christianity, the Swiss Brethren of the same era did establish Scriptural churches.

These events produced extensive growth in population, commerce, industry, and agriculture. By 1600, men were daily discovering new things. And they imagined that man would be able to solve all his own problems. But the world remains corrupted by the sin of man; he can never save himself.

Applying the Lesson

A. Write *true* or *false*.

1. Taking notes promotes concentration because it keeps your mind active.
2. You should be able to write a good summary of an article after you have skimmed it.
3. A good rule for note-taking is "The more, the better."
4. When the teacher writes something on the chalkboard, it is impressed on your mind well enough that you should not need to write it in your notes.
5. Taking notes on facts that are new to you helps you to learn them better.
6. A good summary should preserve the author's original wording as much as practical.
7. Most summaries have two hundred to three hundred words.

B. Write the correct word or phrase for each sentence.

1. Good notes should mirror the (logical order, supporting details) used by a speaker or writer.
2. Notes and summaries are useful for review because they are (brief, detailed).
3. Good notes should include (some, all) of the main points and some of the (interesting, significant) details.
4. For best results, organizing and rewriting of notes should be done (promptly after class, at the end of each week).
5. A summary should *not* include your own (opinions, wording).

C. Take notes on one of the next sermons you hear or on a devotional in school.

D. Summarize the following composition in 200–250 words.

The First Transatlantic Cable (about 600 words)

Cyrus W. Field was a wealthy American merchant who devoted himself to the dream of laying a telegraph cable across the Atlantic Ocean. He probably never imagined how difficult the task would be or how much ridicule and disapproval he would endure because of it.

One great problem was to raise the $1.75 million needed to finance the project. For this purpose, Field went to England and organized the Atlantic Telegraph Company in 1856. Another problem was to design a suitable cable. The planners tried many experiments and saw many failures before a four-inch, brass-bound, insulated copper cable was completed. This cable contained 340,000 miles of wire woven into strands.

The first attempt. The great enterprise was launched in 1857, the same year that the first telegraph was completed across the American continent. In August, the *Niagara* and the *Agamemnon* left Valentia, an island just off the west coast of Ireland. Laying cable and relaying messages to shore went well for more than 300 miles.

Suddenly the messages ceased, but 2½ hours later they resumed. However, the next morning the cable snapped and hope was lost. The ships had to retrace their route.

The second attempt. In June 1858, the *Niagara* and the *Agamemnon* met in the mid-Atlantic, each carrying half of a new cable. Upon successfully splicing the cable, the ships sailed toward opposite shores. But after only 250 miles of cable were laid, it snapped at one ship and then the other. The men returned to England to hear some even more disheartening news. Some of the directors of the Atlantic Telegraph Company were planning to dissolve the company.

The third attempt. Because of the persistence and influence of Cyrus Field, the company continued; and one month later, things were ready for another try. Again the ships met in mid-ocean, and again the men spliced the two cables. But ships were passing too near the sinking cable. Floating icebergs and a passing whale added to the anxiety. Would this attempt also end in failure?

Finally on August 5, 1858, each ship arrived at its harbor with the cable still intact. The transatlantic cable spanned 1,950 miles, and it did transmit electrical signals. But the signals were so weak that when Queen Victoria sent official congratulations to President James Buchanan, it took 67 minutes to transmit her 90-word message.

It soon became evident that the cable's insulation was defective. The signals became more and more feeble, and by October 20 the cable was dead. For over six years, the transatlantic project received little further support or attention.

The fourth attempt. Early in 1865, Field was on the *Great Eastern*—the world's largest steamship at the time—as it left Valentia Island with a new cable. This one measured 3,000 miles long and weighed 7,000 tons. But after 1,186 miles of cable were laid, the cable snapped. The grappling device on the ship was not able to retrieve the four-inch cable some 5,000 feet below on the ocean floor. Once more the crew returned to England.

Success at last. In the spring of 1866, Field was again on the *Great Eastern,* and this time he succeeded in laying a working cable across the Atlantic. The great steamship then traveled to the location of the lost 1865 cable. The men made some thirty attempts with an improved grappling device, and finally they retrieved the cable. They spliced another one to it and then completed the second live cable across the ocean. After nine years of setbacks and frustrations, Cyrus Field had not one but two successful telegraph cables across the Atlantic Ocean.

---

13. Improving Your Editing Skills, Part 2

The standard proofreading symbols provide a neat, efficient way to mark corrections in a manuscript. Anyone who is familiar with the marks will immediately understand what changes are intended. By contrast, look at the marks used to make changes in the following sentence.

```
                  s          an
Suddenly from the Sky came a loud earsplitting roar.
```

It may not be clear that *Sky* is to be changed to *sky,* for uppercase and lowercase *s* both have the same form. And scribbling out an unwanted word does not look neat at all. Can you imagine the unsightly appearance of a whole page full of such sloppy corrections? Consider too that later you may change your mind about a deleted word. How will you retain a word if it has been obliterated beyond recognition? Using the standard proofreading marks is surely much better.

The following table reviews the six proofreading marks from Lesson 7 and introduces six new marks. Below the table is a sample manuscript showing how the new marks are used. The exercises call for the proper use of all these proofreading marks.

Marks Used in Editing and Proofreading

(Introduced in first proofreading lesson)

∨ or ∧ insert (caret)	delete	.... stet (let it stand)
¶ begin new paragraph	lc change to lowercase (small letter)	uc change to uppercase (capital letter)

(Introduced in this lesson)

no ¶ no new paragraph	← move (arrow)	⌐‿⌐ transpose
# insert space	⁀‿ delete space	____ use italics

Explanations

To move a word from one line to another, it may be simplest to circle the word and use an arrow.

Words *I* and *my* are to be italicized.

Transpose symbol is used with words, letters, or punctuation.

"Delete space" symbol means the two words or word parts should be joined.

"No paragraph" symbol means the two paragraphs are to be joined.

Arrow indicates moving indented text left to the vertical line.

Extended line of the symbol # shows exactly where the space is to be inserted.

Sample Manuscript

Nebuchadnezzar did not give God His rightful place, certainly. He filled his speech with I's and my's as he declared, "Is not great this Babylon, that I have built"? For this reason, God cuased the boast ful king to go through a very humiliating experience. no¶

|←Afterward, Nebuchadnezzar said meekly, "Those that walk inpride he [God] is able to abase" (Daniel 4:37).

There are other proofreading marks besides the ones shown in this lesson. But these twelve are the most basic symbols, and they are the ones that best apply to your work. Learn to use them accurately.

Editing Practice

A. Use the proper proofreading marks to correct two spacing errors in each sentence.

1. **The Sermon on the Mount is meant for to day, not just for somefuture age.**
2. **If every one followed Jesus' teachings, noone would knowingly mistreat others.**
3. **True Christians would rather suffer wrong thanuse physical force against an other person.**
4. **Using physical force in cludes taking some one to court.**
5. **Paul rebuked the Corinthians because of their law suits against eachother.**

B. Use the proper proofreading marks to indicate one use of italics and to correct one error of transposition in each sentence.

1. **John Bunyan wrote The Pilgrim's Progress while was he in prison.**
2. **You haven't removed all the unnecessary and's from these paragarphs.**
3. **To spell accommodate, you write must two sets of double letters.**
4. **The book War-torn Valley tells a challenging story abuot nonresistance during the Civil War.**
5. **In 1927, Charles Lindbergh used the Spirit of St. Louis to the make first solo nonstop flight across the Atlantic Ocean.**

C. Use the proper symbols to mark the changes indicated in parentheses.

1. **The children asked if they might eat their lunches under the shade trees outside.** (Move *outside* so that it follows *lunches.*)
2. **Chastening is not pleasant; if we respond properly to it, however, we can benefit from the experience.** (Move *however* and the comma after it to a position after the semicolon.)
3. **Job remained faithful to God in spite of great loss and suffering.** (Use an arrow and a vertical line to move the indented text to the left.)

D. Now try your editing skills on the selection below. You will need to do the following things.

a. Make one correction in each full line. (You will use each proofreading mark at least once.)
b. Show that one word already deleted should be retained.
c. Make the third paragraph begin in line 13 rather than line 12.
d. Show that the term *solar constant* is to be italicized.

Sixteen changes should be marked. Can you find them all?

1. **Suppose man had to pay for all the solarpower that the**
2. **earth receives. At eight cents per kilowatt-hour, the Energy**
3. **recieved every second would cost $4 billion, or about two**

dollars for every living person. Imagine! Each man, woman and child wuld have to pay $120 per minute, which comes to $7,200 per hour or $172,800 per day. how long could your family afford this? ~~Yet~~ God sends solar energy completely free.

Remember too that the earth is but one tinny sphere in the vast the solar system. The sun produces 2 billion times as much energy as what the earth receives.

In fact, the sun produces in one second as much energy as the earth receives in about sixty years. Scientists carefully measure the soler energy reaching the earth. They find that the ~~approximate~~ rate is about 5 million Horsepower per acre. This is called the solar constant, for it has shown hardly any measur able change over the past hundred years.

---

14. Outlining Written Material

Outlining is a valuable skill. It helps a speaker or writer to organize the material he is to present. It helps a listener or reader to comprehend the material he hears or reads.

The Form and Content of an Outline

An outline is an orderly summary of something spoken or written. It shows the title, the main topics, the subtopics, the points, and so forth. An outline may consist of a paragraph summary for each idea, though that is not common. Some outlines have complete sentences to express each idea. Most outlines are topical, with a word or phrase to express each point.

Study this partial topical outline, which illustrates the rules of outline form given below it.

Old Testament Building Projects

I. Noah's ark (Genesis 6)
   A. The purpose
      1. To display God's grace and power
      2. To preserve a godly line

- B. The plan
  - 1. Its size
    - a. 300 cubits (450 feet) long
    - b. 50 cubits (75 feet) wide
    - c. 30 cubits (45 feet) high
  - 2. Other details
    - a. Made with rooms
    - b. Pitched within and without
    - c. Made with three stories
    - d. Made with one window and one door
- C. The building time—about 100 years
  - 1. Because apparently not much help
  - 2. Because took time out to witness
  - 3. So that men had opportunity to repent

II. The tower of Babel (Genesis 11)

- A. The purpose
  - 1. To reach heaven by human effort
  - 2. To make themselves a name
  - 3. To avoid being scattered
- B. The plan

The form and structure of an outline follow a definite pattern. Notice how the sample outline above illustrates these rules.

1. Center the title above the outline.
2. Begin each line with a capital letter.
3. Indent each level equally.
4. Indent each level farther right than the previous level.
5. Put a period after each numeral or letter that marks an item. After you have used periods with *1* and *a* to mark points and subpoints, use parentheses with *1* and *a* if there are further details. On the outline above, details under "Made with one window and one door" would be marked *(1)* and *(2)*. And if those items also had details, they would be marked *(a)* and *(b)*.
6. Have at least two parts when subordinate points come under an item. If there is only one subordinate point, include it with the item above it.
7. Use either all paragraphs, all sentences, or all topics.
8. Use proper end punctuation with paragraph and sentence outlines. Omit end punctuation with topical outlines.
9. Use a logical progression from the beginning to the end of the outline.
10. Use headings that do not overlap in thought.
11. On a topical outline, keep the items of each level as nearly parallel as possible.

In relation to Rule 10, consider the first outline below. Some of the main topics overlap because essay writing includes argumentative essays and expository essays.

The second and third items should be subordinate to "Essay writing," as shown on the second outline.

Poor: Headings overlap

Composition Writing

I. Essay writing
II. Argumentative essays
III. Expository essays
IV. Story writing

Better: Headings restructured

Composition Writing

I. Essay writing
    A. Argumentative essays
    B. Expository essays
II. Story writing

Items that are parallel (Rule 11) are items with a basic similarity. All the items should begin with the same part of speech and be generally similar in structure. Compare the following examples.

Poor: Unparallel items

Meaningful Devotions

I. Reading the Bible
    A. Analyzing the passage
    B. Apply the principles
II. Prayer

Better: Parallel items

Meaningful Devotions

I. Reading the Bible
    A. Analyze the passage
    B. Apply the principles
II. Praying

The first outline lacks parallelism because *Reading* does not match *Prayer,* and *Analyzing* does not match *Apply.* What about *Reading the Bible* and *Praying* on the second outline? These items are not perfectly parallel, but little can be done about this, since *Reading* needs the object *Bible,* but *Praying* needs no object. The outline is acceptable because these two items are as closely parallel as possible.

Outlining as a Study Aid

Outlining is an effective study aid. The very process of outlining requires you to analyze the material you are reading. You must identify the main ideas and the lesser ideas. You must consider how the various details relate to each other. Writing an accurate, thorough outline requires diligent effort and study.

An outline continues to be a valuable aid long after you have completed it. The concentration that went into making the outline impresses the details more deeply upon your mind than if you had merely read the material. The outline also provides a good source for quick review. You can usually pick out main ideas and specific details more quickly on your outline than in your book.

Below is an example of a history lesson, with pointers to direct you through the steps of outlining it.

1. *Skim the paragraphs, and try to identify the main idea.*

Swiss Mennonite Encounters With Indians

The Swiss Mennonite settlers in colonial Pennsylvania suffered very little from the Indians before the French and Indian War. One reason for this may have been that they generally did not live on the frontier lines. By contrast, the Scotch-Irish who settled the frontiers were in frequent conflict with the Indians.

However, the larger factor contributing to peaceful relationships was the nonresistant position of the Mennonites and Amish. These peace-loving settlers treated the Indians with respect and consideration. There is no evidence that they ever used force against the Indians or that they used the forts erected by other settlers for protection. The lengthy poem "The Unbarred Door" portrays the peaceful and trusting relationship between the Indians and the Swiss settlers of the early colonial era.

The Indians who had not migrated north and west of the Blue Mountains were friendly in general. One group of Delaware Indians south of Bethlehem joined the local Mennonite (or Amish) families in their Sunday meetings. In the Lancaster area, Mennonite children played with their Indian neighbors. One of the Indian boys, Cristy, was named after someone in the Mennonite settlement, and he taught the white boys to make bows and arrows. A number of the Indians in the surrounding neighborhoods became Christians. But the Scotch-Irish on the frontier resented these peaceful relationships.

The picture changed after the Walking Purchase of 1737 and the Albany Purchase of 1754, which embittered many of the Indians. They began uniting with the French in conflict against the English settlements. This led to the bloody French and Indian War (1754–63), in which the nonresistant settlers suffered right along with the rest of the people.

One of the first Indian attacks came on October 16, 1755, at Penns Creek near Selinsgrove. The Delaware and Shawnee Indians killed, scalped, or captured all twenty-five of the settlers. Two days later, twenty-five settlers were killed five miles south of Sunbury. The massacres in 1757–58 of Mennonite families in Lebanon County, in Northkill near Hamburg, and in Page County, Virginia, are well-known incidents. On September 7, 1758, the Virginia Mennonites sent a letter to Holland stating that fifty of their number had been killed and two hundred rendered homeless. The Holland brethren gave $376.40 to assist the suffering ones.

According to the record, the early Mennonite settlers were instrumental in winning a number of Indians to the Christian faith. These Mennonites consistently upheld the doctrine and practice of nonresistance under very trying circumstances. They faithfully expressed Christian attitudes toward the Indians, whether friend or foe. Let us also express a Christlike spirit and leave a positive witness in our surrounding society.

Have you identified the main idea? Basically, this lesson discusses the relationship that the Swiss Mennonite settlers experienced with the American Indians.

2. *Read the paragraphs more carefully, trying to recognize the main divisions.* Keep a broad view as you read. Remember, you are looking for main divisions.

You should have recognized two main divisions in the lesson above: (1) the peaceful relationships between the Swiss Mennonites and the Indians before the French and Indian War and (2) the sufferings they experienced during the war. The last paragraph is a conclusion and therefore will not appear on the outline.

3. *Read the lesson again, narrowing your focus this time so that you can identify significant details and see how they relate to the main divisions.* Following these three steps should produce an outline similar to the one below.

Swiss Mennonite Encounters With Indians

I. Peaceful relationships before French and Indian War
  A. Because they did not live on frontier lines
  B. Because they practiced nonresistance
    1. Treated Indians considerately and honestly
    2. Used no force against Indians
    3. Refused protection of the forts
  C. Because the Indians living in their areas were generally friendly
    1. Group of Delawares south of Bethlehem attended Sunday meetings
    2. Mennonite children played with Indians in Lancaster area
      a. Indians named a boy Cristy, after a Mennonite
      b. Cristy taught white boys to make bows and arrows
    3. Indians in surrounding neighborhoods became Christians
II. Sufferings during French and Indian War
  A. Reasons
    1. Indians embittered by Walking Purchase (1737) and Albany Purchase (1754)
    2. Indians united with French to fight English
  B. Examples
    1. October 16, 1755, at Penns Creek—all 25 settlers killed, scalped, or captured
    2. October 18, 1755, south of Sunbury—25 settlers killed
    3. 1757–58 massacres
      a. In Lebanon County
      b. In Northkill, near Hamburg
      c. In Page County, Virginia
    4. September 7, 1758
      a. Letter sent from Virginia to Holland
        (1) 50 massacred
        (2) 200 left homeless
      b. Aid of $376.40 sent from Holland to Virginia

No two people working with the same composition are likely to produce identical outlines. But the outlines should definitely be similar in the main topics and subtopics that they portray.

Applying the Lesson

A. Improve this partial outline. Each starred line has an error.

Basic Steps in Making Bread

*I. Preparing the Dough
  A. Warm a large bowl
    1. Run hot water around inside

*2. drain off water
*B. Pour correct amount of lukewarm water into bowl
*C. Yeast into warm water
D. Add sugar and stir well
E. Cover and set aside
*1. until it foams
*2. Wait until it doubles in volume
*F. Remaining ingredients mixed in well
1. Salt
*2. Add shortening
*3. flour as directed
*G. Adding remaining flour
*1. To make soft, pliable dough
H. Place dough on lightly floured breadboard
II. Kneading the dough
*A. Working with lightly floured hands
B. Knead vigorously
*1. work toward center of dough
2. Turn dough repeatedly
*a. Until dough becomes smooth, springy, and satiny
*C. Shape into a large ball.
*1. Place in warm, greased bowl to rise

B. Write an outline of this composition.

The Island That Exploded

Krakatoa is a volcanic island in the Sunda Strait of Indonesia, between Java and Sumatra. At the beginning of 1883, this island contained about 18 square miles (47 km^2) and was populated by only a few native inhabitants. But later that year, an event occurred on Krakatoa that thousands of people heard of in a very literal way, with effects that were visible around the world for the greater part of a year.

Krakatoa's only known previous eruption had been a moderate one in 1680. But in the spring of 1883, it became clear that the volcano was stirring again. Two new fissures opened, with smoke and steam pouring out. A stream of lava cut a wide swath through the nearby jungle. The Sunda Strait was gradually covered with such a thick layer of floating cinders that by mid-August, ship captains no longer dared to sail through. On the island itself, the ground became so hot that the natives had to seek refuge in their boats.

Deep inside the island, the pressure of volcanic gases was growing more and more intense. On the afternoon of August 26, the huge rock layers in the side of the volcano—beneath the water level—suddenly buckled and broke apart, allowing white-hot lava to burst forth. Ocean water poured into the new fissure, changing instantly into steam as it contacted the hot lava; and soon a tremendous explosion ripped through the rocks. Again and again the ocean rushed into the opening, and time after time the island was rocked by stupendous explosions as the superheated steam shattered more and more of the massive rock layers.

Finally on the morning of August 27, the seawater reached the volcanic center of Krakatoa. The resulting explosion was so powerful that the entire northern two-thirds of the island was blown away. About 5 cubic miles (21 km^3) of rock were blasted as high as 30 miles (50 km) into the air. The noise of the explosion was heard as far away as Australia, 2,200 miles distant (3,500 km); and the resulting waves were observed as far away as Africa, 5,000 miles distant (8,000 km). Clouds of smoke and dust blotted out the sun, plunging parts of Indonesia into darkness for two days.

Along with the noise came great shock waves that traveled around the world in all directions. The first of these reached London, England, some 36 hours after the explosion—arriving from the west. Then a second wave struck the city from the east. Back and forth the shock waves went, convulsing the atmosphere for more than ten days before their energy was spent.

The explosion caused widespread death and destruction. Some 36,000 people drowned when the coastal towns of nearby Java and Sumatra were struck by a wall of water 120 feet high (37 m). Red-hot ashes fell on hundreds of square miles, burying whole towns, turning rice paddies into deserts, and reducing jungles to ash-choked ruins.

Dust from the volcano was carried some 50 miles (80 km) aloft, where it hung in the atmosphere for months. Winds carried the dust over land and sea, drawing a veil across the sun and causing strange sights in the heavens. People around the world saw blue and lead-colored sunsets, green stars, and a green moon.

For months after the explosion, the little that remained of Krakatoa was utterly dead. But slowly life returned, carried by currents of air and water. The wind brought seeds, insects, and birds, and the water carried insect eggs, reptiles, and logs on which were snails and other small creatures. In fact, Krakatoa became an ideal place for scientists to observe how communities of plants and animals develop in a completely dead and isolated place. The government allowed no human visitors there except scientists; and within forty years, the island that had exploded was again teeming with plants and animals of every description.

Review Exercises

A. Write whether each statement about study skills is *true* or *false*. [9–12]

1. Before you can study at your best, you must take an interest in your work
2. After you study a lesson, the rate at which you forget the material increases as time passes.
3. You should begin your study period by doing first what is most enjoyable.
4. Surveying a lesson before reading it gives you a helpful overview of the lesson.

5. You should wait until you have read a lesson before asking questions about it.
6. If you cannot recite answers to your questions about a lesson, you have not mastered that lesson.
7. When skimming a book, you should be sure to look at the preface or introduction.
8. Skillful skimming of a lesson can often take the place of studying the lesson.
9. Note-taking and summarizing promote logical thinking because the person doing these activities must understand the speaker's or writer's development.
10. Good notes should have all the main points and some of the supporting details.

B. Name the five steps in the SQ3R study method. After each one, briefly explain how to apply that step in studying a lesson. [10]

---

15. Outlining the Life Story of a Bible Character: Finding the Main Ideas

Christians often use outlining in their Bible study. Outlining skills serve well in preparing sermons, topics, and devotional meditations; in planning articles; and in studying Bible characters for personal benefit.

An outline of a Bible character's life story highlights the significant details of the person's birth, life, and death. The Bible does not give enough information about every character to always make an extensive outline. On the other hand, the Bible gives so many details about some characters that you would need a very long outline to include them all. Of course, the life story of many Bible characters can be outlined in more than one way. A given outline is not necessarily the only one that is correct.

The Bible study needed to form this kind of outline is not something you can do in a few minutes. First, you must study all the Scriptures that refer to the character whose life story you plan to outline. Use a concordance, topical Bible, Bible dictionary, or other reference books to find and read all those Scriptures. Be alert for name variations and for verses that do not specifically name the person. As you read those passages, think: "What short title would summarize this character's life?"

Then as you read and reflect further on those Scriptures, you must decide on the major divisions you will use. Often the simplest approach is to follow a chronological order, especially if the Bible gives details about the character's birth and childhood, his life, and his death. But the outline may also follow a topical order, emphasizing such things as influences that shaped the person's life, character traits that he illustrates, and contributions that he made to God's work.

To illustrate the kind of outlining in focus, we will use the life of Asa, the sixth king of Judah. You would begin by reading all the verses that refer to him. *Nave's Topical Bible* lists the following references: 1 Kings 15:8–24; 1 Chronicles 3:10; 2 Chronicles 14, 15, 16; and Matthew 1:7. As you read these passages, keep thinking about a good title to use.

The verses in 1 Kings 15 and in 2 Chronicles 14 and 15 will probably impress you with the wonderful way in which King Asa led his people back to the worship of the true God. But the verses in 2 Chronicles 16 present a contrast as they describe Asa's disappointing failures later in life. So we could use this title: "Asa—Revival and Failure."

After you have chosen a title, you are ready to decide whether you will follow a chronological or a topical order of development. Consider all that the Scriptures say about the character. Can you see any general categories into which the details fit? If the Bible account includes many details of the character's life, you will probably choose a chronological order that goes through his early life, his youth, his early adulthood, and so on. If the Bible gives few details of this nature, a topical arrangement will probably be better. In that case, you will need to list the details and consider the relationships among them.

First, let us form a chronological outline of Asa's life. This means looking at his life and dividing it into logical time periods. The first division is fairly easy: his birth and early life. But where do we go from there? Does his adult life show any distinct divisions or changes? Yes, it does. After living faithfully for a number of years, Asa turned away from God. This makes a logical dividing point on our outline: first his years of faithfulness and then the time of his failure.

Asa's failure came when he was near the end of life. The remaining information is mainly about his death and burial. This gives us the following chronological outline.

Asa—Revival and Failure

I. His birth and childhood
II. His faithfulness
III. His failure
IV. His death and burial

Now let us develop a topical outline of Asa's life. We must keep our view broad and general, keeping his whole life in focus. Specific details are important only in relation to more-general observations concerning his life. What general observations can we make? Doubtless, the Bible details about this character could be grouped in a number of different ways. The following topical outline is just one possibility.

Asa—Revival and Failure

I. Influences that shaped his life
II. Characteristics that were evident in his life
III. Contributions that he made to God's cause
IV. Lessons that his life holds for us

If we were forming a topical outline of Abraham's life, one of our main topics would surely refer to his faith. An outline of Moses' life would probably have a main point concerning his meekness, and an outline of Job's life would have one about his patience. Any topical outline of a Bible character's life should definitely include his most outstanding characteristics.

Outlining the life story of a Bible character is a valuable exercise that helps us to gain a clearer overall perspective of that person. It enables us to see truths that we probably would never see by simply reading about him.

Applying the Lesson

A. Prepare to outline the life story of one of the following Bible characters by reading all the verses in the Bible which refer to that character.

1. Jephthah	4. Ruth	7. Noah
2. Esau	5. Balaam	8. Esther
3. Jonah	6. Haman	

B. Begin forming your outline by choosing an appropriate title and listing the major divisions of the character's life. You may use either chronological or topical order.

---

16. Outlining the Life Story of a Bible Character: Filling In the Details

The main topics of your outline give you a sense of direction as you further study the life of a Bible character. These main ideas help you to focus on specific areas of the character's life as you add smaller details to your outline.

With your main divisions written down, read again the verses that relate to the character's life; then you will be ready to fill in the details under each main topic.

Chronological Outline

On the chronological outline of Asa's life in Lesson 15, the first main topic is "His birth and childhood." The Bible gives little information about Asa's early life, but we do find the following details. (For the material about his father, we must expand our research and read about King Abijah.)

Asa—Revival and Failure

I. His birth and childhood
   A. Was the son of Abijah
      1. Abijah's early profession of loyalty to God
      2. Abijah's later failure in true worship and godly living
   B. Was great-great-grandson of King David
   C. Was an ancestor of Jesus Christ
   D. Was born in time of widespread apostasy

Now you are ready to fill in the details under the second main topic, "His faithfulness." As you consider the years when Asa was faithful to God, look for general divisions. You will see three distinct periods: his years of peace, his victory over the Ethiopians, and his leading of the people in revival. We will use these three divisions as subtopics and place the smaller details where they fit under them.

- II. His faithfulness
  - A. Laid a good foundation in years of peace
    - 1. Removed idolatry
    - 2. Commanded the people to seek God
    - 3. Fortified the cities
    - 4. Raised an army
  - B. Led his people to victory over the Ethiopians
    - 1. Faced a formidable army nearly twice as large as his own
    - 2. Cried to the Lord for help
      - a. Recognized God's ability to work through many or few
      - b. Pleaded for God's help
      - c. Expressed complete confidence in God
    - 3. Experienced a miraculous victory
    - 4. Pursued the enemy to complete victory
    - 5. Gained an abundance of spoil
  - C. Led his people in spiritual revival
    - 1. Received encouragement from the prophet Azariah's message
    - 2. Continued to remove idolatry and evil from Judah
    - 3. Renewed true worship
    - 4. Provided a spiritual haven for many who sought the Lord
    - 5. Led the people in an outstanding worship experience
      - a. An offering of 700 oxen and 7,000 sheep
      - b. A renewed covenant to seek the Lord
      - c. A time of great rejoicing
    - 6. Removed his idolatrous grandmother from being queen mother
    - 7. Brought into the temple that which his father and he had dedicated

To complete the outline, we would follow the same procedure for the rest of the main topics. Let us look now at the development of a topical outline.

Topical Outline

The first main topic on our topical outline is "Influences that shaped his life." This thought is related to that of the first main topic of the chronological outline above, but it represents a different viewpoint. Ask yourself: What influences do we find that would have helped to shape Asa's life? One that the Scriptures mention is his parents and grandparents. They certainly were major influences on Asa, so those points belong under this main topic.

What other factors would have influenced Asa? The low spiritual condition of Judah when he was growing up, and his acquaintance with the true God. Arranging these details under our main topic gives us the following outline.

Asa—Revival and Failure

I. Influences that shaped his life
   A. The inconsistency of his father Abijah
      1. Father showed measure of faith and loyalty
      2. Father failed in true worship and godly living
   B. The idolatry of his grandmother
   C. The apostasy of his people
   D. The God of his fathers

Now we are ready to fill in the details under the second main topic, "Characteristics that were evident in his life." As we consider this point, we remember that Asa was faithful for much of his life but then turned away from God. That suggests two divisions under this point, one for his godly qualities and one for the ungodly ones. By examining the Scriptures more closely, we can fill in further details under these two subtopics. Notice these points on our outline.

II. Characteristics that were evident in his life
   A. Godly qualities during most of his reign
      1. Spiritual interest
      2. Alertness
      3. Foresight
      4. Ability to organize
      5. Trust in the Lord
      6. Prayerfulness
      7. Perseverance
         a. In defeating the enemy
         b. In continuing the revival
      8. Courage
      9. Willingness to sacrifice for God's cause
   B. Ungodly qualities in his last years
      1. In his league with Ben-hadad
         a. Failure to trust in the Lord
         b. Confidence in a heathen king
      2. In his treatment of the prophet Hanani
         a. Anger at being rebuked
         b. Rashness in throwing the prophet into prison
      3. In his oppression of the people
      4. In his response to his physical disease
         a. Failure to trust in the Lord
         b. Confidence in the physicians

Once again, we would finish the outline by following the same procedure for all the main topics that are left.

When you have a well-rounded set of details under each point of your outline, check to see that all the points are in logical order. Also make sure you have used good form on your whole outline. Check your headings especially to see that they do not overlap in thought and that the points are as nearly parallel as possible. Finally, write the entire outline neatly.

Applying the Lesson

Follow the method described in this lesson to finish the outline you began in Lesson 15.

---

17. Improving Your Speaking Style, Part 1: Eye Contact

Over the past few years, you have had several assignments in which you went to the front of the classroom and addressed your classmates as an audience. In those assignments, you worked mainly to develop a speech with good content and organization. After all, the most important part of an effective speech is having something meaningful to say.

But having something meaningful to say is not enough. You must also say it in a meaningful way. Your *speaking style* contributes greatly to the effectiveness of what you say. How well do you communicate with an audience if you speak in a mumble? Can you capture the listeners' attention if your eyes are glued to your notes? Will a dead monotone stir an audience to action? Of course not. Interesting and meaningful content requires appealing presentation to make an effective speech. This is the first of three lessons that give pointers on improving your speaking style.

Eye contact with the audience is a vital part of effective public speaking. Because many people feel self-conscious before a group, they tend to look somewhere else—at their notes, the floor, or the back wall. But meeting the eyes of your audience is so important that you dare not neglect it. Eye contact establishes an unspoken link with your listeners. It arrests their attention and shows that you are talking directly to them. It helps you to know whether you are communicating clearly. The listeners' reactions and facial expressions reveal whether you are talking loudly enough, whether your points are clear to them, and whether they enjoy what you are saying. Moreover, eye contact actually helps you to emphasize important points.

This means that you must look directly at your listeners. You are speaking to *people,* not to your notes or the walls. You are speaking to *individuals,* not to an abstract mass called an audience. Merely glancing at the group or running your eyes unseeingly over the audience is not eye contact. Look directly at individual listeners. You will know which person's eyes you meet, but that person will not know whether you are looking at him or at the person beside him. If you meet the eyes of persons in every part of the audience—in the front, in the back, to the left, and to the right—it will help each listener to feel that you have spoken directly to him.

Plan to establish eye contact with your listeners from the very beginning, with your introduction. This immediately communicates that you have something you want to tell them, something you consider worthwhile. Throughout the speech, maintain regular eye contact with your audience. However, you should not act like a programmed machine, raising your head at scheduled intervals. Rather, look at your audience naturally as you look at your friends when you talk to them.

Eye contact is especially important when you want to emphasize a certain point. Suppose in a discussion of honesty, you want to warn against exaggeration. You look down at your notes and carefully read this sentence: "We always weaken what we exaggerate." But imagine how much more effective that statement will be if you look directly at an individual in the group and say, "We always weaken what we exaggerate." Eye contact is an unobtrusive but forceful way of telling your audience, "Now, listen to this."

Finally, you should look at your audience as you conclude your speech. Though it is almost finished and you may be eager to return to your seat, your work is not quite done. Give it your best to the end. Have a well-planned conclusion, give it with fervor, look directly at your listeners—and you will end your speech on a solid, positive note.

You may think, "But I'm too nervous to look up while I'm talking. I'll get all mixed up if I do that." Those feelings are normal. But take your mind off yourself and concentrate on your subject. Think about your listeners and how they will benefit from what you have to tell them. Also remember that they are kind, sympathetic friends, who understand the difficulty you face and who want you to succeed. Like most hard tasks, this one becomes easier once you begin and also as you gain experience.

Your teacher will likely use the chart below to evaluate your speaking style assignments. This lesson introduces eye contact, so this assignment will be evaluated only for that one point of emphasis. In the next speaking style lesson, you will be evaluated on eye contact and the point of emphasis in that lesson. The third lesson will introduce a final point of emphasis, thus giving three items that your teacher will evaluate in your speaking.

Evaluation of Speaking Style

Part		***Points of Emphasis***	
	Eye Contact	*Voice Control*	*Enthusiasm*
1.	———	....	....
2.	———	———	....
3.	———	———	———

G = Good **F** = Fair **P** = Poor

Applying the Lesson

Prepare a talk of three to six minutes on one of the following topics or on another idea approved by your teacher. Think through your topic until it is part of you, so that you can speak confidently and wholeheartedly.

1. An accident or natural disaster experienced by your family
2. Memories of a special trip or an exciting day
3. An enjoyable family or school project

---

18. Chapter 2 Review

A. List from memory the five points of the SQ3R study method.

B. Write *true* or *false* for each sentence.

1. You can develop interest in a subject by studying it as if you were interested.
2. The best time to do the hardest assignments is near the end of a study period.
3. A pleasant environment can help you study more efficiently.
4. Slouching can hinder your study because it reduces the amount of oxygen your brain receives.
5. The rate at which you forget is highest right after you have studied something.
6. The first step in studying a lesson should be to read it carefully.
7. Asking questions before reading a lesson helps you to read more purposefully.
8. Even though you have studied a lesson thoroughly, using the SQ3R method, you will need to review before taking a test.
9. When you read actively, you read to find specific information.
10. Skimming can become an effective substitute for detailed study.
11. Skimming is a good way to evaluate a book without absorbing its wrong influence.
12. When skimming a book, you need not take time to read its preface or introduction.
13. Skimming can be useful when reviewing material.
14. When skimming a book, you should occasionally read a paragraph or two.
15. Taking notes and summarizing help you to listen or read with an active mind.
16. A good rule for note-taking is "The more, the better."
17. A good summary should be written primarily in your own words.
18. A good summary should be about half as long as the original material.
19. Eye contact involves meeting the eyes of individual listeners.
20. Eye contact is important at the end but not the beginning of your talk.

C. Answer these questions about study skills.
   1. Why is interest the most important attitude for effective studying?
   2. What are three ways to develop self-discipline in your studying?
   3. For what two reasons is a regular study time important?
   4. What is meant by reviewing actively?
   5. What are four worthwhile purposes of skimming?
   6. What are some types of significant information that you should write in your notes?
   7. What are the four basic steps in summarizing?

D. Answer these questions about outlining.
   1. How does outlining a lesson force a student to analyze it thoroughly?
   2. What long-term benefits does outlining have?
   3. When outlining the life story of a Bible character, what is the first step you must take after choosing the character?
   4. What are two possible orders you may follow in outlining the life story of a Bible character?

E. Copy this partial outline, correcting all the errors.

The Art of Rug Braiding

I. What are some incentives?
   A. a simple skill to learn
   B. It is a good way to recycle old material.
   C. Can be a means to earn money
      1. High demand
         a. In craft shops
         b. Farmers' markets
      2. Flexible schedule
         a. Can be done in short snatches of time
   D. a worthwhile product to use
      1. They can fit with the décor of almost any room.
      2. come in great variety
         a. Variety of colors
         b. Various materials
         c. In a variety of shapes
            (1) Circles
            (2) In semicircles
            (3) oblongs
            (4) Can be squares
      3. Serviceable
         a. Simple to clean
         b. Reversed easily
         c. Conveniently enlarged
II. Procedures

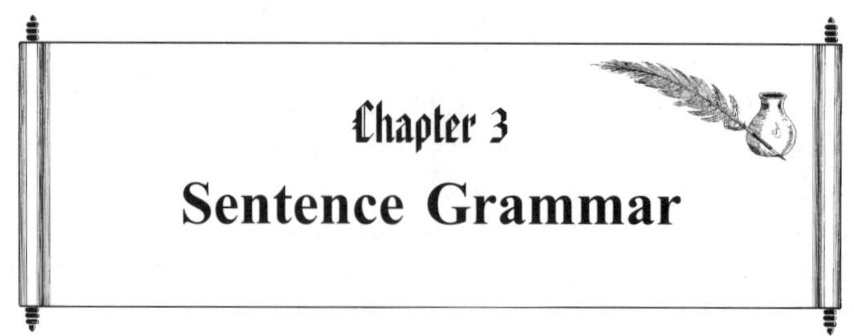

19. Complete Sentences and Sentence Skeletons

The sentence is the basic unit of language. A good grasp of sentence grammar, therefore, is essential to every kind of communication—listening, speaking, reading, and writing.

1. *A sentence is a group of words that expresses a complete thought.* It makes a statement, asks a question, gives a command, or makes an exclamation.

> Jesus Christ is Lord.
> Are we submitting to His lordship?
> Walk faithfully in His footsteps.
> If only all men would bow before Him!

2. *Every sentence can be divided into two parts: the complete subject and the complete predicate.* The complete subject tells *who* or *what* the sentence is about, and the complete predicate tells what the subject *does* or *is.*

> | complete subject | complete predicate |
> The Nelson Crider's, our neighbors for ten years, have moved to Illinois.

Sometimes the complete subject comes after the complete predicate or between parts of the complete predicate. Such a sentence is written in inverted or mixed word order, as you will see in Lesson 25. In the following sentences, the complete subject is underlined once and the complete predicate is underlined twice.

> Toward the heap of lumber streaked Brownie, our small but energetic dog.
> After a short scuffle, he came back, dragging a large woodchuck.

3. *The sentence skeleton consists of the simple subject and the simple predicate.* The simple subject is the basic part of the complete subject. It is always a substantive: a noun or pronoun, or a word, phrase, or clause used as a noun. The simple predicate is the verb or verb phrase. Either or both of these sentence parts can be compound.

4. *A fragment does not express a complete thought.* You can correct a fragment either by joining it to another sentence or by adding words to make it a complete sentence.

Fragments:

> On Sunday we plan to visit Alton Mennonite Church. Where Uncle Harold's attend.
> Two pies cooling on the counter.

Revisions:

On Sunday we plan to visit Alton Mennonite Church, where Uncle Harold's attend.

On Sunday we plan to visit Alton Mennonite Church. That is where Uncle Harold's attend.

Two pies were cooling on the counter.

The two pies cooling on the counter are for the Stutzman family.

5. *An elliptical sentence has one or more parts missing, but it expresses a complete thought because the missing parts are understood.* Most imperative sentences are elliptical because the subject *you* is understood. Also, many sentences with clauses of comparison are elliptical because parts of that clause are understood. Example: The Mississippi River is longer than the Susquehanna River (is long).

Other elliptical sentences are understandable because of the context. Elliptical sentences of this kind occur mainly in dialogue.

"Are you ready to get to work?"

"Where?"

"In the storage room. Mother says we're cleaning it out today."

6. *A run-on error occurs when two or more sentences are joined incorrectly.* You can correct a run-on error in one of the following ways.

a. By inserting a comma and a coordinating conjunction between the two parts. (Inserting only a comma produces a comma splice.)
b. By inserting a semicolon between the two parts.
c. By changing one of the clauses to a dependent clause.
d. By dividing the incorrect sentence into two or more sentences.

Run-on error:

Jesus' enemies tried to trap Him several times, He always put them to silence.

Corrections:

(a) Jesus' enemies tried to trap Him several times, but He always put them to silence.
(b) Jesus' enemies tried to trap Him several times; He always put them to silence.
(c) Though Jesus' enemies tried to trap Him several times, He always put them to silence.
(d) Jesus' enemies tried to trap Him several times. He always put them to silence.

Applying the Lesson

A. Copy the complete subject, draw a vertical line after it, and copy the complete predicate. If the subject does not come first, rewrite the sentence in normal subject–predicate order before marking the division.

1. God's people should be ready to sacrifice to serve others.
2. The welfare of others holds priority over personal welfare.

3. When God's love fills the heart, the child of God finds pleasure in helping others.
4. In the pathway of selfless service lies the way of true joy.
5. By such love for our brethren, the world can see that we love Jesus.
6. If we find selfishness crowding out kindness, we must repent.
7. Through selfishness comes much human heartache.
8. Through the power of the Gospel, every person can realize the joy of selflessness.

B. Copy the simple subject and the simple predicate of each sentence. Draw a vertical line between the two parts. (Watch for compound parts.)
   1. A soft answer turns away wrath.
   2. Angry words stir up bitterness.
   3. A true peacemaker talks and acts in a peaceable manner.
   4. By seeking peace, we can build good relationships with others.
   5. Thoughtfulness and kindness are essential qualities for the peacemaker.
   6. A person seeking peace not only will avoid doing unkind things but also will find ways to express good will.
   7. Feelings of impatience or intolerance can quickly destroy peaceful relationships.
   8. Often politeness and cheerfulness have contributed to peaceableness.
   9. From Great-grandfather Gerber's excellent memory come many old-time stories.
   10. Electricity and telephones came to his rural community in his childhood and dramatically changed life on his father's farm.
   11. With the coming of electricity, farm jobs did often become easier.
   12. With the telephone came various advantages for the farmer and his family.
   13. Both the power of electricity and the convenience of telephones brought great changes and raised difficult questions for God's people.
   14. The value of such new things is determined by their use.

C. These paragraphs have mistakes in joining or dividing sentences. Write the words immediately before and after each mistake, and show how to join or divide the sentences correctly. You may need to insert a conjunction.
   1. The mute swan, quite common in parts of Europe and Asia, is a beautiful, graceful bird. The swan is a large bird. Attaining a length of sixty inches and a wingspan of seventy-five inches. Unlike many birds, the female generally is slightly larger than the male.
   2. Mute swans are primarily herbivorous. Meaning that they feed on plant material. Since they spend most of their time on the water, their diet consists mostly of aquatic plants and roots, they also eat some small fish, frogs, and insects. An adult swan may consume as much as ten pounds of plant material in one day.
   3. The swan's long, graceful neck is not merely ornamental it is essential for feeding. By stretching out its long neck, a swan is able to reach

far underwater to get vegetation. That other waterfowl, such as ducks and geese, cannot reach. In fact, if a swan upends itself, it can reach nearly three feet under the water.

4. Mute swans nest during the months of March through June. The male and the female work together at building the nest on the ground near a body of water. The male brings the sticks and reeds, the female fashions her nest from these materials. The female lays eggs every other day. Until she has from five to eight eggs. After an incubation period of thirty-six days, the cygnets hatch.

D. Show how to correct the fragments and run-on errors in this dialogue, using the same method as in Part C. Do not change elliptical sentences. If a paragraph has no mistake, write *correct.*

1. "Dorothy, will you please slice these loaves of bread? That Sister Bertha gave us?"
2. "Surely," answered Dorothy. "Everyone has been very kind to us while you've been sick, we'll need to watch for opportunities to return their kindness."
3. "Yes, indeed! It's a wonderful privilege to be part of a caring brotherhood."
4. "You're right. I remember when we first attended church here at Locust Point, we've surely learned a lot since then."
5. "Ten years," murmured Mother. "And it's been a happy ten years."
6. "Yes, it has. God has certainly blessed us. In many ways that I can hardly fathom."

Review Exercises

Write correctly each word that should be capitalized. If no capital letter is needed, write *correct.* [1]

1. magellan's ship *victoria*
2. at horst's appliance center
3. the book *in from the wasteland*
4. study bookkeeping II this winter
5. in the years before the civil war
6. see mr. horn's farm in the valley
7. in jesus' sermon on the mount
8. with my father and one of my uncles
9. some halls cough drops for sunday
10. about jeffersonian ideas in history class

---

20. Sentence Complements

A *complement* is a word that *completes* the meaning of a sentence skeleton. There are three basic kinds of complements: subjective, object, and objective complements.

Subjective Complements

A *subjective complement* completes the sentence skeleton by referring to the subject. Verbs before subjective complements must be linking verbs: forms of *be* or verbs that can be replaced by them, such as *taste, look, grow, seem,* and *remain.*

1. A *predicate nominative* is a substantive that follows a linking verb and renames the subject.

> Our Master is the Lord Jesus Christ.
> (*Lord Jesus Christ* renames *Master.*)
> Christians are strangers and pilgrims in this world.
> (Both *strangers* and *pilgrims* rename *Christians.*)

2. A *predicate adjective* follows a linking verb and modifies the subject.

> God is altogether worthy of our worship.
> (*Worthy* modifies *God.*)
> Father's voice sounded calm and confident.
> (Both *calm* and *confident* modify *voice.*)
> Our hearts felt light and cheerful.
> (Both *light* and *cheerful* modify *hearts.*)

Verbs like *look, turn,* and *feel* are not always linking verbs. In some sentences they are followed by adverbs, direct objects, or other sentence parts. A sentence contains a subjective complement only if the main verb expresses being rather than action, and only if the verb is followed by a substantive that renames the subject or an adjective that modifies the subject.

> The clouds turned an inky black.
> (*Turned* expresses being; it can be replaced by *were. Black* modifies *clouds. Black* is a predicate adjective.)
> The storm has turned suddenly toward the south.
> (*Has turned* expresses action; it cannot be replaced by *has been.* Neither *suddenly* nor *toward the south* renames or modifies *storm;* they are adverbs.)

Object Complements

An *object complement* completes the sentence skeleton by receiving the action of a transitive verb.

1. A *direct object* is a substantive that receives the action of a transitive verb directly. In a sentence with a direct object, the subject performs the action, and the direct object receives the action. To find the direct object, say the skeleton and ask *whom* or *what.*

> God created the world out of nothing.
> (*World* receives the action of *created.*)
> God created the heaven and the earth in just six days.
> (Both *heaven* and *earth* receive the action of *created.*)
> God blessed the seventh day and sanctified it as a day of rest.
> (*Day* receives the action of *blessed,* and *it* receives the action of *sanctified.*)

2. An *indirect object* is a substantive that receives the action of a transitive verb indirectly. An indirect object comes between a verb and its direct object. To find an indirect object, say the skeleton with the direct object, and ask *to whom or what* or *for whom or what.*

Sharon has given us some valuable help.
(Sharon has given help *to whom*? *Us* is the indirect object.)
Leon told Kevin and me the plans.
(Leon told the plans *to whom*? *Kevin* and *me* are the indirect objects.)

Objective Complements

An *objective complement* is a noun or an adjective that follows and completes the direct object of a verb which expresses the idea of "making" or "considering." If the objective complement is a noun, it renames the direct object; if it is an adjective, it modifies the direct object. An objective complement is somewhat like a subjective complement. A subjective complement relates to the subject, but an objective complement relates to the direct object. Generally, you can insert the words *to be* between the direct object and the objective complement.

The heavy rains made the creek a raging river.
(*River* is a noun that renames the direct object *creek.*)

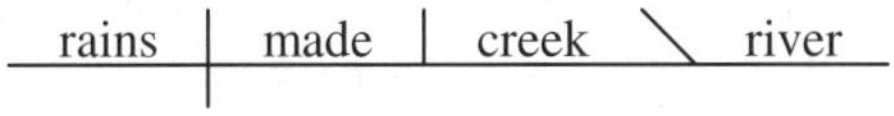

rains | made | creek \ river

Meteorologists had considered a flood quite likely.
(*Likely* is an adjective that modifies the direct object *flood.*)

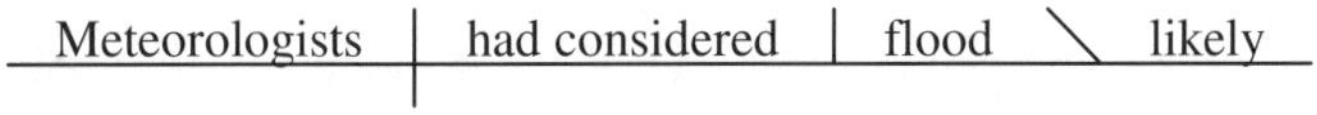

Meteorologists | had considered | flood \ likely

Use the following steps to find an objective complement.

1. Identify the sentence skeleton and the direct object.
2. Determine whether the verb has the idea of "making" or "considering." If it does not, there can be no objective complement. If it does, go to Step 3.
3. Determine whether the sentence has an indirect object. If it does, there can be no objective complement. If it does not, go to Step 4.
4. Determine whether the direct object is followed by a noun that renames the direct object or by an adjective that modifies the direct object. Also determine whether you can insert the words *to be* between the direct object and the noun or adjective.

At first we thought the idea impractical.
Step 1: Skeleton and direct object: *We thought idea.*
Step 2: The verb *thought* has the idea of "considering."
Step 3: There is no indirect object.
Step 4: The adjective *impractical* modifies *idea.* "Thought the idea to be impractical" is sensible. *Impractical* is an objective complement.

Then Father considered several other plans carefully.

Step 1: Skeleton and direct object: *Father considered plans.*

Step 2: The verb *considered* has the idea of "considering."

Step 3: There is no indirect object.

Step 4: *Plans* is not followed by a noun or an adjective that renames or modifies *plans.* There is no objective complement. (*Carefully* is an adverb.)

God has made the earth beautiful.

Step 1: Skeleton and direct object: *God has made earth.*

Step 2: The verb *has made* has the idea of "making."

Step 3: There is no indirect object.

Step 4: The adjective *beautiful* modifies *earth.* "Made the earth to be beautiful" is sensible. *Beautiful* is an objective complement.

God made Adam and Eve coats of skin.

Step 1: Skeleton and direct object: *God made coats.*

Step 2: The verb *made* has the idea of "making."

Step 3: There is an indirect object, *Adam and Eve.* There can be no objective complement.

Are you confused by the terms *subjective complement, object complement,* and *objective complement*? Remember that a subjective complement *refers* to the subject, and an objective complement *refers* to the direct object. An object complement *is* an object—either a direct object or an indirect object. But no subject *is* a complement, so there is no such thing as a subject complement.

Applying the Lesson

A. Copy each subjective complement, and label it *PN* for predicate nominative or *PA* for predicate adjective. If a sentence has no subjective complement, write *none.*

1. The Gospel message will never become outdated.
2. God's message is the answer to every man's needs.
3. Jesus' gracious words must have sounded sweet to the afflicted woman.
4. We should look often into God's Word for encouragement.
5. Two things to look for in each Bible passage are promises and commands.
6. God's Word should be growing precious and meaningful to you.
7. The warnings of the Bible should turn our minds to serious thoughts.
8. Bowser has become Richard's inseparable companion.
9. Aunt Geraldine has been a teacher or a mission worker for twenty years.
10. Judith's flower beds looked beautiful last week and have grown even more lovely since the rain.
11. The heat was high already this morning and became almost unbearable by noon.
12. Evelyn is both my cousin and my schoolmate.

B. Copy each object complement, and label it *DO* for direct object or *IO* for indirect object. If a sentence has no object complement, write *none.*

1. God's people must cultivate the Christian graces.

2. God faithfully describes these qualities in His Word.
3. The Lord gives His servants rich blessings of peace and joy.
4. The waffles turned a golden brown.
5. We children have been gathering walnuts and chestnuts in the pasture.
6. Grandfather Hackman made each grandchild a carved nameplate.
7. We gave Spot and Tippy baths this afternoon.
8. The boys dug potatoes and picked watermelons.
9. This morning Bonita worked on her afghan.
10. Marlene is filling the jelly dishes and the butter trays.
11. Orpha has mashed the potatoes and browned the butter.
12. Willie gave Father and the boys the message.

C. Copy the objective complements in these sentences. If a sentence has no objective complement, write *none.*

1. God's people recognize themselves responsible to live consistently.
2. We should be making our lives useful vessels for God's glory.
3. The trusting soul considers God well able to meet his every need.
4. The exercise of faith will make any trial bearable.
5. Kelvin constructed these rabbit hutches by himself.
6. Has Mr. Daley estimated the price of the job too high?
7. Will Mrs. Foster make this driftwood the centerpiece of her flower arrangement?
8. The girls worked hard all afternoon.
9. The boys thought their work even more difficult.
10. This dog is making himself a nuisance by his constant barking.

D. Copy each underlined complement, and label it *PN, PA, DO, IO,* or *OC.*

1. Do you consider <u>sharks</u> dangerous <u>creatures</u>?
2. Although tiger sharks are known <u>killers</u>, some shark experts actually consider <u>them</u> <u>gentle</u>.
3. God gave the <u>tiger shark</u> powerful <u>jaws</u> and serrated <u>teeth</u>.
4. Tiger sharks have keen <u>eyesight</u>, but two other senses are actually more <u>important</u> to their hunting than eyesight.
5. With its acute sense of smell, the tiger shark is <u>able</u> to detect minute traces of blood in the water.
6. Other creatures' nerve and muscle vibrations send the <u>shark</u> perceptible <u>messages</u> that pinpoint their location.
7. Perhaps the strangest things found in sharks' stomachs have been license <u>plates</u> and gasoline cans.
8. Tiger sharks are both <u>solitary</u> and <u>nomadic</u> in nature.

Review Exercises

For each underlined word, write *yes* or *no* to tell whether it should be followed by a comma. [2]

1. Our God is <u>omnipotent</u> <u>omniscient</u> and omnipresent.
2. Recognizing God's <u>greatness</u> and <u>goodness</u> we serve Him with our whole heart.

3. Sincere obedience not mere lip service demonstrates our love for God.
4. We pray to the Lord with sincere purpose and in simple faith.
5. Lead us our Father by Thy divine grace.

---

21. Retained Objects and Objective Complements

You know that many verbs pass their action to another word in the sentence. If the receiver of the action is an object complement, the verb is usually in the *active voice.* But if the receiver is the subject, the verb is in the *passive voice.* (You will study voice more fully in Chapter 9.) Compare the following sentences.

Active: God has given bountiful blessings.
(*Blessings,* the receiver, is the direct object.)

Passive: Bountiful blessings have been given by God.
(*Blessings,* the receiver, is the subject.)

Retained Object Complements

Can a verb in the passive voice have an object complement? Yes, it can. To show how that is possible, let us first change the sentence above so that it has a direct object and an indirect object.

Active: God has given *mankind* bountiful blessings.

Now let us change this sentence to the passive voice, with the indirect object serving as the subject.

Passive: *Mankind* has been given bountiful blessings by God.

Note that *blessings* still follows the verb and receives its action, the same as in the active voice. So it is still the direct object, even though the verb is in the passive voice. Since the direct object is the same as it was in the active voice, such a sentence is said to have a *retained direct object.*

We can also rewrite the original sentence in the passive voice with the direct object serving as the subject.

Passive: Bountiful blessings have been given *mankind* by God.

Now *blessings,* the direct object, has become the subject; and *mankind,* the indirect object, has been retained in its original position. *Mankind* is now a *retained indirect object.*

As these examples show, either a direct object or an indirect object may be retained. In fact, only a sentence with both kinds of objects in the active voice can have a retained object in the passive voice. A sentence can even have an indirect object without a direct object!

When you need to decide whether a sentence has a retained object, use the following steps.

1. Change the sentence so that the verb is in the active voice. (You may need to supply a subject.)
2. Identify the direct object and the indirect object. If the sentence does not have two kinds of complements, there can be no retained object.
3. See if either of these complements is an object in both active and passive voice constructions.

Problem: Nehemiah was given permission to return to Jerusalem.
Step 1: The king gave Nehemiah permission to return to Jerusalem.
Step 2: Direct object: *permission;* indirect object: *Nehemiah*
Step 3: *Permission* is a direct object in both voice constructions.
Solution: *Permission* is a retained direct object.

Problem: Nehemiah's labors were blessed by God.
Step 1: God blessed Nehemiah's labors.
Step 2: Direct object: *labors;* no indirect object
Solution: There is no retained object.

Problem: Good leadership was given the people by Nehemiah.
Step 1: Nehemiah gave the people good leadership.
Step 2: Direct object: *leadership;* indirect object: *people*
Step 3: *People* is an indirect object in both voice constructions.
Solution: *People* is a retained indirect object.

Retained Objective Complements

Not only object complements but also objective complements can be retained. A retained objective complement is an objective complement that is retained in a passive voice construction. Look at the following sentence. What are the direct object and the objective complement?

God makes His will plain to the sincere seeker.
(*will*—direct object; *plain*—objective complement)

You could rewrite this sentence in the passive voice.

God's will is made plain to the sincere seeker.

With the passive voice, the direct object *will* becomes the subject. What happens to the objective complement? It is retained in its original position, so now it is a *retained objective complement.*

When you need to decide whether a sentence has a retained objective complement, use the following steps.

1. Change the sentence so that the verb is in the active voice. (You may need to supply a subject.)
2. Identify the direct object and the objective complement. If the sentence does not have both a direct object and an objective complement, there can be no retained objective complement.

3. See if the same word is an objective complement in both active and passive voice constructions.

Problem: Our work was made more pleasant by our singing.
Step 1: Our singing made our work more pleasant.
Step 2: Direct object: *work;* objective complement: *pleasant*
Step 3: *Pleasant* is an objective complement in both active and passive voice constructions.
Solution: *Pleasant* is a retained objective complement.

Problem: The work has been done efficiently.
Step 1: We have done the work efficiently.
Step 2: Direct object: *work;* no objective complement
Solution: There is no retained objective complement.

Applying the Lesson

A. Rewrite each sentence so that the verb is in the passive voice. Follow the directions in parentheses for retaining complements. You may omit the *by* phrase at the end of your sentence unless it is needed for clarity.
1. Jesus gave the people many precious truths. (Retain the direct object.)
2. Soon darkness will make the outdoor gathering impractical. (Retain the objective complement.)
3. A young lad presented Jesus a small lunch. (Retain the indirect object.)
4. Jesus gave each person sufficient food. (Retain the direct object.)
5. The multitude considered Jesus a wonderful teacher. (Retain the objective complement.)
6. The people assigned Him the position of an earthly king. (Retain the indirect object.)

B. Copy each underlined complement, and label it *DO, IO,* or *OC.* Also write *ret.* after the label if the object is retained.
1. All creation gives <u>God</u> <u>glory</u> in one way or another.
2. Ungodly men may think <u>themselves</u> <u>independent</u> from God.
3. Yet even their wickedness will finally make God's <u>Name</u> <u>glorious</u>.
4. Every man is given the <u>opportunity</u> to glorify God of his free will.
5. God is brought acceptable <u>honor</u> only by His children.
6. God's judgment upon the wicked brings <u>Himself</u> <u>glory</u> as right is vindicated and wrong is punished.
7. The hot day has been made more <u>comfortable</u> by the breeze.
8. This beautiful set of tea towels was given <u>Mother</u> for her birthday.
9. A thorough housecleaning was given the old <u>cottage</u> by the mothers.
10. The barn was made quite a miserable ruin by years of neglect

C. Copy the retained complement in each sentence, and label it *DO ret., IO ret.,* or *OC ret.*
1. The farmers were given an uneasy feeling by the early cold spell.
2. Our farm is provided an adequate water supply by a large creek.

3. The whole countryside was made a winter wonderland by the freshly fallen snow.
4. A terrible scare was given Martha by a snake in the house.
5. The girls were shown several simple apron patterns by Aunt Louise.
6. We were shown the correct pronunciation of the unfamiliar word.
7. Several options were presented the congregation by the building committee.
8. The little house was made quite attractive by a new paint job.
9. The old wagon shed was made a chicken house by Uncle Laverne's brother.
10. Some good advice was offered the young man.
11. A simple but delicious meal was served the hardworking crew.
12. The report was made very interesting by the colorful details.

Review Exercises

A. Name the punctuation that should follow each underlined word: *colon, semicolon, ellipsis points,* or *none.* [4]

1. Father reverently read the Scripture <u>verses</u> afterward, he led us in prayer.
2. The brightest stars of the Northern Hemisphere include the <u>following</u> Arcturus, Vega, Cappella, and Procyon.
3. "Yes, Audrey, I would like to see your new place, <u>but</u>" Elaine said with a shrug.
4. When half of the corn was husked, the girls and Mother went inside to prepare it for <u>freezing</u> and we boys finished the husking, cleaned up the porch, and then helped in the kitchen.
5. Although he is only four years old, James enjoys taking care of Tabby and Mittens, our two <u>cats</u> Sport, our <u>dog</u> and Fluff, our lop-eared rabbit.

B. Write the letter of the sentence in which the boldface part is correct. [5, 6]

1. a. "Where is the verse, 'Blessed are the **peacemakers?'"** asked Father.
   b. "Where is the verse, 'Blessed are the **peacemakers'?"** asked Father.
2. a. We sang **"Loving Kindness";** that song always inspires me.
   b. We sang **"Loving Kindness;"** that song always inspires me.
3. a. "God loveth a cheerful **giver," (2 Corinthians 9:7)** and He promises to reward such.
   b. "God loveth a cheerful **giver" (2 Corinthians 9:7),** and He promises to reward such.
4. a. The clipper ship **"Thermopylae"** sailed from London to Melbourne, Australia, in 63 days.
   b. The clipper ship ***Thermopylae*** sailed from London to Melbourne, Australia, in 63 days.
5. a. Calvin gave a book report on ***Tips for Woodworkers.***
   b. Calvin gave a book report on **"Tips for Woodworkers."**
6. a. "Let love be without dissimulation **[pretense]**" (Romans 12:9).
   b. "Let love be without dissimulation **(pretense)**" (Romans 12:9).
7. a. "What shall we do **with—?"** Bonita dashed to the door.
   b. "What shall we do **with—"** Bonita dashed to the door.

8. a. Several families will make the **three-hour** drive to the ordination.
   b. Several families will make the **three hour** drive to the ordination.
9. a. This sentence has too many **"of's"** trailing at the end.
   b. This sentence has too many ***of*'s** trailing at the end.
10. a. We received **seventy-five-hundredths** of an inch of rain.
    b. We received **seventy-five hundredths** of an inch of rain.

---

22. Improving Your Writing Style, Part 2: Active Verbs

Imagine for a moment that you are observing a large, magnificent building. You gaze in awe at the large sandstone building blocks. You examine with fascination the massive main entrance with its intricate woodwork, and then you admire the elaborate windows. You tilt your head back, your eyes moving upward.

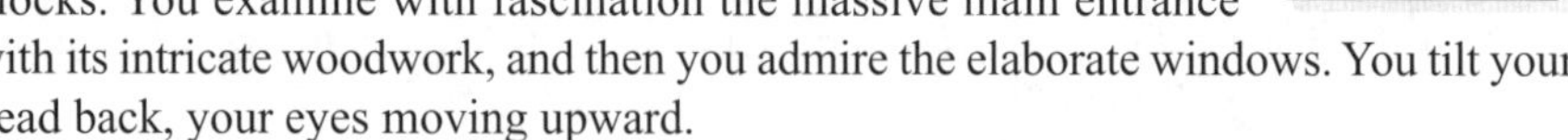

Suddenly a small boy comes running down the sidewalk, followed closely by a barking dog and two other boys. Do you continue admiring the impressive building? Surely not. You turn your head quickly to see what is happening.

The same thing holds true in writing. Action draws attention. For this reason, we must make our writing as active as we can. We need to use plenty of specific action verbs so that the reader can see exactly what is happening.

What about the little verb *be*? It shows up time after time. Do we need this little, inactive verb? Look at these typical sentences in which this verb appears.

> There was much sin in the city of Sodom.
> All evening the children were outside.
> Abraham was a man of great faith.

Used as a main verb, the forms of *be* express no action—only existence. Will this absence of action weaken our paragraphs? Should we root out *be* from all our writing? Or does this verb stand on its own merits as a verb we need, a verb with strength of its own? The following three guidelines will help you to work with this verb.

1. *Beware of using* there *followed by a form of* be. Whenever you spot a sentence beginning with *There is, There are, There was,* or *There were,* plan to revise it. Almost invariably, you can improve such sentences. Consider again the first example above.

> There was much sin in the city of Sodom.

Remove *There was,* and the basic thought of the sentence still remains: *much sin in the city of Sodom.* Now if we add an action verb to go with it, we will have a better sentence.

Sin abounded in the city of Sodom.
Much sin polluted the city of Sodom.
Sin corrupted the city of Sodom.

No longer do these sentences tell us merely that sin *was,* that it *existed* in Sodom. The verbs show what sin *did. Polluted* and *corrupted* go even further than *abounded* by showing how sin affected the city. By replacing *There was* with an active verb, we tell both what existed and what it did.

Here is another example.

During the night there was a heavy rain.

This time *there was* comes later in the sentence, but the problem is the same. If we remove *there was,* we have the subject of the sentence: *a heavy rain.* We must tell what the rain did, and the reader will know that the rain *was* without our saying so.

Heavy rain flooded our garden last night.

You will not find it easy to restructure every sentence that contains *there is* or *there was.* But if you make a special effort to weed out these phrases, you will help your sentences to "stand up and do something" rather than lying idly on the page.

2. *Examine each use of* be *as a main verb.* Surprisingly often, we can replace *be* with an action verb and thereby express the thought of the sentence more effectively. Look again at the second example sentence above.

All evening the children were outside.

So the children *were.* They existed. And they existed outside. But did they do nothing as they existed? Possibly, but not likely! They probably were *playing* or *running* or *talking* outside. Add that information to the sentence, and it takes on more life.

All evening the children played outside.

This does not mean that we must never use *be* as a main verb. In many cases, *be* is just the word we need. Here is the third example from the list above.

Abraham was a man of great faith.

Could we reword this sentence? Yes, we could write *Abraham, a man of great faith,* and add an action verb to tell what he did. We could write *Abraham obeyed God even though he did not know the outcome.* But does this revision really improve the original sentence? Not necessarily. Depending on the surrounding sentences, the revision may fit well and add vigor to the paragraph. Then again, the original sentence may fit effectively and stand in its own right.

The following paragraph concludes with a sentence using *be* as its main verb. Notice how well this sentence fills its place. (All the verbs are underlined.)

> At the call of God, Abraham <u>departed</u> from Ur and <u>moved</u> away, not knowing where God <u>would lead</u> him. He <u>left</u> his father's family at Haran and <u>traveled</u> on to the land of Canaan. Even there he <u>faced</u> great tests. When God <u>commanded</u> him to sacrifice his son Isaac, he <u>obeyed</u> without hesitation. Truly, Abraham <u>was</u> a man of great faith.

3. *When* be *is a linking verb, try to replace it with a more descriptive word.* We have a number of choices in this: *sound, look, appear, taste, feel, smell, become, seem, stay, grow, turn, remain, prove,* and others. Compare the sentences in the following pairs.

Nondescriptive forms of *be:*
Father's prediction of rain <u>was</u> correct.
In days of ease, the hearts of many <u>are</u> cold toward spiritual things.
More descriptive linking verbs:
Father's prediction of rain <u>proved</u> correct.
In days of ease, the hearts of many <u>grow</u> cold toward spiritual things.

Though *proved* and *grow* are still linking verbs, they do suggest action and therefore add strength to the sentence. The small change makes a definite improvement. Now consider this example.

> Although some Scripture verses *may be* difficult to comprehend, the Holy Spirit *is* our Guide into all truth.

We could say that some Scripture verses *may seem* or *may appear* difficult. But this changes the thought, suggesting that the Scriptures are not difficult to understand—they only seem that way. We probably will choose to keep the verb *may be.* And for the verb *is,* no other linking verb replaces it very well. The original sentence appears to have the best wording.

But wait. We can remove the linking verbs completely and reword the sentence with all active verbs!

> Although we <u>may find</u> it difficult to comprehend some Scripture verses, the Holy Spirit <u>guides</u> us into all truth.

How do we know when to revise a sentence and when to let it stand? That is part of the art of writing. We learn by doing, by practicing, by experimenting. Examine your uses of *be,* think of other ways to express the same thought, and then use the wording you consider most effective. Sometimes it will be a new wording with an active verb, sometimes a new wording with a more descriptive linking verb, and sometimes the original sentence.

Your assignment in this lesson will be to explain or illustrate a proverb from the Bible. Below are two examples of such an explanation. Do you see how the active verbs make the second one more direct and forceful?

Paragraphs with many forms of *be:*

"A soft answer turneth away wrath: but grievous words stir up anger" (Proverbs 15:1). The story of David and Abigail is a clear illustration of this proverb. When David's servants asked Nabal for provisions, his answer was one that might have been a record for grievous words. "Who is David?" asked Nabal. "Shall I take the food that I have prepared for my workers, and give it to someone I do not even know?" These words were so insulting to David that he was ready to wipe Nabal and his household from the face of the earth.

As soon as Abigail was aware of Nabal's response, she prepared enough food to feed a small army. Soon she was in the presence of David with her gift, saying, "Upon me, my lord, upon me let this iniquity be"—speaking such gracious words that David immediately was sorry for his murderous plans. By her soft answer, Abigail was able to turn away David's wrath and save the lives of everyone in her household. The impression she made on David was so favorable that after Nabal's death, David sent a proposal to Abigail, and soon she was his wife.

Paragraphs with more active verbs:

"A soft answer turneth away wrath: but grievous words stir up anger" (Proverbs 15:1). The story of David and Abigail clearly illustrates this proverb. When David's servants asked Nabal for provisions, he gave an answer that might have set a record for grievous words. "Who is David?" asked Nabal. "Shall I take the food that I have prepared for my workers, and give it to someone I do not even know?" These words stirred up such anger in David that he made preparations to wipe Nabal and his household from the face of the earth.

As soon as Abigail heard of Nabal's response, she prepared enough food to feed a small army. She hastened with her gift to David, saying, "Upon me, my lord, upon me let this iniquity be"—speaking such gracious words that David immediately repented of his murderous plans. By her soft answer, Abigail turned away David's wrath and saved the lives of everyone in her household. She made such a favorable impression on David that after Nabal's death, David sent a proposal to Abigail, and soon she became his wife.

Work hard to put action into your writing style. Use descriptive, active verbs. Replace *be* if you can use something better. Remember: action draws attention.

Applying the Lesson

In 150–200 words, explain or illustrate a verse from Proverbs. You may use one of the following or choose one yourself. Put special effort into using lively action words. Also work for originality as you studied in Lesson 3.

1. "A good name is rather to be chosen than great riches, and loving favour rather than silver and gold" (22:1).

2. "A word fitly spoken is like apples of gold in pictures of silver" (25:11).
3. "He that passeth by, and meddleth with strife belonging not to him, is like one that taketh a dog by the ears" (26:17).
4. "Pride goeth before destruction, and an haughty spirit before a fall" (16:18).
5. "Wealth gotten by vanity shall be diminished: but he that gathereth by labour shall increase" (13:11).

---

23. Phrases and Clauses

Some sentences consist merely of a sequence of single words, but others include phrases and clauses. Study the following examples.

> The calves bawled.
> The calves in the hutches were bawling for their breakfast before we got out of bed.

The second example has an adjective phrase (*in the hutches*), a verb phrase (*were bawling*), an adverb phrase (*for their breakfast*), and an adverb clause (*before we got out of bed*). By becoming skilled in working with phrases and clauses, you will improve your ability to communicate effectively.

Phrases

A *phrase* is a group of related words without a skeleton.

1. A *prepositional phrase* begins with a preposition (like *to, for,* or *with*), it ends with an object (usually a noun), and it includes all the modifiers of the object. A prepositional phrase is usually an adjective (modifying a substantive) or an adverb (modifying a verb or another modifier). Sometimes it is a noun because it names something.

> The tea in this bed came from Grandmother Petre.
> (*In this bed* is an adjective phrase modifying the noun *tea. From Grandmother Petre* is an adverb phrase modifying the verb *came.*)
> In the other bed is the place where we planted the tea from the meadow.
> (*In the other bed* is a noun phrase that names a place. It is the subject. *From the meadow* is an adjective phrase modifying *tea.*)

2. A *verbal phrase* contains a verb form used as another part of speech. The verbal phrase includes the verbal and all its modifiers and complements.

a. A gerund phrase contains an *-ing* form used as a noun.

> Standing solidly for the right may not always be easy.
> (phrase beginning with the gerund *Standing*)
> We should enjoy serving the Lord.
> (phrase beginning with the gerund *serving*)

b. A participial phrase contains a past form or an *-ing* form used as an adjective. It answers the question *what kind of* about a substantive.

A family serving God together is a great blessing.
(phrase beginning with the participle *serving*)
The family, assembled for morning worship, sat reverently.
(phrase beginning with the participle *assembled*)

c. An infinitive phrase contains a basic verb form preceded by *to* and is used as a noun, an adjective, or an adverb.

(1) When used as a noun, an infinitive phrase must name an action and fill a noun function in the sentence.

Jennie has asked to read this book next.
(phrase beginning with the infinitive *to read* is the direct object of *has asked*)
Virgil's mistake was to depend solely on Leon's story.
(phrase beginning with the infinitive *to depend* is the predicate nominative renaming *mistake*)

(2) When used as an adjective, an infinitive phrase immediately follows the substantive it modifies and usually answers the question *which* or *what kind of.*

An important principle to consider now is that young people have a prime opportunity to establish good habits.
(phrase *to consider now* tells *what kind of* about *principle;* phrase *to establish good habits* tells *what kind of* about *opportunity*)

(3) When used as an adverb, an infinitive phrase may modify a verb or verbal, an adjective, or another adverb. An infinitive phrase that modifies a verb or verbal almost always tells *why.* One that modifies an adjective or adverb immediately follows the word it modifies. Usually it tells *to what degree* or *how;* sometimes it does not answer any specific question but obviously adds to the meaning of an adjective or an adverb.

Before eating, we bowed our heads to pray to our heavenly Father.
(tells *why* about the verb *bowed*)
Pausing to recognize our heavenly Father's providence is only fitting.
(tells *why* about the verbal *Pausing*)
Indeed, only God is able to provide for our daily needs.
(answers no specific question, but adds to the meaning of the predicate adjective *able*)
God loves us too strongly to fail us in any way.
(tells *to what degree* about *too strongly*)

3. A *phrase of a single part of speech* contains several nouns or verbs working together as a unit.

Grandmother Augsburger now is living near Texter Mountain.

Clauses

A *clause* is a group of related words that contains a skeleton.

1. An *independent clause* expresses a complete thought and can stand alone as a sentence. Actually, every simple sentence is an independent clause, but this term is generally used only when a sentence has more than one clause.

> A wild rabbit hopped into the clearing. (simple sentence: independent clause)
> A wild rabbit hopped into the clearing, and we watched it quietly.
> (compound sentence: two independent clauses)
> A wild rabbit hopped into the clearing while we sat quietly watching.
> (complex sentence: first clause is independent; second is dependent)

2. A *dependent clause* does not express a complete thought but must function within an independent clause. It may function as a noun, an adjective, or an adverb.

> Whoever wants God's blessing must obey His Word.
> (dependent noun clause functioning as the subject)
> God, who understands humanity perfectly, directs us how to live.
> (dependent adjective clause modifying *God*)
> Although the Bible reveals God's will, too many people ignore its counsels.
> (dependent adverb clause modifying *ignore*)

Applying the Lesson

A. Label each underlined phrase *prep.* (prepositional), *vb.* (verbal), or *ps.* (single part of speech). Also write the abbreviation for the part of speech that each one is.

1. The [a]Holy Scriptures [b]will guide the believer [c]without fail.
2. [a]To benefit from that guidance, we [b]must seek [c]to understand the message of the Bible.
3. [a]Studying the Bible sincerely certainly requires a willingness [b]to do God's will.
4. God's Word [a]will endure [b]to all generations.
5. Our whole family hiked [a]up Hickory Mountain and found a small clearing [b]with a dilapidated log cabin.
6. [a]Startled by our quiet approach, a doe fled [b]with her fawns to the safety [c]of the denser woods.
7. [a]To watch the wildlife awhile, we sat quietly [b]in the brush beside the clearing.
8. [a]Within five minutes, a buck [b]with majestic antlers had crossed the clearing, and a fat porcupine had waddled [c]down the trail.
9. [a]On such occasions, our goal is [b]to increase our knowledge of nature, and we also gain a renewed appreciation [c]for God's creative power.
10. [a]Observing God's world can be a definite benefit [b]for God's people.

B. Label each underlined clause *I* (independent) or *D* (dependent). If the clause is dependent, also label its part of speech.

1. "A city that is set on an hill cannot be hid."
2. "Whosoever is angry with his brother without a cause shall be in danger of the judgment."

3. "If ye salute your brethren only, what do ye more than others?"
4. "Beware of false prophets, which come to you in sheep's clothing, but inwardly they are ravening wolves."
5. "A good tree cannot bring forth evil fruit, neither can a corrupt tree bring forth good fruit."
6. "If any man will come after me, let him deny himself."
7. "When ye shall see all these things, know that it is near, even at the door."
8. "All they that take the sword shall perish with the sword."

C. Label each underlined word group *phrase* or *clause.* Also label its part of speech.

1. The [a]Caucasus Mountains lie [b]between the Black Sea and the Caspian Sea.
2. The main range [a]of the Caucasus, [b]which runs roughly east and west, stretches nine hundred miles.
3. [a]For centuries, communities [b]have existed high in these mountains.
4. Highland glens, [a]lying between steep ridges, have been populated [b]since very early times.
5. [a]Because these mountains rise rugged and beautiful, they have challenged mountain climbers [b]who have come from all parts of the world.
6. [a]Although the Caucasus Mountains lie between two large bodies of water, only the western part of the range [b]is blessed with abundant rainfall.
7. [a]Whatever Mr. Parks sells is generally a product [b]of high quality.
8. [a]George Keyes has learned [b]that our mud makes miserable roads.
9. [a]Mewing softly, Misty looked up from the corner [b]where she had her nest.
10. Edward's main chore [a]in the mornings is [b]to take care of the calves.
11. [a]To ease our morning schedule, we try [b]to have the lunches packed in the evening.
12. [a]Where Bennie cut his foot should be found [b]so that it does not happen again.

Review Exercises

A. Copy each underlined complement, and label it *PN, PA, DO, IO,* or *OC.* [20]

1. Ceylon became the Republic of Sri Lanka in 1972.
2. From 1948 to 1972, Ceylon had been independent, but it remained a member of the British Commonwealth.
3. A population of over fourteen million gives this island a high population density.
4. The island, containing 25,332 square miles, is somewhat larger than West Virginia.
5. Sri Lanka's equatorial, oceanic location makes its climate tropical.

B. Label each underlined complement *DO ret., IO ret.,* or *OC ret.* [21]

1. By God's grace, your life can be made useful in God's service.
2. Your life can never be given true godly quality by self-help efforts.
3. We are taught the way to true greatness in God's Word.
4. God's Word must be considered authoritative so that we can trust its counsels.
5. No true help is provided man by the world's false philosophies.

---

24. Appositives and Independent Elements

Appositives

An *appositive* is a substantive that identifies or explains another substantive. The appositive may be a substantive standing alone, or it may be a phrase that includes adjective modifiers. An appositive usually follows the substantive that it explains, but sometimes it precedes the other substantive.

> The apostle <u>Paul</u> carried the Gospel message on several missionary journeys. (The appositive *Paul* identifies *apostle.*)
>
> Paul, <u>the apostle to the Gentiles</u>, carried the Gospel message on several missionary journeys. (The appositive *the apostle to the Gentiles* further explains *Paul.*)
>
> <u>The apostle to the Gentiles</u>, Paul carried the Gospel message on several missionary journeys. (The appositive precedes the substantive that it explains.)

1. A *nonrestrictive appositive* merely gives additional information about a substantive, and it is set off by commas. In the example sentences above, the second and third ones contain nonrestrictive appositives.
2. A *restrictive appositive* restricts the meaning of a substantive, and it is not set off by commas. Most restrictive appositives consist of only one or two words. In the examples above, the first sentence contains a restrictive appositive.

Independent Elements

An *independent element* is a word or word group that is not grammatically related to the rest of the sentence. Usually it is set off with commas or other punctuation.

1. A *noun of direct address* names the person or thing to whom one is speaking. It may be a single noun or a noun with modifiers.

> <u>Barbara</u>, I think your bread is ready to put into the oven.
>
> "<u>Men of Israel</u>, and <u>ye that fear God</u>, give audience."

2. An *expletive* introduces a sentence without adding to its meaning. The two words used as expletives are *it* and *there.* You can usually reword the sentence to omit these expletives.

   a. *It* is an expletive when not used as a normal pronoun. When used as a normal pronoun, *it* has an antecedent. When used as an expletive, *it* has no antecedent.

> *It* was kind of Grandfather to give us this new sled.
> (*It* merely introduces. The sentence can be reworded without *It.* To give us this new sled was kind of Grandfather.)
>
> *It* should work well with this snowfall.
> (*It* is the subject; the antecedent is the noun *sled* in the previous example sentence. The sentence cannot be reworded without *It.*)

b. *There* is an expletive when not used as an adverb telling *where.*

There is a strange dog on the porch.
(*There* merely introduces. The sentence can be reworded without *There:* A strange dog is on the porch.)
There it goes across the lawn.
(*There* is an adverb telling *where.* The sentence cannot be reworded without *There.*)

3. An *exclamation or interjection* expresses strong feeling. A few such terms are acceptable, but using them too freely can be a bad habit that mars godly speech. A mild interjection is followed by a comma; an interjection said with strong feeling is followed by an exclamation point, and the next word is capitalized.

Say! Look at that red fox! Oh, I didn't realize they are that small.

4. A *response* such as *yes* or *no* is sometimes used to introduce a sentence.
5. A *parenthetical expression* is a phrase such as *I believe, for example, in contrast,* or *we know.*

Doing evil that good may come, we know, is never God's will.

6. A *nominative absolute* is an introductory phrase consisting of a substantive and a participle. Such a phrase is related to the thought of the sentence but is not grammatically tied to it. That is, a nominative absolute does not serve as a subject, an object, a modifier, or any other sentence part.

Heavy snow blurring his vision, Father drove slowly across the mountain.
(substantive *snow* + participle *blurring*)
The service having already begun, we took seats on the back bench.
(substantive *service* + participle *having begun*)
His sermon being finished, Brother Lynford led the congregation in prayer.
(substantive *sermon* + participle *being finished*)
His sermon finished, Brother Lynford led the congregation in prayer.
(The word *being* is often omitted from a nominative absolute.)

A nominative absolute can easily be changed to a subordinate clause, and sometimes this should be done for the clearest, most direct communication. However, the occasional use of carefully written nominative absolutes can add a special appeal to your writing. The following sentences show how the examples above can be rewritten with subordinate clauses.

Because heavy snow blurred his vision, Father drove slowly across the mountain.
Because the service had already begun, we took seats on the back bench.
After his sermon was finished, Brother Lynford led the congregation in prayer.

Distinguish carefully between nominative absolutes and participial phrases. A *nominative* absolute begins with a *nominative,* but a *participial* phrase begins with a *participle.*

His sermon finished, Brother Lynford led the congregation in prayer. (nominative absolute)
Having finished his sermon, Brother Lynford led the congregation in prayer. (participial phrase modifying the subject)

A nominative absolute does not always come at the beginning of a sentence. It can also be a convenient way to add details at the end of a sentence.

Father drove cautiously over the mountain, the snow falling thickly, the wind blowing briskly, and the temperature dropping rapidly.

7. A *repeated word* may be used for emphasis or for poetic effect. This may be the repetition of the same word or of a word that names the same person or thing.

Patience! We surely need patience in human relationships. (*Patience* is repeated for emphasis.)
"Thy rod and thy staff they comfort me." (*Rod* and *staff* name the same things as *they.*)

Do not confuse this repetition with an improper expression like "Betty she drew that picture." Careless repetition of that kind merely adds clutter to a sentence. Proper repetition is deliberately planned, and it has an appealing literary effect.

Applying the Lesson

A. Copy each appositive, and label it *R* for restrictive or *N* for nonrestrictive. Commas have been omitted.

1. Respect for authority a trait sadly lacking today must characterize any young person who loves the Lord.
2. A young man of deep conviction Joseph showed great respect for Potiphar his master.
3. Daniel another youth of strong character also demonstrated respect in relating to his overseer Melzar.
4. The lad Samuel responded promptly to Eli the priest whom he served.
5. The poem "Respect in Youth" emphasizes several important principles.
6. Nevin Keeto a young man without a Christian upbringing faces many struggles that we cannot fully understand.
7. My sister Yvonne painted this picture a scene from our old place.
8. At the Spanish service we used the songbook *Himnos de la vida cristiana.*

B. Copy each independent element. Include enough words to show any needed capitalization or punctuation.

1. It is a wonderful privilege to know that God answers prayer.
2. God having commanded us to pray we can come to Him in confidence.
3. No Gary the Lord does not promise to answer the prayers of the wicked.
4. Too many people it seems expect God to answer prayer according to their own wishes.
5. Prayer how it strengthens us to face temptation!
6. Whew getting that truck out of the ditch was quite a job.

7. Mud covering us from head to foot we hurried home to clean up.
8. These roads how they try our patience!
9. The weather service I understand is predicting more rain for tomorrow.
10. Yes this is quite typical of our spring Lamar.
11. At all times to be sure we should be considerate of others.
12. Well the car started burning and headed straight toward our house.
13. What did the car actually burst into flames?
14. Father having called the fire department he and Wesley hurried outside to see what they could do the rest of us watching from a safe distance.

C. For sentences 1–6, write whether the underlined part is a *nominative absolute,* a *participial phrase,* or a *dependent clause.* Rewrite sentences 7–10, changing each underlined part to a nominative absolute.
1. The multitude seeking to make Jesus king, He departed to a mountain.
2. Evening having come, the disciples went down to the sea.
3. When they had boarded a ship, the disciples started sailing toward Capernaum.
4. Soon they ran into a storm, the wind arising and the sea becoming rough.
5. The disciples having rowed some distance, they saw Jesus walking on the water.
6. Understanding the disciples' fear, Jesus spoke comforting words to them.
7. Because Peter was imprisoned, the church prayed unceasingly for him.
8. Peter arose at the angel's command while the chains fell from his hands.
9. When the prison door opened of its own accord, the angel led Peter outside.
10. After the angel had departed, Peter went to Mary's house.

Review Exercises

A. Write *true* or *false* for each sentence. [9–12]
1. The most important attitude for good study skills is interest.
2. Removing distractions is usually better than trying to ignore them.
3. The rate at which you forget increases greatly several days after you have studied something.
4. Proper posture helps your body to be physically and mentally alert.
5. Getting a bird's-eye view of a lesson prepares you to read it more effectively.
6. If you use SQ3R faithfully, you will not need to review before taking a test.
7. By skimming, you can master your school lessons without reading them word for word.
8. When skimming, you should read beginning and ending sentences of paragraphs.
9. Taking notes can be an effective help to listening actively.
10. A summary should preserve the author's original wording as much as practical.

B. Name the five steps in the SQ3R study method. After each one, briefly explain how to apply that step in studying a lesson. [10]

25. Classes of Sentences

Classes According to Use

1. *A declarative sentence makes a statement and ends with a period.*

    Jesus Christ is the Son of God. His shed blood provides redemption.

2. *An interrogative sentence asks a question and ends with a question mark.* The subject often follows the verb or comes between two parts of the verb phrase.

    Are you laying a solid foundation for life?

3. *An imperative sentence gives a command or request and generally ends with a period.* The subject is always *you,* and it is usually understood rather than directly stated. Sentences with helping verbs like *shall, should,* or *must* may appear to be imperative; however, the verb in an imperative sentence never includes a helping verb.

    Heavenly Father, help me to grow more like Jesus. (imperative; makes a request)
    We must be growing more like Jesus. (declarative; makes a statement)

4. *An exclamatory sentence expresses strong feeling or emotion and ends with an exclamation point.* It may simply be one of the other three sentence types expressed forcefully and punctuated as an exclamation.

    Praise the Lord! God certainly has great compassion!

Many exclamatory sentences have a special word order. The skeleton may come at the end of the sentence so that a word like *what* or *how* can come first. Or the sentence may have the form of a dependent clause that would be a fragment if it were not exclamatory.

How wonderful is our great God!
If only all men would submit to Him now!

Classes According to Structure

1. *A simple sentence contains one independent clause.* Although it may have compound parts, it has only one skeleton.

    The mockingbird flew to the post and sang a beautiful medley.

2. *A compound sentence contains two or more independent clauses.*

    The mother bird flew to the nest, and the babies' mouths opened wide.

3. *A complex sentence contains one independent clause and one or more dependent clauses.*

    While we watched the nest, the parent birds brought a total of six worms.

4. *A compound-complex sentence contains at least two independent clauses and at least one dependent clause.*

    The raccoons have invaded our sweet corn again, but before another morning breaks, Father hopes to have defeated the invaders.

Classes According to Word Order

1. *In natural word order, the complete subject precedes the complete predicate.* This is the most common word order, which we use most naturally in forming sentences.

A large bull moose splashed across the small lake.

2. *In inverted word order, the complete predicate precedes the complete subject.* Do not separate these two sentence parts with a comma.

Across the small lake splashed a large bull moose.

3. *In mixed word order, the complete subject comes between two parts of the complete predicate.* A comma often precedes the complete subject, especially if an adverb clause or a long adverb phrase begins the sentence. (The whole adverb clause is considered part of the predicate.)

Across the small lake, a large bull moose splashed.
When the moose came out the other side, he galloped away into the bush.

Classes According to Style

1. *A loose sentence gives the main idea first and the details later.* Often such a sentence could end at various points, and the thought would still be complete. The following loose sentence could end after any of the underlined words.

We can know the truth by heeding God's Word in every detail of life, no matter how small.

Since loose sentences are the simplest kind to understand, most of your spoken sentences are naturally of this style. Most of your written sentences should also be of the loose variety.

2. *A periodic sentence gives the details first and saves the main idea until the end of the sentence.* A person must read to the *period* in order to get the main idea. Because the reader must wait, this sentence style helps to impress the main idea forcefully on his mind. Compare the following sentences with the example above. Do you see the increasing emphasis on the main idea?

By heeding God's Word, we can know the truth.
By heeding God's Word in every detail of life, no matter how small, we can know the truth.

An inverted sentence is often short, but you must still read to the end before you get the main idea. So the inverted sentence is also periodic.

Beside the road sat blind Bartimaeus.

Used occasionally, periodic sentences can effectively emphasize key ideas in a paragraph. But too many periodic sentences will make a paragraph sound unnatural.

3. *A balanced sentence has two well-matched clauses.* One kind of balanced sentence has clauses beginning with words like "the more . . . the more" or "the sooner . . . the better." Another kind uses a slight change of wording to produce a

notable or unexpected contrast. Because of its unusual structure, a balanced sentence gives strong emphasis to the idea in focus.

> The more deeply we love God, the more deeply we will hate sin.
> Though God is blessing all our store, we must not store all our blessings.
> We are not called to see through each other; we are called to see each other through.

Note the repositioning of *through* in the last sentence. This is an example of rearranging the words to produce a striking, memorable statement. Such a sentence stands out because of its unusual structure; not many expressions can be reworded in this way. Therefore, the balanced sentence is the least common of the three sentence styles.

Changing the *style* of a sentence may have the same result as changing the *word order* of the sentence. Study the following examples.

> We must keep working until this job is finished.
> (natural word order; loose sentence)
> Until this job is finished, we must keep working.
> (mixed word order; periodic sentence)

Why is the change classified in two different ways? Word order deals mainly with the mechanical arrangement of words in sentences. Its primary concern is whether the subject comes at the beginning, in the middle, or at the end. Style has more to do with the "spirit" of a sentence. Its primary concern is how the message of a sentence is affected by different word arrangements.

Applying the Lesson

A. Label each sentence according to its use (*dec., int., imp., exc.*) and its structure (*S, CD, CX, CD-CX*). End punctuation has been omitted.

1. Do you carefully follow your parents' wishes, or do you do the least amount possible
2. Because respect for parents is very important, your answer to such a question tells much about your character
3. Youth who have never learned to respect their parents have difficulty learning to fear God
4. If you have godly parents, thank God for them; and if you do not, learn to fear God anyway
5. What a shame it is when one turns his back on a godly heritage
6. Did you see the beautiful display of northern lights last night
7. How delicious Mother's dinner looks and smells
8. Call Father for dinner after you have poured the water
9. Before we eat, we give thanks to our heavenly Father for His blessings
10. Do we daily praise God, who gives us our food, or do we often complain

B. Label the word order of each sentence *N* (natural), *I* (inverted), or *M* (mixed).

1. From the barn came the lowing of hungry cattle.
2. Soon we were on the way to the barn.

3. Before we may eat our breakfast, we must take care of the animals.
4. Our morning chores usually take us about one hour.
5. We have our family worship right before breakfast.
6. To our lips spring joyful songs.
7. In confidence we pray to our Lord.
8. As we think upon God's goodness, our hearts are humbled.

C. Label the style of each sentence *L* (loose), *P* (periodic), or *B* (balanced).
1. Before you can study to learn, you must learn to study.
2. I can study more effectively since we have learned about study skills in Chapter 2 of this book.
3. The more carefully I apply the principles of SQ3R, the better I remember the details of a lesson.
4. Even though a study method like SQ3R gives much practical help for studying, effective study remains hard work.
5. Dozens of strong thunderstorms pounded central Pennsylvania as a cold front passed through the region late yesterday afternoon.
6. In the days of youth while you are forming habits and developing character, remember your Creator.
7. Although evil abounds and the love of many waxes cold, sin will have its payday.
8. We will find strength in prayer if we pray for strength.
9. In everything we do, whether seen or unseen, we should exalt God.
10. He who exalts himself shall be humbled, but he who humbles himself shall be exalted.

D. Rewrite sentences 1–4 in mixed order and 5–8 in inverted order.
1. The sun triumphantly announced a new day as it burst over the eastern mountains.
2. Its gentle rays soon warmed the chilled earth.
3. We were ready to shed our jackets by the time we had finished the chores.
4. The temperature had risen to eighty degrees by afternoon.
5. A bald eagle soared high in the sky.
6. Its shrill cry came faintly to our ears.
7. The huge, majestic bird plummeted downward.
8. A red-tailed hawk hung in its talons.

E. Rewrite sentences 1–4 in the periodic style. In each of sentences 5–8, copy the beginning of the second clause and add words to complete the balanced sentence.
1. Conrad suddenly jumped and yelled during our picnic lunch by the creek in our back pasture.
2. We understood his actions after he told us that a bee had stung him on the cheek.
3. We welcomed a break after stacking straw in the overheated barn all afternoon.
4. Grandfather Weinhold stayed with us during the eight weeks of recuperation from his broken leg.
5. We must control our thoughts, or our thoughts . . .

6. The Christian rejects the world and follows Christ; the carnal man…
7. The more impressed we are with God's glory, the less…
8. The more carefully we keep God's Word, the better…

Review Exercises

Label each underlined item *nominative absolute* or *participial phrase.* [24]

1. The dishes washed, we girls hurried to help husk the corn.
2. Kevin was quite pleased, his kite having turned out nicely.
3. Drumming on the tin roof, the rain drowned out our voices.
4. The river having overflowed its banks, we were forced to turn back.
5. I enjoy watching the goats frisking around the pasture.

---

26. Improving Your Editing Skills, Part 3

With the basic proofreading symbols that you have learned, you can mark most of the corrections commonly needed in manuscripts. However, you will soon encounter some situations where you are not sure exactly how to mark the changes. Consider the following example. Which is the best way to show the inserted dash?

```
The energy from the sun but I have mentioned that before.
The energy from the sun-but I have mentioned that before.
The energy from the sun but I have mentioned that before.
```

We could use any of these ways, but we will understand one another's work more easily if we all follow the same pattern. This proofreading lesson and the next one show some specific patterns for using several of the proofreading marks. These patterns are the ones you should use throughout this course.

Marks Used in Editing and Proofreading

˅ or ^ insert (caret)	delete	stet (let it stand)	use italics
¶ begin new paragraph	no ¶ no new paragraph	lc change to lowercase (small letter)	uc change to uppercase (capital letter)
# insert space	delete space	← move (arrow)	transpose

Explanations	Sample Manuscript
Ellipsis points, like periods and commas, are inserted by writing them below the caret. All other punctuation is written above the caret. If there is room, these other marks may be written where they would normally go. If not, they must be written in the space above the words. Loop for delete symbol curves up if there is room in the space above, and down if there is not. Curving down also works well for deleting a word and a comma or period after it. Inserted dash must be long enough to distinguish it from a hyphen.	"For sin shall not have dominion over you: for ye are under grace" (Romans 6:14) What does this verse mean? An Indian in Oklahoma traveled by train to a pastors' conference. The theme of the conference was this subject: "Living Under Grace." A number of prominent speakers were there; and as they delivered profound messages on law and grace, the Indian pastor listened carefully. Afterward he said, "It would seem to me that the ~~those~~ train station represents law ~~law,~~ and this conference represents grace. At the train station, men were ~~are~~ spitting on the floor even though a sign said, 'Do not spit.' Here we have no sign, yet no one spits." This simple-hearted Indian pastor illustrated the truth well—perhaps more clearly than any of the honored speakers.

Editing Practice

A. Use proofreading marks to add the missing punctuation. In each sentence, one mark will go above the caret and one below.

1. "Boys have you finished digging the red beets" asked Mother.
2. John (the only cousin my age will be visiting our farm this coming Saturday
3. "Then Jonah prayed unto the Lord out of the fish's belly" (Jonah 21).
4. You are welcome to eat lunch with us however we have only sandwiches and apples.
5. The fire chief had one main goal to determine, if possible the cause of the fire.

B. Use proofreading marks to insert one hyphen or dash and to make one deletion in each sentence. Make the loop curve down for at least two of your deletions.

1. **I'll show you you, how to prune this young peach tree it's a fairly simple procedure.**
2. **Be sure to use well sharpened shears, for clean cuts heal more readdily than jagged ones.**
3. **A broken branches will be a long term liability; remove it.**
4. **If branches are tangled together this does happen often—leave only the branch that is growing most directly from the trunk off the tree.**
5. **Now trimm, off those high reaching shoots.**
6. **Just a few more cuts, and we will but I see that it's time time to quit.**

C. Use proofreading marks to correct the fourteen errors in these paragraphs. No line contains more than one error.

1. **The universe is so large that our mind's falter when**
2. **we consider its vast extent. To begin, consider the**
3. **number of of individual stars. We can see about 3,000**
4. **stars with the unaided eye; and by using a telescope,**
5. **we can see many, many more. But our galaxie (the Milky**
6. **Way) contains an estimated 200 billion stars—a number**
7. **that defies are comprehension. And scientists calculate**
8. **that there are than more 10 billion galaxies in the**
9. **[illegible] part of the universe.**
10. **When we consider the distances involved in the universe,**
11. **our minds again stagger. Consider this. Even at the grate**
12. **speeds attained by space craft, it takes three days to reach**

the moon. Traveling to Jupiter would take 2 years, and going to Pluto would require 15 years. But these figures pail when we compare the distance to the stars. Reaching Alpha Centauri, the nearest star, would mean a trip almost 100,000 years—and the spacecraft would still be deep inside the Milky way!

No Design is greater than its designer. As we consider the mind boggling size of the universe, we begin to grasp the greatness and power of the God who created it.

---

27. Chapter 3 Review

A. Write the words immediately before and after each mistake in this dialogue, and show how to join or divide the sentences correctly. Add words only where necessary; do not change elliptical sentences.

1. "Father, who was the stranger that came to the barn? And talked with you for a while?" asked Laban.
2. "Right after lunch? That was Mr. Jack, he's a salesman for Hamilton Supply," replied Father.
3. "A new salesman? Is he replacing Mr. Keedy? When he retires in a few weeks?"
4. "Yes, that's what Mr. Jack said. He started to work for Hamilton Supply two months ago. And seems to know his products well."
5. "Good. It's nice to have good salesmen, they've often given us sound advice."

B. Copy the simple subject and the simple predicate of each sentence. Draw a vertical line between the two parts.

1. The Lord is gracious to His children.
2. He is daily pouring out His blessings upon us.
3. From our Father comes every good gift of life.
4. The ungrateful receive good things from God but fail to return thanks to Him.
5. You and I should be filled with thanksgiving to our great God.

C. Copy each complement, and label it *PN, PA, DO, IO,* or *OC.*

1. The sunset is becoming gorgeous; the whole western sky is a display of rich colors.
2. The squirrels are making their nests secure for the coming winter.
3. Brother Yoder found some interesting information and gave us a summary of it.

4. That bird must consider us a threat to her nest.
5. Father gave Leland and me clear instructions.

D. Copy each retained object, and label it *DO ret., IO ret.,* or *OC ret.*
1. A warm welcome was given the visitors from Belgium.
2. These chickens are fed laying mash every day.
3. The children were told a story by Uncle Myron.
4. The story was made especially interesting by his lively style.

E. Copy the appositives, and label them *R* (restrictive) or *N* (nonrestrictive). Commas have been omitted.
1. Joshua Strite a former member of our church gave a report of the mission work in India a land of many contrasts.
2. My brother Lamar plans to accompany Brother Aaron Yoder our bishop on a visit there next month.
3. The story "Where Is Linda?" was captivating.

F. Copy each independent element, and add any punctuation that is needed after it. Also write correctly any other word with which there is an error in capitalization or punctuation.
1. Great this snow I believe will be perfect for sledding!
2. Do you remember Doris what Grandmother used to say in times like these?
3. It is certainly an answer to prayer to hear that Donna is getting better.
4. The electricity having gone off an hour ago Mother could prepare only a cold lunch.
5. These modern conveniences how much we have come to depend on them!

G. Label each underlined word group *prep.* (prepositional phrase), *vb.* (verbal phrase), *ps.* (phrase of a single part of speech), *D* (dependent clause), or *I* (independent clause). Also label the part of speech that each phrase or dependent clause is.
1. The safety bicycle, [a]having equal-sized wheels and pneumatic tires, was developed [b]in the late 1800s.
2. Because such bicycles [a]could be ridden easily by anyone, [b]they quickly became popular.
3. The [a]United States Census Bureau stated [b]that "few articles ever used by man have ever created so great a revolution in social conditions."
4. [a]To supply the demand, over three hundred companies were manufacturing bicycles by 1895; indeed, the largest manufacturer, [b]which operated five factories, produced about one bicycle every minute.
5. The bicycle gave many the freedom [a]to travel greater distances, for [b]one could travel much faster on a bicycle than on foot.
6. [a]Traveling on horseback could also be speedy, but a horseman always needed [b]to feed and water his horse.
7. [a]What helped most for nighttime biking was the 1895 invention [b]of the carbide lamp, which allowed the cyclist to see the ruts and holes [c]in the road.
8. [a]By the turn of the century, the bicycle's popularity waned [b]as electric trains provided efficient transportation between towns and cities.

H. Label each sentence according to its use (*dec., int., imp., exc.*) and its structure (*S, CD, CX, CD-CX*). End punctuation has been omitted.
   1. What a privilege we have to carry our burdens to the Lord in prayer
   2. When we pray in simple faith, God promises to hear and answer us
   3. Cast your burdens on the One who is omnipotent, and trust His gracious care
   4. Did you seek God's blessing today, or did you foolishly step forth in your own strength
   5. If we expect to handle life by ourselves, we are bound to be bitterly disappointed

I. Label the word order of each sentence *N* (natural), *I* (inverted), or *M* (mixed).
   1. Joseph was a truly remarkable young man.
   2. In his life are found many types of Christ.
   3. Because he feared God, he resisted temptation.
   4. Through strange circumstances, God directed Joseph's life.
   5. From his lips came words of good advice for Pharaoh.

J. Label the style of each sentence *L* (loose), *P* (periodic), or *B* (balanced).
   1. It is good to focus on a noble aim; it is better to keep aiming for that focus.
   2. By persevering diligently to the end of life, we can reach our final goal.
   3. Life holds rich meaning to those who follow God in commitment to His will.
   4. The more sincerely we purpose to follow the Lord, the more easily we can follow His purposes.
   5. Although many declare that man is becoming more intelligent, that the world is getting better, and that a utopia lies just around the corner, the human race is actually degenerating.

K. Rewrite these sentences according to the directions in parentheses.
   1. We can see Mount Parnell when the sky is clear. (Change to mixed word order.)
   2. A diamond dewdrop sparkled on every blade of grass. (Change to inverted word order.)
   3. A cat sprang from the bushes just as the little rabbit disappeared into its hole. (Change to periodic style.)
   4. You must cut the glass carefully, or... (Finish as a balanced sentence.)
   5. As we kneel more humbly before God, we can stand more courageously before men. (Change to a balanced sentence beginning with "The more humbly we kneel...")

L. Rewrite each sentence, using a more active verb.
   1. There were a few deer in our bean patch yesterday.
   2. Sometimes Fido is loud at night.
   3. This pie is delicious.

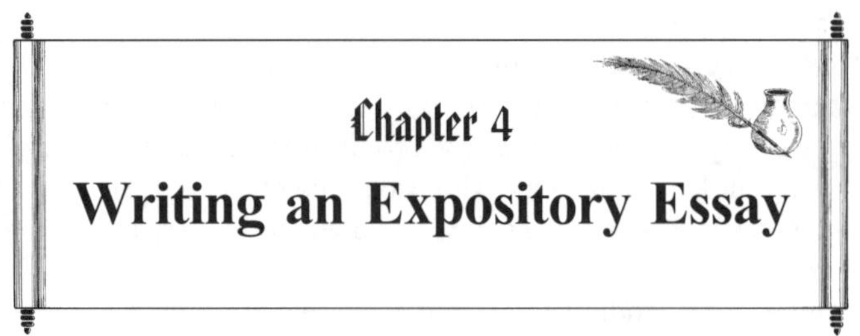

Chapter 4
Writing an Expository Essay

28. Understanding an Expository Essay

An expository essay is an essay that explains. We have all explained—or tried to explain—many things to others. Whether we told our grandparents how we learned to ride a bicycle or informed a friend why an accident occurred or showed a younger brother how to tie his shoe, we were explaining. Actually, giving and receiving explanations has occupied a large part of our lives.

This means writing an expository essay should come naturally, doesn't it? In some ways it probably will. But in other ways, you will benefit greatly from having some specific directions to guide you.

The Nature of an Exposition

The noun *exposition* comes from the verb *expose.* Thus, an exposition is writing that *exposes.* It takes something not seen or understood by others and holds it up to clear view. This immediately suggests a limitation in the topics that are suitable for expository writing. Why explain something that everyone already understands? You are in a position to explain a subject only when you understand things about it that your readers do not. Some of this understanding you gain through personal experience. Some of it you gain through reading and research.

In writing exposition, you must present your topic with complete clarity and precise order. You may report new information (as in your sixth grade report on alligators); you may explain how something works; you may show how to do something; or you may describe the steps in a process. Whatever the topic, you must present everything as clearly as possible. Anything unfamiliar to the reader must be laid out before him in plain language. The goal of all expository writing is to lead the reader to say, "I understand."

Much of your writing in previous grades was exposition. In grade 6, as already mentioned, you wrote a report about alligators. You have also written many single paragraphs of explanation. You will now use your background knowledge and experience to produce a final expository essay.

Below is a sample exposition. As you read it, can you sense that the writer knows what he is talking about? Does the essay present the explanation in a clear and precise manner?"

The Beautiful Nuisance

1 The water hyacinth is a tropical water plant with large, elegant lavender flowers. It floats on air-filled sacs, and it reaches a height of about 2 feet (61 cm) above the surface of the water. When thousands of water

hyacinths grow together, they form a mat so thick that it can support a man's weight.

2 But for all its striking beauty, the water hyacinth has some very ugly behavior. The plants multiply with amazing speed, sometimes doubling in number every ten days. Just 10 plants can increase to a mat of more than 600,000 in one growing season,[1] and the mat continues to spread until it completely covers the surface of the water. In this way, the plant makes itself such a nuisance that it has been called the purple curse.

3 The water hyacinth does its mischief in a multitude of forms. It decreases the oxygen content of water so much that fish suffocate. When canals are choked with hyacinths, boats cannot get through and irrigation water cannot flow freely. The mats make ideal homes for mosquitoes that carry malaria. And high winds will sometimes roll mats of hyacinths into great dams, backing up waterways and flooding the surrounding countryside.

4 Man himself is actually to blame for the purple curse. Water hyacinths grow naturally in South America, where various diseases and insects keep the plant in check. But in 1884 the plant was displayed at the New Orleans Exposition, where gardeners were delighted by its beauty. Some of them took seedlings home for their garden pools, and eventually the plant invaded streams and creeks. By 1900, the water hyacinth had spread all the way from Florida to Texas and as far west as California. Even the Panama Canal has been invaded; it must be cleared regularly to keep the plants from choking off canal traffic.[2]

5 Nor has the water hyacinth limited its domain to the Americas. It reached Australia in 1895 and India around 1900—probably transported by people fascinated with its beauty. A missionary is said to have carried it to Africa around 1950, where it infested the Congo River and then spread rapidly to many other African waterways.[3]

6 People soon discovered that the water hyacinth is no easy enemy to defeat. They fought it first with pitchforks and then with dynamite. They used arsenic, but it killed crops and cattle as readily as hyacinths. Government engineers devised a seagoing "lawn mower" that cut a swath 40 feet wide (12 m), but cutoff pieces floated away and spread the hyacinth to new locations. One scientist even experimented with a flamethrower. The next year, however, the burned plants sprouted first and grew taller than before!

7 Finally in the late 1940s, scientists found that 2,4-D[4] is an effective weapon against water hyacinths. This chemical made it possible to clear thousands of acres of hyacinth-infested water in Florida and Louisiana, and it soon became an important tool for keeping waterways passable in the South. But no one is comfortable with such widespread use of 2,4 D year after year.

8 Because of the chemical danger, scientists are investigating natural methods of control. They have learned that the manatee, or sea cow, is able to eat enough of the plants to keep river mouths clear. Other possibilities include beetles that eat hyacinth leaves, moths that cause rot by boring into the roots, and certain grasshoppers and caterpillars that eat hyacinths.

9 To be sure, the water hyacinth has a few good points. Because the plants are excellent absorbers of chemicals, some scientists think that polluted water might be purified by passing it through tanks full of water hyacinths.[5] Also, a way might be found to make cattle feed from dried hyacinths. But until a safe and effective method is found to control this weed, it will continue to plague tropical waters around the world.

Notes

[1]James Poling, "The World's Most Exotic Nuisance," in *Our Wonderful World of Nature* (Pleasantville, N.Y.: Reader's Digest Association, 1969), p. 109.

[2]*Compton's Encyclopedia,* 1992, article "Panama Canal."

[3]Poling, "Exotic Nuisance," p. 110.

[4]This herbicide has natural hormones that kill broadleaf plants but not grasses.

[5]*World Book Encyclopedia,* 1983, article "Water Hyacinth."

Bibliography

Compton's Encyclopedia. "Panama Canal." 1992.

Poling, James. *Our Wonderful World of Nature.* Pleasantville, N.Y.: Reader's Digest Association, 1969.

World Book Encyclopedia. "Water Hyacinth." 1983.

This essay includes footnotes and a bibliography. The main purpose of footnotes is to show the sources of information in case the reader wants to verify a particular statement. Sometimes a footnote simply gives an added explanation, as illustrated by footnote 4 above. The purpose of a bibliography is to list all the sources from which the writer obtained information for the essay. You will learn more about footnotes and bibliographies in later lessons.

The Structure of an Exposition

1. *The introduction.* Like most compositions, an expository essay consists of three parts: introduction, body, and conclusion. The introduction of a shorter composition may be only a sentence or two. In an exposition of 500–600 words, it will be a complete paragraph. The introduction has several purposes. First, it must appeal to the reader's interest. If it fails to do this, no one will read the essay and it will not explain anything to anyone! Second, it must tell what object or concept will be explained and must introduce it in a general way.

Examine the introductory paragraph in the exposition above. Notice first that it begins with a general statement: *The water hyacinth is a tropical water plant with large, elegant lavender flowers.* This is followed by several other descriptive details about the water hyacinth. These opening sentences do not directly introduce the theme of the essay—that the beautiful water hyacinth has become a serious nuisance. But they give basic information that is needed to understand the essay, and this information is presented in a way that should appeal to the reader's interest.

The sample exposition does not introduce the theme until the beginning of the second paragraph. Other patterns are also possible. You may find the theme at the end of the first paragraph, with the second paragraph going into the first of the main supporting points. Especially in a longer essay, the topic may be such that two paragraphs are required for the basic information. Then the theme may appear at the end of the second paragraph or the beginning of the third.

The introduction of an exposition is like a funnel. It is wide at the beginning—with a general statement—and then it narrows down to the theme of the essay.

2. *The body.* With the main idea introduced, the body of an exposition goes on to develop the explanation. In the body, the writer lays out exact details that will help the reader to understand. Here it is that his exposition succeeds or fails. Therefore, he must be sure to use precise, accurate information and to follow a clear, logical order.

The writer must use specific facts that he finds by careful research. It is not enough to guess and reason; he must provide concrete information so that the reader gains a clear picture of what he is explaining. Each paragraph must develop one aspect of the theme, one step in the process, or some other block of supporting information.

Notice the many specific details in the sample essay. Paragraph 2 does not say merely that a few plants can multiply into thousands in a short time. It says that *10 plants* can increase to *more than 600,000* in *one growing season.* Paragraph 3 says the water hyacinth *decreases the oxygen content of water so much that fish suffocate,* and it gives four other specific forms of mischief. Paragraph 4 states the exact year when the plant was brought to the United States, and paragraph 5 gives the years when it was carried to other continents. Note also the many specific details about the methods used to combat the water hyacinth.

The details in the essay are presented in a clear, logical order. To achieve this, of course, a writer must develop and follow a good outline. You will study this further in later lessons.

3. *The conclusion.* Having stated his theme and explained it as clearly as possible, the writer is ready to close his exposition. How can he bring the essay to a smooth and satisfying conclusion? In the sample essay, this is done by using a contrast. The closing paragraph shows that the water hyacinth is not all bad—again by giving specific details—but then it returns to the idea that the plant is, after all, a serious nuisance. The last sentence is a general statement about the future outlook in relation to water hyacinths.

Other patterns are also possible. A good conclusion might summarize the main points and give a final observation. It might contain a quotation that is especially fitting. Or it might call the reader to some kind of response in relation to the information presented.

Remember that the introduction is like a funnel that narrows down to the theme of the essay. The conclusion is like an inverted funnel, narrow at the beginning and broadening to general ideas. Below is an illustration showing this pattern in the form of a diagram.

Introduction
General ideas narrowing to statement of theme

Body
Supporting details presented and clarified

Conclusion
Theme summarized or otherwise reinforced, followed by general ideas

A good exposition is carefully planned and well organized. It clearly exposes a theme by presenting specific facts in an orderly way. Fix these principles firmly in your mind, and let them guide you in planning and writing your expository essay.

Applying the Lesson

A. Answer these questions about expositions.

1. What is the goal of all expository writing?
2. One specific purpose of an exposition is to report new information. What are three other specific purposes for which expositions may be written?
3. What kind of topic is *not* suitable for an expository essay?
4. Instead of directly stating the theme, what do the opening sentences often provide?
5. Where is a common place to find the statement of the theme?
6. In the body, why must the writer present specific facts rather than guessing and reasoning?
7. How can the writer make sure that he presents his facts in a clear, logical order?
8. How is the introduction like a funnel? How is the conclusion like an inverted funnel?

B. Below are three introductions for expository essays. Tell which one is *good,* which one *has no general opening ideas,* and which one *does not lead to the theme.*

1. **How Airplanes Fly**

One of the four forces affecting an airplane is thrust, which is usually provided by propellers or jet engines. Propellers drive a plane by cutting into air as a screw cuts into wood. Jet engines drive a plane with a powerful exhaust of burning gases. The plane is driven forward with a force equal to that of the gases shooting out the back.

2. **Animals That Hibernate**

Wild animals have various ways of surviving cold winters. Many birds leave their summer homes and fly to warmer regions. Some animals store away food, and a few simply expand their feeding grounds. Wild animals also grow heavier coats to keep warm in winter.

3. **Changing a Flat Tire**

If you are ever a driver, and if your driving experience is normal, you will someday have a flat tire. This event announces itself in various ways. Sometimes you will simply notice a strange vibration or find that steering is difficult. Less frequently—and less fortunately if it occurs at high speed—the tire will go flat with a loud bang. Whatever the circumstances, you will have a great advantage if you know how to change a flat tire.

C. The conclusions below are for the essays introduced in Part B. Note how the conclusions progress from narrow to general ideas. Then write whether a *summary,* a *contrast,* or a *quotation* precedes the general ideas.

1. Not all vehicles affected by thrust and lift will rise from the ground and fly. But when men learned how to use these forces to overcome drag and gravity, they were able to build airplanes of many different types and sizes.
2. In Psalm 36:6, David wrote, "O LORD, thou preservest man and beast." This verse reminds us that God cares for the animals as well as the people in His creation. Hibernation is just one of the many ways that God has designed to preserve wild animals.
3. Though a flat tire is an inconvenience, it is no reason for panic. Just remember to drive well off the road; then jack up the car and replace the flat tire with the spare. You will probably be back on the road in less than thirty minutes.

---

29. Choosing a Limited Topic

Remember that an *exposition* has that name because it *exposes* facts or information to others. It is not a narrative that teaches a lesson by telling a story. Rather, an exposition defines, clarifies, or explains something to help readers understand it more fully.

Choosing a General Field of Information

In many cases, the writer of an exposition does not need to choose his subject. Instead, the subject presents itself through his work or through an incident in his life. He may be asked to write a report to explain a situation or happening to others. A minister may feel the need to write an article explaining a Bible doctrine or clarifying the position of the church on a particular issue. This suggests that church periodicals contain much expository writing.

In this chapter, however, you will need to decide on your own subject. Choose a general field of information that interests you. This matter of interest is important; for without it you will have little motivation, and your work will be dull and tedious.

The range of possible fields of information is as wide as the scope of human knowledge. Are you interested in your father's vocation: farming, carpentry, or mechanics?

Do you have a personal hobby such as crocheting, woodworking, or stamp collecting? Did you especially enjoy a visit to a museum, a cave, or some other point of interest? Has your curiosity been stirred by some detail in a history or science lesson? by some natural phenomenon that you have witnessed? by some invention or discovery? These questions suggest a few of the general fields that you could choose to explore.

A list of all the available fields would be almost endless. However, there are some subjects that may be best not to choose. First, you should avoid a topic that involves only your personal knowledge and experience. You need to be somewhat familiar with the topic, of course, but you should be able to do research and learn something new about it. Second, avoid topics that you can hardly research because they are too uncommon or because you do not have access to sufficient material. Third, avoid topics that are controversial. This essay is to be an exposition, not an argument.

Limiting the Scope of Your Topic

After you have decided on a general field of information, you must limit the topic to an idea that you can cover in an essay of 500–600 words. The topic must be limited enough so that you must do more than state generalities. Your essay must give specific details that will truly inform. On the other hand, you do not want a topic so narrow that you can hardly find enough information.

To limit the topic, think of the more general field of information as the title of a book. But you do not intend to write a book! So you must think of a subtopic that might make a chapter title in that book. Even this may be too broad for your purpose here. You may need to further limit the subtopic to something that could be part of a chapter. Sometimes a topic almost automatically narrows down as you begin reading and researching for your essay. For instance, you may find sufficient information about only one aspect of the topic. Or you may become inspired by a topic that is a little to the side of your original topic.

Note the narrowing process in the following examples. The italicized topics would make suitable titles for an essay such as you will be expected to write.

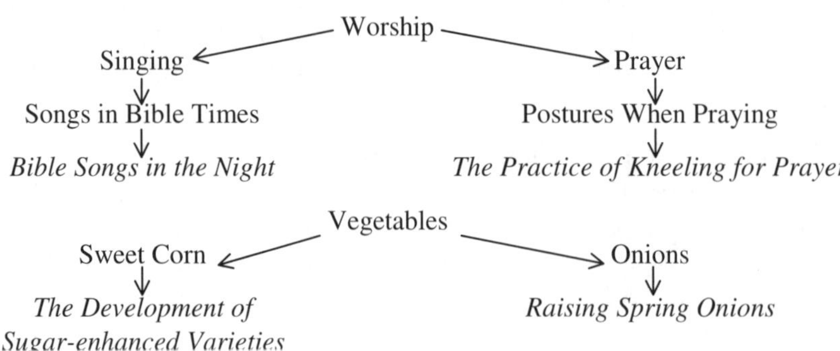

The wording of the limited topic you choose will serve as your working title during the research and early writing stages. Later you might adjust that title or replace it entirely. But you should not spend much time on the title now. Indeed, your research may lead to a slight shift in emphasis that calls for a new title anyway.

Stating the Purpose of the Essay

After you have chosen a limited topic, you should state the purpose of your essay. Even a limited topic could likely be developed in various ways. Your statement of purpose will indicate exactly how you plan to develop your essay. This statement will then help you stay on track as you select information in your research. Study the following examples.

Limited Topic: The Practice of Kneeling for Prayer
Statement of Purpose:
To explain why it is a good practice to kneel for prayer.

Limited Topic: Raising Spring Onions
Statement of Purpose:
To show the steps to be followed in raising spring onions.

The lessons throughout this chapter will develop the following topic and statement of purpose.

Limited Topic: The Pharisees of Jesus' Day
Statement of Purpose:
To explain the significant place of the Pharisees in Jewish life during the time when Jesus was on earth.

Deciding on Main Topics

Often you can determine what main topics your essay will develop even before you begin gathering information. In fact, deciding on those main topics first will be a definite help in guiding your research. For example, in preparing for the topic "The Pharisees of Jesus' Day," you might anticipate finding information that will come under the following main topics.

I. Their origin
II. Their beliefs
III. Their relationship to Jesus

All the steps in this lesson are preliminary. They will not show directly in your final essay. But they will show! The first steps in any process are of major importance, and writing a well-developed expository essay is no exception.

Applying the Lesson

A. For any five of the following topics, write one specific, limited topic that would be suitable for an expository essay of 500–600 words.

1. The Age of Exploration
2. The Inca Indians
3. Weather
4. Small Engines
5. Wildlife in Africa
6. Making Paper
7. History of Virginia (Missouri, etc.)
8. Angels
9. Nonresistance
10. The Bible

B. As you work through this chapter, you will produce an expository essay. Begin now to consider possible topics on which you might write an essay of 500–600 words. Write two limited topics that you would consider using, along with a statement of purpose for each. Then for each topic, make an outline with three to five main topics that would be suitable for your essay.

The score on the essay you write will make up a considerable part of your Chapter 4 test score.

Review Exercises

A. Name the five steps in the SQ3R study method. After each one, briefly explain how to apply that step in studying a lesson. [10]

B. Write whether each of these sentences about studying is *true* or *false.* [9–12]

1. An uncomfortable environment promotes efficient study.
2. Good posture is helpful because it allows an adequate supply of oxygen to reach the brain.
3. Asking questions before reading a lesson helps you to read with purpose.
4. If you use the SQ3R method, you will not need to review before taking a test.
5. When you read actively, you read to find specific information.
6. Skimming can be an effective substitute for detailed study.
7. Skimming can be useful when reviewing material.
8. When skimming a book, you should avoid actually reading any whole paragraphs.
9. Taking notes helps you to listen or read with an active mind.
10. When taking notes, you should be sure to write something from every paragraph in a lesson.

---

30. Taking Notes for an Expository Essay

After you have limited the topic for an expository essay, you must do research. You will need to dig for facts and bring them together. This information is the raw material for your finished product. The quality of that final product depends heavily on the quality of your research and notes.

Reference Sources

You need to find information in a variety of reference sources. The most important source of information is the Bible, for it contains both specific information about many subjects and important principles relating to every subject. Other reference sources include Bible dictionaries, Bible handbooks, encyclopedias, and so forth. Books on your particular topic usually have more details than you will find in general reference sources such as encyclopedias. When looking for information in a book, put to practice the skimming skills that you learned in Chapter 2.

You should plan to use at least two or three different sources of information. Drawing from several sources helps to balance your essay because it gives you a wider scope of details. In addition, blending the details from several sources helps you to express your ideas in your own words. Using several sources of information also helps you to verify the information that you find. If more than one source gives a particular detail, you can be fairly sure that it is accurate. Finally, drawing from several sources helps you to avoid misinterpreting facts. The particular wording in one source may give you a wrong impression that another source may correct.

Guidelines for Taking Notes

1. *Take careful notes.* Include only information that relates directly to your topic, and indicate exactly where you found each item. You will need this later if you write a footnote for that item, or if you want to check the accuracy of your notes. Include the title and page number if the information is from a book, the title of the article if it is from an encyclopedia, and the date of issue if it is from a periodical.

2. *Avoid plagiarism.* It is plagiarism to copy another person's writing and pass it off as your own. Using *ideas* from other people is all right, as long as you express those ideas in your own words. Therefore, your notes should consist primarily of short phrases rather than whole sentences or paragraphs. Of course, you may copy a short quotation from a reference source and use it in your essay if you give proper credit within the text of the essay or in a footnote. Be sure to place exact quotations in quotation marks.

3. *Write sufficient notes.* You need a broad understanding of your subject to write an effective essay. Therefore, you should expect to write more notes than you will actually use, rather than writing barely enough. It is always easier to discard some notes than to go back through your reference sources looking for more information.

Of course, you should also avoid the other extreme. Do not get yourself bogged down by taking far more notes than you can use. With experience, you will develop a sense of when you have enough notes for the purpose at hand.

Below are notes for the topic "The Pharisees of Jesus' Day." These notes are simply shown as a list; you will probably write your notes on note cards as you did in Grade 8.

— began in third century B.C. in resistance to Hellenization (Halley's Bible Handbook, p. 411; Henry H. Halley; Zondervan Publishing House, Grand Rapids, Mich., 1965)
— wanted to keep their national identity intact and to keep alive the strict adherence to Mosaic Law (HBH, p. 411)
— included more adherents and had greater influence than any other Jewish sect (HBH, p. 445)
— mostly "known for their covetousness, self-righteousness, and hypocrisy" (HBH, p. 445)
— arose in time of Maccabeans, chiefly from the scribes, whereas the Sadducees came primarily from the priests (The New Unger's Bible Dictionary, p. 997; Merrill F. Unger; Moody Press, Chicago, Ill., 1976)
— surfaced in Jewish life when Maccabeans no longer stood for loyalty to the Law (NUBD, p. 997)

— some beliefs of the Pharisees: acknowledged judgment upon sinners; resurrection to life for saints (Josephus, *Ant.* 18.1.3; cited in *NUBD*, p. 998)
— recognized cooperation of divine will and human will in human affairs (Schürer, *History of the Jewish People in the Time of Christ*, div. 2, 2:15; cited in *NUBD*, p. 998)
— were primarily a spiritual party, not a political party; involved in politics only when their freedom to obey Law was threatened (*NUBD*, p. 998)
— numbered about 6,000 (*NUBD*, p. 999)
— name first appears in time of John Hyrcanus (Mattathias Maccabeus's grandson) (*Explore the Book*, p. 50; J. Sidlow Baxter; Zondervan Publishing House, Grand Rapids, Mich., 1966)
— were spiritual successors of the Chasidim ("Pious Ones") who had resisted Antiochus Epiphanes's efforts to destroy Judaism 30 to 40 years before (*EB*, p. 50)
— name, which means "Separatists," likely was given by those who despised "their pious but proud and often petty exclusiveness" (*EB*, p. 51)
— admired by common people, who considered them very righteous (*EB*, p. 51)
— most influential in keeping alive the Messianic hope in years before Christ's coming (*EB*, p. 52)
— had influence far greater than numbers would warrant because of popularity with common people (*EB*, p. 52)
— believed in resurrection, angels, and spirits (Acts 23:8)
— practiced frequent fasting (Matt. 9:14; Luke 18:12)
— believed washing of hands and eating utensils to be important (Matt. 15:1–3; Mark 7:1–5)
— basically right in beliefs, but inconsistent in doing right (Matt. 23:3)
— hypocrisy denounced by John the Baptist (Matt. 3:7–10) and by Jesus (Matt. 23)
— made desperate efforts to trap Jesus with questions (Matt. 19:3; 22:15–21; Mark 8:11; Luke 11:54; 20:20; John 8:3–11)
— some followed Jesus (John 3:1; Acts 15:5; Phil. 3:5)

Remember that these notes are the raw material for an essay. In the next lesson, you will study the process of converting this raw material into a meaningful form.

Applying the Lesson

In Lesson 29, Part B, you wrote two limited topics that you would consider using for an expository essay. Decide exactly what topic you will write about, and take notes from at least two sources on that topic. Save your notes for use in the next several lessons.

---

31. Organizing Your Material

Organization is one key to success in writing an expository essay. If an essay is to define, clarify, or explain in a meaningful way, it must follow a logical order. Otherwise, it will be a rambling hodgepodge of ideas that hardly communicates anything worthwhile.

Use the following three steps to organize your material for an expository essay.

1. *Finalize the main topics for your outline.* The main topics that you chose earlier may need adjustment to make them suitable for your essay. Change them in any way necessary so that your notes fit logically under them. The notes in Lesson 30 can be grouped into four main ideas: the Pharisees' origin, their relationship to the Jews in general, their beliefs, and their relationship to Jesus.

2. *Arrange the main topics in a logical order.* Sometimes this is totally arbitrary; you have no specific reason for the order you choose. But often the topic has a natural order of chronology, space, or importance. In what order would you place the four main ideas in the example above? The following order is not the only logical one, but it does make a good arrangement.

I. Their origin
II. Their beliefs
III. Their relationship to Jews in general
IV. Their relationship to Jesus

3. *Fill in the outline with details from your notes.* Again, several different arrangements may be acceptable; but you do need to give careful thought to the order of the details. Try to have a logical reason for the order you choose. Study the following partial outline.

The Pharisees of Jesus' Day

Purpose:

To explain the significant place of the Pharisees in Jewish life during the time when Jesus was on earth.

I. Their origin
  A. The conflict of the Maccabean era
    1. Were spiritual successors of the Chasidim ("Pious Ones") who had resisted Antiochus Epiphanes's efforts to destroy Judaism 30 to 40 years before
    2. Came chiefly from the scribes, whereas the Sadducees came primarily from the priests
    3. Surfaced when Maccabeans no longer stood for loyalty to the Law
    4. Opposed Hellenization
  B. The significance of their name
    1. Appeared first in time of John Hyrcanus (Mattathias Maccabeus's grandson)
    2. Means "Separatists"
    3. Was likely first given by those despising "their pious but proud and often petty exclusiveness"

   C. Their twofold goal
      1. To keep their national identity intact
      2. To keep alive the strict adherence to Mosaic Law
II. Their beliefs
   A. Believed washing of hands and eating utensils to be important
   B. Believed frequent fasting to have definite merit
   C. Acknowledged judgment upon sinners and resurrection to life for saints
   D. Acknowledged the existence of angels and spirits
   E. Recognized the cooperation of divine will and human will in human affairs
   F. Were basically right in beliefs, but were inconsistent in doing right

When such an outline is completed, it provides the framework needed to write a well-organized expository essay.

Applying the Lesson

A. Using the information you gathered in Lesson 30, write a basic outline of three or four main points. Show this outline to your teacher before you do Part B.

B. Use additional information from your notes to make a more detailed outline.

---

32. Writing an Expository Essay

Now that you have gathered your raw material and organized it into an outline, you are ready to start shaping the finished product. As with other compositions you have written, an expository essay consists of three main parts: an introduction, a body, and a conclusion. In an essay of the length in focus here, both the introduction and the conclusion should be short paragraphs. These two parts are not apparent on the outline. Rather, the outline serves as the skeleton for the body—the main part of the essay.

Follow the steps below to write the first draft of your expository essay.

1. *Write an introduction that leads naturally to the theme of your essay.* Remember that the introduction should resemble a funnel, opening with a broad, general statement and then narrowing to the theme of the essay. The first several sentences must catch the reader's attention and lead him to the idea you plan to develop. The last sentence should directly state the theme of the essay. Usually that can be done by weaving in the statement of purpose that you wrote when you chose the topic.

Where can you find ideas for those first sentences? Sometimes they come easily. Other times you must work much harder to develop an opening that you like. You can begin your search for a meaningful opening by looking at the main words in your statement of purpose. What general comment can you make that relates to those key words, that appeals to your readers, and that leads naturally toward your theme?

Below is the statement of purpose for the sample topic being developed in these lessons. The key words are in italics.

To explain the significant place of the *Pharisees* in *Jewish life* during the *time when Jesus was on earth.*

Any of the following sentences could serve as the springboard of the introductory paragraph.

By the time of Jesus' earthly life, the Pharisees had degenerated greatly from their original position.
The religious life of the Jews demonstrated many contrasts in the time of Jesus.
Jesus lived in a time of great religious zeal.

Once you have a broad idea for your opening, you must find a way to move logically from that idea to your specific theme. You may need to try several times before you develop a satisfactory introduction. Do not be surprised at that; rather, approach it as a puzzle to be solved. Enjoy the challenge of making unruly words fall into line. Try and try again until you succeed.

Developing a general statement from key words in the purpose is only one way to begin an introductory paragraph. You can use any opening statement that allows you to move logically toward the theme of your exposition. The limit is your imagination.

Think of it this way. Your introduction is like bait. You are trying to attract your reader so that he will read your exposition. If he does not take the bait, he fails to read your exposition and it will mean nothing to him. So you must make your introduction as appealing as possible!

2. *Write the body of the essay, based on your outline.* For this first draft, write only on every other line so that you can proofread more easily in Lesson 34. Express each important point of the outline in a clear topic sentence. As you develop each paragraph, you may discover that one main idea needs to be developed in several paragraphs. Perhaps each of the subpoints deserves a full paragraph of development.

If your essay is to succeed as an exposition, you must develop your paragraphs with plenty of concrete details. Use specific facts that tell *what,* sound reasons that tell *why,* and clear illustrations that show *how.* Keep inspecting your work for generality and vagueness, the two enemies of good expository writing. Both enemies can be overcome by the use of clear, specific details.

When developing these paragraphs, remember the important qualities of good paragraphs. Keep the paragraphs unified with every sentence clearly developing the topic sentence. Keep the paragraphs coherent with logical order of development, with good use of transitional words, with effective repetition of key words, and with clear pronoun reference. Finally, provide smooth transitions between the paragraphs.

Write brief notations for all direct quotations and for all important statements that you have summarized from your reference sources. Put these notations in parentheses right within the paragraphs, writing just enough for you to recognize the sources. (See the notations in the first draft of "Who Were the Pharisees?" at the end of the lesson text.) When you write the final draft, you will transform these notations into footnotes that come at the end of your essay.

As you write, you may wonder how you can decide when a footnote is needed, since almost every sentence may draw directly from your notes. But you hardly expect to have a footnote for every sentence! The following list will help you to determine when to make a notation for a footnote.

a. *For direct quotations.* Of course, if you credit the source right within the text, no footnote is needed.

b. *For details that the reader might question.* The footnote helps to validate a detail by showing that it is not just your opinion; the idea comes from an established source.

c. *For technical information, such as definitions and statistics.* The footnote will enable the reader to do further research if he so desires.

3. *Write a smooth, satisfying conclusion.* In your introduction, you tried to catch the reader's attention. In the body, you tried to present a clear, logical discussion of your theme. Now in your conclusion, you must wrap up your exposition in a way that impresses the theme upon the reader's mind. Below are some ideas for doing this, illustrated mostly with examples from elsewhere in the chapter.

a. *Summarize the steps, and describe the outcome or finished product.* This is a good way to conclude an exposition when the main points can be condensed into one or two statements. If this cannot be done, a summary can easily become repetitious.

> Though a flat tire is an inconvenience, it is no reason for panic. Just remember to drive well off the road; then jack up the car and replace the flat tire with the spare. You will probably be back on the road in less than thirty minutes.

b. *Emphasize the importance or usefulness of what has been explained.* For example, if you have presented the steps in a process, you could mention a few instances when the process is useful in everyday life. The sample conclusion above points out that a knowledge of the steps described should keep a driver from being seriously delayed by a flat tire.

c. *Use a contrast.* Such a conclusion might describe how things would be in the absence of the thing explained, or it might give a few points that contrast the main emphasis of the essay. Note that using a contrast is one way to conclude an essay by broadening to general ideas.

> To be sure, the water hyacinth has a few good points. Because the plants are excellent absorbers of chemicals, some scientists think that polluted water might be purified by passing it through tanks full of water hyacinths. Also, a way might be found to make cattle feed from dried hyacinths. But until a safe and effective method is found to control this weed, it will continue to plague tropical waters around the world.

d. *Use a quotation.* A fitting Bible verse can be especially effective in the conclusion. An impressive statement from another source may also be suitable if it matches the theme well. For best results, a quotation should be woven smoothly into the closing paragraph.

In Psalm 36:6, David wrote, "O LORD, thou preservest man and beast." This verse reminds us that God cares for the animals as well as the people in His creation. Hibernation is just one of the many ways that God has designed to preserve wild animals.

e. *Call for some kind of response.* The conclusion may call the reader to a specific action in relation to what has been explained. It may simply call him to appreciate the thing explained, or it may urge him not to forget the facts presented.

The next time you start a fire with a simple flick of the wrist, think about our ancestors of a few centuries ago. Remember how hard they worked to light and maintain the fires that gave them light, kept them warm, and cooked their food.

Several of these methods may be combined in the conclusion of an essay. For example, you might combine a summary with a statement of how useful the process can be, as is done in the first sample conclusion above. Or you might combine a quotation with a call for a certain response. Your main goal is to write a smooth, satisfying conclusion that clinches the theme of your essay.

4. *Write an appealing title.* The title of your essay should be short—not more than five words if possible. It should relate directly to the theme of your exposition, and it should catch the reader's interest. Writing a good title is often a challenge all its own. What is the secret of making it fresh and catchy? A good title often has rhyming words, alliteration, or an interesting word combination. Sometimes it is a question. If the title is appealing enough that it causes a person to read the essay, it will have accomplished its purpose.

Look at the following titles. Can you tell why the second one in each pair is better than the first?

(1) a. **Fair:** How to Make an Attractive Birdhouse
b. **Better:** Building Beautiful Birdhouses
(2) a. **Fair:** Bible Happenings in the Jordan Valley
b. **Better:** Bible Highlights of the Jordan Valley
(3) a. **Fair:** Hardships of Early Voyages to America
b. **Better:** Braving the Waves to Reach America

Title (1)b holds definite appeal because of the strong alliteration. But some of its appeal is also in its directness. With a little effort, you can usually improve a title that begins with *How to.* Title (2)b contains an interesting play on words. The essay describes *highlights* about a *low* place. Title (3)b has the appeal of assonance as well as originality. To speak of braving the waves carries an air of freshness and vitality in contrast to the commonplace wording of the first title.

The following paragraphs show the beginning of the first draft of an expository essay based on the outline in Lesson 31. The final draft of the entire essay appears in Lesson 35. Notice that the working title has been changed to a question.

Who Were the Pharisees?

The religious life of the Jews demonstrated many contrasts in Jesus' day. No doubt Simeon and Anna represented a large group of righteous Jews. But we also meet in the Scriptures the worldly-minded Sadducees, promoting their policy of assimilation into the surrounding Greek culture. On the other hand, we read much more about the narrow-minded Pharisees, who clung to a corrupted form of conservatism. Let us take a closer look at these Pharisees. Who were they, and what was their significance in Jewish life at the time of Christ?

To understand that significance, we should first consider the origin of the Pharisees. This group emerged as a distinct sect during the conflict of the Maccabean era. The Pharisees were spiritual successors of the Chasidim, or "Pious Ones," who had resisted Antiochus Epiphanes's efforts to destroy Judaism at least thirty years before. (EB, p. 50) The Pharisees drew primarily from the ranks of the scribes, in contrast to the Sadducees, who came primarily from the priests. Specifically, they surfaced when the Maccabeans no longer stood for loyalty to the Law. They opposed the Hellenizers' goal of adopting Greek culture. (HBH, p. 411)

The very name Pharisee reveals something significant about their origin. The term (which first appears in the time of John Hyrcanus, the grandson of Mattathias Maccabeus) means "separatist." Likely, this name was given by those who despised the "pious but proud and often petty exclusiveness" (EB, p. 51) of the group. These early Pharisees, however, espoused a noble twofold goal. Against the threat of Hellenization, they determined to keep Jewish national identity intact. Closely related, they committed themselves to keeping alive a strict adherence to the Mosaic Law. These two goals, of course, represented every faithful Jew's faith in God and hope for the Messiah.

An expository essay exposes a block of information little by little. You need to work step by step so that your readers will gain a clear and complete view of that information.

Applying the Lesson

Write an expository essay based on the outline you made in Lesson 31.

33. Improving Your Editing Skills, Part 4

For people to communicate successfully, they must use symbols that they understand in the same way. Misunderstandings result when a symbol means different things to different people. Some misunderstandings are humorous. Others are quite serious. For example, suppose you found a box lying along the road, and it was marked with the symbol shown at the right. Would you open the box to see what was inside? You had better not, for this symbol indicates a dangerous radioactive substance!

Failure to understand proofreading symbols could result in serious communication errors. In this lesson you will again see some specific patterns to follow in the use of these symbols.

Marks Used in Editing and Proofreading

˅ or ˄ insert (caret)	delete	.... stet (let it stand)	___ use italics
¶ begin new paragraph	no ¶ no new paragraph	lc change to lowercase (small letter)	uc change to uppercase (capital letter)
# insert space	delete space	← move (arrow)	transpose

Explanations

Symbol for "transpose" may involve items in two different lines.

It may be better to delete and insert than to use the transpose or move symbol.

When a letter is deleted within a word, the symbol for "delete space" may be used to show that no space is to remain—although this is optional.

Transpose symbol may be used with more than two words or letters.

Sample Manuscript

The story is told of a Bible scholar named Bengel, who was lying on his death-bed. One day a friend quoted a Bible familiar verse to him. Actually, He misquoted the verse actually by adding an extra word. "I know in whom I have believed," said the friend.

"No, no," respounded the dyeing man. "Do not allow a preposition even to come between my Savouir and me. 'I know whom I have believed!'"

Editing Practice

A. Correct the two errors of transposition in each sentence. Notes in parentheses give specific instructions for correcting some errors.

1. **On our trip to the Midwest, we visited Colby, Wisconsin, place the where Colby cheees was first made.**
2. **Mr. Zeiger, who has just moved to a nursing home, an old friend, requested that our family him visit often.** (Use delete and insert symbols to make *an old friend* come immediately after *Mr. Zeiger.* Omit the comma after *friend.*)
3. **The above two sentences are both decarlative, not imperative.** (Use the transpose symbol to make *above* follow *sentences.*)
4. **The rich man was albe to buy a new, large, expensive car every year.** (Use the transpose symbol to make *new* come immediately before *car.* Delete the comma after *new.*)
5. **"The secret of faithfulness under test really not is hard to understand", said Brother Arnold.** (Use the transpose symbol to make *is* come before *really.*)
6. **The three couragoues Hebrews simply determined that they would do what was right regradless of the consequences.**

B. Use the "delete space" symbol twice in each sentence. Some uses will be in connection with a letter that you should delete.

1. **When Father returned from South America, he arrived at the air port late on Friday evenning.**
2. **Christians should be grateful for the priviledge to spread the Gospel with out government interference.**
3. **Every one was impressed by the extra ordinary abilities revealed by Pedro's work.**
4. **Our prayers should include petition, praise, confesssion, thanks giving, and intercession.**

C. Use proofreading marks to correct the thirteen errors in the following paragraphs. No line has more than one error.

If our galaxy (the Milky Way) so large that spacecraft would require almost 100,000 years to reach the nearest star, how large is the whole universe. Suppose we could

reduce the known universe one trilion times. This would make the sun the size of a pinhead, and the entire solar system would fit in side your classroom. How close would the nearest star be now? It would be 26 miles (42 km) away. And the Milky Way still be would about 600,000 miles (970,000 km) in diameter!

Let us reduce everything again, this time untill the Milky Way is the size of large pie pan. How big would that make the known universe? The greatest dinstace that man has peered into outerspace would be 30 miles (48 km) away.

What a grate and mighty God we serve! "Thou art worthy, O Lord, to recieve glory and honour and power: for thou hast created allthings, and for thy pleasure they are and were created" (Revelation 4:11.)

---

34. Proofreading an Expository Essay

Almost without exception, producing a good finished essay requires proofreading and rewriting. Check the essay you wrote in Lesson 32, using the following questions to direct you.

Content and Organization

1. Does your essay include the three distinct parts: introduction, body, and conclusion?
2. Does the introduction lead naturally to the theme? Is the theme woven effectively into the introduction?
3. Are the main points in logical sequence?
4. Do the paragraphs of the body develop the main points carefully and completely?
5. Does every paragraph have unity and coherence?
6. Does the thought flow smoothly from one paragraph to the next?
7. Have you made the necessary notations from your reference sources for footnotes?
8. Does the conclusion bring the essay to a positive, satisfying end?
9. Does your essay have an appealing title?

Style

1. Do you see any sentences that you should write with more freshness and originality?
2. Do you see any vague, general terms that you could replace with exact, descriptive words?
3. Do you see any weak or passive verbs that you could make more active?

Mechanics

1. Have you used any unnecessary or repetitious words?
2. Have you omitted any words or phrases that are needed to make the meaning clear?
3. Have you transposed or misplaced any words, phrases, or clauses?
4. Have you misspelled any words? Especially check spellings like *ei* and *ie, ai* and *ia, ent* and *ant,* and so forth. Double-check your use of homonyms like *your—you're* and *their—there—they're.* Make sure that you have spelled technical terms and proper nouns correctly. Pay close attention to words that you have difficulty spelling correctly.
5. Have you used proper capitalization and punctuation?
6. Have you followed the rules of correct grammar and word usage?

Do not imagine that you can evaluate all these points at one time. Since the points under "Content and Organization" form a sequence, you should consider them in the order they occur. For "Style," you will probably need to evaluate your essay on each point separately. For the points under "Mechanics," it will take several readings to do a thorough job. Concentrate first on points 1–3, next on point 4, then on point 5, and finally on point 6.

Applying the Lesson

Proofread the essay that you wrote in Lesson 32.

---

35. Writing the Final Draft

After you have proofread your essay and marked the changes on your first draft, you must rewrite the essay. This essay is to be set up in a formal manner, with footnotes and a bibliography. Follow these guidelines for writing the final draft of your expository essay.

The Standard Layout

Type or recopy the essay according to the following standards.

1. Use 8½-by-11-inch typing paper or standard lined composition paper
2. Type on only one side of a sheet. If writing by hand, follow your teacher's direction about using one or both sides of the paper.
3. If typing, double-space. (Spacing of 1½ lines may be used if the typewriter has that capability.) If writing by hand, use blue or black ink and write on every line.
4. Leave a margin of about one inch along all four edges of each page.

5. Center the title. Allow some extra space between the title and the first line of the essay.
6. Indent paragraphs five spaces for typed copy or one inch for handwritten copy.
7. Beginning with page 2, number each page in the upper-right corner.

The Footnotes

As you write the final draft, change the notations from your reference sources into footnotes. Number the footnote locations throughout the entire essay. The number referring to a footnote should appear immediately after the text to which the footnote applies. Elevate the number slightly from the main text.

The footnotes themselves are commonly listed at the end of the essay. It is also correct to write each one at the bottom of the page to which it applies, but you will probably find it more convenient to list all the footnotes together at the end. If you place them at the bottom of the page, you will need to plan ahead to see how much space your footnotes will require. Begin each footnote with the appropriate number, again elevated slightly. Indent the first line in the normal manner for a paragraph. Each footnote should end with a period, whether or not it is a complete sentence.

The following guidelines give further help for writing footnotes. Pay careful attention to the punctuation of these samples.

1. a. For information from a book or pamphlet, the first reference to a particular source should give the author's name, the title, the place of publication, the publisher, the copyright date, and the page number(s) referred to. (The state is included with a less familiar city such as Grand Rapids, but not with a well-known city such as Chicago.)

   [1]J. Sidlow Baxter, Explore the Book (Grand Rapids, Mich.: Zondervan Publishing House, 1966), p. 50.

   b. Later references to the same source should include just enough information for simple identification. In these later references, write only the author's last name, one or two key words from the title, and the page number(s).

   [2]Baxter, Explore, p. 52.

   c. If the book has been compiled by an editor, use the editor's name instead of the author's name, and write *ed.* after it.

   d. If the author's name is not given, the footnote simply begins with the title.

2. a. For information from an article in a magazine or some other periodical, the first reference to a particular source should list the author's name, the title of the article, the name and date of the publication, and the page number(s) referred to.

   [3]David K. Siegrist, "Basic Map Skills," The Christian School Builder, March 1990, pp. 178, 179.

   b. Later references to the same source should include just the author's last name, one or two key words from the publication name, and the page number(s).

   [4]Siegrist, Builder, p. 183.

3. For information from encyclopedia articles, write the name of the encyclopedia, the edition number or copyright date, and the title of the article.

    [5]Compton's Encyclopedia, 1995, article "Inquisition."

4. For information from the Bible, write the reference in its usual form.

    [6]Matthew 23:3.

5. If part of a reference is included in the text, you do not need to repeat it in the footnote. For example, if the author's name is mentioned in the text, the footnote may begin with the second part of the entry.
6. If a footnote refers to the same source as the preceding footnote, write *ibid.* and the page number(s). This abbreviation stands for the Latin word *ibidem* (ib′·i·dem′), which means "in the same place."

    [7]Henry H. Halley, Halley's Bible Handbook (Grand Rapids, Mich.: Zondervan Publishing House, 1965), p. 411.

    [8]Ibid., p. 445.

7. If a footnote refers to information from some other source within the source you consulted, give the original source first and then the source in which you found it.

    [9]Josephus, Ant. 18.1.3, cited in Merrill F. Unger, The New Unger's Bible Dictionary (Chicago: Moody Press, 1988), p. 998.

8. If a footnote is simply a comment by the author, write it in normal paragraph form.

    [10]The English word martyr comes from a form of the Greek martus, which means "witness."

The Bibliography

Your finished expository essay should include a *bibliography,* a complete listing of all the sources (except the Bible) that you consulted in writing your essay. The bibliography shows all the works from which you obtained information, whether or not you actually quoted from all of them. The following guidelines will help you to write the bibliography correctly.

1. The sources should be listed in alphabetical order according to the last names of the authors. If you used more than one reference source from the same author, group those sources alphabetically by title. If no author's name is given, list the source alphabetically according to the title.
2. Each entry for a book should have the following information in the order given. Place a period after the information for each lettered item below.
    a. The author(s), editor(s), or organization that did the writing. The author's last name should be first.
    b. The title of the book.
    c. The volume number of a book in a series. For an encyclopedia, the title of the article is sufficient.

d. The place of publication, the publisher, and the copyright date. Place a colon between the name of the city and the publisher, and a comma between the other two items. For an encyclopedia, only the copyright date is needed.

3. Each entry for a periodical should have the following information in the order given. Place a period after the information for each lettered item below.
   a. The author(s), editor(s), or organization that did the writing. The author's last name should be first.
   b. The title of the article.
   c. The name of the periodical and the date of issue. Place a comma between these two items.
4. Entries of more than one line are arranged with hanging indents. In a hanging indent, the first line extends to the left and the remaining lines are indented. (This is the opposite of a normal paragraph indent. All the rules in this list are arranged with hanging indents.)

Below is the final draft of the expository essay illustrated throughout this chapter, with the footnotes and bibliography.

Who Were the Pharisees?

The religious life of the Jews demonstrated many contrasts in Jesus' day. No doubt Simeon and Anna represented a large group of righteous Jews. But the Scriptures also tell of the worldly-minded Sadducees, who favored assimilation into the surrounding Greek culture. On the other hand, we read much more about the narrow-minded Pharisees, with their hypocrisy and corrupted form of conservatism. Take a closer look at these Pharisees. Who were they, and what was their significance in Jewish life at the time of Christ?

The Pharisees first emerged as a distinct sect during the conflict of the Maccabean era. They were the spiritual successors of the Chasidim, or "Pious Ones," who had resisted Antiochus Epiphanes's efforts to destroy Judaism at least thirty years before.[1] The Pharisees drew primarily from the ranks of the scribes, whereas the Sadducees came primarily from the priests. Specifically, the Pharisees surfaced when the Maccabeans no longer stood for loyalty to the Law. They opposed the Hellenizers' goal of adopting Greek culture.[2]

The very name Pharisee reveals something significant about their origin. The term (which first appeared in the time of John Hyrcanus, the grandson of Mattathias Maccabeus) means "separatist." Quite likely, this name was given by those who despised the "pious but proud and often petty exclusiveness"[3] of the group. These early Pharisees, however, espoused a noble twofold goal. Against the threat of Hellenization, they determined to keep Jewish national identity intact. Closely related, they committed themselves to keeping alive a strict adherence to the Mosaic Law. These two goals, of course, represented every faithful Jew's belief in God and hope for the Messiah.

From the New Testament Scriptures and from other sources, we can discover the basic beliefs of these Pharisees. We learn, for example, that they placed a strong emphasis on the ceremonial washing of hands and of eating utensils. It also appears that they considered frequent fasting to have definite merit. Furthermore, they acknowledged the reality of judgment upon sinners and of the resurrection to life for the saints. We know that they believed in the existence of angels and of spirits. And they recognized the cooperation of the divine will and the human will in human affairs.[4] Jesus indicated that their beliefs were basically right but that they were inconsistent in doing right.[5]

What was the relationship of the Pharisees to the Jews in general at the time of Christ? First, they were primarily a spiritual party, not a political party. They became involved in politics only when their freedom to obey the Law was threatened.[6] Although they numbered only about 6,000,[7] they apparently included more adherents and held greater influence than any other Jewish sect.[8] They were greatly admired by the common people, who considered them very righteous; therefore, they had an influence far greater than their actual numbers would warrant. Above all, the Pharisees held the strongest influence in keeping alive the Messianic hope in the years before Christ's coming.[9]

More important than the Pharisees' relationship to the Jews in general was their relationship to Jesus. From early in Jesus' ministry until His crucifixion, the Pharisees appear numerous times in the Gospel accounts. On the one hand, Jesus scathingly denounced their hypocrisy. In fact, Matthew 23 records some of the sternest denunciations in the Gospels, leveled against Pharisaic hypocrisy. On the other hand, the Pharisees made desperate efforts to trap Jesus by using trick questions. Yet a few of the Pharisees did follow Jesus. Nicodemus secretly believed in Him before

His crucifixion. The most influential Pharisee to become a follower of Jesus, no doubt, was the apostle Paul. And Acts 15:5 indicates that a sizable number of Pharisees joined the early church.

In summary, the Pharisees constituted a force that figured largely in Jewish life. From their noble origin as defenders of Judaism against Hellenization, they clung to a core of beliefs that were basically right. But their response to Jesus varied from outright rejection to loyal commitment. The Pharisees stand as a reminder that a noble beginning never guarantees that a group will continue on a right course.

Notes

[1]J. Sidlow Baxter, Explore the Book (Grand Rapids, Mich.: Zondervan Publishing House, 1966), p. 50.

[2]Henry H. Halley, Halley's Bible Handbook (Grand Rapids, Mich.: Zondervan Publishing House, 1965), p. 411.

[3]Baxter, Explore, p. 51.

[4]Schürer, History of the Jewish People in the Time of Christ, div. 2, 2:15, cited in Merrill F. Unger, The New Unger's Bible Dictionary (Chicago: Moody Press, 1988), p. 998.

[5]Matthew 23:3.

[6]Merrill F. Unger, The New Unger's Bible Dictionary (Chicago: Moody Press, 1988), p. 998.

[7]Unger, Dictionary, p. 999.

[8]Halley, Handbook, p. 445.

[9]Baxter, Explore, p. 52.

Bibliography

Baxter, J. Sidlow. Explore the Book. Grand Rapids, Mich.: Zondervan Publishing House, 1966.

Halley, Henry H. Halley's Bible Handbook. Grand Rapids, Mich.: Zondervan Publishing House, 1965.

Unger, Merrill F. The New Unger's Bible Dictionary. Chicago: Moody Press, 1988.

Applying the Lesson

A. Write the following footnotes correctly. Use the exercise numbers as footnote numbers.

1. Christian Literature Crusade, Fort Washington, Pa., Made According to the Pattern, page 90, Charles W. Slemming, 1974.

2. Glenn M. Jones, Big Ten Tabernacle Topics, pp. 18–20, Moody Press, Chicago, Ill. 1977
3. Charles W. Slemming, Pattern, p. 93.
4. Moses and the Gods of Egypt, John J. Davis, Grand Rapids, Mich., Baker Book House, 1986, pages 275, 276.

B. Compile a bibliography for the footnotes above.

C. Write the final draft of your expository essay. Include your footnotes neatly and correctly.

D. Compile the bibliography for your essay.

Your teacher may use the following evaluation chart to grade your expository essay. Remember, your score on this essay will make up a considerable part of your Chapter 4 test score.

Evaluation of an Expository Essay

Points possible	Points earned	
Title		
3	____	Short and appealing
3	____	Directly related to theme
Introduction		
3	____	Interesting; catches attention
3	____	Leads naturally to statement of theme
Body		
3	____	All points of exposition are clear
3	____	Consists of well-developed paragraphs
3	____	Gives points in logical order
Conclusion		
3	____	Brings theme into clear focus
3	____	Summarizes or otherwise reinforces main points
3	____	Ends with effective concluding sentence
Style		
3	____	Freshness and originality
3	____	Active verbs and other exact, descriptive words
Mechanics		
3	____	Correct spelling
3	____	Correct capitalization and punctuation
3	____	Correct grammar
3	____	Avoids careless repetition, omitted words, transpositions
48	____	**Total points**

36. Chapter 4 Review

A. Write the correct word or phrase for each blank.

1. An expository essay has that name because it ——— facts or information in order to define, clarify, or explain something.
2. Before you begin doing research, it will help you to select the right information if you write down the ——— of your essay.
3. Three types of information for which you should write footnotes are ———, ———, and ———.
4. For the final draft of your essay, leave a margin of about ——— along all four edges of the pages.
5. In a footnote for a quotation, the first item of information is usually the name of the ———.
6. The abbreviation *ibid.* means ———.
7. A list of the sources of information for an essay is called a ———.

B. Answer these questions.

1. What are three kinds of subjects that you should avoid when choosing a topic for an expository essay?
2. What are three things you can do to make sure you are not guilty of plagiarism?
3. How should the introductory paragraph begin, and how should it end?
4. One good way to develop paragraphs is by using specific facts that tell *what.* What are two other good ways?
5. What are two good ways to conclude an expository essay?
6. In what two places may footnotes appear?
7. When do you *not* need to write a footnote for a direct quotation?
8. What are three general characteristics of an appropriate title?
9. What are three specific ways to make a title appealing?
10. What three guidelines determine the order of the reference sources in a bibliography?

C. Write the following set of footnotes correctly, using the proper form and avoiding unnecessary repetition.

1. <u>The Mennonite Church in America</u>, p. 358, John C. Wenger, Herald Press, Scottdale, Pa., 1966
2. Harry A. Brunk, <u>History of Mennonites in Virginia: 1900–1960</u>, Vol. 2, McClure Printing Co., Inc., Verona, Va., 1972. pages 25–28
3. Harry A. Brunk, <u>History of Mennonites in Virginia: 1900–1960</u>, Vol. 2, McClure Printing Co., Inc., Verona, Va., 1972. pages 505–507
4. Jesse Neuenschwander, <u>The Eastern Mennonite Testimony</u>, "Perpetuating Biblical Nonconformity," December, 1990, p. 6
5. John C. Wenger, <u>The Mennonite Church in America</u>, p. 360

D. Compile a bibliography for the footnotes above.

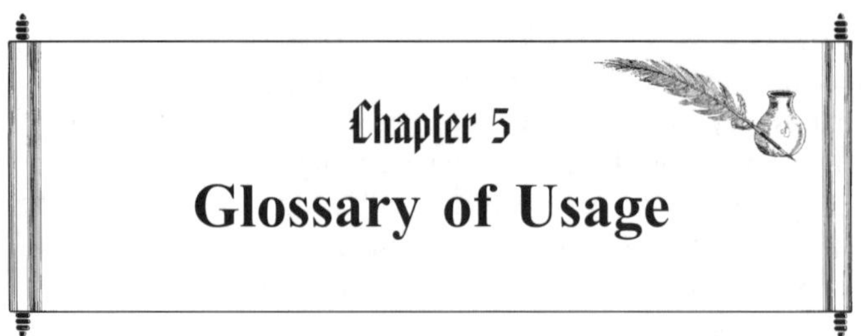

Chapter 5
Glossary of Usage

Book 1 Word List

Part 1
- ability, capacity
- accompanied by, with
- adverse, averse
- affect, effect
- agree to, with
- all the farther, faster
- allusion, illusion
- already, all ready
- altogether, all together
- among, between

Part 2
- and etc.
- anyways, nowheres, somewheres
- as
- at, to (*with* where)
- awful, awfully
- bad, badly
- being as, that
- beside, besides
- better
- but that, what

Part 3
- cannot help but
- complement, compliment
- contend against, for, with
- correspond to, with
- credible, credulous
- different(ly) from, than
- discover, invent
- disregardless, irregardless
- emigrate, immigrate
- envelop, envelope

Part 4
- exalt, exult
- farther, further
- fewer, less
- figure (out)
- formally, formerly
- get
- had (hadn't) ought
- hardly, scarcely
- have got to
- healthful, healthy

Part 5
- hear to
- in, into
- incredible, incredulous
- inferior, superior
- kind, kinds
- later, latter
- learn, teach
- literally
- lot, lots
- mad

Part 6
- mighty
- muchly
- nohow
- nowhere near
- of
- part from, with
- piece
- plus
- pretend like
- principal, principle

Part 7
- real, really
- reckon
- right
- said, same
- sight
- so, such
- sometime, some time
- statue, stature, statute
- suppose
- suspect, suspicion

Part 8
- taunt, taut
- their, there, they're
- to, too, two
- type
- valuable, invaluable
- wait for, on
- want that
- where
- who's, whose
- you all, you'ns, you's

Book 2 Word List

Part 1 (Lesson 37)
above
accept, except
adapt, adopt
advice, advise
ain't
all
all right
allude, elude, refer
almost, most
altar, alter

Part 2 (Lesson 38)
always, all ways
amount, number
angry about, at, with
anymore, any more
as (if), like
awhile, a while
believe, feel
be sure and
burst, bursted, busted
can, may

Part 3 (Lesson 40)
censor, censure
compare to, with
comprehensible, comprehensive
contemptible, contemptuous
continual, continuous
could (should, would) of
council, counsel
differ from, with
dilemma
disinterested, uninterested

Part 4 (Lesson 41)
eminent, imminent, immanent
enormity
enthuse, enthused
everyday, every day
fabulous
flaunt, flout
good, well
haven't but, only
heap, heaps
hopefully

Part 5 (Lesson 42)
how come
impact
imply, infer
in back of
ingenious, ingenuous
its, it's
kind (sort) of
lay, lie
let, leave
loose, lose

Part 6 (Lesson 43)
maybe, may be
momentarily
nice
notable, noted, noteworthy, notorious
OK, okay
over with
persecute, prosecute
perspective, prospective
poorly
precede, proceed

Part 7 (Lesson 45)
propose, purpose
quote
raise, rise
receipt, recipe
respectable, respectful, respective
right along
set, sit
some, somewhat
stationary, stationery
straight, strait

Part 8 (Lesson 46)
than, then
them
this (these) here, that (those) there
transpire
try and
want in, off, out, through
way, ways
what for
worst kind, sort, way
your, you're

37. Correct Word Usage, Part 1

This chapter contains a listing of commonly misused or confused words. Book 1 of this set contains a companion listing of other words. Each lesson includes ten items with brief explanations and illustrations to show how the words should be used.

Some example sentences are marked with labels that indicate levels of usage. *Standard* usage refers to what is proper for all speech and writing. Words and meanings in this category are shown in the dictionary without any special label. *Informal* usage is acceptable for everyday speech and for personal writing (such as friendly letters), but it is not recommended for public speaking or for compositions such as reports and explanations. Compare the following sentences.

Informal: Carl acted like he was enthused about the suggestion.
Standard: Carl acted as if he was enthusiastic about the suggestion.

Many example sentences in this chapter are simply labeled *correct* if they represent standard usage, and *incorrect* if they do not. Study the illustrations below.

Incorrect:
Everyone accept Norman thought the idea would work alright.
Correct:
Everyone except Norman thought the idea would work all right.

Above

Most people have no difficulty with *above* when it is a preposition (*above* the clouds). When used as an adjective, it should follow the noun it modifies (the clouds *above,* the paragraph *above*). Using *above* before the modified noun is proper in legal or business writing, but it should be avoided otherwise. Also avoid using *the above* to mean "something already referred to."

All the statistics above have been verified. (not *the above statistics*)
Read the agreement above before signing your name. (not *the above*)

Accept, Except

Accept is a verb meaning "to receive" or "to agree with." This word has the prefix *ac-,* which is a form of *ad-.* When you *accept* something, you *add* it to what you already have.

Except is usually a preposition meaning "not including." It is sometimes a verb meaning "to leave out; exclude." Note that *except* has the prefix *ex-,* which means "out of."

We must accept responsibility for our actions.
No man except Jesus has ever lived a sinless life.
[illegible] except anyone from the requirements for salvation

Adapt, Adopt

Adapt means "to adjust" or "to make suitable." (The root *apt* means "fitting.")
Adopt means "to accept" or "to make one's own." (The root *opt* means "to choose.")

We adapted the words of the poem for this occasion.
The Swiss Anabaptist immigrants did not readily adopt the English language.
Misty adopted the orphaned kittens and cared well for them.

Advice, Advise

Advice is a noun meaning "counsel." The last three letters spell *ice,* which is also a noun in most cases.

Advise is a verb meaning "to give counsel." It has the same ending as verbs like *revise* and *surmise.* This word may mean "inform" in legal or business writing, but that use is generally not appropriate.

Young people should listen to the advice of those more experienced.
Godly parents advise their children to guard their friendships carefully.
Mother informed us that dinner was ready. (not *advised*)

Ain't

The contraction *ain't* is not standard English. Use *am not, are not (aren't),* or *is not (isn't).*

Incorrect:
I ain't ready yet, and Harvey ain't either.
Correct:
I am not ready yet, and Harvey isn't either.

All

The word *all* should not be used to mean things like "all gone," "all consumed," or "all done."

Incorrect: The sugar in the canister is all.
When the work was all, we went home.
Correct: The sugar in the canister is all gone.
The sugar in the canister is all used up.
When the work was all done, we went home.

All right

The correct spelling is *all right,* not *alright.* (*All right* is the antonym of *all wrong.*)

Incorrect: I feel alright now that I have rested.
Correct: I feel all right now that I have rested.
These answers are all right.

Allude, Elude, Refer

Allude means "to refer to indirectly" or "to hint." When a person alludes to something, he does not identify it specifically because he assumes that the listener or reader is familiar with it.

Elude means "to escape from by evading or avoiding." (The prefix *e-* is a form of *ex-*.)

Refer means "to mention specifically." This word (rather than *allude*) should be used for speaking directly about a person or thing.

> By describing his escape as a "Red Sea experience," Mr. Golitsyn <u>alluded</u> to Israel's deliverance from the Egyptians.
> Several times he <u>eluded</u> the secret police who were pursuing him.
> He often <u>refers</u> to his grandmother, who was a true believer.

Almost, Most

Almost is an adverb meaning "nearly." Avoid using *most* for this definition.

> **Incorrect:** <u>Most</u> everyone has heard of the patience of Job.
> **Correct:** <u>Almost</u> everyone has heard of the patience of Job.

Altar, Alter

Altar is a noun meaning "an elevated structure on which offerings are made." *Alter* is a verb meaning "to change." To alt<u>er</u> something is to conv<u>er</u>t it.

> Abraham built an <u>altar</u> almost everywhere he went.
> God's Word will never <u>alter</u> to suit man's changing ways.

Applying the Lesson

A. Choose the standard expressions in these sentences.

1. When Brother Edward told us not to hide under a juniper tree, he was (alluding, eluding, referring) to the experience of Elijah.
2. We must always be ready to (altar, alter) our ways to follow the Bible way.
3. Although he tried hard, Darius could not (accept, except) Daniel from the penalty that his law decreed.
4. (Almost, Most) every book of the Bible refers to the Messiah.
5. This morning Brother Alvin (advised, informed) us that our memory work is due on Thursday.
6. My assigned work was (all, all finished) before Father returned.
7. Everything seemed (all right, alright) again after Father came home.
8. A careful reading of the (above paragraph, paragraph above) should answer your questions.
9. We (ain't, aren't) getting more cereal until this cereal is (all, all gone).
10. Mr. White (advised, informed) us that the fox which had (alluded, eluded) our traps was now hanging in his shed.
11. The board members discussed the (above, paragraph above) and agreed to (adapt, adopt) it as a statement of their position.
12. Mr. Chadwick (ain't, isn't) here now, but he will probably (accept, except) your offer.
13. It is not enough to have (almost, most) everything on the (altar, alter) of sacrifice.
14. This tropical weather may suit you (all right, alright), but I can hardly (adapt, adopt) to it.

B. Write the standard word or words for the underlined part of each sentence. If it needs no improvement, write *correct.*

1. The worldly wiseman does not except the Bible as God's authoritative Word.
2. We must be cautious lest we adopt the world's values and standards.
3. We know that things will come out all right in the end, for God is on the throne.
4. We can never altar an unpleasant truth by ignoring it or misrepresenting it.
5. No man can allude Satan's snares without godly faith and commitment.
6. The Bible teaches that ignorance does not except a person from accountability.
7. If the cookies are all, please serve the cupcakes.
8. Jerry fell off the wagon, but he thinks he will be alright.
9. Brother Wesley adopted this mobile home to serve as an office.
10. These chickens ain't laying very well anymore.
11. I did not write the above, but I know who did.
12. Brother Philip often eludes to his experiences on the mission field in Guatemala.
13. People who refuse to listen to good advice usually meet disaster.
14. We had almost all the work finished before noon.
15. I ain't sure what Father's surprise is, but he acts as if we will enjoy it.
16. Tell Father that the heifer feed is almost all.
17. Most every calf hutch needs fresh bedding tonight.
18. Father advised us that he has special plans for tomorrow.
19. The apostle Paul mentioned the Athenians' altar "TO THE UNKNOWN GOD."
20. Did you read the above carefully before you tried to answer the questions?

C. Write enough words to show how each sentence should be improved according to the rules you have studied. If a sentence needs no improvement, write *correct.*

1. Oliver Evans, born in 1755, invented several machines that worked alright; but his greatest invention was the high-pressure steam engine.
2. When he was seventeen years old, one of his brothers advised him about something that the blacksmith's son had done.
3. The boy had blocked the touchhole of a gun barrel, put water into it, and plugged the muzzle with wadding—which usually ain't wise at all!
4. Having altared the barrel in this way, the lad put it into the smith's fire; and soon the steam pressure shot out the wadding with great force.
5. Oliver immediately recognized that this idea could be adapted to make a useful steam engine.
6. However, it was most thirty-three years later before his dream materialized, and he completed the first steam-powered vehicle to run on American roads.
7. He named his weird-looking contraption *Orukter Amphibolos,* eluding to its ability to travel both on land and in water.

8. Evans built his machine after excepting a contract to dredge out the Philadelphia harbor.
9. He appealed to President Jefferson for relief when his money was nearly all.
10. We learn from the above that useful ideas sometimes come from unexpected sources.

Review Exercises

Write whether the underlined sentence part is a nominative absolute (*NA*) or a participial phrase (*PP*). [24]

1. The storm having passed, we went outside to see what damage it had done.
2. Looking around, we saw many leaves and twigs on the ground.
3. One tree, having withstood many previous storms, now lay prostrate on the ground.
4. The bark of another tree was split open, the tree having been struck by lightning.
5. God alone having power to control the weather, man must simply accept what comes.

---

38. Correct Word Usage, Part 2

Always, All ways

Always is an adverb meaning "every time," "all the time," "forever," or "at any time."

The expression *all ways* means "every way." It often follows a preposition.

> Myron is always ready to help others.
> God will always be sovereign over His creation.
> The book was attractively designed in all ways.

Amount, Number

Use *amount* with a noun that refers to a single mass—something that cannot be counted. *Amount* goes with the same nouns that *much* (rather than *many*) goes with.

Use *number* with nouns that refer to individual items—things that can be counted. *Number* goes with the same nouns that *many* (rather than *much*) goes with.

> We covered a large amount of material in our history classes this week.
> (Compare: *much material,* not *many material*)
> We covered a large number (not *amount*) of pages in our history classes this week. (Compare: *many pages,* not *much pages*)

Angry about, at, with

A person may be *angry with* another person, *angry about* a situation or an event, and *angry at* an animal or an inanimate object.

God is angry with the wicked every day.
Jonah was angry about the destruction of the gourd.
Balaam became angry at his donkey.

Anymore, Any more

In standard usage, *anymore* is an adverb meaning "any longer" or "at the present," and it occurs mainly in negative constructions and questions. It is used informally to mean "nowadays."

Informal: Anymore, Grandmother Bricker hears very poorly.
Standard: Grandmother Bricker cannot hear well anymore. (negative statement)
Do Eskimos build igloos anymore? (question)

The phrase *any more* should be used only in the sense of "some additional." It should not be used as an adverb.

Incorrect: We do not live in Virginia any more.
Correct: We do not live in Virginia anymore.
We do not have any more maple syrup.

As (if), Like

In standard English, *as* and *as if* are conjunctions and *like* is a preposition. *Like* has become accepted as a conjunction in informal usage.

Informal: God does not treat us like we sometimes treat our fellow men.
Too often we treat others like they have no feelings.
Standard: God does not treat us as we sometimes treat our fellow men.
Too often we treat others as if they have no feelings.
We should conduct ourselves like humble servants of Jesus Christ.

Awhile, A while

Awhile is an adverb meaning "for a short time."

The expression *a while* often follows a preposition. Avoid using the adverb *awhile* as the object of a preposition.

This evening we plan to visit Grandfather awhile.
This evening we plan to visit Grandfather for a while. (not *for awhile*)

Believe, Feel

Believe means "to think" or "to be convinced of." A valid belief is based on fact.

Feel indicates a perception based on emotion or opinion and not necessarily on fact.

Poor: We feel that Sunday is the proper day of worship.
Better: We believe that Sunday is the proper day of worship.
Because of our great privileges, we should feel that we are richly blessed. (Note the emotional aspect.)

Be sure and

The expression *be sure and* should be replaced with *be sure to.*

Incorrect: We must be sure and fix that broken window.
Correct: We must be sure to fix that broken window.

Burst, Bursted, Busted

The three principal parts of the verb *burst* are *burst, burst, burst.* The forms *bursted, bust,* and *busted* are not standard English verbs.

Incorrect: The dam bursted and flooded the valley below.
The water pipes busted during the cold snap.
Correct: The dam burst and flooded the valley below.
The water pipes burst during the cold snap.

Can, May

Can means "to be able to." It refers to ability.

May means "to be permitted to." The distinction between *can* and *may* is illustrated in this sentence: You *may* get a drink if you *can.*

Incorrect: Can I use your pen?
Correct: May I use your pen?

Sometimes *may* indicates possibility. For example, "They may go" could mean "They are permitted to go" or "It is possible that they will go." If the meaning of *may* is uncertain, replace it with *might* or *must* or some other verb.

Unclear:
We may hike in the woods this afternoon.
We may not allow the fear of man to control our actions.

Clear:
We are allowed to hike in the woods this afternoon. (permission)
We might hike in the woods this afternoon. (possibility)
We must not (or *dare not*) allow the fear of man to control our actions.

Applying the Lesson

A. Choose the standard expressions in these sentences.

1. Youth who do (as, like) their godly parents request are (always, all ways) happier than those who insist on their own way.
2. If you feel like becoming angry (about, at, with) someone who has wronged you, be (sure and, sure to) crucify those feelings.
3. God is (always, all ways) able to (burst, bust) our balloon of pride if we exalt ourselves.
4. We (believe, feel) that God hears the prayers of saints, but sometimes His answer does not come for (awhile, a while).
5. Although many do not uphold Bible principles (anymore, any more), we must be (sure and, sure to) keep on obeying God.

6. A large (amount, number) of Bible verses warn us not to live (as, like) the world does.
7. (Can, May) we walk to the back pasture this afternoon?
8. We do not have (anymore, any more) snow on the ground.
9. Grandmother Bicher will live with us (awhile, a while) this winter.
10. Due to an acute ear infection, Melanie's eardrum (burst, bursted, busted).
11. Even though the heifers are contrary, you must not become angry (about, at, with) them.
12. Mother said that we (can, may) make blueberry cobbler for dessert.
13. With only a small (amount, number) of visitors, our little church building is soon full.
14. Job must have (believed, felt) that God had forsaken him; for he said, "Oh that I knew where I might find him!"

B. Write the standard word or words for the underlined part of each sentence. If it needs no improvement, write *correct.*
1. If we desire God's blessing, we must <u>be sure and</u> follow His will.
2. Our heavenly Father is <u>always</u> watching over us lovingly.
3. We may face trials for <u>awhile</u> in life, but heaven will be worth it all.
4. A large <u>amount</u> of songs in the German *Ausbund* deal with the theme of persecution.
5. We should live each day <u>like</u> it might be our last.
6. Do you have <u>anymore</u> prayer requests?
7. The water line <u>burst</u> because the pressure regulator had stuck.
8. Did Brother Alan say that we <u>can</u> eat outside today?
9. Do you <u>feel</u> that kindness is an essential quality for God's people?
10. If you trust in the Lord, you cannot be <u>angry about</u> a change in your plans.
11. Self-pity will cause you to <u>feel</u> that nobody cares about you.
12. I wonder if Aunt Charlotte has <u>any more</u> of those crocheted afghans ready.
13. Suddenly the tire <u>bursted</u> with a tremendous bang.
14. Leslie managed to work in the shop <u>awhile</u> this morning.
15. Viola <u>can</u> go along to the store if she wants to.
16. That strange man seems quite <u>angry at</u> Father.
17. We almost <u>all ways</u> see several deer in this pasture in the evening.
18. Mother wants to <u>be sure and</u> send a get-well card to Sister Annette.
19. We had a record <u>amount</u> of thunderstorms this summer.
20. It seems <u>like</u> many thunderstorms follow the mountain ridge behind our farm.

C. Write enough words to show how each sentence should be improved according to the rules you have studied. If a sentence needs no improvement, write *correct.*
1. During the American Revolution, many items were all ways in short supply.
2. In 1779, at the age of fourteen, Eli Whitney felt that he could supply some of the demand for nails.
3. "Can I make a forge in our workshop?" Eli asked his father.
4. Eli's father let him make a forge like he requested.

5. Soon young Eli could not meet the demand any more.
6. He hired a helper to increase the number of nails he could produce.
7. The war ended in 1783, bringing cheaper nails from England and busting the bubble of his success.
8. Instead of becoming angry with the circumstances, Eli started making hatpins and walking canes.
9. He continued this business only for a while; then at eighteen years of age he began teaching school.
10. Be sure and read more about Eli Whitney's inventive career.

Review Exercises

Write enough words to show how each sentence should be improved according to the rules you have studied. If a sentence needs no improvement, write *correct.* [37, 38]

1. In 1527, George Wagner was arrested at Munich because he refused to adapt the position of the state church on four articles of faith.
2. George was held in prison for awhile as the authorities urged him to recant.
3. An astounding amount of people tried to make George change his mind.
4. Even George's wife and child were brought to the prison to see if they could persuade him to alter his beliefs.
5. However, George felt that he must remain loyal to God if he was to be saved in the end.
6. When the prince finally decided that George would not except deliverance, he condemned him to death.
7. George wanted to be sure and testify about the truth before everyone present at his execution.
8. With a smile, George went bravely to his death; he was not angry with his persecutors.
9. The sheriff, however, did not consider his work to be all; he determined to arrest more of the brethren.
10. But the sheriff could not allude God's judgment, and that night he died in bed.

---

39. Improving Your Writing Style, Part 3: Active Voice

In the previous two writing style lessons, you learned that originality and the use of active verbs characterize good writing style. That is, an effective writer looks for fresh, colorful ways of expressing himself, and he strives to use verbs that put life and action into his writing.

Another element of good writing style is the deliberate use of verbs in the active voice. You should remember that transitive verbs can be active or passive. In the active voice, the subject *performs* the action of the verb. But in the passive voice, the subject merely *receives* the action.

Active voice: The presidents and princes hated Daniel.
They persuaded the king to make a foolish law.
Passive voice: Daniel was hated by the presidents and princes.
The king was persuaded to make a foolish law.

The active voice puts energy into writing because it makes the subject do something. The presidents and princes *hated* Daniel; they *persuaded* the king. In contrast, the passive voice introduces a passive subject that never gets into the action! Daniel did nothing; he simply *was hated.* The king did nothing; he merely *was persuaded.*

This difference between active voice and passive voice makes a great contrast in writing. While the passive voice is dull and sluggish, the active voice is lively and energetic. We can understand this; but unless we think carefully as we write, the passive voice will slip into our sentences and snuff out the action. See how that happens in the following example.

> After feeding the five thousand, Jesus sent His disciples across the Sea of Galilee. Before they reached the other side, however, a mighty tempest arose. The ship and every person in it were being threatened. But Jesus was not neglecting His loved ones! Above the roar of the storm, the Master's voice was heard: "Be of good cheer."
>
> Peter responded, "Lord, if it is You, bid me come to You on the water."

Did you catch it? *The Master's voice was heard.* Why should we record this action with a passive verb? Jesus Himself spoke words of comfort to His distressed disciples. We want to capture that action: Above the roar of the storm, *the Master called,* "Be of good cheer." Or we could say that *the disciples heard a voice.* Either way, we are using the active voice, and the action puts life into the writing style.

You see this, but did you see the other use of the passive voice in the example? *The ship and every person in it were being threatened.* Again we have a subject with no action; the ship and those in it are merely being acted upon. How can we write this in the active voice? To answer that question, consider *what action* was taking place and *who* or *what* was doing it. *The stormy waves were threatening the ship and every person in it.* Now we have action; now we have life.

Of course, the passive voice does exist for a good reason. Sometimes there is no clear doer of the action, and sometimes we deliberately avoid naming the doer. Also, the passive voice may fit well in a sentence that pictures someone as the victim of a tragedy or disaster: *Samson was blinded and imprisoned.* But the passive voice nearly always weakens writing style because it allows a person to write in vague generalities without saying exactly *who* does the things he describes.

For this reason, you need to make a special effort to detect passive verbs in your writing and replace them with active verbs. This point is so important that you will try to avoid the passive voice completely in your written work for this lesson.

Applying the Lesson

A. Read the story below, and do the following exercises in class.

1. Find the one passive verb in each paragraph, and notice how it spoils the action. Suggest how to improve that sentence or clause with a verb in the active voice.
2. Tell whether each underlined expression has a *good* or *poor* effect on the story. If it is good, tell whether it illustrates *originality* or an *active verb.* If it is poor, suggest how to improve it.

How Nevin Helped

(1) Mother sighed as she glanced out the window at the [a]haze-blanketed August sky. "What a day!" she thought as beads of sweat were wiped from her forehead. Father had left early that morning to attend the ministers' meeting. He would not return before evening, so Mother had some of his work to do in addition to her own regular duties.

(2) Mother's shoulders sagged as tomatoes were cut to make tomato juice. She must hurry. [b]There were many jobs pressing upon her. She thought over the many interruptions of the morning. Several times the doorbell had rung. Mother needed to stop her work to see who had come. How [c]many precious minutes fled with each person at the door! How small the heap of cut tomatoes looked beside the big pile awaiting the [d]work of her deft hands!

(3) "Oh!" exclaimed Mother. "That washer has stopped already. How time flies! I guess the wash must be hung up by Nevin."

(4) Mother turned to call her fourteen-year-old son. But then she turned back to the sink. "I promised Nevin that he could work at his pine hutch this afternoon. And this will surely be called a girl's job. [e]I feel just too tired to deal with complaints now. Maybe I can hang up the wash later."

(5) Another juicy red tomato was cut by Mother. Then she shook her head. "No," she decided. "I have a son [f]who can be a helper. And he must learn to help cheerfully."

(6) The button of the intercom was pressed. Hearing no [g]noise, Mother called, "Nevin, would you please come to the house?"

(7) "Sure, Mother," Nevin returned. "Be there shortly. Some clamps on the side panels that I've just glued are being set by me."

(8) "What do you want, Mother?" Nevin asked as the kitchen was entered a few minutes later.

(9) "I'm sorry, Nevin, but your help is needed," Mother told him, [h]a little sunlight coming from her knife. "Please hang up that load of towels for me."

(10) "Sure," Nevin answered. He whistled like a bird as the clean, wet towels were pulled from the washer.

(11) [i]Mother smiled as Nevin's cheerful whistle was heard from the clothesline. "Thank You, Lord, for his cheerful attitude right now when

I'm feeling so pressured," Mother whispered. [k]Some of her tension melted away, and the mountain of tomatoes steadily melted too.

B. Write a story of 200–300 words about a time when you or someone else helped another person, perhaps in a small or hidden way. ***Use no passive voice*** in your writing. Also put special effort into applying the other elements of writing style that you have studied: originality and active verbs.

---

40. Correct Word Usage, Part 3

Censor, Censure

Censor (sen′·sər) means "to examine (speech or writing) and remove objectionable content."

Censure (sen′·shər) means "to express strong disapproval of" or "to condemn harshly."

> Father censored some slang words from the book before he gave it to me.
> The angry woman censured the boy for ruining her flowers.

Compare to, with

Use *compare with* to speak of comparing things in order to observe literal similarities or differences.

Use *compare to* for making figurative comparisons.

> How does your weather in northern Ontario compare with ours here in Alberta?
> The New Testament compares the Christian life to a warfare.

Comprehensible, Comprehensive

Comprehensible means "intelligible; understandable."

Comprehensive means "of a large scope" or "inclusive."

> After I learned the meanings of a few key words, the directions became comprehensible.
> This book gives a comprehensive survey of beekeeping.

Contemptible, Contemptuous

Contemptible means "deserving contempt; despicable." It should generally be used to describe actions rather than people.

Contemptuous means "expressing contempt; scornful." It may describe words, actions, or people.

> Judas committed the contemptible deed of betraying Jesus for money.
> Sanballat spoke contemptuous words when the Jews began rebuilding the wall.

Continual(ly), Continuous(ly)

Continual means "occurring repeatedly at frequent intervals."
Continuous means "occurring constantly without interruption."

> God has blessed us with continual showers this spring.
> It has rained continuously for the past twelve hours.

Could (Should, Would) of

In informal speech, contracted forms like *could've, should've,* and *would've* sound like *could of, should of,* and *would of.* Inexperienced writers sometimes write these verbs with *of* rather than *have.*

> **Incorrect:** We should of started sooner; then we would of been here earlier.
> **Correct:** We should have started sooner; then we would have been here earlier.

Council, Counsel

A *council* is a group of people who serve in some official position, as in a state church or in civil government.

As a noun, *counsel* means "advice" or "an exchanging of ideas." As a verb, *counsel* means "to give advice" or "to exchange ideas."

> The Jewish council sought false witnesses to testify against Jesus.
> Mother counseled me to discuss the question with Father.
> A preparatory service before Communion is often called a counsel meeting. (not *council meeting*)

Differ from, with

Differ from means "to be unlike," usually with no indication of conflict.
Differ with means "to disagree with." It usually refers to people with conflicting ideas.

> The Spanish alphabet differs from the English alphabet in several ways.
> Mr. Hilbert differed with us when we discussed nonresistance.

Dilemma

The primary meaning of *dilemma* is "a circumstance requiring one to choose between two equally undesirable options." (The prefix *di-* means "two.") In standard writing, avoid using *dilemma* to mean simply "problem" or "difficulty."

> Pilate faced a dilemma. Should he crucify an innocent man or risk a riot by the Jews?
> The pioneers met one difficulty after another as they traveled through the mountains. (not *dilemma*)

Disinterested, Uninterested

The primary meaning of *disinterested* is "impartial; having no special preference concerning the outcome of an issue." For example, a good judge is disinterested in the outcome of a trial. His main interest is to have a fair and just trial.

Uninterested means "having no interest in," "not paying attention," or "indifferent."

The neighbors asked a <u>disinterested</u> person to help settle their disagreement.
Mr. Scott appears quite <u>uninterested</u> in the Gospel.

Applying the Lesson

A. Choose the standard expressions in these sentences.

1. Because of the (dilemma, problem) that Moses faced, Jethro suggested that he appoint (disinterested, uninterested) judges to help settle disputes among the Israelites.
2. The Pharisees differed (from, with) the Sadducees because their doctrines differed (from, with) the Sadducees' doctrines.
3. The faithful priests (censored, censured) Uzziah when he offered incense.
4. Ever since his fall, Satan has maintained a (continual, continuous) warfare against God.
5. Ephesians 6 presents a (comprehensible, comprehensive) list of the armor that a Christian should wear.
6. Compared (to, with) the Old Testament, the New Testament upholds the same faith in God but a new way of approaching God.
7. David's (contemptible, contemptuous) sin gave the enemies of the Lord an occasion to blaspheme.
8. Haman built a gallows at his wife's (council, counsel), and Mordecai might (have, of) been hanged on it if Haman's scheme had worked.
9. Paul differed (from, with) Barnabas over the wisdom of taking John Mark on another missionary journey.
10. The (contemptible, contemptuous) children who mocked Elisha were punished severely.
11. Jesus spoke of a rich man who was (disinterested, uninterested) in the welfare of his soul.
12. The school board will (censor, censure) these books before putting them into the library.
13. We have been praying (continually, continuously) for rain.
14. The note was barely (comprehensible, comprehensive), but we understood its main idea.
15. My brother compared the writing (to, with) chicken scratches.
16. We should (have, of) been more careful when we planted these rows of peas.

B. Write the standard word or words for the underlined part of each sentence. If it needs no improvement, write *correct.*

1. Though many people consider the Bible a mysterious book, it is easily <u>comprehensive</u> to those who sincerely want to know God.
2. The prophets <u>censored</u> God's people for their unfaithfulness.
3. Animal sacrifices, <u>continuously</u> offered during the Old Testament years, could not provide full salvation for man.

4. The attitudes of the world <u>differ from</u> those of God's people.
5. Father gave careful, <u>uninterested</u> consideration to both sides of the story.
6. We <u>should of</u> listened more carefully to what Mother said.
7. Anabaptists were often brought before a church <u>council</u> and questioned about their beliefs.
8. The people laughed <u>contemptibly</u> when Jesus said that Jairus's daughter was sleeping.
9. <u>Compared with</u> our farm in Virginia, this farm has much better soil.
10. The fireman faced the <u>dilemma</u> of letting the child perish and saving his own life, or trying to rescue the child and risking two lives.
11. After Brother Wilmer had <u>censured</u> the newspaper clipping, he posted it on the bulletin board.
12. With a casual, <u>disinterested</u> shrug of his shoulders, the man walked away.
13. Even though Mr. Clark was so <u>contemptuous</u>, we need to forgive him.
14. In building our new shop, we faced a number of <u>dilemmas</u> that had no simple solutions.
15. Father often sought <u>counsel</u> from Brother Wayne, an experienced builder.
16. Your recipe <u>differs with</u> mine in only a few details.
17. In Walter's poem, the flowers are <u>compared with</u> smiling faces.
18. I need a more <u>comprehensible</u> concordance than the small one in the back of my Bible.
19. We <u>could of</u> worked a little longer, but we had come to a good place to stop.
20. The fans do not run <u>continually</u>; they are thermostatically controlled.

C. Write enough words to show how each sentence should be improved according to the rules you have studied. If a sentence needs no improvement, write *correct.*

1. In 1792, Eli Whitney arrived in Georgia, where he would of tutored Major Dupont's children.
2. Compared to the salary he had been promised, however, he found that he might receive only half as much money.
3. Whitney moved to a different plantation, where he heard about the dilemma that faced cotton growers in the South.
4. As he listened to the plantation owners' discussions, he gained a comprehensible view of the strong market for cotton and the great need for a speedier process of cleaning cotton.
5. A lady gave this council: "Mr. Whitney can build a machine to clean cotton"; and within two weeks, he had built a cotton gin.
6. Whitney's gin differed with others in several important ways, and it was able to clean the green seed cotton that other gins could not clean.
7. Moving teeth on a roller continuously pulled the cotton through narrow slits that prevented the seeds from coming through
8. A number of dishonest men, seemingly contemptible of patent laws, made cotton gins modeled after Whitney's without paying for the right to do so.
9. In a letter to a fellow inventor, Whitney bitterly censured those who profited at his expense.

10. Although many southern states did authorize payments to Whitney, an uninterested observer will soon recognize that he did not earn what he deserved from this invention.

Review Exercises

Write enough words to show how each sentence should be improved according to the rules you have studied. If a sentence needs no improvement, write *correct.* [37–40]

1. Leonhard Keyser, a Roman Catholic priest, could not be satisfied any more with the corruption in the church.
2. He made quite a comprehensive study of Lutheran, Zwinglian, and Anabaptist doctrines.
3. In 1525, Leonhard joined the Anabaptist movement like many others were doing.
4. He served zealously as a minister among the Anabaptists, all ways undaunted by the severe persecution.
5. After he was arrested, the authorities advised him that he would be burned on the Friday before Saint Lawrence Day.
6. On the way to the execution, the priests spoke to Leonhard in Latin because otherwise the common people would of understood them.
7. Leonhard plucked a flower and told the judge that if they could burn the flower and his body, their way was all right and his was wrong.
8. Twice the executioners built an enormous fire; yet when the wood was all, Leonhard's body and the flower remained unharmed.
9. The executioners then did a contemptible deed: they cut Leonhard's body into pieces and tried to burn them.
10. When the pieces of his body would not burn, the terrified judge resigned his office and moved away; but the judge's servant adapted the Anabaptist faith and lived in godliness until death.

---

41. Correct Word Usage, Part 4

Eminent, Imminent, Immanent

Eminent (em′·ə·nənt) means "high-ranking," "conspicuous," or "prominent."

Imminent (im′·ə·nənt) means "likely to occur at any moment."

Immanent (im′·ə·nənt) means "indwelling" and refers mainly to a person. It has the same root (*man*) as the word *remain.* Note that *imminent* and *immanent* are pronounced alike; they are homonyms.

> Menno Simons was respected as an eminent church leader.
> We must not lose sight of Jesus' imminent return for the saints.
> The immanent Holy Spirit directs the life of a Christian.

Enormity

Enormity means "extremely great wickedness" or "outrageousness." To refer to greatness of size, scope, or influence, use *enormousness* or *immensity.*

> Overwhelmed by the enormity of his sin, David pleaded for God's forgiveness.
> The immensity of outer space boggles our finite minds. (not *enormity*)

Enthused

The word *enthused* is derived by folk etymology from *enthusiasm. Enthused* is informal but undignified because it suggests an outward emotional display. In standard English, it should be replaced by a word such as *excited* or *enthusiastic.*

> **Informal:** The children were enthused about visiting Grandmother.
> **Standard:** The children were enthusiastic (or *excited*) about visiting Grandmother.

Everyday, Every day

The word *everyday* means "daily," "relating to ordinary days," or "commonplace." It is an adjective.

The expression *every day* means "each day." It functions as an adverb.

> My everyday chores include feeding the chickens.
> Pack two sets of everyday clothes for the trip.
> We have family worship every day before breakfast. (not *everyday*)

Fabulous

Fabulous, derived from *fable,* means "incredible," "imaginary," or "known only through fables." It is informal for "outstanding" or "marvelous."

> **Informal:** Myra did a fabulous job on these posters.
> **Standard:** Myra did an outstanding job on these posters.
> The neighbor boy told a fabulous story about killing a wolf barehanded.

Flaunt, Flout

Flaunt means "to make a bold, showy, or defiant display of."

Flout means "to show bold disregard for (a rule or standard)."

> The Pharisees often flaunted their piety before others.
> Many of their practices flouted the clear commandments of God.

Good, Well

Good is an adjective with many meanings, such as "right," "proper," and "satisfactory."

Well usually modifies an action verb by indicating "in a good manner." It is sometimes an adjective meaning "healthy," "proper," or "prudent."

> The children's good behavior made the baby-sitting job a pleasure.
> Listen well so that you will know exactly what to do.

If Aunt Mae feels well enough, she will help us make applesauce.
It is good (or *well*) that you asked for advice.

Haven't but, only

Haven't but is a double negative because *but* has a negative meaning in this construction.

The phrase *haven't only* sometimes occurs in expressions like "we haven't only." This indicates either that we have more than the amount specified or that we have none at all. The correct expression is "we have only."

Incorrect: We haven't but two bushels of apples left, and we haven't only one bushel of pears.
Correct: We have but two bushels of apples left, and we have only one bushel of pears.

Heap, Heaps

A *heap* is a pile. The word is used informally to mean "many," "large amount," or "multitude."

Informal: We had a heap of trouble pushing the van out of the mud.
This area must have had heaps of rain.
Standard: We had great difficulty pushing the van out of the mud.
This area must have had a large amount of rain.
The farmer repaired his lane with stones from the heap of gravel.

Hopefully

Hopefully means "in a hopeful manner." Avoid using *hopefully* as a sentence modifier meaning "it is hoped" or "if all goes well."

Poor:
Hopefully, we will finish harvesting the wheat tomorrow.
Better:
If all goes well, we will finish harvesting the wheat tomorrow.
We looked hopefully at the approaching clouds, but they brought no rain.

Applying the Lesson

A. Choose the standard expressions in these sentences.
1. Because of the (enormity, enormousness) of Israel's sin, God brought severe judgment upon the nation.
2. Although the people of Judah knew about this, they brazenly continued to (flaunt, flout) their own wickedness.
3. The prophets did their work (good, well), but most of the Jews paid little heed to their warnings.
4. Finally the (eminent, imminent, immanent) presence of the Lord departed from the temple.
5. When one is (enthused, enthusiastic) about his assignment, he can work efficiently.

6. We (haven't only, have only) one life to live, so we must live it in godly fear.
7. We have had rain (everyday, every day) so far this week.
8. I think Susan did a (fabulous, remarkable) job on her embroidery patch.
9. If you (flaunt, flout) good advice today, you will regret it tomorrow.
10. The (enormity, immensity) of the ocean amazes me every time I see it.
11. By steady perseverance, the (fabulous, remarkable) tortoise won the race with the hare.
12. Since Mother is not feeling (good, well), she is resting this afternoon.
13. The Alabama coast was in (eminent, imminent, immanent) danger from a violent hurricane.
14. Chasing heifers should not be an (everyday, every day) occurrence, but every dairy farmer will need to chase heifers.
15. The Christian (hasn't but, has but) one overall goal: to please the Lord.
16. Are you as (enthused, enthusiastic) about gaining approval from the Lord as from your friends?

B. Write the standard word or words for the underlined part of each sentence. If it needs no improvement, write *correct.*

1. A Christian has the <u>imminent</u> presence of the Holy Spirit.
2. The Book of Jude describes false teachers who <u>flout</u> Gospel principles and follow their own self-centered ways.
3. God lavishes rich blessings upon us <u>everyday</u>.
4. <u>Hopefully</u>, we remember to praise His Name frequently.
5. The <u>enormity</u> of the dense forest frightened the little children.
6. The destitute refugees <u>hadn't only</u> enough food for one scant meal.
7. Over lunch hour, Market Square is crowded with a <u>heap</u> of office workers.
8. The idea of selling cantaloupes <u>enthused</u> Steven immensely.
9. Those who <u>flaunt</u> their knowledge have a poor concept of true wisdom.
10. Benjamin Franklin, an <u>eminent</u> statesman of his day, published hundreds of wise sayings.
11. According to Miss Orndorf's <u>fabulous</u> account, her parents grew tons of produce every year in their small backyard garden.
12. Do your work <u>good</u> the first time, and you will not need to go back and redo it.
13. Tractor breakdowns have been almost <u>every day</u> occurrences lately.
14. The <u>enormity</u> of the crime shocked the community.
15. We <u>haven't but</u> one load of straw to stack now.
16. Nobody seemed very <u>enthused</u> about dinner because of the high heat and humidity.
17. <u>Hopefully</u>, the temperature will cool down a bit before tomorrow
18. Mr. Eisenberger owns <u>a heap of</u> real estate in this area.
19. Because he has strep throat, Wesley is not <u>good</u> enough to go along tonight.
20. With all the rain this summer, we have a <u>fabulous</u> stand of field corn.

C. Write enough words to show how each sentence should be improved according to the rules you have studied. If a sentence needs no improvement, write *correct.*

1. Cyrus McCormick's father Robert was an immanent man at Walnut Grove, Virginia; he owned over one thousand acres, two gristmills, two sawmills, a limekiln, a distillery, and a blacksmith shop.
2. Robert McCormick had tried for many years to devise a mechanical harvester, but there were heaps of problems to overcome.
3. Although his father gave up, Cyrus remained enthused about the idea.
4. By the age of twenty-two, Cyrus had developed a machine that worked well enough to harvest as much grain in a few hours as three men could cut by hand in a day.
5. Although others had tried to build mechanical reapers before McCormick, none of the other machines worked as fabulously as the McCormick reaper did.
6. At this time the McCormicks invested most of their capital in an iron-smelting venture, which hadn't only begun production when the Panic of 1837 hit.
7. The enormity of their losses plunged them into debt, so Cyrus began building and selling reapers again.
8. So great was his success that within a few years he paid his family's debt and made the reaper an every day piece of machinery on American farms.
9. However, McCormick seemed to enjoy flouting his patent rights in court as he engaged in suing and countersuing his rivals.
10. Hopefully, we can learn from his perseverance without following his ungodly ways.

Review Exercises

Write enough words to show how each sentence should be improved according to the rules you have studied. If a sentence needs no improvement, write *correct.* [37–41]

1. At Kitzbuehl in the province of Tyrol, the authorities arrested a fairly large amount of believers in 1527.
2. The tyranny of the persecutors succeeded so good that a number of the believers recanted.
3. These authorities publicly censured the Anabaptists by saying, "How finely your teachers and pastors now give their lives for you!"
4. Then Thomas Hermann, apparently one of the leaders, bursted from the crowd.
5. He advised the authorities that he had taught the people the truth and that he was ready to testify to the truth with his blood.
6. Thomas excepted his coming death so calmly that on the way to his martyrdom, he composed and sang a hymn.
7. This execution differed with many others, for Thomas's heart would not burn; so his enemies threw it into a nearby lake.

8. The town clerk declared that he would not lay down his head in peace until he had helped exterminate these people; and his vow was fulfilled, but not like he had expected.
9. He was not able to elude God's judgment; for in making a turn with his sleigh, the town clerk was thrown out, and his brains were dashed out against a wall and an oak tree.
10. This account reminds us that God all ways has the last word when men blaspheme Him or persecute His people.

---

42. Correct Word Usage, Part 5

How come

How come is an informal expression for "how is it that?" or "why?"

Informal: How come we never have liver or spinach anymore?
Standard: Why do we never have liver or spinach anymore?

Impact

Impact is often a noun that refers to the force of a collision or an influence. As a verb it means "to strike forcefully" or "to pack in." Avoid using *impact* as a verb with the meaning "to affect or influence."

Poor:
The rising corn prices strongly impacted the farmers in our area.
Correct:
The rising corn prices strongly affected the farmers in our area.
The rising corn prices had a strong impact on the farmers in our area.
I cleaned the impacted mud from the grooves in my shoe soles.

Imply, Infer

Imply means "to express indirectly." Implying is done by a person who is writing, speaking, or acting.

Infer means "to reach a conclusion by reasoning." Inferring is done by a person who is reading, listening, or observing.

Mr. Peterson implied that he appreciated our Gospel signs.
Father inferred from his words that several other neighbors were displeased with them.

In back of

Do not use *in back of* for *behind*. However, it is correct to use *in the back of* when referring to the back part of a place.

Incorrect: We looked in back of the shed for Lela's doll.
Correct: We looked behind the shed for Lela's doll.
In the back of the room is Warren's stamp collection.

Ingenious, Ingenuous

Ingenious (in•jēn′•yəs) means "skillful," "clever," or "resourceful."
Ingenuous (in•jen′•yü•əs) means "simple and trustful; not cunning or suspicious."

An ingenious mechanic is a valuable asset on the mission field.
The ingenuous youth was easily persuaded by the smooth-tongued salesman.

Its, It's

Its is a possessive case pronoun that means "belonging to it."
It's is a contraction for "it is" or "it has."

The angry bull shook its massive head and pawed the ground.
It's high time to get out of here!

Kind (Sort) of

Kind of and *sort of* should not be used to mean "rather" or "somewhat." Also, the article *a* or *an* should not follow *kind of, sort of,* or *type of* when referring to a class of items.

Incorrect: I was sort of surprised that Bennie would say such a thing.
What kind of a goat is this?
Correct: I was rather surprised that Bennie would say such a thing.
What kind of goat is this?

Lay, Lie

Lay is a transitive verb meaning "to put or place (something)." Its principal parts are *lay, laid, (have) laid.*

Lie is an intransitive verb meaning "to rest, recline, or remain in a flat position." Its principal parts are *lie, lay, (have) lain.* One reason for confusing these words is that the form *lay* is the first principal part of *lay* and also the second principal part of *lie.*

If plans carry, we shall lay the linoleum this afternoon.
Apparently this book lay out in the rain all morning.

Let, Leave

Let means "to allow or permit." Its principal parts are *let, let, (have) let.* This verb is always followed by an infinitive without *to,* which tells what is being permitted. Sometimes the infinitive is understood from the context.

Leave means "to depart, go away from, or allow to remain." Its principal parts are *leave, left, (have) left.* Unlike *let,* the verb *leave* is not followed by an infinitive.

Sometimes Father lets me drive the car out the lane to get the mail.
(*Let* is followed by the infinitive *to drive* with *to* omitted.)
I wanted to drive the car into the garage, but Father would not let me.
(The infinitive *to drive* is understood.)
Do not leave the car windows open.

Loose, Lose

Loose is an adjective that means “not tight; not fastened or restrained.” As a verb it means “to release” or “to set free.” This word has the same ending as the rhyming words *goose, moose,* and *noose.* You might also remember that in the phrase “loose tooth,” both words have double *o*’s.

Lose is a verb that means “to be deprived of; to have (something) taken away.” Its past form is *lost;* note that the present and past forms both have just one *o.*

If you carry <u>loose</u> change in your pocket, you are likely to <u>lose</u> some of it.

Applying the Lesson

A. Choose the standard expressions in these sentences.

1. We (imply, infer) that a spirit of self-sufficiency was (behind, in back of) Nebuchadnezzar’s boastful words.
2. To humble Nebuchadnezzar, God (let, left) him become insane and (loose, lose) his kingdom for a time.
3. Jesus was not so (ingenious, ingenuous) that the scribes and Pharisees could trap Him.
4. The disciples were (kind of, rather) weak in faith at times.
5. The labors of the apostle Paul strongly (impacted, influenced) the early church.
6. (Its, It’s) hard to imagine what would have happened to the church without his efforts.
7. I wondered (how come, why) Luann was not helping, but then I saw the cast on her leg.
8. She told me that she had experienced a bad fall on (loose, lose) gravel.
9. During the sultry afternoon, the cattle (laid, lay) under the shade trees or stood in the creek.
10. The brief shower hardly (impacted, affected) the temperature at all.
11. Father said that you should (let, leave) the disabled wagon in the field.
12. (Behind, In back of) Mr. Jenkin’s rough manners, you will find a friendly man.
13. What (kind of, kind of a) turtle is this?
14. Mrs. Stacy (implied, inferred) in various ways that she wished she still lived on a farm.
15. (How come, Why) are we starting the chores early this evening?
16. Using an (ingenious, ingenuous) whistle code, the villagers kept their only Bible hidden from the authorities.
17. (Behind, In back of) even the stormiest clouds shines the sun.
18. When people strive for earthly riches, they often (loose, lose) sight of the riches in heaven.
19. Covetousness, with (its, it’s) related sinful attitudes, robs man of true happiness.
20. The choice to be content or to be covetous (lays, lies) with each person.

B. Write the standard word or words for the underlined part of each sentence. If it needs no improvement, write *correct.*

1. The conduct of older children strongly <u>impacts</u> their younger brothers and sisters.
2. You should not be too <u>ingenious</u>, but neither should you be unduly suspicious.
3. There is no greater loss than to <u>lose</u> one's soul.
4. Be careful not to <u>imply</u> an idea that the speaker did not actually intend.
5. If we have failed, we know the problem <u>lays</u> with us rather than God.
6. Since our family is <u>kind of</u> outdoors-oriented, we enjoy hiking in the woods.
7. Our woods is not large, but <u>its</u> beautiful in all seasons.
8. If warm air rises, <u>how come</u> are mountain peaks cooler than lowlands?
9. The answer <u>lays</u> in the fact that air cools as its pressure decreases.
10. The low pressure of air at the top of a mountain has a direct <u>impact</u> on its temperature.
11. Father did not see the post <u>in back of</u> the truck, so he backed right into it.
12. Marvin <u>let</u> some bags of feed on the truck to unload at the other shed.
13. Wilmer wonders <u>how come</u> this heifer feed is different from that heifer feed.
14. Did you know that the billy goat has gotten out of <u>it's</u> pen again?
15. You should <u>leave</u> the wooden chairs in the house.
16. The man standing <u>in back of</u> Uncle Howard is Brother Silas Wenger.
17. Please <u>lose</u> the horse so that he can go to the watering trough.
18. This article wrongly <u>implies</u> that the United States is a Christian nation.
19. What <u>kind of a</u> government would a Christian nation have?
20. No matter how <u>ingenuous</u> the leaders may be, they cannot set up a truly Christian nation.

C. Write enough words to show how each sentence should be improved according to the rules you have studied. If a sentence needs no improvement, write *correct.*

1. Although rubber fascinated Charles Goodyear when he was yet a schoolboy, he little imagined then how he would impact the development of useful rubber.
2. The practical uses of uncured rubber are sort of limited.
3. Even though its waterproof, uncured rubber is brittle in cold weather and tacky in warm weather.
4. For over six years, the problem of making a useful, all-weather rubber lay heavy on Goodyear's mind.
5. The conviction that the Creator wanted him to devote his life to this pursuit stood in back of his perseverance.
6. In January 1839, Goodyear was heating a compound of rubber and sulfur when he accidentally left some drop onto the hot stovetop.

7. From what he saw, he immediately implied that he had discovered the long-sought key for curing rubber into a consistently useful material.
8. Chemists still cannot explain how come heat and sulfur produce a chemical reaction in rubber that makes it strong and flexible in both heat and cold.
9. After perfecting this process, known as vulcanization, Goodyear did not loose much time in finding ways to use his new rubber.
10. This ingenuous man might have become wealthy if he had received all the royalties that he deserved, but he actually lived and died in poverty.

Review Exercises

Write enough words to show how each sentence should be improved according to the rules you have studied. If a sentence needs no improvement, write *correct.* [37–42]

1. In 1529, seven brethren in southwestern Germany were arrested because their beliefs differed with the doctrines of the state church.
2. Among them was a fourteen-year-old lad who had a fabulous faith.
3. He was kept in prison for most a whole year.
4. During this time the authorities continually tried to persuade him to recant.
5. However, the young man did not leave any of their appeals move him.
6. While he was awaiting execution by the sword, an imminent person rode up to him.
7. This man offered the lad a regular payment of money if he would adapt the teachings of the state church.
8. The youth steadfastly refused to altar his convictions.
9. He would rather have suffered on earth than loose his inheritance in heaven.
10. Like him, we should be more enthused about our heavenly home than about earthly riches.

---

43. Correct Word Usage, Part 6

Maybe, May be

Maybe is an adverb meaning "perhaps" or "possibly."
May be is a verb phrase that expresses possibility.

Maybe Aunt Lela will come tomorrow.
Grandmother may be able to come along.

Momentarily

The primary meaning of *momentarily* is "for a moment; briefly." This word is sometimes used to mean "in a moment" or "soon," but that usage should be avoided because it may be unclear.

Unclear: The clerk promised to wait on us <u>momentarily</u>.
(Would the clerk wait on us for only a moment?)
Clear: The clerk promised to wait on us <u>in a moment</u>. (or *soon*)
I was <u>momentarily</u> blinded by the bright lights.

Nice

Nice is an overworked, vague adjective. Choose more specific and colorful words such as *pleasant, thoughtful, kind, desirable,* and *delightful.*

Poor: The Wallaces have been <u>nice</u> neighbors.
This is a <u>nice</u> day for a hike to the falls.
Better: The Wallaces have been <u>friendly</u> neighbors.
This is a <u>pleasant</u> day for a hike to the falls.

Notable, Noted, Noteworthy, Notorious

Notable, noted, and *noteworthy* mean "famous," "well-known," or "remarkable." *Notorious* means "well-known for an unfavorable reason; infamous."

Gideon won a <u>notable</u> victory over the Midianites.
Boaz was <u>noted</u> for his kindness and benevolence.
David made a <u>noteworthy</u> contribution to Israel's spiritual life.
Abigail admitted that Nabal was <u>notorious</u> for his churlishness.

OK, Okay

OK and *okay* are informal for "all right" or "in good condition."

Informal: After a brief rest, I felt <u>OK</u> (or *okay*) again.
Standard: After a brief rest, I felt <u>all right</u> again.

Over with

Do not use *over with* to mean "over," "finished," or "past."

Incorrect: We were glad when that hard task was <u>over with</u>.
Correct: We were glad when that hard task was <u>over</u>. (or *finished*)

Persecute, Prosecute

Persecute means "to harass or oppress, usually for one's beliefs."
Prosecute means "to take legal action against."

The Jews <u>persecuted</u> the early church.
The attorney general <u>prosecuted</u> the leader of the crime network.

Perspective, Prospective

Perspective means "a visible scene" or "a mental view; an outlook."
Prospective means "of or in the future" or "potential."

The whole valley lay in <u>perspective</u> before us.
From our <u>perspective</u>, the Anabaptists faced very trying circumstances.
Some of you are <u>prospective</u> teachers, writers, and editors.

Poorly

Poorly is an adverb meaning "in a poor manner." It is used informally as an adjective meaning "in poor health."

Informal:

Great-aunt Lucinda has been poorly in recent weeks.

Standard:

Great-aunt Lucinda has been in poor health in recent weeks.
Even with medication, her heart has been functioning poorly.

Precede, Proceed

The basic meaning of *precede* is "to go before" (*pre-,* before, + *cede,* to go). This word uses the most common spelling of the *cede* root, which also occurs in words like *concede, recede, secede, antecedent,* and *intercede.*

The basic meaning of *proceed* is "to go forth or forward" (*pro-,* forth or forward, + *ceed,* an alternate spelling of *cede,* to go). *Proceed, exceed,* and *succeed* are the only English words with the *cede* root spelled *ceed;* in all other words it is spelled *ced* or *cede.*

In the New Testament, the Gospels precede the Epistles.
You may proceed with the special project if all your assignments are completed.

Applying the Lesson

A. Choose the standard expressions in these sentences.

1. Before David came into the camp, Saul's army was too fearful to (precede, proceed) in the battle against the Philistines.
2. David's (notable, notorious) victory, however, produced a marked change.
3. David's (perspective, prospective) was quite different from that of the others because he trusted in the Lord.
4. The giants that we face (maybe, may be) less recognizable than Goliath, but they are no less formidable.
5. The disgruntled man (persecuted, prosecuted) his Christian neighbors in various small ways.
6. Since he did not believe in God, he thought everything would be (okay, all right) in the end.
7. We must remember that no matter how hardened a person may seem, he is still a (perspective, prospective) believer in Jesus.
8. Even a persecutor as (noteworthy, notorious) as Saul became a devoted follower of Christ.
9. The gray skies and the northeast wind suggest that (maybe, may be) a blizzard is coming.
10. The police could not find enough evidence to (persecute, prosecute) their suspect.
11. Prisoner's base is (okay, all right), but I would rather play freeze tag.
12. Sufficient planning must (precede, proceed) the writing of a worthwhile story.

B. Write the standard word or words for the underlined part of each sentence. If it needs no improvement, write *correct.*

1. We must keep a heavenly prospective if we expect to win the race of life.
2. The righteous are often persecuted by wicked people who hate the truth.
3. Many saints have found that glory in heaven is proceeded by suffering on earth.
4. The righteous may not have everything nice, but they do enjoy God's rich blessing.
5. One of the most notorious blessings is a free conscience.
6. It is also a great blessing to know that someday all temptations will be over with.
7. Maybe we recognize that too often we take these blessings for granted.
8. The Cretians were notable for their deceit and slothfulness.
9. The next wagonload of hay should be coming momentarily.
10. Grandmother Boll has been poorly ever since she had a stroke last winter.
11. These pancakes taste okay, but I like whole-wheat pancakes better.
12. There still maybe time to make a batch of cookies this morning.
13. We will miss Uncle Joel's family when their visit is over with.
14. Although the bolt of lightning lasted only momentarily, it started a forest fire that raged for several days.
15. Our congregation made a sunshine box for Caroline Wenger, who has been poorly for several weeks.
16. Except for a few minor difficulties, the work has preceded well.
17. The setting sun spread its nice colors across the western sky.
18. Father is interviewing a perspective hired man today.
19. Although Mr. Harrison has not paid his bill, we will not persecute him.
20. My head was hurting this morning, but I feel okay now.

C. Write enough words to show how each sentence should be improved according to the rules you have studied. If a sentence needs no improvement, write *correct.*

1. In the early life of Samuel F. B. Morse, there maybe little to suggest that he would become an important inventor.
2. Even at the age of thirty-four, when his wife was poorly and then died, he had made no significant mark as an inventor.
3. Both of his parents died within the next three years, and in 1829 he sailed for Europe to renew his courage and precede with his halting career as an artist.
4. On his return trip in 1832, a discussion about electricity provided the inspiration for his most notorious invention: the electric telegraph.
5. When he learned that electricity can travel over long wires, he concluded that messages could be transmitted momentarily over great distances.
6. Immediately after dinner, he started sketching the design of a perspective telegraph system.
7. But it was not until 1836 that he completed a crude device that worked okay.
8. In later years, Morse was not very nice to Professor Joseph Henry, from whom he had often received scientific advice and public support.

9. In fact, Morse and Henry prosecuted each other over patent rights.
10. When the legal battles were over with, Samuel F. B. Morse emerged as the owner of the patent for the telegraph.

Review Exercises

Write enough words to show how each sentence should be improved according to the rules you have studied. If a sentence needs no improvement, write *correct.* [37–43]

1. About 1538, two cousins from Flanders were persecuted for their faith.
2. These youths became enthused about studying the Bible, and soon they were convinced that the Scriptures teach believer's baptism.
3. They went to Germany to seek fellow believers, but they stayed there only for awhile because they could find nobody who shared their convictions.
4. Back home with their parents, these young men sought to live the kind of a life that would please the Lord.
5. However, the authorities suspected that they were heretics, and they imprisoned the young men under conditions most beyond description.
6. When a sister brought them some new shirts, they told her that they could not keep the worms from eating their clothes any more.
7. John Styaerts, one of the youths, was released for a time because he was poorly.
8. He probably could of escaped during that time, but he willingly returned to prison to die with his brother in Christ.
9. When no amount of suffering could change their minds, the young men were put to death by the sword.
10. Hopefully, we shall be able to stand faithfully for the Lord no matter what circumstances we face.

---

44. Improving Your Editing Skills, Part 5

The story is told of a man who walked all the way across the United States, from California to New York City. At the end of his journey, someone asked, "What was the greatest difficulty you encountered on your way? Was it the steep mountains you had to climb?"

"No, it was not that," the traveler assured him.

"Perhaps the swollen rivers that crossed your trail were the greatest hazard," the inquirer suggested.

"It was not that either," replied the traveler. Then after a pause, he said, "What almost defeated me on my journey across the continent was the sand in my shoes."

Many things in real life are just like that. Often we are defeated not by great problems but by little nagging difficulties that we face day after day.

In writing, it is seldom whole sentences and paragraphs that hinder communication. It is usually the little things instead—details like spelling, punctuation, and word usage. Errors in these details are the "sand" that will hinder the message of your writing. That is why you are making a special study of word usage in this chapter.

In this lesson you will again practice the use of proofreading marks. See if you can find *every* mistake in the exercises.

Marks Used in Editing and Proofreading

∨ or ∧ insert (caret)	delete	.... stet (let it stand)	___ use italics
¶ begin new paragraph	no ¶ no new paragraph	lc change to lowercase (small letter)	uc change to uppercase (capital letter)
# insert space	delete space	← move (arrow)	transpose

Editing Practice

A. Use proofreading marks to correct the two capitalization or punctuation errors in each sentence.

1. **In Math we learned that one acre contains 43560 square feet.**
2. **When an inch of rain falls 3,630 cubic feet of water is dumped on one Acre.**
3. **"I have read that the weight of water varies slightly, said conrad.**
4. **One cubic foot of water weighs an average of 62.4 pounds, thus, one inch of rain on one acre weighs about: 113 tons.**
5. **"Can you convert that figure to gallons," asked brother Henry.**
6. **The Total comes to more than 27000 gallons of water.**
7. **"What a tremendous amount of water falls in just a small Spring shower," exclaimed Carol.**

8. **Water is precious to people of desert region's like the sahara.**
9. **One Missionary in africa wrote that even the children knelt in gratitude when he gave them a drink of water.**
10. **"As cold waters to a thirsty soul, so is good news from a far country (Proverbs 25 25).**

B. Use proofreading marks to correct the two usage errors in each sentence.

1. Whitcomb L. Judson was enthused about most any kind of new gadget.
2. He invented a considerable amount of useful every day items.
3. One of his friends had a dilemma that would of been a trial for anyone.
4. Because of his stiff back, this friend all ways had a heap of trouble putting on his shoes.
5. The ingenuous inventor devised a slide fastener that differed with any fastener ever made before.
6. This invention left a person fasten or lose his shoes by using just one hand.
7. Judson's fastener alluded popular notice until an imminent manufacturer used it in a line of boots called Zippers.
8. Be sure and notice that its the slide fasteners rather than the boots that are called zippers today.

C. Use proofreading marks to correct the sixteen errors in the following paragraphs. No line has more than one error.

1. **Early astronomers believed that the earth was at the**
2. **center of the universe. This fit good with their view of man**
3. **and his importance. About A.D. 150, a Greek astronomer name**
4. **Ptolemy produced a work of thirteen volumes on based on**
5. **this theory. He described a stationary earth with the sun,**
6. **the moon and the stars all revolving around it. For nearly**
7. **1,500 years, people considered Ptolemys theory to be fact.**
8. **In 1543, Nicolaus Copernicus propposed that the sun**
9. **rather than the earth was the center of the universe,**

and that the the earth and other planets revolve around the sun. His ideas still were not alright, but they were closer to the truth than Ptolemy's were. This new theory stirred up a storm of opposition. Men who excepted it were charged with heresy, and at least one was burned the at stake. Galileo with his telescope observed four moons of Jupiter revolving around that Planet, which provided further support for the Copernican theory. But in 1633, Roman catholic officials forced Galileo to confess that he was in error!

Astronomers continued to study the haevens until they proved beyond doubt that the planets in deed revolve around the sun. Instead of being at the center, man and his World are a mere speck in the grand universe that God created.

---

45. Correct Word Usage, Part 7

Propose, Purpose

Propose is a verb meaning "to suggest." If an action is proposed, it is generally stated in a *that* clause which follows *propose.*

Purpose is a verb meaning "to determine" or a noun meaning "aim or goal." Either an infinitive or a *that* clause may follow *purpose.*

> I <u>propose</u> that we make a scrapbook for Sister Melody.
> Our <u>purpose</u> would be to cheer her lonely days.
> Like Daniel, we must <u>purpose</u> that we will not defile ourselves.

Quote

Quote is usually a verb. It is used informally as a noun meaning "quotation."

> **Informal:** This <u>quote</u> from Proverbs is especially fitting now.
> **Standard:** This <u>quotation</u> from Proverbs is especially fitting now.

Raise, Rise

Raise is a transitive verb meaning "to cause (something) to go up or grow up." Its principal parts are *raise, raised, (have) raised.*

Rise is an intransitive verb meaning "to get up or go up." Its principal parts are *rise, rose, (have) risen.*

We shall raise our voices to the Lord in joyful song.
As our praises have risen to the Lord, we have received rich blessing.

Receipt, Recipe

Receipt (ri•sēt′) is the noun form of *receive.* It means "the act of receiving," "a quantity received," or "a written acknowledgment that something has been received."

Recipe (res′•ə•pē) means "formula" or "method."

I found the receipt at the bottom of the bag.
This recipe calls for too much sugar.

Respectable, Respectful, Respective

Respectable means "worthy of respect."
Respectful means "showing respect or esteem."
Respective means "individual; particular."

Evan has developed a respectable character in spite of his background.
Darlene gave consistently respectful answers to Mrs. Hawsley's sharp accusations.
Put these peaches, pears, and plums into their respective compartments in the cooler.

Right along

The expression *right along* is used informally to mean "steadily" or "with little hindrance."

Informal:
The work on the new shed has been progressing right along.
Standard:
The work on the new shed has been progressing steadily.

Set, Sit

Set is usually a transitive verb meaning "to put or place (something)." It also has the following intransitive meanings: "to move below the horizon," "to keep eggs warm for hatching," and "to become firm." Its principal parts are *set, set, (have) set.*

Sit is an intransitive verb meaning "to rest or be seated." Its principal parts are *sit, sat, (have) sat.*

Please set the bags of groceries on the table.
The moon has just set beyond the western mountains.
Biddy has been setting for a week.
Has the glue set well yet?
We sat breathlessly watching the deer eat.

Some, Somewhat

The adverb *some* is informal when it has the meaning "somewhat."

Informal:

This tree has grown some taller since we moved here.

Standard:

This tree has grown somewhat taller since we moved here.

Stationary, Stationery

Stationary means "fixed; unmoving." Think of something stationary as standing in a fixed position.

Stationery means "writing materials." Think of stationery as including paper.

We tied the wagon to a stationary post.
Grandmother gave Elaine a box of stationery.

Straight, Strait

Straight is a modifier that means "not curved," "level," "direct," or "directly."

The noun *strait* refers to a narrow stretch of water. *Strait* is also an archaic modifier that means "narrow" or "strict."

We should not expect to travel straight to heaven without facing obstacles.
The Strait of Magellan lies at the southern tip of South America.
"Enter ye in at the strait gate" (Matthew 7:13).

Applying the Lesson

A. Choose the standard expressions in these sentences.

1. We (set, sat) in (respectable, respectful, respective) silence as Father read the Scripture passage.
2. The Bible informs us that nobody can (raise, rise) himself to a (respectable, respectful, respective) standing with God by his own strength.
3. "Did not we (straightly, straitly) command you that ye should not teach in this name?" (Acts 5:28).
4. When the (stationary, stationery) front finally moved out, the weather became (some, somewhat) cooler.
5. I have (proposed, purposed) to acknowledge the (receipt, recipe) of every get-well card that arrives.
6. Louella (proposed, purposed) an interesting plan for helping the Leids.
7. Lolita's new (stationary, stationery) has a beautiful rose design.
8. The prices have (raised, risen) to record highs because of the drought.
9. Caleb finished his chores (some, somewhat) earlier than he had expected.
10. Hold your drill (straight, strait) to drill these dowel holes.
11. The "Never-Fail Cake" was a total failure even though Gloria followed the (receipt, recipe) exactly.
12. For a long time the owl (set, sat) on a branch of the old oak tree.

B. Write the standard word or words for the underlined part of each sentence. If it needs no improvement, write *correct.*

1. Do you know where to find the quote, "Be subject unto the higher powers"?
2. Christians must maintain respective attitudes even toward oppressive civil authorities.
3. Jesus broke the power of sin when He raised from the dead.
4. Jesus Christ is sitting at the Father's right hand to intercede for us.
5. Father proposed that we visit Brother Henry this evening.
6. Although he is feeling some better, Brother Henry still cannot go to church.
7. Our peach harvest is almost finished, and the apple harvest is increasing right along.
8. The speeding truck collided with a stationary car.
9. Neighbors said that the car had been setting there for two days.
10. Mother often bakes cookies without looking at a receipt.
11. In the open Midwest, many roads run strait for miles on end.
12. Cutting off the corn and packing it into freezer boxes is progressing right along.
13. We are some closer to Mother's goal for frozen corn than we had been earlier.
14. "And he straitly charged them that they should not make him known" (Mark 3:12).
15. Airmail stationary is lightweight to keep down the postage price.
16. Donald proposed to improve his penmanship.
17. Mother checked the receipt to make sure it contained no errors in calculation.
18. The smoke from the burning barn raised in a huge cloud, visible for many miles.
19. You should verify this quote from Isaiah 53.
20. God sets the members of the church in their respective places.

C. Write enough words to show how each sentence should be improved according to the rules you have studied. If a sentence needs no improvement, write *correct.*

1. In the early 1800s, even respectful adults often rode hobbyhorses for recreation.
2. These wheeled horses were not stationery as many children's horses are today.
3. A person would set on the horse and push himself along with his feet.
4. A Scottish blacksmith named Kirkpatrick Macmillan decided that the hobbyhorse could be used for a more worthwhile purpose.
5. The receipt, he thought, was to devise a way to turn the wheels with pedals.
6. Macmillan's work progressed right along, and soon he completed a two-wheeled machine that he called a bicycle.
7. This machine had pedals that drove a strait rod connected to the back wheel.
8. In 1840, Macmillan pedaled his bicycle seventy miles in ten hours—an "astounding achievement" according to one quote.

9. But his success was marred some, for he accidentally knocked down a young lady and was jailed for reckless driving!
10. Macmillan's invention raised to such popularity that within his lifetime, thousands of people in different countries were riding bicycles.

Review Exercises

Write enough words to show how each sentence should be improved according to the rules you have studied. If a sentence needs no improvement, write *correct.* [37–45]

1. Two men named George Vaser and Leonhard Sailer, whose lives differed with those of people around them, were passing through Neudorf, Austria.
2. They were arrested and taken to the nearby town of Metling, where they were held in prison continuously for almost a year.
3. Although it seems hardly comprehensive, these brethren had testified boldly on the way to Metling, and the authorities had been too amazed to stop them.
4. Cast into the common prison, these godly men faced the dilemma of enduring the gross wickedness of their fellow prisoners.
5. In fact, they would rather have been forced to set in an offensive dungeon than in that prison with such company.
6. They still were able to impact the lives of the others, for they answered many questions about their faith.
7. These Anabaptists boldly declared that those who flout the teachings of the Bible will face God's wrath.
8. Their fabulous faith gave them a sincere desire to depart, and they manfully and boldly expected death at any hour.
9. Having maintained their faith very good, the two men were marvelously delivered after nearly a year in prison.
10. These notorious brethren came to the church at Trasenhofen, where they were received joyfully.

---

46. Correct Word Usage, Part 8

Than, Then

Than is a conjunction used to introduce the second part of a comparison.

Then is an adverb with meanings that include "at that time," "in that case," "therefore," and "next in time, space, or order."

> Our history test proved easier <u>than</u> I had expected.
> <u>Then</u> why did you not make a better score on your test?

Them

Them should never be used as a demonstrative to replace *those.*

Incorrect: Them apples are deliciously sweet.
Correct: Those apples are deliciously sweet.

This (These) here, That (Those) there

The demonstratives *this, that, these,* and *those* must not be followed by *here* or *there.*

Incorrect: This here rosebush is lovely.
Correct: This rosebush is lovely.

Transpire

Transpire means "to leak out" or "to become known to many people." It has a pretentious tone when used for the meaning "to happen; occur."

Poor:
Walton's accident transpired last evening.
Correct:
Walton's accident occurred last evening.

Water vapor transpires through the leaves of plants.
The news of Aunt Lena's plans to teach school has transpired already.

Try and

The expression *try and* should be replaced with *try to.*

Incorrect:
We should try and finish splitting this wood before dark.
Correct:
We should try to finish splitting this wood before dark.

Want in, off, out, through

An expression like "want in" should be revised so that an infinitive such as *to come* or *to get* comes after *want.*

Incorrect: That cat always wants in at mealtime.
The man on that tractor wants through this gate.
Correct: That cat always wants to come in at mealtime.
The man on that tractor wants to get through this gate.

Way, Ways

Ways is an informal word for "distance." Use *way* or *distance* in standard writing.

Informal.
We have quite a long ways to the mountain from our place.
Standard:
We have quite a long way to the mountain from our place.

What for

The expression *what for* should not be used to mean "what kind of." *What for* can also mean "for what reason," but that meaning is not always clear. It is generally better to use *why.*

Poor:

What for book are you reading?

What are you going outside for?

(Could mean "For what item are you going outside?" or "For what reason are you going outside?")

Better:

What kind of book are you reading?

Why are you going outside?

Worst kind, sort, way

Expressions with *worst* should not be used to mean "very much" or "in the highest degree."

Incorrect:

Linda wants in the worst way to finish sewing her dress before the weekend.

Correct:

Linda wants very much to finish sewing her dress before the weekend.

Your, You're

Your is a possessive pronoun that means "belonging to you."

You're is a contraction for *you are.*

Is this your sweater?

You're supposed to put it away.

Applying the Lesson

A. Choose the standard expressions in these sentences.

1. God has blessed us far more (than, then) what we deserve.
2. If we would (try and, try to) count those blessings, time would fail us.
3. (What for, What kind of) attitudes do you express toward your parents?
4. If (your, you're) insubmissive at home, you cannot be truly happy.
5. Every sincere Christian recognizes that he is a long (way, ways) from reaching perfection.
6. (Them, Those) people who consider themselves superior fail to realize how foolish they are.
7. Do you know when the next solar eclipse is supposed to (transpire, occur)?
8. With godly grandparents living near (your, you're) home, you have a definite privilege.
9. Both sets of my grandparents live a long (way, ways) from my home.
10. Your little brother is crying, but I don't know (what for, why).
11. We shall (try and, try to) start cleaning the school early this evening.

12. If we start early, (than, then) we should be able to finish early.
13. Do you know where (them, those) runaway steers belong?
14. What a strange event (transpired, occurred) last night!

B. Write the standard word or words for the underlined part of each sentence. If it needs no improvement, write *correct.*

1. Our congregation often conducts services at <u>this here</u> rest home.
2. This one has more guests <u>then</u> any other rest home in our area.
3. Nelson and I will <u>try and</u> pick all our tomatoes before the end of the week.
4. Since we had only two days to finish the job, we needed to make <u>them</u> days count.
5. You can drive this car a long <u>ways</u> after the fuel gauge shows empty.
6. Justin wanted <u>in the worst way</u> to run the baler.
7. <u>What for</u> experience has he had with baling hay?
8. Man and animals use the oxygen that <u>transpires</u> from green plants.
9. If <u>you're</u> chores are finished early, we shall leave early.
10. <u>That there</u> new barn is the one Uncle Melvin is building.
11. We all hurried <u>in the worst way</u> so that we would finish in time.
12. Some groundhogs were trying to get through this fence, and it's easy to guess <u>what for</u>.
13. They <u>wanted through</u> so that they could eat our vegetables.
14. When <u>your</u> driving in the West and first see a town ahead, it is still many miles away.
15. <u>Then</u> after a long time, you finally arrive at the town.
16. Even though we had entered Missouri, we were still a long <u>ways</u> from Uncle Walter's house.
17. You will need hot, soapy water to wash <u>them</u> greasy dishes clean.
18. I will <u>try and</u> memorize these verses perfectly.
19. We told the bus driver that we <u>wanted off</u> at the King Street Market.
20. Things <u>transpired</u> so rapidly that we wondered what would happen next.

C. Write enough words to show how each sentence should be improved according to the rules you have studied. If a sentence needs no improvement, write *correct.*

1. In the 1850s, a man named Linus Yale wanted in the worst way to make a good lock.
2. Most locks in them days were crude and fairly easy to open.
3. If a burglar wanted into a house, there was hardly any way to keep him out.
4. What for lock could one make that would be more secure?
5. Yale devised a lock that was much better then all others of his time.
6. That there lock had a cylinder with a number of pins which were all of different lengths.
7. To try and open such a lock, one must use a key with a pattern of notches cut into it.
8. Each notch lifts one pin just a small ways; but if it is too little or too much, the lock will not open.

9. Eventually it transpired that Yale had gotten the idea for his lock from the ancient Egyptians, who had also used locks with pins of varying lengths.
10. Quite likely, many of you're family's possessions are secured by locks based on the principle of the Yale lock.

Review Exercises

Write enough words to show how each sentence should be improved according to the rules you have studied. If a sentence needs no improvement, write *correct.* [37–46]

1. In 1544, an Anabaptist maiden named Maria van Beckum was driven out of her home because her mother would not leave her stay there anymore.
2. She fled to the house of her brother John, whose wife Ursula shared her prospective of faith.
3. When a large group of men came to arrest Maria, she was compelled to raise from bed and face them.
4. Seeing the large amount of people, Maria asked Ursula if she would go along with her.
5. Ursula answered, "I am willing to go if John says that I can."
6. John gave his consent, and them two sisters in the Lord went with the persecutors to face the afflictions that awaited.
7. After enduring many trials and sufferings, Maria and Ursula were sentenced to death by the council in Delden.
8. As the time of their execution drew near, these notorious sisters prayed that God would forgive the judges who would be guilty of their blood.
9. When Ursula stepped up to the stake, the wood was not very stationery, and she almost slipped off.
10. The priest thought that may be she wanted to recant, but Ursula assured him that she would "constantly adhere to Christ"; and thus both sisters remained steadfast until death.

---

47. Chapter 5 Review

A. Choose the standard expressions in these sentences.

1. We must (always, all ways) be ready to (altar, alter) our ways to please the Lord.
2. Others can (imply, infer) much about your character from your (everyday, every day) speech habits.
3. Using a great (amount, number) of interjections and casual expressions shows the lack of a godly (perspective, prospective).
4. (Its, It's) never (all right, alright) to (flaunt, flout) the instruction of godly parents.
5. If you are (disinterested, uninterested) in wise (council, counsel), you will suffer for it.

6. Even though another person may be angry (about, at, with) us, we must (raise, rise) above our natural feelings and treat him (good, well).
7. We (believe, feel) that God will (let, leave) no insurmountable test come our way, so we willingly (accept, except) the most trying circumstances.
8. When we (propose, purpose) to (adapt, adopt) ourselves to God's will (as, like) we should, we have found the (receipt, recipe) for true joy.
9. Many people who do not esteem the Bible (anymore, any more) do (allude, elude) to it in more ways (than, then) they may realize.
10. Mr. Barnes seems to have a (comprehensible, comprehensive) knowledge of (almost, most) every subject, yet he is not (contemptible, contemptuous) toward us common folks.
11. Although Father feels (some, somewhat) better now, he still does not (set, sit) up (continually, continuously) for more than twenty minutes.
12. When we compare our lives (to, with) the lives of many others, we conclude that we are a long (way, ways) from poverty.
13. When we differ (from, with) others in our opinions, we should not (censor, censure) them (as if, like) we are much wiser than they.
14. Even if God does not answer our prayers for (awhile, a while), we must not (loose, lose) faith in Him.
15. It looks as though (maybe, may be) a deer has (laid, lain) here recently.
16. Father said that we (can, may) go to the neighbors for milk if we come (straight, strait) home again.
17. The township supervisors intend to (persecute, prosecute) the persons responsible for the (burst, bursted, busted) water line.
18. When Curvin came home, we (advised, informed) him about the letter that had arrived on the (preceding, proceeding) day.
19. Is the equipment in (your, you're) workshop all run by this (stationary, stationery) engine?
20. The students took their (respectable, respectful, respective) places with (noteworthy, notorious) quietness.

B. Write enough words to show how each sentence should be improved according to the rules you have studied. Every sentence needs two improvements.
   1. If you try and do your best, you may impact others for good.
   2. We faced a dilemma that was intensified because there were heaps of possible solutions.
   3. Grandfather Fox has been sort of poorly for several weeks.
   4. Aunt Mary is recuperating right along since she had that operation and began taking them heart pills.
   5. If you have read the above, you know that Mr. Brian's special offer will soon be over with.
   6. Hopefully Alvin has not become too enthused about buying those rabbits.
   7. He wanted in the worst way to buy them regardless of his older brother's council.
   8. Does anyone know how come the wheelbarrow is in back of the garage?

9. You should be surc and check the accuracy of that quote.
10. We will be there momentarily to see your fabulous stamp collection.
11. The feed is all, and the cattle want out into the pasture.
12. This corn ain't as nice as some that we have sold.
13. I haven't only one picture that shows the enormity of the rock we saw.
14. In spite of the way things transpired, everything turned out okay.

C. Write the correct words for these sentences.
   1. The ——— voice puts more energy into writing than the ——— voice does.
   2. In the ——— voice, the subject is acted upon.
   3. In the ——— voice, the subject does something.
   4. The passive voice may be useful when there is no clear ——— of the action, when we want to avoid naming the ———, or when the subject is the victim of a ———.
   5. Choose the more lively verb in each sentence.
      a. The sun (disappeared, was hidden) behind thick clouds.
      b. Even strong trees (bowed, were bowed) in the fierce wind.

Whatsoever thy hand findeth to do,

do it with thy might.

Ecclesiastes 9:10

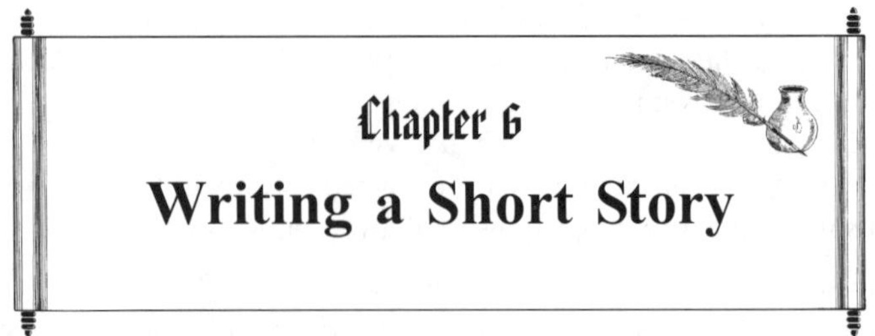

Chapter 6
Writing a Short Story

48. The Writer of a Story

No doubt you have read dozens of stories; and some of them, consciously or subconsciously, you labeled good. You have also read stories that you labeled boring or stiff or unrealistic. What makes the difference? What are the keys to writing a good story? This chapter should help to answer these questions. First, however, we shall take a look at the person who writes the story.

What kind of individual is a storywriter? He is not one with unique experiences that nobody else has, neither does he have a special pen from which fascinating stories flow effortlessly. Instead, he is generally a common person just like you. If a story is especially interesting, it is because the writer has used the time and effort needed to make the story interesting.

The Contribution of a Storywriter

A writer of short stories should understand the important role that stories fill. God chose to reveal much truth through stories in the Bible, and this illustrates the high value that He places on stories. Most of the Old Testament books contain stories. The Gospels and Acts—over half the New Testament—tell story after story about Jesus and His disciples. Even the New Testament Epistles relate a few stories.

A good short story fills an important place because it teaches a worthwhile lesson. The writer who loves God and His kingdom has a higher purpose than merely to entertain. Yes, he seeks to capture the reader's attention, but his most important goal is to communicate a Bible principle or to persuade the reader to pursue a noble course of action.

Furthermore, a story has certain advantages over an essay in presenting truth. Because a reader identifies with the story characters, he may accept truth in story form more readily than if it were expressed in a sermon or an essay. And because the reader's emotions become involved in the story, the truth tends to penetrate deeper and stick longer than if it had been expressed in another way. For instead of presenting an abstract theory, a story shows how truth works in real life. You can probably think of at least one time in your own experience when a story helped you to deal properly with a difficult or perplexing situation.

The Resources of a Storywriter

A short-story writer should cultivate an alertness for story material. Beware of thinking that good stories must be about extraordinary happenings. The fact is that worthwhile stories portray either true or true-to-life experiences. They are easy to identify with. And it is the common, everyday happenings that meet this requirement most naturally.

Where will you find your prospective story material? Remember first of all that every story deals with a problem to be solved. Then watch the actions and reactions of people around you—acquaintances as well as strangers—as they face various problems. Every problem-solving situation has some degree of potential for a story.

The problems and conflicts in your own life are one major resource. Here are some things you may have experienced and forgotten: eating a certain food for the first time, getting calves (or pigs) back into their pen, facing a strong temptation, learning to ride a bicycle, making ice cream, playing with the neighbor children, baking a cake (as a boy), or driving a tractor (as a girl). You can write best about familiar happenings because you know them best.

Of course, you may want to write about other people's experiences. Grandpa may have told you many interesting stories such as the time the horses ran away with three children alone in the wagon, or the time an aunt who was not a Christian wanted to adopt his little sister.

You can also get story ideas from books. They describe things like fighting forest fires in Oregon, farming by the square mile in Australia, nursing in African mission hospitals, and suffering persecution in Anabaptist days. They tell of many people outside your own little circle of friends. Books stir your writing imagination.

But remember, the people and happenings you know best will be the easiest for you to write about. The following story beginning comes from a shopping trip on an ordinary day.

> "Do you see what I see?" Mother pointed to the ignition switch inside the locked car. There hung the car keys. "I guess we can't go home yet, after all. Well, I'll just take this ironing board back to the store and ask them to keep it for us. Then we'll need to find someone to open the door."
>
> An hour later, after a mechanic had used a wire to unlock the car, Mother and Beth were finally on their way home. The town lay three miles behind them when Beth was struck by a sudden thought. "Mother, where is our ironing board?"
>
> "Just where we left it," Mother replied calmly as she stepped on the brake. "In Hodges' Department Store."
>
> So they returned to the store and picked up the ironing board. But just as Mother and Beth settled themselves in the car again, they heard a tapping on the window. Quickly Mother rolled down the window to see what the woman standing there wanted.
>
> "I'd like to know what that white cap is that you're wearing on your head," the woman said.

The writer may base his story directly on a real-life experience. He may use an actual happening as the foundation but then add or adjust details to make the story interesting and instructive. Or he may write a story based entirely on his imagination. However it originates, the story will be most effective if it deals with a practical, true-to-life experience.

The Qualities of a Storywriter

A storywriter needs a large measure of humility. If he is proud, he will find it hard to accept corrections and suggestions for changes from his teacher and later from an editor. Few indeed are the writers whose work is so nearly perfect that an editor accepts it without making changes. Also remember that only what is done in humility can truly bring glory to God. A writer motivated by selfish ambition may write a story that is interesting and even worthwhile, but he will miss the blessing of serving the Lord.

A storywriter also must be willing to work hard at improving his skills. Do you think that you have little or no story-writing ability? Do your best to improve the ability you do have. Do you enjoy writing stories? Do you think that you have already written some good stories? Determine to learn techniques that will make your stories even better. The lessons in this chapter will give specific helps on writing worthwhile, appealing short stories.

Applying the Lesson

A. Do these exercises.

1. How does the Bible show the valuable place of stories?
2. What important goal should a person have in writing a short story?
3. Why can stories often communicate truth more effectively than essays?
4. What are the three sources of story material mentioned in this lesson?
5. This lesson emphasizes that you would probably find it easiest to write about what type of subject: grand, familiar, or mysterious?
6. About which two of the following subjects could an upper grade student probably write the best stories?
   a. kings and castles
   b. family life and daily chores
   c. pioneers and covered wagons
   d. doctors and famous medical discoveries
   e. classrooms and playgrounds
7. For what two reasons is humility essential for writing effective short stories?

B. Write the numbers of the following items that should make good, profitable stories.

1. Ruth overhears one classmate softly telling another that some incorrect answers on a history test were not marked wrong. Should she ignore the incident or talk to the person?
2. Aunt Ellen spends an enjoyable day working in her garden.
3. Three evenings in a row, Nathan's baseball glove is hidden when he is ready to go home. "I know who did it," he thinks, "and I'll think of some way to get even."
4. Seventeen-year-old Oscar hears Linda urgently calling him. Running to the house, he finds little Anthony lying unconscious where he has fallen on the concrete porch. He keenly remembers Father's words as he and Mother left: "Well, Oscar, take care of everything."

5. Katrina enjoys knitting on a grassy place beside the creek. The sound of the flowing water is relaxing, and numerous birds and other wild creatures feed, drink, and play within sight.
6. Arlin is anticipating a trip to the zoo with his family and Uncle Myron's family. But on the evening before the trip, his younger brother makes a careless mistake and breaks his leg.

C. Write three examples of your own for good story possibilities, following the pattern of the good examples in Part B. Save this work for use in later lessons.

Review Exercises

A. Label each sentence according to its use (*dec., int., imp., exc.*) and its structure (*S, CD, CX, CD-CX*). End punctuation has been omitted. [25]
   1. Do you know what dry ice is, and can you explain its formation
   2. Read this simple description of transforming carbon dioxide into dry ice
   3. Gaseous carbon dioxide is cooled at high pressure; this causes the gas to liquefy
   4. After the carbon dioxide is cooled and compressed through several stages, it is allowed to expand quickly, which causes rapid evaporation
   5. What drastic cooling this evaporation causes
   6. The sudden cooling changes about one-third of the liquid carbon dioxide into carbon dioxide "snow," which is pressed into blocks of dry ice; and the remaining two-thirds is returned to the cooling and compressing process

B. Label the word order of each sentence *N* (natural), *I* (inverted), or *M* (mixed). [25]
   1. If our affection is set on heavenly things, we will not pursue the pleasures of this world.
   2. Throughout the fabric of our lives must run the fear of God.
   3. Simple trust in the Lord produces rest and calmness.
   4. By the fruits of our lives, others can discern something about our hearts.

C. Label the style of each sentence *L* (loose), *P* (periodic), or *B* (balanced). [25]
   1. The optimist sees something good in the darkest circumstances; the pessimist sees something bad in the brightest circumstances.
   2. A man of faith believes that God's hand is at work throughout the varied experiences of life.
   3. Even when the sun of God's love seems hidden by gloomy clouds, God cares.
   4. We must overcome evil, or evil will overcome us.

---

49. The Message of a Story

Foundational to every worthwhile story is a worthwhile message. A story without a message would be like an expository essay without a theme. The message is the thread that holds a story together from beginning to end.

Read the two sample stories below. You will refer to them several times in this lesson and in later lessons.

Sample Story 1

Terry's Temper

"Three months to enjoy the farm!" Terry voiced his thoughts to twelve-year-old Walter. The previous day had marked the last day of his ninth year in school. A pleasant mid-May sun smiled on the lush growth of grass. Terry took deep breaths of the fresh, exhilarating air. Brushing his hand across his well-combed hair, he glanced at Walter's unkempt hair.

"This grass sure needs a good haircut. Looks almost as bad as your hair," Terry said. "Wonder if that old mower will last all summer. Father said maybe we'll get a riding mower, and I hope we do soon."

Some time later, Terry was resolutely pushing the old mower back and forth across the Gehmans' spacious yard. The front lawn was nearly finished when the sputtering engine coughed and died.

Terry's temper flared. "You old mower! You belong on the junk heap," he snarled. "Wish Father would buy a decent mower right now."

The gas and oil checked, Terry gave the starter cord several vigorous pulls. Nothing. He checked the spark plug. It looked fine. He looked at the air cleaner. It was clean. Red-faced and grim, he grabbed the starter cord and yanked it again. *Clunk!* Throwing the torn starter cord against the mower, Terry spun around, his face a thundercloud.

"Father's probably in the shop," he muttered to himself as he stalked across the lawn.

"Better calm down a bit," Terry thought uncomfortably as he neared the shop. He took several deep breaths. Stopping at the outside faucet, he splashed cold water over his face.

Forty-five minutes later, Terry was mowing grass again.

One morning several days later, Father said, "Terry, I want you to fill the feed bin for the calves. Walter scraped out the last feed this morning."

This job Terry enjoyed. He thrived on the challenge of mixing the feed precisely, and he enjoyed running any farm machinery. Before long, the auger was carrying the feed from the mixer to the bin with a rhythmical *clankety-clank.*

"Stop! Stop!" Walter's urgent shouts jolted Terry like an electric shock. "The feed is pouring out on the barn floor," Walter gasped. "I forgot to shut the door."

Quickly Terry pulled the lever, stopping the auger. "Walter Jay Gehman! Of all things! You're always forgetting to close the door!"

Sure enough, a mountain of feed covered the floor below the feed bin chute. "Well, you may as well get the feed bags and a shovel," Terry said grimly as he struggled to slide the door shut. "Get to work while I finish emptying the mixer." He threw the words over his shoulder as he stalked away.

Terry was back in a few minutes. "Come on, shovel faster!" he snapped at his brother. "I ought to make you clean it up alone."

"I'm sorry, Terry," Walter said. "The breakfast bell rang just as I finished emptying the bin. Then I forgot all about it," he finished lamely.

"Obviously," stormed Terry.

"Terry." Father's stern voice broke in upon the scene. "You must not talk and act like this."

Turning to Walter, he said, "You are excused for a while."

"Now, son," Father said, and his penetrating gaze searched Terry's face. "Sit down here on this feed bag. Perhaps you can explain what's going on."

Unable to meet Father's gaze, Terry dropped his eyes. "I guess Walter forgot to close the door," he faltered, "and the feed spilled out on the floor, and . . ."

"And what?" Father prompted.

"And—well—I—I guess I got upset at him." Terry's troubled eyes met Father's kind ones.

"Yes. I've noticed recently that you get quite impatient when something doesn't suit you. Have you thought about the selfishness of your impatience? You think everything must suit *you.* And you're not being considerate of other people's feelings. I want you to think about this. And you *must* learn to control your temper.

"Now, you clean up this mess by yourself. And I expect you to apologize to Walter for your unkindness."

The following day, the heifers found a weak spot in the fence and were soon romping in the alfalfa. "Oh, the heifers are out!" Mother dropped her basket of laundry.

"Terry! Walter! The heifers are out!" Mother cupped her hands and called toward the barn.

"Oh, no!" groaned Terry as he and Walter stepped outside the milk house. "Why did those miserable animals—" Terry's voice dripped with annoyance.

"Looks like they're having fun," commented Walter.

"I guess they are having fun!" Terry retorted. "It sure won't be fun for us!"

For a few moments, Terry stood beside the barn, his hands clenched, his jaw set, and his anger rising. Suddenly in his mind's eye, he saw Father's serious but kind face. And he heard Father's words, "You *must* learn to control your temper."

Slowly Terry's anger melted, and he glanced sheepishly at Walter. "Well, I guess there's nothing to do but bring them in.

"Mother, open the gate. You and the girls guard the lane. Come, Walter. Let's circle around and chase the heifers through the back yard and in the gate." Terry's quick mind laid out a plan as the boys dashed across the lane.

But the heifers had other plans. Up went their heads and tails, and away they raced across the field toward the woods.

"Look at those heifers run!" Terry sighed. "We might as well use the tractor. How about it, Walter? Want to drive?"

"Sure," answered Walter, surprised at Terry's offer.

Forty minutes later, two exhausted boys chased the last heifer through the gate just as Father drove in the lane.

The boys rehearsed the story while they helped Father fix the fence. "Well, boys, it sounds as if you had quite a chase. I'm glad you got them all back in," said Father. "But that isn't the best part of the story," he added, looking at Terry. "The best thing I've heard is that you didn't lose your temper."

Sample Story 2

"He Rides Upon the Storm"

My hands were mechanically cutting apples into neat halves when Mother's words burst into my thoughts. "Grandmother Fry called this morning. She asked if it would suit for you to spend the weekend with her. She said you help her to feel secure because she knows you are dependable. There'll be no school Friday, so you could go on Thursday evening. We'd pick you up again on Sunday afternoon."

My mind whirled into high gear. "Of course, I dearly love Grandmother," I thought. "But would she want me to come if she knew how insecure I feel sometimes? What if I can't fit into her schedule? What if . . ."

"Oh, Mother, I don't know what to say," I finally answered.

"Why not? What's wrong, Wanda?" Mother's steady voice calmed my tumultuous thoughts somewhat.

"Well," I began slowly, "well, I suppose it would be all right. But, Mother, didn't she say just the other week that she gets up at four o'clock? Will she expect me to get up that early too?"

"Oh, I doubt it," answered Mother. "She spends some of that time in Bible reading and prayer. In fact," Mother continued, "I remember her saying recently that she eats breakfast at seven o'clock."

"What about her special diet? Will I have to eat without sugar and salt?"

"Would that be so bad?" Mother's voice held a tone of humor. "But, seriously, no. She has sugar and salt that you can add to your food. Just trust in the Lord, and He will be with you."

"I suppose I can try it if you're sure everything will be all right," I finally answered hesitantly.

Friday and Saturday were busy days at Grandmother's house. We made tomato juice, ketchup, and applesauce. But we had time for a leisurely walk over to Uncle Jacob's farm for milk on Saturday afternoon.

After a simple Sunday lunch of potato soup, Grandmother said, "I've surely enjoyed your help and your company these days, Wanda."

"Not more than I've enjoyed being here," I returned. As I looked at Grandmother's neatly veiled, silvery hair shining in the sunlight, love filled my heart. Even her wrinkled face looked more beautiful than ever. "To think I was uneasy about coming," I thought. "But I trusted God, and He blessed me with peace and a pleasant time."

The following Saturday, I hurried from the flower bed I was weeding and burst into the kitchen. "Alta," I gasped, "there's a man coming in the lane. A bushy-haired, scary-looking man! Whatever will we do?" I wailed.

Father's parting words flashed across my mind: "Well, Alta, you'll be in charge for a few hours. Wanda, you pitch in and help take care of the little ones. In case of an emergency, call Uncle Ralph's. Above all, trust in the Lord." Then he and Mother had left to visit Aunt Mattie in the hospital.

Alta glanced out the window. "We'll trust the Lord," she said. The man had nearly reached the house.

"Shall I call Uncle Ralph's?" I asked desperately. But a firm knock sounded just then, sending a shiver down my spine.

"Good morning," said Alta politely. "Can I help you with something?"

"I'm sorry to bother you, ma'am." The soft, polite voice contrasted sharply with the man's appearance. "My car choked off just past your lane, and I can't get it started again. Do you have a phone I could use?"

"Yes," Alta replied. "In fact, my uncle Ralph owns Witmer's Garage just one mile up the road. Should I call him?"

"Sounds great! I'll just walk back to my car then," the man replied. With a bow, he was gone.

"Whew!" I breathed. "I didn't know what to expect. My heart's still racing!"

"But God is with us," answered Alta. "He's well able to care for us, isn't He?"

"Yes, but . . ." I hesitated. "I—I guess I should learn to trust Him more."

That very night I suddenly sat bolt upright in bed, my heart pounding wildly. "What was that?" I wondered bewilderedly. In answer, there came a brilliant flash of lightning, followed closely by a sharp crash of thunder. All sleepiness chased away, I lay down, closed my eyes, and shivered.

Soon one flash after another kept the sky lit almost continuously. Tremendous crashes of thunder rattled the windows and shook my bed. The howling wind whipped the trees outside my window. The rain and the hail combined into one mighty, oceanlike roar.

And there stood Alta at the window, as calm as if she were watching a summer sunset! "Are you awake, Wanda?" she asked, beckoning me to stand beside her.

Hesitantly I climbed out of bed and crossed the room. "Aren't you afraid?" I asked as another streak momentarily blinded our eyes.

"Not really," she answered with her usual calmness. "But I find it awesome to see this display of God's power. Just think! Some people can watch a storm like this and still declare that there is no God!" Alta shook her head.

"I guess I never thought of it that way," I admitted. The storm raged for a while longer. Then as suddenly as it had come, it moved on.

"'What a mighty God we serve!'" I breathed as I climbed back into bed. Then I prayed, "Help me, heavenly Father, to trust Thee more completely."

A Worthwhile Purpose

A story with a worthwhile message must be written for a worthwhile purpose. People write stories for all kinds of purposes, including many that are not profitable. The following paragraphs describe three noble purposes.

1. *To help readers acknowledge their own weaknesses and shortcomings.* A reader may see the fault of a story character and condemn him for it—only to realize that he himself has the same fault. With such an indirect approach, the reader is often able to acknowledge his fault when he might have rebelled at a more direct approach.

In 2 Samuel 12, the prophet Nathan needed to help David acknowledge the great sin he had committed against Uriah and Bathsheba. Rather than confronting the king with a direct rebuke, Nathan began by telling a story from everyday life. David strongly condemned the rich man in the story for his great injustice—only to realize that he himself had done something much worse. The story fulfilled its purpose as David responded by repenting and confessing his sin.

Jesus also told stories to show people their shortcomings. His story of the Good Samaritan made it clear that the Samaritan obeyed God's command to "love thy neighbour as thyself," while the priest and the Levite did *not* obey that command.

2. *To inspire noble ideals and godly living.* Just as an experience in our own lives can inspire and encourage us, so an experience we encounter in a story can serve the same purpose. Through stories we can benefit from the experiences of other people. The following story should inspire greater love for God in all who read it.

Once there was a Christian man who became seriously ill. As he lay in bed, he grew troubled because he felt so little love for God in his heart. He expressed his concern to a Christian brother one day.

"My friend," replied the other, "when I leave here, I expect to go home to my family. We have a baby whom I love more than words can tell. But she loves me little. If my heart were breaking with sorrow, it would not disturb her sleep. If my body were racked with pain, it would not interrupt her play. In fact, if I died, she would forget me in a very short time.

"Even so, there is not enough money in the whole world for someone to buy my baby. Do I say that because she loves me or because I love her? Do I withhold my love until I know she loves me? Do I wait for her to do something worthy of my love before I extend it to her? Of course not! And God loves us in the same way except that His love is infinitely greater."

This illustration so affected the sick man that tears began rolling down his face. "Oh, now I see!" he exclaimed. "It is not my love for God but His love for me that I should be thinking of. And I do love Him now as I have never loved Him before."

3. *To show God at work.* As we go through the daily routines of life, what God does for us may become commonplace. We tend to forget or overlook God's workings in our lives and surroundings. A story can bring the overruling hand of God into sharp focus and clearly remind us of what God does. Consider the following example.

A good many years ago, I was sailing in the desolate seas off Cape Horn, hunting whales. One day we were beating directly south in the face of a hard wind. We had been tacking this way and that all the morning and were making very little headway.

About eleven o'clock, as I stood at the wheel, the idea suddenly came into my mind, "Why batter the ship against these waves? There are probably as many whales to the north as to the south. Suppose we run with the wind instead of against it?"

In response to that sudden idea, I changed the course of the ship and began to sail north instead of south. One hour later, at noon, the lookout at the masthead shouted, "Boats ahead!"

Presently, we overtook four lifeboats in which were fourteen sailors, the only survivors of the crew of a ship that had burned to the water's edge ten days before. Those men had been adrift in their boats ever since, frantically praying to God for rescue; and we arrived just in time to save them. They could not have survived another day.

Consider the two sample stories in this lesson. Which of the three purposes above do those stories fulfill? "Terry's Temper" helps to show readers their own shortcomings as it portrays them in Terry. "'He Rides Upon the Storm'" should inspire trust in God in facing the circumstances of life.

One Central Theme

Another basic part of the story message is a theme—a lesson that the story teaches. A worthwhile theme communicates a specific Bible principle applied to life. Your goal is to convince the reader of the importance of that principle.

A good short story develops only one central theme. After you have decided what it will be, seek to have every detail of your story point to that theme. Every character trait, every description of the setting, and every point in the conflict should contribute to the lesson you want to teach. Although the story may naturally hint at other themes, avoid the temptation to weave them deliberately into the story. A short story is too limited to develop more than one theme effectively. Trying to do so will spoil the unity of the story.

Is your theme thoughtfulness to parents? Then refrain from sticking in little lessons about diligence in school or friendliness to neighbors. These other ideas will detract from the main theme.

Consider again the sample stories in this lesson. Can you identify the theme in each one? They may be stated as follows:

> Learning to control one's temper is an important part of maturing emotionally and spiritually.
>
> Simple trust in the Lord brings peace even in uncertain and frightening circumstances.

Although the theme should run through the entire story, it should not be directly stated in the story. A story is neither a sermon nor an essay; rather, it works in a more subtle way. As the reader follows the main character through the story, he should subconsciously absorb the theme that you have woven in.

Fact and Fiction

A good short story may be either fact or fiction. A factual story develops a specific, actual happening. Very few stories, however, are totally factual. A writer may change the names of characters and places, as well as other details, to avoid embarrassing the people involved. Also, a writer must often use his imagination to supply details of action, dialogue, and thoughts that will carry the story along.

If a story is fiction, it often contains a combination of fact and imagination. A writer may combine details from various events and conversations into one story. Even though every detail may have occurred at one time or another, the story is fiction because those details do not represent one actual event.

An author may also build a story from a snatch of conversation that he hears or a snapshot of action that he observes. In this case again, the story is fiction because it does not describe an actual happening. Of course, a writer may develop a story completely from his imagination. He chooses a story theme that he wants to convey and then creates the characters, events, and dialogue to portray that theme.

The writer of worthwhile fiction must take great care to write realistically. Even though the story is not true, it must be true to life. A reader should not have reason to conclude that the story could not have happened to real people.

Applying the Lesson

A. Do these exercises.

1. List three noble purposes for worthwhile stories.
2. What is a story theme?
3. Why should a short story develop only one central theme?
4. The theme of a good story is not stated directly. Then how does the theme become clear to the reader?
5. What is the difference between a story of fact and a story of fiction?
6. In what ways might a factual story be changed?
7. List several things that may serve as the seed for a story of fiction.
8. What must the writer of fiction be especially careful to do?

B. Write a possible theme for each of the following story openings.

1. Flying snow filled the air as two snow shovels moved steadily. The snowbanks on either side of the drifted lane rose higher.

   "Really deep," grunted Mark, tossing another shovelful of snow.

   "Uh-huh," Jesse agreed. "Packed too. I hope we'll be able to get the lane open before the milk truck comes."

   "I hope so too," said Mark. "I prayed about it."

2. Recess was nearly over. Joyce backed up far beyond second base, prepared to catch a fly ball, for Alvin was coming up to bat. He selected his favorite bat and swung it experimentally. "Think I can hit a home run before the bell rings?"

3. "I wish I could do as I please for once," commented Doris.

   "Oh, I don't think that would make you happy," replied Mother.

   "Well, I think it would. Couldn't we try it, just once?" coaxed Doris.

4. Jonathan whistled a merry tune as he hurried to the barn through the rain. "It surely has rained often this summer," he thought. He glanced at the cornfield, which was already starting to turn yellow. Then his eyes swept across the field of hay that they had planned to bale today. Jonathan was glad when he could step into the warm, dry barn.

   "Good morning," his father greeted him. "Looks like a rainy day today, so the hay will have to wait a little longer."

5. "Oh, David, what could have happened?" I asked with concern. "Edward still isn't home."

   "I can't understand it." David frowned and scratched his head. "Edward said they'd come back early today."

6. "Ernest Swalm?" asked the major as Ernest entered the room.

   "Yes, sir."

   "You refuse to put on your uniform?"

   "Yes, sir. I am a Christian. I cannot kill my enemies, for the Scriptures say, 'Love your enemies.' Nor can I wear the uniform of an organization whose business it is to kill."

C. Choose one of the possibilities you wrote in Lesson 48 as the basis of a story that you will write in this chapter, or another idea approved by your teacher. Write the theme that you will develop in your story. (Save this work for use in later lessons.)

Review Exercises

A. Write whether the underlined sentence part is a nominative absolute (*NA*) or a participial phrase (*PP*). [24]

1. <u>The dishes finally finished</u>, we walked out to the orchard.
2. <u>Walking among the apple trees</u>, we breathed in the sweet smell of ripening apples.
3. <u>Several apples having fallen to the ground</u>, each of us enjoyed a snack.

4. Later we headed back to the house, the air having grown chilly.
5. The mothers visited together for a time, sharing their girlhood memories.

B. Rewrite each sentence, changing the underlined subordinate clause to a nominative absolute. [24]
1. Because the grass has grown tall, Delmar plans to mow the lawn this afternoon.
2. After her first batch of cookies burned, Katrina paid closer attention to the clock.
3. Because Mollie's milk is rich in cream, we make plenty of butter.

---

50. Improving Your Editing Skills, Part 6

When you proofread a composition, you must give full attention to the work at hand. You will not detect errors very well if you have a preoccupied mind or you try to proofread in a distracting environment. This may be the reason that even professional proofreaders occasionally let errors get into print.

Overlooked errors can sometimes be humorous. Someone surely was not concentrating on his work when he allowed the following mistakes to slip through.

In an advertisement for a lawn mower:
"Riding mower, 42′ cut."

In a recipe printed with a magazine article:
"Spoon topping over cake until all is absorbed. Leave cake in pain."

Just one mark or one letter is incorrect in each case. But what a difference those errors make!

In this lesson you will again proofread a number of sentences and paragraphs. Give full attention to your work so that you can find *every* mistake in these exercises.

Marks Used in Editing and Proofreading

∨ or ∧ insert (caret)	delete	.... stet (let it stand)	——— use italics
¶ begin new paragraph	no ¶ no new paragraph	lc change to lowercase (small letter)	uc change to uppercase (capital letter)
# insert space	delete space	← move (arrow)	transpose

Editing Practice

A. Use proofreading marks to correct the two errors of spelling or spacing in each sentence.

1. God has given sevral kinds of fish strange waysof caring for their young.
2. Sum African fish carry their eggs around in their mouths be fore they hatch.
3. In some speceis the male caries the eggs, and in others the female does.
4. The eggs hach in afew days, and the young continue to live in the adult's mouth.
5. Ocassionally the parent fish spits out the young, and they swim near by.
6. When any danger thretens, the young dart back into the adult's protectin mouth.
7. In a few weeks, howver, the little fish grow to large for the parent to carry.
8. The young are than left to care for them selves.
9. During those weaks of caring for their young, the adult fish eats no thing.
10. By the time the young are one their own, the pour adult is quite thin and weak.

B. Use proofreading marks to correct the errors in word order in these sentences.

1. Monsoons are great convectional currents that between winter and summer reverse their direction.
2. During the winter cool months, the oceans remain warmer than the continents.
3. So the winds blow out to the ocean and keep the land dry mostly.
4. When the continent becomes warmer during the summer than the ocean, the winds blow inland from the ocean.

5. These winds bring heavy rain to the land, being laden with moisture.
6. The best-known monsoons occur in India probably.
7. From December through March, a typical dry winter monsoon only brings about five inches of rain to a given region.
8. In April, the winds change and five inches of rain approximately may fall in that month.
9. When the moist summer monsoon blows from May through October, the rainfall may exceed one hundred inches actually.
10. Then as the monsoon changes during November again, another five inches may fall.

C. Use proofreading marks to correct all the errors in this essay. Your corrections should include one use of the stet symbol and one joining of two paragraphs. No line has more than one error.

1. God created the earth "to be inhabited (Isaiah 45:18).
2. This required that the earth have an atmosphere.
3. The atmosphere provides oxygen for breatheing. But
4. that is only a small part of the picture. The atmosphere
5. serves to to regulate the surface temperature of the
6. earth. Like a huge blanket, it surrounds us, allowing
7. sunlight to pass ~~through~~ but preventing heat from escaping
8. freely into Space.
9. By contrast, the atmosphere of Venus traps so much solar
10. heat that the surface tempature of that planet is scorching
11. hot. And the moon, which has no atmosphere, endures blister
12. ing noontime temperatures and freezing nights
13. [illegible]
14. the atmosphere. If this did not ~~really~~ happen, even a small
15. meteoric particel no larger than a dust speck would strike
16. the earth with the force of a shot from a revolver.

Since billions of such particles strike the atmosphere everyday, we surely need its protection!

In addition to these all services, the atmosphere is a shield against deadly radiation from space. Truely, our atmosphere is the handiwork of an all knowing Creator.

---

51. The Structure and Elements of a Story

"Oh, girls." Doris glanced around the warm auditorium and instinctively lowered her voice. "Did you hear the latest news?"

Betty fidgeted self-consciously while several other girls leaned forward eagerly. "What should I do?" Betty wondered.

A short story must get right down to business. This sample beginning does. It hints at the theme of the story, which you studied in Lesson 49. It also pictures the setting briefly, it introduces the main characters, and it suggests the conflict. These are the three main elements of every good story.

The Setting

A short story should include just enough details about the setting to make the story clear. The first few paragraphs should make some reference to the setting. As the story moves along, you may add more details to help explain the story. Often the setting helps a reader to understand why the characters act as they do.

One main part of the setting is *where* the story occurs. You can usually indicate this with incidental details (like "the barn door" or "the kitchen sink") that show whether the story happens at home or elsewhere. Or you can make a brief reference to the geographical location (such as "the Kansas prairie"). Detailed information is necessary only if the reader is probably unfamiliar with the setting and if those details are important to the story. You must be well familiar with the location of the story so that all the details will be consistent.

Another part of the setting is *when* the story occurs. Brief descriptions, such as "a spring morning" or "the setting sun," are usually enough to indicate the time. Specific dates may be important for historical interest or value.

The setting also includes the emotional or spiritual atmosphere in the story. If the moods of significant characters are important to the development of the story, the opening paragraphs should give that information. Often it takes just a few words ("whistled merrily" or "fumed to herself") to indicate whether the atmosphere is pleasant or unpleasant.

The details of the setting often reflect the attitudes or actions of the main character. Is your story about an inner turmoil of conscience? The setting may include turbulent clouds overhead. A setting of morning countryside beauty may reflect the peace of a soul yielded to God. Sometimes, however, the details of the setting differ sharply from the attitudes or actions of the main character. A peaceful setting, by its very contrast, may emphasize the irritability or perplexity of the main character.

Look again at the story opening at the beginning of this lesson. What hints do you find about the place, time, and atmosphere of the story? In the second sentence, the mention of a *warm auditorium* reveals that the story takes place at church, probably in summer. The opening further suggests that the atmosphere is less than ideal, with the two characters displaying opposite moods.

The Characters

Characters are central to the action and conflict of a story. Although you might produce a story with no allusion to a physical setting, you certainly cannot produce a story without characters. In fact, they are so important that the entire next lesson deals with the portraying of story characters.

Story characters must be realistic. If you present the main character as a noble example, he must uphold high ideals. However, he must not be so idealistic that your reader can hardly identify with him. What real-life teenager (or any other person) is so good that he never does anything wrong, never considers a wrong response, and never even faces a strong temptation to do wrong? If you portray such characters in a story, you will destroy its realism and the reader will probably discredit the whole story.

If your story is about people you actually know, you must be especially careful to portray their characteristics fully and clearly. You will tend to interpret details of your story by your background knowledge of the characters, but your reader knows only what you reveal to him in the story. As a result, what seems perfectly clear to you may be confusing or baffling to your reader when he first meets a character. Read the following example.

> Carla had just finished her drawing when Ivan walked into the room. "I'd be ashamed of a picture like that," he declared.
>
> Carla smiled happily and sat up a little straighter.

Are you surprised at Carla's reaction? Surely she heard what her brother said. Is she such a cheerful person that criticism does not bother her? No, Carla is a normal girl; but Ivan has a habit of speaking in irony, and he was actually praising his sister's work. If you had known that, you would have understood Carla's reaction immediately. In the same way, your reader must have all the necessary details about your characters in order to understand why they act as they do.

Story characters must not only be realistic but also remain consistent throughout the story. If conflict in the story changes the main character, the change should generally be in a gradual way and in the same direction. Any sudden or unexpected change should be the result of a crisis in the story, or the character will not seem realistic.

Story characters should also generate an emotional response from the reader. If your main character is a good example, his reactions throughout the conflict should cause your reader to respond with definite approval. If he is a poor example, he should provide reasons for definite disapproval of his reactions. Be sure to portray the characters in a manner that directs the reader's sympathy in the right way. A poor example may actually draw the reader's sympathy to himself if he is constantly ridiculed and mistreated by the other story characters.

The Conflict

A conflict involving the main character must be the framework of your story. This struggle or problem that the main character faces is what holds the reader's interest and makes the story theme live.

This does not mean that you must write about robberies or sinking ships or burning hospitals. Many less dramatic experiences build up interest quite well. The important thing is to tell the story in the right order, making the conflict grow stronger as you go along. For example, Jane looks up from her test and sees Miriam looking in her direction. She knows Miriam would not be trying to copy from her test, so she thinks nothing of it. Later she looks up again, and Miriam is still looking in her direction. After several more glances, she hardly knows what to think because Miriam is still looking. Do you see the buildup?

1. *Types of conflict.* The conflict in a story is one or more of three different types. One common type is conflict between the main character and another character. The story of Isaac and his wells is a familiar Bible story with this kind of conflict. Isaac, the ***protagonist*** (main character), must relate to the unfair demands of the Philistines, who are the ***antagonists*** (persons opposing the main character). Other examples of this type of conflict might include a main character who struggles to appreciate a classmate; one who rejects the advice of an authority figure; or one who resists the wrong influence of another person.

A second type of conflict is that between the main character and his circumstances. For instance, Paul and the other passengers faced this type of conflict when a tempest battered their ship for days and finally destroyed it. Other examples include a main character who must accept a change of plans, who must cope with a handicap or hardship, or who must accomplish some task against contrary circumstances. Although other characters may play a part in the story, this type of conflict is brought on by a circumstance rather than by a person.

A third type is conflict between the main character and himself. This type is illustrated by the story of Moses' hesitation when God called him to lead Israel out of Egypt. Other examples would include a main character's struggles in overcoming a temptation or a bad habit; in clearing his conscience by confessing a wrong or making restitution; or in facing a difficult decision. Sometimes in this type of conflict, you may almost conclude that God is the antagonist opposing the main character. But this is not true; God is rather prompting the main character to respond rightly. The conflict rages between the main character's proper desire to do right and his carnal desire to take the easiest way.

2. *Development of conflict.* The conflict should be introduced as early as possible in the story. Avoid a long introduction that merely gives background or setting

information but involves no action or conflict. Suppose your story is about strange guests who appeared at bedtime asking for a place to sleep. You do not need to tell what you had for supper that evening or what your family discussed at the table. Start the story with the timid knock on the front door.

"But," you say, "I have to start back in the afternoon so that the setting is clear. Father was not at home, because he was away at a meeting. He said that he wouldn't be back until late, and he told us not to disturb Mother unless it was positively necessary. She was in bed with a bad sore throat."

What you can do is begin with the action of the story and slip those facts in later as a flashback. There may be several flashbacks, each one introducing background information as it is needed. The flashbacks in the following example are underlined.

> There we were, with strangers on the front porch asking for lodging. Wilbur, Helen, and I looked at each other questioningly.
>
> "Oh, I wish Mother could be up," I sighed. <u>"But she just told me that her sore throat isn't much better than it was this morning."</u>
>
> "We can make out this time without her help, can't we?" Wilbur replied. "<u>Father did say we shouldn't disturb Mother unless it's really necessary.</u> Remember?"
>
> "Sure we can manage," Helen said cheerfully. Wilbur returned to the door to invite the guests inside.

Once you have started with a good conflict, keep the story moving. Increase the intensity of the conflict throughout the main part of the story. Unless the story is very short, the main character should face his conflict at least two times before it is resolved. Each incident of the conflict should involve stronger emotion than the preceding incident. This, along with the recurrence of the conflict, increases the reader's suspense as the story progresses. The most intense incident of the conflict is the climax, at which point the main character's response brings either victory or defeat.

After the conflict is resolved, a short conclusion should round out the story and clinch the theme. The reader is satisfied. He knows how the problem was solved and is ready for the story to end. And the theme of the story should be clear to him. If it is not, a direct statement will only dull the point and spoil his interest. So if the lesson is vague, revise your story until you do not need to explain the theme at the end. Your closing should contain just enough to tie the story together, like this:

> The rain had slowed to a fine drizzle when Mr. Smith dumped the last bucket of water down the drain. "People say I procrastinate," he muttered, "but I know one job I'm not going to put off again. I'm going to be up on the roof patching those leaks bright and early tomorrow morning."
>
> He looked at the clock.
>
> "Not tomorrow," he said. "Today."

Applying the Lesson

A. Do these exercises.

1. Where should the setting of a story be portrayed?
2. What three things make up the setting of a story?
3. Why is it important to make story characters realistic?
4. In a story about actual people, why might a writer neglect to portray the characters clearly enough for his reader?
5. If a main character changes in a sudden, drastic way, how can you make the change seem realistic?
6. What is the story conflict?
7. What are the three common types of story conflict?
8. Where should the conflict begin?
9. What is the purpose of a flashback?
10. What should happen to the conflict as the story unfolds?
11. What two things cause a buildup of intensity in the conflict?
12. What two things should the conclusion do for the story?

B. Answer these questions about the sample story "Terry's Temper" in Lesson 49.

1. What information about the place and time do the first two paragraphs provide?
2. Is the setting a reflection of or a contrast to the conflict?
3. The main character changes in this story. How is that change kept realistic?
4. What is the conflict in the story?
5. Which of the three types of conflict does the story portray?
6. How many incidents of conflict occur in the story?
7. What are some things that make the climax (final incident) the most intense?
8. How does the conclusion clinch the story theme?

C. Answer these questions about the sample story "'He Rides Upon the Storm'" in Lesson 49.

1. What information about the place, time, and atmosphere is given in the first three paragraphs?
2. What is the conflict in the story?
3. Which of the three types of conflict does this story portray?
4. How many incidents of conflict occur in the story?
5. How does the conclusion clinch the story theme?

Review Exercises

Do these exercises on expository essays. [28–32]

1. What is the general purpose of an expository essay?
2. Write the letters of the two topics that are limited enough for an expository essay.
   a. Weather Systems
   b. The Formation of Hurricanes
   c. Effects of Weather on Agriculture
   d. Weather Patterns in Canada
   e. Typical Blizzards of the Great Plains

3. Write whether each statement about expository essays is true (*T*) or false (*F*).
   a. A good set of notes draws from at least two sources.
   b. A good set of notes contains no direct quotations from reference sources.
   c. Good notes include many sentences and paragraphs.
   d. The introductory paragraph should begin with a statement of the theme.
   e. Credits for direct quotations are noted in the bibliography.
   f. The conclusion should summarize or otherwise reinforce the main points of the essay.

---

52. Characterization in a Story

A story lives if its characters live. Therefore, a writer must pay close attention to his characters and portray them in a way that shows their traits as clearly as possible. The process of portraying story characters is *characterization.*

Three Classes of Characters

Every story character fits into one of three classes: major, minor, and background. The *major characters* carry the development of the story conflict. They are the ones that the reader should come to know by reading the story. Every story has at least one major character—whom you have known before as the main character. Another name for this main character is *protagonist.* The entire story generally comes to the reader through the protagonist's eyes. Many stories also include a second major character, the *antagonist.* The antagonist is the protagonist's opponent. (Note the prefix *ant-,* meaning "against.")

The number of major characters in a short story must be strictly limited. Since each one deserves to be characterized clearly, the story simply does not have room for more than three major characters. For example, the story of David killing the giant has two major characters: David and Goliath.

The *minor characters* contribute to the development of the conflict without carrying it directly. These are generally named, and they should be characterized only as much as necessary. Normally, this means the portraying of only one character trait.

The *background characters* are simply a part of the setting; they do not contribute to the actual story conflict. So they should not be characterized, and usually they should not even be named. Background characters often occur in groups. For example, siblings referred to in a family setting or students in a school setting are background characters. Even in writing a factual story, you are not required to [illegible] in order to be honest. [illegible] writing a story, [illegible] giving a *report.*

The story of David and Goliath illustrates these three classes of characters. David and Goliath, of course, are the major characters—the protagonist and the antagonist. Saul, Jesse, and Eliab are the minor characters. The background characters include David's unnamed brothers, the Israelite soldiers, and the Philistine soldiers.

Direct and Indirect Characterization

Direct characterization generally uses adjectives to tell what story characters are like. Here are two examples of direct characterization.

> Mary Jane was very active.
> Susan was quiet and gentle.

In a good story, however, things need to keep moving. The characters must engage in specific actions and say specific words. They will seem lifeless if you paint portraits of them! Direct characterization slows the forward movement of a story. Any sentence that merely *tells* what a character is like will hinder the action of the story.

Furthermore, direct characterization tends to be dull. Why say that Mary Jane *is* active or that Susan *is* quiet and gentle? The reader wants to know what is *happening.* So the value of direct characterization in stories is very limited. It is usually effective only for minor characters, and only if it is a brief description important to the story.

Much more effective is indirect characterization, which *shows* what story characters are like. This is accomplished by including the characterizing right with the flow of the story action. As a further advantage, indirect characterization gives the reader the satisfaction of drawing his own conclusions by reading between the lines.

> Mary Jane came skipping down the steps, humming to herself.
> I looked up to see Susan rearranging the flowers on the table. "Why, I didn't even hear you come downstairs," I said.

Methods of Characterization

You can use five basic methods to accomplish your goal of indirect characterization. Not every story will include all five; but as you write, you should look for ways to include as many of them as possible.

1. *Show the character's actions.* Jesus said, "By their fruits ye shall know them." A character's actions are a significant part of that fruit. Carefully chosen words that show how a character walks, works, plays, or drives can paint vivid pictures of your character's traits. A proud person would strut down the sidewalk, while a rebellious person might swagger and a determined person might stride. A careful driver will accelerate smoothly and use his turn signals, but a hostile one might go roaring down the road with his tires squealing.

2. *Show the character's speech.* Again Jesus said, "Out of the abundance of the heart the mouth speaketh." In similar circumstances, one character might complain while another gives thanks, thus displaying contrasting character traits. A character who uses polite, respectful, or gracious words reveals much about his true self.

In addition to *what* a character says, the explanatory words that tell *how* he spoke are also revealing. Compare the following examples. What does each one reveal about the speaker?

> "I'll show him what happens to people who cross my path," growled the man.
>
> "We must forgive as Christ did," the man said gently. "We must always forgive."

3. *Show the character's thoughts.* This method is used far less than the previous two. In fact, many stories do not show the characters' thoughts at all. But thoughts are one of the best indicators of what a character is really like. "As [a man] thinketh in his heart, so is he."

In the following paragraph from the second sample story, the main character's thoughts reveal her tendency to be anxious and fearful.

> My mind whirled into high gear. "Of course, I dearly love Grandmother," I thought. "But would she want me to come if she knew how insecure I feel sometimes? What if I can't fit into her schedule? What if . . ."

4. *Show the character's appearance.* Again, this method is used only occasionally. But a passing comment about a character's tousled or neatly combed hair, about his dirty or clean clothes, or about his stern or friendly face can certainly add to the total picture of a character's inner traits.

5. *Show the character's reputation.* This method is used the most infrequently of all. However, the words and actions of others in relation to a certain character can help the reader to understand that character and see why other characters respond to him as they do. Consider the following example from the Book of Acts.

> And there was a certain disciple at Damascus, named Ananias; and to him said the Lord in a vision, Ananias. And he said, Behold, I am here, Lord.
>
> And the Lord said unto him, Arise, and go into the street which is called Straight, and enquire in the house of Judas for one called Saul, of Tarsus: for, behold, he prayeth. . . .
>
> Then Ananias answered, Lord, I have heard by many of this man, how much evil he hath done to thy saints at Jerusalem: and here he hath authority from the chief priests to bind all that call on thy name.
>
> But the Lord said unto him, Go thy way: for he is a chosen vessel unto me, to bear my name before the Gentiles, and kings, and the children of Israel.

We know that a person's reputation is not a foolproof indication of his character. A reputation may match a person's true character, or it may not (as in the example above). And a skillful writer can make good use of this very fact. The contrast between a character's reputation and his true self can make a strong impression about that character.

Know Your Characters Well

Obviously, if you are to portray your story characters effectively, you must know them well before you write the first sentence of the story. If the story is about real people whom you know, choose one or two specific traits that best match your story theme. Then stick to them, and emphasize only those traits. If your story is fiction, you must gain a clear mental image of the characters that will make up the story. Visualize the kinds of persons who will develop your theme effectively. Then list details about each major and minor character's appearance and inner traits to make them true to life.

Be sure to keep these details consistent. Some of the details in your list will never be mentioned in the story. But you still need to write them down so that you yourself will have a well-rounded picture of the characters. Unless you have such a picture, you may write something inconsistent about a character without even realizing it.

Applying the Lesson

A. Do these exercises.

1. What is characterization?
2. Explain the terms *protagonist* and *antagonist.*
3. Write *major, minor,* or *background* to tell which class of characters fits each description.
   a. Should be named but not characterized very much.
   b. Should be no more than three in number.
   c. Should be characterized fully.
   d. Are often grouped together.
   e. Have an effect on the conflict, but do not carry it.
   f. Are part of the setting rather than the conflict.
   g. Carry the development of the conflict.
4. What is the difference between direct and indirect characterization?
5. Which two methods of characterization should you use in every story?
6. Name three other methods that you might use occasionally.

B. Do these exercises on the sample story "Terry's Temper" in Lesson 49.

1. List all the story characters, grouped in the three classes.
2. Give specific example details that characterize Terry, as indicated below.
   a. Two examples of action. (Identify each one, and describe the trait revealed.)
   b. Three examples of speech. (Identify each one, and describe the trait revealed.)
   c. One example of thoughts. (Identify it, and describe the trait revealed.)
   d. Two examples of appearance. (Identify each one, and describe the trait revealed.)
3. Give specific examples that characterize the following characters, as indicated below. Your answers should follow the same pattern as in exercise 2.
   a. Walter: one example each of action and appearance.
   b. Father: one example each of speech and appearance.

C. Do these exercises on the story "'He Rides Upon the Storm'" in Lesson 49.
  1. List all the story characters, grouped in the three classes.
  2. Give specific examples that characterize Wanda, as indicated below.
     a. Two examples of action.
     b. Three examples of speech.
     c. Three examples of thoughts.
     d. One example of reputation.
  3. Give specific examples that characterize the following persons, as indicated.
     a. Mother: two examples of speech.
     b. Alta: one example of action and two examples of speech.

---

53. The Point of View and Plot of a Story

Two different artists painting the same farm could produce pictures that look quite different. How is that? Suppose one painter stood to the northwest on a small hill, and the other stood to the southeast at a place level with the farm. Their pictures might look so different that you could hardly recognize them as portraying the same place.

Likewise, two people could tell entirely different stories about the same event. The story told by a ten-year-old child would be so different from that of a forty-year-old father, that it might be hard to imagine how they could represent the same incident. In both illustrations, the contrast results from a difference in the painters' or storytellers' point of view.

Point of View

Every story is written from a certain perspective, or ***point of view.*** The three most common points of view are first person, third person, and omniscient.

1. *First person point of view.* With this viewpoint, the main character is the author himself. He uses first person pronouns like *I, me, us,* and *our* in referring to himself; and the reader may not find out what his name is in the story until another character speaks to him. Of course, other characters may also use *I* and *me* in direct quotations, but then the pronouns do not refer to the storyteller.

The main advantage of the first person point of view is its strong impression of reality. The writer has firsthand information. He was really there. On the other hand, this point of view also has several disadvantages because the writer must limit himself to the view of the character-narrator. First, he can include only what this character (the *I* in the story) can realistically see, hear, or know. Second, since the main character is the narrator, he has the difficulty of portraying his good qualities without appearing to be proud.

The story "'He Rides Upon the Storm'" (Lesson 49) is written from the first person point of view. The narrator is the main character, Wanda. The story reveals Wanda's thoughts several times, but it does not reveal any other character's thoughts. What you know of the other characters is only what Wanda herself can observe. So the author can write the first of the example sentences below; for as Wanda saw it, Alta did seem to be enjoying the scene. In contrast, the author would not have been consistent if he had presented any detail from Alta's viewpoint, as in the second example below.

Consistent with first person point of view:
There stood Alta at the window, apparently enjoying the scene.
Not consistent with first person point of view:
There stood Alta at the window, pondering the greatness of God.

2. *Third person point of view.* This is like the first person point of view in that the author must limit himself to the viewpoint of the main character in the story. He must always stay at that character's side, as it were, portraying the things he observes but omitting anything he cannot observe. Because the author is not writing about himself, he can more easily reveal the good qualities of the main character.

The story "Terry's Temper" (Lesson 49) is written from the third person point of view. This story is portrayed through Terry's eyes. What you know of the other characters is totally from Terry's viewpoint. So the author can write the first example sentence below, but not the second.

Consistent with third person (Terry's) point of view:
"Better calm down a bit," Terry thought uncomfortably as he neared the shop.
Not consistent with third person (Terry's) point of view:
"I forgot to shut the door," thought Walter.

3. *Omniscient point of view.* With this viewpoint, the author writes as an outside observer, seeing everything as God does in the real world. Since the happenings are not presented as seen through any one character's eyes, the author has the advantage of being able to describe events at various places. For example, he may describe what is happening at home while Mother is in the hospital. Then he might change the scene to the hospital and show what is happening there. However, this viewpoint tends to be impersonal because it does not bring the reader to identify with any character in the story.

The following examples illustrate how the same incident can be presented with these three different viewpoints.

First person:
I picked up the telephone and dialed Mrs. Perry's number. "Hello," came our neighbor's voice across the line. She sounded more cheerful than when I had called the day before.
Third person:
Cheryl picked up the telephone and dialed Mrs. Perry's number. "Hello," came the neighbor's voice across the line. She sounded more cheerful than when Cheryl had called the day before.

Omniscient:

Cheryl picked up the telephone and dialed Mrs. Perry's number. "Hello," the neighbor lady answered brightly. She had just come inside from a walk in the bright spring sunshine, and she was feeling more cheerful than usual.

4. *Subjective and objective viewpoints.* The third person and the omniscient viewpoints can be either subjective or objective. With the third person subjective point of view, the author sees into the mind of the one character through whose eyes the story unfolds. He reveals the thoughts of that character but not of any other character in the story.

With the third person objective point of view, the author does not see into the mind of any character. He goes with the main character through the story, portraying his words and actions but not his thoughts. Since it is difficult to write in this way, very few stories represent the third person objective point of view.

With the omniscient subjective point of view, the author writes about the thoughts of any character. If he uses the objective approach, he does not write about any character's thoughts.

The sample story "Terry's Temper" is written in the third person subjective point of view. The following examples show a portion of that story written in two other viewpoints. Compare the underlined words with the sample story.

Omniscient subjective:

"Stop! Stop!" Walter's urgent shouts <u>jolted Terry like an electric shock</u>. "The feed is pouring out on the barn floor," Walter gasped. <u>"Because I forgot to shut the door," he thought. "Wonder what Terry will say now?"</u>

Quickly Terry pulled the lever, stopping the auger. "Walter Jay Gehman! Of all things! You're always forgetting to close the door!". . .

Terry was back in a few minutes. "Come on, shovel faster!" he snapped at his brother. <u>To himself he tumed, "I ought to make him clean it up alone."</u>

Omniscient objective:

"Stop! Stop!" Walter's urgent shouts <u>made Terry jump</u>. "The feed is pouring out on the barn floor," Walter gasped. <u>"I forgot to shut the door."</u>

Quickly Terry pulled the lever, stopping the auger. "Walter Jay Gehman! Of all things! You're always forgetting to close the door!". . .

Terry was back in a few minutes. "Come on, shovel faster!" he snapped at his brother. <u>"I ought to make you clean it up alone."</u>

The following chart summarizes the points of view that stories can have.

First Person	Limited to the viewpoint of the author, who is the main character. Uses the pronouns *I* and *me.* Gives a strong impression of reality.
Third Person	Limited to the viewpoint of the main character. Can reveal the main character's good qualities. *Subjective:* Reveals the thoughts of the main character only. *Objective:* Does not reveal the thoughts of any character.
Omniscient	Views happenings as an outside observer. Tends to be impersonal. *Subjective:* Reveals the thoughts of any character. *Objective:* Does not reveal the thoughts of any character.

Plot

A short story should develop a plot. The plot is the overall development of the story conflict. Most short stories have either a complication plot or a loose plot.

With a ***complication plot,*** the conflict builds up to a definite climax. This is the type of conflict that you worked with in the previous books of this series. The story "Terry's Temper" illustrates the complication plot. Below is a brief outline of a complication plot.

1. A brief beginning introduces the main character, establishes the setting, and presents an opening problem that hints at the theme.
2. The middle includes the main part of the story. The main character faces his conflict in a series of episodes, each increasing the suspense. The suspense builds to the climax, in which the main character either prevails or fails.
3. A brief conclusion shows the outcome of the conflict and leaves the main character with the results of his climaxing decision.

With a ***loose plot,*** the conflict moves through several incidents relating to the problem in the story, without building to a definite climax. The story "'He Rides Upon the Storm'" illustrates the loose plot.

A story with either kind of plot has a beginning, a middle, and a conclusion. With the loose plot, however, there is only a loose connection between the incidents in the middle of the story. Each incident also resembles a miniature story in itself, with the conflict basically resolved before the story moves on. The loose plot tends to represent real life more accurately than the complication plot, for most everyday problems do not involve a buildup that parallels a complication plot in a short story.

Applying the Lesson

A. Do these exercises.

1. What is meant by the point of view of a story?
2. Write *first, third,* or *omniscient* to identify the point of view described by each statement. For some, you will need to write two answers.
   a. The author writes as if he is constantly with a certain character in the story.
   b. The main character is the author himself.
   c. The author writes as if he can see all aspects of the story at once.
   d. The story seems especially realistic because it shows what the author actually observed.
   e. The author can write either subjectively or objectively.
   f. The author may find it awkward to portray the main character's good qualities.
   g. The main character's actual name may be hard to find.
   h. The author is limited to one character's perspective.
3. What is the difference between a subjective and an objective point of view?
4. What is the plot of a short story?
5. Write *complication, loose,* or *both* to tell which kind of plot is described in each statement.
   a. The story has a beginning, middle, and conclusion.
   b. The story is particularly true to life.
   c. Each incident increases the buildup of suspense.
   d. Each incident resembles a miniature story.

B. Name the point of view used in each of these excerpts. Include *objective* or *subjective* if it applies.

1. "You could never guess who I saw in town last week." My sister Millie dropped this challenge into the middle of our chicken-dressing project. Her eyes were sober when she raised them to mine.

   I paused for a moment with my knife in midair. "No, I probably couldn't. How about a hint?"

   "I saw an old friend of yours; one you haven't seen for years. And it wouldn't make you happy to see her now."

2. "So it's true!" Alvin mused as he lay across his bed, his thoughts going back to the close of the prayer service held that evening. He thought again of Brother Mark's announcement that the Martin Weaver family would soon move to the new area into which their congregation was expanding.

   "That means Titus and I won't be together as much," he realized. "Forty miles really isn't very close." He stopped as a new thought dawned upon him. "Brother Mark mentioned that an ordained brother would be asked to move there also! What if that is Uncle Wilbur's? If they move, no other boy my age will live here anymore!"

3. "Will you come out to church some Sunday?" Faith invited. "We would be happy to have you." For a moment Joyce again stared dumbfounded and then replied, "I have a church to attend." . . .

After walking up and down the hospital hallway a few minutes to relieve tired, aching muscles, Faith returned to her room and spent the day with her mother, and in prayer for Joyce. "Help her find the way. Give me more opportunities and the right words to speak," she prayed. Joyce's troubled face had impressed her with the deep need in her life, the unsatisfied longings, and the lack of peace with God. . . .

At home that evening, Joyce felt restless and discontented. A new longing possessed her to find the way to God. An entirely new concept of God had been awakened in her heart. . . .

Joyce's thoughts were in a turmoil. "She's just trying to convert me to her religion," she decided.

4. An hour later Calvin was again on the steps at the side porch. "We're finished now," he announced when Dorie came to the door. "And here's the bill."

"What!" exclaimed Dorie. "It's higher than last time."

"That's because we trimmed the hedge this time," reminded Calvin gently.

"Well, okay then; just wait a minute till I get the money." When she returned, she handed the money to Calvin and then closed the door without a word.

The boys loaded their equipment and soon left. But Lloyd, the boys' employer, received a call from Dorie Baner just a few hours later.

"Those boys of yours!" she said angrily. "They can do all right sometimes, but this time they didn't. I just knew there couldn't be any boys around that are always good as gold!"

C. Read this story, and do the exercises after it.

Twenty Pounds

"Grandmother is very sick, and I must go over to stay with her," Mother told the children.

"Please take us all along. We can sleep on the kitchen floor," twelve-year-old Timothy pleaded.

"No, son, not this time," Mother said firmly. "You must be brave. You are the oldest. Little Joseph is too sick to be taken out on a cold night like this, and the girls are scarcely over the whooping cough. You must stay at home and help Donna take care of the little ones."

The two oldest children listened attentively to the directions and sadly nodded their heads.

"Remember, God is with you," Mother whispered as she went to the door after the four youngest had fallen asleep. "Now you two go to bed and try to sleep. I will be only a few hundred yards away. If anything happens so that I need to come home, just turn the porch light on, and I should soon see it. I am sure I won't sleep much, the way Grandmother is."

"If only their father were with us, how different it would be," Mother thought wistfully as she went on her way. Her faithful Christian husband had died two years earlier.

The night hours dragged, and the sick woman did not sleep much. Toward morning she became more rational but also weaker. Her voice was scarcely more than a whisper.

"Marla," the sick woman called tremulously, "I will not be here much longer. God has been good to me. Trust Him. He has been my faithful companion, and He will be yours." Her eyes rested lovingly on her only daughter. "I know you have seen hard times and will likely see more. I have nothing to leave you but this small house with the half acre of land. Maybe you will be able to sell or rent it to someone."

Marla knew it was doubtful that anyone would buy or even rent the small rundown, two-room house so near their own.

"Marla," her mother continued when she had rallied enough strength to talk more, "over there on the table is a coffee can; in it you will find a twenty-pound note. It has been dedicated to the Lord. Take it to the bank, cash it, and send the money to that faithful little mission in Scotland. God laid it on my heart to send it to them. I know you could use it, but it is the Lord's money. Send it as I have requested, and the Lord will return it to you a hundredfold."

"Twenty pounds!" thought Marla. "My mother does not know that her own dear grandchildren have not had sufficient food these past months, that there is no food in the house for breakfast and no flour to bake bread, and that they haven't had milk or eggs for weeks. If only I could ask her to lend it to me to feed my family, just until I could earn enough to pay it back."

Marla waited quietly for her mother to finish her instructions, but that was all. She lay perfectly motionless. Marla bent forward. Her mother was not breathing; she had quietly slipped away to her reward.

The first streaks of red were glowing in the eastern sky as Marla softly pulled the covers up over the dear form on the bed, so lifeless and still. She tiptoed out of the room and closed the door. Tears streamed down her cheeks as she hurried home.

The children were all sleeping quietly when she arrived. As Marla gazed upon their peaceful faces, the note came again to her mind. "Twenty pounds! Would it be wrong to keep it? Could the mission in Scotland possibly need it as badly as my own family does? Couldn't they wait? Surely sometime I could pay it back."

Softly Mother called, "Timothy, Timothy."

The lad stirred on his cot beside Joseph's crib.

"Come out in the hall so we don't wake the baby," Mother said as the boy sat up and rubbed his eyes.

Donna awoke too and joined them in the hall, stretching and yawning sleepily. "Is it morning?" she asked.

"Yes," replied Mother. "Grandmother suffered a lot and was very weak. Early this morning God took her home to her eternal reward.

"Timothy," Mother added, "I want you to harness Old Steady and ride over to the Millers. They are our nearest neighbors who have a telephone. I'll write them a note, telling them whom I want them to call about Grandmother. Donna, when the children awake, dress them and tell them that Mother will soon be home with some breakfast for them," Mother instructed as she prepared to return to Grandmother's little cottage.

At Grandmother's house, Mother looked around and sized up the situation. She and Timothy could carry Grandmother's cot over for Donna to sleep on so that all four girls would not have to sleep in one bed. Then there was Grandmother's old rocker and the table. Oh, yes, there was the coffee can. She must take care of the twenty-pound note.

"Twenty pounds!" Mother sighed wistfully. Her mind pictured the milk and eggs and flour and many other things her family desperately needed. "Oh, what shall I do?" her troubled thoughts raced. "Is it right to neglect my dear children? Couldn't I use the money for now and give it to the mission later?"

"No, this will never do." Quickly Mother stuffed the twenty-pound note into her apron pocket. Of course, she would obey her mother's parting instructions.

"The Lord will return it to you a hundredfold," Grandmother had said. That was hard to understand.

Immediately after breakfast, Mother saddled Old Steady and hurried into town. In obedience to her mother's directions, she obtained a money order for the twenty pounds and sent it to the mission in Scotland. She never told the children about that money or the gift to Scotland.

Work was not easy to find, and the family's condition grew worse. The children tried to help all they could. Mother often thought of her own mother's last words: "I know you could use it, but it is the Lord's money. Send it as I have requested, and the Lord will return it to you a hundredfold."

Mother's heart was broken when Timothy rejected her faith, took his own way, and joined the army. "I can't find any way to help you support the family here. At least this way you will have one less mouth to feed," he justified himself.

The sad and weary mother grieved and wept and slaved for the sake of her children. She prayed constantly for Timothy, as her wayward son was traveling somewhere far away. She had not heard from him for many months.

She often envisioned that little piece of paper, a money order dated 1935, sent to the mission in Scotland. Oh, how she needed that money! As time went on and things grew worse, doubts stormed her mind. "Did I do the right thing? If only I had that twenty pounds now!" Often she did not know which way to turn, but God always supplied their need in some way.

One day a letter came, postmarked in Scotland. Mother's mind turned immediately to the faithful mission in Scotland and, along with it, to the twenty-pound note. The handwriting looked familiar.

Inside was a single sheet. Her eyes ran quickly to the signature at the bottom. *Timothy* stood out in bold letters, along with *Mother, I love you.*

Her heart leaped for joy as her oldest son explained how he had come under conviction after he had wandered into a little mission in Scotland. There the truth of God's Word was taught exactly as his own dear mother had taught him at home, and there he had received salvation. Timothy would soon be returning home.

The last paragraph especially gripped her attention. "Mother, this little mission has been here for fifty years," wrote Timothy. "They told me it nearly closed down nine years ago. The country was in such desperate straits, and there was no money to pay the rent to keep the mission open. The pastor wept and prayed all night, pleading with God for funds to keep it open. Many souls had been saved there. He asked God for the twenty pounds they needed, and God sent it from some foreign country—he couldn't remember where—but he knew it was sent from God to keep the mission open. He said, 'Had that twenty-pound money order not arrived in the winter of 1935, there would be no mission here today.' Suppose it had been closed," he added. "I wouldn't be writing this letter today."

The letter ended with these words: "I thank God for that faithful giver who lives somewhere, though I will probably never know who it was."

Mother felt that she could stand no more. Her joy overflowed in tears of humility and gratitude. A twenty-pound money order in the winter of 1935, sent to the mission in Scotland! A son saved, for whom she had labored in tears and prayers! And her mother's words!—"Send it as I have requested, and the Lord will return it to you a hundredfold."

"Ah, my dear mother could have said a millionfold, and that would not have been enough," said Mother. "For this one soul is worth more than the whole world."

1. Identify the point of view from which the story is written. Include *subjective* or *objective* if it applies.
2. Choose the letters of the three main incidents of conflict in the story. Also write the letter of the climax, and circle it.
   a. Mother thinks of her faithful husband and wishes he were still with her.
   b. Mother is tempted to keep the twenty pounds immediately after Grandmother's death.
   c. Mother needs to tell the children about Grandmother's death.
   d. Mother is tempted to keep the twenty pounds when she gathers some of Grandmother's things for her family.

e. Mother sends the twenty pounds to the mission in Scotland.
f. Mother is heartbroken when Timothy rejects her faith and joins the army.
g. Mother struggles for years with doubts about the twenty pounds sent to the mission.
h. Mother's doubts melt away when she learns of how the twenty pounds contributed to her son's salvation.
i. Mother acknowledges that one soul is worth more than the whole world.

---

54. Developing a General Plan for a Story

Now that you have studied the different aspects of a short story, it is time to put your understanding into practice. Before you begin writing, however, you must make a plan. This lesson will guide you in writing a general plan for your story. In the next lesson, you will fill in the details.

Follow these steps in developing a general plan for a short story. Refer to the first sample story in Lesson 49, "Terry's Temper," as you study these steps.

1. *Write a theme for your story.* If you are writing a factually based story, you must determine what particular theme (perhaps out of several possibilities) you want to emphasize. If your story is fiction, choosing a theme is a good place to begin. In either case, you must have a definite goal for the story if you expect to write something worthwhile.

This statement of your theme will never actually appear in the finished product, but it is essential to the unity of the story. Then as you plan and write, you should review your theme several times. Otherwise, your story is likely to wander from that theme.

The theme of "Terry's Temper" may be stated like this:

Theme:

Learning to control one's temper is an important part of maturing emotionally and spiritually.

2. *Determine the age level of your reading audience.* You need to do this because the main character should usually be about the same age as the readers for whom you write the story. In your school assignments, you will write to your own age level unless otherwise directed. You are naturally most familiar with the interests and characteristics of your own age group.

Writing for children of a younger age level is a special challenge. You need to thoroughly familiarize yourself with their mannerisms and vocabulary. Give your descriptions of the appearance and behavior of children on their own level, not as it appears to you. For example, be careful about calling them *little, cute, silly,* and so forth. Children like to think of themselves as big, and they do *not* consider themselves silly.

Whether you write to your own age level or to a different age level, you must plan and write consistently. Ask yourself frequently, "Will my readers be able to involve themselves in this story?" The age level for the first sample story may be written like this:

> **Age level:**
> early and mid teens

3. *Determine the basic identity of the major characters.* With rare exceptions, you should put the main character on the age level of your intended audience. This is an important part of aiming your story at your audience. Do not attempt to describe these characters at this point. In fact, you need not even name them now.

The basic identity of the major characters in the first sample story may be written as follows:

> **Major characters:**
> a fifteen-year-old boy, his twelve-year-old brother, and his father

4. *Decide from what point of view you will write the story.* Consider the advantages and disadvantages of each point of view that you studied in Lesson 53; they are summarized below. Also decide whether you want your story to be subjective or objective.

> **First person:**
> Gives strong impression of reality; limits writer to one character's viewpoint; makes it difficult to portray the main character's good qualities.
>
> **Third person:**
> Limits writer to one character's viewpoint; makes it easier to portray the main character's good qualities.
>
> **Omniscient:**
> Allows writer to report on different characters at various places; does not bring the reader to identify with any character in the story.

5. *Write a sentence summarizing the conflict.* This sentence should not describe the individual incidents in the conflict; it should merely give a general view of the conflict. A suitable conflict must be typical of the age level you are writing to. It should also appear difficult for the main character to handle. Remember that a suitable conflict does not need to be something unusual or dramatic. Here is a statement of conflict for the first sample story.

> **Conflict:**
> Terry struggles to overcome his tendency to become angry when things do not go as he wishes.

Developing a general plan like this will force you to take an overall view of your story. This overall view, in turn, will help you to produce a unified, smooth-flowing story. The following example brings together all the points in the general plan for the first sample story.

Theme:

Learning to control one's temper is an important part of maturing emotionally and spiritually.

Age level:

early and mid teens

Main character:

a fifteen-year-old boy

Other major characters:

boy's twelve-year-old brother and boy's father

Point of view:

third person, subjective

Conflict:

Terry struggles to overcome his tendency to become angry when things do not go as he wishes.

Applying the Lesson

Write a general plan for the story possibility you chose in Lesson 49, which will be the basis of a story that you will write in this chapter.

---

55. Planning the Details of a Story

The general plan you developed in Lesson 54 represents an important beginning to your story writing. But you still are not ready to write the actual story. You need to do the more detailed planning that this lesson describes.

Use the following steps to plan the details of your short story.

1. *Write descriptions of all the major characters.* For each character, you will make two lists. In the first one, list some details about the character's appearance. Look each character over carefully in your mind's eye, and then describe him in detail. Is he tall or short? muscular or slight? What color is his hair? Is it neatly combed? Not all of these details will receive even a passing comment in the story, but you should list them to give yourself a well-rounded view of your character, especially if the story is fictitious.

In your second list, write some traits of inner character. Is the person shy? impulsive? greedy? diligent? honest? The more familiar you are with the characters of your story, the more realistically you will be able to have them act in the story. Be careful, though. The traits you list must give a consistent picture of a real life or true-to-life individual.

If your characters are real people whom you know, this step may be quite easy. However, you could consider changing some details about a character's appearance or even his inner traits if you wish to conceal the true identity of the characters. If they are fictitious, you will need to spend extra time learning to know them in your mind.

Here is this part of the detailed plan for the first sample story, "Terry's Temper."

Appearance:	**Inner traits:**
Light brown hair	Diligent
Blue eyes	Tends toward being perfectionistic
Strong, muscular build	Not very talkative
Medium height	Sensitive

2. *Plan the opening.* Write a short description of the setting. Include the time, place, and atmosphere. Briefly describe the opening scene. Begin as near to the first scene of conflict as possible. Remember, you can often include important background information in a flashback more effectively than in the opening. And do not forget to hint at the theme and the conflict of the story.

Here is a plan for the opening of the first sample story.

Setting:

A south-central Pennsylvania farm, on a pleasant day in mid-May. A fine Christian family atmosphere.

Opening scene:

Terry and Walter are outside on the first day of summer vacation. Terry comments that the lawn needs to be mowed and then that their worn-out mower might not last the whole season.

3. *Plan each scene in the conflict.* In a brief paragraph, describe the basic events of each scene and the outcome of that scene. Be sure these incidents grow directly out of the conflict, that they develop the theme, and that they reveal the characters' traits. If you are using a complication plot, arrange the scenes in order of increasing importance to the final outcome and of increasing difficulty for the main character to solve.

Give special attention to the climaxing scene, for this is the most critical point in the story. At this point, the main character makes his final decision for or against the right course. Here is a plan for the scenes of conflict in the first sample story.

Incident 1:

The mower quits working before Terry finishes mowing. He becomes angry and jerks the starter cord so hard that it tears.

Incident 2:

Walter forgets to close the door to the feed bin chute after emptying the bin. When Terry tries to fill the bin, a huge pile of feed spills out on the barn floor. Terry scolds his brother harshly, but Father hears him and rebukes him.

Incident 3:

The heifers get out and give Terry and Walter quite a chase. Terry is strongly tempted to become angry, but he overcomes the temptation and responds properly.

4. *Plan the ending.* Briefly describe the main character's actions in carrying out the climaxing decision. Then in closing, describe the final outcome. Show and impress upon the reader the story theme through the main character's responses. If any important questions about the major characters have not been answered, briefly dispose of them. Do not include distracting remarks about minor characters or about later events involving the main character.

Here is a plan for the ending of the first sample story.

Ending:

Father comes home just as the boys are getting the last heifer back in. He commends Terry for keeping his temper under control.

Below is the complete plan for the details in the sample story "Terry's Temper."

Appearance:

Light brown hair
Blue eyes
Strong, muscular build
Medium height

Inner traits:

Diligent
Tends toward being perfectionistic
Not very talkative
Sensitive

Setting:

A south-central Pennsylvania farm, on a pleasant day in mid-May. A fine Christian family atmosphere.

Opening scene:

Terry and Walter are outside on the first day of summer vacation. Terry comments that the lawn needs to be mowed and then that their worn-out mower might not last the whole season.

Incident 1:

The mower quits working before Terry finishes mowing. He becomes angry and jerks the starter cord so hard that it tears.

Incident 2:

Walter forgets to close the door to the feed bin chute after emptying the bin. When Terry tries to fill the bin, a huge pile of feed spills out on the barn floor. Terry scolds his brother harshly, but Father hears him and rebukes him.

Incident 3:

The heifers get out and give Terry and Walter quite a chase. Terry is strongly tempted to become angry, but he overcomes the temptation and responds properly.

Ending:

Father comes home just as the boys are getting the last heifer back in. He commends Terry for keeping his temper under control.

Applying the Lesson

Write a detailed plan for your story, following the steps in this lesson.

56. Writing a Story

Now that you have planned your story in detail, you are ready to write. But remember that your plan is a guide, not a set of ironclad rules. You may well discover in the actual writing process that you need to add or delete ideas in some parts of the story. You may find that the incidents are not in the best order and should be rearranged. You may even decide that a certain incident in the story needs to be completely reworked. Make whatever changes are needed, shaping and reshaping the story as you work.

Use the following steps in writing your story.

1. *Write your opening scene.* If the first paragraph is dull, a reader may lay your story aside without even reading it. So begin with action, dialogue, or an unusual statement. Read again the opening paragraphs from the two sample stories in Lesson 49. Notice how each one begins.

Begins with dialogue:

> "Three months to enjoy the farm!" Terry voiced his thoughts to twelve-year-old Walter. The previous day had marked the last day of his ninth year in school. A pleasant mid-May sun smiled on the lush growth of grass. Terry took deep breaths of the fresh, exhilarating air. Brushing his hand across his well-combed hair, he glanced at Walter's unkempt hair.

Begins with an unusual statement:

> My hands were mechanically cutting apples into neat halves when Mother's words burst into my thoughts. "Grandmother Fry called this morning. She asked if it would suit for you to spend the weekend with her. She said you help her to feel secure because she knows you are dependable. There'll be no school Friday, so you could go on Thursday evening. We'd pick you up again on Sunday afternoon."

Besides attracting attention and interest, the opening paragraphs should also introduce the main character. In fact, the first character to speak, to do something, or to be introduced should usually be the main character. Look again at the opening paragraphs in the examples above. The main character is speaking in the first example and acting in the second.

Sometimes the opening paragraphs weave in a few details of the setting. In the first example, you learn that the story occurs on a farm in mid-May. In the second example, you can deduct that the story occurs in a kitchen (that is the most likely place to be cutting apples into halves) in the fall (apples are a fall crop and school has begun). The second example also hints at the emotional mood by using the words *mechanically* and *burst.*

2. *Write the scenes in the conflict.* Be careful to characterize the story characters consistently. Refer to your detailed descriptions of the major characters before writing each incident in the conflict. Keep asking yourself, "Are these characters' words, actions, and appearances consistent with the way I have described them?"

Provide smooth transitions from one incident to the next. For example, in the story "Terry's Temper," the second incident begins with the words "One morning several days later." This shows the relationship between the two incidents. The third incident begins with the words "The following day." In the story "'He Rides Upon the Storm,'" the second incident begins with the words "The following Saturday." And the third incident begins with the words "That very night." Each of these transitions helps the reader to move from one incident to the next without confusion.

Use occasional flashbacks to provide important background information. "'He Rides Upon the Storm'" has a flashback at the beginning of the second incident. It is underlined in the following excerpt.

> The following Saturday, I hurried from the flower bed I was weeding and burst into the kitchen. "Alta," I gasped, "there's a man coming in the lane. A bushy-haired, scary-looking man! Whatever will we do?" I wailed.
>
> Father's parting words flashed across my mind: "Well, Alta, you'll be in charge for a few hours. Wanda, you pitch in and help take care of the little ones. In case of an emergency, call Uncle Ralph's. Above all, trust in the Lord." Then he and Mother had left to visit Aunt Mattie in the hospital.
>
> Alta glanced out the window. "We'll trust the Lord," she said. The man had nearly reached the house.

3. *Write the ending.* After the climax, the reader should be satisfied. Bring your story to a prompt close. Make the ending *show* the theme of the story; do not directly state it. If the reader has not caught the theme throughout the story, he will not be impressed by a direct statement at the end. The following sentence would *not* be a good one to include in the last paragraph of the second sample story: "These experiences helped to teach me that simple trust in the Lord brings peace even in uncertain and frightening circumstances."

4. *Write an interesting title.* The title should hint at the story theme without giving away the outcome. It should be short, generally not more than five words, and it should be fresh and original. Alliteration, rhyming words, and unusual word combinations can increase the appeal of titles. Compare the following titles for the stories in this chapter.

Good titles:	**Poor titles:**
Terry's Temper (is short; uses alliteration)	Terry Learns to Control His Anger (is long; gives away outcome) Terry's Misplaced Energy (misses story theme)
"He Rides Upon the Storm" (uses an interesting quotation) Worrying Wanda (is short; uses alliteration)	"Above All, Trust in the Lord" (is long; states theme too directly) Wanda Learns to Trust (gives away outcome)
Twenty Pounds (is short; is appealing because *pounds* can mean different things)	Mother's Faith Is Rewarded (gives away outcome) How Twenty Pounds Became Worth a Million (is long; gives away outcome)

Applying the Lesson

Write the first draft of your story, following the steps in this lesson. Write on every other line to allow room for revising. Your story should have 700–1,000 words.

Be sure to save this first draft. You will do further work with it in Chapter 8.

---

57. Improving Your Speaking Style, Part 2: Voice Control

In Lesson 17 you learned that eye contact is one important element of an effective speaking style. Look directly at individuals in your audience. Establish eye contact early in your speech, use eye contact to emphasize major points throughout the speech, and close the speech on a solid note with eye contact.

Your *voice control* also affects your speaking style. Actually, your voice reveals many things about you. It shows whether you are careless or careful, tense or relaxed, timid or confident. This becomes especially important when you speak to a group. The listeners should sense that you are eager to communicate something worthwhile to them. If your voice suggests that you are bored with your subject, the listeners will be bored too!

The following paragraphs discuss four important elements of proper voice control.

1. *Articulation.* You need to open your mouth well and pronounce each word distinctly, for your talk will lose its effect if the listeners cannot understand you. They may be able to miss a considerable number of sounds and still understand what you mean; but the greater the number of sounds missed, the greater the chance of misunderstanding.

Of course, you must also avoid the extreme of exaggerated articulation. Your voice sounds best when it is clear, natural, and relaxed.

2. *Volume.* This is probably the first thing you think of when you consider voice control. Be sure to speak loudly enough so that your listeners need not strain to hear you. No matter how many other good qualities your voice may have, your talk will not be effective if the audience cannot hear what you say.

On the other hand, speaking too loudly is just as ineffective as speaking too softly. Your voice must not be so loud that your listeners feel uncomfortable. Rather, you should have a pleasant variety, using the greatest volume for your most important points. This variety will help you to avoid a boring manner of speech.

Look at the following sentences. What pattern of volume would be appropriate for each one?

> Does this mean that we should compromise principle for peace? God forbid! God forbid that we ever compromise principle for peace.

> Sometimes we may feel like compromising. But true peace is never gained that way.

The first example should begin with moderate volume and build up to strong volume for the words *God forbid.* The reverse pattern should be used in the second example—beginning loud and gradually becoming softer. In the third example, the volume should increase through the word *compromising* and then decrease. These differences in volume help to put proper emphasis where it belongs.

3. *Pitch.* This aspect of the voice is directly affected by emotions. When you are calm and confident, your voice pitch is generally lower than when you are excited or anxious. Therefore, make a deliberate effort to relax and use the lower tones in your voice range.

You must modulate your pitch according to what you are saying. In everyday speech, do you state a fact, ask a question, and make an exclamation with every word at the same pitch? Of course not—and neither should you do that in speaking to a group. Raise and lower the pitch of your voice to communicate as you would in a normal conversation. Few things deaden a talk more than a voice droning on and on in a monotone.

Pitch and volume generally go together, with high pitch accompanying strong volume and lower pitch accompanying lower volume. Notice how this is true as you again read the sample sentences above. When you do use falling pitch and volume (especially at the end of a sentence), be careful not to reduce them too much. Otherwise, your listeners will fail to catch the last words.

4. *Speed.* Regulating your flow of speech is another aspect of voice control. Try to speak at the same comfortable speed that you use in conversation. You should not have long, awkward pauses, but neither should you try to fill in pauses by using *uh*'s and *ah*'s. Try to use a natural variety, speaking faster to express excitement or enthusiasm and slowing down to emphasize major points.

Which of the following sentences should be spoken slowly? Which should be spoken more rapidly? The answers should be obvious.

> To understand that significance, we should first consider the origin of the Pharisees. (major point)
>
> The Pharisees drew primarily from the ranks of the scribes, in contrast to the Sadducees, who came primarily from the priests. (supporting detail)

Some voices just naturally sound more pleasant than others; there is little we can do about that. But regardless of the natural sound of your voice, you will communicate at your best if you speak clearly and use a variety of volume, pitch, and speed. A well-modulated voice is constantly changing to express the meanings known and *felt* by the speaker. If you follow these guidelines and put your heart into your message, you will communicate well with your audience.

Applying the Lesson

A. Two sample stories appear in Lesson 49: "Terry's Temper" and "'He Rides Upon the Storm.'" Practice reading paragraphs from these stories in class, with good voice control as taught in the lesson.

B. Choose a story that you know well and that you can tell in three to five minutes. It may be from your own experience, or it may be an incident you have heard or read. After your teacher approves your story, prepare to tell it to your class. Concentrate on effective voice control, and remember also to maintain eye contact with your listeners.

---

58. Chapter 6 Review

A. Write the correct words to complete these statements.

1. The most important goal for writing any short story should be to ———.
2. You will find it easiest to write about ——— subjects.
3. A short story does not need to be about some ——— subject; it can deal with common, everyday happenings.
4. The lesson a story teaches is the ——— of the story.
5. A short story should develop ——— theme rather than several themes.
6. The setting should be introduced in the ———.
7. The setting includes the ———, the ———, and the ———.
8. The struggle or problem that the main character faces is the story ———.
9. If the main character struggles to overcome the habit of gossip, the story conflict is between the main character and ———.
10. If the main character struggles to accept the handicap of a crippling disease, the story conflict is between the main character and ———.
11. If the main character must resist the wrong influence of some worldly cousins, the story conflict is between the main character and ———.
12. The overall development of a story conflict is the ———.
13. With a complication plot, the conflict should ——— as the story progresses.
14. The process of portraying story characters is called ———.
15. The main character of a story is sometimes called the ———.
16. A person opposing the main character is called the ———.
17. Characters that should be named but not characterized very much are ——— characters.
18. Characters that should be clearly characterized are ——— characters.
19. Characters that are often not even named are ——— characters.
20. Every story portrays the characters by their ——— and ———.
21. In addition to the methods above, characters may be portrayed by their ———, ———, or ———.
22. The perspective from which an author writes a story is the ——— of that story.
23. When the author writes as if he is able to see every character equally well, he is writing from the ——— point of view.
24. When the author uses *I* and portrays himself as the main character, he is writing from the ——— point of view.

25. When the author follows one particular character through the story, he is writing from the ——— point of view.
26. The ——— point of view carries a strong impression of reality.
27. If a story reveals any character's thoughts, its viewpoint is ———.
28. If a story does not reveal any character's thoughts, its viewpoint is ———.
29. The four elements of voice control are ———, ———, ———, and ———.
30. You should have variety in all the elements of voice control except ———.

B. For each of these samples, write a suitable theme that it would be likely to develop.

1. A few minutes' work by the experienced woodsmen brought the giant maple crashing down, shaking the earth beneath their feet. Then suddenly John and his crew found themselves listening to the greatest torrent of profanity that they had ever heard from Graham McIntosh. The huge tree was hollow; and Graham was expressing his displeasure.

   Brother John slowly moved over to stand beside Graham. When the volley of vulgar words finally ended, John turned to face him. "Graham, why do you swear?" he asked simply.

   "Why, I—I—I—" Graham's face flushed, and his hands went in and out of his pockets. "I—I—I don't swear near as much as some men do. And, anyhow—well—what does it matter how I talk, anyway?"

   "Did you know," John asked softly, "the Bible says that 'every idle word that men shall speak, they shall give account thereof in the day of judgment'?"

   Graham had nothing further to say, and after a few moments of silence, John returned to his chain saw. Graham watched the men for a few minutes more; and then, with his usual call of "Don't work too hard," he left.

   A week later, John and his wife were driving through a neighboring town when they saw Graham on the sidewalk. He raised his hand in friendly greeting as they passed.

   "You know," John mused, "Graham has really seemed different the last while. Especially since he's so careful about his language when we're working for him."

2. Thomas walked briskly as he headed toward the barn. It seemed that extra jobs always awaited him on the family dairy farm. So this Saturday he planned a head start for next week. And a prompt start would mean more time this evening for the Sunday school lesson.

   "Father and Mother have an errand to run today. He suggested that I use the day at my discretion. That points to the calf pens. Their cleaning is overdue. I can hustle through the Saturday chores by nine o'clock and finish the pens by midafternoon. Then if I finish writing that story before milking time, I won't have to take the time from next week," Thomas thought as he mentally planned his day.

Whistling cheerfully, Thomas finished washing the milkers. He trotted through the barn, grabbed a straw bale with each hand, and began bedding the heifers. The rumble of a car motor alerted his thoughts. "Likely a neighbor passing; no reason to stop and look." But the sound did not move on. "Well, I'll have to check," he decided, reluctantly dropping his bale.

Yes, it was Mrs. Berry, their widowed neighbor.

"Good morning," he greeted.

"My goat is out again." Her aging voice trembled. "I was wondering if you had time to help me catch her."

"Certainly," agreed Thomas. "I'll be right over."

3. Breathing a prayer for wisdom and patience, I went to the door. "Good afternoon, Mr. Daley," I said pleasantly as a cool fall breeze blew in.

"Good afternoon, nuthin'!" Mr. Daley thundered. His six-foot, three-hundred-pound frame towered above me on the porch. Disheveled hair, tobacco-stained beard, and grimy clothes accentuated the harsh voice. "Think you gonna put your fence three feet on my side of the line, eh? Well, you just take those posts off my property 'fore mornin', or else!"

"I'm sorry, Mr. Daley," I answered, trying hard to keep my voice calm. "I'm putting the fence exactly where it was before."

"Yep, I know. That fence's always been on my side of the line, and I'm tired of it. I won't have a new fence put there. Leastways not by a Bible-quoting sissy of a Mennonite!"

"Well, Mr. Daley, if you have a few minutes, let's just go right down there now and mark where that line should be," I suggested.

4. Debra blinked, but the tears multiplied faster than she could blink them away. "If only I could hike along with the other girls tomorrow up to Vista Peak. Wish Father would be more reasonable."

But then her conscience smote her. "That's not fair to your father. You know quite well that with Mother ill, you're needed at home. What about that verse you read this morning about honoring your parents?"

"Oh, I know." At Debra's voice, Princess perked up her ears and wagged her tail. "Lord, help me to be respectful," Debra prayed as she looked up to the beautiful mountains that rose abruptly behind the family farm.

"Well, Princess, I'd better get back in the house and finish the dishes." Debra gave her pet a final caress and resolutely strode for the kitchen. Soon her voice swelled with the words "Count your many blessings."

Through Mother's bedroom door came the sound of Debra's melodious voice. "Praise the Lord!" Mother said to herself. "That sounds like Debra's usual, cheerful self again." The lines on her face relaxed, and soon she was sleeping peacefully.

C. Answer these questions about the setting of the samples in Part B.
   1. a. What is the day of the week in sample 2?
      b. In what season of the year does sample 3 occur?
      c. Does sample 4 occur during warm weather or cold weather?
   2. What do you learn about the place of sample 4?
   3. How would you describe the atmosphere of sample 4?

D. For each sample in Part B, write whether the main character's conflict is with *another person, circumstances,* or *himself.*

E. Do these exercises about the characters of the samples in Part B.
   1. In sample 1, who is the main character? Who is another major character? Who are the background characters?
   2. In sample 2, who is the main character? Who is the minor character? Who are the background characters?
   3. Give two specific examples of characterization by actions. (Give the characters, the actions, and the traits revealed.)
   4. Give three specific examples of characterization by speech. (Give the characters, the speech, and the traits revealed.)
   5. Give two specific examples of characterization by thoughts. (Give the characters, the thoughts, and the traits revealed.)
   6. Give one specific example of characterization by appearance. (Give the character, the appearance, and the trait revealed.)
   7. Give two specific examples of characterization by reputation. (Give the characters, the reputation, and the traits revealed.)

F. For each sample in Part B, write which point of view is used. Include *subjective* or *objective* where applicable.

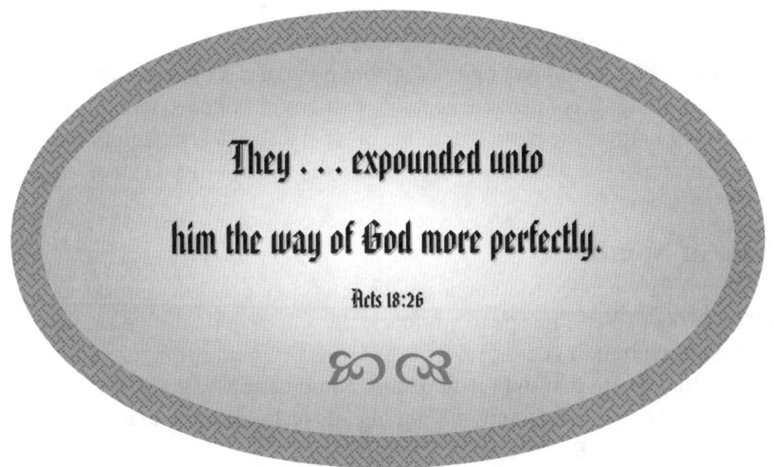

They . . . expounded unto
him the way of God more perfectly.
Acts 18:26

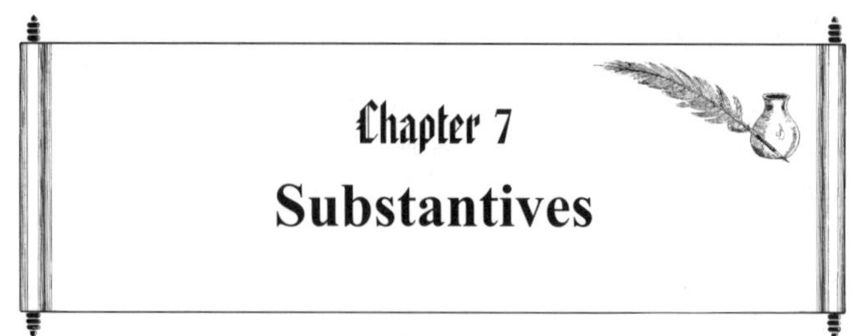

59. Identifying Nouns

As you have known for years, a noun is the name of a person, place, thing, or idea. Nouns constitute the backbone of language. To a large extent, we use nouns to express the main ideas in our communication.

Concrete and Abstract Nouns

A noun names a person, place, thing, or idea. Nouns are either concrete or abstract. A concrete noun names a person, place, or thing, usually with physical substance that we can perceive through the senses. An abstract noun names an idea that does not have physical substance and that we cannot perceive through the senses.

Concrete:

carpenter	church	grass
Edward	Potter County	automobile

Abstract:

job	mercy	courage
parable	humility	righteousness
idea		

Names referring to God, spiritual beings (like *cherubim*), and spiritual places (like *paradise*) are also concrete nouns. Although they do not have physical substance that we can perceive through our senses, they are real persons, places, and things.

Common and Proper Nouns

Nouns are either common or proper. A common noun is the general name of a person, place, or thing. It is the name *common* to a group of items, and it is not capitalized. A proper noun is the particular name of a person, place, or thing. It is the name *proper* for one specific item, and it is capitalized. In Lesson 1 you studied ten groupings of proper nouns.

Gender of Nouns

All nouns have gender. Masculine gender refers to persons or animals that are male (*boy, father, buck*). Feminine gender refers to persons or animals that are female (*girl, mother, doe*). Common gender refers to persons or animals that are either male or female, or to a group that may include any combination of genders (*child, parent, deer*). Neuter gender refers to nonliving objects or to abstract nouns, which can be neither male nor female (*door, river, cheerfulness*).

Noun-forming Suffixes

Many nouns, especially abstract nouns, end with noun-forming suffixes. The following are common noun-forming suffixes: *-ment, -ity, -ness, -ion, -ation, -dom, -ance, -ence, -ude, -al, -ship, -hood, -er, -or,* and *-ar.* The pairs of words below illustrate how these suffixes are used to form nouns from other parts of speech or from other nouns.

appoint—appointment	solitary—solitude
free—freedom	deprive—deprival, deprivation
continue—continuation, continuance	child—childhood

Other Words Used as Nouns

A word is classified as a certain part of speech not only because of its basic meaning but also because of how it is used in a sentence. When used with their normal meanings, some words are always nouns, some are never nouns, and some may be either nouns or other parts of speech. Can you place each of the following words into one of those three categories?

right	apple	near	calmness
sweetly	reliance	look	retain

Calmness and *reliance* are always nouns. *Sweetly, near,* and *retain* are never nouns. *Right, apple,* and *look* are sometimes nouns and sometimes other parts of speech.

Perhaps you notice that *apple* can actually serve as an adjective sometimes, as in *apple tree.* But dictionaries generally do not label *apple* as an adjective. This is an example of an attributive noun—a noun that precedes another noun and functions as an adjective. In its basic essence, however, such a word is a noun.

Applying the Lesson

A. Copy each noun, and label it *C* (concrete) or *A* (abstract).

1. Sincere worship and praise ascend to God like the sweet incense that Aaron offered.
2. The true believer feels his unworthiness and insufficiency.
3. A careful study of the Scriptures increases our spiritual understanding.
4. Faithful characters of the Old Testament are an inspiration to us today.
5. While the dough was slowly rising, Mother heated the oven.
6. After dinner the boys will cut the thistles in the pasture.
7. As we entered the damp cave, an uneasy feeling caused our hearts to beat more rapidly.
8. The confidence of our guide soon dispelled our fears.

B. Copy each noun, and write *M* (masculine), *F* (feminine), *N* (neuter), or *C* (common) to label its gender.

1. In humble devotion, Mary approached her beloved Master.
2. Breaking her alabaster box, she poured precious ointment on His feet.

3. The disciples thought that the act of this worshiper was a great waste.
4. She could have sold her gift and used the money to help the poor.
5. Jesus praised the woman for her noble sacrifice of such a great gift.
6. At the request of Balaam, King Balak offered seven bullocks and seven rams on seven altars.
7. The aged bishop addressed the members of the church with tender affection.
8. The matron at Grand View Children's Home supervises the activities of the children.

C. Add a noun-forming suffix to each word in parentheses so that it fits in the sentence.
1. Thomas Edison, a famous (invent), possessed great (determine) and (persevere).
2. His (develop) of the light bulb came only after thousands of (fail) and (disappoint).
3. Scientists had made the (declare) that the (construct) of Edison's light was an (impossible).
4. Edison's (hard) were repaid when he and his assistants watched in (elate) the gentle (radiate) of the first successful bulb.
5. In the (Create), God produced (illuminate) by His simple (command) that there be light.
6. God did not need to exercise (persevere), for through His infinite (able) He could make light immediately without a single (err).
7. Edison's first (achieve) of success produced a light that burned about forty-five hours; but God's light (produce), the sun, has been in (exist) for nearly six thousand years.
8. In (compare) to the work of God, Edison's light fades into (pale) and (insignificant).

D. Write whether each word is *always, never,* or *sometimes* a noun.

1. idea	7. solidify
2. contrast	8. preacher
3. swallow	9. spoken
4. contain	10. generally
5. salvation	11. cook
6. jump	12. childhood

Review Exercises

A. Identify the structure of each sentence as simple (*S*), compound (*CD*), complex (*CX*), or compound-complex (*CD-CX*). [25]
1. Beware of a person who says he hates gossip.
2. By perseverance the snail reached the ark.
3. A lie travels around the world while truth is putting on her shoes.
4. Confess that you were wrong yesterday; it will show that you are wiser today.
5. Carry an appetite to God's house, and you will be fed.

B. Identify the word order of each sentence as natural (*N*), inverted (*I*), or mixed (*M*). [25]
1. Christ's soldiers fight best on their knees.
2. When everybody talks, nobody hears.
3. After the cup of affliction comes the cup of consolation.
4. Guilt on the conscience puts grief on the countenance.
5. On a long journey, even a straw is heavy.

C. Identify the style of each sentence as loose (*L*), periodic (*P*), or balanced (*B*). [25]
1. Children may make a rich man poor, but they make a poor man rich.
2. If you want a boy to move fast, say, "Now, my man!"
3. Do not leave your heart at home when you go to worship.
4. Holiness is not the way to Christ, but Christ is the way to holiness.
5. The best book about Christ is His living biography, written out in the words and actions of His people.

---

60. Verbals and Clauses as Nouns

Most nouns are single words or compound words whose normal, basic meanings make them nouns. Sometimes, however, other words and word groups serve to name persons, places, things, or ideas. The most common of these are verbals, verbal phrases, and clauses. Study the following sentences. In each one, the subject is underlined.

> <u>Faith</u> is essential to a life that pleases God. (simple single word)
> <u>To believe</u> is not enough in itself. (infinitive)
> <u>Obeying the Bible</u> must complement a profession of faith. (gerund phrase)
> <u>How a person lives</u> determines the truth of his profession. (noun clause)

Verbals as Nouns

Verbals hold two jobs. On the one hand, they are verb forms that have many characteristics of verbs. On the other hand, they function in a sentence as some other part of speech. Two kinds of verbals can function as nouns: the gerund and the infinitive. When the gerund or the infinitive has adverb modifiers or complements, the word group is a verbal phrase. The entire verbal phrase then functions as a noun.

1. *Gerunds and gerund phrases.* A gerund is the present participle (the *-ing* form) of a verb used as a noun. It functions as the subject of a sentence, as a verb complement, or as the object of a preposition. Rather than expressing action, as a verb does, the gerund *names* an action.

> <u>Studying</u> requires a great deal of concentration.
> (The subject *Studying* names an action; it is a gerund.)

Aunt Thelma enjoys painting these colorful scenes.

(The direct object *painting these colorful scenes* names an action; it is a gerund phrase.)

Grandfather Weaver's hobby is carving.

(The predicate nominative *carving* names an action; it is a gerund.)

Brother Elmer added a room to his shop for storing lumber.

(The object of the preposition, *storing lumber,* names an action; it is a gerund phrase.)

Sentence diagrams can help you to evaluate the place that a verbal or verbal phrase fills in a sentence. Remember that a verbal used as a noun is diagramed on a pedestal. Observe specifically the noun position filled by each gerund.

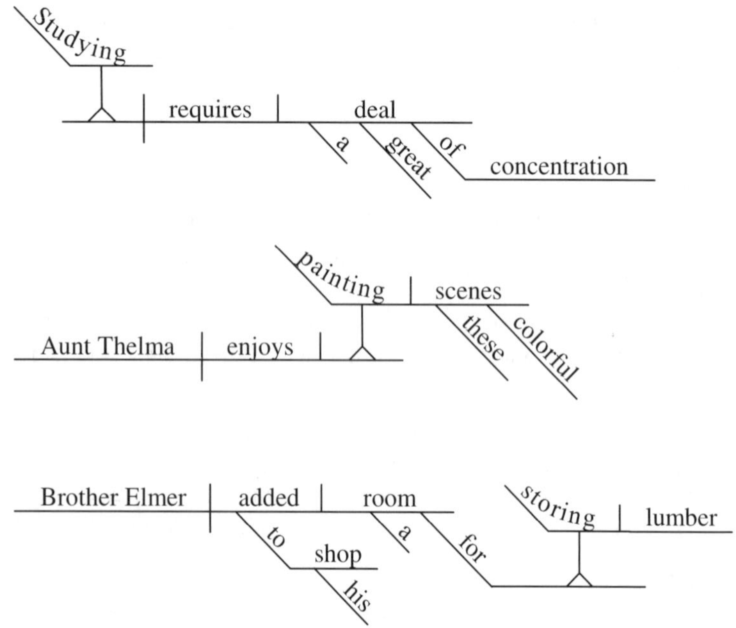

Be especially careful that you do not confuse a gerund functioning as a predicate nominative with the present participle form of a true verb. In both cases the *-ing* form may follow a form of *be.* If the word is a gerund, however, it must name an action and rename the subject. If the word is part of the verb phrase, it will express the action that the subject is performing. Examining the meaning of the sentence and reading the skeleton should help you decide which it is.

Sister Ruth's main responsibility at the rest home is keeping the residents' rooms clean. (*Keeping the residents' rooms clean* renames the subject *responsibility;* it is a gerund phrase.)

Her job certainly is keeping her busy.

(*Keeping* does not rename the subject *job;* it expresses the action that the subject is performing; it is part of the verb phrase.)

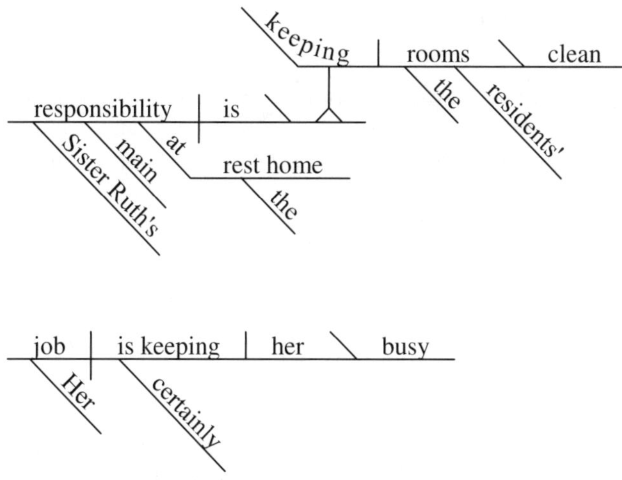

2. *Infinitives and infinitive phrases.* An infinitive is the basic form of a verb preceded by *to.* An infinitive is a noun when it names an action and fills a noun function in the sentence.

> To persevere requires determination and endurance.
> (The subject *To persevere* names an action; it is an infinitive.)
>
> God promises to bless His faithful servants.
> (The direct object *to bless His faithful servants* names an action; it is an infinitive phrase.)
>
> God's desire has always been to preserve a people for Himself.
> (The predicate nominative *to preserve a people for Himself* names an action; it is an infinitive phrase.)

Notice on each diagram how the infinitive fills the place of a regular noun in each sentence.

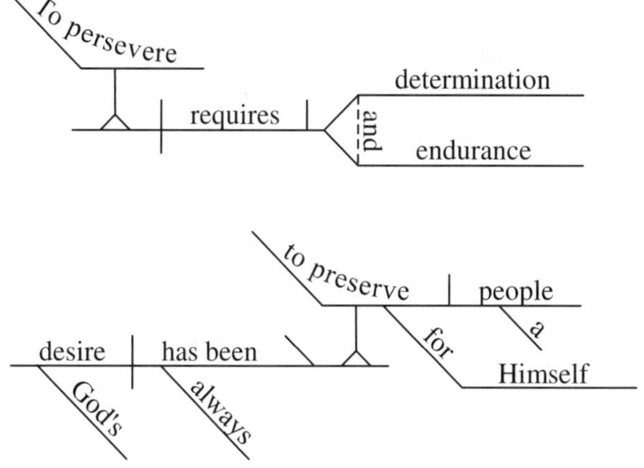

Do not confuse infinitives with prepositional phrases that begin with *to*. *To* plus the basic form of a verb makes an infinitive. *To* plus a noun or pronoun makes a prepositional phrase.

Nancy plans to bake bread, and she will take some to Grandmother Smith.
(*To bake bread* is *to* plus a basic verb form; it is an infinitive phrase. *To Grandmother Smith* is *to* plus a noun; it is a prepositional phrase.)

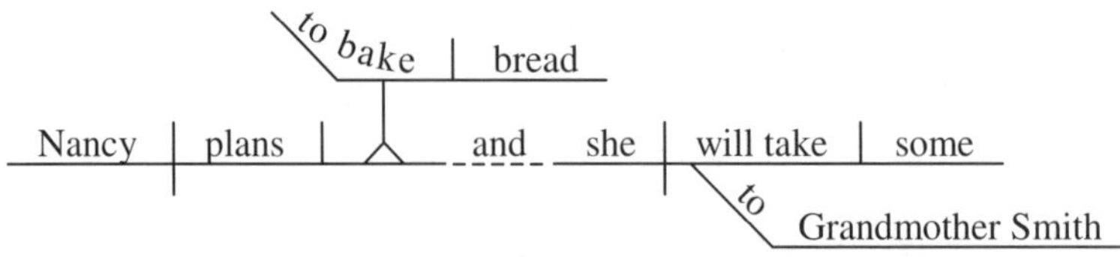

Noun Clauses

A noun clause is a dependent clause with a noun function in a complex sentence. Unlike an adjective or an adverb clause, a noun clause is a basic part of the independent clause except when it serves as the object of a preposition. In a complex sentence containing a noun clause, therefore, the two clauses are sometimes hard to identify.

When a sentence contains a noun clause used as a verb complement, the two clauses are usually quite easy to identify. Especially obvious are the clauses that function as direct and indirect quotations. Almost always they are noun clauses used as direct objects. In the following sentences, the noun clauses are in brackets and the skeletons of both clauses are underlined.

Grandfather said [that his arthritis was bothering him].
(The clause in brackets is the direct object of *said.*)

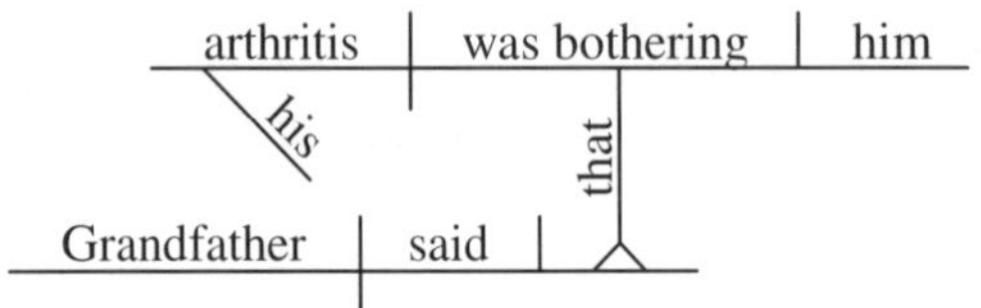

Mrs. Kendig offered [whoever was thirsty] a drink of cold tea.
(The clause in brackets is the indirect object of *offered.*)

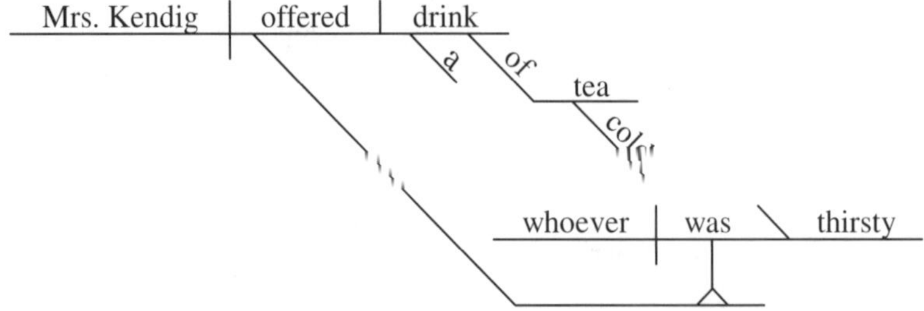

This rain is [what the crops desperately needed].
(The clause in brackets is a predicate nominative renaming *rain.*)

When a sentence contains a noun clause used as a subject, the two clauses may be difficult to identify. The entire noun clause serves as the subject of the independent clause; therefore, the skeleton of that independent clause may be difficult to detect. In the following sentences, the noun clauses are again in brackets. The skeletons of the noun clauses are underlined, and the verbs of the independent clauses are underlined.

[Whoever wants salvation] must believe the Gospel.
(The clause in brackets is the subject of the independent clause.)

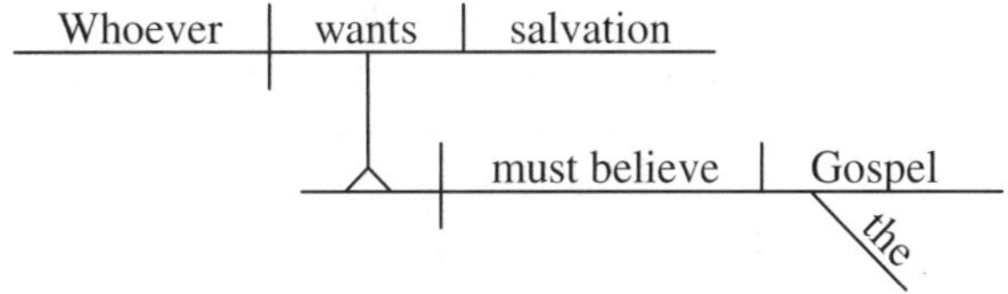

[Whose sweater this is] remains a mystery to us.
(The clause in brackets is the subject of the independent clause.)

A noun clause functioning as the object of a preposition is not a basic part of the independent clause. Therefore, the two clauses should be easy to identify. The following sentences show the noun clauses in brackets, with the skeletons of both clauses underlined.

Louis Pasteur took a great interest in [what causes diseases].

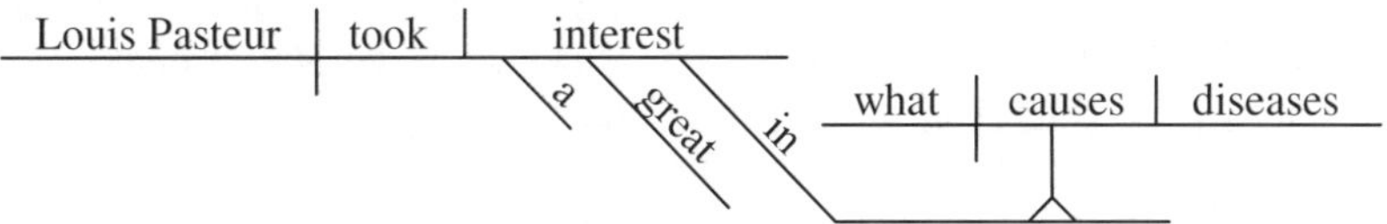

Today we benefit greatly from [what he discovered].

Applying the Lesson

A. If the underlined item is a noun phrase, identify its function by writing *subject, direct object, predicate nominative,* or *object of a preposition.* If it is not a noun phrase, write *none.*

1. The ultimate purpose for every created being is to glorify the Creator.
2. Peace with one's own self and with others requires living in peace with the Lord.
3. Overcoming temptation in our own strength is a foolish endeavor.
4. The only way to victory over sin is through the power of the Lord.
5. A godly man wants to receive the wisdom of God.
6. To view life from God's point of view means that we must take our eyes off self.
7. However, too many people are thinking too much of themselves.

8. True fullness of life comes by <u>emptying ourselves of all that is selfish</u>.
9. We can find true happiness in <u>seeking the happiness of others</u>.
10. The Christian's greatest joy will be <u>seeing his Saviour face to face</u>.

B. Copy each verbal or verbal phrase, and write whether it is a gerund (*G*), a gerund phrase (*GP*), an infinitive (*I*), or an infinitive phrase (*IP*).

1. Stacking those boxes that high is not wise.
2. The lame horse has finally managed to stand.
3. This evening Maryann's job will be to wash the dishes.
4. Helping in Grandfather's small-engine shop is Nevin's chief delight.
5. We can often learn many things by listening.
6. To sleep is to refresh the body's energy and alertness.
7. Working can often relax a body that is tired from study or nervous strain.
8. By thinking ahead, we can often spare ourselves the pain and shame of foolish mistakes.
9. To procrastinate is rarely a reasonable option for facing difficult circumstances.
10. Sledding is practically unknown in this flat country.

C. If the underlined word group is a noun clause, identify its function by writing *subject, direct object, indirect object, predicate nominative,* or *object of a preposition.* If it is not a noun clause, write *none.*

1. Mortal man will never fully understand <u>how the physical world works</u>.
2. <u>Whoever considers himself wise</u> knows nothing yet as he ought to know.
3. Your character is <u>what your choices have made it to be</u>.
4. By now you should recognize <u>why even life's little choices are important</u>.
5. We should seek to glorify God by <u>whatever we do, say, or think</u>.
6. <u>Whenever a person goes against better knowledge</u>, he damages his conscience.
7. We give <u>whoever sent this gift of food</u> our sincere thanks.
8. This truck is <u>what we call a rattletrap</u>.
9. <u>How long it will keep working</u> remains to be seen.
10. Give this message to <u>whomever you can find in the shop</u>.
11. We shall leave <u>when everyone is ready</u>.
12. Our loud noises must have given <u>whatever was disturbing the chickens</u> a good scare.

D. Copy each noun clause.

1. How Cousin Alvin can paint with his arthritic hands is truly amazing.
2. He will put into rich color and exquisite detail a scene of what you describe to him.
3. Have you discovered whose dog was chasing your sheep?
4. The outside dimensions of the bookcase must be whatever fits well in that corner.
5. Michael gave whichever calf was coughing a shot.
6. Whose idea this was is not hard to guess.
7. I could not read the chalkboard from where I was sitting.

8. Although confined to a wheelchair, Grandfather Horning gives whoever visits him more inspiration than they give to him.
9. A good time to visit him can be when you are feeling discouraged.
10. The visitor could not remember if he had met any of us before.

Review Exercises

For each underlined word, write *yes* or *no* to tell whether it should be followed by a comma. [2]

1. Gertie our pet goat is a most frolicsome creature.
2. Grazing out in the meadow she looks as placid as a sheep.
3. Let the boys play out in the meadow however and you will see what a tease she can be!
4. If they play tag you can be sure that Gertie enjoying herself immensely will run and jump with them.
5. The game that she enjoys most is hide-and-seek.

---

61. Plural and Possessive Nouns

Plural Forms

Most one-word nouns show number; that is, their form shows whether they are singular or plural. The following rules will help you to write the plural forms of nouns correctly.

1. *General rules.*
   a. To form the plurals of most nouns, add -*s*.

      paper—papers
      stream—streams
      state—states
      explanation—explanations

   b. To form the plural of a noun ending with *s, sh, ch, x,* or *z,* add -*es*. You may need to double a final *s* or *z*.

      gas—gases *or* gasses
      church—churches
      tax—taxes
      quiz—quizzes

2. *Nouns ending with* y.
   a. To form the plural of a noun ending with *y* after a vowel, add -*s*.

      bay—bays
      chimney—chimneys
      envoy—envoys

b. To form the plural of a noun ending with *y* after a consonant, change the *y* to *i* and add *-es*.

   cherry—cherries
   enemy—enemies

3. *Nouns ending with* f *or* fe.
   a. For many nouns, change the *f* to *v* and add *-s* or *-es*.

      wolf—wolves
      sheaf—sheaves

   b. For other nouns, simply add *-s*.

      strife—strifes
      gulf—gulfs
      chief—chiefs

   c. For most nouns ending with *ff,* simply add *-s*.

      bluff—bluffs
      plaintiff—plaintiffs

   d. Sometimes either ending is correct for a word.

      hoof—hoofs *or* hooves
      handkerchief—handkerchiefs *or* handkerchieves

4. *Nouns ending with* o.
   a. To form the plural of a noun ending with *o* after a vowel, add *-s*.

      patio—patios
      portfolio—portfolios
      zoo—zoos

   b. To form the plural of a noun ending with *o* after a consonant, add *-s* or *-es*. Sometimes either ending is correct.

      tomato—tomatoes
      silo—silos
      zero—zeros *or* zeroes

   c. For most musical terms ending with *o,* simply add *-s*.

      soprano—sopranos
      trio—trios

5. *Compound Nouns.*
   a. In general, change the most important word to the plural form.

      daughter-in-law—daughters-in-law
      inspector general—inspectors general
      bondwoman—bondwomen

b. Simply add *-s* to nouns ending with *-ful.*

mouthful—mouthfuls bucketful—bucketfuls

c. For a few nouns, each part of the compound word is made plural.

manservant—menservants
womanservant—womenservants

6. *Nouns with irregular plural forms.*
   a. In only seven nouns, the internal vowels are changed for the plural forms. Of course, if a compound word contains one of these roots, the plural is formed in the same way.

   foot—feet; tooth—teeth; goose—geese
   (forefoot—forefeet *but* mongoose—mongooses)
   louse—lice; mouse—mice (dormouse—dormice)
   man—men; woman—women (fireman—firemen)

   b. Four plural nouns have an archaic *-en* ending.

   child—children; ox—oxen (still used today)
   brother—brethren (used within the church, but archaic otherwise)
   hose—hosen (archaic; found once in the King James Bible)

   c. Some nouns have the same form whether singular or plural.

   trout—trout sheep—sheep
   deer—deer series—series

7. *Nouns with foreign plural forms.*
   A number of nouns borrowed from foreign languages have retained their foreign plural forms. In addition, the regular English pattern is often acceptable.

Singular Ending	Plural Ending	Example
-is	-es	oasis—oases
-ex *or* -ix	-ices	apex—apices *or* apexes
-a	-ae	vertebra—vertebrae *or* vertebras
-us	-i	narcissus—narcissi *or* narcissuses
-um *or* -on	-a	paramecium—paramecia

Possessive Forms

Possessive nouns show possession or ownership. The following rules will help you to write possessive forms correctly.

1. *Singular nouns.*
   a. Make the possessive form of most singular nouns by adding *'s.* This includes nouns that end with a single *s* sound.

   the visitor's question James's reputation

b. If a singular noun contains two *s* or *z* sounds in the last syllable, add only an apostrophe. Adding a third *s* or *z* sound makes the word awkward to pronounce.

Jesus' disciples   Xerxes' rule

2. *Plural nouns.*

a. If a plural noun does not end with *-s,* add *'s.*

the women's waterpots   the deer's tails

b. If a plural noun ends with *-s,* add only an apostrophe.

the girls' purses   the monkeys' antics

3. *Compound nouns and noun phrases.*
Make the last word in the compound possessive.

his mother-in-law's kindness   the passerby's wave

Usage of Possessive Nouns

1. Normally, only nouns naming persons or animals are written in possessive forms. For inanimate objects, you should generally use a prepositional phrase. Exceptions include poetic or figurative language and various common expressions, such as those used for measures of time or money.

a spider's web
the hands of the clock (*not* the clock's hands)
a day's wages; a moment's delay; five dollars' worth

2. Show joint ownership of several nouns by making only the last noun possessive. Show separate ownership by making each noun possessive.

Joint ownership:
Have you ridden Samuel and Aaron's bicycle?
(one bicycle owned by two boys together)
Separate ownership:
Have you ridden Samuel's and Aaron's bicycles?
(two bicycles owned by two boys separately)

3. A noun coming before a gerund should usually be possessive. To see why, replace the gerund with a regular noun form. It is clear that the preceding noun should be possessive.

Moses' interceding turned away God's fierce wrath.
(*Interceding* was what turned away God's wrath. *Moses'* modifies *interceding* by telling whose. Compare: Moses' intercession, *not* Moses intercession.)
John's studying for the test enabled him to make a perfect score.
(*Studying* was what enabled him. *John's* modifies *studying* by telling whose. Compare: John's preparation, *not* John preparation.)

Do not confuse this with a noun followed by a participle.

We all saw <u>John</u> studying for the test.

(The sentence does not mean that we saw *John's studying,* but that we saw *John* in the action of *studying.* The participle *studying* modifies the direct object *John.*)

Applying the Lesson

A. For each noun, write the singular possessive, the plural, and the plural possessive forms. Use the foreign plural spellings for numbers 31–40. If possessive forms should generally not be used, write *none.*

1. sheriff
2. company
3. post office
4. calf
5. child
6. embargo
7. brother (church)
8. lioness
9. family
10. manservant
11. placebo
12. trout
13. alloy
14. spoonful
15. alto
16. kinsman
17. roof
18. Angeleno
19. sheep
20. mongoose
21. bondservant
22. titmouse
23. son-in-law
24. inspector general
25. goose
26. clef
27. bush
28. valley
29. louse
30. ox
31. emphasis
32. appendix
33. nebula
34. cactus
35. bacterium
36. basis
37. vertex
38. formula
39. octopus
40. criterion

B. Write correctly each phrase that has an error. If it is correct, write *correct.*

1. Judas' desire for money
2. Matthew's and Mark's Gospels
3. strife between Abram and Lot's herdsmen
4. the corn's ears
5. the blind mans plea
6. her mother's-in-law's direction
7. disobeyed Samuel's orders
8. for a day's wages
9. the two prophet's miracles
10. sprinkled handfuls of ashes
11. James's, Joses', Judas's, and Simon's brother
12. foretold Peter denying his Lord
13. went to Zacchaeus's house
14. the tabernacle's coverings
15. found Jesus talking with the Jewish teachers
16. married seven hundred wifes
17. six potsful of water
18. grieved by the children's mocking
19. at the years end
20. three mens' visit to Abraham

Review Exercises

A. Identify each underlined word as a direct object (*DO*), an indirect object (*IO*), a predicate nominative (*PN*), a predicate adjective (*PA*), or an objective complement (*OC*). [20, 21]

1. No one considered my plan <u>workable</u>.
2. Brother Mark always gave us sufficient <u>time</u> to do our lessons.
3. A good beginning is an important first <u>step</u> in any project.
4. The children showed <u>Sister Mary</u> a spider in the garden.
5. John, your shoes are <u>muddy</u>.
6. The Bible calls hatred a terrible <u>sin</u>.

B. Identify each underlined word as a retained direct object (*DO ret.*), a retained indirect object (*IO ret.*), or a retained objective complement (*OC ret.*). [21]

1. After the fire, Brother Albert was given much <u>assistance</u> by the church.
2. Outside work was made <u>difficult</u> by the bitter wind.
3. The answer to the riddle was told <u>us</u> by little Jacob.
4. The harmless water snake was declared a dreadful <u>creature</u> by our visitors.
5. Christian women are asked numerous <u>questions</u> about their veilings.
6. Bread and meat were provided <u>Elijah</u> by the ravens.

---

62. Personal and Compound Personal Pronouns

A *pronoun* is a word that takes the place of a noun. The noun to which a pronoun refers is its *antecedent.* This lesson reviews two of the six classes of pronouns, and the next lesson deals with the other four classes.

Personal Pronouns

Personal pronouns are words like *he, you,* and *them,* which often refer to persons. The pronouns in this class are probably the first ones that come to your mind when you think of pronouns. Personal pronouns have different forms to show person, number, case, and gender.

1. *Person.* The person of a pronoun shows the relationship between the pronoun and the speaker. First person pronouns (*I, me, my, mine, we, us, our, ours*) refer to the speaker himself. Second person pronouns (*you, your, yours*) refer to the person that the speaker is talking to. Third person pronouns (*he, him, his, she, her, hers, it, its, they, them, their, theirs*) refer to the person or thing that the speaker is talking about.

2. *Number.* The number of a pronoun shows whether it is singular or plural. First and third person pronouns have different forms according to number, but second person pronouns do not.

3. *Case.* The case of a pronoun relates to its use in the sentence. The three cases in the English language are nominative, objective, and possessive.

The *nominative case* pronouns are as follows: *I, you, he, she, it, we, they.* These pronouns function as subjects, predicate nominatives, or appositives to one of these. Be especially careful to use the nominative case in compound structures of these sentence parts.

Titus and I raked the leaves in the front yard. (subject)
The visitors, Audrey and she, are signing the guest book.
(appositive to subject)
We girls will help Aunt Mary clean her house.
(subject followed by appositive)
The men to serve on the building committee would be they.
(predicate nominative)

The King James Bible uses the archaic forms *thou* (singular) and *ye* (plural) as second person pronouns in the nominative case.

"When thou hast brought forth the people out of Egypt, ye shall serve God upon this mountain."

The *objective case* pronouns are as follows: *me, you, him, her, it, us, them.* They function as object complements, objects of prepositions, or appositives to any of these. Be careful to use the objective case in compound structures of these sentence parts and with appositives.

The teacher commended Laura and her for their interesting essays.
(direct object)
Brother Robert has given you and me an interesting assignment.
(indirect objects)
The request came from us boys.
(object of preposition followed by an appositive)

The objective case is also used as the *subject of an infinitive.* This is a new grammatical construction for you, but since you are familiar with infinitives, you should find it easy to understand. Begin by considering this sentence with a simple infinitive phrase.

Father wants to paint the woodshed.

Father wants what? *To paint the woodshed.* The infinitive phrase is the direct object in the sentence. Look at the diagram of this sentence.

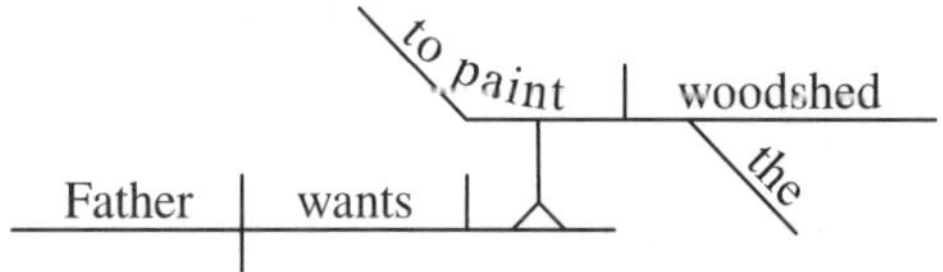

To this same sentence we will add one more word.

Father wants *me* to paint the woodshed.

Now find the direct object. Father wants what? *To paint the woodshed?* No, he wants *me* to paint it! *Me to paint the woodshed* is clearly the thing that Father wants—the direct object. *Me* is the subject that will perform the action of the infinitive. A diagram may help to show this more clearly.

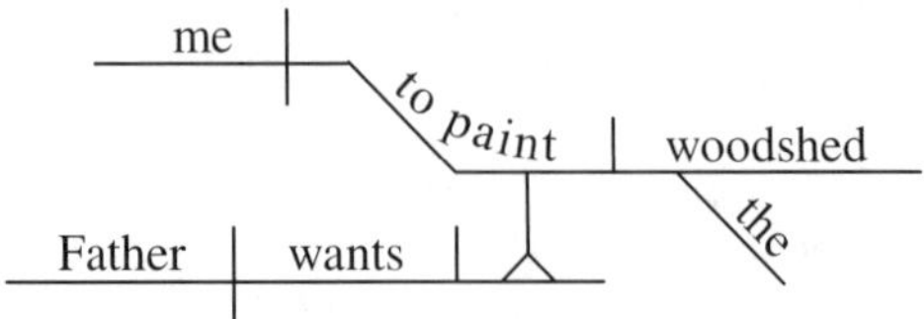

The direct object in each of the following sentences is an infinitive phrase with a subject. Notice that each of these subjects is in the objective case, not nominative.

> Brother Myron told <u>him to open the windows</u>.
> Aunt Matilda is teaching <u>us to knit slippers</u>.
> Mother let <u>me try another recipe</u>.

In the last sentence above, the main verb is *let* and the word *to* is understood: *let me (to) try another recipe.* (Compare "allowed me to try another recipe.") In former years you learned that *let* is always used with another verb form that tells what action is permitted. This verb form is always an infinitive with a subject and with *to* understood.

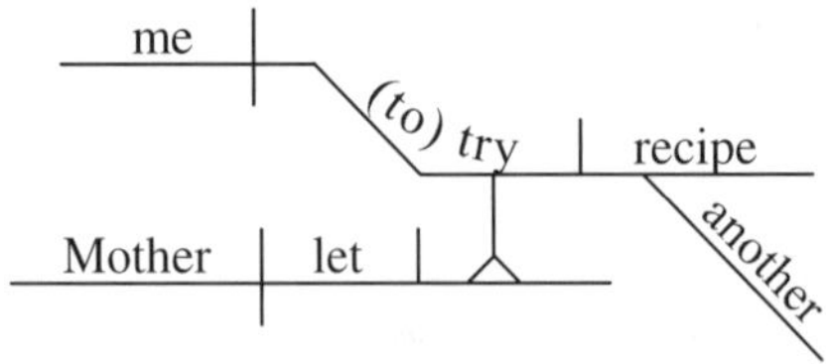

The King James Bible uses the archaic forms *thee* (singular) and *you* (plural) as the second person pronouns in the objective case.

> "And the eye cannot say unto the hand, I have no need of <u>thee</u>: nor again the head to the feet, I have no need of <u>you</u>."

The *possessive case* pronouns are as follows: *my, mine, your, yours, his, her, hers, its, our, ours, their, theirs.* These pronouns show ownership. Most possessive case pronouns function as adjectives, modifying the nouns they precede. Absolute possessive pronouns function as substantives, representing both the possessor (the antecedent) and the thing possessed (the understood noun that could be stated).

> Their farm is more productive than <u>ours</u>.
> (*Their* functions as an adjective modifying *farm. Ours* is an absolute possessive pronoun that stands for *our farm,* thus representing both the speaker and the speaker's farm.)

The King James Bible uses the archaic forms *thy* and *thine* as second person singular pronouns in the possessive case. *Thy* precedes consonant sounds, and *thine* precedes vowel sounds. In archaic usage, *my* also precedes consonant sounds, and *mine* precedes vowel sounds.

"Thy prayers and thine alms are come up for a memorial before God."
"Thou knowest my downsitting and mine uprising."

4. *Gender.* The gender of a pronoun is *masculine, feminine, neuter,* or *common.* This is the same as for nouns, as you studied in Lesson 59. Only third person singular pronouns have specific forms for gender. They are as follows: *he, him, his* (masculine); *she, her, hers* (feminine); *it, its* (neuter). All other personal pronouns are of common gender.

5. *Agreement of pronouns and antecedents.* A pronoun must agree with its antecedent in person, number, and gender. In the following sentence, the pronouns are underlined and the antecedents are italicized.

Felix Manz lost his life because he opposed the *Zwinglians* and their teachings. (*His* is third person singular, masculine gender, to agree with *Felix Manz. Their* is third person plural, common gender, to agree with *Zwinglians.*)

Compound Personal Pronouns

The compound personal pronouns end with *-self* or *-selves.* Below is a table showing the nine compound personal pronouns (including one archaic form).

	Singular	Plural
First person:	myself	ourselves
Second person:	yourself (thyself)	yourselves
Third person:	himself, herself, itself	themselves

Be sure to use the correct forms of compound personal pronouns. The following forms should be avoided: *ourself, themself, hisself, theirselves.*

A compound personal pronoun can serve in two ways. If it is *intensive,* it serves to add intensity or emphasis to another noun or pronoun. Such a pronoun serves as an appositive, emphasizing a person or thing by referring to it a second time.

If a compound personal pronoun is *reflexive,* it shows an action done by the subject to itself. In this use, the pronoun functions as the direct object, the indirect object, or the object of a preposition and shows an action *reflected* back to the subject.

Intensive: We *ourselves* are responsible for this predicament.
The girls *themselves* put up the new curtains.
The girls put up the new curtains *themselves.*
Reflexive: Roger gave *himself* a severe scolding. (indirect object)
You boys may take a short hike by *yourselves.*
(object of preposition)

Usage of Personal and Compound Personal Pronouns

1. *Use the proper case when a pronoun follows* than *or* as. Such a pronoun is either a subject or an object in an elliptical clause. Therefore, you must consider what the completed construction of the clause would be, and choose the correct pronoun case to fit that construction. Sometimes either case is correct, depending on the meaning.

> Sandra is more artistic than I.
> (Completed construction: than *I am artistic. Me* does not fit.)
> We meet the Millers more often than them.
> (Completed construction: more often than *we meet them.*)
> We meet the Millers more often than they.
> (Completed construction: more often than *they meet the Millers.*)

2. *Never use apostrophes with personal pronouns in the possessive case.* The possessive forms of some other classes of pronouns require apostrophes. With personal pronouns, however, use apostrophes only to form contractions.

> He's doing his assignments, but yours and hers are completed already.

3. *When you speak about another person and yourself, refer to the other person first and yourself last.* This not only represents correct grammar but also complements the Bible principle, "In honour preferring one another."

> Mr. Totter, our neighbor, wants Brian and me to shovel his snow this winter.

4. *Do not use compound personal pronouns to replace personal pronouns.* Use them only as intensive or reflexive pronouns, as illustrated above.

> **Incorrect:** Harry and myself turned out a baseball bat on the old lathe.
> Cleon's family and ourselves traveled together to Niagara Falls.
> **Correct:** Harry and I turned out a baseball bat on the old lathe.
> Cleon's family and we traveled together to Niagara Falls.

Applying the Lesson

A. Copy each personal pronoun, including any possessive form used as an adjective. Label its person (*1, 2, 3*), number (*S, P*), case (*N, O, P*), and gender (*M, F, N, C*).

1. When Samuel heard God's voice, he thought Eli was calling him.
2. At the people's request, Aaron made them a golden calf, and they worshiped it.
3. Jesus said, "I am the way, the truth, and the life: no man cometh unto the Father, but by me."
4. The man who displays his giving receives from the world its applause and praise.
5. Our good deeds can never gain for us a position in heaven.
6. We know that the woman who touched Jesus' garment was healed because of her faith in Jesus.
7. If you sow wild oats, my friend, they will grow to produce a bitter harvest.
8. Children, treat your parents with utmost respect, for they deserve it.

B. Write a personal pronoun to fit each description.
1. first person, plural, objective case
2. third person, plural, nominative case
3. second person, possessive case (2 forms)
4. first person, singular, possessive case (2 forms)
5. third person, singular, objective case, feminine gender
6. third person, singular, possessive case, neuter gender

C. Copy each compound personal pronoun, and write whether it is intensive (*I*) or reflexive (*R*).
1. We continually reminded ourselves of the warm house we would find at the end of the hike.
2. Mother said herself that she planned to invite company on Sunday.
3. Jacob hurt himself when he slipped on the wet floor.
4. The girls prepared the entire meal by themselves.
5. We owe everything we have to God Himself.
6. The Nile River itself was turned to blood.
7. If you find yourself groping for answers, ask for advice.
8. We must forbear with others, for we have some shortcomings ourselves.

D. Diagram these sentences, which contain infinitives with subjects.
1. Father asked Henry to hold the wrench.
2. The children watched him tighten the bolts.
3. He let them start the motor.
4. Then they helped him to mow the lawn.

E. Find the errors in pronoun usage, and write the correct words or phrases. If a sentence has no error, write *correct.*
1. Brother Melvin prepared for the demonstration by hisself.
2. The students gathered theirselves around his desk.
3. He told ourselves that the bowl contained water.
4. He then asked I to connect the wires to a battery.
5. We saw for ourself that the test tubes were filling with gas.
6. As different students asked questions, Brother Melvin answered them himself.
7. Me and Jeffrey noticed that one tube had collected twice as much gas as the other one.
8. Brent declared that the tube with more gas contained oxygen; Stephen was not as sure as him about that.
9. The teacher asked Brent and he to tell us the formula for water.
10. They did not have their books, so Miriam loaned them her's.
11. When us students heard the formula H_2O, we began to understand.
12. Brother Melvin hisself explained, "Every decomposed water molecule produces twice as much hydrogen as oxygen."
13. Was there any way for him to prove which gas was which?
14. Us girls were extremely curious as he collected the gases in two new test tubes.

15. The ones who held the tubes were Paul and him.
16. The boys themself helped to get a wood splint burning.
17. Brother Melvin blew out the splint and said, "Paul, I'm ready for your's."
18. When he inserted the glowing splint into the tube, everyone except me and Elizabeth heard a distinct bark.
19. "Hydrogen is known as the barking gas," he said; so we were all as sure as him that this tube had contained hydrogen.
20. The ones who tested the other tube were George and him; this time the glowing splint burst into flame.

Review Exercises

A. Write the letters of the correct plural forms in each sentence. [61]

1. From the ([a]chimneys, [b]chimnies) poured huge ([a]puffs, [b]puffes) of smoke.
2. The ([a]editors in chief, [b]editor in chiefs) carefully examined the ([a]leafs, [b]leaves) of the books.
3. Many huge ([a]bison, [b]bisons) thundered across the prairie with pounding ([a]hoof, [b]hooves).
4. Before ([a]workmans, [b]workmen) could complete the Panama Canal, they had to reduce the great numbers of ([a]mosquitoes, [b]mosquito).
5. Please put out two ([a]cupsful, [b]cupfuls) of seed for those ([a]titmouses, [b]titmice).
6. For one measure in the song, the ([a]sopranos, [b]sopranoes) rested while the ([a]altos, [b]altoes) carried the melody.
7. Our ([a]familys, [b]families) attend Bible-believing and Bible-obeying ([a]churchs, [b]churches).
8. The ([a]neighbors, [b]neighbores) spend many hours relaxing on their ([a]patioes, [b]patios).

B. Write the letter for the correct foreign plural form of each singular noun. [61]

1. nova	a. novae	b. novum
2. vortex	a. vorta	b. vortices
3. thesis	a. thesae	b. theses
4. hippopotamus	a. hippopotami	b. hippopotama
5. podium	a. podia	b. podii
6. appendix	a. appendi	b. appendices

---

63. Other Pronoun Classes

Demonstrative Pronouns

The four demonstrative pronouns (*this, that, these, those*) point out specific persons or things. A demonstrative pronoun is a pronoun only when it functions as a substantive. If it precedes and modifies a noun, it is an adjective telling *which* rather than a pronoun.

God has always rewarded faith in Him, and *that* will never change.
(subject of clause: pronoun)
This truth gives us hope for the future.
(precedes and modifies a noun: adjective)

Two rules for correct usage of demonstrative pronouns deserve special mention.

1. Never use *them* as a demonstrative pronoun.
2. Do not say *this (these) here* or *that (those) there.*

Incorrect: Them are outstanding heroes of faith.
We must be like those there men.
Correct: Those are outstanding heroes of faith.
We must be like those men.

Relative Pronouns

There are six relative pronouns: *who, whom, whose, which, what, that.* You learned in previous years that a relative pronoun introduces an adjective clause which modifies the antecedent of the relative pronoun.

Noah, *who feared God,* built an ark on dry ground.
(The relative pronoun *who* introduces an adjective clause that modifies *Noah,* the antecedent of *who.*)

You have learned that the same pronouns may introduce noun clauses. They are also classed as relative pronouns when they function in that way. A relative pronoun has no antecedent when it introduces a noun clause.

Do you know *what motivated him in that hard task*?
(The relative pronoun *what* introduces a noun clause that is the direct object of *you Do know.* There is no antecedent for *what.*)

That is a relative pronoun only when it has a substantive function. If it simply introduces a clause, it is a conjunction.

The apples that we bought are Golden Delicious.
(direct object in adjective clause: relative pronoun)
I think that they were picked too green.
(no substantive function; simply introduces noun clause: conjunction)
I think that spoils their taste. (subject in noun clause: relative pronoun)

Correct usage of the relative pronouns requires that *who* and *whom* refer only to people, *which* refer only to things, and *that, what,* and *whose* refer to either people or things. In the King James Bible, however, *which* often refers to people.

Youth who can resist temptation have learned a valuable lesson.
(not *youth which*)
Those two kittens, which we found on our front porch, have entertained the children for hours. (not *kittens who*)
The man that was blind possessed an understanding that the Pharisees lacked.
"Come, see a man, which told me all things that ever I did" (John 4:29).

Three of the relative pronouns actually are different forms of the same word, used to show different cases. *Who* is nominative, *whom* is objective, and *whose* is possessive.

> Andrew Smith, who painted our house, has thirty years of experience.
> (nominative *who* for subject of clause)
> Mrs. Graham, from whom we buy our eggs, keeps a small flock of chickens.
> (objective *whom* for object of preposition)
> I do not know whose shoes are making these black marks.
> (possessive *whose* for adjective)

Compound relative pronouns are formed by adding *-ever* or *-soever* to simple relative pronouns. They introduce only noun clauses.

> Whoever drinks of the water of life has inner peace in whatever circumstances he faces.

Interrogative Pronouns

The interrogative pronouns (*who, whom, whose, which, what*) introduce questions. Each of these pronouns also serves a specific function in the sentence, such as a subject or a direct object. When *who, whom, whose,* and *which* are interrogative pronouns, the same usage rules apply as when they are relative pronouns. The only exception is that the interrogative pronoun *which* can refer to persons as well as things.

> Who is coming down the stairs?
> (*Who* acts as a subject and refers to a person.)
> Whom shall we invite for dinner?
> (*Whom* acts as a direct object and refers to a person.)
> Whose can we borrow? (*Whose* acts as a direct object and refers to a person.)
> Which is your brother? (*Which* acts as a subject and refers to a person.)
> What is she asking for?
> (*What* acts as the object of a preposition and refers to a thing.)

Indefinite Pronouns

The indefinite pronouns, as their name suggests, do not refer to definite persons, places, or things. Unlike most other pronouns, they often have no specific antecedents. Many indefinite pronouns are always singular: *each, either, neither, one, another, anybody, anyone, anything, everybody, everyone, everything, somebody, someone, something, nobody, no one, nothing.* Most of the pronouns in this group contain the singular word element *other, one, thing,* or *body.*

When one of these singular pronouns functions as a subject, a prepositional phrase with a plural object often comes between the subject and the verb. Be careful to make the verb agree with the subject, not with the object of the preposition. If any other pronoun refers to the singular subject, it must also be singular.

> Each of the articles presents *its* message clearly and effectively.
> Everyone in our churches has *his* personal responsibilities to fulfill.

A few indefinite pronouns are always plural: *both, few, many, others, several.* Use plural verbs with these pronouns, and use plural pronouns in referring to them.

> Several of the farmers were selling *their* produce at local markets.

A few indefinite pronouns may be either singular or plural: *some, any, none, all, most.* The number of the pronoun depends on the number of its antecedent. When one of these pronouns is used as a subject, that antecedent often occurs in a prepositional phrase between the subject and the verb. If the antecedent is singular, the indefinite pronoun is singular because it refers to a certain portion of that one thing. If the antecedent is plural, the indefinite pronoun is plural because it refers to certain individual items in that set of things.

> Some of this *market* is in the open air.
> (A portion of this one thing is in the open air.)
> Some of these *markets* are in the open air.
> (Some items in this set of things are in the open air.)

> None of this *fruit* comes from another state.
> (No portion of this one thing comes from another state.)
> None of these *fruits* come from another state.
> (No items in this set of things come from another state.)

Make the possessive forms of indefinite pronouns by adding *'s*. This is different from the possessive forms of personal pronouns, which do not have apostrophes.

> Everyone's composition is lying on his desk.

The words listed as indefinite pronouns are pronouns only if they have a substantive function in a sentence. Many of these words also function as modifiers, and then they are adjectives.

> I ate both of the buns for breakfast. (pronoun used as direct object)
> I ate both buns for breakfast. (adjective modifying direct object)

Applying the Lesson

A. Copy each pronoun, and write whether it is personal (*P*), compound personal (*CP*), demonstrative (*D*), indefinite (*ID*), interrogative (*IR*), or relative (*R*). Include the possessive pronouns used as adjectives.

1. We show ourselves to be good or poor sports by many of our actions on the playground.
2. One must play graciously, without scolding his teammates for the errors that they make.
3. Who enjoys playing with someone who has not learned this?
4. Let others play their parts by themselves; that allows everyone to enjoy the game.
5. Even when you are winning, control yourself and guard against comments which could make someone on the other team feel bad.

6. Which is more important to me, winning the game or helping all to enjoy themselves?

B. Choose the correct words in parentheses.
1. Both of my parents (was, were) advising me to try.
2. Each of the ministers (take, takes) part in the morning service.
3. One of the brethren (lead, leads) the singing.
4. Most of us (have, has) a priceless Christian heritage.
5. Everyone (enjoy, enjoys) the fellowship during and after the service.
6. Have you ever met anybody who considers (himself, themselves) indispensable?
7. Some of my friends (think, thinks) the work is too difficult.
8. Several of these cauliflower heads (is, are) beginning to turn brown.
9. (Is, Are) any of the cake left for me?
10. (Have, Has) all of those cakes been eaten already?
11. Either of your suggestions (offer, offers) a reasonable solution.
12. Another of the trees (have, has) been blown over.

C. Write one or two words to show how to correct each error. If the sentence is correct, write *correct.*
1. Brother Mahlon is the man who you should ask about the oil leak.
2. You will ruin that there engine if you run it without oil.
3. The mechanic which serviced your car did not tighten the drain plug.
4. We can avoid most mistakes if everyone does his work carefully.
5. This composition is full of life, but them use the passive voice too much.
6. I have a very good idea whom the writers were.
7. All of my aunts and uncles are planning to be at the reunion.
8. Should a nonresistant Christian have a dog who would viciously attack an intruder?
9. We should bear one anothers burdens.
10. Them are my books, but you are welcome to borrow a few.
11. I have no idea whom the author is.
12. Mr. Morgan is a salesman who you can trust.

Review Exercises

Write the letters of the correct forms in each sentence. [61]
1. When Brother ([a]Amos', [b]Amos's) neighbor visited our church, he especially enjoyed the ([a]congregation, [b]congregation's) singing.
2. After ([a]a moment's hesitation, [b]the hesitation of a moment), Ellen lifted ([a]the trap's arm, [b]the arm of the trap) and removed the dead mouse.
3. The ([a]boy, [b]boy's) talking to your brother is as tall as ([a]Wanda's, [b]Wandas') father.
4. ([a]Womens', [b]Women's) purses and ([a]girls', [b]girls's) shoes are on sale this week.
5. ([a]Brother Edgar, [b]Brother Edgar's) and Sister Marie's family will be helping to clean ([a]Aunt Alice, [b]Aunt Alice's) and Sister Carol's houses this fall.

6. ([a]Ruth's, [b]Ruths') faithfulness was ample reward for all her ([a]mother's-in-law, [b]mother-in-law's) sacrifices.
7. Brother Levi asked his ([a]ministers's, [b]ministers') advice before he agreed to his ([a]son, [b]son's) serving in Guatemala.
8. It is ironic that the Jews cried for ([a]Jesus', [b]Jesus's) crucifixion and accepted ([a]Barabbas', [b]Barabbas's) release.

---

64. Improving Your Writing Style, Part 4: Using Poetic Devices

To develop an effective writing style, you must put much time and effort into your work. You need to look for ways to weave original, creative expressions into your sentences. And you must take special care to put energy into your verbs—by choosing lively action verbs instead of linking verbs, and by using the active voice rather than the passive voice.

Yet another way to add appeal to your writing is by the use of poetic devices. The words of poetry have a distinct musical quality. By borrowing a few devices from poetry, we can put some of that music into our prose writing. Three of these devices are described below.

1. *Alliteration.* This is the repetition of beginning consonant sounds. Poems often use this repetition to produce a musical effect. Feel the music in the example below.

> Day is dying in the west,
> Heaven is touching earth with rest;
>   Wait and worship while the night
>   Sets her evening lamps alight
> Through all the sky.

Just as alliteration adds appeal to poetry, it can add appeal to prose. For the most striking effects, weave alliteration into the more significant words of your sentences. Also consider that different sounds add different musical tones. The repetition of sharp, cutting sounds like /b/, /d/, or /k/ can add a tone of harshness and increase the tempo of a sentence. On the other hand, the repetition of slow, soft sounds like /f/, /m/, or /s/ can add a note of mildness and slow the speed of a sentence.

Read the following sentences. Each pair says basically the same thing, but note the music in the second set of sentences because of their alliteration.

Without alliteration:

Bitterness damages the hearts of those it controls.
Grandmother's pleasant face gives cheer wherever she goes.

With alliteration:

Bitterness becomes a blight on the inner being of those it controls.
(The repetition of the hard /b/ matches the idea of bitterness.)

Grandmother's smiling face spreads sunshine wherever she goes.
(The repetition of soft /s/ sounds matches the idea of cheer.)

2. *Rhyming words.* We can also borrow from poetry the music of rhyme. We will not do this often; but in the few places where it is suitable, rhyme will add a few notes of melody to our writing. The rhyming words should come fairly close together for the best effect. As with alliteration, we need to choose significant words for the rhymes.

Read the following pairs of sentences. Observe how rhyme adds to their appeal.

Without rhyming words:

Christians commit themselves to obey truth and to share it with others.

Godly fear and worldly mirth never abide in the same heart.

With rhyming words:

Christians commit themselves to live and to give the message of truth.

Godly fear and worldly cheer never abide in the same heart.

3. *Onomatopoeia* (on′·ə·mat′·ə·pē′·ə). This is the use of a word having an imitative sound. Onomatopoeia appeals especially to children, but a limited use of it can contribute to an effective style in any type of writing.

Can you hear the music added to each of these sentences by their onomatopoeia? (The last example uses both rhyme and onomatopoeia.)

Without onomatopoeia:

The boasting of pride and the complaining of self-pity war against the soul.

Let nothing turn you aside, whether it be the world's approval or disapproval.

With onomatopoeia:

The blustering of pride and the murmuring of self-pity war against the soul.

Let nothing turn you aside, whether it be the world's hooting and jeering or its clapping and cheering.

Your assignment in this lesson will be to write a paragraph of description. In such a paragraph, the topic sentence should give a brief, basic sketch of what is being described. The rest of the paragraph should expand the topic sentence by giving details that clarify or illustrate it.

Read the following paragraph. Can you see how the poetic devices add musical appeal to the description?

The children huddled around the fireplace, trying to keep warm as the blizzard raged. It howled and growled, rattling the windows, rumbling in the chimney, and rocking the small cabin. Snow swished against the walls and sifted through cracks around the door. Mother had set one kerosene lamp on a windowsill, but it was only a feeble light in the dark night. Before going to bed, the family knelt and prayed that Father would find his way home safely.

Applying the Lesson

A. Improve the style of the following sentences by using alliteration, rhyming words, and onomatopoeia. Be ready to compare your work with that of your classmates, to see the various things that can be done.

1. The market resounded with the sounds of dogs, sheep, and cattle.
2. In order to live as you should, you must forsake wrong.
3. Amid the noisy activities of daily life, do not forget to enjoy the sounds of the wind and the brook.
4. Faith perceives the unseen, accepts the unbelievable, and obtains the impossible. (The second and third verbs should rhyme with *perceives,* and all the direct objects should begin with *i.*)
5. To do things "decently and in order," do them readily, correctly, and patiently. (Use three adverbs beginning with *p.*)

B. Write a paragraph of description on one of the following topics. Put special effort into using poetic devices and applying the other elements of effective writing style that you have studied.

1. the family car
2. the kitchen (or another room) in your home
3. the woods (or another outdoor place) where you live

Review Exercises

Write the letters of the sentences with the better writing style. [3, 22, 39]

1. a. The gentle rain made the flowers look brighter again.
   b. The gentle rain washed the dainty face of each flower.
2. a. I wish I had given my tongue a vacation.
   b. I wish I had not talked so much.
3. a. The plumber thanked me profusely for helping him carry his tools to his truck.
   b. The plumber heaped upon me a truckload of unmerited thanks for helping him convey his occupational equipment to his work vehicle.
4. a. The setting sun was making the waves sparkle like diamonds.
   b. The setting sun was skipping stars across the waves.
5. a. Soon the evening sky was a shining pink and gold.
   b. Soon the evening sky glowed with pink and gold.
6. a. The visiting speaker gave numerous illustrations from nature.
   b. Numerous illustrations from nature were given by the visiting speaker.

65. Identifying Substantives

Nouns and pronouns have specific functions in sentences: subjects, direct and indirect objects, predicate nominatives, and so forth. Words, phrases, or clauses that you would not necessarily identify as nouns or pronouns can also function in these ways. The term *substantive* is used for any word or word group that names something and serves as a noun or pronoun.

1. *Single-word nouns and compound nouns are substantives.* This includes all the words that obviously name persons, places, or things. You would recognize them as nouns without knowing how they were used in a sentence.

<u>Jesus Christ</u> gave His <u>life</u> for the <u>sins</u> of <u>mankind</u>.

2. *Pronouns are substantives.* This includes the words in all six classes of pronouns that you reviewed in Lessons 62 and 63. However, a possessive pronoun that modifies a noun is not considered a substantive, for it functions as an adjective.

<u>We</u> serve a God <u>who</u> reveals His power in <u>everything</u> <u>He</u> created.
(*His* is an adjective, not a substantive.)

3. *Infinitives and infinitive phrases may be substantives.* An infinitive is the basic form of a verb preceded by *to.* When an infinitive has a subject, the subject is part of the substantive. Infinitives and infinitive phrases used as adjectives or adverbs are not substantives.

<u>To listen</u> is a good way to learn many things.
(*To listen* is an infinitive used as a subject. *To learn many things* is an infinitive phrase used as an adjective.)
The doctor told <u>Mother to rest for several days</u>.
(*Mother to rest for several days* is an infinitive phrase with a subject; it is used as a direct object.)

4. *Gerunds and gerund phrases are substantives.* A gerund is the present participle of a verb (the *-ing* form) used as a noun. But remember that the present participle can also be used as a main verb or as an adjective.

Our family enjoys <u>singing</u> when we are traveling.
(*Singing* is a gerund used as a direct object. *Traveling* is a main verb.)
Lester's favorite pastime, <u>reading history books</u>, gives him a growing understanding of the present. (*Reading history books* is a gerund phrase used as an appositive to the subject. *Growing* is an adjective.)
The giggling girls failed to realize the seriousness of <u>being too lighthearted</u>.
(*Being too lighthearted* is a gerund phrase used as the object of a preposition. *Giggling* is an adjective.)

5. *Prepositional phrases may be substantives.* Such a phrase names a place or a thing and usually functions as the subject of a sentence with a linking verb.

<u>In the furnace room</u> is a good place to dry your gloves.
(prepositional phrase used as a subject)

6. *Noun clauses are substantives.* A noun clause is a dependent clause that functions as a substantive in a complex sentence.

> Whatever we do should be done as unto the Lord. (clause used as a subject)
> Even a child is known by what he does.
> (clause used as the object of a preposition)
> The slothful man wishes that he would not need to work.
> (clause used as a direct object)

7. *Any item used as a subject of discussion is a substantive.* Such an item is not being used in its normal sense; it is referred to as a symbol, a letter, a word, or a word group. Remember that a word or a letter used as a subject of discussion should be italicized (underlined).

> Three *e's* are buried in the word *cemetery*.
> (The first underlined item is the subject, and the second is an appositive.)
> Should I pronounce *vehement* with a silent *h*?
> (The first underlined item is the direct object, and the second is the object of a preposition.)

8. *Any title is a substantive.* Such a substantive may also be called a noun phrase.

> "My Old Bible" is my favorite poem about the Bible. (title used as a subject)
> The book *When Father Was a Boy* describes the growing-up years of Edward Sanger. (title used as an appositive to the subject)

The term *substantive* is a convenient label that includes nouns, pronouns, and any other expressions that serve as nouns. When you look for substantives in a sentence, first find the largest elements (the clauses) and then look for verbals and other kinds of noun phrases. Last of all, find the nouns, pronouns, and other small elements that serve as substantives.

Applying the Lesson

A. Copy all the words (including noun phrases) that function as substantives in these sentences.

1. All who view Niagara Falls are confronted with clear evidence of a mighty Creator.
2. Christians share God's love and mercy with those in need.
3. *Mississippi* has four *i*'s, yet it can see nothing.
4. We found some of this information in *Nature Friend,* a magazine for children.
5. What were the causes of the accident on Ridge Avenue?
6. Which is the most strongly accented syllable in the word *ambiguity*?

B. Copy the phrases and verbals that function as substantives in these sentences.

1. By imitating those around him, a small child quickly learns to do many things.
2. To read the preface of a book is a good way to evaluate its contents.
3. In the incinerator is the best place for sweepstakes offers.

4. To have students who enjoy learning makes teaching a highly rewarding occupation.
5. Most people like to read, but they need more time to do it.
6. Before 6:00 is the best time to call Brother Harlan.

C. Copy the clauses and titles that function as substantives in these sentences.
1. The book *Our Solar System* tells how the gravity of the moon affects the earth.
2. According to what I have read, its pull causes the earth to flex.
3. What really surprises me is that the earth keeps its shape more rigidly than steel.
4. "The Planet Earth" is a good article for whoever wants to find more interesting facts.

D. Copy all the substantives in these sentences. Do not list separately a substantive within another substantive phrase or clause.
1. During the presidency of Richard M. Nixon, American astronauts amazed the world by landing on the moon.
2. Who would have thought that men could do such a thing?
3. They had left the earth itself and gone out into the heavens.
4. The president of the United States declared that it was the greatest event in history.
5. Neil Armstrong called the first small step which he took on the moon a giant leap for mankind.
6. Does anyone know the message on the plaque that the astronauts placed on the moon?
7. "We came in peace for all mankind."
8. Reading that message may remind us of something that happened long ago.
9. Jesus Himself left the heavens to come down to the earth.
10. The purpose of His coming was to bring peace and goodwill to men.
11. We know how the world rejected Jesus, and His mission seemed like a failure.
12. On the cross was a shameful place for Him to die.
13. Now I want you to answer a question.
14. Which of these two events was greater?

Review Exercises

A. Choose the correct words in these sentences. [62]
1. Brother Mark appointed Harvey and (he, him) as editors for our school newspaper.
2. He also wants Martha and (she, her) to help proofread the articles.
3. The artists for this project will be (me and Sidney, Sidney and I, Sidney and me).
4. Brother Mark said that the principal and (he, himself) will need to approve all the articles.
5. (We, Us) students will surely be busy now.
6. Since the students at Maple Hill School began their paper two weeks sooner than (we, us), their paper will be finished before (ours, our's).

B. Choose the correct words in these sentences. [63]

1. We meet many people (who, which) have poor listening habits.
2. Too many are like sponges, (who, which) soak up everything they meet.
3. The problem is that (these, these here) people absorb the bad as well as the good.
4. On the other hand are those people (who, whom) we might call funnel-listeners.
5. (They, Them) are at fault because they do not catch anything—it all goes right through!
6. And surely none of us (want, wants) to be sieve-listeners, catching the bad while all the good passes through.
7. If each of these (is, are) so bad, how then shall we listen?
8. Make your mind like a colander in which all of the good things (remain, remains) while the unprofitable things drain away.

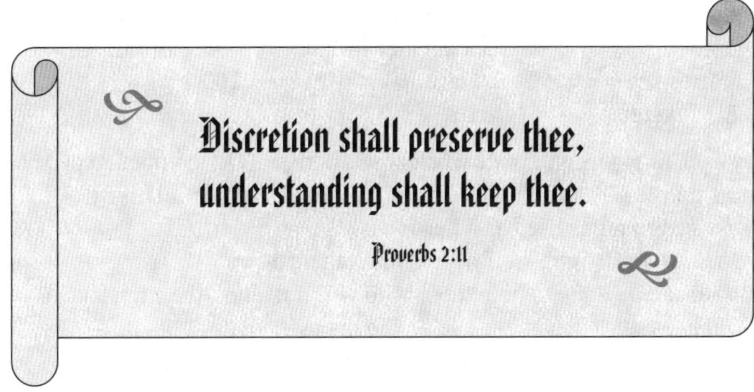

Discretion shall preserve thee,
understanding shall keep thee.
Proverbs 2:11

66. Chapter 7 Review

A. Copy each noun, and write whether it is concrete (*C*) or abstract (*A*). Also label its gender (*M, F, N, C*).

1. Margaret was writing a story about the childhood of her grandmother.
2. Through the years, my teachers have demanded the best of all their students.
3. If a person will not do a humble task, he is not worthy of greater responsibilities.
4. Adam's sin in the Garden of Eden brought eternal consequences.
5. The widow of Nain received her son raised to life again.
6. In Galatians, Paul referred to Hagar and Sarah in his discussion of spiritual freedom.

B. Write the plural form of each noun. Use the foreign plural spellings for numbers 15–24.

1. grief
2. species
3. attorney at law
4. tornado
5. eyetooth
6. footman
7. child
8. mother-in-law
9. turkey
10. brother (two forms)
11. solo
12. pocketknife
13. trout
14. panoply
15. phenomenon
16. antenna
17. diagnosis
18. thesaurus
19. index
20. crisis
21. curriculum
22. vertex
23. fungus
24. memorandum

C. Write the possessive form of each noun.

1. Ulysses
2. geese
3. giraffes
4. chief of staff
5. hostess
6. daughter-in-law
7. visitors
8. Josephus
9. patrolman
10. king

D. Copy each pronoun, and write whether it is personal (*P*), compound personal (*CP*), demonstrative (*D*), indefinite (*ID*), interrogative (*IR*), or relative (*R*). Include the possessive pronouns used as adjectives.

1. One never raises himself by pushing others down.
2. What can be done to help those who will not admit their mistakes?
3. You had better keep your eye on the man whom dogs distrust.
4. Few of our inconveniences are as serious as we often think.
5. That is not what I was expecting.
6. This must be done by some of the girls themselves.

E. Copy each substantive in these sentences, and label it *N* (one-word or compound noun), *Pron.* (pronoun), *G* (gerund or gerund phrase), *I* (infinitive or infinitive phrase), *Prep.* (prepositional phrase), *C* (clause), *T* (title), or *S* (subject of discussion). If a substantive is within a substantive phrase or clause, or within a title, do not list it separately.

1. The moderator said that Brother Jason would conduct our devotions.
2. He sought to inspire us with the greatness of God.
3. *Uncle Ben's Quote Book* contains many short, forceful quotations.
4. By displaying Gospel tracts, we offer help to whoever may be seeking.

5. The word *bullheaded* suggests refusing stubbornly to change one's mind.
6. "Loving Kindness" is the song which Uncle Jerry selected, and we plan to sing it now.
7. In the attic is our starting place; Mother wants us to find her old diary.
8. Before your test is the time to learn the spelling of the word *ambidextrous.*

F. Write the underlined items correctly. If an item has no error, write *correct.*

1. The Americans fighting a Civil War was a great calamity, and each of the battles were a tragedy.
2. Angela and me learned that this country of our's experienced much anguish and suffering.
3. There were over 600,000 men which died in the war, and most of the Southern families were bereft of a father, son, or brother.
4. The Northerners theirselves had offered a position of leadership to Robert E. Lee, who the South chose as their commander.
5. Me and Herman discovered that this was the first time photographers followed a war's progress.
6. This here opened the eyes of the nation to the horrors of war, even though none of the photographs was of actual battle scenes.
7. Since a subject had to hold hisself motionless for several minutes, Matthew Brady's and others' photographs were of soldiers posing between battles.
8. At a battle's end, they took pictures of the dead, often after some of the bodies were rearranged to make the pictures more striking.
9. Even though these here pictures shocked men and women, selfish and sinful men continue to fight those who they cannot get along with.
10. When Gerald's and Jolene's teacher goes to Bible school, we do not know whom the substitute will be.
11. Everyone except Sharon and herself was working faster than me.
12. Me and Julia made these cookies, but them were made by someone else.
13. Father bought these brown coats for Samuel and me, and that blue one is your's.
14. Even though the old tree's nectarines were knotty and bitter, the hogs who ate them were soon looking for more.
15. I don't know who raised these cantaloupes, but them on the truck came from New Jersey.
16. Sheila and myself have never done as well in algebra as him.

G. Write the correct words for these sentences about writing style.

1. Poetic devices have a ——— quality that adds appeal to writing.
2. The repetition of beginning consonant sounds is ———.
3. Repetition of sharp sounds like /b/ and /k/ will (increase, decrease) the tempo of a sentence, while repetition of soft sounds like /m/ and /s/ will (increase, decrease) the tempo.
4. A phrase like "believing and receiving" uses ——— to add appeal to writing.
5. The use of words having an imitative sound is ———.

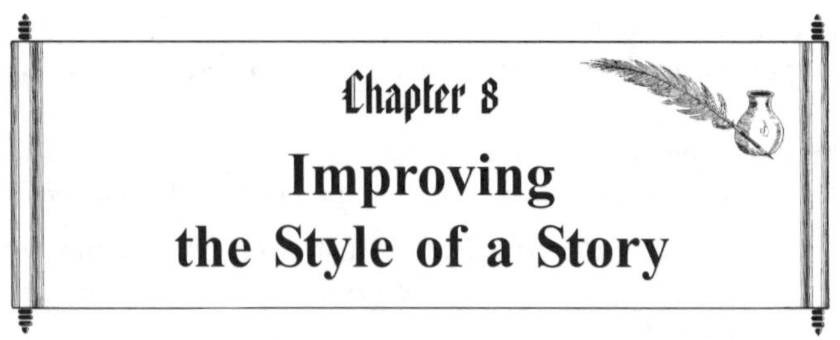

67. Make a Story Live

To be interesting, a story must contain an appealing plot and conflict. Even if these things are present, however, a story may fail to appeal to readers if its style is poor. This chapter will teach you a number of methods for improving the style of stories you write. At the end of the chapter, you will apply those methods to the first draft of the story you wrote in Chapter 6.

A writer's style can make his story live or die. If his story lives, readers will reach out to receive its message. If his story dies, they will lay it aside and its message will have no effect on them. This lesson will help you to add vigor and energy to your story.

Use Natural Dialogue

Dialogue is an important element of effective stories. Without dialogue, a story becomes a mere account—much like a report or description. But just having the story characters communicating with each other is not enough. Their dialogue must sound natural—the way real people talk. Below are three points that will help you to write natural-sounding dialogue.

1. *Keep the tone informal.* Few people speak in the formal tone that marks an essay. Can you imagine visiting with your friends after school and talking like this?

> "That was a very difficult history test, was it not?" asked Marlene.
>
> "It certainly was a very difficult test!" declared Susan. "I am almost sure that I will have some wrong on those matching sets. Those essay questions were hard too! I could not remember even one thing for that last question!"
>
> "Oh, I know those essay questions were hard." Marlene sighed. "I will be afraid even to look at my test when Brother Marcus returns it."

No, that is hardly the way you talk to your friends. Rather than using carefully structured, complete sentences, everyday speech contains contractions, interruptions, and elliptical sentences. The conversation above would be much more likely to sound like this:

> "Quite a history test, wasn't it?" asked Marlene.
>
> "Certainly was!" declared Susan. "I'm almost sure I'll have some wrong

on those matching sets. And those essay questions! I couldn't remember a thing for that—"

"Oh, I know." Marlene sighed. "I'll be afraid to even look at my test when Brother Marcus hands it back."

Establishing an informal tone, however, does not mean that you must use poor grammar, sloppy language, and slang. You might use poor grammar or sloppy language sparingly to characterize a specific person as being careless and unconcerned. But otherwise, such language is beneath the dignity of Christian writing.

2. *Change speakers frequently.* When people speak together, one person usually does not talk on and on. Instead, one person says a few things; then another asks a question or makes a comment, and so forth. Especially in a story, keep the quotations short. Long quotations stall the forward movement of a story.

3. *Use descriptive explanatory words.* Although *said* and *asked* are good words to use sometimes, a great variety of other terms can express *how* the characters said or asked their words. For example, words like *shout, call, demand, whisper, murmur, mutter, mumble, comment, prompt, agree, continue, answer, inquire,* and *question* can make an otherwise mediocre dialogue come alive.

Explanatory words must refer to things that can actually be done with words. People can *invite* with words, and they can *beg, call, shout, argue,* and so on. But no one can *hum, whistle, pause, point, smile,* or *frown* with words.

Incorrect:

"Come right on in," smiled Father.

"Well, I just came to ask if I may borrow your tractor," paused Mr. Nelson.

Correct:

"Come right on in," Father invited with a smile.

"Well, I just came to ask if I may borrow your tractor." Mr. Nelson paused.

(In the last sentence, *paused* is correct because it tells what Mr. Nelson did, not how he spoke. Note that it is in a separate sentence.)

Although explanatory words often contribute to the descriptiveness and smoothness of a story, they are not necessary in every paragraph of an extended dialogue. If the identity of the speakers is clear without stating who is speaking and you do not need to describe how they spoke, you may well omit the explanatory words altogether. The following example illustrates this point.

Late that night Mervin heard a loud knock at the door. He jumped out of bed and ran to his parents' bedroom. "Father!" he gasped. "There's someone at the door!"

Quickly Father got up, dressed, and hurried downstairs. Turning on the porch light, he saw a policeman standing outside!

Father opened the door. "Good evening; what can I do for you?" he asked.

> "Who's shooting around here?" demanded the policeman.
>
> "I don't know," replied Father calmly.
>
> "Do you have any boys?"
>
> "Yes, six."
>
> "Are they home?"
>
> "Yes, they are all in bed. But Mervin heard the shooting. If you want to talk with him, I can call him."

Use Straightforward Language

Clear, straightforward language also adds life to the writing style. But if your story contains many uncertain expressions, it will appear weak to your readers. Notice the underlined words in the following excerpt.

> "Melvin, you must take care of that boy of yours." Mr. Winters, the neighbor man, spoke in a loud, harsh-sounding voice. "Last evening he was down here throwing stones at my horses."
>
> "Well," replied Melvin rather uneasily, "I know he does things like that sometimes. I guess I'll have to talk with him." He shuffled around a bit as if somewhat unsure of what to do next.

It is easy to see that Melvin is a weak and indecisive father. You may use indefinite expressions in the speech of a character like that, but be careful not to let them creep into the narrative itself. Compare the following version of the excerpt above.

> "Melvin, you must take care of that boy of yours." Mr. Winters, the neighbor man, spoke in a loud, harsh voice. "Last evening he was down here throwing stones at my horses."
>
> "Well," replied Melvin uneasily, "I know he does things like that sometimes. I guess I'll have to talk with him." He shuffled around as if unsure of what to do next.

Here is a list of uncertain expressions and endings that you should treat with suspicion.

a little (a bit)	fairly	probably	-ish
about	maybe	rather	-looking
almost	perhaps	seemed	-seeming
around	possibly	somewhat	

These expressions do have a proper use, of course, but you must exercise good judgment. For example, suppose you are writing about Nelson, whose height is 5 feet 11 inches. You may well describe him as being "almost six feet tall," since *six feet* is an exact measure. But if you describe him less precisely, say that he is "tall," not "somewhat tall." The word *tall* is already inexact, and *somewhat* only makes it more so. A story with numerous expressions like these cannot convey a clear, forceful theme.

Use Fresh, Original Language

You need to avoid clichés in the narrative parts of a story—the parts that describe what is happening. As you saw in Lesson 3, a cliché is an expression which has been repeated so often that it no longer has its original force. Though the expression had once been vivid and sparkling, it is now weak and dull.

Many clichés are worn-out figures of speech. If you find such an expression in your writing, replace it with an original figurative comparison. Otherwise, use clear, direct language to express your idea.

Poor: Uses clichés

Though his face was as white as a sheet, George tried to make his voice to sound as bold as a lion.

Better: Uses an original comparison and direct language

Though his face was as pale as a wax figure, George tried to make his voice to sound strong and bold.

Remember, though, that people often use clichés in everyday speech. So it is proper to include a limited number of clichés in dialogue. In fact, a cliché is sometimes the best choice because an original expression may sound unnatural. Consider the following examples.

"That screw had been right here on the bench, as plain as day," Arnold declared. "Trying to find it now will be like looking for a needle in a haystack." (Clichés sound natural in dialogue.)

"That screw had been right here on the bench, as plain as a clock on the wall," Arnold declared. "Trying to find it now will be like looking for one grain of oats in a wheat bin." (Original expressions often sound unnatural in dialogue.)

This does not mean that you should purposely use clichés to make your story dialogue sound natural. It simply means that you may have a story character use a cliché if that is the most natural expression for a given situation.

Appeal to the Five Senses

Close your eyes and plug your ears. Now try to enjoy a conversation with your friends. Try to enjoy the outside scenery. Try to enjoy *anything* happening around you. Your chances of succeeding are quite low, for we learn about the world around us through our senses. Without them, we would lose touch with our surroundings.

Remember this when you are writing a story, and strive to stimulate the senses of your reader. Appeal to his sense of sight by giving clear and vivid descriptions. Appeal to his sense of hearing by portraying the sighs and screeches and other sounds of your story. Show the smells and describe the tastes that go along with the action. Make the reader feel the heat or shiver with cold.

When the reader lives with your story characters—seeing, feeling, smelling, hearing, and tasting along with them—your story comes to life. Notice how this is accomplished in the following paragraphs. The parts that especially appeal to the senses are underlined.

These descriptions show graphically the warmth and the cold. The reader can hardly help feeling with Fred as he faces the bitter elements outside.

Not only does the writer mention the smells, but he goes on to describe them so temptingly that we feel as if we are stepping into the warm kitchen with Fred.

With a glance toward the barn two hundred feet away, Fred resolutely stepped out of the cozy comfort of the house. Immediately the cold north wind bit into the exposed flesh of his face. It knifed through his heavy coat. It stung his nose and burned his lungs.

Two hours later, delicious breakfast smells welcomed Fred back into the snug house. He could almost taste the bacon sizzling in the cast-iron frying pan as it filled the atmosphere with its aroma. More faintly, the fragrance of freshly baked cornmeal muffins floated across the room.

Here is another paragraph, this one appealing to the reader's sense of hearing.

Crash and *tinkling* help the reader to hear the same sounds that poor Edna heard.

Suddenly Grandma Kramer's prized platter slipped from Edna's hands. It landed with a crash, followed by the tinkling of myriad pieces of china. Edna blinked back tears as she stared in horror at the ruins.

Remember: Have your characters speak with true-to-life expressions. Use straightforward language without *maybe*'s and *somewhat*'s. Think for yourself and avoid clichés. And aim for the five senses of your reader. The added life in your stories is well worth your extra efforts.

Applying the Lesson

A. Rewrite this story excerpt, following as many points of the lesson as possible to make the dialogue more natural. For one change, have Mother interrupt the speaker's detailed explanation in the third paragraph.

"What is wrong?" I asked as Mother replaced the telephone receiver.

In a tremulous voice, she said, "Keith has had an accident. Where is Father?"

"He is seeding alfalfa," I said. "That is what he said yesterday that his plans are. He would like to finish today because tomorrow it is supposed to rain."

"Take the pickup, and tell Father that Keith is in the hospital," Mother said.

"Thank You, Lord," I said in a whisper as I saw Father coming toward the near side of the alfalfa field.

Leaping from the truck, I sprinted across the field. "Father!" I said. "Keith is in the hospital. They have just transferred him to Springfield Medical Center."

B. Rewrite the underlined parts of these paragraphs, removing or replacing the clichés and indefinite expressions. If an underlined item needs no improvement, write *correct.*

"Young man." The gentleman addressed Ralph [1]in a fatherly-sounding voice. "Young man, the world has a place for talented, decent people like you. Have you ever considered going to college?" He surveyed Ralph [2]with kind-looking eyes.

"Well—ah—sir . . ." Ralph [3]hesitated a little and then [4]spoke somewhat more firmly. "Well, sir, I'm a Christian. I—"

"Of course," the man [5]answered as quick as a flash. "That's exactly why you could serve the world. You haven't ruined your life [6]in sowing wild oats as so many young people are doing today."

"It's only by the grace of God," replied Ralph, thinking of [7]his fairly sheltered life in a godly home. "But, sir, as for having a place in this world, I am not looking for that. I simply want to do God's will as faithfully as I can." Ralph had no desire to [8]blow his own horn; he would let the Lord choose the place where he should serve.

C. Follow the instructions to improve these story excerpts.

1. Rewrite to add appeal to the sense of hearing. (Add several words to indicate sounds.)

   Darla stirred in her sleep. Then she sat bolt upright. "Is someone knocking at the door?" she wondered. Sure enough, the knocking sounded again.

   Darla quickly crossed the hall and stood at her parents' bedroom door. "Father, Mother," she called, "someone's knocking at the front door."

2. Rewrite to add appeal to the sense of sight. (Add sentences describing what Father saw.)

   Father looked anxiously at the clouds gathering in the west. Glancing back over the pepper patch, he urged, "Boys, we'd better hurry. Looks like a thunderstorm brewing."

3. Finish the second paragraph to describe Wendell's lunch in a way that appeals to the sense of taste. (Add sentences giving details of what Wendell enjoyed as he ate the lunch.)

   When the sun stood high overhead, Grandpa said, "Time to eat, Wendell." Leaning their axes against the pile of split wood, the two made their way to the sugaring shack to eat lunch.

   After a prayer of thanks to the Provider of life, health, and daily food, Wendell opened his lunch bag.

D. You wrote the first draft of an original story in Chapter 6. In Chapter 8, you will either write the second draft or write a new story. As you learn in this chapter how to improve stories, think of specific ways to apply those methods to your own story. (You may want to write down some ideas.) Your score on the second draft of the story will make up a considerable part of your Chapter 8 test score.

Review Exercises

A. Write the correct term to match each description. [28–30]

1. Copying another's writing and passing it off as your own.
2. The main point of an essay.
3. A list of the sources used in preparing an essay.
4. A comment about a detail in the essay.

bibliography
exposition
footnote
plagiarism
theme

B. Write *true* if the statement is true, or *false* if it is false. [28–35]

1. The purpose of an exposition is to convince the reader of your idea or viewpoint.
2. The introductory paragraph of an exposition should resemble a funnel, with general ideas narrowing to a statement of the theme.
3. If a topic is too general, an essay is likely to be too detailed.
4. The abbreviation *ibid.* means "in the same place."
5. The entries in a bibliography should be numbered.
6. You should write a footnote for every detail that you draw directly from your notes.

---

68. Keep the Action Flowing

A well-written story picks up the reader right at the beginning, carries him at a comfortable speed through the entire story, and sets him down with a satisfied feeling at the conclusion. Therefore, an important element of an effective story is a smooth flow of action. This lesson describes four ways to keep the action flowing.

Use Lively Action Verbs

Verbs are the engines of sentences. If you use sluggish engines, your story will move sluggishly. But powerful engines will make your story move briskly and energetically. In previous books of this series, you learned that verbs in the active voice give much more life and vigor to sentences than do linking verbs and passive verbs.

Linking verbs convey no movement. They suggest stationary characters and events. Passive verbs do express action, but they weaken its force because things happen automatically—the story characters do little or nothing. Read the following paragraphs, noticing how the underlined linking and passive verbs deaden the action.

The sky was perfectly cloudless. Since there was not even the slightest breeze, the atmosphere was heated to an almost unbearable temperature by the blazing sunshine. The bean rows appeared almost endless.

"I am dreadfully thirsty," sighed Dennis.

"Yes," agreed Father, "the work certainly is made harder in this heat." Their progress was surveyed briefly, and then a welcome announcement was made. "Time for a break, boys."

Verbs in the active voice, as well as many intransitive complete verbs, do much better at keeping things brisk and interesting. Furthermore, using these strong verbs tends to draw out picturesque details in a way that linking verbs do not. As you read the following paragraphs, you should feel the stronger sense of movement produced by the active verbs.

Not a single cloud graced the sky. Not the slightest breeze moderated the blazing sunshine, which heated the atmosphere to an almost unbearable temperature. The bean rows stretched endlessly across the produce patch.

"I am dreadfully thirsty," sighed Dennis.

"Yes," agreed Father, "this heat certainly makes the work harder." He surveyed their progress briefly and then announced, "Time for a break, boys."

Notice that the improved version retains one linking verb: "I *am* dreadfully thirsty." Linking verbs portray a state of being, which is certainly true here. To rewrite this sentence with an active verb would produce a strained effect ("I have dreadful thirst").

Active voice and intransitive complete verbs generally make stronger engines than other verbs, but not all such verbs have equal "horsepower." So choose the most dynamic and descriptive verbs that fit the context. Compare the following examples.

Poor: Weak Verbs

"Wherever can that water be coming from?" asked Dawn.

"The bathroom!" Lois Ann called over her shoulder as she went up the steps two at a time. She pushed open the bathroom door with a *whoosh.*

A stream of warm water from the base of the faucet was running over the floor. Lois Ann waited but a moment; then she put her hand under the sink and turned the hot water shutoff valve.

Better: Strong Verbs

"Wherever can that water be coming from?" asked Dawn.

"The bathroom!" Lois Ann flung the words over her shoulder as she raced up the steps two at a time. She threw open the bathroom door with a *whoosh.*

A stream of warm water from the base of the faucet was spraying over the floor. Lois Ann hesitated but a moment; then she reached under the sink and twisted the hot water shutoff valve.

Limit Static Description

Every story includes a certain amount of static description. This is description that does not move the story forward, such as details about the setting or characters. A good story has as few such details as necessary. When static description is needed, try to slip it into a phrase or clause within a sentence that does carry the story action. Compare the following examples.

Poor: Too much static description

Terry stood outside the barn on the dairy farm where he lived, and twelve-year-old Walter stood nearby. The previous day had marked the last day of Terry's ninth year in school. Today was a pleasant day in mid-May. The air was fresh and exhilarating, and the sun shone brightly on the lush growth of grass. Terry's hair was neatly combed, but Walter had unkempt hair.

Better: Description woven into action

"Three months to enjoy the farm!" Terry voiced his thoughts to twelve-year-old Walter. The previous day had marked the last day of his ninth year in school. A pleasant mid-May sun smiled on the lush growth of grass. Terry took deep breaths of the fresh, exhilarating air. Brushing his hand across his well-combed hair, he glanced at Walter's unkempt hair.

Both paragraphs contain the same details (underlined), but note the contrast in how they are presented. In the better description, Terry *voiced his thoughts* rather than merely standing outside the barn. A pleasant mid-May sun *smiled* on the grass, and Terry *took deep breaths* of the fresh air. Terry was *brushing his hand* across his well-combed hair, and he *glanced* at Walter's unkempt hair. This is much more appealing than merely saying that it *was* a pleasant day, the air *was* fresh and exhilarating, Terry's hair *was* neatly combed, and so on. As much as possible, include such details in the action rather than presenting them as static description.

Avoid Arrested Action

A subtle snare that stalls story action is to have characters *begin* or *start* to do things rather than actually doing them. If Mother washed the dishes, do not write that she merely *began washing* them. If Susan swept the floor, avoid saying that she *started to sweep.* True, doing something always includes a beginning; but if you say that a story character merely *began* to do something, you arrest the action. Consider the following example.

Nolan whistled cheerily as he climbed the ladder to the haymow. At the top, he swung his leg over the beam and pulled himself onto the hay. Then he walked across the mow, grabbed a bale in each hand, and came back toward the edge of the mow.

"I'd better be careful," he said to himself. "Don't want to knock these end bales loose."

But even as he spoke, Nolan felt the bales shift beneath his feet. He threw himself backward and grabbed desperately for a handhold, but the entire edge of the mow had given way. With a sickening lurch, he plunged over the edge and landed with the hay bales on the floor below.

Father was just outside the milk house when he began to hear Nolan calling for help. He started running toward the barn as fast as he could.

Did Father actually hear Nolan, or did he only *begin* to hear him? Did he run to the barn or merely *start* running? Poor Nolan needed help, and we surely hope that Father indeed ran all the way to the barn. The following sentences keep the story moving without arresting the action.

> Father was just outside the milk house when he <u>heard</u> Nolan calling for help. He <u>ran</u> toward the barn as fast as he could.

Of course, *begin* and *start* do have valid uses. Sometimes an action is truly interrupted. And sometimes you may want to emphasize the time when an action began.

> Father <u>began to plow</u> the back field, but a hydraulic hose burst.
> Since Father <u>began plowing</u> the back field soon after lunch, he should be almost finished.

Match the Pace to the Action

On some occasions, things happen rapidly and time flies. On others, the activity around us almost stops and time seems to crawl. This difference shows up in stories too. Things happen at different speeds. As we write about these circumstances, we must match our story style to the speed of the action.

For example, suppose we are writing about a busy Saturday morning scene. A telephone call has just announced unexpected visitors for lunch. Suddenly much work must be done in a very short time. How can we write in a way that creates the feeling of hustle-and-bustle that would be present on such an occasion? As you read the following paragraphs, try to identify what it is that makes the action move rapidly.

> "All right, then. We'll be glad to see you folks again." As Father hung up the telephone receiver, all eyes focused on him.
>
> "Well, this is going to change our morning plans drastically," announced Father. "Brother Abner Krahn's are on their way to Lancaster County. Their trip went better than they had expected, and they want to visit with us for a few hours. They'll be here for lunch."
>
> "Oh, dear," wailed Melanie. "How will we ever get ready for company that fast?"
>
> "And whatever will we do with all those apples?" asked Ferne.
>
> "Some of them may just wait until Monday," Mother replied calmly to Ferne. "And," turning to Melanie, "we can easily prepare for company in four hours!"
>
> "Yes," agreed Father. "Everyone finished with breakfast? You're all excused. Clarence, finish feeding the stock. Nevin, mow the grass. James and Dallas, clean up around the house and barn. Then check with Mother."
>
> Suddenly the kitchen became a beehive of activity. The boys dashed outside. Father followed at a brisk walk. Melanie whisked the plates and cups off the table. Ferne plopped the dishpans and the draining rack into place. And Mother snatched the cookbook off the shelf.

Notice how short most of the sentences are. In the entire selection, the average is about eight words per sentence. But in the last two paragraphs, the sentences average only six words each. These short sentences give a distinct feeling of bustling activity.

In addition to the shortness of the sentences, the author's choice of words in the last paragraph pictures speed, energy, and excitement. Note the words *beehive, dashed, whisked, plopped,* and *snatched.*

Now suppose we are writing about a very different Saturday morning scene. Father and Mother had left for the hospital before breakfast because Grandfather was sick. The rest of the family is at home, waiting for news about Grandfather. How can we write in a way that emphasizes the slower action and dragging time on such a morning? Read the following paragraphs, noting how they differ from the example above.

> "Well, that's the latest breakfast I ever remember eating." Clarence sighed as he glanced around the table.
>
> "That's for sure," agreed Nevin. "Guess I didn't realize how much work Father does." He smiled sheepishly as he pushed his chair back from the table.
>
> Melanie nodded understandingly. "Same thing here in the kitchen, wasn't it, Ferne?"
>
> "Yes," answered Ferne. "I'm glad Mother isn't gone every morning." She paused and cleared her throat; then she added, "I sure wonder how Grandpa is doing."
>
> "So do I," stated Clarence. "But Father will call as soon as he has anything to report, so we may as well get started with the morning work. We have too many things to do to just sit here and talk."
>
> He rose from his chair and scratched his head thoughtfully. "Nevin, if you help me feed the livestock, you can start mowing while I do the other chores at the barn. James and Dallas should clean up around the house and barn. Do you girls have any work for them after that?"
>
> "Yes, they'll be a big help to us," replied Ferne.
>
> Listlessly the boys got up from the table and headed for their various chores. With a long sigh, Melanie picked up her cup and stacked it with the others. Ferne pulled the dishpans out from under the sink. Gazing out the window, she idly sloshed her hands in the water that slowly filled the dishpan.

Notice how much longer these sentences are than in the previous sample. In the entire selection, the sentences average about eleven words each. In the last three paragraphs, the average is thirteen words per sentence.

Again, the author's choice of words contributes to the pace of the story. Note the words *paused, listlessly, long sigh, idly,* and *slowly.*

As you can see, short sentences and lively words speed up the action of a story; but long sentences and sluggish words slow down the action. By using these devices, we can create a mood and pace that matches the action in a story.

Applying the Lesson

A. Rewrite this story excerpt, removing as many linking verbs and passive voice verbs as practical.

"Sure, Mrs. Nelson," Father responded. "Splitting and stacking your wood was enjoyed by the boys."

"Well, their work was greatly appreciated again. You folks are helpful to me in so many ways. Yet you're never fully repaid for your kindness." These words were spoken with deep emotion.

"Oh, but you're mistaken, Mrs. Nelson," Father said softly. "We are well rewarded by the Lord. Your praise should be given to Him."

On the way home, Father's statement was pondered by two tired boys. Finally the thoughts on their minds were expressed by Raymond. "Father, I wish Mrs. Nelson's offer to pay us for our work would be accepted. That would be better than the reward you talked about."

"Why, Raymond!" Father exclaimed. "That was surely said without thinking. How can anything be more valuable than the blessing of the Lord?"

B. Find each sentence with an example of arrested action, and write enough words to show how it can be improved.

1. [a]"Well, girls," Mother declared after breakfast, "we must start cleaning the house and preparing dinner. [b]Uncle Lamar's will be here before we're ready."

   [c]"Yes," agreed Father as he began to push his chair back from the table. [d]"You boys have plenty to do too in the furniture shop. [e]Fred, you start working at cleaning up the finishing room. [f]Mervin, I want you to start turning that stock for McKee's order. [g]It must be finished by tomorrow."

2. [a]"Mother, this iron is starting to give me trouble again," Melinda called. [b]"It isn't staying hot like it should."

   [c]Mother began to sigh. [d]"Oh, no," she said. [e]"If the iron quits working too, what will we do?" [f]But she had barely spoken when she began to think of some Bible promises assuring the saints of God's care.

3. [a]I was at the far end of my trapline when I started to notice that the previously bright sunshine was dimming fast. [b]I glanced at the sky and checked the wind. [c]A cold deeper than the rising wind at the sub-zero temperature began to grip my heart. [d]A blizzard was brewing, and I had been too absorbed in my work to notice!

   [e]"Dear Lord," I prayed as I began to hurry homeward, "protect me if it be Thy will."

C. Rewrite these story excerpts, following the directions for each.

1. This scene contains a number of static descriptions (underlined). Rewrite the scene to include those details within sentences that carry the story action. Begin your paragraph with the starred sentence.

   <u>It was a pleasant day in June. The uncles and aunts and cousins were sitting around the picnic tables at Uncle Raymond's farm.</u>

*A solemn hush fell over the group as Grandfather Bender stood and lifted his hand for silence. His hair was snow-white, and his hands were shaky. "It is a pleasure to come together like this again," he said. His voice was tender, and it trembled a bit more than usual. "The Lord has richly blessed us. We have a godly heritage. And we have plenty of food and clothing. Let us bow our heads and give thanks to our heavenly Father."

2. For this scene, suppose that Grandmother had just called and asked for Nancy's help in the afternoon. Rewrite the scene to change the slow-moving action to the more rapid action that would result. Change and add details to make things consistent.

"Now what shall I do next?" Nancy murmured to herself. Staring at the clock, she stifled a sigh. "Only ten o'clock!" Her words echoed in the kitchen that usually bustled with family activity.

"I never imagined that I would become so lonely this soon!" she declared to herself. Her mind went back to the morning two days before when Father and Mother and all the children except Abigail and her had left for New York. "Well, this is Saturday." Nancy sighed. "So it's just today and Monday to spend alone here, doing all the work. I guess I'd better get started with making the butter."

Review Exercises

A. Write the correct term to match each description. [49–53]

1. The lesson that a story teaches.
2. The process of portraying story characters.
3. The perspective from which an author writes a story.
4. The main character of a story.
5. The struggle or problem that the main character faces.
6. The time, place, and atmosphere of a story.

antagonist
characterization
conflict
point of view
protagonist
setting
theme

B. Write *true* if the statement is true, or *false* if it is false. [48–53]

1. Many effective stories are written about common, everyday happenings.
2. The first person point of view carries the strongest impression of reality.
3. The two most common methods of portraying characters are showing their actions and their appearance.
4. In the third person point of view, the author writes as if he were able to see every character equally well.
5. In a subjective point of view, the author reveals the thoughts of characters.
6. Background characters may be named, but they should not be characterized.

69. Paint Descriptive Details

A good story holds the reader's interest. While this is often due to the nature of the story and the development of its plot, the writer's choice of words also plays a major part. For just as a painter needs brilliant, sharp colors to make an attractive painting, so an author needs descriptive words to write an effective story.

Exact, Descriptive Words

Vagueness clouds writing and obscures its message. The only way to avoid such haziness is to use exact, descriptive words. Pay special attention to nouns and verbs, the two most important parts of speech. Whenever possible, use a precise noun or verb rather than a general word with modifiers. Your dictionary or thesaurus will help you to find the best possible word choices.

Compare the following sentences. Notice the precise nouns and verb forms that are underlined in the second example.

> **Vague:** The men forcefully threw the burning things from the building.
> **Clear:** Father and Uncle Charles flung the flaming rags from the shop.

Although modifiers are not as basic to our communication as nouns and verbs, they are also important. You need to choose colorful adjectives and adverbs to make the picture as clear as possible. Notice in the sample above that *burning* is changed to *flaming* because that paints a sharper picture. We could also add adjectives to describe *shop.*

> Father and Uncle Charles flung the flaming rags from the crowded furniture shop.

Remove every weak modifier. If a sentence would benefit from additional details, change the weak modifier to an appropriate adjective or adverb, or choose a more precise noun or verb. Be especially suspicious of the following weak modifiers.

anyway	exactly	really	some
certainly	just	right	such
definitely	maybe	so	very
even	quite		

Now compare the following sentences. Notice the improvement made by deleting or replacing the weak modifiers.

Weak modifiers:

> Because the boys were very much involved in their game, they definitely failed to notice the really black clouds gathering in the west.

Exact modifiers:

> Because the boys were deeply involved in their game, they failed to notice the inky clouds gathering in the west.

Simple, Familiar Words

Occasionally, a writer falls into the trap of thinking that many large and unusual words add to effective description. That is not necessarily true. In fact, simple, familiar words are generally the best. These words the reader will readily understand. If you do use an occasional larger or less familiar word, be sure the context makes the word easy to understand.

Here are two versions of a paragraph from the story "'He Rides Upon the Storm'" in Chapter 6. Observe the difference in the underlined words.

Poor: Uses uncommon words and expressions

That very night I suddenly sat bolt upright in bed, my heart beating apace. "What was that?" I wondered bewilderedly. In rejoinder, there came a resplendent flash of lightning, followed instantaneously by a sharp crash of thunder. All slumber having departed, I reclined, closed my eyes, and shivered.

Good: Uses simple, familiar words

That very night I suddenly sat bolt upright in bed, my heart pounding wildly. "What was that?" I wondered bewilderedly. In answer, there came a brilliant flash of lightning, followed closely by a sharp crash of thunder. All sleepiness chased away, I lay down, closed my eyes, and shivered.

Imagery

Imagery includes similes, metaphors, personification, and hyperboles. By making apt, striking comparisons, these figures of speech paint vivid word pictures. They are high-powered tools of descriptive writing. In the discussion below, the examples are from stories in Chapter 6.

A simile makes a figurative comparison by using *like* or *as.*

Walter's urgent shouts jolted Terry like an electric shock.
The rain and the hail combined into one mighty, oceanlike roar.

A metaphor makes a figurative comparison without using *like* or *as.* Some metaphors contain a form of *be* and say that one thing is another thing when that is not literally true. Other metaphors use literal terms to describe something that happens only in a figurative sense.

"This grass sure needs a good haircut."
Throwing the torn starter cord against the mower, Terry spun around, his face a thundercloud.
He threw the words over his shoulder as he stalked away.
Terry's voice dripped with annoyance.
My mind whirled into high gear.

In personification, a thing or quality is pictured as if it had the characteristics of a living creature

The front lawn was nearly finished when the sputtering engine coughed and died.

A hyperbole is what might be called an artistic exaggeration. It gives an overstated description—not to deceive someone, but to create a vivid picture in the mind.

Sure enough, a mountain of feed covered the floor below the feed bin chute.

Challenge yourself to make your story so clear and colorful that readers feel as if they are personally involved in the action.

Applying the Lesson

A. Write words that are more exact and descriptive, which could replace the underlined words in this story excerpt. If an underlined item should be deleted, show that by writing the words immediately before and after it.

Grandmother always seemed happy, using her [1]equipment to [2]work on clothes for others. She was sitting there when I stepped into the [3]room.

With a [4]tired sound, I [5]sat down on a nearby chair. "What do you do, Grandmother, when someone [6]just deliberately tries to [7]make you feel bad?"

Calmly Grandmother finished the [8]line of stitches. Then she turned to look at me. "Is Trudy Walters [9]getting after you again?"

"Yes. I [10]really don't understand why she should [11]be against me. I'm [12]just sure I've never done anything to [13]cause her resentful feelings."

"From what you've said before, Arlene, I wonder if [14]maybe Trudy's problem is that your [15]good testimony is [16]making her feel guilty."

B. Write simple, familiar words that could replace the underlined words in this story excerpt.

"Does your head still feel [1]congested?" Mother asked [2]solicitously as she turned to face her oldest daughter. "If it does, I can [3]transport you to the doctor and go shopping while I wait."

"That would be [4]charitable," Rhoda answered. "I surely would [5]take no pleasure in driving today."

The waiting room was [6]overpopulated. Rhoda [7]anticipated a long wait as she [8]traversed the room to find an [9]unoccupied chair. About an hour passed before a nurse [10]summoned her to see the doctor.

C. Write suitable figures of speech that could replace four of the underlined expressions in this story excerpt.

Carla stood on the porch a few minutes, gazing about [1]with an expression of awe. "How I enjoy this secluded valley with the mountains [2]all around us," she whispered. "And the beautiful blue sky with the [3]fluffy white clouds." As she stood there [4]gazing at the beauty, a Carolina wren [5]expressed itself in a sweet song. "Thank You, Lord, for the beautiful world You have made," Carla whispered again.

"Carla, hang up that wash!" Mother's harsh voice shattered Carla's reverie. "You have too much work to do to stand there gawking!"

"Yes, Mother," responded Carla quietly. "This beauty impressed me so greatly that I had to praise the Creator."

[6]Her heart felt heavy as she hurried out to the clothesline. "If only Mother were a Christian," Carla said with a sigh.

---

70. Improving Your Editing Skills, Part 7

As the title of this lesson indicates, editing involves a number of skills—things that you must practice in order to do them well. One important skill is to see what is actually written on the page, rather than what you expect to see. Consider the following example.

Two scientists in Europe, working separately, discovered oxgyen in the 1770s.

Is everything in order? The proper noun is capitalized, *separately* is spelled properly, and the independent element and *1770s* are punctuated correctly. But there is one mistake! If you did not catch it, you saw the misspelled word *oxgyen* as *oxygen.* It is because proofreaders see what they expect to see that they sometimes overlook mistakes—even if they think they are fully concentrating on their work.

When you proofread, you need to inspect each word and punctuation mark separately. Put special effort into seeing what is actually written so that you can correct *every* mistake.

Marks Used in Editing and Proofreading

˅ or ^ insert (caret)	delete	.... stet (let it stand)	use italics
¶ begin new paragraph	no ¶ no new paragraph	lc change to lowercase (small letter)	uc change to uppercase (capital letter)
# insert space	delete space	← move (arrow)	transpose

Editing Practice

A. Use proofreading marks to correct the two capitalization or punctuation errors in each sentence.

1. **A new commission for patents was established shortly before the thirteenth State signed the constitution.**
2. **The first commission consisted of: Thomas Jefferson, Henry Knox and Edmund Randolph.**
3. **Opening for business on april 10, 1790 this commission required a working model with each application for a patent.**

4. **An unmanageable number of models had accumulated by 1807, therefore, a new Law specified that the commissioner would determine whether a model was needed.**
5. **It appears, however that the commissioner felt inadequate to decide, for the accumulation of models didnt decline.**
6. **Because of the large number of models the patent office had been moved to Blodgett's hotel in 1810.**
7. **When the British burned the capital city during the war of 1812 this was the only government building spared.**
8. **Dr William Thornton headed the patent office at that time and he deserves the credit for saving its treasures.**
9. **News of the danger to the office raised Thorntons ire so much that he ignored self interest and raced to the city.**
10. **He dissuaded the British from burning the building—what a waste that would have been! by comparing such an action to the Turks destruction of the Alexandrian Library.**

B. Use proofreading marks to correct the one or two usage errors in each sentence.
1. If we maintain a heavenly prospective, we will continue to feel that the Bible always applies to present-day living.
2. Read often in the Book of Proverbs, and leave those practical precepts influence your life.
3. If your not enthused about a job, do the best you can anyway.
4. For three days a stationery front set over the region, producing heavy rains.
5. Loretta's answer implied that she is progressing right along with her work.
6. Father is doing some better, but the doctor said that he will be in bed for awhile yet.
7. I wonder how come Duchess wants out of her pen so much.
8. Our neighbor's dog is notable for continually disturbing the neighborhood chickens, lambs, and other animals.

9. Milford's idea surely differed with mine, but I know he is more familiar with those there tools than I am.
10. There is nothing in back of you, so you should back strait to the loading dock.

C. Use proofreading marks to correct all the errors in this essay. Your corrections should include one use of the stet symbol and one joining of two paragraphs. No line has more than one error.

Our sun is an average-sized star. That is, in comparing it to most other stars in the universe, we find that it is similar in size. But lets consider a star that is not average—one that is much more larger than the sun.

Scientists classify Betelgeuse (bēt′·əl·jüz′), a bight star in the constellation Orion, as a red supergiant. The star is red (rather than yellow like the sun because its surface temperature is half only as hot. This star goes through cycles of expanding and shrinking. With an average diameter 460 times that of the sun, it has an enormity that we can hardly fathom.

If this star could be placed in the center of our solar system, it would ~~completely~~ engulf the orbits of Mercury, Venus, earth, and Mars!

The diameter of Betelgeuse, varies by about 100 million miles, which is more than the distance from the earth to the sun. If our sun were a variablestar like that, life as we know it would~~n't~~ hardly be possible. Truly we can be glad for the Sun as God made it—a steady star that provides a constant, depend able supply of heat and light.

71. Proofreading and Rewriting the Story

You probably put much time and effort into the first draft of the story you wrote in Chapter 6. In the present chapter, you have studied various methods by which a story can be improved. Now you will put those methods to practice in proofreading and rewriting your story.

Proofreading

In proofreading the first draft of your story, use proofreading marks to show your corrections. The following checklist can help in this process.

1. Does the story have a worthwhile theme?
2. Does the story open effectively with action, dialogue, or an unusual statement?
3. Does the opening promptly introduce the main character, establish the setting, and hint at the theme and conflict? Does the story open as near to the first scene of conflict as possible?
4. Does it portray the characters effectively and consistently?
5. Is the conflict clear and forceful? Does it build up to a climax that occurs near the end of the story?
6. Is the conclusion brief and satisfying?
7. Does the story have a fresh, original title that does not give away the outcome?
8. Have you consistently adhered to the point of view that you have chosen?
9. Does the story have smooth transitions between scenes?
10. Does it have natural dialogue, straightforward expressions, and fresh, original language? Does it appeal to the five senses?
11. Have you kept the action moving by using lively action verbs, by limiting static description, and by avoiding arrested action?
12. Have you used exact, descriptive words while avoiding large unfamiliar words?
13. Have you used apt figures of speech?
14. Are there any awkward sentences that you should reword?
15. Have you used correct spelling, punctuation, and grammar?

Rewriting

The final step, of course, is to rewrite the story, incorporating the corrections and changes you have made in your proofreading. For the final draft, you should write on every line. Strive for a neat paper: use your best penmanship, keep the left margin straight, and keep the right margin as straight as practical.

Applying the Lesson

A. Do one of the following things.

1. Proofread the first draft of the story that you wrote in Lesson 56. Use the questions listed in this lesson, and mark changes by using the proofreading symbols you have learned.

2. Start over by writing a new story, following the pattern taught in Chapter 6. Lay your story aside for a day or so, and then proofread it as described in number 1 above.

B. Write the second draft of your story, making the improvements that you marked. Use every line, write as neatly as you can, and keep neat margins. Your teacher may use the evaluation chart below to grade your story. Remember, your score on this story will make up a considerable part of your Chapter 8 test score.

Evaluation of a Story

Points possible	Points earned	
Title		
2	____	Short and appealing
2	____	Relates to theme without revealing the outcome
Theme		
3	____	Introduces theme in an interesting way
3	____	Worthwhile; evident without being directly stated
3	____	Consistent throughout story
Structure		
3	____	Opens effectively with action, dialogue, or unusual statement
3	____	Has at least three incidents of conflict
3	____	Conflict intensifies or consists of satisfactory individual incidents
3	____	Has consistent point of view throughout story
3	____	Ends with a satisfying conclusion
Characterization		
3	____	Major characters portrayed consistently throughout story
3	____	Uses several methods of characterization
3	____	Minor and background characters presented appropriately
Style		
3	____	Natural dialogue, straightforward language, appeals to five senses
3	____	Active verbs; other exact, descriptive words; avoidance of unfamiliar words
3	____	Apt figures of speech
Mechanics		
3	____	Correct spelling
3	____	Correct capitalization and punctuation
3	____	Correct grammar
3		Avoidance of careless repetition, omitted words, transpositions
58	____	**Total points**

72. Chapter 8 Review

A. Write the correct words for these descriptions.

1. Words like *said, asked,* and *exclaimed.*
2. The voice of verbs that adds life and vigor to a story.
3. A figurative comparison that uses *like* or *as.*
4. A figurative, artistic exaggeration.
5. Imagery that uses literal terms to describe something that happens only in a figurative sense.
6. Imagery that pictures a thing or quality as having the characteristics of a living creature.
7. A once-vivid expression that has become stale through overuse.
8. The error of having story characters merely *begin* or *start* to do things.

B. Rewrite this story excerpt, making the dialogue more natural as you studied in Lesson 67.

"Oh, Tina," said Lillie, "you ought to read *Caught in the Web.* It is quite interesting."

"Should I really read it?" said Tina. "Is it your book?"

"No, it is not mine," said Lillie. "It belongs to my cousin Suzanne. Do you remember her? She is from Pennsylvania. She was at church last summer when her family visited us."

"Yes, I remember her." Tina said thoughtfully. "She was rather worldly, was she not?"

"Well, yes, she was a bit worldly," Lillie said. "But this book is a good, Christian story."

"What is the story about?" said Tina.

"It is about a Christian girl who grew cold spiritually, ran away from home, and got tangled up in some wrong things," Lillie said. "Toward the end of the book, she repented and got things straightened out again."

"It does sound interesting," Tina said. "Of course, I would want my parents to review it first."

C. Rewrite the numbered phrases, replacing the clichés, removing the indefinite expressions, and making a stronger appeal to the five senses. Several notes in brackets give specific directions.

"This spot is beautiful," declared Fred [1]in rather awed tones. "That waterfall sounds [2]really loud." [Use a simile.]

"I'd like to go down closer," suggested Melvin.

"We can't climb down here," returned Fred. He pointed toward [3]the steep-looking bank.

"I know a path we can take," offered Albert. "It's almost as steep as a ladder. But if you watch your step, it's not too bad."

[4]As quick as a wink, the boys were clambering down the trail. [5]They made a beeline for the waterfall [6]almost as soon as they reached the bottom.

"Look at this pool!" exclaimed Melvin. "The water [7]is really clear." [Use a simile.]

[8]"I can feel the spray from the waterfall way out here," Fred commented. [Have Fred tell how the spray feels.]

D. The following excerpt contains several linking verbs and passive verbs. For each numbered sentence, write enough words to show how to improve those sentences with lively action verbs.

[1]"Yes, Allen is a hard worker," stated Sister Arlene. "I'm not sure how I would get along without his strong arms. Since Paul passed away . . ."

[2]"His dedication is deeply appreciated by all of us," she was assured by Sister Brenda.

[3]"Nearly all the farm work is managed by him now," Sister Arlene commented further. [4]"Uncle Dale is here occasionally to check on things. [5]He is called by Allen whenever there is a problem."

[6]The conversation was ended by Allen's sudden appearance. [7]"Good afternoon, Sister Brenda," the visitor was addressed politely. "This is surely a warm day, isn't it?"

E. Rewrite this story excerpt, removing all examples of arrested action. Also remove the static descriptions, or include them within sentences that carry the story action.

Mildred Lefever was sixteen years old. She had blue eyes and blond hair. She had been crippled in a car accident and was now confined to a wheelchair. On this warm June day, she was soaking in the warmth of the sunshine as she sat on the spacious front porch.

"Oh, how nice!" Mildred's face began to light up with joy as Uncle William's car drove up the lane. "An afternoon with Louise and Alma will be wonderful!"

Before long, the two cousins had started setting up a small folding table for a game of Scrabble.

F. Write more exact and descriptive words that could replace the underlined words.

Paul [1]took the [2]tool and [3]moved it swiftly through the air. *Crack!* The sharp blade [4]divided the wood neatly. Quickly he [5]put another [6]piece in place. *Crack!* That one too was soon split.

"At this rate," he said to himself as he wiped the [7]moisture from his [8]face, "I'll finish [9]this job by noon. Then I can work on my [10]project for a while."

G. Write simple, familiar words that could replace the underlined expressions.

"This large [1]institution of learning is quite different from the small one we were [2]accustomed to [3]heretofore," Priscilla commented as she and Edward [4]ambulated homeward.

"I [5]concur with that," Edward replied. [6]"Gaining acquaintance with all these students is [7]intimidating, but I will enjoy the recesses."

"Yes, and the class [8]dialogues will be [9]far superior too. Back at Walnut Valley, it was quite [10]infrequent to have more than four students in one class."

As the two reached the top of the last [11]prominence in the road, they broke into a run for their [12]residence.

H. Write suitable figures of speech that could replace the underlined expressions.

Vernon glanced up from his book as the wind [1]blew vigorously outside. It [2]made wild noises around the corners of the house, and it [3]blew the deep snow into intricate shapes.

In the center of the room stood the cast-iron stove, [4]warming the house. Through its glass doors, Vernon watched the flames [5]moving upward around the oak logs. As his gaze [6]passed over his surroundings, Vernon's heart filled with thanksgiving.

"Thank You, Lord," he breathed, "for a cozy house. Thank You even more for a fine Christian family."

Then his thoughts turned to the Swartz family down the road. He remembered Sylvan's longing words, "You fellows have it so nice. Every time I'm with you, why, it seems so very peaceful. The atmosphere in my home is [7]tense."

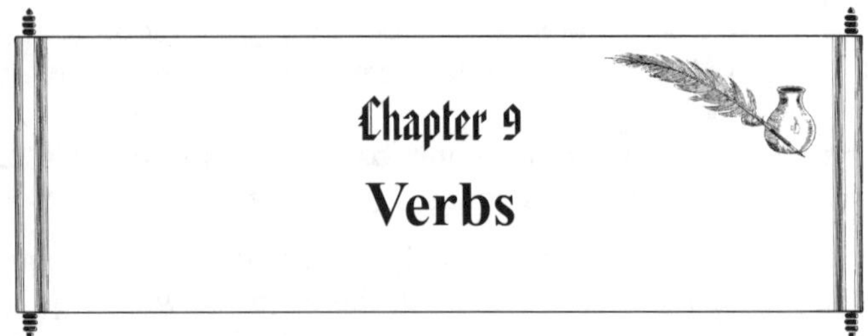

Chapter 9
Verbs

73. Verbs and the Principal Parts of Verbs

Nouns and verbs make up the core of language. Nouns give substance to language by naming persons, places, things, and ideas. Verbs are the engines of language, making the nouns act or exist in specific ways.

Basic Facts About Verbs

1. *A verb expresses action or being to tell what the subject does or is.* The verb joins with the subject to make the basic framework, or skeleton, of a sentence.

> Isaac willingly gave up his wells.
> Isaac is an example for us.

2. *Every clause has a verb, which is the simple predicate of the clause.*

> The Philistines had mistreated Isaac.

In an elliptical clause, the verb may be understood. Elliptical sentences are found mainly in dialogue.

> Which two Bible characters never died?
> Enoch and Elijah. (Enoch and Elijah never died.)

3. *Many simple predicates are verb phrases, consisting of the main verb and one or more helping verbs.* The main verb always comes last in a verb phrase.

Other words often interrupt a verb phrase. Many of these are adverbs like *not, never, hardly, always, ever,* and *surely.* In a contraction like *don't,* the *n't* is also an adverb. In a question, the subject often comes between the helping verb and the main verb.

> Elaine has surely increased her typing speed this year.
> She hasn't managed to type without numerous errors.
> Does she really deserve a good score on this paper?

4. *Sometimes the simple predicate is a compound verb, in which two or more verbs are joined by a conjunction.* The parts of a compound verb share the same subject. They may also share the same helping verb, which may appear only before the first main verb.

> The students sat tensely and waited for the starting signal.
> Soon they were typing rapidly, trying to avoid errors, and listening for the signal to stop.

Principal Parts of Verbs

5. *Verbs have three principal parts, which are used to form the different tenses: the first principal part (present form), the second principal part (past form), and the third principal part (past participle).*

Present	Past	Past Participle
walk	walked	(have) walked
ring	rang	(have) rung

6. *The first principal part is the basic form of a verb—the form you would use with* to.

walk see ring build run

7. *The second and third principal parts of most verbs are formed by adding* -ed *to the first principal part.* Other spelling changes may also be necessary. If the verb ends with *e,* drop the *e* before adding *-ed.* If the verb ends with *y* after a consonant, change the *y* to *i.* If a one-syllable verb ends with a single consonant after a short vowel, double the final consonant.

Present	Past	Past Participle
comb	combed	(have) combed
bake	baked	(have) baked
carry	carried	(have) carried
chop	chopped	(have) chopped

8. *The second and third principal parts of some verbs have irregular forms.* The correct forms of a few of the commonly misused ones follow. Use an English handbook or a dictionary to find the correct forms whenever you are in doubt.

First *(Present)*	Second *(Past)*	Third *(Past Participle)*	First *(Present)*	Second *(Past)*	Third *(Past Participle)*
awake	awoke	(have) awoke	know	knew	(have) known
	or awaked	(have) awaked	lay	laid	(have) laid
bid	bade	(have) bidden	leave	left	(have) left
	or bid	(have) bid	let	let	(have) let
blow	blew	(have) blown	lie	lay	(have) lain
bring	brought	(have) brought	raise	raised	(have) raised
burst	burst	(have) burst	rise	rose	(have) risen
come	came	(have) come	see	saw	(have) seen
creep	crept	(have) crept	set	set	(have) set
dig	dug	(have) dug	shrink	shrank	(have) shrunk
do	did	(have) done		*or* shrunk	(have) shrunken
drag	dragged	(have) dragged	sit	sat	(have) sat
drink	drank	(have) drunk	swim	swam	(have) swum
drown	drowned	(have) drowned	swing	swung	(have) swung
forbid	forbade	(have) forbidden	tag	tagged	(have) tagged
	or forbad	(have) forbid	take	took	(have) taken
go	went	(have) gone			

9. *In addition to the three principal parts, most verbs have two other forms—the present participle and the* -s *form.* The present participle, which ends with *-ing,* is used in progressive verb forms. The *-s* form is used with third person singular subjects in the present tense.

Mother is baking bread today. She bakes ten loaves every week.

Applying the Lesson

A. List all the verbs and verb phrases. Underline the main verb in each verb phrase.

1. "The words of a talebearer are as wounds, and they go down into the innermost parts of the belly."
2. "A good man obtaineth favour of the LORD: but a man of wicked devices will he condemn."
3. "Trust in the LORD with all thine heart; and lean not unto thine own understanding."
4. "Counsel in the heart of man is like deep water; but a man of understanding will draw it out."
5. A Christian driver will be obeying the traffic laws and showing courtesy to other motorists.
6. He dims his lights for oncoming traffic, follows other cars at a proper distance, and keeps his vehicle in a safe condition.
7. Did you stop completely at that intersection?
8. Has Harold been studying for his driver's test?

B. Write the correct form of each underlined verb; do not change the tense. If it is correct, write *correct.*

1. After the water pipes had froze, we needed to carry water in buckets.
2. The students raised their hands to volunteer for the job.
3. When the dog seen me coming, he started to bark fiercely.
4. These stockings have shrank so much that I can no longer wear them.
5. I was sure that I had laid the knife beside my plate.
6. Howard tug three of the prisoners and set them free.
7. The wind is so strong that it has blew down several of our pine trees.
8. It looks as if Mrs. Walters has came for some more eggs.
9. The allurements of evil have drawn many away from the Lord.
10. By this time most of the robins have flew north for the summer.
11. Our neighbor lady planned to visit our church, but her husband forbad it.
12. After you have hanged the wash on the line, sweep off the porch.

C. Write the correct past form of each verb in parentheses. Use the past participle only if there is a helping verb in the sentence.

1. You have again (forget) to close the door.
2. We (throw) the empty box into the incinerator.
3. After everyone had (shake) hands, we sat down to visit.
4. The congregation has (kneel) for prayer.
5. David (slay) Goliath with the giant's own sword.
6. The boy who has (steal) a penny will likely steal much larger things.

7. Slowly and quietly, we (creep) toward the large bullfrog.
8. Never before had we (ride) in a jet.
9. The borrower is servant to the man who has (lend) him money.
10. Mary polished the apple until it (shine).

Review Exercises

Write the letters of the correct forms in each sentence. [61]

1. When Jesus fed the five thousand, twelve ([a]basketsful, [b]basketfuls) of food were left after the ([a]people's, [b]peoples') hunger was satisfied.
2. The three ([a]bailiff's, [b]bailiffs') terms lasted until ([a]the decade's end, [b]the end of the decade).
3. We put ([a]ten dollars' worth, [b]the worth of ten dollars) of gasoline into ([a]the car's tank, [b]the tank of the car).
4. Both of my ([a]brother-in-laws, [b]brothers-in-law) know what a ([a]day's laborer, [b]day laborer's) life is like.
5. An ([a]individual's, [b]individuals') looks and intelligence are not reliable ([a]indicae, [b]indices) of his character.
6. The ([a]dormice, [b]dormouses) disappeared into the ([a]bushes' leaves, [b]leaves of the bushes).
7. Some brook ([a]trout's, [b]trouts') bodies are as much as eighteen ([a]inches, [b]inches') long.
8. Ancient ([a]Roman's, [b]Romans) served the tongues of ([a]flamingo's, [b]flamingos) as a delicacy.
9. In both ([a]gentlemen's, [b]gentlemens') opinions, these ([a]analysa, [b]analyses) are fair and accurate.
10. The ([a]nuclea, [b]nuclei) of all the ([a]amoebae, [b]amoebi) were clearly visible in the photograph.

---

74. Simple and Perfect Tenses

Verbs have different forms to indicate action or existence in the past, present, or future. English verbs have three simple tenses and three perfect tenses.

Simple Tenses

1. *The present tense shows action or existence in the present.* It also records a statement of general truth, even if the context of the sentence is past. Present tense uses the first principal part (present form). The third person singular form ends with *-s.*

> Jonathan Burkholder, who lives next door, is a minister at our church.
> Jesus testified that He is the Son of God.

2. *The past tense shows action or existence in the past.* It uses the second principal part (past form).

> Daniel Kauffman edited the book *Doctrines of the Bible.*

3. *The future tense shows action or existence in the future.* The future tense uses the first principal part (present form) with the helping verb *shall* or *will.* In formal writing, use *shall* for first person subjects and *will* for second and third person subjects. In general usage, *will* is acceptable for all three persons.

I shall call you tomorrow if you will be home then.

To show determination, strong desire, or promise, reverse the normal pattern of *shall* and *will* in formal English.

I shall go now, and you will come later. (simple future tense statement)
I will go now, and you shall come later. (statement of determination)

The King James Bible uses formal English. Understanding the distinctions between *shall* and *will* contributes to a clear understanding of many Bible verses. Study the following examples.

"Moses said unto the people, Ye have sinned a great sin: and now I will [strong desire] go up unto the LORD; peradventure I shall [simple future] make an atonement for your sin" (Exodus 32:30).

"Now I will [determination] come unto you, when I shall [simple future] pass through Macedonia: for I do pass through Macedonia" (1 Corinthians 16:5).

Perfect Tenses

4. *The present perfect tense shows an action or a condition that began in the past and is completed as of the present or continues into the present.* This tense uses the third principal part (past participle) with the helping verb *have* or *has.*

Both the simple past and the present perfect tenses refer to things that happened before the present. The simple past, however, merely indicates that an action or existence occurred at some past time. The present perfect indicates that what began in the past is now completed or is still continuing.

Simple past: The boys split the firewood yesterday.
Present perfect: The boys have split all the firewood.

Simple past: Brother Heisey answered many questions.
Present perfect: In his years of teaching, Brother Heisey has answered many questions.

5. *The past perfect tense shows an action or a condition that was completed by a certain time in the past.* This tense uses the third principal part (past participle) with the helping verb *had.*

The past perfect tense requires that two past actions or conditions be expressed or implied. That which was completed first must be expressed in the past perfect tense.

Incomplete: Only one past action
It had snowed for several hours.

Complete: Two past actions stated
It had snowed for several hours before darkness fell.
Complete: One past action stated and one implied
It had snowed for several hours before dark.

Use the past perfect tense either to clarify which of two past actions or conditions occurred first or to emphasize that one action or condition was completed at the time of the other. Compare the differences in meaning and emphasis in the following sentences.

Unclear: Sounds as if the two actions occurred at the same time
We opened our Bibles to the passage that Brother Harold announced.
Clear: Clarifies that the announcing came first
We opened our Bibles to the passage that Brother Harold had announced.

Completed action not emphasized: Both verbs in simple past tense
Brother Harold read all the verses before he explained them.
Completed action emphasized: First action in past perfect tense
Brother Harold had read all the verses before he explained them.

6. *The future perfect tense shows an action or a condition that will be completed by a certain time in the future.* This tense uses the third principal part (past participle) with either *shall have* or *will have* as helping verbs.

The future perfect tense requires that two future actions or conditions be expressed or implied. That which will occur first or whose completion is to be emphasized must be expressed in the future perfect tense; the other may be expressed in the simple future or simple present tense.

Incomplete: Only one future action
Our school will have operated for twenty-six years.
Complete: One future condition implied and one future action stated
By the end of this school term, our school will have operated for twenty-six years.

The future perfect tense serves a function similar to that of the past perfect tense. Use it either to clarify which of two future actions or conditions will occur first, or to emphasize that one action or condition will be completed at the time of the other. Compare the differences in meaning and emphasis in the following sentences.

Unclear: Sounds as if we shall travel *after* the stated time
At the end of our trip, we shall travel two thousand miles.
Clear: Clarifies that our traveling will be completed at the stated time
At the end of our trip, we shall have traveled two thousand miles.

Completion of action not emphasized: Both verbs in simple tenses
Before this week ends, we shall sing at the rest home.
Completion of action emphasized: Completed action in future perfect tense
Before this week ends, we shall have sung at the rest home.

A *conjugation* is a listing of certain forms of a verb. Here is a conjugation of *help* in the simple and perfect tenses.

Help

Person	***Singular***	***Plural***
	Present Tense	
First:	I help.	We help.
Second:	You help.	You help.
Third:	He helps.	They help.
	Past Tense	
First:	I helped.	We helped.
Second:	You helped.	You helped.
Third:	He helped.	They helped.
	Future Tense	
First:	I shall help.	We shall help.
Second:	You will help.	You will help.
Third:	He will help.	They will help.
	Present Perfect Tense	
First:	I have helped.	We have helped.
Second:	You have helped.	You have helped.
Third:	He has helped.	They have helped.
	Past Perfect Tense	
First:	I had helped.	We had helped.
Second:	You had helped.	You had helped.
Third:	He had helped.	They had helped.
	Future Perfect Tense	
First:	I shall have helped.	We shall have helped.
Second:	You will have helped.	You will have helped.
Third:	He will have helped.	They will have helped.

Applying the Lesson

A. Copy each verb or verb phrase, and write which tense it is.

1. Father has sharpened the chain saw, and soon he will fill the fuel tank.
2. That old locust tree is not dead, but it leans over the driveway.
3. After Father had examined the tree, he noticed some nearby wires.
4. The wires run along the driveway, but they seem a safe distance away.
5. Before Father cuts down the tree, he will have checked more carefully.
6. The tree easily cleared the wires just as Father had expected.
7. Locust wood burns well, but we have no need for firewood.
8. The neighbor will bring his truck this evening; by then we shall have sawed the wood into two-foot pieces.

B. Write the correct verb form for the tense shown in italics.

1. If you memorize one Bible verse each day, you (memorize) over three hundred verses by the end of the year. *future perfect*

2. Remembering Scripture passages (require) frequent review. *present perfect*
3. By the time I was in ninth grade, I (gain) a great store of Bible verses. *past perfect*
4. By the middle of January, the students (finish) chapter 15. *future perfect*
5. Most of our visitors this month (comment) on the attractive bulletin board. *present perfect*
6. I was encouraged by the comment that the teacher (write) on my paper. *past perfect*

C. In each sentence, changing one verb to a perfect tense would make the meaning clearer or would put more emphasis on the completion of one action. Write that verb in the correct perfect tense.
1. The wise men followed the star for many miles before they came to Jerusalem.
2. King Herod learned from them that an infant king came into his domain.
3. We shall read about the conflict between these two kings before our devotional period ends.
4. When the wise men arrive at Bethlehem, they will follow the star to the end of their search.
5. The diligent seekers worshiped the King that they found.
6. Joseph took Jesus and His mother to Egypt before Herod killed the children in Bethlehem.
7. I shall read the rest of the account when I reach the end of Matthew 2.
8. When we learn to submit cheerfully, we shall gain a valuable character trait.

D. Write short sentences for these descriptions, using pronouns and the correct verb forms.
1. First person singular, present tense of *think.*
2. Second person, present perfect tense of *ride.*
3. Second person, future tense of *go.*
4. Third person plural, past tense of *wring.*
5. Third person singular, feminine, past perfect tense of *forget.*
6. First person plural, present tense of *keep.*
7. First person plural, future perfect tense of *seek.*
8. First person singular, past perfect tense of *shut.*
9. Third person plural, past tense of *eat.*
10. Third person singular, masculine, future perfect tense of *cut.*

Review Exercises

Write the letter of the correct form in each sentence. [61]
1. ([a]James and John's, [b]James's and John's) mother came to Jesus with a special request.
2. She asked Jesus for the favor of her ([a]sons, [b]sons') sitting at His right hand and left hand in His kingdom.
3. Jesus first asked about the ([a]brothers, [b]brothers') being able to drink of the cup that He would drink.

4. Then He said that His Father, not Jesus Himself, would be the ([a]one, [b]one's) granting that position.
5. At the Last Supper, Peter objected strongly to ([a]Jesus, [b]Jesus') washing his feet.
6. ([a]Peter and John's, [b]Peter's and John's) ideas about the heavenly kingdom were much clearer after Pentecost than before.
7. The apostles continued boldly preaching the Gospel even after the Jewish council prohibited ([a]their, [b]them) speaking in the Name of Jesus.
8. We stayed at my ([a]aunt's and uncle's, [b]aunt and uncle's) home while Mother was sick.
9. While she recuperated, Mother liked to listen to the ([a]birds, [b]birds') singing cheerily outside.
10. She especially enjoyed the ([a]bluebird and robin's, [b]bluebirds' and robins') songs.

---

75. Moods of Verbs

A *mode* is a manner of doing something. When people want to go somewhere, they can choose among several different modes of travel. They can walk, ride a bicycle, drive a car, or travel by plane—to name a few possibilities. They choose the mode that best fits their purpose.

Just as there are different modes of travel, there are different modes of verbs. However, we generally use the term ***mood*** instead of *mode* when referring to verbs. The mood of a verb is its manner of communicating, as determined by the intention of the speaker or writer. For example, a preacher during his sermon communicates in several different ways. The following sentences are some of the things he might say; each underlined verb is in a different mood.

> Abraham showed remarkable faith in offering his son Isaac.
> Open your Bibles to Genesis 22.
> If I were Abraham, could I pass such a test?

In the first sentence, the speaker intends simply to state a fact. So he uses a declarative sentence, which declares that something is true. The mood of this verb is indicative (in•dik′•ə•tiv) because it indicates a fact about Abraham.

In the second sentence, the speaker intends that his listeners do something. He expresses his intention by using an imperative sentence. Since the sentence is imperative, the verb is in the imperative mood.

What is the speaker's intention in the third sentence? He is making no request; neither is he indicating that something is true. In fact, he is expressing an idea that could *not* be true: "If I were Abraham" (when obviously he is not Abraham). The verb in this clause is in the subjunctive mood.

These examples illustrate the three moods of English verbs: indicative, imperative, and subjunctive.

The Indicative Mood

The ***indicative mood*** states a fact or asks a question. Since we generally use language to *indicate* real actions or conditions, we use the indicative mood far more often than any other mood. The verbs in most declarative and interrogative sentences are indicative.

> Great Britain became the northernmost province of the Roman Empire.
> What peoples invaded Great Britain after the Romans left?

The Imperative Mood

The ***imperative mood*** gives a command or makes a request. The verbs in all imperative sentences are imperative.

> Find more information about this invasion.
> Please tell us what you have discovered.

A verb in the imperative mood may appear to ask a question even though it actually makes a request. A sentence with such a verb ends with a period rather than a question mark because the verb is imperative.

> Will the owner of this pickup please move his truck away from the doors.
> Shall we kneel for prayer.

The Subjunctive Mood

You have probably used the ***subjunctive mood*** even if you have never heard of it before. Have you ever made a statement like this one?

> If I were you, I would try to finish by noon.

Why do you say "I were"? Have you not learned that the correct expression is "I was"? Yet here it is—"if I were you"—and it sounds quite natural. You use the form *were* because this verb is in the subjunctive mood.

The subjunctive mood does not tell or ask about something that actually happens. Rather, it often expresses a condition contrary to fact, as in the example above. I am not you, and I can never be you. I will always be me! The subjunctive mood may also express a doubt, a wish, or a recommendation.

The subjunctive mood is much less common today than it was long ago. It is still required in a few expressions like "if I were you," and it may be used in certain other phrases. But today we often use helping verbs like *would* and *should* for ideas that formerly were expressed with the subjunctive mood.

You have studied verbs in the indicative and imperative moods ever since you studied declarative and imperative sentences. So these moods generally pose no problem for you. But the subjunctive mood requires more careful attention because a few of its forms are less familiar to you.

Subjunctive Verb Forms

Actually, almost all the subjunctive verb forms are identical to those of the indicative mood. There are only three places where they differ. Learning the correct subjunctive verb forms for these three exceptions will help you to use the subjunctive mood properly. The following paragraphs describe these three situations.

1. *The verb* be *in the present tense.* In the indicative mood, we must use three different forms for the verb *be* in the present tense. In the subjunctive mood, however, we use only the form *be.* Notice this difference on the chart below. (The conjunction *if* is included with the subjunctive forms because subjunctive verbs are common in *if* clauses.)

Present Tense *(Indicative Mood)*		**Present Tense** *(Subjunctive Mood)*	
I am	we are	(if) I be	(if) we be
you are	you are	(if) you be	(if) you be
he is	they are	(if) he be	(if) they be

Again, note that the subjunctive mood uses the word *be* no matter what the subject. Here are some examples of this usage.

"And I, if I be lifted up from the earth, will draw all men unto me."
(subjunctive *I be* rather than indicative *I am*)
"Will ye plead for Baal?… If he be a god, let him plead for himself."
(subjunctive *he be* rather than indicative *he is*)

2. *The verb* be *in the past tense.* Here the indicative mood uses *was* and *were.* As with the present tense, the subjunctive mood again uses a single form, this time *were.* Study the difference between the two forms in the chart below.

Past Tense *(Indicative Mood)*		**Past Tense** *(Subjunctive Mood)*	
I was	we were	(if) I were	(if) we were
you were	you were	(if) you were	(if) you were
he was	they were	(if) he were	(if) they were

Here the subjunctive mood is the same as the indicative mood except for two places: *I were* and *he were.* These may sound strange; but in examples such as the following, you will probably recognize that you have heard and even used them yourself.

If I were at home right now, I would be doing my chores.
(subjunctive *I were* rather than indicative *I was*)
"If this man were not of God, he could do nothing."
(subjunctive *man were* rather than indicative *man was*)

3. *Third person singular verbs in the present tense.* In the present tense, indicative mood, verbs always add *-s* for the third person singular. He *eats.* He *sees.* He *thinks.* The subjunctive mood, however, does not add this *-s.* The following chart shows the forms for the verb *go.*

Present Tense *(Indicative Mood)*		**Present Tense** *(Subjunctive Mood)*	
I go	we go	(if) I go	(if) we go
you go	you go	(if) you go	(if) you go
he goes	they go	(if) he go	(if) they go

He go is the only place the subjunctive mood is different. Following this pattern with other verbs, we would have *he eat, he see, he think,* and so forth. Such usage is not as common as the subjunctive uses of *be,* yet these examples should have a familiar ring to them.

> "If thy presence go not with me, carry us not up hence."
> (subjunctive *presence go* rather than indicative *presence goes*)
> If Mother go away for a month, how would we manage?
> (subjunctive *Mother go* rather than indicative *Mother goes*)

For the second example, we may be more likely to say, "If Mother were to go away for a month." Even then we would be using the subjunctive mood, *Mother were,* rather than the indicative mood, *Mother was.*

The English of the King James Bible follows the rules of formal usage. Also, the subjunctive mood was used much more in the 1600s than it is today. For these reasons, the King James Bible contains many examples of subjunctive verbs. Understanding the subjunctive verb forms described above will help you to understand some of the "unusual" verb forms in the King James Version, and thus it will make the Bible clearer to you.

Using the Subjunctive Mood

1. *Use the subjunctive mood in the following situations.* The subjunctive mood occurs most often in a clause introduced by *if, whether, as if, as though,* or *that.* In the example sentences below, the underlined verbs are in the subjunctive mood.

   a. Expressing doubt or uncertainty.

      "All men mused in their hearts of John, whether he were the Christ, or not."
      "Now therefore, if it displease thee, I will get me back again."

   b. Expressing a wish or desire.

      "Peace be with thee." I wish he were more careful.

   c. Expressing a supposition, a condition contrary to fact, or something unlikely.

      I would be cautious too if I were in his shoes.
      "If Satan rise up against himself, and be divided, he cannot stand."

   d. Expressing recommendation, request, command, or necessity in a *that* clause.

      I move that the trustees be authorized to repair the roof.
      The doctor recommended that Grandfather have a checkup.

2. *In a* that *clause expressing recommendation, request, command, or necessity, use the present subjunctive form even if other verbs in the sentence are in a different tense.*

> Father will request that he be exempted from jury duty.
> (*Be exempted* is present tense even though *will request* is future tense.)

God has directed that the Christian live in holiness.

(*Live* is present tense even though *has directed* is present perfect tense.)

The Lord commanded that Abram move out of Ur.

(*Move* is present tense even though *commanded* is past tense.)

3. *Use the subjunctive mood to avoid unnecessary* would *phrases.* When a sentence has a dependent *if* or *that* clause, the main clause often uses *would* as a helping verb. *Would* may seem to fit in the dependent clause too, but that is not a standard usage. You will avoid repeating *would,* and you will express your idea more concisely, if you use the subjunctive mood in the *if* or *that* clause. Study these examples and explanations.

Two *would* phrases:

If I would be you, I *would* set my alarm a bit earlier.

Improved with subjunctive:

If I were you, I *would* set my alarm a bit earlier.

(Subjunctive form *I were* fits in a statement that is contrary to fact.)

Two *would* phrases:

I *would* like to suggest that Brother James would be appointed as the leader.

Improved with subjunctive:

I *would* like to suggest that Brother James be appointed as the leader.

(Subjunctive form *be appointed* is used in a recommendation. Also note that the recommendation is given in the present tense.)

Two *would* phrases:

If you would have gotten up sooner, you *would* not need to hurry so much.

Improved with subjunctive:

If you had gotten up sooner, you *would* not need to hurry so much.

(*If you had gotten up sooner* is a statement contrary to fact. This requires using the subjunctive mood. Is *had gotten* a subjunctive form? Yes, because the subjunctive and the indicative forms are exactly the same. Remember, subjunctive mood differs from indicative mood only in the three situations listed earlier in this lesson.)

The verbs in most sentences are in the indicative mood—the mood that tells or asks about things as they really are. But a verb in the imperative mood is necessary for telling someone to do something, and a verb in the subjunctive mood is useful for speaking of something that is doubted, wished, or supposed.

Applying the Lesson

A. Copy each underlined verb, and write whether its mood is indicative (*ind.*), imperative (*imp.*), or subjunctive (*sub.*).

1. God commands that everyone obey His Word.
2. If I were not trusting in the Lord, these temptations would overwhelm me.

3. Raise your hand if you have a question or comment.
4. "If God be for us, who can be against us?"
5. A proud person often acts as if he were entitled to the last word.
6. Never act as if God were on vacation.
7. The Lord preserve you from all evil.
8. Will you please clean up this clutter.
9. If I be at fault, I want to know.
10. I move that the chairman appoint a committee to study the problem.
11. That bull sounds as if he were ready to charge.
12. The government inspectors recommend that major repairs be made to the bridge.
13. Suppose your little brother were to find this knife on the floor.
14. If indeed the work be finished, I shall go home.

B. Choose the words that are correct for the subjunctive mood.
1. Suppose this (was, were) your last opportunity to visit Grandfather Stauffer.
2. Our neighbor worked as if he (was, were) afraid of having a heart attack.
3. The company recommends that the equipment (be, is) serviced annually.
4. God's grace (be, is) with you until we meet again.
5. If any man (hear, hears) God's voice, let him pay close heed.
6. I wonder if indeed this (be, is) the best explanation.
7. If he (do, does) his best, I will be satisfied.
8. Lazarus would not have died if Jesus (was, had been) present, but He received more glory by raising Lazarus from the dead.
9. That rooster acts as if he (was, were) the king of the barnyard.
10. If Sheila (was, were) to help us, we could finish in a few minutes.
11. The teacher required that everyone (be, was) prepared.
12. If this work (prove, proves) successful, I shall be surprised.
13. The building inspector requested that the electrician (make, made) a small change.
14. I wish that Duke (was, were) more friendly to the children.
15. Even if David (would have made, had made) an unreasonable request, Nabal should have responded more courteously.
16. If Abigail (would not have taken, had not taken) prompt action, Nabal's whole household would have been destroyed.

C. Write a subjunctive verb or verb phrase to replace each underlined *would* phrase.
1. We would leave at three o'clock in the morning if that would be practical.
2. I would appreciate if these directions would be a little clearer.
3. I move that the secretary would mail out copies of the minutes.
4. Brother Alvin asked that the noise level would be lowered.
5. If we would have made better plans, things would not have turned out this way.
6. If Grandfather would have been able, he would surely have come to the services.

Review Exercises

A. Choose the correct words in these sentences. [62, 63]
1. I am older than my brother Carl, but he is a little taller than (I, me).
2. One day Father told (we, us) boys to burn some trash.
3. He had often warned Carl and (I, me) to be careful with fire.
4. I started the fire by lighting some gasoline-soaked rags from (someones, someone's) cleanup project.
5. The flames roared up very suddenly, almost burning (me, myself) in the face.
6. It was a good lesson for (me and Carl, Carl and I, Carl and me).

B. Choose the correct words in these sentences. [62, 63]
1. Elijah was a man (who, which) had feelings and desires just like ours.
2. (This, This here) was the prophet who prayed that rainfall would cease in Israel.
3. All of us generally (prefer, prefers) prosperous times.
4. But (them, those) were days when the people had become extremely wicked.
5. Elijah so greatly desired that (they, them) return to the true God, that he was willing to endure a great drought along with the sinful people.
6. Each of us (need, needs) to care about other people as Elijah did.

---

76. Transitive and Intransitive Verbs

Verbs are classified according to their tense, their form, and their mood. They are also classified as either transitive or intransitive.

Transitive Verbs

The word *transitive* comes from a Latin word that means "passing over." A transitive verb passes its action to a substantive in the sentence. Transitive verbs are in the *active voice* or the *passive voice,* depending on the receiver of their action.

1. *A transitive verb in the active voice passes its action to the direct object.* The subject performs the action, and the direct object receives the action. A verb with a direct object may also have an indirect object or an objective complement.

God answered Solomon's prayer for wisdom.
(*Prayer* is the direct object of *answered.*)
God gave Solomon wisdom to rule his kingdom.
(*Wisdom* is the direct object of *gave,* and *Solomon* is the indirect object.)
God made Solomon wise above all other men.
(*Solomon* is the direct object of *made,* and *wise* is the objective complement.)

The direct object may be a verbal, a verbal phrase, or a noun clause.

Every Christian needs <u>to pray</u>. (verbal)
Every Christian needs <u>to pray without ceasing</u>. (verbal phrase)
Every Christian realizes <u>that he needs to pray without ceasing</u>. (noun clause)

2. *A transitive verb in the passive voice passes its action to the subject.* In the passive voice, the subject receives the action rather than performing it. Often the doer of the action is named later in the sentence, by a substantive in a phrase beginning with *by.* A verb in the passive voice consists of the past participle with a form of *be* as a helping verb.

Solomon's prayer for wisdom was answered by God.
(*Prayer* receives the action of *was answered.*)
Wisdom to rule his kingdom was given to Solomon by God.
(*Wisdom* receives the action of *was given.*)

Intransitive Verbs

Just as *transitive* means "passing over," so *intransitive* means "not passing over." An intransitive verb does not pass its action to a substantive in the sentence. Intransitive verbs divide into two groups: intransitive complete and intransitive linking.

1. *An intransitive complete verb expresses action but does not pass the action to a receiver.* The meaning of the skeleton is complete without a complement.

During the night, two inches of snow fell.
In silence we waited for his answer.

Some intransitive complete verbs may seem to pass their action to the subject. However, both the meaning of the sentence and the form of the verb show that the subject actually is performing the action.

Slowly the ice cube in my cup melted.
(intransitive complete; *melted* means the ice cube turned to liquid; subject performs this action; verb is simple past form)
The ice cube was melted by the warm water.
(transitive verb in the passive voice; subject receives the action performed by the *warm water;* verb consists of a past participle with a form of *be* as a helping verb)

Some verbs may be either transitive or intransitive complete, depending on their use in a sentence. Most dictionaries give specific definitions for both transitive and intransitive uses of such verbs.

We learned three new songs in music class.
(transitive; *songs* receives the action)
The students learned very rapidly.
(intransitive complete; no receiver of the action)

2. *An intransitive linking verb expresses a condition or a state of being.* Such a verb often has little meaning of its own; it serves mainly to link the subject to the subjective complement. The subjective complement may be either a predicate nominative, which renames the subject, or a predicate adjective, which modifies the subject.

The most common linking verbs are the forms of *be: am, is, are, was, were, be, been, being.* Linking verbs also include verbs of sense (*taste, feel, smell, sound, look, appear*) and some other verbs (*grow, seem, stay, become, remain, turn, prove*).

> Joseph Funk <u>was</u> an early Mennonite music teacher.
> (*Teacher* is a predicate nominative renaming *Joseph Funk.*)
> His introduction of shaped notes <u>proved</u> very beneficial.
> (*Beneficial* is a predicate adjective modifying *introduction.*)

Do not confuse a linking verb followed by an adjective with an intransitive complete verb followed by an adverb or with a transitive verb in the active or passive voice. Except for the forms of *be,* most of the linking verbs can also function as transitive verbs or as intransitive complete verbs. A verb is intransitive linking only when it expresses a condition or a state of being rather than an action.

> Students sometimes <u>grow</u> restless in the springtime. (*Grow* expresses a condition; it links *Students* and *restless. Grow* is intransitive linking.)
> Many students <u>grow</u> rapidly during the year. (*Grow* expresses action; there is no receiver of the action. *Grow* is intransitive complete.)
> My brothers <u>grow</u> watermelons to sell at the market. (*Grow* expresses action; *watermelons* receives the action. *Grow* is transitive active.)
> These watermelons were <u>grown</u> on our own farm. (*Grown* expresses action; *watermelons* receives the action. *Grown* is transitive passive.)

A sentence diagram can help you to quickly tell whether a verb is transitive or intransitive. If a direct object follows the verb, it is a transitive verb in the active voice. If the verb is a past participle with a form of *be* as a helping verb, it is a transitive verb in the passive voice. If the verb is not passive and it has no complement, it is an intransitive complete verb. And if a predicate nominative or predicate adjective follows the verb, it is an intransitive linking verb.

Transitive active:

brothers | grow | watermelons

Transitive passive:

watermelons | were grown

Intransitive complete:

students | grow

Intransitive linking:

Students | grow \ restless

Applying the Lesson

A. Copy each verb and the substantive that receives its action. Label the verb *active* or *passive.*

1. Early in his ministry, Daniel Kauffman visited the Sugar Creek congregation in Wayland, Ohio.
2. His supper was eaten at the home of the bishop, Sebastian Gerig.
3. During the meal, very little was said by Kauffman.
4. Because of this, Bishop Gerig's hired man did not expect a very forceful sermon that evening.

5. On the way to church, young Kauffman expressed indecision about what to use for his subject.
6. Several simple texts were suggested by the somewhat uneasy bishop.
7. To Brother Gerig's surprise, the subject of the resurrection was used for that night's message.
8. Kauffman's powerful sermon made a vivid impression on the congregation.

B. Write whether each underlined verb is transitive (*T*) or intransitive complete (*IC*).
1. Our visitor <u>had</u> very poor hearing.
2. In each ear he <u>wore</u> a hearing aid.
3. As he explained how they work, we <u>listened</u> with interest.
4. When only one hearing aid <u>was operating</u>, he could not identify the direction from which a sound came.
5. Why <u>do</u> we <u>need</u> two ears?
6. A sound <u>rings</u> more loudly in the ear closer to the source.
7. The sound also <u>arrives</u> a little sooner in that ear than in the other ear.
8. Our brain <u>uses</u> the difference in volume and time to discern the direction of the sound.

C. Copy each linking verb and the words that it links.
1. The Book of Psalms has always been a source of great inspiration.
2. This book was the hymnal of the Jewish people.
3. To the New Testament saint, it remains fresh and meaningful.
4. The parallelism of Hebrew poetry is truly beautiful.
5. Some of the psalms are acrostics.
6. The psalms have grown sweet to many Bible readers.

D. Copy each verb, and label it *TA* (transitive, active voice), *TP* (transitive, passive voice), *IC* (intransitive complete), or *IL* (intransitive linking).
1. The Hans Herr House is the oldest building in Lancaster County, Pennsylvania.
2. Hans Herr, a Mennonite minister, came to Pennsylvania from the German Palatinate.
3. The Mennonites first settled in Lancaster County in 1710.
4. Actually, this house was built by Hans Herr's son Christian.
5. The stone above the door bears the date 1719.
6. This house served as a residence and as a Mennonite meetinghouse.
7. Its construction follows the style of Swiss–German architecture.
8. The roof of this stone house is very steep.
9. A long fireplace and large chimney are located in the center of the house.
10. The raised floor of the fireplace kept children out of the fire.
11. For about one hundred years, the house was a neglected structure.
12. It was restored during the years 1970–1972.

Review Exercises

Name the tense of the underlined verb in each sentence. [74]
1. By the early 1700s, Isaac Newton <u>had</u> already <u>demonstrated</u> that sunlight contains the seven colors of the rainbow.

2. To this day, however, scientists have not been able to explain light fully.
3. Light is a form of energy that travels even through a vacuum.
4. Light leaving the sun will have passed through millions of miles of vacuum by the time it reaches the earth.
5. Since vibrating molecules carry sound, it cannot pass through a vacuum.
6. Sound passing through air will travel about 1,100 feet every second.
7. An echo is the reflection of a sound that occurred just a moment earlier.
8. When lightning has struck, its one brief discharge sets off a series of echoes that we call thunder.

---

77. Forms of Verbs

All verbs have six tenses—three simple and three perfect. Within these tenses, verbs also have three different forms that give them slightly different shades of meaning. The three forms are *simple, progressive,* and *emphatic.* We use these different verb forms to give precise expression to the ideas we want to convey.

Verb Forms in the Active Voice

1. *The simple form of a verb expresses an action or a condition as simply as possible.* The only helping verbs used with the simple form are *shall* and *will* (for the simple future tense) and forms of *have* (for the perfect tenses). The simple form is the one you immediately think of when you are asked to give a particular verb in any tense. In all the previous lessons of this chapter, the focus has been on the simple form of verbs.

Simple form:

Present: I help my father.
Past: I helped my father.
Future: I shall help my father.
Present perfect: I have helped my father.
Past perfect: I had helped my father.
Future perfect: I shall have helped my father.

2. *The progressive form uses the present participle with a form of* be *as a helping verb.* In contrast to the simple form, the progressive form emphasizes that an action or a condition is in progress. Each of the six tenses has a progressive form.

Progressive form:

Present: I am helping my father.
Past: I was helping my father.
Future: I shall be helping my father.
Present perfect: I have been helping my father.
Past perfect: I had been helping my father.
Future perfect: I shall have been helping my father.

3. *The emphatic form uses the first principal part with a form of* do *as a helping verb.* As its name suggests, this form gives added emphasis, perhaps in response to a question or a doubt. Only the present and past tenses have emphatic forms, because sentences like "I do will help" and "I did had helped" would be extremely awkward.

Emphatic form:
Present: I do help my father.
Past: I did help my father.

The helping verbs *do* and *did* are also used in questions and negative statements. The verb form in such a sentence is simple rather than emphatic.

Do you help your father? (present tense, simple form)
I did not help my father. (past tense, simple form)

Verb Forms in the Passive Voice

4. *The simple form of a verb in the passive voice is the past participle with a form of* be *as a helping verb.* This is the simplest verb form that will pass an action to the subject of a sentence.

Simple form:
Present: I am helped by my brother.
Past: I was helped by my brother.
Future: I shall be helped by my brother.
Present perfect: I have been helped by my brother.
Past perfect: I had been helped by my brother.
Future perfect: I shall have been helped by my brother.

5. *The progressive form of a verb in the passive voice is made with the addition of* being *as a helping verb.* As in the active voice, the verb phrase contains a present participle—but the *-ing* is added to *be* rather than the main verb. Such a verb phrase contains two forms of *be:* a form like *am, is,* or *was* for the passive voice, and *being* for the progressive form. In the passive voice, the progressive form commonly occurs only in the present and past tenses. The other forms are too awkward because of the many helping verbs required.

Progressive form:
Present: I am being helped by my brother.
Past: I was being helped by my brother.

(Forms seldom used because of their awkwardness)
Future: I shall be being helped by my brother.
Present perfect: I have been being helped by my brother.
Past perfect: I had been being helped by my brother.
Future perfect: I shall have been being helped by my brother.

6. *The emphatic form never occurs in the passive voice, because it is too awkward and illogical.* The emphatic form would require constructions like *I do am helped* and *I did was helped.*

Study the following chart, which compares the three forms of verbs in both the active voice and the passive voice.

Comparison of Verb Forms

Active Voice

	Simple Form	*Progressive Form* Made with a form of *be* and *-ing*	*Emphatic Form* Made with a form of *do*
Present:	I help.	I am helping.	I do help.
Past:	I helped.	I was helping.	I did help.
Future:	I shall help.	I shall be helping.	(too awkward)
Pr. perf.:	I have helped.	I have been helping.	
Past perf.:	I had helped.	I had been helping.	
Fut. perf.:	I shall have helped.	I shall have been helping.	

Passive Voice

	Simple Form Made with a form of *be* and a past participle	*Progressive Form* Made with two forms of *be* and a past participle	*Emphatic Form* (not used at all)
Present:	I am helped.	I am being helped.	
Past:	I was helped.	I was being helped.	
Future:	I shall be helped.	(too awkward; seldom used)	
Pr. perf.:	I have been helped.		
Past perf.:	I had been helped.		
Fut. perf.:	I shall have been helped.		

Applying the Lesson

A. Identify the form of each underlined verb as *simple, progressive,* or *emphatic.*

1. I do believe that a storm is coming soon.
2. The birds that come to the feeder have been fighting more than usual.
3. That blue jay has chased all the other birds away and does not let them come back.
4. We invited Mr. Smith to our services, and he will be coming next Sunday.
5. The boys did lock the gate, but somehow the heifers pushed it open.
6. Have you heard that Sister Dorcas broke her arm?

B. Write the progressive form and the emphatic form of each underlined verb. If such a form is awkward or nonexistent, write *none.* Do not change the tense of the verb.

1. Amos hopes to finish the job by noon.
2. Our neighbors plan to move to Indiana in the spring.
3. Henry was questioned by the officer about his accident.
4. Tomorrow the students will take their science test.
5. No one has tried successfully to solve this equation.
6. Before the window had been washed, we could hardly see through it.

C. Identify the tense, voice, and form of each underlined verb.

1. "In the beginning God created the heaven and the earth."
2. We have been receiving heavy rains for several days.

3. I do believe that your brother is learning to be patient.
4. While the book was being written, the author did more research.

D. Copy the chart below, and fill in the blanks with all the forms for the following two skeletons.
   1. He finds.
   2. You hear.

Verb Forms

Active Voice

	Simple Form	*Progressive Form*	*Emphatic Form*
Present:	________	________	________
Past:	________	________	________
Future:	________	________	
Pr. perf.:	________	________	
Past perf.:	________	________	
Fut. perf.:	________	________	

Passive Voice

	Simple Form	*Progressive Form*	*Emphatic Form*
Present:	________	________	
Past:	________	________	
Future:	________		
Pr. perf.:	________		
Past perf.:	________		
Fut. perf.:	________		

Review Exercises

A. Write whether the underlined sentence part is a nominative absolute (*NA*) or a participial phrase (*PP*). [24]
   1. Mild weather having come, we heard geese honking already in January.
   2. Flying in great V formations, the geese were heading northward.
   3. Surprised to see geese so early, we wondered how they would fare if frigid weather came.
   4. God having promised His care, we should not worry as much as we sometimes do.

B. Rewrite each sentence, changing the underlined subordinate clause to a nominative absolute. [24]
   1. Because the creek had flooded, we had to find a different way home.
   2. Soon we had to change our course again because a tree had fallen across the road.

3. Since our route extended over twice the normal distance, the trip took much longer than usual.
4. After my homework was finished, I played with my little brother for a while.

---

78. Subject–Verb Agreement

For the vast majority of sentences, you have very little problem with subject–verb agreement. Some situations, however, do deserve special attention. The following rules give you specific direction in these problem areas.

1. *When the verb precedes the subject, think ahead to the subject and make the verb agree with it.* In many questions and in most sentences beginning with *there* or *here,* the verb or a part of the verb phrase precedes the subject.

> Are the women washing all the windows?
> There was a steady rain falling throughout the day.

2. *Make the verb agree with the subject, not with some other substantive in the sentence.* Be especially careful when a prepositional phrase comes between the subject and the verb, and when a subject and its predicate nominative differ in number.

> A huge flock of blackbirds has landed in the wheat field.
> The emu, along with the ostrich and the penguin, is a bird that cannot fly.
> One attraction at the Baltimore zoo is the monkeys.
> The monkeys are an irresistible attraction to the children.

3. *Use a contraction as you would use the words it represents.* Be especially alert to the contractions *here's, there's, how's, what's,* and *don't.*

> **Incorrect:** Here's (Here is) the answers to our questions.
> This cow don't (do not) give much milk.
> **Correct:** Here are the answers to our questions.
> This cow doesn't give much milk.

4. *Use a plural verb with a compound subject joined by* and. The conjunction *and* means that the verb expresses action or condition for all parts of the subject.

> Sodium and chlorine combine to form salt. (Two elements combine.)
> A stone and a sling were the only weapons David needed.
> (Both were weapons.)

Sometimes a compound subject names only one person or thing, as when one person holds two positions or one dish is composed of two foods. In this case, the verb is singular and an article or a possessive pronoun is used only before the first noun. In contrast, if the compound subject names two different persons or objects, the verb is plural and an article or a possessive pronoun is used before each of the nouns.

The farmer and minister was humbly serving the Lord.
(One man was serving the Lord.)
The farmer and the minister were discussing Sunday's sermon.
(Two men were discussing the sermon.)
Macaroni and cheese is a favorite at our house. (One dish is a favorite.)

5. *Follow these rules for compound subjects joined by* or *or* nor.
   a. If both subjects are singular, use a singular verb.

      Neither fire nor sword is able to stop the Gospel message.

   b. If both subjects are plural, use a plural verb.

      Cruel trials or angry mockings do not deter Christians from their purpose.

   c. If one subject is singular and one is plural, make the verb agree with the subject that is nearer to the verb.

      Neither Joseph nor his brothers were aware of God's purposes.
      Neither his brothers nor Joseph was aware of God's purposes.

6. *Use a singular verb with a singular indefinite pronoun.* These pronouns are as follows: *each, either, neither, one, another, anybody, anyone, anything, everybody, everyone, everthing, somebody, someone, something, nobody, no one, nothing.*

Neither of the prisoners was able to interpret his dream.
Nothing is impossible when we trust in God.

7. *Use the correct verb with indefinite pronouns that may be either singular or plural.* These include *some, any, none, all,* and *most.* Such a pronoun is singular if its antecedent is singular. (The antecedent is usually stated in a prepositional phrase after the pronoun.) The indefinite pronoun then means a certain portion of that one thing and takes a singular verb. But the pronoun is plural if the antecedent is plural. Then the indefinite pronoun means certain individual items in that set of things, and it takes a plural verb.

Most of the lawn has been mowed.
Most of the lawns have been mowed.

8. *Use a singular verb with a noun that is plural in form but singular in meaning.* This includes nouns like *news* and *gallows,* names of diseases like *measles* and *mumps,* and words ending with *-ics* like *civics* and *ethics.*

For many years checkers has been a favorite game.
Mathematics is one of our most important school studies.

9. *Usually a plural verb is used with a noun that names an item made of paired parts.* This includes words like *shears, trousers, pliers, glasses, tweezers,* and *tongs.*

If the subject is *pair* followed by one of these nouns in a prepositional phrase, the verb must agree with the singular *pair.*

> Mary's new glasses have helped to relieve her headaches.
> Mary's new pair of glasses has helped to relieve her headaches.

10. *If a collective noun refers to a group acting as a unit, use a singular verb. If a collective noun refers to individual members of the group acting separately, use a plural verb.* A collective noun names a collection of individuals. Some common collective nouns are *group, family, congregation, herd, flock,* and *swarm.* In many sentences, a word like *its* or *our* helps to show whether the group is acting unitedly or separately.

> The class is studying about the early Indians of Central America.
> (Class acting as a unit, doing the same thing.)
> The class are preparing their reports about the early Indians of Central America.
> (Class members acting individually, doing different things; note the plural *their.*)

11. *Use a singular verb with a title or a word that is a subject of discussion.*

> *Fire Among the Zurich Hills* tells of early Swiss Anabaptists.
> *Emphases* is the plural of *emphasis.*

12. *Use a singular verb with a subject that is plural in form but which indicates a quantity or is regarded as a unit.*

> Five dollars was missing from her purse.
> (This amount was missing from her purse.)
> Eight miles is too far to walk tonight. (This distance is too far to walk tonight.)

13. *Make the verb after a relative pronoun agree with the antecedent of the relative pronoun.*

> Our farm has a small spring which gives clear, pure water.
> Our farm has several springs which give clear, pure water.

Sometimes a relative pronoun follows a phrase like *the only one.* Then the antecedent is singular, and the verb in the relative clause should be singular.

> Judas was the *only one* of the disciples who was a traitor.
> (*Who was a traitor* modifies *one;* the antecedent of *who* is the singular *one.* The sentence indicates that only one disciple was a traitor.)
> Peter was *one* of the disciples who were with Jesus in the garden.
> (*Who were with Jesus in the garden* modifies *disciples;* the antecedent of *who* is the plural *disciples.* The sentence indicates that several disciples were with Jesus in the garden.)

14. *For words like* plenty, abundance, *and* rest *and for fractions followed by a phrase beginning with* of, *the object of the preposition following the subject determines the number of the subject.*

The rest of the day was spent cultivating the corn.
The rest of the days were spent cultivating the corn.

Three-fourths of the work is done.
Three-fourths of the jobs are done.

Applying the Lesson

A. Choose the correct word or phrase.

1. (There's, There are) many truths we can learn from the tabernacle of Moses.
2. One of the things that (impress, impresses) us is the single opening in the outer court.
3. Neither man nor woman (come, comes) to God through any way other than the one He has designed.
4. Many of the sacrifices (was, were) brought to the brazen altar.
5. A clear type of Christ (is, are) the many blood sacrifices that were offered here.
6. Our class (is, are) studying some Bible lessons about the tabernacle.
7. The cleansing of believers (is, are) portrayed by the priests' washing at the laver.
8. Some of the tabernacle types (relate, relates) to the different kinds of metals.
9. *Big Ten Tabernacle Topics* (indicate, indicates) that the gold was typical of Christ's deity.
10. An abundance of types (shine, shines) forth from the furniture of the holy place.
11. There (have been, has been) a few differences of opinion on some of these things.
12. Neither Herod nor his soldiers (was, were) able to destroy the Christ child.
13. Some of Jesus' worshipers (was, were) wise men from the East.
14. Simeon and Anna (stand, stands) as godly saints who rejoiced to see their Saviour.
15. A host of enemies (have, has) tried numerous ways to get around their accountability to a holy God.
16. Many teachings of the Bible (come, comes) to us from simple things.
17. The ant or the coney (teach, teaches) us to prepare ahead of time.
18. The spider (don't, doesn't) give up even after its web is destroyed by enemies.
19. The locusts, which (have, has) no king, challenge us to work together in humility and unity.
20. One of the differences between the twins (is, are) their personalities.
21. Our neighbor and accountant (fill, fills) out our tax returns each year.
22. The chickadees or titmice (visit, visits) our feeder each morning.
23. Eleanor's glasses (have, has) so many scratches that she needs new ones.
24. My trousers (seem, seems) too short since Mother washed them the last time.

25. You are the only one of my cousins who (was, were) not told about the accident.
26. Five days (pass, passes) very slowly when you are sick in bed.
27. Neither sickness nor other hardships (mean, means) that God has forsaken us.
28. Civics (was, were) very important to Mr. Johnson.
29. In my opinion, fifty dollars (is, are) an exorbitant price to pay for that purse.
30. *Arthropods* (was, were) the answer the teacher expected.
31. Each of my brothers (work, works) at home on our farm.
32. Stella is the only one of the students who (type, types) more than fifty words per minute.
33. Song leaders and moderators (fill, fills) an important place in our services.
34. A visit or a letter often (mean, means) very much to shut-ins.

B. Rewrite each sentence, following the directions in parentheses and changing the verb as needed to agree with the subject. Do not change the tense of the verb.

1. The heavy spring showers were flooding our garden. (Begin the sentence with *Each of.*)
2. Mr. Springfield is one of our neighbors who work on Sunday. (Insert *the only* before *one.*)
3. Neither my brothers nor my sister remembers Grandfather Martin. (Reverse the order of the subjects.)
4. There's a swarm of bees in the cherry tree. (Change *a swarm* to *thousands.*)
5. Most of these years have been unusually wet. (Change *these years* to *this year.*)
6. The family was eating a quiet dinner together. (Change the ending to *telling about their various experiences of the day.*)
7. This pair of trousers has a torn pocket. (Change *This pair of trousers* to *These trousers.*)
8. These stories haven't been revised yet. (Insert *One of* before *These.*)
9. The car and the truck use too much oil. (Change *and* to *or.*)
10. I have read all of the book that tells about Fanny Crosby's life. (Change *book* to *library books.*)
11. Two-thirds of the work is completed. (Change *work* to *chores.*)
12. This pair of pliers is broken. (Change *This pair of pliers* to *These pliers.*)
13. Susan is one of those girls who make friends easily. (Insert *the only* before *one.*)
14. Most of these boys know how to change a flat tire. (Change *these boys* to *this group.*)
15. The visitors that were present paid close attention. (Change *visitors* to *visitor.*)
16. Henry and Emma gather the eggs. (Change *and* to *or.*)
17. There's excellent cooperation among the students. (Change *cooperation* to *relationships.*)
18. Either the driver or the passengers were watching for the hidden lane. (Reverse the order of the subjects.)

19. These vehicles don't use much fuel. (Insert *One of* before *These.*)
20. The rest of my friends were just around the corner. (Change *friends* to *luggage.*)
21. The softball team were taking their places on the field. (Change the ending to *winning the game by four runs.*)
22. These alarm clocks wake a sound sleeper. (Insert *Neither of* before *These.*)

Review Exercises

Choose the words that are correct for the subjunctive mood. [75]

1. It would be a great blessing if every person (was, were) a student of the Bible.
2. If a man (know, knows) not where to find truth, he is indeed in great darkness.
3. We could have attended every service if the meetings (would not have been, had not been) so far away.
4. Some people were acting as if it (was, were) cold in the auditorium.
5. Brother David requested that someone (turn, turns, turned) up the heat.
6. The chairman recommended that the decision (be, is, was) postponed until the next meeting.
7. He considered it important that each board member carefully (think, thinks, thought) through the proposal.
8. If the captain (would have known, had known) about the danger, he would have tried to prevent the accident.
9. An accused man should be set free if he (be, is) found innocent.
10. If every person (was, were) completely honest, court trials would be unnecessary.

---

79. Improving Your Editing Skills, Part 8

We use alarm clocks to waken us in the morning. As long as we get up when the alarm rings, the system works well. But we all know what happens to a person who ignores his alarm clock. The more often he turns the alarm off and goes back to sleep, the less sensitive he becomes to its warning. Finally, the time will come when he continues to sleep while the alarm continues to ring!

Your editing skill works in an amazingly similar way. The more careful you are to use correct English in everyday speech and writing, the sharper you become in detecting errors. But if you excuse your errors and say or write things you know are incorrect, you will grow less sensitive. Do you allow yourself to use expressions like "Him and I plan to go" or "That don't matter" or "I seen him yesterday"? If so, you will find it hard to catch all the mistakes when you are editing—especially those that involve a fine detail of English grammar.

Whenever you become aware of an error in your use of English, you need to consciously raise yourself to a proper use of the language. This is the only way to develop a high degree of skill in editing.

Marks Used in Editing and Proofreading

∨ or ∧ insert (caret)	delete	.... stet (let it stand)	——— use italics
¶ begin new paragraph	no ¶ no new paragraph	lc change to lowercase (small letter)	uc change to uppercase (capital letter)
# insert space	⁀‿ delete space	← move (arrow)	transpose

Editing Practice

A. Use proofreading marks to correct the ten spelling or spacing errors in this selection.

George R. Brunk was an influental Mennonite bishop in Virginia. He served the church faith fully until his death in 1938. In one of his sermons, he denouced the infidel ity of men like Robert G. Ingersoll, a promanent agnostic. After the service, one of the brethern from the audience came to Brother Brunk with an intresting question. He

asked if it was allright to buy an Ingersoll watch. The quick-thinking bishop smiled and replied, "Certianly; Ingersoll will do for time, but not for eternity."

B. Use proofreading marks to make these corrections in the paragraph below.

a. Divide the selection into two paragraphs.
b. Correct two errors in sentence division.
c. Improve the word order in two places.

George Brunk was visiting one day a brother who was lying in the hospital, after speaking to him words of comfort, the minister turned to a man in a bed nearby and asked him about the state of his soul. The man replied gruffly, "If God wants me, let Him come and

6. get me!" "Listen," said Brother Brunk. "If you don't
7. concern yourself about your soul's salvation and do
8. something about it. Somebody will come and get you—
9. and it won't be God either."

C. Use proofreading marks to correct all the errors in these paragraphs. No line has more than one error.

1. Whereas some stars are much larger then the sun, others
2. are much more smaller. One of these is Sirius B, which is a
3. companion of the bright star called Sirius (the Dog Star).
4. Scientists classsify Sirius B as a white dwarf. Because
5. of its white color, they think its surface temperature is
6. hoter than that of the sun.
7. Though the diameter of Sirius B appears to be about
8. equal to that of the earth. Scientists believe its total
9. mass is equal to that of the sun. Compressing so much
10. mass into such a small sphere produces a extremely great
11. density. According to one estimate, a brick made of
12. substance from Sirius B weigh would thirty tons. That
13. is the weight of six full grown elephants!
14. According to scientists, the reason for differences in
15. stars is that they are in different stages of developement.
16. White dwarfs, they say, are millions of years older than
17. "young stars" like the gaint Betelgeuse. The Bible teaches
18. that God made all the stars on the forth day of Creation.
19. It also says, "One star differeth from another star in
20. glory (1 Corinthians 15:41). The stars are different, not
21. because they are in variuos stages of evolution, but
22. because God made them that way.

80. Chapter 9 Review

A. Copy each verb or verb phrase, and write which tense it is. Also write whether it is *simple, progressive,* or *emphatic* in form.
1. Over the years men have used water for many different things.
2. We do drink water, of course, and we are continually washing ourselves and our clothes.
3. We shall always need water for our plants.
4. Have you been thinking about its use for transportation?
5. Oh, yes, I had forgotten about its use in baptism.

B. Most of these sentences have mistakes in the use of verb principal parts. Write the correct verb, or write *correct.*
1. The dam at Johnstown had bursted after days of heavy rainfall.
2. I seen the mistake as soon as he handed me his paper.
3. Nobody else had did as much of the work as little Samuel.
4. I do believe that this shirt has shrunken with every washing.
5. As soon as you have tug someone else, he will be it.

C. Rewrite each sentence, changing one verb to a perfect tense so that the meaning is clearer or a completed action is emphasized.
1. Before we saw the other car, it crashed into our back fender.
2. By the time you finish your homework, the rest of the family will go to bed.
3. When I ate my lunch, I went outside to play.

D. Copy each underlined verb, and write whether its mood is indicative (*ind.*), imperative (*imp.*), or subjunctive (*sub.*).
1. Ahab <u>coveted</u> the vineyard of his neighbor Naboth.
2. How he wished that he <u>were</u> the owner of the land.
3. Always <u>guard</u> against an envious spirit.
4. <u>Do</u> you <u>think</u> that Ahab really needed the vineyard to be happy?
5. Jezebel ordered that Naboth <u>die</u> so that the king could have what he wanted.

E. Choose the words that are correct for the subjunctive mood.
1. "If God (is, be) for us, who can be against us?"
2. The doctor recommended that Grandfather (take, takes) a stress test.
3. Brother Sanford moved that the trustees (fix, fixed) the roof.
4. If we (were, would be) earlier, we would stop and visit Sister Emma.
5. Suppose this car (was, were) to run out of fuel.

F. Copy each verb, and label it *TA* (transitive, active voice), *TP* (transitive, passive voice), *IC* (intransitive complete), or *IL* (intransitive linking).
1. Three different arks are mentioned in the Scriptures.
2. The first one is Noah's large boat.
3. Next Moses' mother built a very small ark.
4. The ark of the covenant comes third.
5. The materials used for each ark were different.
6. Different items were placed into each of the arks.

7. Each ark served as an instrument of preservation.
8. Like an ark today, the Christian home protects its inhabitants from many surrounding dangers.

G. If the underlined verb or contraction does not agree with the subject, write the correct form. If it does agree, write *correct.*

1. Brother Brendon or Brother Wesley are scheduled to conduct the Wednesday devotional period.
2. The apple tree and the pear tree needs pruning this spring.
3. This pair of shears are too dull to do the job well.
4. Fifty pounds is the average weight of a fertilizer bag.
5. Approximately one-third of our watermelon plants wilts if we fail to spray them.
6. Nothing about his comments suggest that he felt mistreated.
7. *Thrilling Escapes by Night* recounts the experiences of William Tyndale.
8. Does your mother's parents still live near Mount Aetna?
9. English is the only one of my subjects that seem fairly easy.
10. My favorite breakfast is pancakes and syrup.
11. The family was working at their hobbies last evening.
12. He declares that it don't make any difference whether he comes or not.
13. Most of the building has been destroyed by the fire.
14. Neither the lettuce nor the onions appeals to my sense of taste.
15. All of the wall that was painted should have a second coat.
16. My friend and helper are holding the board in place.
17. The nail clippers were lost somewhere in the drawer.
18. Baby sheep or goats adds a great deal of interest around a place.
19. Our class has just finished a study of the Great Pyramid of Egypt.
20. There's no dull moments when Uncle Henry is present.

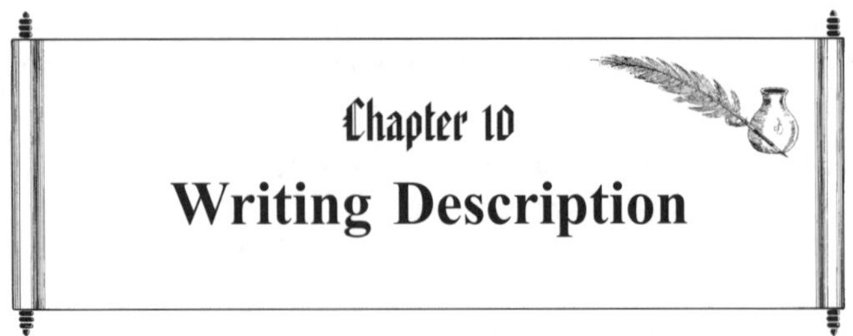

Chapter 10
Writing Description

81. Employing Descriptive Language

A writer of description uses words to sketch the details of a scene or an event. In describing a scene, he depicts the details of a particular place. In describing an event, he portrays the points of a particular happening. The more skillfully he draws his word pictures, the more appealing and fascinating they will be to the reader.

Almost invariably, writers weave descriptive writing into their stories, expositions, and arguments. Without it, the paragraphs would be flat, dull, and lifeless. Occasionally, however, a writer may produce an entire essay of description. Such an essay has as its purpose to paint a distinct picture in the reader's mind. You will produce such an essay in this chapter. But first, in this lesson, you will review the qualities that make writing truly descriptive.

Rich Detail

Effective description consists of rich detail. A paragraph of fuzzy generalities is about as satisfactory as a photograph that is out of focus. Clear details produce a sharp, meaningful picture.

What can you do to ensure that your writing contains that richness of detail? Above all, you must develop an eye for detail in the things around you. Look at things as if you had never seen them before. Analyze them carefully and thoroughly. Instead of taking a sweeping view, stop and consider exactly what you are seeing. Notice the people, their faces, their clothes, their postures. Notice specific objects and their variations of color, shape, and size. Pay attention to the things that are happening around you. You cannot hope to add rich detail to your writing unless you first exercise keen observation.

Consider this example, apparently written by a traveler in a Central American country.

> Looking at each other dubiously, we boarded the old, rickety bus. Soon we were jolting down the rough road.

The writer has described his experience simply, clearly, and honestly. But before he lays his pencil down, he should answer a few questions. How could he tell that the bus was old? By recognizing it as a 1945 model? By its faded paint? What was rickety about the bus? Was it missing a hood? Were the windows cracked and rattly? Did the floor have holes? And can he show us that the road really was rough?

If he fills in these answers, he will produce a description with rich details that stimulate our imagination and help us enjoy what he has observed. Read the description below, with these details added.

> Looking at each other dubiously, we boarded the dented, rust-eaten bus. The door sagged on its hinges, and we soon noticed that it refused to close completely. What padding the seats may have contained in some ancient past had disappeared or compacted so tightly that the seats felt more like knotty boards than bus seats worthy of the name. The engine coughed and almost died as the driver coaxed the bus to drag itself forward. Each bump and pothole (of which there were many!) made its whole rheumatic body twist and groan with pain.

Vivid, Concrete Words

Effective description uses vivid, concrete words. Exact nouns paint a sharper picture than general nouns modified by adjectives. Why write *huge rock* when *boulder* makes the picture clear? Or why write about a *sudden, heavy downpour* when *cloudburst* paints a sharp image? Look at the exact nouns in the paragraph above. The writer chose the word *padding* rather than *soft material.* He wrote *driver,* not *the man who was driving.* These exact nouns contribute to the descriptiveness of the paragraph.

Expressive verbs also add to the sparkle of the word picture. As much as practical, use strong, vivid action verbs. Linking verbs, passive verbs, and weak action verbs tend to tarnish a description. Compare the underlined verbs in the following sentences with the ones used in the paragraph above.

> We <u>got</u> onto the dented, rust-eaten bus.
> The door <u>was</u> crooked and <u>was</u> impossible to close completely.
> What padding there <u>may have been</u> in the seats in some ancient past <u>was gone</u>.
> The bus <u>was coaxed</u> to drag itself forward.
> Its whole rheumatic body <u>was caused</u> to twist and groan with pain.

Truly picturesque modifiers can add further color and sharpness to exact nouns and expressive verbs. The paragraph about the old bus contains a number of such picturesque words. Notice the italicized modifiers in the following expressions from that paragraph: Looking at each other *dubiously,* refused to close *completely,* in some *ancient* past, like *knotty* boards, its whole *rheumatic* body.

Imagery

Similes, metaphors, hyperboles, personification, and onomatopoeia help to make a description especially appealing. A skillful sprinkling of these figures throughout your composition adds spice and freshness that tickle the taste buds of a reader's mind. How many of these kinds of imagery caught your attention in the sample paragraph?

Simile:

> the seats felt more <u>like knotty boards than bus seats worthy of the name</u>

Hyperbole:

What padding the seats may have contained <u>in some ancient past</u>...

Personification:

The door... <u>refused to close completely</u>.

The engine <u>coughed and almost died</u> as the driver <u>coaxed the bus to drag itself forward</u>.

Each bump... <u>made its whole rheumatic body twist and groan with pain</u>.

Onomatopoeia: twist and <u>groan</u> with pain

Used with discretion, onomatopoeia adds a special appeal to descriptive writing. Unless the writing is geared to young children, you should use very few onomatopoeic exclamations like *Crash!* and *Moo!* or expressions like "the box rolled *bumpity-bump* down the steps." Rather, use more subtle forms of onomatopoeia like *groan* in the sample paragraph.

Appeal to the Five Senses

What is true for story writing (Chapter 8) is just as true for description: sensory details help the reader to live what the author is describing. Most descriptive writing appeals primarily to the sense of sight. But put forth special effort to include details that appeal to the other senses. In the description of the bus, the writer deliberately included details that appeal to three of our senses.

Sight: It was a dented, rust-eaten bus.
The door sagged on its hinges and did not close tight.
The padding of the seats was worn thin.

Sound: The engine ran rough and almost choked off.
The bus made groaning sounds as it bounced over the rough road.

Feeling: The seats were hard and lumpy.

Applying the Lesson

A. From these paragraphs, write examples that illustrate the indicated elements of description.

Suddenly the Sunday afternoon peace was shattered by screams of pain and fright. Father and I dashed outside to see three-year-old Bennie racing for the house with all the speed he could muster. Like a windmill gone berserk, his arms were flailing at his face, his stomach, and his legs. Around him swarmed an army of yellow jackets, furiously injecting their red-hot, poisoned needles into his flesh.

Grabbing a nearby water hose, Father dispersed most of the army. Quickly he and I removed Bennie's shirt, killing several more of the zealous warriors. Then Father picked up the little boy, who was swelling rapidly, and raced for the house. "[illegible]," he shouted, "get the van out of the garage. We must go to the hospital!"

1. An exact noun for loud noises.
2. An exact noun for clothing.
3. A verb that describes vigorous whirling motions.

4. Five other clear, vigorous verbs or verbals.
5. Two picturesque adjectives.
6. Two picturesque adverbs.
7. One simile.
8. Three metaphors.
9. Two details that appeal to the sense of sight.
10. Two details that appeal to the sense of hearing.

B. Write a more descriptive word for each underlined expression in this paragraph. Use personification in two of your answers, as noted in brackets.

The mountain road went on and on, sometimes [1]going around hairpin curves and sometimes [2]going swiftly downward [personification] into narrow ravines. Then a [3]very lovely view presented itself. Almost directly below us, a huge lake [4]showed an image of the bright blue heavens. A few small fishing boats [5]moved lazily on its [6]undisturbed surface. Several small farms [7]were in the verdant valley beyond the lake. In the distance, [8]nice hayfields [9]went up [personification] the slope for only a short distance before another mountain range abruptly cut them off.

C. Write a descriptive paragraph about two of these scenes or events. Include as many of the elements of description as practical.

1. Your younger siblings playing school.
2. The view from your house.
3. A place of interest that you have visited.
4. Your classroom at lunchtime.
5. Several puppies (kittens, lambs) playing together.
6. The aftermath of a flood (hurricane, tornado).

---

82. Selecting and Arranging the Details

Imagine that you are drawing a picture of your schoolroom. To make the picture accurate, will you draw everything that you can see? Indeed not! You will not draw all the cracks between the boards in the floor. Neither will you include all the lines of the wood grain in the teacher's desk, nor every speck and irregularity on the chalkboard. If you try to draw everything you can observe, you will succeed only in producing a grand and ungracious clutter.

Now imagine that you are writing a description of your schoolroom. Will you include everything that you can see, hear, smell, and feel? The lines in the floor? The rustling of papers? The squeaking of shoes? The smoothness of your desk top? No, of course not. Such a description would become a meaningless assortment of trivial details.

Whether drawing a picture with lines or with words, we must limit the details that we include.

Selecting the Details

To write effective description, you must select details carefully. First you must learn to recognize the important details. Which items in the scene catch your attention? Which other items fit with them to create the scene? Or which movements in an event stand out most? Which other movements blend with them as the significant happenings? Since you cannot use every detail, you must choose those that are central to your description.

In essence, every detail in a description should contribute to one specific impression. This is the theme of the description. In Lesson 81, for example, the paragraph about the rickety bus focuses only on the rundown condition of the bus. The author did not include details about how crowded it was or about the dust blowing in the open windows. He did not describe the driver, the cattle on the road, or anything else outside. The paragraph is intended to impress the reader with the condition of the bus itself; therefore, any other details would detract from that theme.

Two descriptions may give two different impressions about the same scene or event. For example, compare the following paragraphs, which describe the same kitchen scene.

> As usual, the kitchen extends a cozy welcome to each family member on this blustery winter evening. From its place in the corner, the large wood stove cheers the whole room with its friendly warmth. A large kettle on its surface diffuses the spicy aroma of hot apple cider. Eli and Conrad sit on the floor, playing contentedly with their tractors and farm animals. The three older girls enjoy the comfort of the sofa. Dorcas is engrossed in the experiences of *War-torn Valley.* A steady stream of words issues from Esther's pen as she writes to one of her friends. And the skein of yarn at Sarah's feet gradually takes shape as a sweater for baby Miriam, who coos and giggles from her walker. I turn back to the English lesson waiting patiently on the kitchen table. A warmth more precious than that of the cozy kitchen fills my heart as I thank God for my Christian home.

> As usual, the kitchen presents a busy but orderly appearance on this blustery winter evening. Mother has banished any dirt that was bold enough to gather on the floor. Her zeal is also evident in the sparkle of the wood stove standing in the corner. Now Mother's industrious needle is steadily changing a basketful of torn items into neat stacks of mended clothing. All the children are busily occupied too—the younger ones with their toys, and the older ones with reading, writing, and knitting. The books on the library shelves stand stiff and straight in orderly array. The sink and countertops smile at me with the joy of cleanliness. Once more the scene thrills me as I return to work on my English lesson.

Do you see the difference? In the first paragraph, the focus is on the warm pleasantness of the kitchen. So this paragraph presents details to match that theme, such as the friendly warmth of the wood stove, the spicy aroma of hot apple cider, and the amusement of two small boys. The second paragraph deals with the "busy but orderly" aspects of the kitchen. It develops that theme by mentioning things like Mother's banishing of dirt, her polishing of the wood stove, and the busyness of the children. Thus the paragraphs convey two different impressions even though they describe the same scene.

Arranging the Details

Once you have selected the details, you must consider how you will arrange them. For most descriptive paragraphs, you will choose either spatial or chronological order. Use spatial order to describe a scene. You may move from left to right, from near to distant, from a central figure to the less important details, or in any other logical progression. The sample paragraphs above follow spatial order.

Be sure to maintain a consistent point of view in your description. For example, if you are viewing a barn from the front, you must describe everything as seen from there. You could not tell about the back of the building. If you were to describe the barn as you walk around it, however, it would be appropriate to describe the back of the barn as your circuit takes you there.

Use chronological order to describe an event. In Lesson 81, the description about Bennie and the yellow jackets is in chronological order.

Applying the Lesson

A. Read this descriptive paragraph, and do the exercises that follow.

Aunt Viola's garden stands as a monument to her industry. In the left half is her bed of strawberries, forming a plush carpet that covers about a fourth of the garden. They are bearing exceptionally well this year, and a multitude of berries smile out from their leafy homes. Beyond the strawberries, a number of tomato plants gaze in wonder at the huge cages surrounding them. In the right half, a number of rows run the full length of the garden, as straight as latitude lines. They include a luscious stand of peas supported by four-foot-high poultry wire, as well as lettuce, carrots, beets, onions, radishes, green beans, and lima beans. Throughout the entire garden, not a single weed is bold enough to thrust its head into view.

1. Summarize the main impression about Aunt Viola's garden that this paragraph conveys.
2. Copy the first three words of the sentence that should be deleted because it does not contribute to that impression.
3. Name the order of development that is used in this paragraph.

B. Write two paragraphs describing the same scene or event, creating two different impressions. The following suggestions may help you.

1. An old barn: its neat simplicity, its sturdiness, its great size.
2. Sawing firewood: its noisiness, its bustling activity, its danger.
3. A cleaning day at church: its efficiency, its improvements, its large amount of work.
4. Moving day: its disorder, its excitement, its uncertainties.
5. A deep snow: its beauty, its hindrances to work, its chill.

83. Writing Description Within Other Compositions

When we find out that someone we know has just purchased a farm or a car, or has simply gotten another dog, we immediately want more information. Where is the farm? How big is it? Or, what kind of car did he buy? What year? And the dog—is it full-grown, or is it only a puppy?

Just as descriptive information adds meaning to real life, so it adds to writing. Description fills an important place in narrative essays (stories), expository essays, and argumentative essays. However, descriptive writing does not often stand alone as separate paragraphs in these other kinds of writing. It is usually woven right into the compositions.

Description Within Narratives

Description fills a vital role in narratives. The story setting represents descriptive information about the time, place, and mood of the story. The story incidents themselves should involve ample use of the elements of description. And the process of characterization relies heavily on the elements of descriptive writing.

Indeed, description is so important to narratives that in Chapter 8 you had several lessons devoted specifically to various elements of description in improving the style of a story. Notice the many descriptive details in the following excerpt.

> Being new in the area, Alfred was apprehensive about his first venture to the village. He stepped quietly under the awning of the blacksmith shop, and through the open door he surveyed its smoky interior. Scraps of iron and various crude works of art cluttered the corners. A great forge stood to one side. It crackled and belched smoke as the smith's assistant piled on fresh coal. Scattered here and there were various implements awaiting repair. Mr. Davis himself was hammering out a piece of steel destined to be part of a plow.
>
> Remembering his errand, Alfred stepped timidly into the shop and approached the men. The assistant jerked his thumb toward the smith. "He'll see to you shortly. Just sit and watch a spell." With that, he continued pumping the old leather bellows vigorously. Alfred watched as sparks leaped upward in the furious heat of the forge.

Description Within Exposition

Exposition often employs description. In writing exposition, you explain how something works or what something consists of. To do that effectively, you must include illustrations, examples, and other details. And that means you must write descriptively. Furthermore, to write your exposition interestingly, you should employ the various elements of description.

You will remember the following paragraphs from the exposition in Lesson 28. Notice now how much description the writer used in explaining what the water hyacinth is like.

The water hyacinth is a tropical water plant with large, elegant lavender flowers. It floats on air-filled sacs, and it reaches a height of about 2 feet (61 cm) above the surface of the water. When thousands of water hyacinths grow together, they form a mat so thick that it can support a man's weight.

But for all its striking beauty, the water hyacinth has some very ugly behavior. The plants multiply with amazing speed, sometimes doubling in number every ten days. Just 10 plants can increase to a mat of more than 600,000 in one growing season, and the mat continues to spread until it completely covers the surface of the water. In this way, the plant makes itself such a nuisance that it has been called the purple curse.

In Lesson 81 you studied four elements of description. See how the writer incorporated them in the paragraphs above.

1. Rich detail. Notice some of the specific details. Water hyacinths float on air-filled sacs and reach a height of about two feet. Water hyacinths sometimes double every ten days, and a mere ten plants can increase to 600,000 plants in one growing season. These details add to the quality of the exposition, for they help you to see exactly what the author is writing about.

2. Vivid, concrete words. The paragraphs use exact nouns: *mat, beauty, nuisance.* Notice the expressive verbs: *grow, form, support, multiply, increase.* They add more strength than would verbs of being or passive voice verbs. And several colorful modifiers make their contribution as well: *elegant, lavender, striking, amazing.*

3. Imagery. The second paragraph begins by attributing some *very ugly behavior* to this beautiful plant. Plants do not behave, of course, but we enjoy this imaginative description of what the plant does. The concluding sentence also suggests that the plant *makes itself a nuisance.* Again, the suggestive implication adds interest and appeal.

4. Appeal to the five senses. These paragraphs include language that appeals to your sight. In fact, those visual details constitute the very essence of the exposition. As you see those details, you understand the exposition. Since none of the other senses are involved in observing the hyacinth, the essay includes no details that appeal to them.

Clearly, the inclusion of descriptive writing has helped to make the exposition about the water hyacinth clear, effective, and interesting.

Description Within Argument

Arguments may also include description. True, the strength of an argument lies in its sound reasoning and its supporting facts. But the supporting evidence includes illustrations, examples, and other details that involve description. As with exposition, that description again contributes greatly to the overall effectiveness of the essay.

Notice the descriptive details in the following paragraphs from an argumentative essay.

Owning a small flock of laying hens assures your family a steady supply of eggs. For their room and board, twenty good layers pay between fifteen and eighteen eggs a day for two to four months. During those peak months, that accumulates to nine or ten dozen cartons of economical nutrition every week. This should provide breakfast several times a week for a family with six to eight children, in addition to supplying plenty of eggs for cooking and baking. Even when production declines to only ten eggs a day, you should still be gathering about six dozen eggs per week. Your family will seldom suffer an egg shortage if you have a small flock of layers.

A small flock of laying hens will also give your family the assurance of knowing that you are eating fresh eggs. Unfortunately, eggs from the store can hardly make any reasonable claim to freshness. Indeed, most of those eggs have probably spent several weeks in storage before they get their first glimpse of a store shelf. By the time they are sizzling in your frying pan, they are definitely suffering from old age. But you can trust your own eggs. You know when you gathered them. So a family flock of layers makes sense for people who prefer eating fresh eggs.

All four elements of descriptive language shine in these paragraphs. They are categorized below, along with examples from the essay.

Specific details: twenty good layers, between fifteen and eighteen eggs a day, two to four months, nine or ten dozen cartons, six to eight children, several weeks in storage

Vivid, concrete words: small flock, peak months, breakfast, cooking and baking, egg shortage, fresh eggs, frying pan, old age

Imagery: their room and board, nine or ten dozen cartons of economical nutrition, their first glimpse of a store shelf, suffering from old age

Appeal to the five senses: sizzling in your frying pan

Some description is written purely to give the reader a mental picture of what the writer has observed. Within other kinds of composition, descriptive writing adds color and interest to the narrative, exposition, or argument.

Applying the Lesson

Read the following essay, and show how to make it more descriptive by following the directions below. (Exercise letters correspond to the letters of sentences in the essay.) You need to write only enough of the appropriate sentences to show your improvements.

1. Include the following specific details in the sentences indicated.
   f. The pool of Siloam has an oblong shape.
   h. The water in the pool has a somewhat brackish taste.
   n. The underground conduit is 1,750 feet long.

2. Replace each of the following expressions with a specific noun.
   i. steep face of rock
   l. effort to capture the city by surrounding and blockading it
   o. words inscribed
3. In sentences *c, d, i,* and *k,* replace the passive verbs and linking verbs with more expressive verbs in the active voice.
4. Replace the following expressions with imagery.
   i. rises above (personification)
   n. travels a twisted course (personification)

The Pool of Siloam

[a]In a notable display of His power, Jesus healed a man who had been born blind. [b]But He did not merely speak the word of healing as He usually did. [c]Rather, clay was made and was spread on the man's eyes. [d]Then the blind man was commanded, "Go, wash in the pool of Siloam" (John 9:1–7).

[e]Archaeologists and Bible scholars generally identify the pool of Siloam with the modern Birket Silwan, southeast of Mount Zion. [f]This pool is in a basin about fifty-three feet long, eighteen feet wide, and nineteen feet deep. [g]It lies partly in hewn rock and partly in masonry construction. [h]The water in the pool of Siloam comes from the Gihon Spring. [i]Flowing from the steep face of rock that rises above the Kidron Valley, this spring was the only unfailing source of fresh water for ancient Jerusalem. [j]The spring flows intermittently, however, sending its tribute to the pool from three to five times daily in winter, about twice a day in summer, and about once a day in autumn.

[k]Because of the strategic importance of this spring, an extraordinary feat of excavation was performed by men of ancient times. [l]Apparently in preparation for the Assyrian effort to capture the city by surrounding and blockading it, Hezekiah "stopped the upper watercourse of Gihon, and brought it straight down to the west side of the city of David" (2 Chronicles 32:30). [m]In the words of 2 Kings 20:20, "he made a pool, and a conduit, and brought water into the city." [n]This underground conduit travels a twisted course through solid rock. [o]According to the words inscribed on the channel wall near the pool of Siloam, workmen using picks dug from both ends and met in the middle.

---

84. Planning a Descriptive Essay

You saw in the previous lesson that descriptive writing adds color and interest to narratives, expositions, and arguments. But sometimes a whole essay consists of description. Such an essay has the general purpose of giving the reader a mental picture of what the writer has observed, and the specific purpose of giving a certain impression about the scene or event described.

As with other kinds of writing, a descriptive essay calls for careful planning. The following five steps will help you to plan a descriptive essay.

1. *Choose a scene or an event to describe.* This should be something familiar that interests you. You cannot write a good descriptive essay about something you have never observed unless you write about an imaginary scene or event. A description is not an exposition that presents facts about a subject. It is rather a word picture, giving specific details that will paint in the mind of the reader the picture that the writer sees.

The subject of a good description need not be something extraordinarily beautiful or exciting. With a little imagination and writing skill, you can make interesting descriptions even of everyday scenes and events. For example, you could probably give quite an interesting description of your family at the dinner table.

2. *Decide on the theme of your description.* Remember that the theme is the main impression you want to convey. With many scenes, you can write a description focusing on one of several different impressions. For example, the essay in Lesson 85 emphasizes the great size of Grandfather Hoover's farmhouse. The author could have included details about the neatness of the house or the simplicity of its structure and furnishings. But an essay is better if it focuses on only one theme.

3. *List details about the scene or the event.* Look for details that will paint concrete word pictures. List details that appeal to as many of the five senses as practical. Generally, details that appeal to the sight come quite naturally. But you should also put special effort into capturing details that appeal to the other senses.

If you have already decided on the theme of your description, you will limit the details to those that convey the impression you want. If you have not yet decided, list all the details that are outstanding to you. Your list should be helpful in deciding on a suitable theme.

4. *Examine your list of details, and delete any that do not contribute to the theme.* Even if you have been selective in making your list, you will probably find some details that are insignificant or that are not as well related as you had thought earlier. The following list shows some details that could be written for an essay about a large farmhouse. Notice how the deleted details do not fit. Although they are interesting, they do not develop the impression of the great size of the house.

Massive front door—7½ feet by 4 feet
Five-foot-wide hallway through length of house
Wide spiral stairway in center of hallway
~~Paintings of old farm machinery on two parlor walls~~
Kitchen wood stove ~~with well-padded rocking chair beside it~~
Half-bathroom in corner of kitchen

5. *Organize your details into an outline.* A description of a scene should follow spatial order, and you must be consistent with your point of view. A description of an event should follow chronological order.

Study the following outline for a descriptive essay about a large farmhouse.

Room for Sixteen Children

I. Entrance
   A. Massive front door—7½ feet by 4 feet
   B. Stone walls nearly two feet thick
   C. Five-foot-wide hallway running length of house
   D. Wide, spiraling stairway in center of hall
II. Parlor
   A. Stale odor from little use
   B. Ten-foot ceiling
   C. Echoing sound from paneling and hardwood floor
III. Master bedroom
   A. Large bed in center of far wall
   B. Wide dresser with large round mirror along right wall
   C. Cedar chest in near right corner
IV. Kitchen
   A. Countertop with double sink and spacious cabinets along left wall
   B. Half-bathroom in far left corner
   C. Countertop along a third of right wall
   D. Wood stove in far right corner
   E. Door to living room centered in right wall
   F. Extension table in center
V. Living room
   A. Study in near right corner
      1. Desk at far wall
      2. Bookshelves along both walls to left
   B. L-shaped living room itself
      1. Plants along wall to left
      2. Recliner in far left corner
      3. Walnut hutch along wall beyond
      4. Toy box and table along opposite wall
VI. Second story and attic
   A. Five rooms on second floor—three on left, two on right
   B. Center room on left—bathroom and storeroom
   C. Attic over entire floor space of lower two stories
   D. Attic ceiling—six feet high at peak, four feet at eaves

Applying the Lesson

A. In the next lesson, you will be asked to write a descriptive essay. Choose a scene or an event to describe, and decide what impression you want to convey about it.

B. List a number of details about the scene or event you have chosen to describe, and organize the details into an outline. The score on your finished essay will make up a considerable part of your Chapter 10 test score.

85. Writing a Descriptive Essay

Writing a descriptive essay is much like writing any other essay. You gather and organize information, and then you write the first draft. Later you proofread and revise your essay, and finally you write the second draft.

A descriptive essay contains the same three parts found in other essays: an introduction, a body, and a conclusion. However, the introduction and the conclusion may consist of only a single sentence each—one to introduce the theme (general impression) and one to clinch the theme.

In writing a descriptive essay, follow your outline. The outline should keep you on track in the proper spatial or chronological order. It will also help you to include all the important details that you have observed. Your outline, of course, is your guide for writing the essay.

In each paragraph, describe one general section of a scene or one connected movement in an event. Generally, each main topic on your outline (I, II, III, . . .) should constitute one paragraph in your essay. If a main topic includes many details, each subtopic (A, B, C, . . .) might constitute a separate paragraph. But if a main point has only a few supporting details, all the subtopics may be covered in a single paragraph. You can see actual examples of this by comparing the essay below with the outline in Lesson 84.

Your essay will also need a title. The title should be short (five words or less), and it should relate to the theme in an appealing way.

Read the following essay. The first sentence is the introduction, the last is the conclusion, and all the material in between is the body. Then compare the essay with the outline in Lesson 84. Notice how it describes the entrance to the house in the first paragraph, the parlor in the second, the master bedroom in the third, and so forth. The last paragraph describes both the second story and the attic because so little detail is given about those parts of the house.

Room for Sixteen Children

Grandfather Hoover's live in an old farmhouse that dwarfs any other house I have ever entered. To begin our tour, we shall enter the front door—a massive oak slab measuring seven and one-half feet by four feet. As we move through the doorway, we notice that the stone walls are almost two feet thick! We have stepped into a great hallway five feet wide, running the whole length of the house. Every footstep echoes in the vast, almost empty space. Our eyes immediately focus on a wide stairway in the exact center of the hallway. It spirals from the ground floor all the way to the attic.

To the left of the hallway are two large rooms: the parlor and the master bedroom. A slightly stale odor greets us as we enter the parlor, for it is used only when a large number of visitors come. As in all the rooms of the first and second stories, the ceiling of the parlor soars above us at an altitude of ten feet. So in spite of the padded parlor furniture, the wood paneling and the hardwood floor make this room an effective resonator, echoing every sound.

Now we step into the master bedroom. A large bed is centered on the far wall, but the room is so spacious that the bed almost looks small. Along the wall on our right, a wide dresser with a large round mirror surveys the scene. Squatting beside it in the near corner is a small cedar chest—or does it only look small? A full bathroom completely fills the near corner to our left.

Across the hall from the master bedroom, we come to the kitchen—which I usually consider the most important room of the house. Along the wall to our left is a long countertop with a large double sink in the center and with spacious cabinets above and below. A half-bathroom occupies the far left corner. Another large countertop embraces a third of the wall to our right, and the old wood stove beams a warm welcome from its place in the far right corner. Centered along the wall to our right is the door to the living room. Today the shrunken table huddles forlornly in the space directly before us. But when the table spreads its broad back to bear the food at our family gatherings, it fills the center of the kitchen quite comfortably.

We pass through the door from the kitchen to the living room. Shortly after he was ordained forty years ago, Grandfather walled off the entire corner to our right for his study. As we step through its doorway, which stands immediately to our right, we see his large desk sitting solemnly along the far wall. Grandfather's extensive library fills both walls to our left.

Now we step back into the L-shaped living room. Even with one corner walled off, this room still makes us feel small. The broad wall to our left is loaded with Grandmother's plants—cherry tomatoes, small strawberries, and a great variety of flowers—enough to start a fair-sized garden. In the corner beyond the plants, a recliner bids a pleasant welcome to anyone who yearns to sit back and relax. Centered between this chair and the hallway door, a wide walnut hutch stands almost like a throne, with a pair of heavy wooden chairs guarding its two sides. Along the opposite wall sits a large toy box and a long table, where we grandchildren often play games.

We go through the hall door and climb the steps to the second story. Here we find five large rooms, three on the left of the hallway and two on the right. Years ago, Grandfather divided the center room on the left into a spacious bathroom and storeroom. The mammoth attic sprawls over the entire floor space of the lower two stories, but its ceiling is only six feet high at the peak and four feet at the eaves. As we descend the long stairway, we are again impressed with the immensity of this house in which Grandfather Hoover's raised their sixteen children.

As you write, strive to employ the four qualities of descriptive writing that you studied in Lesson 81: rich detail; vivid, concrete words; imagery; and appeal to the five senses. Use descriptive language throughout your essay to clearly show the details you are portraying.

Applying the Lesson

Write the first draft of your descriptive essay, following the steps in this lesson. Write on every other line to allow room for revising. Your essay should have 500–700 words.

---

86. Improving Your Editing Skills, Part 9

Many English words have a variety of meanings and uses. In most cases, we can combine words in more than one way to communicate our thoughts. But occasionally a certain word combination can produce an *ambiguous* sentence. Such a sentence may be seriously misleading—or embarrassingly humorous.

The following item once appeared as a headline in a newspaper.

TWO CARS COLLIDE, ONE SENT TO HOSPITAL

The ambiguity, of course, results from the different ways in which *one* can be used. We often use this pronoun to mean "one person." But in the headline, *one* appears to mean "one of the cars." Are we expected to think that a car was actually sent to the hospital? We know better.

This time we can smile and pass on. But some ambiguous statements are confusing or misleading, so you need to make it your responsibility to detect and change such statements. A person should not need to be a detective to understand what he is reading.

In this lesson and in all your proofreading, make sure every sentence is clear and easily understandable.

Marks Used in Editing and Proofreading

˅ or ˄ insert (caret)	delete	.... stet (let it stand)	use italics
¶ begin new paragraph	no ¶ no new paragraph	lc change to lowercase (small letter)	uc change to uppercase (capital letter)
# insert space	delete space	← move (arrow)	transpose

Editing Practice

A. Use proofreading marks to correct the two errors of capitalization or punctuation in each sentence.

Leopards are large members, of the Cat family. They live throughout most of Africa, the middle East, southern Asia and eastern Asia. When a leopard is born it weighs only about one pound, and is quite helpless. A young leopard generally stays with its Mother until it is two years old; then it becomes self supporting.

did you know that people are a greater danger to leopards than leopards are to people. Actually these animals seldom attack human-beings. But after they discover that people are easy victims: they may become a serious threat to Man. Poachers, herdsmen and shepherds have ruthlessly hunted leopards, however, the species is protected today.

B. Use proofreading marks to correct the fifteen usage errors in these paragraphs, according to the rules you studied in Chapter 5.

Have you ever considered the enormity of the assignment that Noah excepted from God? Because the Flood was immanent, he needed to build an ark of fabulous size. Also, he and his family had to stand all alone in a society that flaunted the principles of godliness. A quote from 2 Peter infers that Noah warned his fellow men while he worked, but they were disinterested in his message. Apparently none of them wanted into the ark.

What are some notorious lessons that we can learn from this here account? First, Noah felt that God's words would surely come to pass. He did not loose his faith even though many years passed before the Flood came. Second, Noah committed himself to obeying God regardless of what transpired. It is all ways best to believe and obey God, no matter what other people may do.

C. Use proofreading marks to correct all the errors in these paragraphs, including the ones that are specifically mentioned below. No line has more than one error.

a. In the first sentence of paragraph 1, "more and more elaborate telescopes" could mean "a greater and greater number of elaborate telescopes." Make it clear that the telescopes are becoming more and more elaborate.

b. In line 12, change the position of *only* so that its meaning is clear.

c. In the first sentence of paragraph 3, it sounds as if the mirror was *hauled* at an altitude of 7,200 feet. Make it clear that *Cerro Tololo* is at that altitude.

In their effort to learn more about the heavens, men have built more and more elaborate telescopes. The great telescope at the Cerro Tololo Inter-American Observatory in chile is one outstanding example. This huge instrument has a mirror with a diameter of 4 meters (158 inches)—more then 13 feet!

When the molten glass was poured for this mirror; its total wait was 25 tons. The huge mass first had to be cooled for many months—very gradually, to keep it from cracking. Then work men began to grind the glass into a concave shape. They labored for 2½ years, and they remove so much material that the finished mirror only weighed 17 tons. In the perfecting process, technicians used a laser so accurate that it detect ed irregularities as slight as 5 millionths of an inch.

The finished mirror was hauled to Cerro Tololo, at an altitude of 7,200 feet (2,200 m). Scientists chose this place because of its clear stable air and because of its location South of the equator. The site is ideal for studying the centeral portions of the Milky Way galaxy, which are best observed from the Southern Hemisphere.

87. Proofreading and Rewriting a Descriptive Essay

As with other types of writing, you need to give the first draft of your descriptive essay a thorough evaluation. Check the essay that you wrote in Lesson 85, using the following questions to help you find ways to improve it.

Content and Organization

1. Does the description give a clear mental picture of the scene or event? (If possible, have someone else read your first draft and give his comments.)
2. Does the description give details in a logical order?
3. Is the description full of rich detail and vivid, concrete words? Does it use effective imagery? Does it appeal to the five senses?
4. Is the point of view consistent?
5. Are the paragraphs unified and coherent? Is there smooth transition between paragraphs?
6. Does the essay have an introduction, a body, and a conclusion?

Style

1. Do you see any sentences that you should write with more freshness and originality?
2. Do you see any vague, general terms that you could replace with exact, descriptive words?
3. Do you see any passive verbs that you could change to the active voice?

Mechanics

1. Have you used any unnecessary or repetitious words?
2. Have you omitted any words or phrases that are needed to make the meaning clear?
3. Have you transposed or misplaced any words, phrases, or clauses?
4. Have you misspelled any words? Especially check spellings like *ei* and *ie, ai* and *ia, ent* and *ant,* and so forth. Double-check your use of homonyms like *your—you're* and *their—there—they're.* Make sure that you have spelled technical terms and proper nouns correctly. Pay close attention to words that you have difficulty spelling correctly.
5. Have you used proper capitalization and punctuation?
6. Have you followed the rules of correct grammar and word usage?

Do not imagine that you can evaluate all these points at one time. You could begin by checking your essay with the points under "Content and Organization," in the order they appear. Next, you could review your essay for improvements by using the points under "Style." For the points under "Mechanics," you might concentrate first on points 1–3 and then on points 4–6.

Applying the Lesson

A. Proofread the descriptive essay that you wrote in Lesson 85.

B. Recopy your essay in your best handwriting. Your teacher may use the following evaluation chart to grade your essay. Your score on this essay will make up a considerable part of your Chapter 10 test score.

Evaluation of a Descriptive Essay

Points possible	Points earned	
Title		
3	____	Short and appealing
3	____	Directly related to theme
Introduction		
3	____	Introduces theme in an interesting way
Body		
3	____	Clear mental pictures
3	____	Consistent point of view
3	____	Well-developed paragraphs
3	____	Logical order (spatial or chronological)
Conclusion		
3	____	Clinches theme effectively
Elements of description		
3	____	Single theme
3	____	Effective imagery
3	____	Rich details that appeal to the five senses
Style		
3	____	Freshness and originality
3	____	Active verbs and other exact, descriptive words
Mechanics		
3	____	Correct spelling
3	____	Correct capitalization and punctuation
3	____	Correct grammar
3	____	Absence of careless repetition, omitted words, transpositions
51	____	**Total points**

---

88. Chapter 10 Review

A. Write the correct word or phrase for each blank.

1. The author of description paints ———.
2. Effective description employs the vivid language of ——— nouns, ——— verbs, and ——— modifiers.
3. The careful use of ——— makes meaningful comparisons and adds color to a description.

4. By appealing to the ———, a writer can help the reader to live what he has described.
5. A description of a scene usually follows ——— order; a description of a happening usually follows ——— order.
6. The ——— of a description is the one main impression that it emphasizes.

B. Answer these questions.
1. What two important considerations must you remember as you select the details for a descriptive essay?
2. Why must you choose a familiar subject when you plan a descriptive essay?
3. What three parts should a descriptive essay have?
4. If a whole essay consists of description, what is its general purpose? What is its specific purpose?

C. Read this description, and do the exercises that follow.

Kate did not run across that railroad bridge. She did not even walk. She crawled! On hands and knees, she fought physical and mental terrors as she pushed ahead for about five hundred feet to the far side of the bridge, groping through darkness, her lips trembling in prayer. From time to time, her skirt became entangled in spikes, nearly toppling her off balance. Other spikes and splinters cut and bruised her hands and knees. Every moment she was fearful of seeing the headlight of the eastbound train shine full in her face.

Panic gripped Kate when, about halfway across, she saw a huge tree, its roots thickly matted with earth clods, bearing down upon her like a giant battering ram. The tree was so big that she felt sure it would engulf and drag her down to a watery grave when it smashed the bridge. But somehow it passed harmlessly between the piers, spraying her with leaves and spume; and she continued to creep toward the end of the bridge, which appeared so very far away.

1. Write exact nouns that are used instead of the following general words or phrases.
   a. great fears
   b. large nails
   c. sudden overwhelming fear
   d. chunks of material sticking together
   e. supporting posts
   f. watery foam
2. Write expressive verbs or verbals that are used for the following actions.
   a. Kate was feeling her way.
   b. Her skirt got caught.
   c. She almost fell over.
   d. Fear came forcefully upon her.
   e. The tree would have struck the bridge with crushing force.
3. Copy the phrase that more expressively communicates this idea: enclose her and pull her down and drown her.
4. Copy the picturesque modifiers that describe these words.
   a. lips
   b. tree
   c. roots
   d. passed
5. Copy the simile that is used.

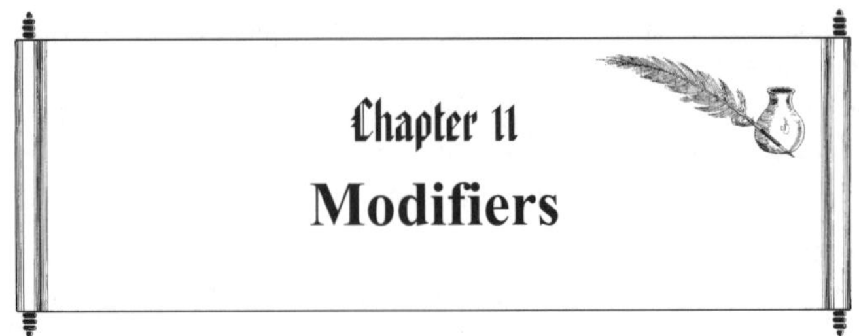

89. Recognizing Adjectives

To modify something is to change it. Teachers modify their lesson plans to fit the needs of different classes. Weather forecasters modify their reports as weather patterns change. Hog farmers modify their feeding program in an effort to make their hogs grow faster. Students modify their reports to make them clearer and more interesting.

In grammar, too, we are familiar with modifiers. Adjectives and adverbs modify the meanings of other words to make them more descriptive and more precise. Adjectives modify substantives by telling *which, whose, how many,* or *what kind of.* These modifiers include two main classes: limiting and descriptive.

Limiting Adjectives

A *limiting adjective* limits a substantive by telling *which, whose,* or *how many.* The following six groups of words may function as limiting adjectives.

1. *The articles are always limiting adjectives. A* and *an* are indefinite articles because they indicate no specific nouns. *The* is a definite article because it indicates a specific noun.

    a minister of the Gospel (any minister)
    the minister of the Gospel (a certain one)

2. *Number words are often used as limiting adjectives.*
    a. Cardinal numbers (*one, two, three,* and so forth) tell *how many.*

        one Lord   three psalms

    b. Ordinal numbers (*first, second, third,* and so forth) tell *which.*

        first day   fourth king of Israel

3. *Indefinite pronouns are sometimes used as limiting adjectives.* These words are adjectives only when they precede substantives to tell *which* or *how many.* When they stand alone and function as substantives, they are pronouns.

    every promise   several questions

4. *Demonstrative pronouns are sometimes used as limiting adjectives that tell* which.

    that mistake   these mountains

5. *The interrogative pronouns* whose, which, *and* what *are sometimes used as limiting adjectives.*

which rivers　　what lakes

6. *Possessive nouns and pronouns are often used as limiting adjectives that tell* whose. Remember to use apostrophes with nouns and indefinite pronouns, but not with personal pronouns.

Herbert's essay　　somebody's heifers
the families' contributions　　books that are ours

Descriptive Adjectives

Descriptive adjectives describe substantives by telling *what kind of.* These are the words that shade and shape our language. Descriptive adjectives can be classified according to their structure.

1. *Some words in their simplest form are descriptive adjectives.*

brilliant sunsets
simple truths

2. *Some descriptive adjectives can be identified by adjective-forming suffixes.* The following list includes some of the most common of these suffixes.

-ish:	foolish, greenish	**-less:**	toothless, tasteless
-al:	parental, tidal	**-like:**	Christlike, summerlike
-ic:	basic, academic	**-ous:**	momentous, bulbous
-ive:	elusive, subjective	**-some:**	winsome, troublesome
-y:	steamy, marshy	**-ant, -ent:**	tolerant, absorbent
-ful:	bountiful, masterful	**-able, -ible:**	replaceable, accessible
-ary:	primary, customary	**-an, -en:**	European, earthen

3. *Some descriptive adjectives are formed by changing the spellings of nouns.* In general, adjectives of this kind are proper nouns.

Switzerland—Swiss
Wales—Welsh

4. *Nouns are often used as descriptive adjectives without any spelling change.* These are known as attributive nouns.

country store　　window frame
tin roof　　Gothic letters

5. *Present and past participles may be used as descriptive adjectives.*

running water　　written message

6. *Infinitives may be used as descriptive adjectives.* Such an infinitive immediately follows the substantive it modifies.

a promise to keep　　a story to write

Remember to separate with commas two or more descriptive adjectives used in a series and having equal rank. If necessary, review the specific details of this rule in Lesson 2.

Several warm, sunny days melted the late snow quickly.

Positions of Adjectives

An adjective may occur in three positions relative to the substantive it modifies. An *attributive adjective* precedes the substantive it modifies. The adjective *attributes* (assigns) a quality to the substantive that follows. Most adjectives appear in this position.

A small, neat school squatted under a mighty oak.

An *appositive adjective* follows the substantive it modifies. This places special emphasis on the adjectives. Appositive adjectives often come in pairs, in which case they are set off by commas.

Each classroom, simple yet attractive, breathes an atmosphere of dignity.

A single adjective may also follow the substantive, especially when it refers to position or when it is modified by an adverb phrase.

An open playroom downstairs is used on rainy days.

The playground, small by some standards, serves the school well.

In the first example above, *downstairs* is an adjective because it tells which playroom. (Compare "the downstairs playroom.") Since *downstairs* tells which, it is a limiting adjective.

A *predicate adjective* follows a linking verb and modifies the subject. You can usually tell that it is a predicate adjective because the word would also fit in the attributive position, before the subject.

The new furnace is quiet and efficient.
(Compare: quiet and efficient furnace)

Applying the Lesson

A. Copy each underlined adjective. First label it *L* (limiting) or *D* (descriptive); then label it *AT* (attributive), *AP* (appositive), or *PR* (predicate).

1. Your character, invisible to man's view, displays itself in the little, everyday actions of life.
2. Noble conduct, displaying wholesome character, earns the respect of others.
3. Acceptable words will be truthful and gracious.
4. Many Bible characters, facing severe temptations to compromise, endured in godly fear.
5. Three boxes to fill are standing beside that pile of wood scraps outside.
6. Which picture above shows the first tractor that Grandfather bought for this thriving farm?

B. Copy each adjective and the word that it modifies.
1. Our Father above continually showers us with numerous gifts.
2. Some gifts, common and often overlooked, still are great blessings.
3. We should be thankful for abundant food to eat and for work to do.
4. The daily ration of many people is several ounces of rice.
5. Multitudes do not have any regular income because they are sick or have no jobs.
6. Simply having fresh air to breathe is a notable blessing.

C. Copy these sentences, replacing each *L* or *D* with a limiting or descriptive adjective other than an article. Add commas as needed.
1. *L* cookies *D* and *D* make a *D* treat.
2. *L* lambs, *D* in the *D* meadow, seem quite *D*.
3. William is making *D D* mottoes in the *D* woodshop *L*.
4. The *D D* water flows from the spring *L* to this *D* pond.
5. The *D* snowdrifts, *D* into *D* shapes, look *D*.
6. Although *L D* mountain looks *D,* it is actually quite *D*.

D. For each word in parentheses, write an adjective form that fits in the sentence.
1. The (office) name of the southernmost (Scandinavia) country is the Kingdom of Denmark, which correctly indicates its (presence) form of government.
2. The Danes have a (constitution) monarchy, with a (parliament) system actually (response) for the (base) governing.
3. The land of Denmark includes a (prominence) peninsula, (know) as Jutland, as well as hundreds of islands of (vary) sizes.
4. The (prevalence) features on Jutland are the long, (roll) hills that are often quite (knob).
5. Many (finger) fiords, (break) up the coastline, give Denmark several (size) seaports that contribute to the country's (prosper) fishing industry.
6. Most regions of Denmark contain (product) grainfields, (fruit) produce farms, or (luxuriate) pastures.

Review Exercises

Write the correct word in each set of parentheses. [62, 63]
1. We know that God is much wiser than (we, us).
2. Anyone who thinks (he, they) can direct (his, their) life without God's wisdom is deceived.
3. Only the person (who, which) trusts the Lord can walk safely the highway of life.
4. God's power is infinite, but (ours, our's) is limited.
5. (Who, Whom) but God can we trust for power to overcome our enemy?
6. God and (I, myself) can be victorious, but I alone cannot be.
7. God's Word contains many promises and warnings, and (them, these) are powerful helps for us.
8. (Everyones, Everyone's) faith would be strengthened if he were to rely wholly on the Lord.

9. If (these, these here) small trials shake our faith, what shall we do when we face severe tests?
10. We live daily with things of this world, but we must love heaven more than (they, them).

---

90. Adjective Phrases and Clauses

Not only single words but also phrases and clauses can function as adjectives in a sentence. Adjective phrases come in a variety of forms: prepositional, participial, and infinitive.

Prepositional Phrases

A prepositional phrase consists of a preposition and its object, along with any modifiers of the object. When a prepositional phrase serves as an adjective, it usually comes right after the substantive it modifies.

> Men of faith consider the order within the universe a testimony to God's creative skill.

Participial Phrases

The present and past participles of most verbs end with *-ing* or *-ed.* (A few past participles end with *-t* or *-en,* such as *lost* and *hidden.*) These verb forms are called participles when they serve as adjectives. If a participle has modifiers or complements, it is a participial phrase. A participial phrase may come before or after the word it modifies.

> Even unbelievers, observing that order, have come to humble submission before God.
>
> Convinced of God's existence, a man may come to trust in Jesus as his Saviour.

Participles can show three different tenses. Use the present participle to express action or being that occurs at the same time as that of the main verb in the sentence.

> The rain, pouring down in torrents, flooded the low-lying areas.
> (The rain flooded the areas at the same time it poured down.)

The past participle can also express an action that occurs at the same time as that of the main verb. In addition, it may express a completed action.

> The streams, affected immediately by the downpour, rose rapidly.
> (The streams were affected at the same time they rose rapidly.)
>
> The river, swollen by heavy rains earlier in the week, soon overflowed its banks. (The river was swollen before and during the time it overflowed.)

The present perfect form indicates that the action or being occurs before that of the main verb in the sentence. The present perfect form consists of the past participle preceded by *having*.

> Having risen rapidly, the flooded streams caught many travelers by surprise. (Indicates that the streams had risen before they caught travelers by surprise.)
>
> Having been warned not to drive through high water, the driver went a different way. (Indicates that the driver was warned before he went a different way.)

Infinitive Phrases

An infinitive phrase, consisting of an infinitive and its modifiers and complements, can be used as an adjective. (Infinitives can also be used as substantives or adverbs.) An infinitive used as an adjective immediately follows the substantive it modifies, and it usually tells *which* or *what kind of.*

> The Bible passage to memorize this week is Romans 12:1–5. (The infinitive phrase tells *which* passage.)
>
> The best way to remember Bible verses is to review them often and put them to practice. (The infinitive phrase tells *what kind of* way.)

Adjective Clauses

An adjective clause is a dependent clause that modifies a substantive. Either a relative pronoun or a relative adverb introduces an adjective clause. The relative pronouns are *who, whom, whose, which,* and *that;* the relative adverbs are *when, where,* and *why.* These words are called relative pronouns and relative adverbs because they *relate* the adjective clause to the substantive that the clause modifies. Therefore, adjective clauses are sometimes called relative clauses.

> Those people whom Father helped had never heard of people who practiced nonresistance.
>
> The town where they live has several churches but apparently few consistent Christians.

Sometimes the relative pronoun or the relative adverb is omitted, making the clause harder to identify.

> The story Great-grandfather told was about a time he went to town on horseback. (Compare: story that Great-grandfather told; time when he went to town on horseback)

The words listed as relative pronouns and relative adverbs do not always introduce adjective clauses. Relative pronouns may also introduce noun clauses, and *when* and *where* may introduce noun or adverb clauses.

> When I walked past the old shed, I saw that wild morning glories are taking over. (*When I walked past the old shed* is an adverb clause telling *when* about *saw. That wild morning glories are taking over* is a noun clause serving as the direct object of *saw.*)

Restrictive and Nonrestrictive Modifiers

Participial phrases and adjective clauses may be restrictive or nonrestrictive. If the phrase or clause restricts the meaning of a substantive by identifying *which one,* it is restrictive. A restrictive phrase or clause is essential to the meaning of the sentence and is not set off with commas.

> That big dog running around our yard belongs to the family who lives across the road.

In the example above, the participial phrase restricts the meaning of *dog* by telling *which one.* Not all the dogs belong to that family—only the one running around our yard. The adjective clause restricts the meaning of *family* by telling *which one.* The sentence is not referring to all the families—only the one across the road. The underlined modifiers are not set off with commas, for they are necessary to the meaning of the sentence.

If the modifying phrase or clause simply gives additional information about the substantive, it is nonrestrictive. A nonrestrictive phrase or clause does not identify a substantive by telling *which one.* Since it is not essential to the meaning of the sentence, it is set off with commas.

> Rising to his feet, Eugene offered his chair to Grandfather, who had just entered the room.

In this example, the participial phrase does not identify *Eugene* by saying "the Eugene rising to his feet." It simply gives additional information about *Eugene.* The adjective clause does not identify *Grandfather* by saying "the Grandfather who had just entered the room." It simply gives additional information about *Grandfather.* The underlined modifiers are set off with commas, for they are not necessary to the meaning of the sentence.

Modifiers Within Other Modifiers

One adjective phrase or clause may contain other adjective phrases or clauses. The object of a preposition, the complement of a participle or an infinitive, and any substantive in an adjective clause may have a phrase or clause modifier. Study the following sentences, in which arrows point from the underlined modifiers to the words modified.

> The owl that is hooting from yonder tree wants a meal for the young ones in its nest.
>
> Filled with many examples of noble character, this book is a treasured gift from my grandfather who recently passed away.

The ability to understand adjective phrases and clauses will help you to construct sentences that express your thoughts clearly and precisely. Learn to recognize and use them well.

Applying the Lesson

A. Copy each adjective phrase. If a phrase is part of a longer phrase, include it with the longer phrase and also copy it separately. Label each phrase *prep.* (prepositional), *part.* (participial), or *inf.* (infinitive).

1. Recognizing God's sovereignty, we do not fear those things disturbing the natural man's tranquillity.
2. Self-worship, also labeled as pride, never fulfills man's need to worship God.
3. True worship, centered on God alone, gives man the motivation to become more godly.
4. The commitment required for steadfastness through trial can be a reality known to all.
5. Our plans to visit our neighbors down the road might provide an occasion to learn some new things about Switzerland.
6. The family's move to a new country has brought many changes, but their desire to find a Bible-believing church may bring the greatest changes.
7. Their faith, having grown over the past several years, is finding a new opportunity to flourish freely.
8. Having found this home in our community, the Muellers have recognized their need to obey the entire Bible and are taking steps to adopt a Biblical lifestyle.

B. Copy the correct participles in parentheses.

1. The bread (rising, having risen) sufficiently, Mother slid it carefully into the oven.
2. The King James Bible, (proving, having proved) itself over several centuries, holds for us a place of high appreciation.
3. (Roasting, Roasted) to juicy tenderness, the chicken made a delicious meal for us.
4. The pork chops, slowly (barbecuing, barbecued) over the charcoal, will soon be finished.
5. (Being, Having been) fed, the puppies lay down to sleep.
6. (Sliding, Having slid) into the ditch, Mother climbed out of the car and went for help.

C. Copy each adjective clause.

1. Anyone who loves the Lord must renounce certain things that this world highly esteems.
2. The Holy Bible, which is God's message to mankind, sanctifies all whose hearts are open to its message.
3. In homes where God's Word holds its rightful place, you will discover that peace reigns.
4. The letter Mother just read stated that Uncle Myron's had two feet of snow last week.

5. The visiting preacher, whom I remember hearing before, was Sue Troyer's grandfather.
6. In the days when Grandfather was young, many modern conveniences were unknown.

D. Write whether each underlined phrase or clause is restrictive (*R*) or nonrestrictive (*N*). Also copy each word that should be followed by a comma, and add the comma.

1. The spotted hyena which lives in the region south of the Sahara is a badly misunderstood animal.
2. Its howl which sounds like eerie laughter helps to make it one of Africa's most-hated creatures.
3. The notion that hyenas follow lions to eat their leftovers is also quite common.
4. The Dutch scientist Hans Kruuk studying hyenas in the wild learned much about these mysterious nocturnal animals.
5. Soon the determined scientist whose equipment included binoculars, cameras, and a sturdy station wagon observed a group of hyenas as they killed a zebra.
6. Several lions, however, seized the kill that these hyenas had made.
7. Kruuk also played into the night air recordings made of hyenas at a kill as well as some of lions at a kill.
8. His lion recording played near a group of hyenas created not the least stir of interest.
9. But lions hearing the recorded sound of hyenas at a kill came on the run.
10. So the animal widely viewed as a thief is actually the victim.

Review Exercises

A. Identify each underlined complement by writing *PN, PA, DO, IO,* or *OC.* [20]

1. This rain will give our gardens and fields a much-needed boost.
2. I consider the miracle of growing things a testimony of the Creator's skill.
3. The rooster's crowing sounded haughty and challenging.
4. Brilliant sunshine warmed the earth and cheered our spirits.
5. The busy schedule challenged us at first but soon became a familiar routine.

B. The underlined words are retained complements. Identify each one by writing *DO ret., IO ret.,* or *OC ret.* [21]

1. A kind helping hand has been given us through this time of trial.
2. Our burdens have been made lighter by the help of so many friends.
3. Their help has been considered a blessing from the Lord.
4. We have been given many encouragements by the Lord.

91. Recognizing Adverbs

Though adjectives modify the substantives in sentences, adverbs modify—or change the meanings of—other words to make them more descriptive and more precise. The points in this lesson and the next will help you to recognize adverbs.

1. *Adverbs modify verbs.* Most adverbs modify verbs by telling *how, when,* or *where* something happened or existed.

> We can continually serve the Lord faithfully, for Jesus ever lives to intercede for us.

The words *not, never, ever, almost, always, hardly, scarcely,* and *seldom* are always adverbs. Often they qualify verbs by limiting or altering their meanings. Even if the word *not* is compounded with *can* in *cannot* or joined with a verb in a contraction ending with *n't,* it is an adverb.

> Man cannot resist the devil in his own strength; moreover, he isn't able to subdue his own carnal nature.

2. *Adverbs modify adjectives and other adverbs.* Adverbs of this kind are often called adverbs of degree because they tell *to what degree.* Almost without exception, they come immediately before the words they modify. The following words are commonly used as adverbs of degree.

almost	especially	quite	thoroughly
completely	extraordinarily	rather	too
dangerously	extremely	so	unusually
definitely	greatly	somewhat	very
entirely	partly	surprisingly	

Study the following sentences. Note especially how the underlined words are diagramed.

> We should be deeply grateful to the Lord, for He has blessed us very richly.

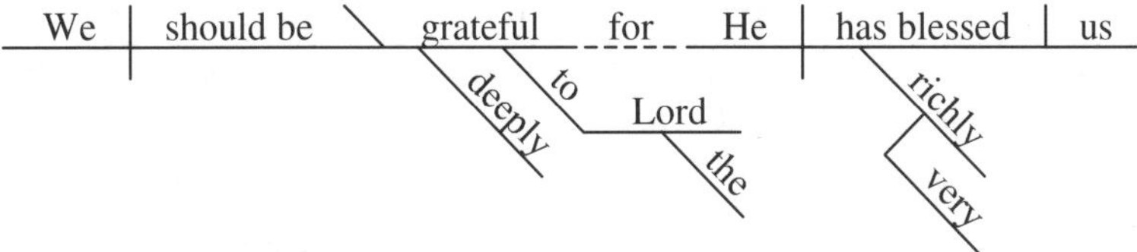

> The formerly eminent man is almost completely unknown now.

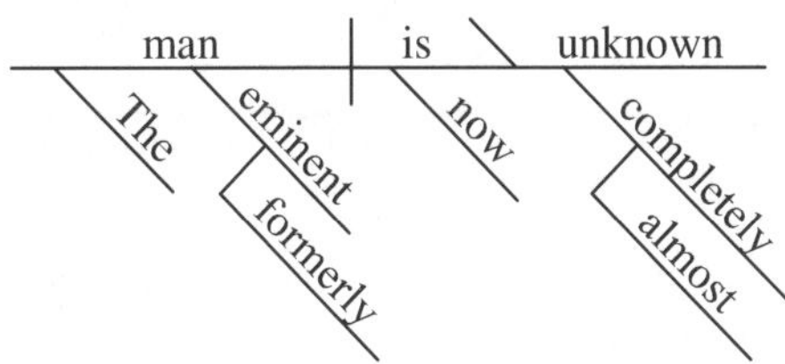

3. *Adverbs modify verbals.* These adverbs tell *how, when, where,* or *to what degree* about the action or existence indicated by the verbal. Remember that verbals include gerunds, infinitives, and participles. In the following examples, the verbals are italicized and the adverbs modifying the verbals are underlined.

> *Flying* gracefully overhead, the swans soon disappeared.
> (*Gracefully* tells *how* and *overhead* tells *where* about the participle *Flying.*)

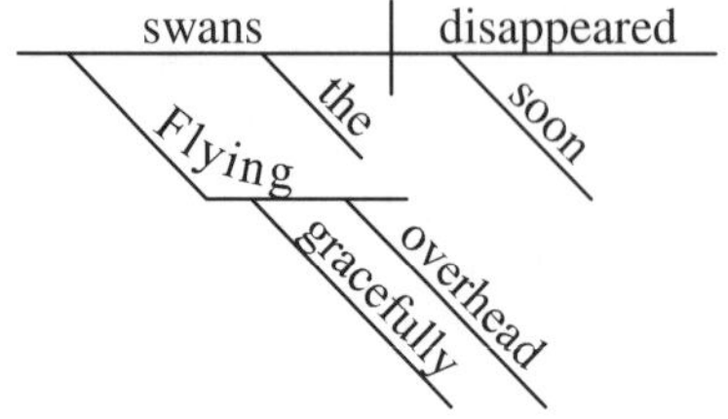

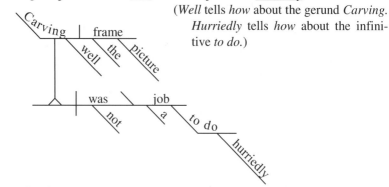

> *Carving* the picture frame well was not a job *to do* hurriedly.
> (*Well* tells *how* about the gerund *Carving. Hurriedly* tells *how* about the infinitive *to do.*)

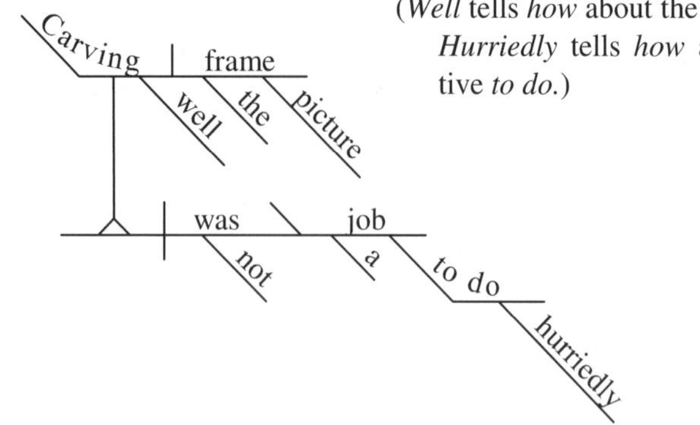

Forms of Adverbs

Many adverbs are adjectives to which the suffix *-ly* has been added. However, an *-ly* ending is not a sure indicator of an adverb, because some words ending with *-ly* are other parts of speech. And some words *not* ending with *-ly* are adverbs—especially those that tell *when* or *where.* You must observe how a word is used in a sentence before you can decide what part of speech it is.

> Those who zealously stand for truth will surely face temptations to compromise.
> If we always trust in the Lord, we shall move forward in His will.
> (In both examples above, all the underlined words are adverbs.)
> A lowly attitude toward self gives one a friendly outlook toward others.
> (The underlined words are adjectives.)

Many adverbs can also function as adjectives or prepositions, without any change in form.

> Last night was quite cold, but tonight the temperature might drop even lower.
> (*Lower* is an adverb modifying *might drop.*)

These <u>lower</u> temperatures may be common <u>up</u> north, but they are unusual here. (*Lower* is an adjective modifying *temperatures; up* is a preposition.)
The weathermen expect the temperature to move <u>up</u> again tomorrow. (*Up* is an adverb modifying *to move.*)

When there are two adverb forms like *quick* and *quickly,* the *-ly* form is usually better in standard English.

Informal: "Come <u>quick</u>," Laura shouted.
Standard: Blizzards can descend very <u>quickly</u> on a prairie region.

Infinitives can be used as adverbs. An infinitive that modifies a verb almost always tells *why.*

The family gathered reverently <u>to worship</u>. (*To worship* tells *why* about *gathered.*)
<u>To pray</u>, they always knelt at their places. (*To pray* tells *why* about *knelt.*)

An infinitive that modifies an adjective usually follows the adjective and tells *to what degree* or *how* (that is, *in what way*). Sometimes it may not answer any specific question, but it definitely modifies the adjective by telling *to do what* about it.

Anyone who is determined <u>to endure</u> must put on the whole armor of God. (*To endure* modifies the predicate adjective *determined* by telling *in what way.*)
The Bible contains many warnings important <u>to consider</u>. (*To consider* modifies the adjective *important* by telling *to do what* about it.)
Too numerous <u>to count</u>, God's blessings should inspire us to faithfulness. (*To count* tells *to what degree* about the adjective unit *Too numerous.*)

In the last example, note that the infinitive modifies the unit *Too numerous.* These words are considered a unit because it is not logical to say that the infinitive modifies either word separately ("Too *to count*" or "numerous *to count*"). Below is the diagram of this sentence.

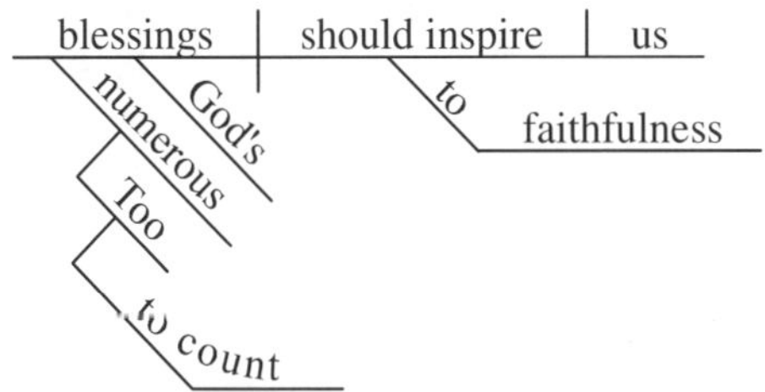

An infinitive that modifies an adverb usually follows the adverb and tells *to what degree* or *how.* Again, the infinitive may merely qualify the adverb by telling *to do*

what about it. And the infinitive almost always modifies an adverb unit similar to that in the last example above.

> You have spoken too softly to understand.
> (*To understand* tells *to what degree* about the adverb unit *too softly. Too* is also an adverb modifying *softly.*)
>
> Perhaps you did not stand close enough to hear.
> (*To hear* qualifies the adverb unit *close enough. Enough* is also an adverb modifying *close.*)

Applying the Lesson

A. Copy each underlined adverb, and write whether it modifies a verb (*v.*), an adjective (*adj.*), an adverb (*adv.*), or a verbal (*vbl.*).

1. God promises His abundantly sufficient grace to all who sincerely seek His face.
2. Man naturally thinks that he is well able to handle the circumstances of life effectively.
3. Man certainly cannot live without God's help, yet he too often resents God's will.
4. The Christian who very humbly looks to God continually receives divine grace.
5. Standing motionlessly in the water, a great blue heron peered downward, waiting patiently for a fish to swim near.
6. Scattered profusely over the hillside, the beautifully blooming wildflowers made a most lovely sight.
7. To raise produce profitably requires a significantly large investment in hard work, coupled with God's blessing.
8. The girls are working unusually fast today, and by noon should be done sufficiently well to be excused.
9. Did those wild animals know in some way impossible to explain that the storm would strike so severely?
10. God has marvelously provided them with the ability to sense keenly some things that man cannot perceive.

B. Copy each adverb, and write the word or words that it modifies.

1. Unexpectedly seeing a wild turkey in a forest glade is a highly interesting experience.
2. A tom turkey often struts stiffly and gobbles noisily as if boldly declaring that he owns the forest.
3. Wild turkeys frequently gather to feed contentedly under the relatively peaceful shade of the trees.
4. The swan's gracefully curved neck contributes quite definitely to its overall beauty.
5. God obviously designed the swan to swim, and it swims almost constantly.
6. The swan's relatively short legs make it a very awkward bird on land.
7. The boys are still looking for Daniel's truck that disappeared overnight.

8. Snow fell thickly today, yet the roads stayed mostly clear and safe to travel.
9. As dusk settled in, the temperature dropped slightly; but the wind later shifted suddenly to the northwest, causing the temperature to drop sharply.
10. Can we accurately measure this wildly drifted snow that unexpectedly blanketed the earth?

Review Exercises

A. Identify the form of each underlined verb as simple (*S*), progressive (*P*), or emphatic (*E*). [77]

1. The Lord does remember those who put their trust in Him.
2. I believe the promises of God.
3. We should be seeking to grow in the qualities of righteousness.
4. Do you consider yourself perfect?
5. I do know that I have much room for improvement.

B. Change each underlined verb to the form shown in italics. Do not change the tense. [77]

1. The day swiftly comes to a close. *progressive*
2. We recognize that the time to labor for the Lord is now. *emphatic*
3. Jesus promised His continual presence with the faithful. *emphatic*
4. We look for the eternal morning to dawn. *progressive*
5. Jesus has prepared a place for us. *progressive*

---

92. Recognizing Other Adverbs

In Lesson 91 you saw that adverbs modify verbs, adjectives, adverbs, and verbals. These are the most common functions of adverbs. This lesson covers less common functions of adverbs. In fact, the last two points of the lesson introduce functions of adverbs that you likely have never considered before.

1. *Adverbs introduce questions.* Such adverbs also modify the verb in the question.

> Where are Uncle Sherman's moving?
> When can we visit them?

2. *Adverbs join independent clauses.* When adverbs function in this way, they are called conjunctive adverbs and always modify the verb of the second clause. You will study conjunctive adverbs further in Chapter 13.

> The sunflower seeds and suet are attracting many birds; indeed, we have already counted over twenty different kinds at the feeding station.
> (*Indeed* connects two clauses and modifies *have counted,* the verb of the second one.)

3. *Adverbs modify prepositions and conjunctions.* Both prepositions and conjunctions show relationships between words. But sometimes a connecting word alone does not express the relationship accurately enough; a modifier is needed to show it more precisely. Then an adverb may be used to modify the conjunction or preposition. Observe how this is done in the following examples.

Henry's ball landed in the water almost beyond Father's reach.
(The preposition *beyond* is not precise enough because the ball did not actually land beyond Father's reach. *Almost* modifies *beyond* and helps to show the exact relationship between the landing of the ball and Father's reach.)

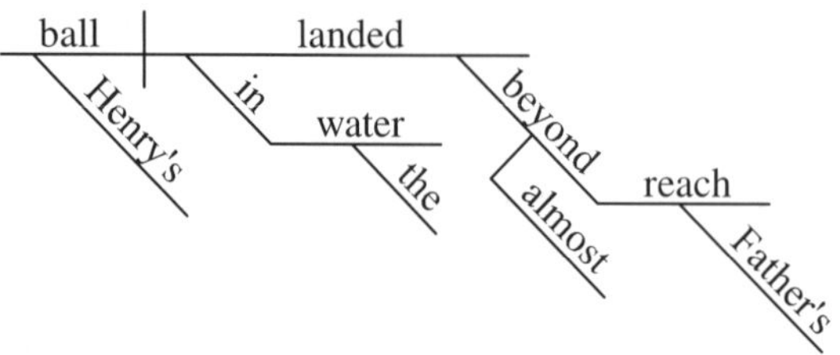

The salesman came right after Father left.
(The conjunction *after* is not precise enough to indicate that Father had barely left when the salesman came. *Right* modifies *after* and helps to show the exact relationship between Father's leaving and the salesman's coming.)

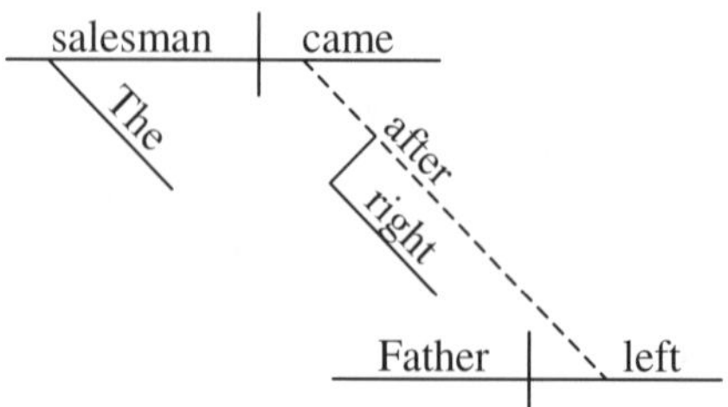

4. *Adverbs modify whole sentences.* An adverb does not always modify a specific word. Sometimes it modifies an entire sentence. Study the following example.

Clearly, the stranger misinterpreted our words.
(*Clearly* modifies the entire sentence, *the stranger misinterpreted our words,* by indicating that its idea is clear. To say that it modifies *misinterpreted*—"misinterpreted clearly"—would not be sensible.)

Here are some adverbs that can modify whole sentences.

certainly	providentially	surprisingly
clearly	regrettably	tragically
interestingly	sadly	understandably
obviously	strangely	

Note that when an adverb modifies a whole sentence, it is usually the first word. But an introductory adverb can also modify just the verb. How can you tell the difference? Here is a method that you should find helpful.

Change the introductory adverb to its adjective form, and use that form in the following expression: "It is ——— that..." Continue with the rest of the original sentence. If the resulting sentence means the same as the original, the introductory adverb modifies the entire sentence. If the meaning is different, the introductory adverb modifies only the verb.

Problem: Strangely, many can behold the wonders of creation and still deny God.
Think: It is strange that many can behold the wonders of creation and still deny God. (This sentence has the same meaning.)
Solution: *Strangely* modifies the entire sentence.

Problem: Sadly the old man told his story of woe.
Think: It is sad that the old man told his story of woe. (This sentence has a different meaning.)
Solution: *Sadly* modifies the verb *told.* (The old man told his story sadly.)

Problem: Sadly, the whole store burned to the ground.
Think: It is sad that the whole store burned to the ground. (This sentence has the same meaning.)
Solution: *Sadly* modifies the entire sentence.

Applying the Lesson

A. Copy each underlined adverb, and write whether it modifies a verb (*v.*), a preposition (*p.*), or a conjunction (*c.*).

1. When will the first strawberries ripen if we had snow and cold almost into May?
2. Just as the capering calf was heading for its hutch, little Jason shouted; consequently, we had another ten-minute chase.
3. The forecasters did not know exactly where the hurricane would strike, but it seemed nearly beyond a doubt that it would hit the East Coast sometime on Wednesday.
4. Why does Shep bark and growl far into the night so often?
5. Soon after Grandmother arrived to spend a few weeks with us, she became quite sick; however, in a few days she was feeling much better again.
6. The deer bounded high over the fence and straight into the forest.

B. Each sentence has two adverbs that modify prepositions or conjunctions. Copy those adverbs, and write *p.* or *c.* after each to tell what part of speech it modifies.

1. Immediately after Jesus was born, angels brought a heavenly message directly to the shepherds.
2. Almost before they realized it, these lowly men were heading straight toward Bethlehem.

3. God's wisdom is not slightly above man's comprehension; it extends far beyond the highest of man's wisdom.
4. Man tries to delve deep into the mysteries of life, but he shall stop exactly where God decrees.
5. Lee is speaking exactly as I believe, but Lamar thinks his ideas are somewhat beside the point.
6. We had battled the fire nearly to the point of exhaustion, but a fresh breeze fanned the flames just as we thought we were winning.
7. The car was heading straight for the ditch, but the driver regained control just before it was too late.
8. Uncle Lester's came soon after ten o'clock, but they had to leave long before nightfall.

C. Write whether each underlined adverb modifies a *verb* or an entire *sentence.*
1. Obviously, man's natural inclinations stand opposed to God's holy purposes.
2. Sadly Father described the end of those who reject God's way.
3. Gladly the Lord will pardon every sinner who turns to Him in true penitence.
4. Regrettably, few backsliders return to the Lord and seek His forgiveness.
5. Strangely, no one saw the fire until most of the building was aflame.
6. Providentially, the fire did not spread to the paint store.
7. Tragically the waifs told their story.
8. Understandably, our hearts were deeply touched by their pathetic story.

Review Exercises

A. Name the punctuation that should follow each underlined word: *colon, semicolon, ellipsis points, dash,* or *none.* [4, 6]
1. At the root of most sin lies one evil pride.
2. "Man really has no basis for being proud," Father mused, "but still"
3. Pride began with Lucifer's attempt to dethrone God it will cease when Satan and all his followers are cast into the lake of fire.
4. We receive much encouragement to humility through the teaching of the Bible, the counsel of our parents, and the example of the godly.
5. "Everyone should strive to be more humble than well, no, that doesn't make sense," said Elmer.
6. We do not strive to be more humble than others however, we do seek to become more humble than we have been.

B. Write the letter of the sentence in which the boldface part is correct. [5, 6]
1. a. "Were you living up to the Bible standard to be subject 'for conscience **sake'?"** asked Father.
   b. "Were you living up to the Bible standard to be subject 'for conscience **sake?'"** asked Father.
2. a. "The powers that be are ordained of **God (Romans 13:1),"** and we should not speak evil of them.
   b. "The powers that be are ordained of **God" (Romans 13:1),** and we should not speak evil of them.

3. a. The chapter **“Nonconformity to the World”** gives much practical help on the subject.
   b. The chapter ***Nonconformity to the World*** gives much practical help on the subject.
4. a. This **all purpose** glue works remarkably well.
   b. This **all-purpose** glue works remarkably well.
5. a. Thomas Jefferson said, “The hole and the patch should be commensurate **[of corresponding size].**”
   b. Thomas Jefferson said, “The hole and the patch should be commensurate **(of corresponding size).**”
6. a. Because of the flu epidemic, nearly **one-third** of the students are absent.
   b. Because of the flu epidemic, nearly **one third** of the students are absent.
7. a. “Did Father ask, ‘Is everyone ready for family **worship’?”**
   b. “Did Father ask, ‘Is everyone ready for family **worship?’ ”**
8. a. The ***Titanic,*** at first a symbol of man’s ability, has become a symbol of man’s foolish pride.
   b. The **“Titanic,”** at first a symbol of man’s ability, has become a symbol of man’s foolish pride.
9. a. As soon as we saw the **mud-covered** truck, we knew why Father was late.
   b. As soon as we saw the **mudcovered** truck, we knew why Father was late.
10. a. You had too many **“ah’s”** in your speech.
    b. You had too many ***ah*’s** in your speech.

---

93. Adverb Phrases and Clauses

Like adjectives, adverbs come not only as single words but also as phrases and clauses. Adverb phrases may be either prepositional or infinitive.

Prepositional Phrases

A prepositional phrase may be an adverb. When such a phrase modifies a verb or a verbal, it answers questions like *how, when, where,* and *why.*

> God has revealed Himself <u>through His Word</u> <u>for man’s eternal well-being</u>.
> (*Through His Word* tells *how* about the verb *has revealed; for man’s eternal well-being* tells *why* about the verb *has revealed.*)
>
> God’s Word, forever settled <u>in heaven</u>, shall continue to guide God’s people <u>until the eternal age</u>. (*In heaven* tells *where* about the participle *settled; until the eternal age* tells *when* about the infinitive *to guide.*)

A prepositional phrase that modifies an adjective or an adverb tells *to what degree, how,* or *how much.* It usually comes immediately after the word it modifies.

Sometimes an adverb prepositional phrase modifies an adjective or an adverb unit like *too friendly* or *too quickly.*

Saul, jealous in the extreme, pursued David even though he was innocent of any wrong. (*In the extreme* tells *to what degree* about the adjective *jealous. Of any wrong* tells *how* about the adjective *innocent.*)

Saul served the Lord too halfheartedly for any lasting usefulness.
(*For any lasting usefulness* tells *to what degree* about the adverb unit *too halfheartedly.*)

Some sentences have several prepositional phrases in succession. Sometimes these phrases are a series of adverb phrases, each modifying the same word independently of the others. Study the following sentence, in which arrows point from the underlined modifiers to the word modified.

Great-grandfather Weber often traveled across the mountain on foot in favorable or unfavorable weather.

At other times, the first preposition introduces the whole string of prepositional phrases, which work together as one adverb. Each of the other prepositional phrases is an adjective modifying the object in the previous phrase. When prepositional phrases occur in succession, you must think carefully about each one to decide whether it is an adjective or an adverb phrase.

Great-grandfather Weber served as the bishop over three congregations in this valley.

Infinitive Phrases

An infinitive phrase, consisting of an infinitive and its modifiers and complements, can be used as an adverb. (Infinitives can also function as substantives and as adjectives.) An infinitive that modifies a verb almost always tells *why.*

We should rise in the presence of the elderly to give them due respect.
(*To give them due respect* tells *why* about *should rise.*)

To give due honor to the Lord, we must give due honor to our fellow men.
(*To give due honor to the Lord* tells *why* about *must give.*)

An infinitive that modifies an adjective or an adverb tells *to what degree* or *how.* Usually, it immediately follows the word it modifies. Again, these infinitives sometimes modify a unit like *too loud.*

Grandmother Wenger is always glad to help us with our work.
(*To help us with our work* tells *how* about the predicate adjective *glad.*)

This bread dough is rather stiff to handle nicely.
(*To handle nicely* tells *how* about the adjective unit *rather stiff.*)

Finally the wind is blowing hard enough to spin the windmill.
(*To spin the windmill* tells *to what degree* about the adverb unit *hard enough.*)

Adverb Clauses

An adverb clause is a dependent clause that modifies a verb, an adjective, or another adverb. An adverb clause begins with a subordinating conjunction. The following list contains some of the most common subordinating conjunctions.

after	even if	than	when
although	even though	that	whenever
as	how	though	where
as if	if	till	wherever
because	since	unless	whether
before	so that	until	while

Just like single-word adverbs and adverb phrases, adverb clauses can modify verbs, verbals, adjectives, or adverbs. Many adverb clauses answer the basic adverb questions *how, when,* and *where.* In addition, they can answer the questions *why, how long, how much, to what degree, in spite of what,* and *under what condition.* Adverb clauses can also modify adjective or adverb units like *as soon* or *so long.*

You should form noble habits while you are still young.
(*While you are still young* tells *when* about the verb *should form.*)
Youth must develop conviction to do right even though others are doing wrong.
(*Even though others are doing wrong* tells *under what condition* about the verbal *to do.*)
A Christian, joyous although hardships beset him, is the truly happy person.
(*Although hardships beset him* tells *in spite of what* about the adjective *joyous.*)
We should strive to live so faithfully that others can find no fault with us.
(*That others can find no fault with us* tells *to what degree* about the adverb unit *so faithfully.*)

When *as* or *than* introduces an adverb clause of comparison, the clause is often elliptical.

Norma does not write poems as often as stories.
(as often *as she writes stories*)
Glenford can run a little faster than Lowell.
(a little faster *than Lowell can run*)

Punctuation With Adverb Phrases and Clauses

Use a comma after an introductory adverb phrase or clause (unless it is a short prepositional phrase). An adverb clause at the end of a sentence needs no comma. If an adverb clause comes in the middle of a sentence, use a comma before and after it. Only a short clause should occur in the middle; a long clause usually mars sentence coherence.

With several feeders on the trees behind our house, we feed many wild birds.
To bring in a large number of birds, hang out several feeders.

If you put different types of seed in the feeders, you should attract a wide variety of birds.
These many birds, when snowy weather comes, flock to the feeders.
We enjoy feeding the birds while their natural food supply is limited. (no comma)

Applying the Lesson

A. Copy each prepositional phrase used as an adverb, including any adjective phrase that may be in it. Write the word or word group that the phrase modifies.
1. In six days of creative work, God made the world, complex beyond man's understanding.
2. After centuries of investigation, many facts continue to baffle man by their complexity in spite of man's scientific advances.
3. Accepting the Bible account by simple faith provides the only foundation solid enough for true scientific understanding.
4. Evolutionary theories are detrimental to man's learning process; indeed they are responsible for many foolish conclusions among the worldly-wise.
5. Many additional responsibilities fell on Charlotte's shoulders during Mother's illness, but she handled them quite well for a sixteen-year-old girl.
6. Warm weather had stayed in our region for a long time, but yesterday the temperature dropped too low for comfort.

B. Copy each infinitive phrase used as an adverb, and write the word or word group that the phrase modifies.
1. We must develop God's point of view to understand anything properly.
2. To develop God's point of view, we must become well acquainted with His Word.
3. Creation speaks of God's glory clearly enough to convince any honest person of His existence.
4. However, many are too proud to accept their accountability before God.
5. A wise person is slow to accept new ideas.
6. Sometimes new ideas are too impractical to prove themselves valuable.
7. Sound wisdom includes the discretion necessary to test new ideas.
8. The Bible warns us against deception often enough to spur us to great carefulness.

C. Copy each adverb clause, and write the word or word group that the clause modifies.
1. If you look at a physical map of South America, the Andes Mountains stand out more sharply than any other feature does.
2. This mountain range, greatly varying as it extends along the west coast, passes through many degrees of latitude.
3. The Andes range, much wider than it appears on a map, is so rugged that it makes an effective barrier.
4. The southern Andes lie where the west winds carry much moisture from the Pacific, but the moisture condenses thoroughly enough that little remains for the lands beyond.

5. Early explorers faced the laborious task of traversing the Andes when the only roads across were steep, narrow paths.
6. Although highways and railroads cross the Andes today, they follow paths so tortuous that they require much patience.

D. Copy each word that should be followed by a comma, and add the missing comma. If no comma is needed, write *correct.*
1. To be a noble example to others we must follow our perfect example—Jesus Christ.
2. Youth because they are inexperienced should especially look for noble examples to follow.
3. We can never truly love the Lord if we love the things of this world.
4. Within the boundaries of God's will for our lives we find true satisfaction.
5. Whenever a person chafes at God's purposes he becomes vulnerable to evil suggestions.
6. We must daily die to self so that we might live unto God.
7. Brother Alvin though he is eighty years old is still quite active and healthy.
8. As spring slowly chases away the winter cold we anticipate the first fresh strawberries.
9. On the far edge of this stand of trees we often pick raspberries and blackberries.
10. To be ready in time for church we shall start chores early.

Review Exercises

A. Write whether the mood of each underlined verb is indicative (*ind.*), imperative (*imp.*), or subjunctive (*sub.*). [75]
1. If it <u>be</u> too late, we <u>shall wait</u> until tomorrow.
2. Brother Gerald <u>requested</u> that each person <u>walk</u> more quietly in the hall.
3. If Spot <u>were</u> more aggressive, <u>imagine</u> how many groundhogs he could have caught.
4. Barbara <u>has been acting</u> as if she <u>were</u> too busy to help Margaret with the cleaning.
5. <u>Suppose</u> everyone <u>were</u> as careless as you.
6. <u>Shall</u> we <u>rise</u> for the benediction.

B. Write the words that are correct for the subjunctive mood. [75]
1. If the stranger (be, is) a Mexican, your Spanish will be useful.
2. That raccoon acts as if it (was, were) rabid.
3. The police officers demanded that everyone (stand, stood) back.
4. If the dictionary (approves, approve) your pronunciation, I shall be surprised.
5. I wish the neighbor man (was, were) more respectful toward God.
6. If he (had been, would have been) more alert, this accident would likely not have happened.

94. Improving Your Writing Style, Part 5: Sentence Rhythm

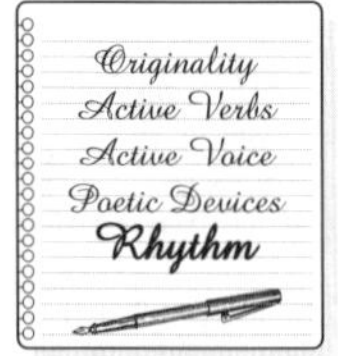

You have studied several different ways to make your writing style more effective. First you considered the importance of putting a touch of originality into your writing. You learned next to harness the energy of lively action verbs and of verbs in the active voice. Then you studied several poetic devices like alliteration, rhyme, and onomatopoeia, which add a musical touch to writing.

A fifth element of effective writing style is sentence rhythm. Now you may immediately think, "Rhythm belongs to poetry, not prose." And poetry does use strong, regular rhythm. Good prose, however, also has a certain rhythm. Though it is not the regular meter found in poetry, it is nevertheless a pleasing flow of sounds and syllables.

Ordinarily, most people speak and write smooth-flowing, rhythmic sentences. We have a natural feel for what sounds right and what sounds awkward. Most of the time, therefore, sentence rhythm poses no problem. But just as we make mistakes in other areas of life, we sometimes construct sentences that have a disturbing lack of rhythm. One of the best ways to identify such problems in our writing is to read it aloud. What looks fine on paper may sound jarring to the ear.

Consider two points that affect sentence rhythm.

1. *Beware of unintentional repetition of similar or identical syllables or words.* The previous writing style lesson directed you to use repetition by means of poetic devices like alliteration and rhyme. These add appeal to writing. But sometimes we repeat words or sounds without realizing it, and then it can be a problem. Such repetition of sounds is often more awkward than appealing.

If you did not purposely use repetition, then you will not even realize it is there. How can you recognize it? Here is where it becomes especially helpful to read aloud what you have written. As you study the following examples, read them aloud for the best understanding.

> **Poor:** Sometimes the repetition of a sound sounds awkward.
> **Better:** Sometimes the repetition of a sound becomes awkward.

Here two forms of *sound* occur in immediate succession. This repetition does not please the ear. Further disrupting the sentence is the fact that the first form of *sound* is a noun and the second is a verb, requiring the reader to switch definitions in mid-sentence.

> **Poor:** Jesus taught beside the seaside outside the city.
> **Better:** Jesus taught along the seaside near the city.

By the time a reader gets past these three *sides*—*beside, seaside, outside*—he may be *side*tracked from the meaning of the sentence. This repetition would be fine if the identical syllables occurred in some kind of parallel relationship, as in the series "the left side, the right side, and the upper side." But since the repetition is obviously unplanned, it is clumsy and distracting.

Poor: The accident happened probably only an hour ago.
Better: Probably the accident happened only an hour ago.
The accident happened probably no more than an hour ago.

This example illustrates the common problem of two *-ly* words occurring next to each other. While the resulting rhythm is not intolerable, it does lack strength. A similar problem is the occurrence of two *-ing* words together, as in "*practicing spelling* words."

In the examples above, the first rewording separates the *-ly* words so that the repeated syllable is no longer noticeable. The second simply replaces one of the *-ly* words.

2. *For words or phrases in a compound construction, you can often improve the rhythm by having the longer item come second.* A different arrangement is not necessarily awkward, but the rearrangement often stands as an improvement.

Fair: The Israelites could trust in God, or they could rely on their own warriors and wits.
Better: The Israelites could trust in God, or they could rely on their own wits and warriors.

Warriors and wits does not actually sound bad, but *wits and warriors* has an increased smoothness that sharpens the sentence. This along with alliteration produces a very pleasing rhythm.

Fair: James 5 gives encouragement to fervent prayer and patience.
Better: James 5 gives encouragement to patience and fervent prayer.

Here again, the rearrangement improves the rhythm because the longer item comes second. This arrangement also makes it clear that *fervent* modifies only *prayer;* the phrase does not mean "fervent prayer and fervent patience."

In some ways, sentence rhythm is like the arrangement of furniture in a room. Not everyone will agree on what is most appealing, and some people will like what others consider poor. Yet there are certain combinations that everyone will agree should not be used. So read your sentences aloud, evaluate them to the best of your ability, and change the wording when you spot a construction that sounds rough or distracting.

Applying the Lesson

A. Improve the style of the following sentences according to the guidelines in this lesson. Be ready to compare your work with that of your classmates, to see the various possibilities for improvement.

1. Brother Milford's charitable, wise words have often proved full of insight and fitting.
2. Nothing on earth can equal the glories of heaven, but many will miss this bliss because of sin.
3. Usually the scene of a gold find finds many undesirable prospectors present.
4. The two friends met with a hearty and hale handshake.
5. What we laugh about says much about what our character is all about.

6. This picture shows a boat afloat in the moat surrounding a city.
7. With temperatures so low, no snow will melt very fast.
8. By the edge of the hedge sat a discouraged, poor orphan.

B. The following paragraphs have poor sentence rhythm in a number of places. Find at least five of those places, and write enough words to show how to improve the rhythm.

[1]On a windy, cold day you may need to take deliberate steps to prevent frostbite. [2]Understanding frostbite right might be the best way to avoid it. [3]This condition most often occurs in the nose, ears, cheeks, fingers, and toes. [4]Therefore, usually simply covering the body well will prevent frostbite.

[5]Preventing frostbite also means avoiding hindering the proper circulation of blood. [6]Ill-fitting and tight clothes sometimes cut off circulation to the extremities. [7]Keeping moving is important if you must go outside in extremely cold weather. [8]This will help to fight frostbite by increasing the flow of blood to the muscles.

C. Write a brief narrative on one of the following topics or a different subject that your teacher approves. Underline at least four phrases that you consider to have good rhythm. Remember also to apply the other elements of effective writing style that you have studied.

1. Elijah praying for rain on Mount Carmel
2. Jesus stilling the storm on the Sea of Galilee
3. Your first hour (or day) in a new school
4. Enjoying the task of chopping wood (or some other job)
5. Your activities on a snow day (or another vacation day)

Review Exercises

Write *originality, active verbs, active voice,* or *poetic devices* to tell why the second sentence in each pair has a better style than the first. [3, 22, 39, 64]

1. a. There are many promises in the Bible that are inspirational.
   b. The Bible contains many promises to inspire us onward.
2. a. The Bible should remove our fears and cause us to have an unwavering trust in God.
   b. The Bible should dispel our fears and impel us to an unwavering trust in God.
3. a. A jet made a line as straight as an arrow across the sky.
   b. A jet was writing across the sky in disappearing ink.
4. a. The noise of chain saws and axes indicated that the brethren were transforming Sister Ada's pile of logs into a neat stack of firewood.
   b. The buzzing of chain saws and the ringing of axes proclaimed that the brethren were transforming Sister Ada's pile of logs into a neat stack of firewood.
5. a. With so many willing hands, the job was finished in two hours.
   b. The many willing hands finished the job in two hours.

95. Forms of Comparison for Modifiers

Basic Definitions and Forms

Many adjectives and adverbs have three degrees of comparison: positive, comparative, and superlative. The following chart illustrates these three degrees.

Positive	Comparative	Superlative
near	nearer	nearest
dim	dimmer	dimmest
friendly	friendlier	friendliest
precious	more precious	most precious
bountifully	more bountifully	most bountifully

The positive degree describes without comparing. This is the simplest form of a modifier.

Alan's dart struck close to the bull's-eye.
Sheba is a friendly dog.
Our gardens yielded bountifully this year.

The comparative degree compares two items. For regular modifiers, it ends with *-er* or includes the word *more.* Use *-er* with most one-syllable and some two-syllable words. If necessary, double the final consonant or change a final *y* to *i* before adding *-er.* For most two-syllable words and for all longer words, use *more.* Use the word *less* for negative comparisons of all words.

Mervin's dart struck closer to the bull's-eye than Alan's did.
Princess is even friendlier than Sheba.
Our gardens yielded more bountifully this year than they did last year.

The superlative degree compares more than two items. For regular modifiers, it ends with *-est* or includes the word *most.* Follow the same rules for using *-est* and *most* (or *least*) as those for the comparative degree.

Of all the darts, Wilmer's struck closest to the bull's-eye.
Tippy is the friendliest dog I know.
Our gardens yielded the most bountifully this year of all the past five years.

Some common modifiers have irregular forms of comparison.

Positive	Comparative	Superlative
good, well	better	best
bad, badly, ill	worse	worst
far	farther	farthest
much, many	more	most
little (amount)	less	least
little (size)	littler	littlest

Grandfather felt ill this morning, but he feels even worse this evening.
We had little rainfall this summer, Oakdale had even less rainfall, and Mapleton had the least rainfall in our county.

Usage Guidelines

As you work with forms of comparison, observe the following guidelines.

1. *Avoid the common mistake of using the superlative form to compare only two items.*

Incorrect: I can hardly decide whether Linda's or Wanda's cookies are the most delicious.
Both Frank and Henry worked hard at shoveling, but Henry shoveled the most.

Correct: I can hardly decide whether Linda's or Wanda's cookies are more delicious.
Both Frank and Henry worked hard at shoveling, but Henry shoveled more.

2. *Do not make a double comparison.*

Incorrect: Jezebel was much more bolder in doing evil than Ahab was.
Correct: Jezebel was much bolder in doing evil than Ahab was.

3. *A modifier that expresses an absolute quality cannot logically have degrees of comparison.* The following adjectives (and their adverb forms) are some examples of modifiers that may express absolute qualities: *square, straight, round, fatal, dead, perfect, true, unanimous, unique.*

Incorrect:
The moon is rounder tonight than it was last night.
This is the most unique book that I have ever read about the Flood.
(If something is truly unique, it is the only one of its kind.)

Correct:
The moon is more nearly round tonight than it was last night.
This is the most remarkable book that I have ever read about the Flood.

Some of the words listed above may express qualities that are not absolute, and then they may logically have degrees of comparison. For example, the phrase *more perfectly* is correct when it means "more fully" or "in greater detail." This is its meaning in the following verse.

"And he said, The Jews have agreed to desire thee that thou wouldest bring down Paul to morrow into the council, as though they would enquire somewhat of him more perfectly" (Acts 23:20).

4. *When comparing one thing with a group of which it is part, do not omit the word* other *or* else. If you omit these words, you will say that something is bigger or better than itself.

Illogical: I enjoy geometry better than any branch of mathematics.
To love God and our neighbor is more important than anything.

Logical: I enjoy geometry better than any other branch of mathematics.
To love God and our neighbor is more important than anything else.

5. *Do not change an adverb to an adjective when using a comparative or superlative form.* This is something rather common that people do with *-ly* adverbs. Some tend to drop the *-ly* and add *-er* or *-est* to the *adjective* form of the word.

Incorrect: You must play <u>quieter</u> while Brenda is napping.
Correct: You must play <u>more quietly</u> while Brenda is napping.

Applying the Lesson

A. Write the comparative and superlative degrees of these adjectives and adverbs.

1. little (size)
2. far
3. badly
4. little (amount)
5. carefully
6. lowly
7. slim
8. masterful
9. happy
10. hot

B. Write the correct form of each modifier in parentheses.

1. Apparently Daniel purposed in his heart (firmly) than did many of his fellow Jewish youth.
2. Certainly his life was (holy) than those who compromised to please the king.
3. God blessed Daniel so that he became the (good) of the king's wise men.
4. Even in the (grim) circumstances of all, Daniel prayed faithfully to his God.
5. Christ came as one of the (lowly) of men so that all could be saved.
6. It is (bad) to never try than to try and fail.
7. Worldly pleasures should have (little) appeal to us than do the glories of heaven.
8. Unless we are (zealous) for truth than for self-satisfaction, we will not make wise decisions.
9. Even with the medication, Bossy is (thin) than she was last week.
10. She is breathing (weakly) this morning than she did last evening.
11. Our goal of weeding this corn before noon seems (attainable) now than it did a while ago.
12. Of all the ones in Father's family, we live the (far) from Grandpa Seibel's farm.

C. Write 1–3 words to show how to correct the mistake in each sentence.

1. In 1990, both Illinois and Iowa produced over one million bushels of grain corn, but Iowa's production was highest.
2. Texas has more farms than any state in the United States.
3. This is the most loveliest mock orange bush I have seen in a long time!
4. We sang the third verse of the song softer than the other verses.
5. Eleanor's test score was more perfect than mine.
6. Sister Elizabeth is one of the most saintliest persons I know.
7. The kitchen corner beside the wood stove is warmer than any spot in the house.
8. Of the two boys' plans, I think Wilmer's will prove most workable.
9. The second half of the school term often seems to go fastest.
10. We succeeded in making the second flower bed rounder than the first.

11. I have been trying to write neater for my school assignments.
12. Aunt Miriam has given me two of her painted mottoes, and I like this one best.

Review Exercises

A. Write whether the underlined sentence part is a nominative absolute (*NA*) or a participial phrase (*PP*). [24]

1. Satan's purposes having been defeated at Calvary, we know that his ultimate defeat is sure.
2. Our faith resting firmly in Christ Jesus, the storms of life cannot unsettle us.
3. Clinging firmly to God's Word, we are well fortified against the wiles of the devil.
4. The Christian stands justified by faith, his sins having been purged by the blood of Christ.
5. The Christian should refuse to waste time in foolishness, knowing that life is short.

B. Rewrite each sentence, changing the underlined subordinate clause to a nominative absolute. [24]

1. After the bell sounded, we gathered up our books to go home.
2. Because the radiator had sprung a leak, the engine soon overheated.
3. Since the temperature was falling rapidly, we prepared for a killing frost.

---

96. Chapter 11 Review

A. Copy each underlined adjective. First label it *L* (limiting) or *D* (descriptive); then label it *AT* (attributive), *AP* (appositive), or *PR* (predicate).

1. What specific goals, high yet attainable, have you set for your character development?
2. Every honest person intent on pleasing God admits that he has numerous important areas to improve.
3. If you truly seek that improvement, you must possess lowly attitudes, godly zeal, and living faith in the Lord.
4. Those old German tools outside are worn but usable because the Germans made their products to last for many years.
5. With plentiful rainfall throughout the growing season, we are now enjoying a fall harvest bountiful beyond our expectations.

B. Copy each adjective phrase or clause. If a phrase is part of a longer phrase or clause, include it with the longer item and also copy it separately. Label each item *prep.* (prepositional phrase), *part.* (participial phrase), *inf.* (infinitive phrase), or *cl.* (clause).

1. Artesian wells, found rather commonly in western North America, overflow because of the pressure of underground water.

2. Can you describe the factors that cause artesian wells?
3. An area where artesian wells can occur must have water-filled subsoil trapped between two rock layers, and that subsoil must slope away from an opening that absorbs the water.
4. Gravity, pulling the water down the slope, causes a buildup of pressure in the water.
5. A well drilled into subsoil of that kind will have the pressure to overflow as an artesian well if all the conditions are right.

C. Copy the correct participle for each sentence.
1. Grandmother Horst, (memorizing, having memorized) many Scripture verses, can meditate on the Word even though she is blind.
2. (Roasting, Roasted) slowly since late last night, the turkey should be well done by noon.
3. (Breaking, Broken) above the knee, John's leg is causing him a great deal of pain.
4. (Soaring, Having soared) at a high altitude, the hawk swept the valley below with his keen eyes.

D. Label each underlined phrase or clause *R* (restrictive) or *N* (nonrestrictive). Also copy each word that should be followed by a comma, and add the comma.
1. Solomon [a]blessed with many advantages began his reign as a king [b]who loved the Lord.
2. His father, David [a]who was a man after God's own heart surely inspired him to a faith [b]that should have remained intact.
3. Yet the course [a]pursued by Solomon led him to the place [b]where he actually turned from God to idolatry.

E. Copy the single-word adverbs, including infinitives, and the word or word group that each one modifies. Write *sentence* if it modifies the whole sentence.
1. Where can we always find wisdom for the dangerously perplexing temptations we face?
2. Certainly, we need to pray daily to the Lord, who understands our needs perfectly.
3. Quite often, zealously seeking God's wisdom is easy to neglect; however, prayer is a definitely needed response for those who would be wise.
4. Though problems may bring us almost to desperation, they will never baffle the Lord.
5. Indeed, He perfectly understands every answer long before man can even recognize his need.

F. Copy each adverb phrase or clause, including any that occurs within another phrase or clause. Also write the word or word group that the adverb modifies.
1. The banyan tree, growing natively in India, is classified by scientists as a fig tree.
2. To gain its needed external support, the banyan often begins its life as an epiphyte.

3. An epiphyte grows on some other object until it develops its own support.
4. As the tree develops, aerial roots grow from its branches to support and nourish the tree.
5. When a banyan tree is full grown, its main trunk may have a diameter of thirteen feet, and its secondary trunks, grown from its aerial roots, may have an almost equal diameter.
6. A long-standing legend states that Alexander the Great used a single banyan tree—a forest in itself—to provide shelter for his entire army.

G. Copy each word that should be followed by a comma, and add the missing comma. If no comma is needed, write *correct.*
1. To live in true contentment we must remove all selfishness from our hearts.
2. Because man is carnal by nature he is far more prone to covetousness than to contentment.
3. We must consciously develop contentment if we would possess this rare virtue.
4. As we recognize God's great provisions our hearts will overflow with joy and thanksgiving.
5. To enrich our lives as God intends contentment must be our daily companion.

H. Write the correct form of each modifier in parentheses.
1. All these mottoes are painted well, but I think this one is (good).
2. Myron must like his food (salty) than I do.
3. We should be (tolerant) of others' faults than of our own.

4. If you oversleep, you will probably take (little) time for your devotions than you should.
5. To remain faithful, we need to be (determined) than Samson was to avoid temptation.

I. Write 1–3 words to show how to correct the mistake in each sentence.
1. The Book of Psalms is longer than any book of the Bible.
2. Psalm 23 is one of the most loveliest of all the psalms.
3. Linford cut the corners of his motto more square than I cut the corners of mine.
4. Time seems to be going more rapid this year than it did last year.
5. Whose eyesight is worst, Mark's or Matthew's?

J. Write whether each statement is *true* or *false.*
1. Both poetry and prose have rhythm, but the rhythm of prose is less regular.
2. Reading a sentence aloud helps to reveal phrases that lack rhythm.
3. Repetition of the same sounds or syllables should be avoided as much as possible.
4. Placing the longest phrase of a series last often contributes to smooth sentence rhythm.

K. Rewrite the following sentences, improving the rhythm.
1. Although he was not downright forthright, he was too upright to be outright dishonest.
2. Many people are totally selfishly pursuing their own way today.
3. I am enjoying looking at this mountain scenery, but the many turns turn my stomach.
4. All day the tempestuous, cold wind blew across the wide-open, flat prairie.

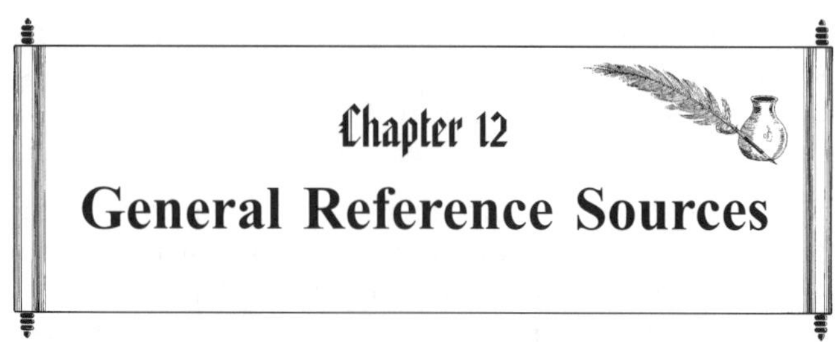

Chapter 12
General Reference Sources

97. Using a Dictionary

The dictionary ranks among the most useful reference books you will ever open. It puts at your fingertips a wealth of information about the English language. It may also contain one or more of the following: a history of the English language, a section listing information about famous persons, a section listing major place names and their pronunciations, a list of common abbreviations, tables of measures, and lists of rhyming words.

In your studies, you may use a variety of dictionaries. All these dictionaries are similar in certain ways, yet each one is also unique. Therefore, you should read the explanatory notes at the beginning of a dictionary that you use frequently. In fact, you should become familiar with your dictionary from beginning to end so that you can use all its features effectively.

Guide Words

Guide words help you to locate words in a dictionary quickly. Printed at the top of the page, these guide words show the first and last entries on a page. Any word coming between them in alphabetical order will be on that page.

Entry Words

Each word defined in a dictionary has an entry that begins with the entry word. An entry word shows two basic things about a word.

1. *Correct spelling.* If a word has more than one correct spelling, the dictionary shows both. If the two spellings are alphabetically close together (such as *neighbor* and *neighbour*), the dictionary lists them together with the more common spelling as the entry word. Otherwise, each spelling is entered separately (such as *gage* and *gauge*). The entry for the less common spelling (like *gage*) refers to the more common spelling, which has a complete entry. The entry for the more common spelling (like *gauge*) shows the alternate spelling. In many dictionaries, the word *also* precedes a spelling that is definitely less common.

> **neighbor** or **neigh·bour** (nā′·bər) *n.* **1.** A person who lives near another. **2.** A person, place, or thing located near another. **3.** A fellow human being.
>
> **gage** (gāj) *n.* & *v.* Var. of **gauge.**
>
> **gauge** *n.* **1.** A standard or scale of measurement. **2.** A standard dimension, quantity, or capacity. **3.** An instrument for measuring or testing. **4.** A means of estimating or judging; a test. Also **gage.**

Correct capitalization is an element of spelling. If a word is always capitalized, the entry word shows it that way. If a word is capitalized only for certain definitions, the dictionary either lists two separate entries or specifies the definitions that require capitalization.

> **phar·i·see** (far′·i·sē) *n.* **1. Pharisee.** A member of an ancient Jewish sect that emphasized strict observance of the Mosaic Law. **2.** A self-righteous or hypocritical person.

2. *Correct syllabication.* A space or raised dot shows each syllable division, where a hyphen may be used to divide a word at the end of a line of writing. Because you should not divide a word so that a single letter is left at the beginning or end of a line, some dictionaries do not show such syllable divisions in the entry word.

Word Information

Information given after an entry word includes much more than the meaning of the word. Notice the different kinds of information given.

1. *Correct pronunciation.* A complete pronunciation key is printed near the front of the dictionary. Most dictionaries also print a short key at the bottom of each right-hand page. Pronunciation symbols vary considerably, so you must familiarize yourself with the key of the dictionary you are using.

Dictionaries show variant pronunciations in different ways, so check the explanatory notes in the front of your dictionary. For some dictionaries, the first option is the preferred or most common pronunciation; in others, that is not necessarily so. If only part of the word has varied pronunciation, only those syllables with variations may be shown. Sometimes a regional label shows where the variation is commonly heard. Any pronunciation following the word *also* is definitely less common.

> **tran·sient** (tran′·shənt, -zhənt, -zē·ənt)
> **clerk** (klėrk; *British* klärk)
> **scourge** (skėrj *also* skōrj)

2. *Parts of speech and definitions.* An abbreviation before the definition indicates the part of speech. Verbs include a label for transitive or intransitive. Definitions for different parts of speech are usually listed either in one grouping in an entry or under separate, numbered entries.

Dictionary A:

> **barb** (bärb) *n.* **1.** A sharp point projecting backward from the main point of a weapon or tool, as on an arrow or a fishhook. **2.** A cutting remark. **3.** *Zoology.* One of the parallel spines projecting from the main shaft of a feather. **4.** *Botany.* A short, sharply hooked bristle or hairlike projection. **barb** *tr.v.* **barbed, barb·ing, barbs.** To provide or furnish with a barb.

Dictionary B:

> **barb**[1] (bärb) *n.* **1.** A sharp point projecting backward from the main point of a weapon or tool, as on an arrow or a fishhook. **2.** A cutting remark. **3.** *Zoology.* One of the parallel spines projecting from the main shaft of a feather. **4.** *Botany.* A short, sharply hooked bristle or hairlike projection.
> **barb**[2] *tr.v.* **barbed, barb·ing, barbs.** To provide or furnish with a barb.

Separate, numbered entries are used for words with the same spelling but different meanings and etymologies.

> **let**[1] (let) *v.* **let, let·ting, lets.** —*tr.* **1.** To give permission to; allow. **2.** To cause to; make. **3.** Used as an auxiliary in the imperative to express a command, request, or proposal, or to give a warning or threat. **4.** To rent or lease: *let rooms.* —*intr.* **1.** To become rented or leased. **2.** To be or become assigned, as to a contractor. [Middle English *leten*, from Old English *lǣtan*.]
>
> **let**[2] (let) *n.* **1.** Something that hinders; an obstacle. **2.** *Sports.* An invalid stroke that must be repeated, as in tennis and other net games. —**let** *tr.v.* **let·ted** or **let, let·ting, lets.** *Archaic.* To hinder or obstruct. [Middle English *lette,* from *letten,* to hinder, from Old English *lettan*.]

3. *Inflections.* These are changes in a word to show things like number and tense. The inflections most commonly shown are irregular plural forms of nouns, irregular principal parts of verbs, and irregular forms of comparison for adjectives and adverbs. Do not confuse inflections with derivatives (see point 6 below).

> **ver·tex** (vėr′·teks′) *n., pl.* **ver·tex·es** or **ver·ti·ces** (-ti·sēz′).
> **fly** (flī) *v.* **flew** (flü), **flown** (flōn).
> **love·ly** (luv′·lē) *adj.* **love·li·er, love·li·est.**

4. *Usage labels.* Not all words are proper to use in every context. Words labeled *nonstandard, substandard,* or *illiterate* should be avoided because they represent poor English. The label *vulgar* indicates that a word should be avoided altogether because of its association with evil. The label *slang* indicates words coined by people trying to say things in unique ways. Because many of these expressions come from the "street language" of immoral people, we should avoid the new, catchy expressions that are constantly showing up. Our speech should rather complement our entire lifestyle as the simple, modest, and holy people of God.

A number of labels limit the proper use of words. *Informal* words are acceptable in everyday speaking and in everyday writing, such as notes to yourself or friendly letters. However, they should not occur in formal speech (giving a topic or preaching a sermon) or in formal writing (schoolwork, articles for publication, or legal papers). Informal words include *barrel* for "a great quantity" and *grill* for "to question relentlessly."

The labels *regional* and *dialectal* mark words used in relatively small areas or by a limited group of people. Some dictionaries even specify regions where people use certain words. The labels *archaic* and *obsolete* designate words that are no longer in general use. Some dictionaries also use other descriptive labels, such as *poetic, technical, mathematics,* and *botany.*

5. *Etymology.* This information about the origin of a word usually appears within brackets either before the definitions or at the end of the entry. Etymologies are valuable for comparing words of similar origin. Study the explanatory notes of your dictionary to learn what the various abbreviations and symbols mean. Here is a typical etymology with an explanation of its meaning.

evade [< Fr *évader* < L *ēvādere* : *ē-*, *ex-*, out + *vādere,* to go.]

Meaning: *Evade* comes from the French word *évader,* which came from the Latin word *ēvādere,* which consists of the word elements *ē-* (from *ex-*, meaning "out") and *vādere* (meaning "to go").

6. *Derivatives.* These are related words, usually of different parts of speech, that are made by adding various suffixes to the entry word.

crisp (krisp) *adj.* —**crisp′·ly** *adv.* —**crisp′·ness** *n.* —**crisp′·y** *adj.*

7. *Synonyms and antonyms.* These are found mainly in advanced dictionaries and only for selected words. Along with the synonyms, some dictionaries give helpful pointers on their proper use. The next lesson deals more specifically with synonyms and antonyms in a thesaurus.

8. *Other information.* Some advanced dictionaries give biographical and geographical information, abbreviations, and foreign words and phrases. These types of information are found either in the main body of the dictionary (under the appropriate entry words) or in separate sections of the dictionary.

Applying the Lesson

A. Write another spelling for each word. If it follows the word *also,* underline it.

1. caldron
2. carousel
3. vise
4. likable
5. softy
6. programmer

B. Copy all the pronunciations for each word. If a pronunciation follows the word *also* or any label that limits the acceptability of the pronunciation, underline it.

1. learned (adj.)
2. nausea
3. financier
4. niche
5. thither
6. pastoral

C. Write a dictionary definition or a synonym that gives the meaning of each underlined word.

1. Though much of the world's art does not appeal to the Christian, he is no <u>Philistine</u>; he does enjoy noble, worthwhile art.
2. This field, having a slight <u>declivity</u> toward the south, yields excellent crops.
3. Mr. Tilley wears a <u>gauntlet</u> when he works at the rotary oven, where the metal handles are heated before they receive a plastic coating.
4. I hardly understand this article well enough to <u>abstract</u> it clearly.
5. For an interesting project, we will <u>found</u> some lead in science class today.
6. As I was smoothing out a mortise, the <u>tang</u> of my chisel cracked.
7. A few <u>pigs</u> remained at the site of the abandoned iron furnace.
8. The group of refugees slowly wended through the dangerous <u>defile</u>.
9. For many years, those who lived in the <u>marches</u> between France and Germany found their governance alternating between the two powers.
10. By late afternoon, our energies were seriously <u>flagging</u> in the intense heat.
11. Some of the photo albums have rich, thick <u>flock</u> on the covers.
12. Can we <u>prize</u> the door with a crowbar?

D. Copy the inflected forms that your dictionary gives for these words.

1. espy
2. evanesce
3. bacillus
4. bad
5. far
6. moldy
7. glad
8. lasso

E. Copy any usage labels your dictionary gives for these words.

1. argent
2. cheesy
3. nohow
4. leasing
5. gangway
6. typo

F. Write out the etymology of each word, using no abbreviations.

1. orient
2. alligator
3. hieroglyphic
4. circumference

Review Exercises

Label each underlined verb *TA* (transitive, active voice), *TP* (transitive, passive voice), *IC* (intransitive complete), or *IL* (intransitive linking). [76]

1. Joseph Funk, a prominent Mennonite of Virginia, greatly influenced the music of the Mennonite Church.
2. His introduction of shaped notes has proved especially helpful.
3. An eight-tone scale with seven different syllable names was promoted by this outstanding music teacher.
4. Although the scale then in use (do, re, mi, fa, sol, la, si, do) differed slightly from the modern scale, it is easily recognizable.
5. In the fifth edition of his *Harmonia Sacra,* Funk used the seven note shapes that are common today.

---

98. Using a Thesaurus

In writing, do you sometimes find it hard to think of exactly the right word to express an idea? Suppose you have related an incident to illustrate how a misspelled word may cause a serious misunderstanding. Then you write, "This illustration (gives prominence to) the importance of always checking your spelling." But you do not like the phrase in parentheses. What is the best word to use as a replacement? You think of *shows, emphasizes,* and *stresses,* but none of those words says exactly what you mean. What can you do?

The thesaurus (thi·sôr′·əs) is a book designed for the very purpose of solving such a problem. Derived from the Greek word for *treasury,* this name refers to a book that is indeed a treasury of related words. Each entry word is followed by one or more groups of synonyms and, in many cases, of antonyms. By using the thesaurus, you should be able to find exactly the word you want.

In the case above, you may look up *emphasize* and find the synonyms *stress, accent, highlight,* and *underscore.* Ah, there it is! You choose the word *highlight* because it fits your sentence exactly.

Understanding the Arrangement of a Thesaurus

Many modern thesauruses follow an easy-to-use alphabetical order. Using an alphabetical thesaurus is a simple matter of looking up the word you want to replace and searching the lists of synonyms for a suitable word. Some alphabetical thesauruses have cross-references at the end of many entries, directing the user to other entries with related words. However, if the word you look up is not a main entry, you will need to find a synonym that is a main entry.

Some thesauruses follow the original classification of words established by Peter Mark Roget (rō•zhā′), a British physician (1779–1869) who developed the first known English thesaurus. Over a period of fifty years, Roget collected thousands of words and classified them into six main categories: abstract relations, space, matter, intellect, volition, and affections. He further divided each of these categories into sections as shown below.

Class I. Abstract Relations
- Section I. Existence (1–8)
- II. Relation (9–24)
- III. Quantity (25–57)
- IV. Order (58–83)
- V. Number (84–105)
- VI. Time (106–139)
- VII. Change (140–152)
- VIII. Causation (153–179)

Class II. Space
- Section I. Generally (180–191)
- II. Dimensions (192–239)
- III. Form (240–263)
- IV. Motion (264–315)

Class III. Matter
- Section I. Generally (316–320)
- II. Inorganic (321–356)
- III. Organic (357–449)

Class IV. Intellect
- Section I. Formation of Ideas (450–515)
- II. Communication of Ideas (516–599)

Class V. Volition
- Section I. Individual (600–736)
- II. Intersocial (737–819)

Class VI. Affections
- Section I. Generally (820–826)
- II. Personal (827–887)
- III. Sympathetic (888–921)
- IV. Moral (922–975)
- V. Religious (976–1000)

Under these sections, Roget listed his words in one thousand numbered entries. The numbers in parentheses above show the range of numbered entries in each section. Of course, in a modern *Roget's Thesaurus,* many new words have been added and many outdated words removed. The numbering has also been changed somewhat. However, a thesaurus that bears Roget's name still uses a classification system based on the one devised by Peter Mark Roget.

Without an index, you would have great difficulty in finding treasures in Roget's thesaurus—unless you were to memorize its basic structure. A thorough index, therefore, is a standard part of the thesaurus. In fact, in many thesauruses the index covers nearly as many pages as does the body. To use a thesaurus of this kind, find a word in the index, turn to the numbered entry or entries that are given, and look through the lists of synonyms there.

A fully alphabetized thesaurus is convenient because you can go directly to synonym lists without needing to use an index first. But Roget's numbering system also has some advantages. The main advantage is that at most entries, you can find other words with related or opposite meanings in the entries before and after the one you looked up.

Choosing Synonyms Effectively

The thesaurus is a valuable aid in communicating expressively. As you dig into this treasury, you will find exact words that will add clarity and sparkle to your writing and speaking. By using the thesaurus regularly, you will enrich the treasury of your personal vocabulary. However, you must always use the thesaurus with discernment. Very few English synonyms are interchangeable in every context. So when you look at the list of synonyms, you must carefully choose a word that means precisely what you want to say. The following points will help you use a thesaurus effectively.

1. *Consider both the denotation and the connotation of the words.* The words *joy, delight, glee, bliss, ecstasy, mirth,* and *gaiety* are all synonyms of *happiness.* Study the definitions of these seven synonyms.

joy, (1) Intense and especially ecstatic or exultant happiness. (2) The expression or manifestation of such feeling. (3) A source or an object of pleasure or satisfaction.

delight, (1) Great pleasure; joy. (2) Something that gives great pleasure or enjoyment.

glee, Jubilant delight; joy.

bliss, (1) Extreme happiness; ecstasy. (2) The ecstasy of salvation; spiritual joy.

ecstasy, (1) Intense joy or delight. (2) A state of emotion so intense that one is carried beyond rational thought and self-control.

mirth, Gladness and gaiety, especially when expressed by laughter.

gaiety, (1) A state of joyful exuberance or merriment; vivacity. (2) Merry or joyful activity; festivity.

A thesaurus will likely list these seven words as synonyms, yet you can see that each word is different from the rest. Part of that distinction results from differences in the denotation—the strict, exact meanings of words. Notice that the first three words above have relatively general meanings of strong happiness. The last four, however, incorporate other specific ideas within the definitions. *Bliss* denotes spiritual joy; *ecstasy,* an irrational or uncontrolled happiness; *mirth,* a happiness expressed by laughter; and *gaiety,* vivacious and festive happiness.

In addition to denotation, each word has its unique connotation—the "personality" of the word or the feeling it conveys. Consider the three synonyms above with similar denotations: *joy, delight,* and *glee.* Do they have the same connotation? If you are not sure, read the following sentence, using a different one of these words each time.

> Imagine our ——— when Grandfather Stoner's said they were coming to visit for a week.

Either *joy* or *delight* fits well, but *glee* definitely does not have the right connotation. Although by definition, it means "jubilant delight" or "joy," its connotation is too lighthearted for this sentence. Notice how that connotation makes it fit well in the following sentence.

> The little children laughed with glee as the puppies tumbled about on the lawn.

This means that you must be well familiar with the words you choose, lest you say or write an absurd statement. Suppose, for example, that a writer wants to replace the word *regularity* in one of his sentences, and in a thesaurus he finds the following synonyms: *rhythm, alternation, pulsation, routine, steadiness.* He chooses *pulsation* and writes the following sentence.

> We have always appreciated Todd's pulsation in performing his duties on the farm.

To avoid using wrong words, be sure to study all the definitions in a reliable dictionary. If the entry includes phrases or sentences showing how to use the word, study them carefully. Checking several dictionaries often proves helpful in developing a full-fledged understanding of a word. If possible, use an unabridged dictionary, which gives a complete listing of possible shades of meanings for each word.

2. *Consider the level of formality of the words.* Words labeled *informal* in the dictionary are acceptable only in everyday speaking and writing. However, some words not labeled *informal* may still have a more informal tone than other words with similar meanings. For example, one definition of *gush* is "to make an excessive display of sentiment or enthusiasm." Because of the relatively informal tone of this word, it would fit all right in the following sentences from a friendly letter.

> Marta, our little fresh-air girl, arrived last week. You should have heard her gush over the little calves!

But if you wrote a sentence about a Christian rejoicing over the blessing of God in his life, the word *gush* would definitely be unsuitable.

3. *Consider the range of application of the words.* The words *remuneration, salary,* and *earnings* are synonyms of *wages,* but each word has its own specific range of use. *Remuneration* covers a broad range of payments for goods provided, services rendered, or losses incurred. It may well include nonmonetary payments. *Earnings* also covers a broad range, referring not only to payments to an employee but also to profits from a business or an investment. *Wages,* on the other hand, generally refers to monetary payments to an employee. *Salary* refers to a regular, fixed payment to an employee.

> As a carpenter during the Great Depression, Grandfather often accepted food as <u>remuneration</u> for his services.
>
> Father's <u>wages</u> include both a <u>salary</u> and <u>earnings</u> based on the total sales in his department.

Do not be content with stale or mediocre words. Examine the gems in your treasury of English words, and choose fresh, precise words that will make your writing attractive and effective.

Applying the Lesson

A. Using a thesaurus, write at least five synonyms for each of these words.

1. painful	3. obstruction	5. atone
2. think	4. mixture	6. tidy

B. Write the synonym with the best denotation and connotation for each sentence.

1. The passengers and crew (abandoned, relinquished, renounced) the sinking ship.
2. During the war, several men (abandoned, relinquished, renounced) their citizenship and joined the ranks of the enemy.
3. King Solomon built a (gaudy, magnificent, pretentious) temple for the Lord.
4. Balaam grew (furious, peeved, pugnacious) when his donkey repeatedly went against his wishes.
5. Jesus rebuked His disciples for their (arguments, conversations, discussions) about which of them would be the greatest.
6. After a lengthy (argument, conversation, discussion), the brethren agreed to vote on the matter.
7. Grandma was (ecstatic, glad, satisfied) when she finally found her lost eyeglasses.
8. Hebrews 3 clearly (declines, refuses, repudiates) the idea that Moses was superior to Christ.
9. Many slaves had a life that was full of (effort, strain, toil) from sunrise until sunset.
10. Our science book explains that by applying (effort, strain, toil) to a lever, we can raise a heavy object.
11. Those who begin smoking usually find it an extremely difficult (custom, habit, routine) to break.
12. Bowing is a traditional (custom, habit, routine) in Oriental countries.

C. Replace each underlined item with a synonym appropriate for formal writing.
1. You can easily see that this fossil is not confined to one <u>layer</u> of rock.
2. Obviously, the fossil did not form over long <u>eras</u> as evolutionists claim.
3. The intense forces present in the Flood offer a <u>reasonable</u> explanation for such fossils.
4. Diligence in everyday work helps to develop the <u>perseverance</u> needed for spiritual victory.
5. One who loves God does not find Biblical discipleship <u>burdensome</u>.
6. A <u>prudent</u> person will flee those situations that bring temptation.
7. We should never <u>overlook</u> the seriousness of trying to hide wrongdoing from those in authority over us.
8. As we hold to the unchanging Word, the <u>uncertainty</u> of life will never overwhelm us.
9. Only the power of God's grace can <u>free</u> sinful man from bondage to sin.
10. We need a <u>perceptive</u> view of life, or we will be sidetracked by the world's allurements.

Review Exercises

A. Copy the correct participle for each sentence. [90]
1. The hay, (drying, dried) rapidly in this heat, should be ready to bale before noon.
2. These huge drifts, (forming, formed) by yesterday's blizzard, will keep us snowed in for several days.
3. (Working, Having worked) at Grandfather's mill long ago, Matt Findley has remained a family friend.
4. Ye Olde Gristmill, (standing, having stood) at the edge of town, offers stone-ground wheat and rye flour as well as a variety of bulk foods.

B. Copy each word that should be followed by a comma, and add the comma. If the sentence needs no comma, write *correct.* [90, 93]
1. Forming as raindrops refract sunlight a rainbow consists of concentric arcs of red, orange, yellow, green, blue, and violet.
2. If the raindrops are quite small the rainbow will be pale.
3. A rainbow formed by large raindrops will be more vivid and may be accompanied by a secondary rainbow.
4. This secondary rainbow which results from refraction and reflection within the raindrops always has the colors reversed from the primary rainbow.
5. If a person stands at ground level he will never see more than a semicircle of a rainbow.
6. You might see the complete circle of a rainbow when you are flying in an airplane.

C. Write enough words to show how to correct the mistake in each sentence. [95]
1. We have had pleasanter weather today than we have had for a while.
2. My sister Elaine is better at math than anyone in our family.

3. These strawberry plants are deader than I expected them to be.
4. Which of these two mottoes do you like best?
5. The rain has been falling more steady for the last hour than it had been earlier.
6. Duke is one of the most friendliest dogs I have ever known.

---

99. Using Reference Books of General Information

Dictionaries and thesauruses are among the most valuable reference books, for they help you to use words properly and effectively. Sometimes you need other kinds of information. What are the land and the climate of Andorra like? When did Vasco Núñez de Balboa live? What lands did he explore? How far apart are San Francisco and New York City? In what nation does nuclear power account for the highest percentage of the total electricity produced? For these and countless other questions, you will probably turn to reference books of general information. These books include encyclopedias, atlases, and statistical almanacs.

Encyclopedias

An encyclopedia contains articles on a wide range of subjects. In fact, the word *encyclopedia* comes from two Greek words: *enkyklios,* meaning "general," and *paideia,* meaning "education." And certainly that is a fitting name for these sets of volumes: they contain a general summary of much of the knowledge that man has gained.

1. *A useful tool for research.* A number of features make the encyclopedia valuable for research on a subject. First, cross-references at the end of some entries give titles of other articles in the set that contain related information. For example, the article about rubber may end with the following cross-references.

Elasticity	Indonesia (picture)
Faraday, Michael	Latex
Firestone, Harvey S.	Plastics
Goodrich, Benjamin F.	Polymerization
Goodyear, Charles	Tire

Second, some encyclopedia articles may include a bibliography, which refers you to books that give more detailed information on the subject. The article about rubber may have the following bibliography.

Gait, A. J., and Hancock, E. G. *Plastics and Synthetic Rubbers.* Pergamon, 1970.
Le Bras, Jean. *Introduction to Rubber.* Rev. ed. Hart Publishing Co., 1969
Morton, Maurice, ed. *Rubber Technology.* 2nd ed. Van Nostrand, 1973.

A third valuable feature for research is the index. Usually the last volume of an encyclopedia is a comprehensive index, which lists all the information that the encyclopedia contains on a certain subject. The index is much more thorough than the cross-references because it lists not only titles of articles that focus on related information but also titles of articles that may contain only a few sentences dealing with the subject.

The index will also help you to find information about a topic on which the encyclopedia has no specific article. For example, an encyclopedia may have no article about chloroprene. However, the index entry may look like this:

Chloroprene [chemical]
Acetylene (Other Uses) **A:22**
Rubber (The Chemistry of Synthetic Rubber) **R:469**

A fourth aid in research that you will find in encyclopedia sets is the annual yearbooks. Because new events and new discoveries constantly change man's knowledge, most encyclopedia publishers offer yearbooks to update their encyclopedias.

2. *A tool to be used with caution.* Although encyclopedias are a valuable resource, you must use them with discretion. First of all, learn to detect the errors commonly found in encyclopedias. The writers of these volumes generally hold a secular, humanistic philosophy of life. Therefore, the articles reflect a point of view that glorifies man and his achievements. They will laud warfare and ungodly movements. They will present as fact the erroneous teachings of philosophies like evolution, environmentalism, and humanism. Conspicuously absent is any acknowledgment of God and of the principles in His Word.

How important that you learn to compare all that you read with the standards of the Bible! Only in God's eternal Word do we find the principles by which we can know what is truth and what is error. Your parents and teachers will help you to identify false teachings as well as theories that are unproven.

A second important caution is to remember that an encyclopedia article does not provide an exhaustive coverage of a particular subject. This is a "general education" reference source—general both because it covers a wide range of information and because it does not thoroughly cover the precise details of the subject. Do not miss the bountiful fruits of broad research by limiting yourself to the encyclopedia. By reading any one of the books listed in the bibliography above, you will learn much more about rubber than by reading the encyclopedia article.

Atlases

An atlas is a book of maps. A world atlas has detailed maps showing all the regions of the world geographically and politically. Geographical maps portray such things as topography, vegetation, land use, rainfall, climate patterns, and population density. Political maps show the boundaries of nations, states, and provinces. But political changes occur frequently, and man is constantly building new roads, dams, and canals. Therefore, an atlas becomes outdated rather quickly.

A road atlas is a guide for traveling and an aid for learning many geographical facts. Such an atlas shows roads, airports, national parks, and similar items of interest to travelers. The atlas may also have information about climate, topography, and history for places that travelers may want to visit.

An atlas usually has an index, listing place names shown on the maps. Each index entry indicates which maps show that place, along with a key to locate the place on the maps.

Statistical Almanacs

Statistical almanacs provide factual information about the world today. The *World Almanac and Book of Facts* and the *Information Please Almanac* are two of the most popular ones. Published annually, these volumes contain a wide variety of information. They provide current statistics and information about things like agriculture, science, industry, and astronomy. They include historical and current political, geographical, and social information about nations, states, and provinces. And they contain articles on significant happenings and issues of the previous year.

Applying the Lesson

A. Using the index of an encyclopedia, list all the volumes and page numbers where you could find information on the following subjects.

1. Muscle
2. Waldenses
3. Hudson River
4. Millard Fillmore
5. Atmospheric pressure
6. Solomon Islands
7. John C. Calhoun
8. Kalahari Desert

B. Answer these questions by using one of the reference books described in this lesson. Give the source of information for each answer.

1. What were the lowest and the highest temperatures ever recorded in Hawaii?
2. Which state in the United States produces the most wheat?
3. Where do marsh deer live?
4. Which is farther north: Portland, Oregon, or Toronto, Ontario?
5. If both the President and the Vice President of the United States were removed from office in any way, what official is next in line to succeed to the Presidency?
6. What is the highest elevation in Tuvalu?
7. What is the most populous city in West Virginia?
8. How long is the Congo River?
9. What are three things for which gutta-percha is used?
10. What is one thing for which David Rittenhouse was well known?
11. What are the chief agricultural crops in Kansas?
12. What north–south interstate highway could a traveler use to reach Des Moines, Iowa? What east–west interstate highway?
13. What interstate highway connects New York City to San Francisco?
14. What three major roads would you use to travel from Greenville, South Carolina, to Clemson, South Carolina?

Review Exercises

A. Name the five steps in the SQ3R study method. After each one, briefly explain how to apply that step in studying a lesson. [10]

B. Write whether each statement about studying is *true* or *false.* [9–12]

1. The rate at which you forget material that you have studied increases as time passes.
2. Surveying a lesson before reading it gives you a helpful overview of the material.
3. In a study period, it is generally best to do the hardest and least enjoyable assignments first.
4. Slouching tends to subconsciously tell your mind to relax.
5. Skillful skimming of a lesson can be a good substitute for the SQ3R method.
6. When you skim a book, you should first look over the table of contents.
7. Taking notes helps promote logical thinking.
8. When summarizing, you should try to preserve the original wording as much as possible.
9. Asking questions before reading a lesson helps to prepare you to read effectively.
10. Reading to find specific answers is the heart of meaningful study.

---

100. Improving Your Speaking Style, Part 3: Enthusiasm

What do you need to remember for effective public speaking? Good eye contact with your audience, for one thing. You should establish eye contact early in your discourse and maintain it throughout your talk. Good voice control is also important. Pronounce your words clearly, use a comfortable volume, and speak at a pitch and speed appropriate to what you are saying.

Conveying a sense of enthusiasm is another important part of an effective speaking style. Your enthusiasm definitely affects both the quality of your speech and the attention of your audience. On the one hand, a proper sense of enthusiasm helps you to put your best efforts into the speech. On the other hand, it will help to stimulate in your audience an enthusiasm that enables them to listen and understand you more easily. It may even make it easier for them to agree with you.

Developing Enthusiasm

Enthusiasm should not be something that you just put on for the need of the moment; rather, it should grow and develop within you. How can you cause it to grow? Can everyone attain this? You should be able to develop an enthusiasm for communicating with others if you do the following things.

1. *Choose a subject that interests you.* This is of utmost importance. How could you talk with enthusiasm about selling produce if you despise waiting on customers and counting out the correct change? By contrast, someone who thoroughly enjoys selling produce will be in an excellent position to give a talk about his family's vegetable stand.

Sometimes you will easily think of a good subject for your speech. You may know just what you want to talk about as soon as you receive the assignment. At other times you must explore numerous possibilities before you find something that appeals to you. Beware lest you throw out every idea you encounter, just because it fails to strike you with great force. Students often find that after a bit of study, a subject is much more interesting than they had thought it would be.

2. *Become thoroughly familiar with your subject.* You can hardly speak with enthusiasm about a subject that you do not know well. You become familiar with a subject by personal experience, by discussing it with others, and by reading about it. Do not cheat yourself. Study your subject until you know it well, until you find an enthusiasm for it growing within you.

3. *Organize your material.* It is essential that you plan your talk carefully. How will you begin? What main points will you present, and in what order will they come? How will you close? Few things dampen enthusiasm more effectively than standing before a group with only a vague idea of what you will say and how you plan to say it.

Make your plans carefully, and then practice giving your talk. As you do this, you will feel a growing confidence about your talk, and your enthusiasm will grow with it. You will actually begin looking forward—though perhaps still with apprehension—to sharing your information with the group. But if you still feel absolutely no spark of enthusiasm, you are doing something wrong! You must make a change somewhere, either in your subject or in your preparation. For as long as a subject fails to stir your own enthusiasm, it has no chance of stirring the enthusiastic attention of your listeners.

Expressing Enthusiasm

Having gained a genuine enthusiasm for your subject, you next face the challenge of communicating it to your listeners. To some degree this will happen automatically because enthusiasm in your heart will show on your face and in your actions. However, you as a speaker should pay deliberate attention to the following things, which help to add life and force to your words.

1. *Eye contact.* You will find it easier to look your listeners in the eye if you have an enthusiastic interest in your subject. This is true because you will be thinking more about your subject than about yourself. You will be confident that your subject is worthwhile and that your audience will also find it interesting. Meeting your listeners eye to eye will help you to communicate effectively as you move through the talk.

2. *Voice inflection.* What you feel will show in your voice. Remember the little boy who has just come home after receiving a lollipop from the doctor. You can hear his voice even now as he exclaims excitedly, "Father, look! A lollipop!" Contrast that with the same boy when he finds a not-so-cherished food on his plate. You now hear the same voice in quite a different tone saying, "Mother, must I eat all this?"

Be assured that your own enthusiasm or lack of it shows through just as clearly when you give a talk. Seek to develop a strong enthusiasm, and then let your voice naturally convey that feeling to your audience.

3. *Facial expression.* You need to show your enthusiasm by looking enthusiastic. Again, this is not a matter of putting something on, but of showing on the outside what you feel on the inside. Gain an enthusiastic interest in your subject, and then let it show on your face.

4. *Gestures.* The gestures you use help to express your enthusiasm. If you are not interested, you probably will use few if any gestures. If you are too self-conscious, you may use some gestures but they will not reinforce the points you make. But if you are truly interested in your speech, your gestures will take on life and meaning. They may indicate size, shape, or direction. They may help to emphasize a major point. Or they may simply reinforce what you are saying.

Of course, gestures can be overdone. You do not need to act out a story in order to tell it effectively. But appropriate gestures, used with reserve and discretion, will definitely add appeal to your presentation.

5. *Posture.* Enthusiasm will motivate you to stand up straight as you speak before the class. It will keep you from shuffling your feet and slouching your body. It will prompt you throughout your speech to maintain the dignity of standing with your weight evenly balanced on both feet and your shoulders straight. Your posture definitely communicates the degree of your enthusiasm.

Your assignment in this lesson will be to describe something of interest to you, such as an animal, a plant, or a place that you have seen. In order to do this in a fresh, appealing way, you must do more than talk about the item in a humdrum manner. You will need to think of specific reasons why the item is interesting to you. If it is an animal, are you impressed by its size? its appearance? its actions? Exactly what makes it impressive and interesting? You may need to do a little research to find exactly how tall, how long, or how heavy it is, or what purpose is served by its spots or other unusual features.

After you have considered the details themselves, you must decide how you will present them. Think of appealing ways to portray the thing you are describing. Was the building so tall that your neck hurt as you tried to see the top? Were you impressed by the hollow, echoing sounds or the damp, chilly feeling of the interior? Remembering exactly what you saw, heard, and felt will help you to describe your subject with interest and enthusiasm.

Applying the Lesson

A. Choose an interesting animal, plant, or place that is familiar to your class. On the board, list specific details that would be included in a description of it. Then work together at thinking of ways to present those details in fresh, creative ways.

B. Think of something interesting to describe, and prepare to give a talk of four to six minutes about it. Your talk should be based mainly on your personal knowledge, though you may use reference sources to obtain specific facts. The following ideas may stimulate your thinking.
   1. An interesting animal
   2. An unusual plant
   3. A place your family has visited

4. A hobby
5. A family project
6. A summer project of your own

Try to develop and show a genuine enthusiasm for your topic. Also remember to practice eye contact and voice control, as you studied in earlier lessons.

---

101. Using the Public Library

"Of making many books there is no end" (Ecclesiastes 12:12). Indeed, many thousands of books come off printing presses in a year's time. Public libraries provide the general public with access to a wide selection of books at little or no cost.

Value of the Public Library

A public library is a valuable source of information. On its shelves you will find numerous books of fiction and nonfiction. Fiction books contain stories made up by their authors. Even if a story is based on historical facts, it is fiction if the writer put it together by using his imagination. Nonfiction books are based on fact. They include biographies, reference books, and books on topics such as science, history, and language.

The library also contains a wide variety of magazines, newspapers, language records, and other literary materials. For a small fee, many libraries offer interlibrary services, giving you access to materials from other area libraries. Furthermore, the librarians are generally willing and able to help you locate hard-to-find information.

You should use a library only when you have a good purpose. It is not wise to browse at length through the materials in a public library—especially not through the books of fiction. However, there are occasions when a public library can offer you worthwhile services. You might need more information for a specific school assignment such as an English composition, a science report, or a history project. Or you might need further information for personal use on practical subjects, such as quilting, caring for a pet, building a doghouse, or starting plants in a cold frame. You might wish to research some local history or some points of interest in an area you plan to visit. Even a small public library contains information on any of these subjects.

Courteous Use of the Public Library

A public library has rules so that it can effectively serve everyone who uses it. You should show your appreciation for its services by obeying the rules courteously. In a library you should be quiet. You will probably not be the only one using the library. The others who have come to read or study need quietness for their concentration. Show respect for them and for the library by walking softly and talking quietly.

Be careful with the books. Remember that you are handling other people's property, so you should be even more careful than you would be with your own books. Turn the pages without creasing or tearing them. Lay the books down gently; never toss them or let them drop. When you remove a book from the shelf, remember where it was so that you can replace it correctly.

Be punctual. If you borrow a book, note carefully the return date and have it back to the library on time. If you discover that a book is overdue or that you have lost one, make the required payment promptly and courteously. Showing appreciation for the library by quietness, carefulness, and punctuality is a small fee to pay for all the privileges the library offers to you.

Prudent Use of the Public Library

Use a library prudently. Go to a public library only with your parents' supervision, and be sure you have your parents' approval before you read a book from a public library. Christians have little or no use for the vast majority of books in a public library. Many books of fiction reflect a lifestyle and value system that is contrary to godliness. Although they may have a limited value in helping you to understand people of other times and cultures, the unwholesome influences often outweigh any benefit. Even nonfiction books pose certain danger to our minds. As noted in Lesson 99, many reference books glorify man's achievements while ignoring God, and many teach false ideas, such as evolution.

Only a full knowledge of God and His Word can keep you from being harmed by finding untruths in the books you read. God's Word is the most important and the only perfectly safe "library" in the world. Although it does not contain every detail of information, it does reveal basic principles that relate to every aspect of human knowledge. Fill your mind with the truth of the Bible, and you will have a standard with which to compare all other books. With this perspective, you will know which books to reject as having a harmful effect and which to accept as providing helpful information.

Applying the Lesson

A. Answer these questions.
   1. What is the difference between fiction and nonfiction?
   2. How might you as a school student make good use of a public library?
   3. How might you or others in your family make good use of a public library for interests other than school matters?
   4. What are three rules for using a library courteously?
   5. Why is it important to be quiet in the library?
   6. What are some guidelines for handling library books carefully?
   7. Why must you use a public library prudently?
   8. Why is it important to compare all books from a public library with the library of God's Word?

B. Write *fiction* or *nonfiction* for each book title.
   1. *Glimpses of Mennonite History and Doctrine* (history of the Mennonite Church and a survey of her important teachings)
   2. *Hyenas* (descriptions of various species of hyenas)
   3. *The Chronicles of Mansoul* (allegory depicting the spiritual conflict for man's soul)

4. *Faithfully, George R.* (story of a prominent Mennonite Church leader)
5. *The True Christian* (practical teaching on the Sermon on the Mount)
6. *Carmi of Judea* (story of a Jewish lad in the time just before Jesus' birth)
7. *War-Torn Valley* (realistic story about Mennonites in Virginia during the Civil War)
8. *A Sower Went Forth* (story of Ralph Palmer's service for the Lord)
9. *The Mighty Whirlwind* (account of tornadoes in several states on Palm Sunday, 1965)
10. *"Whom Shall I Fear?"* (portrays in story form the severe tests that the Anabaptists faced)

Review Exercises

Write whether each underlined adverb modifies a *verb,* a *verbal,* an *adjective,* an *adverb,* a *preposition,* a *conjunction,* or an entire *sentence.* [91, 92]

1. God created some plants to survive indefinitely even in dry environments.
2. Generally, such plants are called succulents because they store amazingly large amounts of water in their leaves or in their stems.
3. The word *succulent* actually comes from a Latin root meaning "juice."
4. Obviously, God created the succulents so that they retain water quite effectively.
5. Some succulents, like the cacti, look almost as though they were fully armored water barrels.
6. Why do so many people ignore this plain evidence of the Creator's skill?

---

102. Understanding the Library Filing System

If your school has a small library, the books may be arranged in alphabetical order by title. But a public library, with its thousands of books, needs a more detailed system of arrangement than that. Although libraries use various methods for arranging books, the one you are most likely to encounter is the Dewey decimal system.

The Dewey Decimal System

The Dewey decimal system is named after Melvil Dewey (1851–1931), the man who organized it. From his childhood, mathematics fascinated young Melvil. It was said that while still in the lower grades, Melvil could solve an arithmetic problem in his head more quickly than others could on paper. Another of his delights was arranging things according to a system. He organized his mother's pantry, classifying all its contents.

At twelve years of age, Melvil walked eleven miles to purchase a Webster's unabridged dictionary. The cost was ten dollars, a large sum for a boy in 1863. The book was so heavy that he needed help to carry it home! Melvil's interest in books led him to visit libraries frequently. But he was disturbed by the lack of organization that he saw. In some libraries the books were placed in alphabetical order. In others they were numbered in a "fixed location" system according to the room, tier, and shelf where the books chanced to stand on the day they were numbered!

At twenty-one years of age, Melvil Dewey devised the classification system that bears his name. This system arranges all books into ten main categories of subjects. Study the basic outline of the Dewey decimal system below. The number and subject name of each classification are shown in boldface, followed by several examples of the types of books in that category.

000–099 General Works

Encyclopedias	Periodicals	Book lists

100–199 Philosophy

Nature of truth	Psychology	Logic

200–299 Religion

Bible	Science and the Bible
Church history	Non-Christian religions

300–399 Social Sciences

Statistics	Government	Economics
Customs	Political science	Education
— Holidays	— International relations	— Curriculum
— Etiquette	— Parliamentary practice	— Instructional methods

400–499 Language

Nature of language	Sign language
English language	Romance languages
— Dictionaries	— Latin
— Grammar	— Spanish (and others)

500–599 Pure Sciences

Astronomy	Biology	Chemistry
Geology	Mathematics	Zoology

600–699 Applied Sciences

Home economics	Business	Manufacturing
— Cooking	Engineering	Medical science
— Sewing	Agriculture	— Medicine
Construction	— Field crops	— Health and hygiene
— Carpentry	— Fruit culture	— First aid
— Masonry	— Domestic animals	

700–799 Arts and Recreation

Architecture	Photography
Painting	Sculpture
Music	Recreation and hobbies
Drawing and lettering	— Hunting and fishing
Landscaping	— Indoor and outdoor games

800–899 Literature

Study and criticism of literature	English literature
— Prose and poetry	American literature
— Drama (and other literary types)	

900–999 Geography and History

Geography
— Atlases
— Travel information
Biography
Ancient history
World history
European history
American history

In the Dewey decimal system, each of these ten categories can be broken down indefinitely into ever more precise divisions and subdivisions. The following outline illustrates how this system works.

200–299 Religion

- 210–219—Natural religion
- 220–229—Bible
  - 220.00–220.99—General
  - 221.00–224.99—Old Testament
  - 225.00–229.99—New Testament
    - 226.00–226.99—Gospels and Acts
      - 226.10–226.19—Harmonies
      - 226.20–226.29—Matthew
      - 226.30–226.39—Mark
      - 226.40–226.49—Luke
      - 226.50–226.59—John
      - 226.60–226.69—Acts
      - 226.70–226.79—Miracles
      - 226.80–226.89—Parables
      - 226.90–226.99—Lord's Prayer
    - 227.00–227.99—Epistles
    - 228.00–228.99—Revelation
    - 229.00–229.99—Apocrypha

How does this classification system help to find one book among many? Each book in the library is given a specific *call number* based on this system. You know, for example, that the 700s relate to arts and recreation. The division 720 is assigned to architecture. In the library you may find a book titled *The Dome People,* which describes how a group of teenagers built a geodesic dome building. This book may be assigned the call number 721.042.

Since the Dewey decimal system has a call number for each book, and since each call number is recorded in the library computer used for finding books, you do not need to memorize each small part of the system. You should, however, remember the ten main classes.

Special Arrangements

Using the Dewey decimal system, librarians can classify every book in the library. But three groups of books—reference, fiction, and biography—are so large that they have special locations in the library, separate from the other books in the Dewey decimal system.

1. *Reference books.* Some books are not to be read from cover to cover; rather, we refer to them for specific bits of information. These reference books include any book in the 000–099 group. (Some are included in other groups, such as dictionaries and handbooks in the 400–499 group.) Reference books usually have a three-line spine tag. The first line is simply *R* for *reference,* and the second line is the Dewey decimal call number. The third line has a capital letter indicating the author's last name, a *Cutter number,* which is a number that libraries assign to a particular author or compiler, and a small letter for the first important word in the title. The following illustration shows the spine tag that may appear on the book *How to Organize and Operate a Small Library,* by Genore H. Bernhard.

R ← for Reference
025 ← Dewey decimal number
B745h ← for *How to Organize and Operate a Small Library*
(745) ← Cutter number (745)
(B) ← for Genore H. Bernard

2. *Fiction.* Books of fiction are part of the 800–899 group in the Dewey decimal system. They usually have only a two-line spine tag. The first line is *F* for *fiction,* and the second line follows the same pattern as the third line on a reference book. No Dewey decimal system number is shown. Fiction books are arranged on the shelves alphabetically by the last name of the author. If an author has more than one book, those books are arranged alphabetically by title. *The Pilgrim's Progress,* by John Bunyan, might have the spine tag shown below.

F
B259p (*B* stands for Bunyan, the author; 259 is the Cutter number; *p* is the first letter in the first important word in the title.)

3. *Biography.* The 920–929 group of the Dewey decimal system consists of biographies. Like fiction books, they have a two-line spine tag. The first line is *B* for *biography* or the number 92, representing the Dewey decimal group for biographies. These books are arranged on the shelves in alphabetical order according to the name of the person they are written about. Books about the same person are grouped together and arranged alphabetically by the authors' last names. The book *David Livingstone,* by Mrs. J. H. Worcester, Jr., might have the following spine tag.

B
L4962w (*L* stands for Livingstone; 4962 is the Cutter number; *w* stands for Worcester, the author.)

In addition to the reference, fiction, and biography sections, many libraries have a special section with books written for younger readers. Books in this section may have simple call numbers that include the letter *J* (for *juvenile*). Below is the spine tag that may appear on *The Rainbow Book of American History,* by Earl Schenck Miers.

J
973 (Dewey decimal number)
Mie (for Earl Schenck Miers)

Applying the Lesson

A. Write the Dewey decimal number and subject name for the category in which each book belongs, such as *000–099 General Works* or *100–199 Philosophy.*

1. *The British Empire and Commonwealth of Nations* (history from the fifteenth century through the late twentieth century)
2. *Pets* (handbook on the care and understanding of all kinds of pets)
3. *Smiles, Nods, and Pauses* (activities for enriching children's communication skills)
4. *A History of the German Baptist Brethren in Europe and America* (history of German Baptists from their beginning through the late nineteenth century)
5. *The Art of Fine Baking* (general information on baking and a collection of recipes)
6. *Come Along to Saudi Arabia* (history of the kingdom of Saudi Arabia)
7. *Endeavor of Faith* (account of a conservative Mennonite provision for voluntary service during the time of a military draft)
8. *Echoes From My Heart* (collection of poetry)
9. *Why We Believe in Creation, Not in Evolution* (detailed illustrations from nature that cannot be explained by evolution)
10. *An Introduction to Music* (elementary and intermediate instructions in music rudiments)
11. *Century Readings in English Literature* (collection of English literary works grouped chronologically)
12. *Beyond Instinct* (debate between a Christian Russian peasant and an educated, atheistic Communist on creation versus evolution)

B. Tell whether each item speaks of *reference, fiction,* or *biography.*

1. Books arranged alphabetically by the name of the person written about.
2. Books arranged alphabetically by the last name of the author.
3. Books that may be placed in more than one category of the Dewey decimal system.
4. Belong to the 920–929 group of the Dewey decimal system.
5. Mostly belong to the 000–099 group of the Dewey decimal system.
6. Belong to the 800–899 group of the Dewey decimal system.
7. May include a few books from the 400–499 group of the Dewey decimal system.
8. Imaginary stories.
9. Books of general information.
10. Stories about the personal lives of individuals.
11. Books used for looking up facts.
12. May have the number 92 instead of a Dewey decimal number.

Review Exercises

A. Write the correct term to match each description. [49–53]

antagonist	conflict	protagonist
characterization	plot	setting
climax	point of view	theme

1. The main character in a story.
2. The overall development of the story conflict.
3. The time, place, and atmosphere of a story.
4. The lesson that a story teaches.
5. The struggle or problem that the main character faces.
6. The process of portraying story characters.
7. The point where the main character's response brings either victory or defeat.
8. The perspective from which an author writes a story.

B. Write *true* if the statement is true, or *false* if it is false. [48–53]
1. The most effective stories are written about unusual, outstanding events.
2. An effective short story must develop only one main theme.
3. The opening paragraph of a story should give a detailed picture of the setting.
4. If the main character struggles to overcome a bad habit, the conflict is between the main character and his circumstances.
5. The story conflict should increase as the story progresses.
6. The major story characters should be characterized fully.
7. The minor story characters should not even be named.
8. Most stories portray the main characters by their speech and their actions.
9. In the omniscient point of view, the author poses as the main character.
10. When the author writes objectively, he reveals the thoughts of the main character.

---

103. Using the Indexes of a Library

Even a small public library contains thousands of books, magazines, newspapers, and other materials. Although these are arranged logically, very few people memorize all the major subdivisions of the Dewey decimal system, let alone all the further subdivisions. Without a good system of indexes to the locations of the books and other materials, the usefulness of a library would be greatly limited.

The Card Catalog

The card catalog, which is often located near the librarian's desk, is a special cabinet with many small drawers. Each drawer is labeled with one or more letters, and it contains hundreds of index cards. You will find three kinds of cards in this index system: title cards, author cards, and subject cards. These cards are arranged alphabetically so that you can easily find books of any title, by any author, or about any subject.

1. *Title cards.* Sometimes you might go to the card catalog to find a specific title. A title card shows the title, centered on the first line. Look for the first word of the title (except *a, an,* or *the*) in alphabetical order. Study the following title card for the book *Patent Laws and Legislation.*

Patent Laws and Legislation—United States
346.7304
Rosenbaum, David G. 1956–
Patent Laws and Legislation—United States
Chelsea House Pub., Philadelphia, 1997
115p.

Patents, trademarks, and copyrights: practical strategies for protecting your ideas.

Notice the information that the card provides.

1. The title. Since this is a title card, the title is centered in the first line.
2. The call number. This is the Dewey decimal number, which tells you exactly where to find the book.
3. The author. The dates of his birth and death may be shown after his name. (If there is more than one author, the following form is used: Jones, Harold and Smith, Carl.)
4. The title, the publisher, and the place and date of publication.
5. Number of pages. If the book contains illustrations, the label *illustrated* or *illus.* indicates that.
6. A brief description.

Any other information at the bottom of the card is for library personnel.

2. *Author cards.* Perhaps you do not know the title of the book. You only know that someone had referred to a book about patents, written by David G. Rosenbaum. So you would go to the card catalog and look for an author card. You know that people's names are alphabetized according to the last name, so you look in the drawer that includes words beginning with *Ro.* Every library book that David G. Rosenbaum wrote will have an author card with the book title beneath his name. This card gives the same information as the title card, but the heading of the card is the author's name instead of the book title.

Rosenbaum, David G. 1956–
346.7304
Patent Laws and Legislation—United States
Chelsea House Pub., Philadelphia, 1997
115p.

Patents, trademarks, and copyrights: practical strategies for protecting your ideas.

3. *Subject cards.* Perhaps most often you will go to the card catalog, not looking for a specific book title or author's name, but for information on a particular subject. Then you look for subject cards. Most subject cards look just like the title and author cards, except that the subject heads the card. Some subject cards are cross-references, directing you to more specific or otherwise related subjects. A book of fiction, however, has no subject card.

> **Patent Laws**
> 346.7304
> Rosenbaum, David G. 1956–
> *Patent Laws and Legislation—United States*
> Chelsea House Pub., Philadelphia, 1997
> 115p.
>
> Patents, trademarks, and copyrights: practical strategies for protecting your ideas.

Most modern libraries no longer have card catalogs. They use microfilm or computer systems instead, but the information is basically the same. If you know how to use the card catalog, you will be able to use the other systems as well.

The *Readers' Guide to Periodical Literature*

A public library has magazines as well as books. Since the world's magazines contain much ungodly material, we generally have little use for them. But sometimes a writer needs up-to-date facts, which he may be able to find in one of the informational magazines available. Then he can use the *Readers' Guide to Periodical Literature,* an index to the contents of more than 150 magazines.

The *Readers' Guide* formerly consisted of booklets published throughout the year, but modern libraries have this index on computer. To use it, a person types in the subject on which he wants information, and the available articles on that subject will appear on the screen.

Remember that you must be prudent in using a public library. Many of the books are unsuitable for godly people, and some will do lasting harm. But if you have parental supervision and a mind filled with Bible truth, you can receive benefit by using a public library.

Applying the Lesson

A. Do the following exercises for each of the catalog cards shown.
   a. Name which kind of card this is.
   b. Write the subject of the main class in the Dewey decimal system to which this book belongs.
   c. Write the author's full name in normal order. If there is more than one author, list each.

d. Write how many pages the book contains.
e. Write whether the book is *illustrated* or *not illustrated.*

1.

Sign Language
419.045
Humphries, Tom
Sign Language—Study and Teaching
T. J. Pub., Silver Spring, Md., 1989, c.1980
280p. illus.
A basic course in American sign language.

2.

Grow, Lawrence
728.3
Cottages—Designs and Plans
Main Street Press, Pittstown, N.J., 1987
127p. illus.
The old house book of cottages and bungalows.

3.

Man Against Germs
614.4
Baron, A. L., Ph.D.
Man Against Germs
E. P. Dutton & Co., Inc., New York, 1957
320p.
The dramatic story of man's war against cholera, tuberculosis, leprosy, bubonic plague, syphilis, typhoid, dysentery, poliomyelitis, smallpox, yellow fever, influenza, typhus, rickettsia.

B. Draw three rectangles on your paper to represent catalog cards. Make one each of the three kinds of cards for the following book.

Title: *The House of Saud* Other: 560 pages; illustrated
Call number: 953.8 Subject: Asian History
Authors: David Holden and Richard Johns
Publisher and date: Holt, Rinehart and Winston, New York, 1981
Description: The rise and rule of the most powerful dynasty in the Arab world.

Review Exercises

Write *true* if the statement is true, or *false* if it is false. [81–85]

1. Careful research in reference books provides the necessary details for effective description.
2. A well-rounded description emphasizes several different impressions.
3. A description of an event usually follows chronological order.
4. Showing the details of a scene of action, rather than telling about them, produces the most effective description.
5. An effective description should give a general, overall view of a scene or an event.
6. The descriptive writer should use exact nouns, expressive verbs, and picturesque modifiers.
7. Descriptive writing is often woven into other kinds of essays.
8. By appealing to the senses, the descriptive writer helps the reader to experience what the author has described.
9. Imagery contributes to description both by making meaningful comparisons and by adding rich color.
10. A descriptive essay is different from other compositions in that it has no introduction or conclusion.

---

104. Chapter 12 Review

A. Write the correct term for each description.

1. Words with similar meanings.
2. A brief history of a word.
3. The "personality" of a word.
4. The changes in a word to show number, tense, and so forth.
5. Words formed from root words by adding suffixes.
6. The strict, exact meaning of a word.
7. A system of classification for arranging books in a library.
8. The number that a library assigns to a book, based on the Dewey decimal system.
9. Words with opposite meanings.

B. Do these exercises on dictionary use.

1. Why does a word like *die* have more than one numbered entry?
2. What three types of inflections do most dictionaries show?
3. Name the usage labels that fit these descriptions. If more than one label fits, a number in parentheses indicates how many you should have.
   a. Words to avoid because of their association with evil.
   b. Words no longer in general use. (2)
   c. Words coined by people trying to say things in unique ways.
   d. Words to avoid because they represent poor English. (3)
   e. Words used in relatively small areas or by a limited group of people. (2)
   f. Words acceptable only in everyday speaking and everyday writing.

4. Find *league* in the dictionary.
    a. Give the meaning of the original Latin word for the *league* that means "a unit of measure."
    b. Give the meaning of the original Latin word for the *league* that means "an association or alliance."
5. Find the entry for the word *excise* with the meaning "a tax on the production, sale, or consumption of a commodity within a country."
    a. Write the phonetic spelling of this word.
    b. What part of speech is it?
    c. From what language does this word come?
6. Find the entry for the word *excise* with the meaning "to remove by or as if by cutting."
    a. Write the phonetic spelling of this word.
    b. What part of speech is it?
    c. From what language does this word come?
    d. What inflections are shown for this word?
7. What usage labels are given in the entries for these words?
    a. even
    b. poke
    c. snag
    d. irregardless

C. Do these exercises on using reference books.
1. What three things should you consider when choosing a synonym from a thesaurus?
2. What advantage does a Roget's thesaurus have over an alphabetical thesaurus?
3. Name four research aids found in many encyclopedias.
4. What two important cautions should you remember about using encyclopedias?
5. What is the difference between a geographical and a political map?
6. Using the index, list all the volumes and page numbers where you could find information on the following subjects in the school encyclopedia set.
    a. moon
    b. Alexander Graham Bell
7. Using an encyclopedia or a statistical almanac, write answers to these questions.
    a. What nation has the largest number of nuclear power plants for electricity?
    b. What is another nation that produces much electricity with nuclear power?
    c. What type of livestock is most important in Oklahoma agriculture?
    d. Where is Niihau Island located?
    e. Where is the day lily a native flower?

D. Do these exercises about libraries.
1. What are the three important rules for using a library courteously?
2. Why must you use a library prudently?
3. List the numbers and the subjects of the ten main groupings in the Dewey decimal system.
4. What are the two main indexes of a library?

5. What three types of cards will you find in a card catalog?
6. Classify each item as *reference, fiction,* or *biography.*
   a. Books arranged alphabetically according to the name of the person written about.
   b. Belong mostly to the 000–099 group of the Dewey decimal system.
   c. Imaginary stories.
   d. Books that may be placed in more than one category of the Dewey decimal system.
   e. Includes some books from the 400–499 group of the Dewey decimal system.
   f. Stories about the personal lives of individuals.
   g. Belong to the 800–899 group of the Dewey decimal system.
   h. Books used for looking up facts.
   i. May have the number 92 instead of a Dewey decimal number.
   j. Belong to the 920–929 group of the Dewey decimal system.
   k. Books of general information.
   l. Books arranged alphabetically by the last name of the author.
   m. Have no subject cards.

E. Draw a rectangle to represent an index card. Make a title card for the following book.

   Title: *Fishes and Their Young*
   Call number: 597.14
   Author: Alan Mark Fletcher
   Other: 47 pages, illustrated
   Publisher and date: Addison-Wesley Publishing Company, Inc., Reading, Mass.; 1974
   Description: Describes fascinating ways in which several kinds of fish care for their young.

F. Answer these questions about speaking style.
   1. What are three ways to develop enthusiasm before you speak to a group?
   2. What is one thing that can greatly dampen your enthusiasm?
   3. What are five things that will demonstrate your enthusiasm as you speak to a group?

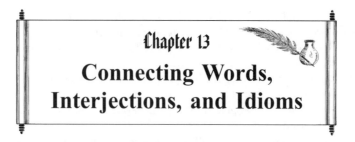

Chapter 13
Connecting Words, Interjections, and Idioms

105. Prepositions and Prepositional Phrases

We use many prepositions to show relationships between substantives and other words in sentences. Prepositions express relationships so precisely that changing a preposition can completely change the meaning of a sentence. Working *with* someone is quite different from working *against* someone. And falling *on* the ice is quite different from falling *through* the ice! A study of these simple but useful words will help you to express your ideas in a clear and meaningful way.

1. *A preposition is a word that shows the relationship between its object and some other word in the sentence.* The following tables show the prepositions used most commonly.

Common Prepositions

aboard	at	by	inside	outside	under
about	before	concerning	into	over	underneath
above	behind	despite	like	past	until
across	below	down	near	since	unto
after	beneath	during	of	through	up
against	beside	except	off	throughout	upon
along	besides	for	on	till	with
among	between	from	onto	to	within
around	beyond	in	out	toward	without
as	but				

Common Compound Prepositions

according to	by means of	in spite of	out of
along with	due to	instead of	owing to
aside from	in addition to	next to	prior to
as of	in front of	on account of	with regard to
because of	in place of		

2. *A prepositional phrase includes the preposition, its object, and any modifiers of the object.* The object of a preposition is the substantive that the preposition relates to another word. You can find it by saying the preposition and then asking *whom* or *what.* If two substantives answer the question, the preposition has a compound object.

The following sentence contains three underlined prepositional phrases. The second one has a compound object, and the third has a compound preposition.

If the well of our heart is filled with pure thoughts and desires, only pure words will come out of our mouth.

3. *A preposition normally precedes its object, except when the object is an interrogative or a relative pronoun or is modified by one of these.*

The trust which the poet wrote about is the key to true peace.
(*About which* modifies *wrote.*)
What key is this song written in? (*In what key* modifies *is written.*)

4. *The object of a preposition is usually a noun or pronoun, but it may also be a verbal, a verbal phrase, or a noun clause.*

After picking five bushels of peas, we were quite ready for a break.
(The object of the preposition *After* is the verbal phrase *picking five bushels of peas.*)
We must show respect to whomever God grants authority.
(The object of the preposition *to* is the noun clause *whomever God grants authority.*)

5. *Prepositional phrases can function as adjectives, adverbs, or nouns.* An adjective prepositional phrase usually comes right after the substantive it modifies.

A brother from our church operates the garage next to Grandfather Bergey's farm.

When an adverb prepositional phrase modifies a verb, it can often be placed at different locations without changing the meaning of the sentence. A phrase that modifies an adjective, an adverb, or a verbal usually comes right after the word it modifies.

Before breakfast we have our family worship in the living room.
(The underlined phrases can be moved to other positions.)
By trusting in God, the martyrs could be courageous beyond their enemies' comprehension. (The underlined phrases cannot be moved to other positions.)

A noun prepositional phrase names a place or a thing and is usually the subject of a sentence with a linking verb.

In the kitchen is not a good place for those muddy boots!
(*In the kitchen* names a place for muddy boots not to be; it is the subject of the sentence.)
After seven o'clock will be a good time to arrive.
(*After seven o'clock* names the time for arriving; it is the subject of the sentence.)

6. *Several prepositional phrases in succession can be either a series of independent phrases or one unit of phrases.* In a series of independent phrases, each phrase modifies the same word. In a unit of phrases, each successive phrase is actually part of the first phrase, modifying the object in the previous prepositional phrase. Study the following examples.

The chickens are scratching in the dirt for food.

(*In the dirt* and *for food* are independent modifiers of *are scratching.*)

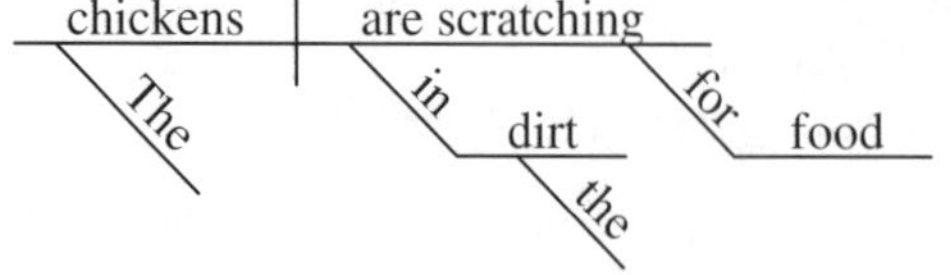

We ate our lunch in the shade of a huge willow beside the river.

(*In the shade of a huge willow beside the river* is a unit modifying *ate; of a huge willow* modifies *shade; beside the river* modifies *willow.*)

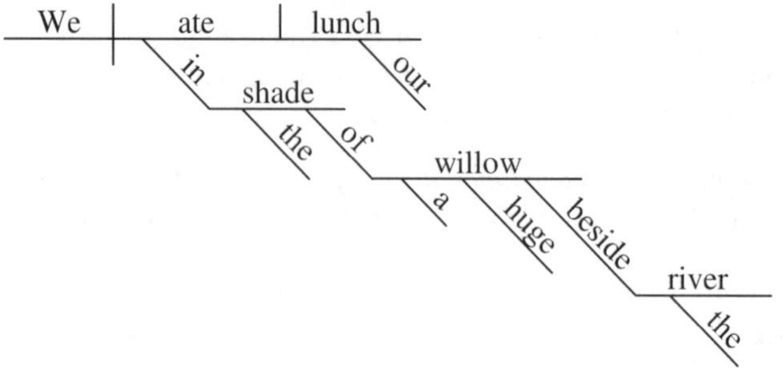

7. *Do not confuse prepositions with adverbs.* If the word is used alone to tell *when* or *where,* it is an adverb. It can be a preposition only if it has an object.

Adverbs:

We should get off at the next station.

We looked inside, but we could not find Timothy.

Prepositions:

We should get off the train at the next station.

We looked inside the garage, but we could not find Timothy.

8. *Do not confuse prepositional phrases beginning with* to *with infinitives. To* is part of an infinitive when a verb form follows it. *To* is a preposition when a substantive follows it.

Sharon hurried to the kitchen to prepare a quick lunch.

(*To the kitchen* is a prepositional phrase; *to prepare a quick lunch* is an infinitive phrase.)

Applying the Lesson

A. Copy each prepositional phrase. If a phrase is part of a longer phrase, include it with the longer phrase, and also copy it separately. Label each phrase *adj., adv.,* or *n.*

1. Throughout human history, men have sought by various means to ignore their accountability to the Creator.
2. Deceived by the devil, many have vainly tried to cast God down from His throne.
3. Under God's blessing is the only place of true safety and satisfaction.
4. Whom shall we look to in difficult times when we face problems beyond our ability to solve?
5. The narrow valley between these two mountain ridges includes several farms with fertile fields.
6. Before sunrise is my favorite time to get up.
7. William H. Prescott, the son of a wealthy judge in Massachusetts, became a historian worthy of admiration.
8. In the middle 1800s, Prescott published four major histories in spite of being nearly blind.
9. Because of his handicap, his secretary read for him the resource materials that he used.
10. To write his notes in somewhat legible form, Prescott used a noctograph—a frame with guide wires across its width.
11. After taking his notes, Prescott had his secretary recopy them in large letters.
12. At some times, he was able to read those notes; but usually his secretary read them repeatedly until Prescott had them fixed in his memory.
13. The remarkable power of his memory is also evident in his writing method; he wrote each paragraph mentally until an entire chapter had taken shape within his mind.
14. On his noctograph, Prescott swiftly wrote the chapter; then his secretary read the copy, corrected it according to Prescott's directions, and recopied it in its final form.

B. Copy each underlined word, and label it *adv.* or *prep.*
1. We climbed <u>aboard</u> the train, and soon after leaving the station <u>behind</u>, we were speeding <u>across</u> the prairie.
2. A bitter wind blew <u>down</u> from the mountains, driving cold air <u>through</u> the thin walls of the cabin and bringing snowflakes <u>inside</u>.
3. The beautiful weather <u>outside</u> matches the joy <u>inside</u> my heart.
4. The Bible verse <u>over</u> the clock helps to lift our thoughts <u>above</u> to the eternal realities.

Review Exercises

A. Copy each underlined verb or verb phrase, and write whether its mood is indicative (*ind.*), imperative (*imp.*), or subjunctive (*sub.*). [75]
1. Brother Leland <u>requested</u> that each of us <u>pray</u> for his elderly mother.
2. <u>Will</u> you please <u>clean</u> up the water that you <u>spilled</u>.
3. If I <u>were</u> to give you too much help, <u>consider</u> how little you would actually learn.
4. Even if a man <u>live</u> to be a thousand years old, he <u>can</u> never <u>learn</u> all there is to learn.

B. Write the words that are correct for the subjunctive mood. [75]

1. Biblical discipleship requires that the Christian (keep, keeps) himself free from worldliness.
2. We would be completely snowed in if this rain (was, were) all snow.
3. When Father was a boy, Grandfather required that his hired hand (go, went) to church.
4. If this cat (is, be) truly the queen of the barn, let her keep the mice under control.

C. Write a subjunctive verb or verb phrase to replace each underlined *would* phrase. [75]

1. The whole family would attend cousin Lucinda's wedding if that <u>would be</u> possible.
2. I move that a committee <u>would be appointed</u> to investigate the possibility of purchasing land to enlarge our parking lot.
3. Grandmother would appreciate if Sharon <u>would be</u> available to help her with housecleaning on Saturday.
4. Mrs. Williams would have come to the meeting if we <u>would have told</u> her about it.

---

106. Coordinating Conjunctions

Coordinating conjunctions usually are small words, but they may join major sentence parts together. The joined parts are *coordinate;* that is, they have a definite equality. Coordinating conjunctions join sentence parts so that they can work unitedly together.

1. *Coordinating conjunctions join sentence parts and show the relationships between those parts.* The common coordinating conjunctions are *and, but, or, for, nor, yet,* and *so. And* shows addition or continuing thought; *but* and *yet* show contrast or unexpected outcome; *or* and *nor* show choice or option; *for* and *so* show cause and effect.

2. *Coordinating conjunctions join sentence parts of parallel structure and function.* Parallel structure means that the joined parts are both words, prepositional phrases, gerund phrases, dependent clauses, and so forth. Parallel function means that the joined parts both function as subjects, verbs, predicate nominatives, adverbs, and so forth.

> *Faith* <u>and</u> *works* complement each other in true Biblical obedience.
> (*And* joins single words used as subjects.)
>
> People *trusting themselves* <u>or</u> *ignoring Bible teaching* cannot be saved.
> (*Or* joins participial phrases used as adjectives.)
>
> *The obedience of faith is a concept easy to grasp,* <u>yet</u> *many stumble at its simplicity.* (*Yet* joins independent clauses.)

Sometimes writers or speakers use a coordinating conjunction to join a word to a phrase or a phrase to a clause. This is improper because the structure of the two parts is different. Correct the mistake either by making the joined parts parallel or by rewriting the sentence.

Incorrect:

The wind, *bitterly cold* and *showing furious strength,* piled the snow into deep drifts. (word joined to phrase)

Correct:

The wind, *bitterly cold* and *furiously strong,* piled the snow into deep drifts.

Showing furious strength, the bitterly cold wind piled the snow into deep drifts.

3. *When a coordinating conjunction joins the clauses in a compound sentence, a comma is usually needed before the conjunction.* If the two clauses are very short and closely related, you may omit the comma. If one or both of the clauses already have several commas, you may need to use a semicolon to show clearly the division between the clauses. Study the following sentences.

Our words should be wholesome, and our tone of voice should be gracious. (normal compound sentence)

Kind words bring cheer but harsh words bring grief. (short clauses; no comma needed)

If we frequently let idle or thoughtless words slip from our tongue, we should examine our heart; for when the heart is well guarded, the tongue does not slip. (other commas; semicolon used)

4. *Correlative conjunctions are coordinating conjunctions that work in pairs.* Like the common coordinating conjunctions, correlative conjunctions show how the joined items are related. *Both—and* shows addition or continuing thought; *not only—but also* shows addition, with greater emphasis on the second item; *either—or, neither—nor,* and *whether—or* show choice or option.

5. *Be careful to place correlative conjunctions just before the sentence parts that they join.* If you put them in the wrong place, they will appear to join unparallel parts.

Incorrect:

This finishing job both *requires* sandpaper and *steel wool.*

Either *you* pushed down too hard or *sanded* across the grain on this piece.

Correct:

This finishing job requires both *sandpaper* and *steel wool.*

You either *pushed* down too hard or *sanded* across the grain on this piece.

6. *When using* not only—but also, *be careful not to omit the word* also.

Incorrect: This cake is not only *moist* but *tasty.*

Correct: This cake is not only *moist* but also *tasty.*

7. *With the correlative conjunction* whether—or, *the second item is often elliptical.* Because of the missing words, the joined sentence parts may appear to have unequal structure when in fact they are parallel.

> Margaret is not sure whether *to make spice cake* or *pound cake.*
> (Meaning: whether to make spice cake or to make pound cake)
> Whether *the service begins at 7:00* or *7:30,* we should start chores early.
> (Meaning: whether the service begins at 7:00 or the service begins at 7:30)

8. *Conjunctive adverbs function as both conjunctions and adverbs.* The following words are often used as conjunctive adverbs.

accordingly	henceforth	namely
afterward	however	nevertheless
also	indeed	otherwise
anyway	instead	still
besides	likewise	then
consequently	meanwhile	therefore
furthermore	moreover	thus
hence		

Conjunctive adverbs join independent clauses and show specific relationships between the clauses. A semicolon always precedes the conjunctive adverb, and a comma often follows it. If the sentence reads smoothly without a pause after the conjunctive adverb, you may omit the comma.

> Our carnal nature pulls us toward the world; nevertheless, we can choose to surrender our will to God's will.
> When we trust in the Lord, we receive power to overcome sin; then we can be more than conquerors.

Conjunctive adverbs are not considered true conjunctions, for they can be moved to different positions in a sentence. (True conjunctions must come between the sentence parts they join.) In one sense, a sentence with a conjunctive adverb simply has two clauses joined by a semicolon, with the conjunctive adverb modifying the verb in the second clause. Consider the following examples.

> The day was quite warm, yet a light breeze brought us welcome relief.
> (*Yet* cannot be moved; it is a true conjunction.)
> The day was quite warm; however, a light breeze brought us welcome relief.
> The day was quite warm; a light breeze, however, brought us welcome relief.
> (*However* can be moved; it is not a true conjunction. It modifies *brought.*)

Applying the Lesson

A. Copy the conjunctions, and label them *CC* (common coordinating conjunction), *Cor* (correlative conjunction), or *CA* (conjunctive adverb).

1. A mirage is an illusion that can occur either on land or on water.

2. The most common mirage is the deceptive appearance of water; indeed, many a weary desert traveler has been fooled by a mirage.
3. When the atmosphere is clear, calm, and dry, the heat of the earth warms a layer of air near the earth; however, the air at a person's eye level remains a bit cooler.
4. These layers of air have both differing temperatures and differing optical densities, so the light rays are refracted as they pass from one layer to another.
5. The mirage is actually light rays from the sky, but those rays appear to originate on the ground because of the way they are refracted.
6. Another kind of mirage can occur over cold water and is called a looming.
7. The air next to the water is colder than the air higher up; consequently, refraction causes a reversing of the image that results.
8. A ship beyond the horizon not only becomes visible but also appears in the sky, upside down!

B. Write enough of each sentence to show how to correct the mistake in it.
1. We should trust the Lord simply and without reserve.
2. We cannot direct our own steps but God will direct us if we trust Him.
3. If we truly trust the Lord, we will neither fear the threats nor the power of the enemy.
4. The Lord is well able to direct our steps in our youth and as we grow older.
5. God is well able to meet all our needs, moreover, He delights to do us good.
6. We either allow God to provide for us, or our deepest needs remain unmet.
7. The little children played quietly and without fighting.
8. Uncle Curvin sent me not only a birthday card but an interesting letter.
9. This story both illustrates a good plot and effective characterization.
10. If it does not rain tomorrow, we shall plant corn, otherwise we shall need to wait.
11. Glenda has gone to prepare lunch so Gordon and I will have to finish picking these beans.
12. This afternoon, the boys should either hoe the corn or the lima beans.
13. Uncle Brandon writes both poems and composes music.
14. The boys not only washed the outside of the car but cleaned the inside.

Review Exercises

Write whether each underlined adverb modifies a *verb,* a *verbal,* an *adjective,* an *adverb,* a *preposition,* a *conjunction,* or an entire *sentence.* [91, 92]

1. The muskellunge is an <u>unusually</u> large freshwater fish <u>often</u> sought by anglers.
2. <u>Perhaps</u> you are more familiar with the term *muskie,* a nickname used <u>quite</u> commonly.
3. Muskellunge live <u>only</u> in three North American watersheds: the Great Lakes–St. Lawrence, the upper Mississippi River, and the Ohio River.
4. A <u>fully</u> mature muskie may weigh sixty pounds and grow <u>nearly</u> to a length of six feet.

5. Obviously, hooking this fish is not something to take lightly!
6. Muskellunge feed freely on almost any food they can swallow; indeed, they have been known to swallow muskrats.
7. How does this large fish catch its prey?
8. A muskellunge will lie quietly in a shaded spot; then almost before you can see what is happening, the muskie rushes out, snapping up the unsuspecting prey.

---

107. Subordinating Conjunctions and Interjections

A subordinating conjunction joins clauses of unequal rank. The clause it introduces is *subordinate* to the rest of the sentence; that is, its function is less important than that of the main clause. The clause that a subordinating conjunction introduces cannot stand alone but has meaning only in relation to the rest of the sentence.

Subordinating Conjunctions

1. *A subordinating conjunction joins a dependent adverb clause to the independent clause in a complex sentence.* The following list shows a number of the most common subordinating conjunctions. Many of these words may also be used as adverbs or prepositions. They are subordinating conjunctions only when they introduce dependent clauses.

after	even if	so that	when
although	even though	than	whenever
as	how	that	where
as if	if	though	wherever
as though	in order that	till	whether
because	provided	unless	while
before	since	until	

2. *A subordinating conjunction shows a specific relationship between the dependent clause and the independent clause.* These relationships include *when, where, how, why, under what condition, in spite of what,* and *to what degree.*

We should treat others *as we want them to treat us.*
(*As* links the dependent clause to the independent clause by telling *how* about *should treat.*)

Even though others mistreat us, we should return good for evil.
(*Even though* links the dependent clause to the independent clause by telling *under what condition* about *should return.*)

The Lord Jesus suffered more intensely *than we ever have.*
(*Than* links the dependent clause to the independent clause by telling *to what degree* about *more intensely.*)

3. *A subordinating conjunction often provides a more effective link between clauses than does the coordinating conjunction* and. The word *and* provides a quick and handy way to join words and word groups. But *and* merely indicates one idea added to another, whereas subordinating conjunctions allow you to express a great variety of more specific relationships.

Vague: Merely adds one idea to another
Douglas will fetch the ax, and Dennis will start stacking the smaller pieces of wood.

Specific: Shows exact time relationship
While Douglas fetches the ax, Dennis will start stacking the smaller pieces of wood.

4. *When a dependent clause comes at the beginning of a complex sentence, a comma separates it from the independent clause.* Two commas are used if the dependent clause comes in the middle. But if the clause comes at the end of the sentence, no comma is needed.

<u>If we can remember</u>, we should call Grandmother and tell her the news.
We should call Grandmother, <u>if we can remember</u>, and tell her the news.
We should call Grandmother and tell her the news <u>if we can remember</u>.

Interjections

1. *An interjection is a word that expresses strong feeling.* The cry or exclamation of an interjection may express pleasure, admiration, adoration, surprise, pain, or any other feeling. The following list shows some common interjections.

ah	good	lo	well
aha	ha	oh	what
alas	hallelujah	ouch	whew
amen	ho	say	why
behold	hurrah		

Lo, our tender Shepherd guides us faithfully.
Ah, what a privilege to trust His all-wise care!
Alas! How often we tend to take our own way!

Words that represent sounds also frequently serve as interjections. Such a word is followed by an exclamation point or a period, depending on the intensity of the sound. Also, the word is italicized because it is "quoting" a sound. No italics are needed when such a word simply names a sound, as in the fourth example below.

<u>Crack!</u> A large branch suddenly gave way under its heavy load of ice.
<u>Knock, knock.</u> Who would be at the door this early in the morning?
<u>Ring! Ring!</u> The telephone interrupted my thoughts.
The loud <u>ring</u> of the telephone startled me.
(a noun that names a sound; no italics needed)

Actually, almost any word can function as an interjection if it is used as an independent exclamation. But if a verb gives a one-word request or command, it is a complete sentence, not an interjection.

> Salt! No, I do not want salt on my watermelon. (interjection)
> Run! I was so frightened that I could not even move! (interjection)
> Run! A rainstorm is coming! (one-word command; a complete sentence)

2. *The use of commas and exclamation points with interjections depends on the degree of emotion intended by the writer.* Exclamation points mark strong interjections. The words *amen, hallelujah, hurrah, ouch, what,* and *whew* are usually strong exclamations, and so are words that represent sounds. If you use an exclamation point, capitalize the next word. Commas mark mild interjections. Many interjections can be used either way.

> Well, this job might take you boys a half hour of hard work.
> Well! You boys must have worked really hard if the job is finished already.

If the whole sentence shows strong feeling, you may use a comma after the interjection and an exclamation point at the end of the sentence. You may also use two exclamation points as in the second example below. But you must not overdo this in writing, for exclamation points should be used sparingly.

> Oh, if only we had not been so careless!
> Oh! If only we had not been so careless!

If an interjection comes in the middle of a compound sentence, set it off with commas.

> In the darkest hour, we can look to the Lord; and, lo, He is there.

3. *Use interjections cautiously and sparingly.* They can easily become idle words of which we must give an account, and they can even fall into the category of profanity. Avoid the following kinds of interjections:

   a. The name of God or any alteration of it.
   b. Words that refer to characteristics of God.
   c. Words that refer to hell, Satan, or any part of his kingdom.
   d. Common words used as interjections that have nothing to do with their normal meanings. Words such as *boy, man,* and *rats* are sometimes used in that way.

Even interjections that are proper in themselves can be used in a wrong way. For example, it is improper to use *amen* and *hallelujah* in a light or carnal way. Also, the Bible commands us to control our emotions and our words. We need to avoid any exclamation of anger or disgust, no matter how acceptable the word itself may be.

Applying the Lesson

A. Copy each dependent clause, and underline the subordinating conjunction.

1. Although godly children have always honored their mothers, the idea of a nationally recognized Mother's Day is more recent than you might suppose.

2. Anna Jarvis was born in 1864 at Grafton, West Virginia; however, when her father died in 1902, her mother moved the family to Philadelphia to live with relatives.
3. After her mother died in 1905, Anna was grief stricken.
4. Though she was apparently an exemplary daughter, Anna felt as if she had not honored her mother sufficiently.
5. She pondered those feelings for two years until they bore fruit in the first public call for a national Mother's Day.
6. Because the second Sunday of May marked the anniversary of her mother's death, Miss Jarvis chose that day for a meeting with her friends so that she could introduce her proposal.
7. If she harbored any doubts about her plan, they were dispelled as her friends enthusiastically supported the idea.
8. As Miss Jarvis desired, her church held a large Mother's Day service one year later in Grafton, West Virginia.
9. The idea of an annual Mother's Day became popular more quickly than some other proposed holidays have.
10. Because it gained such strong support, in 1914 President Wilson signed legislation designating the second Sunday of May as Mother's Day.

B. Rewrite each sentence, joining the clauses with a suitable subordinating conjunction instead of with *and.* Be sure to use commas correctly. You may change the order of the clauses if you wish.
1. We need to catch a glimpse of God's holiness, and we can live before Him in righteousness.
2. We truly love God, and we do not hanker after the things of the world.
3. God is love, and He will judge all wickedness.
4. Jesus Christ lived as a man upon earth, and He manifested the Father.
5. Brother Clyde's had left, and we discovered that they had left Sister Bonnie's purse behind.
6. We are remodeling our house, and Grandfather will come to live with us.
7. The new song was a little hard to learn, and we sang the melody several times.
8. We climbed the high hill behind Uncle Arlen's place, and we could see the whole valley.

C. Copy each interjection, the word before it (if there is one), and the word after it. Use correct capitalization and punctuation, and underline any word that should be italicized.
1. Lo our heavenly Father tenderly cares for us in every experience of life.
2. When we hardly know what to do, we can turn to God; and behold He will always be there.
3. Hallelujah our God will never fail us!
4. What shall we doubt a promise of the Lord God?
5. Though the enemy oppose God's children, he cannot prevail; and lo God always makes a way for them.

6. Astronomy this field of science has impressed me in a new way with God's infinite greatness.
7. Whoosh the snow sliding off the roof startled the entire family.
8. Ouch that low-hanging pipe gave my head quite a blow!
9. Wonderful we are planning a trip to Alberta this summer!
10. Caw the startled crow complained noisily about my intrusion.

Review Exercises

Label each underlined verb *TA* (transitive, active voice), *TP* (transitive, passive voice), *IC* (intransitive complete), or *IL* (intransitive linking). [76]

1. A new day has dawned to God's glory.
2. God has graciously tended our restful hours, giving us peaceful sleep.
3. The eastern sky grows brighter as the moment of daybreak nears.
4. The clouds in the east are being painted in brilliant shades of pink, magenta, and purple.
5. Every sunrise is a testimony to God's faithfulness.

---

108. Idioms

Have you ever said, "I am going to stay at home"? What did you mean? Where are you *going* if you intend to *stay*? This expression is quite familiar to any fluent speaker of the English language, and it is a perfectly acceptable English construction. Yet if you analyze it word by word, you will find that it makes no sense. Welcome to the fascinating study of idioms.

An ***idiom*** is an expression that cannot be explained grammatically or logically, yet it is an established part of a language. We learned English idioms naturally as we learned to speak the language. In fact, if a person makes errors in the use of common idioms, it is a sign that he does not know the language well.

Many idioms contain common words like *come, put, up,* and *down.* These words provide a handy way to communicate ideas that may require clumsy or unnatural wording to express in any other way. Read the examples below, with special attention to the natural, everyday tone of the sentences in the first group.

Sentences With Idioms:

How did you come up with that idea?

Wilma came down with a severe cold.

One boy fainted but soon came to.

Yesterday's work really put us to it.

Who put your little brother up to say that?

Sentences Without Idioms:

How did you devise that idea?

Wilma became sick with a severe cold.

One boy fainted but soon regained consciousness.

Yesterday's work really taxed us.

Who prompted your little brother to say that?

The stress was <u>bearing down on</u> Mr. Neal.	The stress was heavily burdening Mr. Neal.
Still, he <u>turned down</u> our offer to help.	Still, he refused our offer to help.
We stayed inside until the rain <u>let up</u>.	We stayed inside until the rain ceased.
Do not get <u>worked up</u> over such a trifle.	Do not get agitated over such a trifle.
Father <u>cut up</u> the tree to make firewood.	Father cut the tree in pieces to make firewood.

The illogical nature of many idioms is illustrated especially well by the last sentence. When we turn a tree into firewood, we first *cut it down* and then we *cut it up*! There are dozens of other idioms that are no more logical than these. Here are just a few of the many that you use in your everyday speaking and writing.

Other Idiomatic Expressions:

Mother asked me to <u>keep an eye on</u> the younger children. (watch carefully)

<u>By the way</u>, who was that lady on the back bench? (incidentally)

The clerk seemed to be <u>out of sorts</u> for some reason. (irritable)

Daniel <u>made up his mind</u> to be faithful at any cost. (determined)

Idiomatic Usage

The proper use of prepositions is often a matter of correct idioms. In other words, certain prepositions are "correct" or "incorrect" not because of their meanings but simply because of what is established as proper usage. This is the basis for a number of rules in the "Glossary of Usage" (Chapter 5). Here are three examples.

A person may be angry <u>with</u> another person, angry <u>about</u> a situation or an event, and angry <u>at</u> an animal or an inanimate object.

When observing literal similarities or differences, we compare one thing <u>with</u> another. When making figurative comparisons, we compare one thing <u>to</u> another.

One thing may differ <u>from</u> another. One person may differ <u>with</u> another.

Use the dictionary when you are not sure about an expression. Many advanced dictionaries have run-in entries that show established idioms. For example, the entry for *line* may include the following run-in entries at the end.

— **line up,** (1) To form a line. (2) To organize: *line up some people to help.*

— **down the line,** (1) Throughout. (2) In the future: *expect a harvest down the line.*

— **in line for,** Next in order for: *in line for spending the weekend with Grandfather.*

— **on the line,** (1) Ready for immediate payment. (2) In jeopardy: *put his life on the line.*

Applying the Lesson

A. Each of these sentences contains an expression that is not in natural, everyday language. Copy that phrase, and after it write an idiom with a form of *fall,* which could replace it.

1. The heavy snow caused many roofs to collapse toward the inside.
2. During a power outage, we can resort to using our coal furnace.
3. Because of a dispute over land, the neighbors ceased being friendly with each other.
4. Do not be deceived by that salesman's glowing promises.
5. If you miss many days of school, you will fail to keep current in your work.
6. We had hoped that all the cousins could travel together, but our plans met with failure.

B. Write the meaning of each underlined expression. You may use a dictionary.

1. Father has reminded us time and again to be careful with fire.
2. The secretary summed up the discussion in the minutes of the meeting.
3. Do not pick holes in your brother's ideas just because he is younger than you.
4. The second blizzard came right on the heels of the previous one.
5. This new bypass should do away with much of the congestion in the city.
6. The hunter stayed on his guard for wolves and panthers.
7. The teacher pointed out my mistake without beating around the bush.
8. Though the church building is not finished, it is well under way.

C. Rewrite each sentence so that it expresses the same thought without an idiom.

1. We could hardly make out what the sign said.
2. The rescue workers had to pick their way through the rubble.
3. It seemed like a hopeless situation, but the leader's suggestion carried the day.
4. Aunt Tina's remark made us wonder what plans she had up her sleeve.
5. If we all dig in right away, doing these dishes will not take long.
6. Every Christian should live up to his profession.
7. When our car engine blew a head gasket, we were out on a limb because we still had two hundred miles to go.
8. When planning any trip, you should take into account the possibility of unexpected delays.
9. I only lent you my special pocketknife; I did not give it to you for keeps.
10. When Brother Stephen became sick, Brother Dale filled his shoes very well.

Review Exercises

A. Copy the correct participle for each sentence. [90]

1. (Running, Having run) smoothly hour after hour, the generator is providing us electricity while the blizzard rages.
2. (Spending, Having spent) over an hour searching for Betsy's lost kitten, we finally gave up.
3. These pancakes, (frying, fried) to perfection, are delicious.
4. The bacon, (sizzling, sizzled) in the pan, is filling the house with an appetizing aroma.

B. Copy each word that should be followed by a comma, and add the comma. If the sentence needs no comma, write *correct.* [90, 93]
1. Clinging thickly to everything the hoarfrost turned the countryside into a dazzling wonderland.
2. Our visitors from the South were especially impressed when they saw the lovely scene.
3. All the students who failed this test must do some remedial work.
4. After they have completed those exercises they will take another test on this material.
5. This old farmhouse built by Great-grandfather Lutz has some huge stones in the walls.
6. Leon Wagner whose farm borders ours on the west is a kind, helpful neighbor.

C. Write enough words to show how to correct the mistakes in adjective and adverb comparisons. [95]
1. Most things are more cheaper at Springway Grocery Outlet than at other area stores.
2. Theodore is doing his work more careful now than he did when he first worked here.
3. James is the oldest of the two tenth grade boys in our school.
4. With a score of 98%, Lisa had the most perfect grade of all us students.
5. Canada is larger than any nation in North America.
6. The weather is delightfuller today than it has been all week.

---

109. Improving Your Writing Style, Part 6: Review

In your previous writing style lessons, you have studied five elements of an effective writing style. This lesson reviews those elements.

1. Originality

You should not always use the first wording that comes to your mind. Rather, look for fresh, creative ways of expressing yourself—ways deliberately designed to add appeal. Sprinkle your creativity like salt throughout your writing, always remembering to keep your imagination within proper bounds. The added life in your compositions will be well worth the extra time and effort.

In your pursuit of originality, beware that you do not merely use clichés—expressions that once were clever but that now have lost their sparkle through too much use. Surely you do not want your writing to be *as dead as a doornail* because you have written everything *off the top of your head*!

2. Active Verbs

Remember to examine your use of the verb *be.* Whenever practical, reword sentences containing *there is, there are, there was,* and *there were,* as well as sentences with *be* as a main verb. Every time you replace *be* with an action verb, you add more life to your writing. If the verb in a sentence must *be* a linking verb, it will *grow* more appealing if you replace it with a linking verb that suggests action (*sound, look, remain,* and so forth).

3. Active Voice

Deliberately use verbs in the active voice. Passive verbs produce dull writing because they turn a scene of activity into a place where things happen but nobody makes them happen. Verbs in the passive voice *can be replaced* in almost every sentence—but that will happen only if *you replace* such verbs.

4. Poetic Devices

A sprinkling of alliteration, rhyme, and onomatopoeia can add a melodious appeal to your sentences. You have *surely seen* the *rich rewards* that these literary devices offer a writer.

5. Rhythm

Read your sentences aloud to judge whether they have a pleasant, smooth-flowing rhythm. Avoid the careless repetition of similar or identical syllables or words. *Un*planned repetition will *un*doubtedly produce *un*rhythmic, *un*pleasant sentences that will *un*settle your readers. If a sentence contains a compound part, place the shorter part first. Doing these things will give your sentences a smoothness that adds to the rhythmic appeal of your writing.

Work hard to incorporate these devices as you write. They will help you to produce compositions that others find enjoyable and impressive. As you read the following essay, notice how the writer has used the elements of effective style to make his composition appealing.

Mountain Musings

	Man has a love for the mountains, but most of that
Repeated words	love is mere spectator love. He enjoys watching the west-
Figurative language	ern mountains extinguish the fires of the day. He thrills
Picturesque language	at the heart-stopping splendor of the snowcapped peaks.
Balanced sentence	But as long as a mountain does not hinder a man, the
	man usually does not bother the mountain.
	Life contains mountains other than those massive
Alliteration	mounds of rocks and ice. It contains peaks of danger,
	difficulty, and discouragement. These are the real moun-
	tains of life; and though they are less charming, they are
Repeated syllables	just as challenging. God intends these mountains as tests
	and contests to make us mountaineers for Him.

Repeated syllables Alliteration Repeated syllables Rhyme	Mountains have the ability to prove and improve our strength. God does not intend us to skirt them but to scale them. He expects us to face life's challenges as "more than conquerors." He has promised that no mountain will ever be insurmountable. With that assurance and with firm endurance, we shall conquer any peak.
   Alliteration and assonance Repeated syllables Alliteration and assonance	From a mountain summit, we have a clearer perspective of life. We can better place where we are and plot our course for the future. It is a time of triumph over trials and delight over defeat—a foretaste of the future. We often speak of these as our mountaintop experiences. But remember, it is only the mountaineer who stands at the mountaintop. We shall never gain the summit by gazing at it from the valley.
  Alliteration and assonance	Mountains make us more like our Maker. The trifles of life will grow dim in the distance as we rise to higher ground. The upward trail is rough and rugged, but it leads ever homeward to God. When we finally stand on that holy hill of Zion and look back on the heights we have climbed, we shall surely sing, "It has been worth it all."

—Selected and adapted

Applying the Lesson

Write a composition of 150–200 words, using one of the following titles. Put special effort into applying the five elements of effective writing style that you have studied.

1. Voices of the Valley (Show parallels between valleys and the humiliating experiences of life.)
2. Drawn by the Dawn (Show parallels between the dawn and our forward look.)
3. Secrets of the Snow (Draw spiritual lessons from the snow.)
4. Lessons From Man's Best Friend (Show parallels for developing friendships. The following proverb may stimulate your thinking: "A dog is man's best friend because he wags his tail and not his tongue.")
5. Taught by the Trees (Draw lessons from trees, such as their standing upright in spite of storms.)
6. Leaf Lessons (Show parallels between our own lives and the life of a leaf. For example, a small leaf works with many others to accomplish great good.)

110. Chapter 13 Review

A. Copy each prepositional phrase. If a phrase is part of a longer phrase, include it with the longer phrase and also copy it separately. Label each phrase *adj., adv.,* or *n.*

1. Through the power of Christ, we can overcome the world and the forces that work within our own lives.
2. In addition to personal zeal, the power to resist evil requires a full surrender to whatever God's Word teaches.
3. Through God's enabling grace, we can live in complete victory over evil.
4. Below zero degrees is bitterly cold for working in this high wind!
5. Throughout the day, cold drafts came in around the rattly windows of the old house.

B. Copy the conjunctions, and label them *CC* (common coordinating conjunction), *Cor* (correlative conjunction), *SC* (subordinating conjunction), or *CA* (conjunctive adverb).

1. When James Smith moved his family from Quebec and opened a restaurant in Poughkeepsie, New York, he probably had no thought of marketing the first cough drops in America.
2. The following winter, both coughs and sore throats were quite common, so Smith recognized the need for a cold medication.
3. Smith, a candymaker before he moved, was offered a recipe for a good cough remedy; therefore, he paid five dollars for the formula.
4. Before the winter had passed, news of his cough lozenges had spread not only throughout Poughkeepsie but also to neighboring towns.
5. James's sons, Andrew and William, became the famous Smith brothers, whose faces have appeared either on glass jars or on cardboard boxes for nearly 150 years.
6. Various competitors produced cough drops similar both in formula and in name; nevertheless, the Smith brothers saw their production soar from five pounds a day to five tons a day.

C. Write enough of each sentence to show how to correct the mistake in it.

1. Mocking another person is evil for that reproaches the Creator.
2. We must avoid not only the profane words but the seemingly innocent idle words.
3. Our carnal nature gives rise to selfish thoughts and words, however we must choose by God's grace to cultivate noble thoughts that will produce noble words.
4. Our speech reveals much about our attitudes and what we consciously think.
5. Our words either reveal a godly character or a carnal character.

D. Rewrite each sentence, joining the clauses with a suitable subordinating conjunction instead of with *and.* You may change the order of the clauses if you wish.

1. Peter has been complaining about his meals so often, and he shall have only water and a piece of dry bread for lunch today.

2. He is eating his meager lunch, and he should think about the many who would be glad to have the foods he complained about.
3. This dog is very friendly, and he likes to jump up on people.
4. My sister Vera teaches school at Glendale, and she will board with Uncle Lewis's.
5. Father must leave to teach at Bible school, and we hope to have the unloader fixed.

E. Copy each interjection, the word before it (if there is one), and the word after it. Use correct capitalization and punctuation, and underline any word that should be italicized.
   1. Hallelujah the Lord has answered our prayers.
   2. Before this week, we hardly knew what to do; but lo God has clearly shown us the answer.
   3. What you have not heard the perplexing predicament that Father is facing?
   4. Strange the accusations he faced made no sense at all.
   5. Well after a little investigation, the authorities recognized that the accusations were false.
   6. Bang the door slammed in my face.

F. Rewrite each sentence so that it communicates the same idea without an idiom.
   1. That peacock likes to show off his bright colors.
   2. I was tempted to give a sharp reply, but I held my tongue.
   3. Father walked ahead, and the children brought up the rear.
   4. It is usually best to take your time in making a major decision.
   5. Your kitten looks for all the world like a baby leopard.
   6. This cold lemonade really hits the spot.
   7. For some reason, the newcomer seemed to have it in for me.
   8. If your expenses exceed your income, you will soon be in the hole.

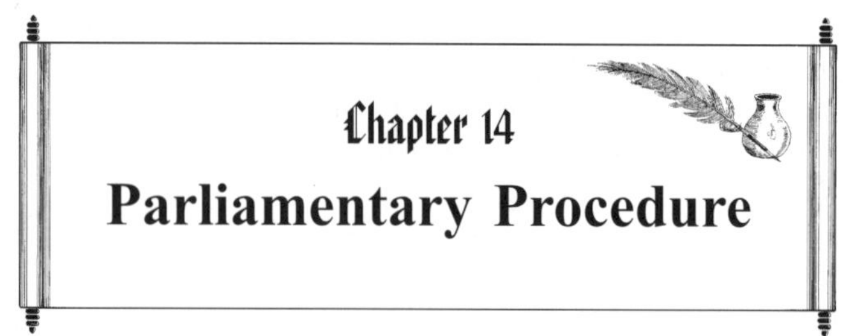

111. Introduction to Parliamentary Procedure

Any group, committee, board, or congregation needs an orderly way to conduct business and make decisions. This order gives them an efficient method for planning and discussing matters to determine the will of the group on any given issue. ***Parliamentary procedure*** is a set of rules providing an orderly way to transact group business. Parliamentary procedure serves four basic purposes.

1. To determine the true intent of the assembly.
2. To allow full, free, and frank discussion.
3. To give a fair hearing to the minority.
4. To assure that the will of the majority is done.

Parliamentary procedure is a courteous, democratic way to accomplish business and to make decisions, but it is *not* the means of determining principles of truth. The Bible is the final authority for sound doctrine. Parliamentary procedure can be used to decide policies or practices that harmonize with Scriptural principles, but it can in no way establish, change, or abolish divine truth.

In this chapter, you will learn some of the basic things involved in parliamentary procedure. These lessons present the proceedings as followed in standard, formal practice. In our church committees and boards, however, we use a less formal version of parliamentary procedure.

Conducting a Meeting With Parliamentary Procedure

A formal meeting begins when the chairman stands before the group and calls the meeting to order. The following example portrays the upper grade students at Yorktown Mennonite School using parliamentary procedure to conduct a business meeting. For the sake of practice, they are imagining that they are responsible for the operation of the school. The teacher is the chairman; and rather than addressing him with the formal *Mr. Chairman,* the students call him *Brother Clyde.*

CHAIRMAN: The meeting will now come to order. Darwin Eberly will lead us in an opening prayer. [Darwin leads in prayer.]

CHAIRMAN: The secretary will now read the minutes of the last meeting.

SECRETARY: The upper grade class of Yorktown Mennonite School held a meeting in the classroom on Friday, March 3, 20—, at 2:00 P.M. Brother Clyde, our teacher, presided.

The minutes of the previous meeting were read. Richard Steiner noted that the secretary had recorded the date of the last meeting incorrectly. The minutes were approved as corrected.

Dean Martin moved that we purchase more stones for our parking area. Ronald Heath proposed an amendment to specify fine stones. The amendment carried. The motion carried as amended.

Kenneth Bucher moved that the meeting be adjourned. The motion carried.

Respectfully submitted,
Brian Hostetter, Secretary

CHAIRMAN: Are there any additions or corrections to the reading of the minutes? [Pause.] The minutes stand approved as read.

Brian Hostetter has been serving as our secretary. His term expired on the last day of March, so our first item of business today is to elect a new secretary. Nominations for secretary are now in order.

KENNETH: [rising] Brother Clyde.

CHAIRMAN: Kenneth.

KENNETH: I nominate Gary Lehman.

DEAN: [rising] Brother Clyde.

CHAIRMAN: Dean.

DEAN: I nominate Lynn Shank.

NEVIN AND MARCUS: [rising] Brother Clyde.

CHAIRMAN: Nevin. [The chairman called on Nevin because he recognized him first.]

NEVIN: I nominate Dean Martin.

CHAIRMAN: Marcus. [Marcus had remained standing.]

MARCUS: I move that nominations cease.

KENNETH: [remaining seated] I second the motion.

CHAIRMAN: It has been moved and seconded that nominations cease. All those in favor, raise your right hands. [Pause.] Those opposed, raise your right hands. [Pause.] The motion is carried. Richard and Kenneth will hand out the ballots and serve as tellers. The nominees for secretary are Gary Lehman, Lynn Shank, and Dean Martin. Write the name of one of these on your ballot. Then turn your ballot over and pass it to the front. [The tellers collect and count the votes.]

Lynn Shank has been elected as secretary.

There is no old business to dispose of. Is there any new business?

ARNOLD: [rising] Brother Clyde.

CHAIRMAN: Arnold.

ARNOLD: I move that we patch the cracked plaster on our classroom walls, and that we repaint the walls a light green.

BRIAN: I second the motion.

CHAIRMAN: It has been moved and seconded that we patch the cracked plaster on our classroom walls, and that we repaint the walls a light green. Is there any discussion?

DEAN: [rising] Brother Clyde.

CHAIRMAN: Dean.

DEAN: It seems to me that the plaster is in rather poor shape. That corner beside the bookshelves is not merely cracked; a piece of plaster is missing. I wonder if just patching the plaster will be satisfactory.

RICHARD: [rising] Brother Clyde.

CHAIRMAN: Richard.

RICHARD: I agree with Dean. After all, this plaster has been on the walls for a long time. I move that we replace the aging plaster on our classroom walls, and that we paint the walls a light green.

CHAIRMAN: Your motion is out of order, Richard, because a main motion is pending.

KENNETH: [rising] Brother Clyde.

CHAIRMAN: Kenneth.

KENNETH: I move that the motion be amended to say that the plaster be replaced instead of being patched.

RICHARD: I second the motion.

CHAIRMAN: It has been moved and seconded that the motion be amended to say that the plaster be replaced instead of being patched. Is there any discussion?

NEVIN: [rising] Brother Clyde.

CHAIRMAN: Nevin.

NEVIN: Are we sure we want to remove and replace all that old plaster? That could become quite expensive.

DEAN: [rising] Brother Clyde.

CHAIRMAN: Dean.

DEAN: I hadn't considered the expense. We should perhaps check some prices.

WAYNE: [rising] Brother Clyde.

CHAIRMAN: Wayne.

WAYNE: I really don't think most of the plaster is in such bad shape. Those few places where it is chipped out can be repaired quite easily. [A number of students nod their heads. The chairman waits a bit for more discussion.]

CHAIRMAN: Since there is no more discussion, we are now ready to vote. It has been moved and seconded that the motion be amended to say that the plaster would be replaced instead of patched. Those in favor, say "Aye." [A few say, "Aye."] Those opposed, say "Nay." [An obvious majority says, "Nay."] The motion is defeated.

The original motion is again on the floor, that we patch the cracked plaster on our classroom walls, and that we repaint the walls a light green. Is there any further discussion?

RONALD: [rising] Brother Clyde.
CHAIRMAN: Ronald.
RONALD: I move that we refer the question to the Maintenance Committee to investigate and report back with specific plans and cost estimates at our regular May meeting.
LYNN: I second the motion.
CHAIRMAN: It has been moved and seconded that we refer the question to the Maintenance Committee to investigate and report back with specific plans and cost estimates at our regular May meeting. Is there any discussion? [Pause.] Those in favor of the motion, raise your right hands. [Pause.] Those opposed, raise your right hands. [Pause.] The motion carries.
MARCUS: [rising] Brother Clyde.
CHAIRMAN: Marcus.
MARCUS: I move that the meeting be adjourned.
KENNETH: I second the motion.
CHAIRMAN: It has been moved and seconded that the meeting be adjourned. Those in favor, say "Aye." [Pause.] Those opposed, say "Nay." [Pause.] The motion carries, and the meeting is adjourned.

The Basic Order of Business

A meeting should follow a basic order of business. This will vary somewhat according to the nature of the meeting and the level of formality required. Here is a typical order of business.

1. *The chairman calls the meeting to order.* Depending on the nature of the meeting, the chairman will call on a member to have a devotional meditation, to lead in an opening prayer, or to lead the group in singing. A good chairman tries to call the meeting to order promptly at the announced time, for this helps to establish a businesslike atmosphere that contributes to order and efficiency throughout the meeting.
2. *The chairman asks for the reading of the minutes.* After they are read, the chairman gives an opportunity for additions or corrections. Then he should rule that "The minutes stand approved as read" or that "The minutes stand approved as corrected."
3. *The chairman calls for the treasurer's report.* After the report, he should ask if anyone has any questions about it. The group is not asked to approve the treasurer's report, for the members would probably not have any way of knowing whether it was accurate.
4. *The chairman calls for any committee reports.* A standing, or permanent, committee has an ongoing work; its report often takes the form of a progress report. A special committee may be formed to investigate or make plans relating to a given matter. Its report is a summary of the recommendations they have prepared.
5. *The chairman brings any old business to the floor.* Old business includes any matters unresolved at the adjournment of the previous meeting and any business that had been postponed to the current meeting. Usually, these items are mentioned in the minutes of the previous meeting.

6. *The chairman opens the meeting for new business.* This is the time for members to introduce matters that the group has not considered previously.

7. *The chairman adjourns the meeting.* Adjournment may occur after a motion to adjourn has passed. Or, if all items on the agenda have been properly disposed of and no member presents any more new business, the chairman may simply declare the meeting adjourned.

Applying the Lesson

A. Write the answers.
1. What is parliamentary procedure?
2. Why is order important when a group makes decisions?
3. List the four basic purposes of parliamentary procedure.
4. Why is parliamentary procedure not a safe way to determine truth?
5. How should the members address the chairman of the meeting according to strict parliamentary law? in a Christian assembly?
6. When may a member properly speak without rising?
7. Why should the chairman call the meeting to order at the scheduled time?
8. Why does the chairman not request approval for the treasurer's report as for the minutes?
9. What is old business? new business?

B. Write the seven points in the basic order of business, and memorize them.

C. Study the procedure that was used to elect a secretary in the sample meeting. Be prepared to participate in a meeting for the election of a vice-chairman, a secretary, and a treasurer.

Review Exercises

A. Write the correct term to match each description. [28–32]

bibliography	footnote	theme
exposition	plagiarism	

1. A comment about a detail in an expository essay.
2. The main point of an essay.
3. Copying another's writing and passing it off as your own.
4. A list of the sources used in preparing an essay.

B. Write *true* if the statement is true, or *false* if it is false. [28–35]
1. The purpose of expository writing is to define, clarify, or explain something.
2. The introduction to an exposition should begin with a statement of the theme.
3. Both the introduction and the conclusion should resemble a funnel—starting out with general ideas and ending with specific ideas.
4. You should avoid controversial topics for expositions.
5. After you have done thorough research for your exposition, you should write a statement of purpose to guide your writing.
6. Using at least two sources of information helps to make an essay more complete and more accurate.
7. The abbreviation *ibid.* means "from an anonymous source."

8. You should list the entries in a bibliography in alphabetical order.
9. You should write a footnote for every detail that you draw directly from your notes.
10. You should include in the bibliography every source from which you obtained information, even if you did not directly quote from it.

---

112. Fundamentals of Parliamentary Procedure

Realizing the value of decency and order, men have set up the system known as parliamentary procedure to aid group decision making. For parliamentary procedure to be an efficient process, each participant must understand well his role in the meeting. An orderly meeting illustrates the Scriptural command, "Let all things be done decently and in order" (1 Corinthians 14:40).

The Various Offices

If a meeting is to function smoothly, the group must have qualified persons in the various offices. The four most common offices are chairman, vice-chairman, secretary, and treasurer. The *chairman,* often called simply *the chair,* bears the primary responsibility for the overall progress of a meeting. He calls the meeting to order and asks for reports from the secretary, the treasurer, and any committee with business to report.

The most important part of the chairman's responsibility is presiding over the actual business of the meeting. He guides the discussion by giving members ***the floor*** (the right to address the assembly); he conducts the voting and announces the outcome; and he adjourns the meeting. Generally, the chairman reserves his right to vote for those occasions when he wishes to make or break a tie vote. In all these responsibilities, the chairman must make sure that the group observes the rules of parliamentary procedure as well as the constitution and bylaws of the specific organization.

The *vice-chairman* is the chairman's assistant. He presides over the meeting when the chairman is absent or when an action involves the chairman, as when he is nominated to serve on a committee.

The *secretary* handles the records and correspondence of the group. At the chairman's direction, the secretary writes and answers letters that pertain to the business of the group. His main responsibility, however, is to write the ***minutes*** of each meeting. (They are called minutes because they summarize the small details of the business transacted.)

The minutes stand as the official record of the meeting. Since the secretary does not have time to write everything in full during the meeting, he must learn to take good notes. He should write the complete minutes as soon after the meeting as practical, while the details are still fresh in his mind.

Although the form of the minutes may vary from one organization to another, the minutes should be a brief summary of the actual proceedings of the meeting. The secretary should strive for conciseness and clarity in writing the minutes.

The minutes should follow a consistent pattern so that members can easily find the information they want. The first paragraph should state the name of the organization; the kind of meeting (regular or special); the place, date, and time of the meeting; the person presiding; and a statement regarding the reading of the minutes.

Depending on the nature of the organization, the next several paragraphs may contain the treasurer's report and reports from various committees. Each report should be given in a separate paragraph.

The bulk of the minutes should record the various items of business transacted during the meeting. Each item of business should be recorded in a separate paragraph. These paragraphs should contain the name of each member who makes a motion, the wording of the motion, and the way in which the motion was disposed of (passed, defeated, or postponed). But they should not include any details of the discussion about the motion or any personal views of the secretary.

The minutes should tell how the meeting was adjourned, and should end with the secretary's signature. The following example shows the form of the minutes read at the meeting described in Lesson 111.

> The upper grade class of Yorktown Mennonite School held a meeting in the classroom on Friday, March 3, 20—, at 2:00 P.M. Brother Clyde, our teacher, presided.
>
> The minutes of the previous meeting were read. Richard Steiner noted that the secretary had recorded the date of the last meeting incorrectly. The minutes were approved as corrected.
>
> Dean Martin moved that we purchase more stones for our parking area. Ronald Heath proposed an amendment to specify fine stones. The amendment carried. The motion carried as amended.
>
> Kenneth Bucher moved that the meeting be adjourned. The motion carried.
>
> Respectfully submitted,
> *Brian Hostetter, Secretary*

The *treasurer* is responsible for the finances of the group. He receives any income and pays any bills associated with the function of the group. He keeps a careful record of all such transactions in an account book. An ***audit*** of these books is made at least once a year. In auditing the books, two or more members of the organization check the accuracy of the treasurer's work. Sometimes one person serves as both secretary and treasurer.

The Work of the Group

The chairman, vice-chairman, secretary, and treasurer fill important roles. The efficiency of a meeting, however, depends also upon the work of each member in the group. The group as a whole, not just the officers, makes the decisions. A ***quorum*** is the minimum number of members that must be present to transact business, as stated in the constitution of the organization. When a quorum is present, the group can conduct its business—make ***motions*** (formal proposals), discuss them, offer ***amendments*** (changes) to motions, and vote on them. The members of the group serve on committees and make nominations.

Whatever your responsibility in a business meeting, try to understand it and do your best to fulfill it. If you have been appointed to leadership, fill that place to the best of your ability. If your place is found with the majority of the group, do your part in thinking seriously about the decisions to be made. Participate in group discussions so that others know your feelings and preferences. And whether you agree or disagree with the decisions of the group, do your best in giving them your support.

Voting Procedures

The whole idea of making motions and discussing them is to prepare the group for a final decision about a matter. When the chairman thinks that the group has amply discussed an issue and knows what decision they intend to make, he calls for a vote to be taken. The chairman can use any one of several specific methods of voting.

1. *Vote by general consent.* The chairman may use this method of voting when he can sense the general agreement of the group, especially on a procedural matter. For example, after the secretary reads the minutes, the chairman asks, "Are there any additions or corrections to the reading of the minutes?" If there are additions or corrections, they should come from the assembly then. In essence, those who remain silent are giving their consent to the minutes as they were read, and those who offer additions or corrections will give their consent after the minutes are changed. Using this basis for general consent, the chairman simply rules, "The minutes stand approved as read" or "The minutes stand approved as corrected."
2. *Vote by acclamation.* Those in favor say "Aye" (pronounced like *eye*); then those opposed say "Nay." This method is used mainly when the chairman knows that the vote will be unanimous or nearly unanimous. It cannot show the will of the group if the vote is close (nearly a tie).
3. *Vote by a show of hands.* Those in favor raise their right hands; then those opposed raise their hands. This allows the chairman to make an exact count of the vote, which is important when the vote is close or when a member questions the ruling of the chairman. The show of hands is the most common method for taking an exact vote on general matters.
4. *Rising vote.* Those in favor rise to their feet; then those opposed rise to their feet. Like the show of hands, this allows the chairman to make an exact count of the vote.
5. *Vote by secret ballot.* The chairman either hands out ballots or appoints tellers to do so. Each member writes his vote on a ballot. In a large assembly, this is the simplest way to establish an accurate count of the votes. It is also appropriate for electing officers and voting on sensitive issues. In a vote by secret ballot, the chairman may vote during the balloting, but he may not vote after the ballots are counted.

Most motions require a simple majority to pass. A simple majority occurs when the ayes have at least one more vote than the nays. A few motions require a two-thirds majority vote to pass. In particular, a two-thirds majority vote is required to pass a motion that would limit the free discussion of the group. For example, after some discussion on a matter, a member may move that the discussion be closed and the matter be brought to a vote. His motion will pass only if a two-thirds majority votes in favor of it.

A motion does not pass if the vote is a tie. In the event of a tie, the chairman may cast a positive vote to break the tie, thus causing the motion to pass. Or if a motion were to pass by only one vote, the chairman may cast a negative vote to create a tie and defeat the motion. If ballots are used, however, the chairman may not cast a vote to change the outcome after the ballots are counted.

Main Motions

A motion is a proposal to discuss or act upon an item of business. Any member except the chairman may make motions. The person making a motion should state it clearly and specifically. A wide variety of motions is available for the members to use in pursuing the business of the assembly. The chart in Lesson 114 summarizes the motions used most often.

Main motions carry the primary business in a meeting. Look at the sample in Lesson 111 as you study the following steps in making and disposing of a main motion. Arnold's motion to patch the cracked plaster is an example of a main motion.

1. A member stands and addresses the chairman to get his attention. If more than one person stands at the same time, the chairman calls on the one he recognizes first.
2. The member states his motion and sits down. He should say, "I move that…" or "I move to…" He should not say, "I make a motion that…"
3. Another member must second the motion. Requiring a second ensures that more than just one person in the assembly supports the idea. If a motion receives no second, it dies for lack of support, and a new motion may come to the floor.
4. The chairman repeats the motion in its original wording.
5. The assembly discusses the motion. Members should express their opinions freely so that the group can reach a proper understanding before voting.
6. After the members have adequately discussed the motion, the chairman repeats the motion and puts it to the assembly for a vote.
7. The chairman announces the result of the voting.

Applying the Lesson

A. Write the correct term for each description.
1. A formal proposal for the group to consider.
2. A change in the wording of a proposal.
3. The minimum number of members that must be present to transact business.
4. The [illegible] record of the time and place of a meeting, and of the business transacted.
5. A check of the accuracy of the treasurer's records.
6. The right to address the assembly.
7. A proposal of the kind used primarily to carry the business of an assembly.

B. For each description, write *chairman, vice-chairman, secretary, treasurer,* or *group.*

1. Keeps account of money matters of the group.
2. Presents motions and makes up the main voting body.
3. Calls the meeting to order.
4. Keeps detailed records of the meetings.
5. Takes the place of an absent chairman.
6. Adjourns the meeting.
7. Discusses motions and amendments.
8. Designates who shall have the floor.
9. Writes and answers letters pertaining to the business of the group.
10. Is primarily responsible to see that the rules of parliamentary procedure and the constitution and bylaws are observed.
11. Receives any income and pays any bills.

C. Write *general consent, acclamation, show of hands, rising,* or *secret ballot* for each description. Some require more than one answer.

1. Is especially suited for elections and sensitive issues.
2. Is used primarily for procedural matters, such as approving the minutes.
3. Allows the chairman to take an exact count.
4. Cannot show the will of the group if the vote is close.
5. Is used when the chairman senses that the group is largely in agreement.

D. Do these exercises.

1. Why must the chairman be well acquainted with the rules of parliamentary procedure?
2. Write the letter of the statement that is *not* true about the minutes of a meeting.
   a. They should include the wording of each motion that was acted upon.
   b. They should express facts about the meeting, not opinions of the secretary.
   c. They should include details about the time and place of the meeting.
   d. They should include specific details about the discussion on each motion.
   e. They should have a separate paragraph for each item of business recorded.
3. If you are a member of the group, how can you help to make the meeting a profitable one?
4. What should you do if the group decision is different from the way you preferred?
5. If twenty members vote on a motion, how many ayes are needed for it to pass by a simple majority?
6. When is a two-thirds majority vote required for a motion to pass?
7. Why would a chairman cast a vote to cause a tie vote?
8. Why would he cast a vote to break a tie vote?

E. Conduct a parliamentary meeting, using the following imaginary situation. Your teacher will appoint specific students to fill the various roles. Each student should act as a secretary and write minutes for the meeting.

CHAIRMAN: Calls the meeting to order, and calls for the reading of the minutes.

SECRETARY: Reads the following minutes:

The monthly meeting of the Room 4 students at Brockton Valley Mennonite School was held in the classroom on January 5, 20—, at 2:15 P.M. Brother Bradley, our teacher, served as chairman.

The minutes of the previous meeting were read and approved.

Raymond Steffy moved that we ask Wadel's Woodshop to make a new Ping-Pong table. Noah Weber moved to amend the motion by specifying a new folding Ping-Pong table. The amendment carried. The motion carried as amended.

Clarence Oberholtzer moved that we buy two new snow shovels for clearing the walks and steps outside. The motion carried.

Since there was no further business, the meeting was adjourned.

Respectfully submitted,
Leonard Brubacher, Secretary

CHAIRMAN: Takes proper action on the reading of the minutes. Opens the meeting for new business.

STUDENT A: Following proper form, moves that the upper grade boys use a series of art periods to design and make two racks for holding Ping-Pong paddles and balls.

STUDENT B: Properly seconds the motion. [Open discussion follows.]

STUDENT C: Suggests that perhaps they should ask Wadel's Woodshop to make them.

STUDENT D: Replies that this project is small enough to be manageable for the students at school.

STUDENT A: States that this would make an interesting and worthwhile project for the boys.

CHAIRMAN: When discussion lags, calls for a vote by a show of hands; announces the result; asks for any other new business.

STUDENT E: Moves that while the boys work on their project, the girls have knitting lessons.

STUDENT D: Seconds the motion. [Open discussion follows.]

STUDENT F: Comments that Sister Matilda enjoys knitting and would probably be willing and able to come and teach the girls.

STUDENT B: States that it sounds like a good idea.

CHAIRMAN: Calls for a vote by acclamation; announces the result; asks for any other new business. When no other business comes to the floor, adjourns the meeting.

Review Exercises

A Name the tense of the underlined verb in each sentence. [74]

1. In 1898, H. Cecil Booth <u>watched</u> a demonstration of a new machine that forced air down into a carpet, causing dirt to billow up into an attached box.
2. When he asked the operator about the possibility of sucking the dust up, the man replied, "You <u>may try</u> it, but no one has yet succeeded with the idea."

3. After he <u>had thought</u> about the idea for several days, he experimented by sucking on the back of a plush seat in a restaurant.
4. Although he choked violently on the dust, he <u>was inspired</u> to try his idea.
5. He declared to himself, "I <u>shall experiment</u> with various fabrics to serve as dust collectors."
6. As he lay at home sucking at his carpet with various fabrics over his lips, he may have thought, "I shall choke to death before I <u>shall have found</u> a way to make a suction sweeper."
7. Before such a calamity, however, he discovered that a tightly woven cloth handkerchief <u>traps</u> dust well as it allows air to pass through it freely.
8. The world <u>has benefited</u> greatly from Mr. Booth's invention of the vacuum cleaner.

B. Identify the form of each underlined verb as simple (*S*), progressive (*P*), or emphatic (*E*). [77]
1. The first vacuum cleaners that Mr. Booth <u>made</u> were huge machines the size of modern refrigerators, and soon they <u>were extracting</u> large amounts of dirt from numerous buildings.
2. When Booth <u>was cleaning</u> the Westminster Abbey for the 1901 coronation of Edward VII, his machine extracted so much dirt that he <u>did receive</u> stares of amazement from the cleaning staff.
3. During World War I, Booth's machine <u>received</u> even greater publicity at London's Crystal Palace, where naval reserve men <u>had been dying</u> at epidemic rates from spotted fever.
4. The doctors <u>did</u> not <u>know</u> how to stop the epidemic, but they <u>did express</u> their suspicion that dirt in the palace was harboring disease germs.
5. The epidemic <u>did come</u> to an end after fifteen of Booth's vacuum cleaners <u>were used</u> to clean the palace.
6. Workers <u>hauled</u> away twenty-six truckloads of dirt before the authorities <u>declared</u> the building clean.

---

113. Improving Your Editing Skills, Part 10

"Among all this people [the soldiers of Benjamin] there were seven hundred chosen men lefthanded; every one could sling stones at an hair breadth, and not miss" (Judges 20:16). When we read this verse, we say, "What amazing skill!" These men did better with slings than many people do today with rifles having high-powered scopes! How did they develop that kind of skill? Certainly they did not attain it in one day or even one year. These men must have practiced constantly, day after day and month after month. As the familiar saying goes, "Practice makes perfect."

You have worked through nine lessons on editing skills. You have practiced your proofreading skills on various composition lessons. Perhaps you have also used these skills on other occasions. Do you now qualify as an expert proofreader? Probably not. But like the Benjamites with their slings, you have practiced and your ability has improved. This editing lesson will be a final test of the skills you have developed.

Marks Used in Editing and Proofreading

∨ or ∧ insert (caret)	delete	.... stet (let it stand)	——— use italics
¶ begin new paragraph	no ¶ no new paragraph	lc change to lowercase (small letter)	uc change to uppercase (capital letter)
# insert space	⁀‿ delete space	← move (arrow)	transpose

Editing Practice

A. Use proofreading marks to correct the ten spelling or spacing errors in the following paragraph. Some lines have more than one error, and some have none.

The praying mantis, a wellcome guest in any garden, can destroy alarge number of harmful insect pests. While it pateintly waits for a meal, the mantis holds its claws in a position that resembles a person praying. The mantis flies occasionally, but it spends most of its time on geen plants were it is nearly invisible. Standing motion lessly for long periods of time, the mantis waits until an unsuspecting insect comes to near. Suddenly the mantis's fore legs snap out; and the next instant, the mantis is holding a victem tightly in its grip.

B. Use proofreading marks to make these corrections in the paragraph below.

a. Divide the selection into two paragraphs.
b. Correct two errors in joining or separating clauses.
c. Improve the word order in two places.

A dormant twig is interesting to observe. Even though it looks completely bare. One thing you can see is the signs of present life. At the end of each healthy, undamaged

4. twig is a terminal bud, which causes the twig to grow in
5. length. You will also along the sides see numerous lateral
6. buds, which will develop new stems, flowers, or leaves.
7. Another thing you can observe is the evidence of life in
8. previous growing seasons. Bud-scale scars form at irregular
9. intervals rings around the stem, showing where each year's
10. growth stopped. The age of any branch equals the number
11. of these bud-scale scars. As you look over the branch,
12. you should also see lighter patches, or nodes, on the
13. bark. Each node indicates a place where a leaf had grown,
14. each one has a rim of tiny scars that mark where the sap
15. flowed from the stem to the leaf and back again.

C. Use proofreading marks to correct all the errors in this essay. No line has more than one error. Move the word *only* in line 11 to a different place in the sentence. Also join the paragraph beginning in line 14 to the preceding paragraph.

1. Is there inteligent life somewhere in this vast universe
2. other than on the earth. This question intrigues many
3. astronomers as they investigate the broad expanse of outer
4. of space. Assuming that man came into being by chance, they
5. wonder if chance has produced life some where else too.
6. These men do more than wonder; they are busy searching.
7. They think that discovering life elsewhere would give man
8. kind a new purpose and a greater faith in the future.
9. One of their search methods, is to monitor the radio
10. waves from the heavens, watching for patterns that could
11. only be produced by intelligent beings somewhere beyond us.
12. The child of God has different thoughts as turns his
13. eyes heavenward.
14. He has no interest in receiving messages from unknown,
15. illusory Beings. He has already received a message from
16. the heavens—the inspired word of God!

The Christian finds purpose in life by excepting and submitting to this message he gains an unshakable faith in the future by believing its promises. "Blessed the is man that trusteth in the Lord, and whose hope the Lord is (Jeremiah 17:7.

---

114. Parliamentary Motions

There are four categories of parliamentary motions. In Lesson 112 you studied the main motion, which is in a category by itself. But sometimes a question demands attention before the main motion is disposed of. Such a question may or may not be directly related to the motion under discussion. When such questions arise, the assembly uses motions from the other three categories: privileged motions, subsidiary (səb·sid′·ē·er′·ē) motions, and incidental motions.

The Precedence of Motions

The motions that may come to the floor must follow a definite order. This order is called the ***precedence*** of motions, and it is determined by the rank of motions in relation to each other—that is, the order in which they must come to discussion and vote. Only one main motion may be ***pending*** (on the floor) at any given time. Depending on circumstances, however, one or more motions of the other three categories may be brought to the floor while a main motion is pending.

Whenever a motion is pending, only a motion that ranks higher in precedence may be presented. On the chart on the next page, each motion has precedence over all the ones below it. For example, suppose a main motion (number 11 on the chart) is on the floor. It would be allowable for someone to move to refer the motion to a committee (number 9). At this point another member could move to take a recess (number 3). This places three motions on the floor for consideration.

These motions must now be disposed of according to their precedence, from highest to lowest rank—number 3 first, number 9 second, and number 11 third. This is exactly the reverse of the order in which they were presented.

The chart on pages 440–441 summarizes the main details about a number of parliamentary motions. The chart lists the motions in order from highest to lowest rank. The motions that are most likely to contribute to efficiency in church business meetings and other church-related work are shaded for ready reference. Additional comments about these selected motions are given below.

Further Comments on Selected Motions

1. *Question of privilege.* This motion generally deals with unfavorable conditions in the meeting room. For example, a member might rise to a question of privilege if he cannot hear a speaker, if there is some disturbance among the members, or if the

room needs better ventilation. If the matter requires immediate attention, a member may interrupt a speaker with this motion.

2. *Point of order.* A member rises to a point of order when he observes a violation of a rule of parliamentary procedure that the chairman does not correct. He would use this motion, for example, if the chairman allowed two main motions on the floor at the same time. The member should immediately rise to his feet, interrupting the meeting if necessary, and say, "Mr. Chairman, I rise to a point of order." The chair should say, "You may state your point." After the member explains his point and sits down, the chairman states his decision on the matter.

3. *Lay on the table.* This motion sets aside a pending motion until the assembly votes to bring it back to the floor. If a motion is laid on the table, all other motions attached to it are automatically laid on the table as well. A tabled motion cannot be brought back to the floor during the same meeting in which it was tabled unless at least one other item of business has been disposed of. If the tabled motion is not brought back to the floor by the end of the next meeting, the question dies. In that case, the subject must be reintroduced as an altogether new main motion before it can be considered again.

4. *Previous question.* The term *previous question* refers to the most recently stated motion, the motion that is presently on the floor. Many people misunderstand the proper order of events when someone moves the previous question. One member's calling for the previous question does not force the pending motion to an immediate vote. Rather, this motion requires a second and a two-thirds affirmative vote to pass (because it limits the discussion of the group). If the vote on the previous question passes, the chair must immediately call for a vote on the pending motion. If the vote on the previous question is defeated, the group may continue debate on the pending motion.

5. *Postpone to definite time.* This motion postpones the pending motion to a definite hour, day, or meeting. However, the motion cannot be postponed beyond the next session of the assembly. Unlike the motion to lay on the table, this motion means that the question must again be brought to the floor at a specified time and without a vote to do so. If it is postponed to the next meeting, it automatically comes up as unfinished business in the reading of the minutes then.

6. *Refer to committee.* This motion refers the pending motion to a committee for further investigation before the motion comes to a vote. When a motion is referred to a committee, the following questions need to be answered:

   a. Is the motion referred to a standing committee, a special committee, or the committee of the whole? (The committee of the whole is the same as the assembly, but it allows more informal rules of discussion than the assembly does.)

   b. If the motion is referred to a special committee, how many members shall the committee comprise, and how shall the members be selected? (Members of a committee may be appointed by the chairman, they may be chosen by nominations and voting of the assembly, or they may be named by the person making the motion.)

   c. What is the committee's specific assignment, and when shall it report back to the assembly?

Parliamen

	May Interrupt Speaker	Second Required	Debatable	Amendable	Vote Required	M R si
Privileged Motions						
1. Adjourn to a certain time	No	Yes	No	Yes	Maj.	
2. Adjourn	No	Yes	No	No	Maj.	
3. Take a recess	No	Yes	No	Yes	Maj.	
4. Question of privilege	Yes (1)	No	No	No	(2)	
Incidental Motions (These motions have no rank among themselves.)						
Closing nominations	No	Yes	No	No	2/3	
Withdrawal of a motion	No	No	No	No	(3)	Y
Point of order	Yes	No	No	No	None	
Subsidiary Motions						
5. Lay on the table	No	Yes	No	No	Maj.	
6. Previous question	No	Yes	No	No	2/3	
7. Limit or extend debate	No	Yes	No	Yes	2/3	
8. Postpone to definite time	No	Yes	Yes	Yes	Maj.	
9. Refer to committee	No	Yes	Yes	Yes	Maj.	Y
10. Amend	No	Yes	Yes	Yes	Maj.	
11. **Main Motion**	No	Yes	Yes	Yes	Maj.	
Specific Main Motions						
Take from the table	No	Yes	No	No	Maj.	
Reconsider	Yes	Yes	Yes	No	Maj.	

(1) If it requires immediate attention.
(2) Chair usually decides; majority if put to a vote.
(3) If chair has stated the motion, a majority vote is required if a
member objects to the withdrawal.
(4) Negative vote only.

ns

Purpose	Acceptable Forms
ne for the next meeting.	"I move that when we adjourn, we adjourn to [specific time]."
eting.	"I move that we adjourn."
n intermission during a pro- neeting.	"I move to take a recess for [specific time]."
mmediate action relating to rights, or privileges.	"I rise to a question of privilege."
r nominations.	"I move that nominations cease."
ember who stated a motion aw it from the floor.	"I withdraw my motion." "I request permission to withdraw my motion." (5)
ion to a violation of a rule.	"I rise to a point of order."
he pending question until the tes to return it to the floor.	"I move to lay the question on the table."
ate and brings the pending to an immediate vote.	"I move the previous question." "I move to vote immediately on the motion."
r lengthens the time agreed the debate of a motion.	"I move to limit [extend] debate until [specific time]." "I move to limit [extend] the speaker's time to [specific time]."
the pending question to a time.	"I move to postpone the question until [specific time]."
uestion to a committee for tion before vote. (7)	"I move to refer the question to a committee." (7)
e content of motion.	"I move to amend the motion by [specific change]."
new business.	"I move that [to] . . ."
bled motion to the floor.	"I move to take from the table the motion to . . ."
notion that has been acted he floor.	"I move to reconsider the vote on . . ."

) If chair has stated the motion, member says, "I request permission to withdraw . . ."

) If the committee has not begun its work.

) May specify a standing committee or assign the chair to appoint a committee.

A member may simply move to refer the question to a committee and allow the group to decide these other details. If he prefers, he may specify some or all of the details in his motion. Here is an example of a motion to refer to a committee.

> "I move that we refer the question to a committee of three members to be appointed by the chairman. They shall bring carpet samples and prices to our next meeting."

7. *Amend.* This motion to alter another motion is probably the most common one used after the main motion. There are two kinds of amendments: a primary amendment, which is attached to any amendable motion; and a secondary amendment, which is attached to a primary amendment. A secondary amendment cannot be further amended.

An amendment may change the original motion by adding words, removing words, or substituting words. A motion to amend may call for the replacement of an entire paragraph, an entire section, or the complete original motion.

Applying the Lesson

A. Write the name of the specific motion that fits each description.

1. Closes debate and brings the assembly to a vote on a motion.
2. Used if a member notices a violation of a rule that the chairman does not address.
3. Sets a question aside until the assembly votes to bring it back to the floor.
4. Is probably the most common motion other than the main motion.
5. Used if a member cannot hear the speaker.
6. Sets a question aside until a specific time.
7. Alters the wording of a motion.
8. Used if the assembly feels that a subject needs to be investigated further before voting on it.

B. Write the letter of the correct choice.

1. If a motion is pending,
   a. it has been laid aside until later.
   b. it is currently under discussion by the assembly.
2. If a member wishes to set a question aside for debate at the next meeting, he should move to
   a. table the question.
   b. postpone the question to a definite time.
3. If a member moves the previous question, he wishes to
   a. bring the question on the floor to a vote.
   b. raise a question about the last speaker's comments.
4. Suppose the previous question has been moved and seconded. According to the principle of precedence, another member may now move to
   a. amend the motion. b. take a recess.
5. Two motions are on the floor: a motion to take a recess and a motion to lay the question on the table. According to the principle of precedence, which motion must be acted on first?
   a. Take a recess b. Lay on the table

6. Which motion requires a higher percentage of votes to pass?
   a. Closing nominations
   b. Referring to a committee

C. Conduct a parliamentary meeting, using the following imaginary situation. Your teacher will appoint specific students to fill the various roles. Each student should act as a secretary and take minutes of the meeting. Each student should be free to rise to a point of order at any appropriate time. (There will be no reading of minutes from a previous meeting in this exercise.)

CHAIRMAN: Calls the meeting to order and opens the floor for new business.
STUDENT A: Moves to install an exhaust fan to help ventilate the school.
STUDENT B: Seconds the motion. [Open discussion follows.]
STUDENT C: Comments that some exhaust fans are quite noisy.
STUDENT D: States that squirrel-cage fans run more quietly and work more efficiently than many other kinds.
STUDENT E: Proposes amendment to change "an exhaust fan" to "a squirrel-cage exhaust fan"
STUDENT F: Seconds the motion. [Open discussion follows.]
STUDENT D: Questions whether anyone in the group has an idea of what it would cost to purchase and install such a fan.
STUDENT B: Says that he wondered about that too and thinks the group needs more information before making any decision.
STUDENT G: Moves to refer the question to a committee, appointed by the chairman, to investigate the costs of purchasing and installing a squirrel-cage exhaust fan. (Remember to specify how many shall be on the committee and when they shall report back to the group.)
STUDENT A: Seconds the motion. [No open discussion follows immediately.]
STUDENT C: Makes a motion of the previous question.
STUDENT E: Seconds the motion.
CHAIRMAN: Calls for a vote by show of hands, and rules on the vote.
CHAIRMAN: Calls for a vote on the main motion, and rules on the vote.
CHAIRMAN: Appoints proper number of students to the committee.
STUDENT F: Moves to adjourn.
STUDENT G: Seconds the motion.
CHAIRMAN: Calls for a vote and announces the result. Adjourns the meeting.

---

115. Chapter 14 Review

A. Give the parliamentary term that fits each description.
   1. Another term for the chairman.
   2. A set of rules providing an orderly way to conduct the business of a group.
   3. Items of business that remain unresolved or postponed from the previous meeting.

4. The principle that determines the order in which motions are disposed of.
5. A check of the accuracy of the treasurer's accounts.
6. A formal suggestion or proposal.
7. A change in the wording of a motion.
8. The minimum number of members that must be present to transact business.
9. One of the motions that carry the primary business in a meeting.
10. The state of a motion when it is on the floor.
11. The official record of the business of a meeting.
12. Items of business that have not previously come before the group.
13. The right to address the assembly.

B. Write the letter of the best answer.

1. Before stating a main motion, a member must
   a. rise to his feet.
   b. address the chairman.
   c. wait for the chairman to call his name.
   d. do all the things above.
2. A member may remain seated to
   a. call attention to a point of order.
   b. second a motion.
   c. nominate someone for election to an office.
   d. do any of the things above.
3. The minutes of a meeting should include all the following *except*
   a. details about the time and place of the meeting.
   b. separate paragraphs for each item of business.
   c. details about the discussion on each motion.
   d. the wording of each motion that was acted upon.
4. The principle of precedence means
   a. that a main motion is put on hold if a member moves to take a recess.
   b. that a member could move to adjourn while a motion to amend is on the floor.
   c. that a motion to lay on the table must come to a vote before a motion to refer to a committee.
   d. all the things above.
5. A motion to amend can
   a. add words to the original motion.
   b. remove words from the original motion.
   c. completely replace the wording of the original motion.
   d. do any of the things above.

C. For each description, write *chairman, vice-chairman, secretary, treasurer,* or *group.*

1. Discusses motions and amendments.
2. Keeps detailed records of the meetings.
3. Receives any income and pays any bills.
4. Presents motions and makes up the main voting body.
5. Takes the place of an absent chairman.
6. Writes and answers letters that pertain to the business of the group.

7. Keeps account of money matters of the group.
8. Determines who may have the floor.

D. Write *general consent, acclamation, hands, rising,* or *secret ballot* for each description. Some require more than one answer.
   1. Allows the chairman to take an exact count.
   2. Is used when the chairman senses that the group is largely in agreement.
   3. Cannot show the will of the group if the vote is close.
   4. Is especially suited for elections and sensitive issues.
   5. Is used primarily for procedural matters, such as approving the minutes.
   6. Is one of the most common methods for taking an exact vote on general matters.

E. Name the motion to be used for each of these purposes.
   1. To address a violation of a rule when the chairman does not address it.
   2. To assign several members to investigate a question before the group votes on it.
   3. To set a time for the next meeting.
   4. To introduce new business.
   5. To change the wording of a motion.
   6. To give a question more or less time on the floor.
   7. To put off further debate on a motion until a specific later time.
   8. To close a meeting.
   9. To keep additional names from being added to a list for an election.
   10. To put off further debate on a motion until the group votes to return it to the floor.
   11. To give the group a break during a long meeting.
   12. To bring back to the floor a motion that had earlier been voted on.
   13. To request action relating to a member's comfort, rights, or privileges.
   14. To take a motion off the floor after you proposed it.
   15. To bring a tabled motion back to the floor.
   16. To end debate on a motion and bring it to a vote.

F. Do these exercises.
   1. List the four basic purposes served by parliamentary procedure.
   2. Why can we not use parliamentary procedure to determine what is truth?
   3. Arrange the following steps in the basic order of a business meeting: treasurer's report, new business, call to order, adjournment, old business, reading of the minutes, committee reports.
   4. List at least three things you should do to help make a meeting flow smoothly and profitably.
   5. What kind of motions can pass only by a two-thirds majority vote?
   6. Why would a chairman cast a vote to break a tie? to make a tie?
   7. Most properly stated motions begin with what words?

Year-end Reviews

116. Final Review 1 (Chapters 1–5)

A. Write correctly each word that has an error in capitalization. For errors in punctuation, write the word before the error and add or omit the mark involved. Each sentence contains three mistakes. (A set of commas or a title counts as one item.)

1. Jesus spoke the following promise to his disciples "But when the Comforter is come, he shall testify of me" (John 15:26).
2. When God called Saul to be an Apostle He promised to do great things through this man
3. Spread the truth of the gospel o Lord over all the world.
4. Jesus' best-known prayer the Lord's Prayer holds a special place in many people's minds nevertheless relatively few live by its principles.
5. Ah these principles to be sure make strong demands on our carnal selfish nature.
6. My Grandfather's house which is a commodious dwelling serves as home to Lily Hoverdale, a young Christian who had to leave her parental home; Sandra Smith, the lower grade teacher at our school, and Martha Boll, a volunteer helper at the Pineville Rest Home.
7. Our Geography books point out how natives in the arctic live quite differently from those who live farther South.
8. Our library here at Lincolnshire Mennonite school has the book *The Way Down is the Way up,* but i have not read it yet.
9. William F. Gockley Sr owns a small machine shop at Johnsonville Illinois.
10. How zealously he serves the lord in his personal affairs, in his business life and in the church
11. Trusting the Lord to watch over us Father drove cautiously on but the storm grew worse, and made driving even more perilous.
12. In the latter part of the eighteenth century many americans were becoming increasingly hostile toward King George's Rule.
13. At our church cleaning is done weekly by the church families Mr. Long rather than by a paid Janitor.
14. Was Ferne glad to have aunt Abigail teach her Sunday School class

B. Each sentence below contains three errors in the use of quotation marks (and related capitalization), italics, dashes, parentheses, brackets, apostrophes, or hyphens. Write enough of each sentence to show the corrections. (A set of marks counts as one item.)

1. The Lord God alone there is no other true God is all powerful, declared Brother Jerry.
2. See then that ye walk circumspectly (accurately; carefully), not as fools, but as wise Ephesians 5:15.
3. "Great aunt Hattie Rutt will turn eighty nine years old this weekend," noted Father, "So I think we as a family should plan to sing for her on Sunday afternoon."
4. You should get the book Our Northern Neighbors and read the chapter The Seal Hunt; its sure to give you some good ideas for your report on seal hunting by the Eskimos.
5. The word anoint does not have two consecutive ns.
6. The soon to be completed highway it will connect Elkdale to Mooseville will certainly be better than the present traffic congested road.
7. In the summer of 97, we took a two week trip to the mission in Guatemala to visit Fathers cousin who is serving there.
8. As the Silver Spray moved slowly up the river, the passengers heard one and two-minute recordings about the pre Columbian ruins that they passed.
9. The rain washed flowers how theyve grown these warm days! are smiling brightly in the morning sunshine.
10. Do you think well get the timing right in the song In Heavenly Love Abiding? asked Keith.

C. Do these exercises on study skills.
1. Why is interest the most important attitude for effective studying?
2. Name three ways to develop self-discipline in your studying.
3. What three noble purposes should motivate your study?
4. Why is having a regular study time valuable?
5. What two types of assignments should you tackle first in a study period?
6. Name at least three qualities of a suitable study environment.
7. How does good posture relate to effective studying?
8. List the five points of the SQ3R study method.
9. What is meant by reviewing actively?
10. List four worthwhile purposes of skimming.
11. What types of information should you include when taking notes on a speaker's topic?
12. How does outlining a lesson force a student to analyze it thoroughly?

D. Copy this outline correctly. Each starred line has at least one mistake.

Magnifying Christ in Our Bodies (Philippians 1)

*I. Paul's Prayer for the Philippians
   A. His personal exercise of prayer
      *1. constancy (vv. 3–5)
      *2. Confident prayer (v. 6)
      *3. Having compassion (vv. 7, 8)

- *B. The pointed expressions he gave
  - 1. Abound in love (v. 9)
  - *2. That they would approve what is excellent (v. 10)
  - *3. Attain full maturity (vv. 10, 11)
- *II. How Paul served Christ
  - *A. He endured persecution
    - *1. in bonds (v. 13)
    - *2. Suffered afflictions (vv. 15, 16)
    - *3. Jeopardy of death (v. 20)
    - *B. The purpose
    - 1. Commitment to the Gospel (v. 17)
    - *2. Desired that Christ be magnified (v. 20)
    - *3. He was surrendered to Christ (vv. 21–26)
    - *4. consistent in life (vv. 27–30)
  - *C. The prize
    - *1. exultation at the spread of the Gospel (vv. 12, 18)
    - *2. He inspired others to speak out (vv. 13, 14)
    - *3. Anticipated a victorious death (v. 21)

E. Label each numbered word group *S* (complete sentence), *F* (fragment), *R* (run-on error), or *E* (elliptical sentence).

[1]"It looks as if it might rain tonight or tomorrow," said Father. [2]"We should try hard to get the corn planted today. [3]If we expect to be selling sweet corn by the middle of July."

[4]"Right. [5]The ground should be in excellent condition now," agreed Timothy. [6]"With a good rain, the seeds should germinate quickly, things should be in good shape in July."

F. Label each underlined word, using the following abbreviations.

S—subject	IO—indirect object
V—verb	OC—objective complement
PA—predicate adjective	OP—object of preposition
PN—predicate nominative	AP—appositive
DO—direct object	DA—noun of direct address

1. [a]Young person, developing a fear of God is extremely [b]important.
2. Indeed, godly fear makes [a]life truly [b]meaningful.
3. True godly fear, the [a]combination of devotion and reverence, has always been an essential [b]foundation for a satisfying life.
4. Without this quality, no [a]man can truly give God His rightful [b]place.
5. When a person fails to give [a]God His rightful place, sin takes control of his [b]life.
6. [illegible]

G. Label each underlined word group *prep.* (prepositional phrase), *vb.* (verbal phrase), *ps.* (phrase of a single part of speech), *D* (dependent clause), or *I* (independent clause). Also label the part of speech for each item (except independent clauses).

1. Many short, simple words [a]<u>in our English language</u> hide amazing word histories [b]<u>that a study of etymologies can uncover</u>.
2. [a]<u>Examining the simple word *barn,*</u> for example, reveals a term [b]<u>deriving from two Old English words</u>.
3. [a]<u>The Old English word *bere* meant "barley,"</u> and the word *ærn* meant "place"; therefore, [b]<u>in the *bere-ærn*</u> was where an Old English farmer stored his barley.
4. By using a dictionary [a]<u>to examine the history of *about,*</u> we can find the meaning of this word [b]<u>when it was first used</u>.
5. [a]<u>In Old English days</u>, the word *about* [b]<u>had been</u> *onbūtan,* meaning "on outside."
6. [a]<u>What was "on the outside"</u> was not far away; hence the word has come to mean "nearby," "nearly," or "around" [b]<u>in Modern English</u>.

H. Label each sentence according to its use (*dec., int., imp., exc.*) and its structure (*S, CD, CX, CD-CX*). End punctuation has been omitted.
1. Will Mother come home from the hospital today, or must she stay for further observation
2. Her speedy recovery has surprised everyone, including her doctor
3. If only the doctor would recognize that the prayer of faith has been effective
4. When he heard about the anointing service, he said nothing; but the look on his face betrayed his skepticism
5. Pray for him, that this experience might lead him toward faith in God

I. Label the word order of each sentence *N* (natural), *I* (inverted,) or *M* (mixed).
1. By her commitment of faith, Ruth the Moabitess found rest among God's people.
2. Along with Ruth's decision to stay with Naomi went her commitment to Naomi's God and Naomi's people.
3. When she left Moab, she made a complete break with her heathen past.
4. The Lord, under whose wings Ruth came to trust, richly rewarded her faith.

J. Label the style of each sentence *L* (loose), *P* (periodic), or *B* (balanced).
1. Faith in prayer is good, but prayer in faith is better.
2. The prayer of faith can work miracles because it links a mortal man to the omnipotent God.
3. If a person truly believes in God's ability and willingness to bless, he will pray regularly.
4. The more we pray about circumstances, the less we will worry about them.

K. Do these exercises on expository essays.
1. What is the goal of all expository writing?
2. How should the introductory paragraph begin, and how should it end?
3. Name three types of concrete details that the writer of exposition should use in developing his paragraphs.

4. What are three good ways to conclude an expository essay?
5. Why should you state the purpose of your essay before you begin doing research?
6. List four reasons why it is wise to use more than one reference source in researching for an essay.
7. What is plagiarism?
8. When taking notes, what three things can you do to help avoid plagiarism?
9. For what three types of information should you write footnotes?
10. What are three important characteristics of an appropriate title?
11. What does the abbreviation *ibid.* mean?
12. What is a bibliography?

L. Choose the standard expressions in parentheses.

1. Abraham demonstrated his (noted, noteworthy, notorious) faith by (almost, most) (always, all ways) building an (altar, alter) when he stopped in his sojourning.
2. Abraham's failure to (raise, rise) such a place of worship during his sojourn in Egypt (implies, infers) that his faith was weaker (than, then) it should (have, of) been.
3. Father (proposed, purposed) a plan to (adapt, adopt) the machine to our needs by using this (ingenious, ingenuous) device, and it (maybe, may be) that his idea will work.
4. Uncle Lewis thinks that (its, it's) (alright, all right) to (precede, proceed) with the plan, but Father is (kind of, somewhat) afraid it will not work.
5. Sometimes one (looses, loses) much time (setting, sitting) in a traffic jam, but in (them, those) times we must be sure (and, to) maintain a patient manner.
6. Rather than (flaunting, flouting) (your, you're) supposed wisdom, you should be willing to (accept, except) the (advice, advise) of others.
7. The influence of one youth with (respectable, respective) behavior goes a long (way, ways) toward helping others to have a right (perspective, prospective) and to behave (good, well).
8. The (comprehensible, comprehensive) data in the (eminent, imminent, immanent) scientist's report (lets, leaves) little doubt (anymore, any more) about the dangers of using tobacco.
9. Although this book was (some, somewhat) better than the other one, Father had to (censor, censure) a small (amount, number) of words from it; now I (can, may) finally read it.
10. (How come, Why) was the bicycle (laying, lying) (behind, in back of) the car, where someone might back (straight, strait) over it without seeing it?

117. Final Review 2 (Chapters 6–9)

A. Write the term that fits each description.

1. The lesson that a story teaches.
2. The struggle or problem that the main character faces.
3. The point of highest intensity in the main character's struggle.
4. The process of portraying story characters.
5. Another name for the main character.
6. A name for a person who opposes the main character.
7. The perspective from which an author writes a story.
8. A perspective in which the author poses as the main character and uses *I* and *me.*
9. A perspective in which the author writes as if he were able to see every character equally well.
10. A perspective in which the author follows one particular character through the story.

B. Answer these questions about short stories.

1. Why can stories often communicate truth more effectively than essays?
2. What three things does a story setting include?
3. What three types of conflict do short stories commonly develop?
4. What are five ways in which the story characters may be portrayed?
5. What is the difference between a subjective and an objective point of view?
6. What are three things that help to make titles appealing?

C. Copy each noun, and label it *concrete* or *abstract.* Also label its gender (*M, F, N, C*).

1. The ten boys and twelve girls in our classroom had the opportunity to sing for Brother Henry's aged grandfather.
2. Many neighbors offered their assistance when our barn burned.
3. These kittens are enjoying their new liberty as they explore the world beyond their nest.

D. Write the plural form of each noun. Use the foreign plural spellings for numbers 8–12.

1. proof-of-purchase
2. knife
3. chimney
4. sheep
5. bluff
6. trio
7. tooth
8. nebula
9. apex
10. oasis
11. criterion
12. cactus

E. Rewrite each expression, using possessive forms. If it is better not to use a possessive form, write *X* after the number.

1. the aprons of the girls
2. the doors of the shed
3. the betrayal of Judas
4. the rapid spread of the fungi
5. the kittens of Abigail and Sheryl (joint ownership)
6. the chores of Curtis and Olen (separate ownership)

F. Copy all the pronouns, including possessive pronouns. Label each one *P* (personal), *CP* (compound personal), *D* (demonstrative), *ID* (indefinite), *IR* (interrogative), or *R* (relative).

1. Who watches over us daily and is well able to deal with anything that we may face?
2. God Himself watches over each of His children, and that is a comforting thought to everyone who trusts Him.
3. Every morning you should commit yourself anew to the Lord's care, which provides the only true security that is available in this world.

G. Copy each substantive in these sentences, and label it *N* (one-word or compound noun), *pron.* (pronoun), *G* (gerund or gerund phrase), *I* (infinitive or infinitive phrase), *prep.* (prepositional phrase), *C* (clause), *T* (title), or *S* (subject of discussion). If a substantive is within a substantive phrase or clause or within a title, do not list it separately.

1. At Bible school, my brother bought the book *The Swiss Anabaptists* for his class.
2. Studying those lessons gave him a renewed appreciation for our faithful heritage.
3. Above ninety degrees is what the weatherman predicts for today.
4. To understand the Biblical use of *mansion,* you need to find an archaic definition.

H. Write each underlined item correctly. If an item has no error, write *correct.*

1. The responsibility was not our's, and we did not know who we should tell.
2. I could not understand that there algebra problem, but Elmer figured it out hisself.
3. Sue Ellen and myself could not seem to work as efficiently as she.
4. This week is Amos's and Alvin's turn to milk the cows, so me and Gerald will do the feeding and take care of the hogs.
5. We should be friendly to the visitors which come to church even though we do not know who they are.
6. This calf coughing indicates a serious problem that them in the other hutches do not seem to have.

I. Answer these questions about the style of short stories.

1. What are three ways to keep story dialogue natural?
2. Why do words like *perhaps, seemed,* and *somewhat* tend to mar the style of a story?
3. What are clichés, and where might you properly use them in a story?
4. Why should a story appeal to the reader's five senses?
5. Why should a story contain more verbs in the active voice than linking verbs and verbs in the passive voice?
6. What is static description, and how should it be included in a story?
7. What is arrested action?
8. What three categories of words should you use to paint descriptive details in your stories?

J. Choose the correct expressions in parentheses.
1. The wickedness of Sodom had (rose, risen) to God.
2. Apparently one of Abraham's visitors (was, were) the Lord Himself.
3. (Don't, Doesn't) God's Word warn us to remember Lot's wife?
4. Ten righteous people (represent, represents) a small remnant, but Sodom had fewer than that.
5. Jesus certainly (did, done) more for us than we can ever repay.
6. Christian ethics (call, calls) us to complete honesty in our dealings with others.
7. All of these issues (demand, demands) careful forethought.
8. *Brethren* (is, are) an archaic plural form that we use commonly within the church.
9. The crew of workers (have, has) scattered to their specific assignments.
10. The crew of workers (have, has) finished its work for the day.
11. Grandfather Ebb's have (went, gone) to India to visit Uncle Fred's family.
12. The shears (cut, cuts) much better since Father sharpened the blades.
13. Neither my book nor my papers (is, are) where I thought I put them.
14. About four-fifths of the peach harvest (have, has) been lost in the late freeze.
15. Josephine, along with her younger sisters, (do, does) Sister Arlene's cleaning.
16. Jelly and peanut butter (is, are) a common sandwich.
17. The jelly and the peanut butter (have, has) been put on the table.
18. Obed is the only one of us children who (is, are) left-handed.
19. Has the cattle hauler (took, taken) Big Bill to the auction yet?
20. Either Connie or Jennifer (make, makes) these pillow tops.

K. Name the tense of each underlined verb. Also write whether the verb is *TA* (transitive, active voice), *TP* (transitive, passive voice), *IC* (intransitive complete), or *IL* (intransitive linking).
1. Little white lambs <u>are frisking</u> in the meadow.
2. Grazing contentedly on the lush grass, the ewes <u>watched</u> their offspring.
3. This year our peas <u>had been planted</u> before the first day of spring.
4. Before the last day of school, we <u>shall have picked</u> peas several times.
5. The rains <u>have been</u> quite adequate so far this spring.
6. Father <u>will look</u> for some extra help during the busiest part of the season.

L. Write the correct subjunctive verb for each sentence.
1. We desire that God (grant, grants) us wisdom to live consistently in a wicked world.
2. Praise (be, is) to the Name of Jesus forever.
3. The officials urge that everyone (take, takes) special precautions against the coming storm.
4. If we (would not have, had not) trusted God, we too would have panicked.
5. Suppose a devastating storm (was, were) to destroy our house!

118. Final Review 3 (Chapters 10–14)

A. Answer these questions about descriptive essays.

1. What is the goal of descriptive writing?
2. What three types of words contribute to vivid language in descriptive writing?
3. What two important considerations must you remember as you select the details for a descriptive essay?
4. What two orders of development are used in descriptive essays, and what type of essay uses each order?
5. You do not usually find an entire essay of descriptive writing. Then where do you find most descriptive writing?
6. Why must you choose a familiar subject when you plan a descriptive essay?
7. What is the theme of a descriptive essay?

B. Copy each underlined adjective. First label it *L* (limiting), or *D* (descriptive); then label it *AT* (attributive), *AP* (appositive), or *PR* (predicate).

1. Two fragrant lilac bushes grace the front yard.
2. We listened to the mockingbird singing, and that song certainly was a beautiful one to hear.
3. These German paintings, colorful and detailed, look lovely.

C. Copy each underlined adverb and the word or word group that it modifies. Write *sentence* if it modifies the whole sentence.

1. Mother could not stop on the treacherously icy roads, and the car went almost over the bank, dangling dangerously on the edge.
2. If the roads are nearly too slippery for a short drive, how will Father go to Greenville to preach?
3. Understandably, the strangers entered the church somewhat hesitantly.
4. After the service, the visitors became pleasantly relaxed.

D. Label each underlined word group *prep.* (prepositional phrase), *part.* (participial phrase), *inf.* (infinitive phrase), or *cl.* (clause). Also label each *adj.* or *adv.*

1. Newton's third law of motion, [a]which states that for every action there is an equal and opposite reaction, gives the scientific basis [b]for jet propulsion.
2. You can use a balloon [a]filled with air [b]to illustrate this principle.
3. [a]While the opening is held shut, there is no action and the balloon does not move [b]in any direction.
4. [a]When you release the balloon, its rubber sides, [b]stretched tightly, perform the action of forcing air rapidly out.
5. This action [a]in one direction causes a reaction that gives the balloon a tendency [b]to move in the opposite direction.

E. Label each underlined phrase or clause *R* (restrictive) or *N* (nonrestrictive). Also copy each word that should be followed by a comma, and add the comma.

1. Jet engines [a]which propel many large airplanes operate on the same principle [b]described in the preceding sentences.

2. In the front part is a powerful compressor [a]forcing air into the engine; in the back is the combustion chamber [b]where rapid burning of the fuel creates tremendous pressure.
3. The pressure [a]that has been described is an action; it produces a reaction of equal force [b]which moves the engine and the airplane through the air.

F. Write enough of each sentence to show how to correct the errors in using forms of comparison.
   1. Of my two brothers, Gordon has the curliest hair.
   2. The calf in the first hutch seemed sick yesterday, and today it is much worser.
   3. You can make a circle rounder by using a compass than by drawing it freehand.
   4. With modern technology, we can do many chores easier than our grandparents could.
   5. We spend far littler time doing the basic jobs than they did.
   6. Of the boomerangs we four boys made, Vernon's goes the fartherest.
   7. Today's weather is more pleasanter than we have had all week.
   8. The temperature will probably rise higher today than on any day of this week.

G. Do these exercises on using reference books.
   1. Why does a word like *post* have more than one numbered entry?
   2. What three types of inflections do most dictionaries show?
   3. Read these sample dictionary entries, and do the exercises that follow.

      sound[1] (sound) *n.* **1.** Vibrations transmitted through a solid, liquid, or gas, which usually can be heard with the ears. **2.** A distinctive noise. **3.** The distance over which something can be heard. —**sound** *v.* **sound·ed, sound·ing, sounds.** —*intr.* **1.a.** To make or give forth a sound. **b.** To be given forth as a sound. **2.** To give a particular impression. —*tr.* **1.** To cause to give forth or produce a sound. **2.** To summon, announce, or signal by a sound. [Middle English *soun*, from Old French *son,* from Latin *sonus*.]

      sound[2] (sound) *adj.* **sound·er, sound·est. 1.** Free from defect, decay, or injury; in good condition. **2.** Having a firm basis; unshakable. **3.** Financially secure or safe. **4.** Based on valid reasoning. —**sound** *adv.* Thoroughly; deeply: *sound asleep.* [Middle English, from Old English *gesund*.] —**sound·ly** *adv.* —**sound·ness** *n.*

      a. What two parts of speech is entry 1? entry 2?
      b. From what language does entry 1 come? entry 2?
      c. What inflections are given for each entry?
      d. What derivatives are given for entry 2?
   4. Name the usage labels that fit these descriptions. If more than one label fits, a number in parentheses tells how many you should have.
      a. Words acceptable only in everyday speaking and everyday writing.
      b. Words used in relatively small areas or by a limited group of people. (2)
      c. Words to avoid because they represent poor English. (3)
      d. Words invented by people trying to say things in unique ways.
      e. Words no longer in general use. (2)
      f. Words to avoid because of their association with evil.

5. What is the etymology of a word?
6. What are word inflections?
7. What is the difference between the denotation and the connotation of a word?
8. Why is it important to consider the connotations of words you might choose from a thesaurus?
9. What two important cautions should you remember about using encyclopedias?
10. What is the difference between a geographical and a political map?

H. Do these exercises about libraries.
1. What are the three important rules for using a library courteously?
2. Why must you use a library prudently?
3. What is a common system of classification for arranging books in a library?
4. What is the call number of a book?
5. Name the primary index for the books within a library.
6. Classify each item as *reference, fiction,* or *biography.*
   a. Imaginary stories.
   b. Stories about the personal lives of individuals.
   c. Books used for looking up facts.
   d. May have the number 92 instead of a Dewey decimal number.
   e. Books arranged alphabetically according to the name of the person written about.
   f. Books of general information.
   g. Books arranged alphabetically by the last name of the author.
   h. Some books in more than one category of the Dewey decimal system.

I. Label each underlined word *prep.* (preposition), *CC* (common coordinating conjunction), *Cor* (correlative conjunction), *SC* (subordinating conjunction), or *CA* (conjunctive adverb).
1. [a]<u>If</u> we have not quiet in our minds, outward comfort will do no more for us than a golden slipper [b]<u>on</u> a gouty foot. (John Bunyan)
2. Thought and theory must precede all [wholesome] action, [a]<u>yet</u> action is nobler in itself than [b]<u>either</u> thought <u>or</u> theory. (William Wadsworth)
3. A man can fail many times; [a]<u>however</u>, he isn't a failure [b]<u>until</u> he begins to blame somebody else. (John Burroughs)
4. [a]<u>In</u> this world, it is not what we take up, [b]<u>but</u> what we give up, that makes us rich. (Henry Ward Beecher)

J. Write enough of each sentence to show how to correct the errors in using conjunctions.
1. Every Christian must both pray for wisdom and for strength if he is to endure.
2. Saving faith involves not only believing with the mind but obeying in life.
3. Many believe that faith only will save, however, the Bible clearly teaches that faith must be accompanied by obedience.
4. He who trusts in God can relate to life's uncertainties calmly and without fear.
5. We know that God rules over all with benevolent care so we trust our lives to Him.

K. Copy each interjection, the word before it (if there is one), and the word after it. Use correct capitalization and punctuation, and underline any word that should be italicized.

1. Alleluia the Lord our God reigns with sovereign power.
2. Oh how restful to commit our cares and perplexities to Him!
3. In every age, God calls men to simple faith in Him; and behold the very ability to believe is a gift of His love.
4. Salt we thought this was the sugar bowl.
5. Buzz the sound of those hornets put wings on my feet!

L. Rewrite each sentence so that it communicates the same idea without the underlined idiom.

1. Do not allow yourself to be <u>out of sorts</u> simply because something did not please you.
2. We failed to <u>take into account</u> how hard-packed the earth would be.
3. This scroll saw has surely <u>lived up to</u> its promised performance.
4. We have <u>turned down</u> many invitations to buy new products.

M. Do these exercises on parliamentary procedure.

1. What is parliamentary procedure?
2. List the four basic purposes of parliamentary procedure.
3. Why can we not use parliamentary procedure to determine what is truth?
4. What is meant by having the floor in a meeting?
5. What are the minutes of a meeting?
6. What is a quorum?
7. What method of voting is used for procedural matters, such as approving the minutes?
8. What is voting by acclamation?
9. When is a two-thirds majority vote required to pass a motion?
10. Why would a chairman cast a vote to break a tie? to make a tie?
11. What is the purpose of main motions in a parliamentary meeting?
12. Most properly stated motions begin with what words?
13. When several motions are properly presented at the same time, what principle determines the order in which the motions are disposed of?
14. Explain the expression "A motion is pending."

Index

B

C

D

E

O

P